Walking in SCOTLAND

Sandra Bardwell
Nancy Frey
Jose Placer
Gareth McCormack
Helen Fairbairn

LONELY PLANET PUBLICATIONS
Melbourne • Oakland • London • Paris

SCOTLAND

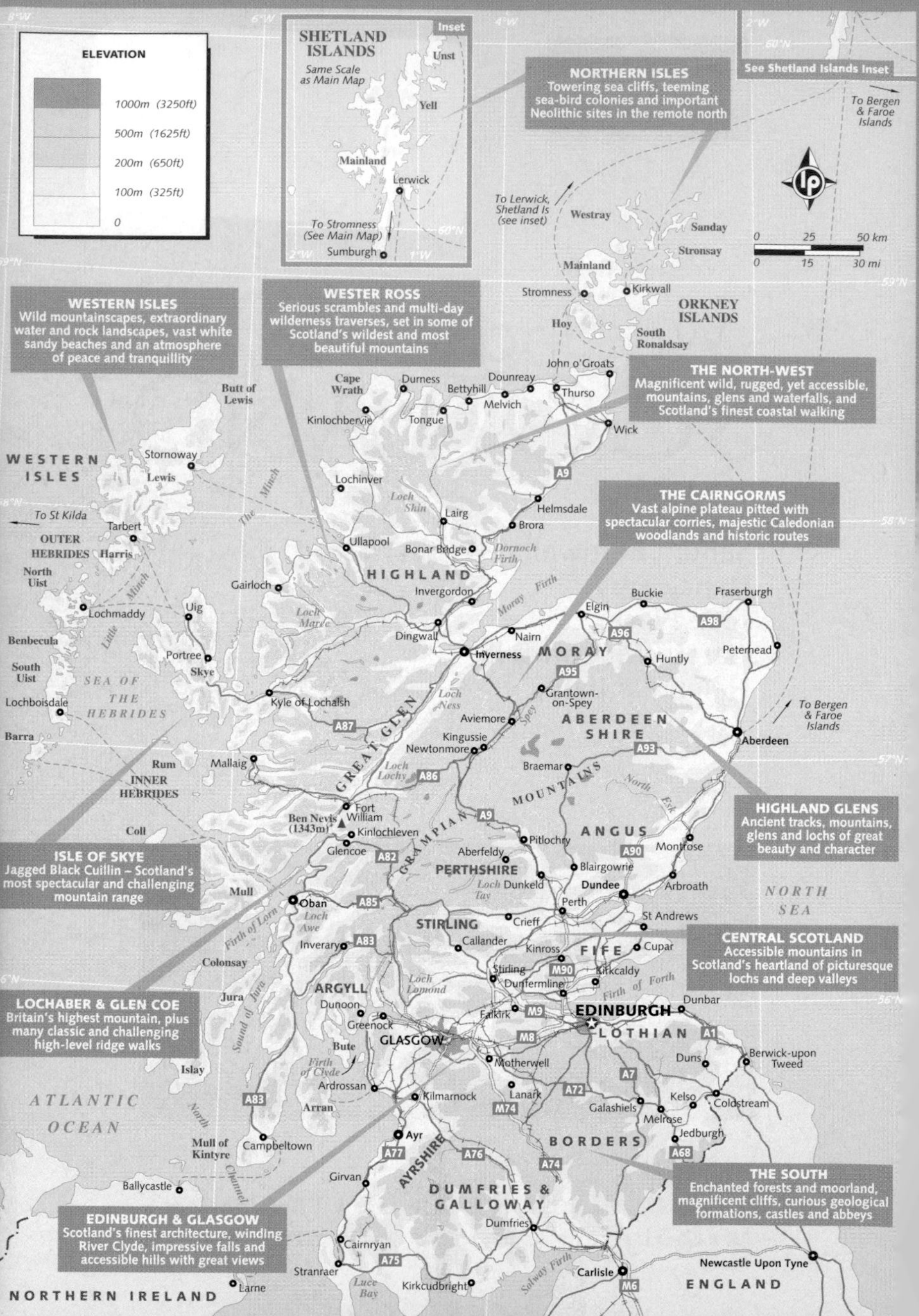
ELEVATION
1000m (3250ft)
500m (1625ft)
200m (650ft)
100m (325ft)
0
SHETLAND ISLANDS
Inset
Same Scale as Main Map
Unst
Yell
Mainland
Lerwick
To Stromness (See Main Map)
Sumburgh
See Shetland Islands Inset
To Bergen & Faroe Islands
NORTHERN ISLES
Towering sea cliffs, teeming sea-bird colonies and important Neolithic sites in the remote north
To Lerwick, Shetland Is (see inset)
Westray
Sanday
Stronsay
Mainland
Kirkwall
Stromness
Hoy
South Ronaldsay
ORKNEY ISLANDS
0 25 50 km
0 15 30 mi
WESTERN ISLES
Wild mountainscapes, extraordinary water and rock landscapes, vast white sandy beaches and an atmosphere of peace and tranquillity
WESTER ROSS
Serious scrambles and multi-day wilderness traverses, set in some of Scotland's wildest and most beautiful mountains
THE NORTH-WEST
Magnificent wild, rugged, yet accessible, mountains, glens and waterfalls, and Scotland's finest coastal walking
Cape Wrath
Durness
Bettyhill
Dounreay
John o'Groats
Thurso
Melvich
Tongue
Kinlochbervie
Wick
Butt of Lewis
WESTERN ISLES
Stornoway
Lewis
Lochinver
Loch Shin
Lairg
Helmsdale
Brora
The Minch
To St Kilda
Tarbert
OUTER HEBRIDES
Harris
Ullapool
Bonar Bridge
Dornoch Firth
HIGHLAND
North Uist
Gairloch
Invergordon
Moray Firth
THE CAIRNGORMS
Vast alpine plateau pitted with spectacular corries, majestic Caledonian woodlands and historic routes
Lochmaddy
Uig
Little Minch
Loch Maree
Dingwall
Nairn
Elgin
Buckie
Fraserburgh
Benbecula
Portree
Skye
Inverness
MORAY
Huntly
Peterhead
South Uist
SEA OF THE HEBRIDES
Lochboisdale
Kyle of Lochalsh
Loch Ness
Grantown-on-Spey
Aviemore
ABERDEEN SHIRE
To Bergen & Faroe Islands
Barra
GREAT GLEN
Kingussie
Newtonmore
Aberdeen
Rum
INNER HEBRIDES
Mallaig
Loch Lochy
Braemar
North Esk
MOUNTAINS
Fort William
Ben Nevis (1343m)
Kinlochleven
Glencoe
GRAMPIAN
Coll
Pitlochry
ANGUS
Montrose
HIGHLAND GLENS
Ancient tracks, mountains, glens and lochs of great beauty and character
ISLE OF SKYE
Jagged Black Cuillin – Scotland's most spectacular and challenging mountain range
Aberfeldy
PERTHSHIRE
Blairgowrie
Loch Tay
Dunkeld
Dundee
Arbroath
Mull
Oban
Loch Awe
Perth
NORTH SEA
Crieff
St Andrews
STIRLING
Firth of Lorn
Inverary
Callander
Kinross
FIFE
Cupar
CENTRAL SCOTLAND
Accessible mountains in Scotland's heartland of picturesque lochs and deep valleys
Colonsay
Stirling
Kirkcaldy
Dunfermline
ARGYLL
Loch Lomond
Firth of Forth
Jura
Sound of Jura
Dunoon
Greenock
Falkirk
EDINBURGH
Dunbar
LOTHIAN
LOCHABER & GLEN COE
Britain's highest mountain, plus many classic and challenging high-level ridge walks
GLASGOW
Bute
Motherwell
Duns
Berwick-upon Tweed
Islay
Firth of Clyde
Ardrossan
Lanark
Kelso
Coldstream
Galashiels
Melrose
ATLANTIC OCEAN
Kilmarnock
Arran
Jedburgh
North Channel
Ayr
BORDERS
Mull of Kintyre
Campbeltown
AYRSHIRE
Girvan
Ballycastle
DUMFRIES & GALLOWAY
THE SOUTH
Enchanted forests and moorland, magnificent cliffs, curious geological formations, castles and abbeys
EDINBURGH & GLASGOW
Scotland's finest architecture, winding River Clyde, impressive falls and accessible hills with great views
Dumfries
Cairnryan
Stranraer
Luce Bay
Kirkcudbright
Solway Firth
Carlisle
Newcastle Upon Tyne
ENGLAND
Larne
NORTHERN IRELAND

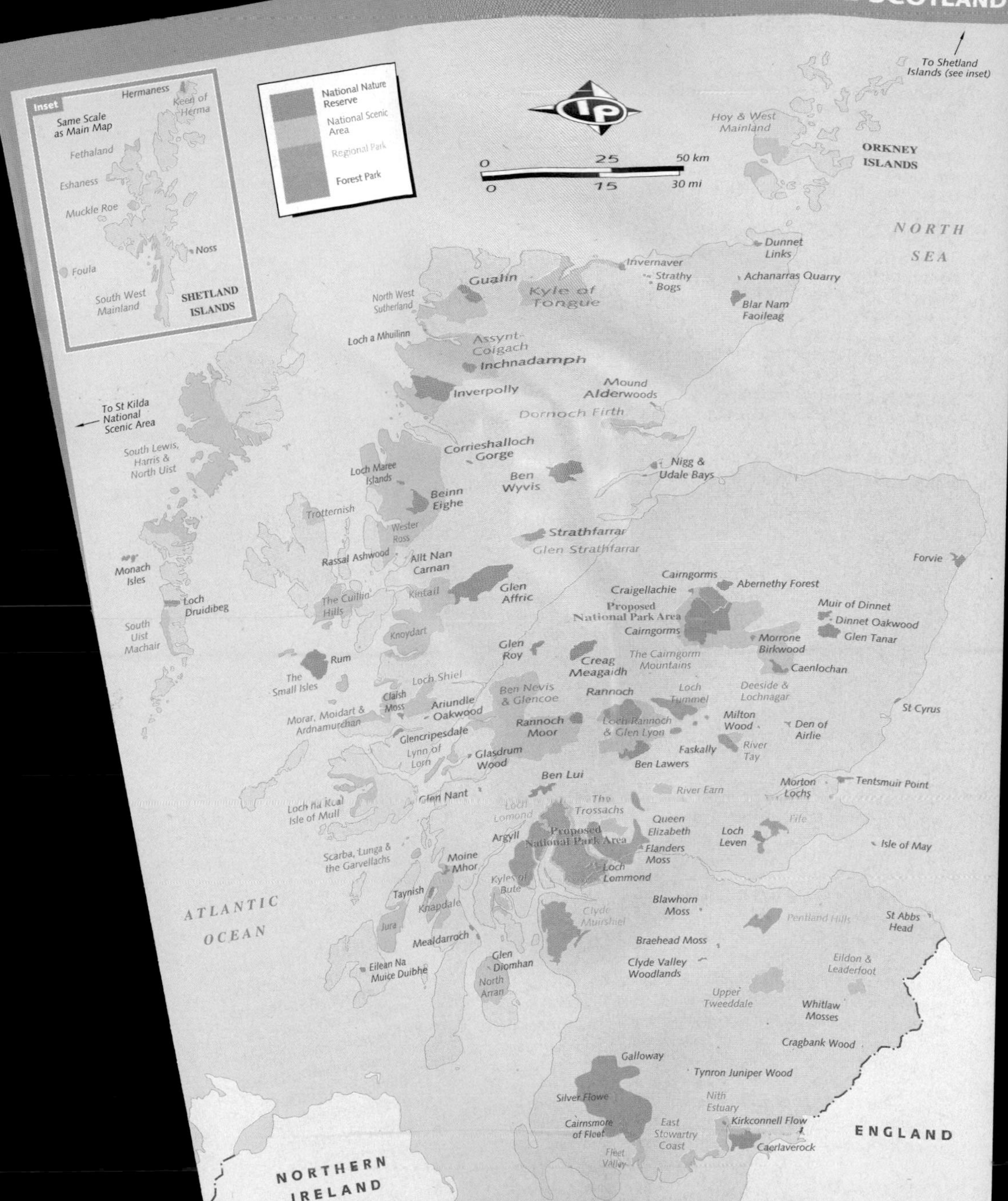

Inset
Same Scale as Main Map
Hermaness
Keen of Herma
Fethaland
Eshaness
Muckle Roe
Noss
Foula
South West Mainland
SHETLAND ISLANDS
National Nature Reserve
National Scenic Area
Regional Park
Forest Park
0 25 50 km
0 15 30 mi
To Shetland Islands (see inset)
Hoy & West Mainland
ORKNEY ISLANDS
NORTH SEA
Dunnet Links
Invernaver
Strathy Bogs
Achanarras Quarry
Blar Nam Faoileag
Gualin
Kyle of Tongue
North West Sutherland
Loch a Mhuilinn
Assynt-Coigach
Inchnadamph
Mound Alderwoods
Inverpolly
Dornoch Firth
To St Kilda National Scenic Area
South Lewis, Harris & North Uist
Corrieshalloch Gorge
Nigg & Udale Bays
Loch Maree Islands
Ben Wyvis
Beinn Eighe
Trotternish
Wester Ross
Strathfarrar
Glen Strathfarrar
Rassal Ashwood
Allt Nan Carnan
Monach Isles
Forvie
Cairngorms
Abernethy Forest
Craigellachie
Glen Affric
Loch Druidibeg
The Cuillin Hills
Kintail
Proposed National Park Area
Muir of Dinnet
Dinnet Oakwood
Cairngorms
Glen Tanar
Knoydart
Morrone Birkwood
South Uist Machair
Glen Roy
The Cairngorm Mountains
Rum
Creag Meagaidh
Caenlochan
The Small Isles
Loch Shiel
Ben Nevis & Glencoe
Rannoch
Loch Tummel
Deeside & Lochnagar
Claish Moss
Ariundle Oakwood
St Cyrus
Morar, Moidart & Ardnamurchan
Rannoch Moor
Loch Rannoch & Glen Lyon
Milton Wood
Den of Airlie
Glencripesdale
Lynn of Lorn
Glasdrum Wood
Faskally
River Tay
Ben Lawers
Ben Lui
River Earn
Morton Lochs
Tentsmuir Point
Glen Nant
Loch Lomond
The Trossachs
Loch na Keal Isle of Mull
Fife
Queen Elizabeth
Argyll
Proposed National Park Area
Loch Leven
Isle of May
Scarba, Lunga & the Garvellachs
Moine Mhor
Flanders Moss
Loch Lomond
Kyles of Bute
Taynish
Knapdale
Blawhorn Moss
ATLANTIC OCEAN
Jura
Clyde Muirshiel
Pentland Hills
St Abbs Head
Mealdarroch
Braehead Moss
Glen Diomhan
Eilean Na Muice Duibhe
Clyde Valley Woodlands
Eildon & Leaderfoot
North Arran
Upper Tweeddale
Whitlaw Mosses
Cragbank Wood
Galloway
Tynron Juniper Wood
Silver Flowe
Nith Estuary
Cairnsmore of Fleet
East Stewartry Coast
Kirkconnell Flow
Caerlaverock
ENGLAND
Fleet Valley
NORTHERN IRELAND

Walking in Scotland
1st edition – November 2001

Published by
Lonely Planet Publications Pty Ltd ABN 36 005 607 983
90 Maribyrnong St, Footscray, Victoria 3011, Australia

Lonely Planet Offices
Australia Locked Bag 1, Footscray, Victoria 3011
USA 150 Linden St, Oakland, CA 94607
UK 10a Spring Place, London NW5 3BH
France 1 rue du Dahomey, 75011 Paris

Photographs
Many of the images in this guide are available for licensing from Lonely Planet Images.
e lpi@lonelyplanet.com.au
w www.lonelyplanetimages.com

Main front cover photograph
Dawn over Loch Scavaig, Isle of Skye (Gareth McCormack)

Small front cover photograph
Climber atop Beinn Mheadhoin, Cairngorms (Graeme Cornwallis)

ISBN 1 86450 350 5

Printed by SNP SPrint (M) Sdn Bhd
Printed in Malaysia

...tents

OF W...

The Walks	Duration	Standard	Transport
Edinburgh & Glasgow			
Edinburgh City Walk	4–4½ hours	easy-medium	T B C
Pentland Hills Circuit	6 hours	medium	B C
Glasgow City Walk	4 hours	easy	T B C
Greenock Cut	4 hours	easy	C W
Clyde Walkway	4 hours	easy	T B C W
Tinto – Fire Mountain	2½ hours	easy-medium	B C
The South			
Southern Upland Way	9 days	medium-hard	T B C F
The Merrick	4–4½ hours	medium-hard	C W
Grey Mare's Tail & White Coomb	5 hours	medium-hard	B C
Peebles Circuit	5 hours	easy-medium	T B C
Eildon Hills	4 hours	easy-medium	T B C
Burnmouth to St Abb's Head	6 hours	easy	B C
Central Scotland			
A Goatfell Circuit	6–7½ hours	medium-hard	F C
Cock of Arran	3½–4 hours	easy-medium	F C W
The Cobbler	5 hours	medium-hard	T B C W
Ben Lomond	4½–5 hours	medium	F C
Ben A'an	2½ hours	easy	B C
Ben Ledi	4 hours	medium-hard	B C W
Ben Lawers	5 hours	medium-hard	B C
Schiehallion	4 hours	medium	B C W
West Highland Way			
West Highland Way	7 days	medium	T B C
Lochaber & Glen Coe			
Ben Nevis via the Mountain Track	6–8 hours	medium-hard	B C W
Ben Nevis via Carn Mór Dearg Arête	8–9 hours	hard	B C W
Ring of Steall	7–8 hours	medium-hard	B C W
The Road to the Isles	6–8 hours	medium	B T W
Buachaille Etive Mór	5–6 hours	medium-hard	B C
Glen Coe & Glen Etive Circuit	5 hours	medium	B C
Bidean nam Bian	6–7 hours	medium-hard	B C
Aonach Eagach	7–8 hours	hard	B C
The Cairngorms			
Cairn Gorm High Circuit	4½–5 hours	medium-hard	B C
Chalamain Gap & the Lairig Ghru	6–6½ hours	medium-hard	B C W
Linn of Dee Circuit	6½–7 hours	medium	B C
Glen Tilt & Glen Feshie	2 days	medium	T B C
Blair Atholl to Glenmore	2 days	medium-hard	T B C
Jock's Road	6–6½ hours	medium	B C W
Lochnagar	6–6½ hours	medium	C

T Train B Bus C Car F Ferry W W

Best Time	Features	Page
all year	Explore city highlights, including the Royal Mile and Arthur's Seat	102
all year	Circular ridge and valley walk through a regional park	104
all year	Circuit exploring important districts and monuments	108
all year	Great family walk with unbeatable views of the Firth of Clyde	112
all year	Flat stroll along wooded river with spectacular three-waterfall finale	114
all year	Ascent of 'Fire Mountain' to an ancient lookout	117
April–Oct	Long and challenging rollercoaster walk from coast to coast	122
April–Nov	Classic walk up Galloway's highest mountain along a scenic trail	132
all year	Superb loop combining a spectacular waterfall and panoramic ridge	134
all year	Easily accessible loop passing ancient forts and a riverside castle	138
all year	Circuit taking in an abbey, Roman settlement and the River Tweed	140
all year	Magnificent coast walk rich in geological sites and marine wildlife	142
May–Sept	Climb rocky ridges to the Isle of Arran's spectacular highest point	151
May–Sept	Discover historic features of Arran's peaceful, scenic north coast	154
Mar–Oct	Highly scenic walk to this famous craggy, three-pronged summit	156
May–Sept	Enjoy magnificent views of Loch Lomond from a popular summit	159
all year	Route up a little mountain with big personality and great views	162
May–Oct	Circuit via lovely Stank Glen for views of the surrounding Trossachs	163
May–Oct	Reach the highest peak on a 12km range above a picturesque loch	167
May–Oct	Walk up the celebrated mountain that inspired cartographers' contours	169
April–Nov	Britain's most popular long-distance path; moors and mountains	174
June–Sept	Steep ascent to the summit of Britain's highest mountain	192
June–Oct	Connoisseur's route up Ben Nevis; thrilling ridge and superb views	195
June–Oct	Challenging mountain horseshoe in The Mamores	198
April–Nov	Spectacular gorge and wild moorland on a remote, low-level walk	200
June–Oct	Fine ridge walk on one of Scotland's most distinctive mountains	206
April–Nov	Tough terrain and mountain passes on a scenic walk	208
June–Oct	Glen Coe's finest walk; stunning mountain and beautiful valley	209
June–Oct	Thrilling ridge-line scramble demanding skill in spectacular situations	211
May–Sept	Outstanding mountain walk across a sprawling alpine plateau	220
May–Sept	Energetic walk into the finest mountain pass in Scotland	221
May–Sept	Southern exploration of two long-distance routes with superb views	227
April–Oct	Magnificent walk through remote glens bordering the uplands	229
May–Sept	Walk across the Cairngorms through woodlands and low passes	233
May–Sept	Historic route over a high pass and beside beautiful Loch Callater	235
May–Sept	View a spectacular panorama, dramatic waterfall and serene loch	238

B F **limited, seasonal or with walking required to the trailhead**

The Walks *continued*	Duration	Standard	Transport
Highland Glens			
Great Glen Way	4 days	medium	T B C
Glen Affric	2 days	medium	B C W
Five Sisters of Kintail	6¾–7½ hours	hard	B C
Gleouraich	5–5½ hours	medium-hard	B C
Creag Meagaidh	7–7½ hours	hard	B C
Isle of Skye			
Bruach na Frithe	6–8 hours	medium-hard	B C
Red Cuillin Horseshoe	6–7 hours	medium-hard	B C
Coast & Cuillin	2 days	medium	B C
Bla Bheinn	6–7 hours	medium-hard	B C
Sgurr Dearg & Coire Lagan	5½–6½ hours	hard	B C
The Storr	4–5 hours	medium	B C
Trotternish Ridge	7–8 hours	medium-hard	B C W
The Quiraing	4–5 hours	easy-medium	B C W
Wester Ross			
The Fannichs	7–8 hours	medium-hard	B C
An Teallach	7½–8½ hours	hard	B C W
Beinn Dearg Mhór	2 days	medium-hard	B C W
The Great Wilderness Traverse	2 days	medium	B C W
Slioch	8 hours	medium-hard	B C W
Beinn Eighe Mountain Trail	2½–3½ hours	easy-medium	B C W
Beinn Alligin	6½ hours	medium-hard	B C W
Liathach	7–8 hours	hard	B C W
Coire Mhic Fhearchair	4½ hours	medium	B C W
Western Isles			
Tolsta to Ness	4–4½ hours	medium	B C W
Rhenigidale Path	4 hours	medium	B C W
Clisham	3½–4 hours	medium	B C W
Eaval	3½–4 hours	medium	B C W
Hecla	7–7½ hours	hard	C
Heaval	4–4½ hours	medium	B C W
The North-West			
Sandwood Bay & Cape Wrath	6½–7 hours	medium	B C W
Ben Loyal	6–6½ hours	medium	B C W
Eas a' Chùal Aluinn	5¾–6¼ hours	medium-hard	B C
Ben More Assynt	7–7½ hours	hard	B C
Glen Canisp	6½–7 hours	medium-hard	B C W
Northern Isles			
Old Man of Hoy	2 days	medium	F
Skara Brae & the Yesnaby Coast	7–8 hours	easy-medium	B C
West Westray Way	5–6 hours	easy-medium	C W
Hermaness & Muckle Flugga	3 hours	easy	C W
Muckle Roe	4–5 hours	easy-medium	B C W
Eshaness Coastal Circuit	5 hours	easy-medium	B C

T Train B Bus C Car F Ferry W W

Best Time	Features	Page
Feb–Dec	Magnificent walk beside suberb lochs and along historic canal	248
May–Oct	Finest walk through beautiful Glen Affric and across dramatic pass	255
May–Sept	Classic ridge walk along a narrow path with awesome views	262
May–Sept	Exhilarating and spectacular traverse of a narrow mountain ridge	264
May–Sept	Strenuous but rewarding, scenic mountain circuit	267
May–Oct	Strenuous mountain walk with spectacular views of the Black Cuillin	277
May–Oct	Demanding mountain horseshoe with expansive views of Skye	280
May–Nov	Spectacular, low-level route to Loch Coruisk in the Black Cuillin	282
May–Oct	Strenuous ascent to an impressive Black Cuillin summit	285
May–Oct	Exhilarating and spectacular ascent on the main Black Cuillin ridge	287
May–Nov	Beautiful route around one of Skye's iconic landmarks	291
May–Nov	Rewarding ridge walk exploring the best Trotternish landscapes	293
April–Nov	Exploration of weird and wonderful pinnacles on Trotternish ridge	294
May–Oct	Mountain circuit on the highest peak in Wester Ross	300
May–Oct	Impressive and challenging scramble along an airy, pinnacled ridge	303
May–Oct	A long and challenging circuit of a remote and spectacular peak	306
May–Nov	Scenic, low-level walk through the heart of The Great Wilderness	308
May–Oct	Beautiful approach along Loch Maree to mountain horseshoe	313
April–Nov	Trail exploring beautiful woodland and wild mountain terrain	315
May–Oct	Enjoyable scrambling on a classic Torridon ridge	319
May–Oct	Sensational but serious route on a challenging mountain	321
April–Nov	Beautiful, low-level walk to an impressive corrie	323
April–Sept	Spectacular coastal scenery, shieling villages and abundant seabirds	331
April–Oct	Historic path through magnificent scenery to an isolated hamlet	335
April–Oct	Steep, rocky ascent to the Western Isles' highest peak	339
April–Oct	Route to North Uist's highest peak with a superb panoramic view	340
April–Oct	Challenging but rewarding walk to South Uist's second-highest peak	343
April–Oct	Climb Barra's highest peak for unsurpassed ocean and island views	347
Mar–Nov	Fine coastal walk through an area of great beauty and wilderness	352
Mar–Nov	Steep climb to an attractive and interesting peak	357
May–Oct	Ruggedly scenic walk to the top of Scotland's highest waterfall	361
May–Sept	Strenuous walk to the highest peak in the far north-west	364
May–Sept	Scenic walk across moorland, past Canisp and Suilven landmarks	365
all year	Magnificent coastal walk along some of Scotland's highest sea cliffs	373
all year	Explore Europe's best-preserved Neolithic village and a wild coastline	376
all year	Coastal walk along vertical sea cliffs teeming with seabirds	378
all year	Circuit of seabird colonies and British Isles' northernmost point	384
all year	Rugged and intricate coastal walk with excellent views	386
all year	Beautiful coastal circuit with good cliff scenery	388

B F limited, seasonal or with walking required to the trailhead

The Maps

Lerwick
Shetland Islands

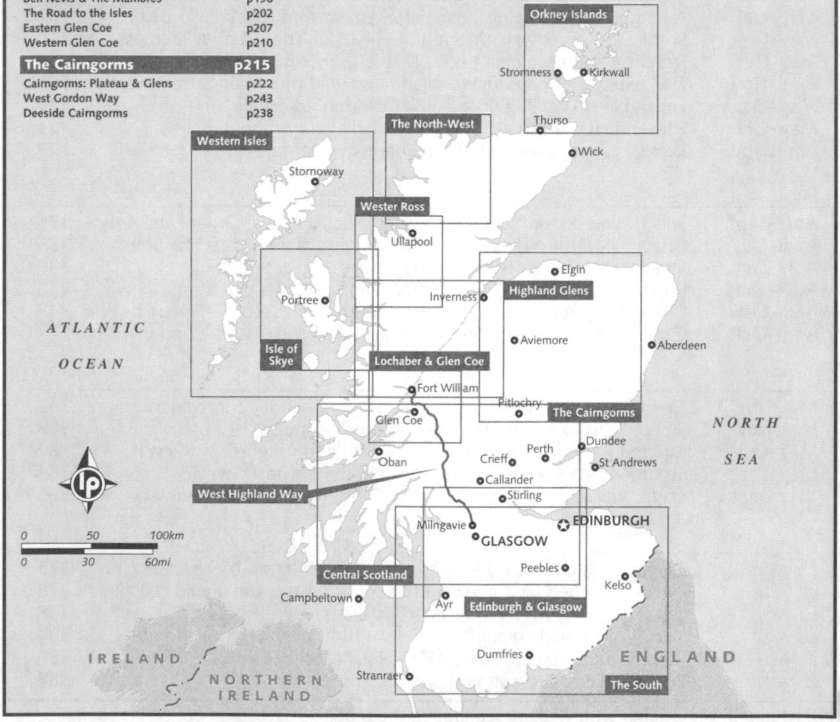

Orkney Islands
Stromness
Kirkwall
Thurso
Wick
The North-West
Western Isles
Stornoway
Wester Ross
Ullapool
Elgin
Highland Glens
Inverness
Portree
Aviemore
Aberdeen
ATLANTIC
OCEAN
Isle of Skye
Lochaber & Glen Coe
Fort William
Pitlochry
The Cairngorms
Glen Coe
NORTH
SEA
Dundee
Perth
Crieff
Oban
St Andrews
Callander
West Highland Way
Stirling
0 50 100km
0 30 60mi
Milngavie
EDINBURGH
GLASGOW
Peebles
Kelso
Central Scotland
Campbeltown
Ayr
Edinburgh & Glasgow
IRELAND
NORTHERN IRELAND
Dumfries
ENGLAND
Stranraer
The South

The Authors

Sandra Bardwell

After graduating with a thesis on the history of national parks in Victoria, Sandra worked as an archivist and then as a historian for the National Parks Service. She has been a dedicated walker since joining a bushwalking club in the early 1960s, and became well known through a newspaper column and as the author of several guidebooks on the subject. In 1989 Sandra and her husband Hal retired to the Highlands of Scotland where they live in a village near Loch Ness. For several years she worked as a monument warden for Historic Scotland, until Lonely Planet took over her life. She has walked extensively in Australia and Britain, and for Lonely Planet in Italy, Ireland, France and, even more extensively, in Australia. Now, researching this book, Sandra has renewed her enthusiasm for Scotland's hills and glens.

Nancy Frey & Jose Placer

Nancy and Jose met while in the Pyrenees. Nancy was researching why thousands of people now walk the medieval Camino de Santiago pilgrimage road across the north of Spain for her doctoral dissertation in cultural anthropology (at the University of California, Berkeley, 1996). This six-year project developed into her first book: *Pilgrim Stories: On and Off the Road to Santiago*. Jose was coming from the Alps and had decided to walk the 450mi Camino, after abandoning his law career. Since their fateful encounter they have not stopped walking together. They've enjoyed the heights of many European countries, North Africa, the Middle East and Nancy's native California. They now run their own company, On Foot in Spain, and lead educational walking tours to the Iberian Peninsula's most enchanting hidden corners. They live in Gallicia and have an adorable son, Jacob.

Gareth McCormack

After finishing a degree in law in 1995, Gareth travelled, walked and climbed his way across Asia, Australia and New Zealand for 18 months. This trip inspired a radical career turnaround and he is now a writer and photographer based in Ireland. He is a regular contributor to the magazine *Walking World Ireland* and coauthored Lonely Planet's *Walking in Ireland*, *Walking in France*, *Walking in Australia* and *Walking in Britain*. Every year he tries to spend several months photographing wild and beautiful parts of the world.

Helen Fairbairn

A year spent teaching English on the French Caribbean island of Guadeloupe convinced Helen of the benefits of life in the sun. She regularly escapes the winters of Ireland to rekindle her relationship with things more exotic. A mountain-lover and dedicated kayaker, the wild areas of the world seem to hold a particular attraction for her. This is Helen's second book for Lonely Planet.

FROM THE AUTHORS

Sandra Bardwell Thanks are due to the helpful staff at Ballater, Castlebay, Inverness, Lochinver, Stornoway, Tarbert and Tomintoul TICs; the Countryside Rangers at Cairngorm, The Bennachie Centre and at Balmoral Estates; Jim Strachan (Speyside Way Ranger) and Alasdair Macleod (Great Glen Way Ranger) for freely giving of their time; Will Boyd-Wallis (the John Muir Trust's man at Sandwood), Calum Macfarlane (Scottish Natural Heritage) and Malcolm Wield (Forest Enterprise) for information and advice; the warden at Kendoon Youth Hostel for a helping hand; Martin Rodgers for his infinite patience behind a photocopier; Chrissie Beaton for generous hospitality on Barra; and Roddy Maclean for valued advice about Gaelic. At LP in Melbourne, Lindsay's and Mike's advice, Jennifer's guidance and Andrew's help have made things much easier. It's been great fun working with Nancy and Jose, and sharing enthusiasm for Scotland's hills with Gareth and Helen. Hal's companionship and support are deeply appreciated.

Nancy Frey & Jose Placer We encountered countless knowledgable and friendly people on the trails to whom we owe much anonymous thanks. We'd like to dedicate the Ben A'an walk to a valued companion, Sir Paul of Ben A'an, and to the memory of his wife, dog and climbing partner. Staff in many TICs went out of their way to answer our questions, especially in Glasgow (Mike Malcolm), Eyemouth, Melrose, Peebles and Lanark. Also, staff from the Argyll Forest Park, Galloway Forest Park and Glen Trool Visitor Centres were very helpful. Thanks also to Lindsay Munro and the staff at Killin's Outdoor Centre. Deeply felt thanks go to our well-organised and meticulous coordinating author, Sandra Bardwell, and to Lindsay Brown at LP in Melbourne. We must also thank Lela and Titan for tending the home fires and our little rascal Jacob, while we ran up and down the Scottish hillsides. Finally, thanks to our trusty steed Ding-Ding.

Gareth McCormack First of all thanks to Helen for taking on the walks my poor knee couldn't face – and making the sandwiches a disproportionate number of times; such is the existence of an LP walking-guide author. Thanks also to the Clancys for company in Glen Coe and to Sandra Bardwell for correspondence and advice.

Helen Fairbairn First of all huge thanks are due to Gareth, who was like a light shining into all the murky corners of LP writing jargon. I'm sure it would have been much harder on my own! Thanks also to Nick and Sandra for very positive back-up support. Cheers to Kate and Cian for coming over from Ireland and entertaining us for the weekend – we'll get you up Aonach Eagach next time! Huge appreciation also to my sister Mags, whose very comfortable flat in Edinburgh offered a much-needed recovery haven.

This Book

Scrambling o'er hill, through glen and along loch, the adventurous team of authors responsible for this first edition of *Walking in Scotland* were Sandra Bardwell (coordinating author), who wrote the introductory chapters as well as The Cairngorms, Highland Glens, Western Isles and The North-West, and parts of The South and Central Scotland. Gareth McCormack & Helen Fairbairn compiled the West Highland Way Special Section, and the Lochaber & Glen Coe, Isle of Skye, Wester Ross and Northern Isles chapters. Nancy Frey & Jose Placer tackled Edinburgh & Glasgow, and wrote parts of The South and Central Scotland chapters. Some material for this book was sourced from Lonely Planet's *Scotland* and *Walking in Britain*.

From the Publisher

Back at the bothy, the LP clan responsible for assembling all the adventures included Andrew Smith (coordinating cartographer/designer) and Jennifer Garrett (coordinating editor). Assisting with the multitude of maps were Jarrad Needham and Karen Fry. The spectacular color sections were created by Andrew Smith and Birgit Jordan. Helping with proofing were Anne Mulvaney, Andrew Bain (who also put the index together) and Emily Coles, while David Andrew cast an expert eye over the Fauna & Flora section. The imaginative illustrations were coordinated by Matt King and the chapter ends drawn by Martin Harris. The language chapter was put together by Emma Koch. Assembling and assisting with slides was the crew from Lonely Planet Images (LPI). The distinctive cover was designed by Jamieson Gross. Handling administration duties was Fiona Siseman. Making sure everything was up to LP standard and responsible for final checks were Glenn van der Knijff (senior cartographer/designer) and Sally Dillon (senior editor). All deserve a wee dram of Scotland's finest for a job well done!

Foreword

ABOUT LONELY PLANET GUIDEBOOKS

The story begins with a classic travel adventure: Tony and Maureen Wheeler's 1972 journey across Europe and Asia to Australia. Useful information about the overland trail did not exist at that time, so Tony and Maureen published the first Lonely Planet guidebook to meet a growing need.

From a kitchen table, then from a tiny office in Melbourne (Australia), Lonely Planet has become the largest independent travel publisher in the world, an international company with offices in Melbourne, Oakland (USA), London (UK) and Paris (France).

Today Lonely Planet guidebooks cover the globe. There is an ever-growing list of books and there's information in a variety of forms and media. Some things haven't changed. The main aim is still to help make it possible for adventurous travellers to get out there – to explore and better understand the world.

At Lonely Planet we believe travellers can make a positive contribution to the countries they visit – if they respect their host communities and spend their money wisely. Since 1986 a percentage of the income from each book has been donated to aid projects and human rights campaigns.

Updates Lonely Planet thoroughly updates each guidebook as often as possible. This usually means there are around two years between editions, although for more unusual or more stable destinations the gap can be longer. Check the imprint page (following the colour map at the beginning of the book) for publication dates.

Between editions up-to-date information is available in two free newsletters – the paper *Planet Talk* and email *Comet* (to subscribe, contact any Lonely Planet office) – and on our Web site at W www.lonelyplanet.com. The *Upgrades* section of the Web site covers a number of important and volatile destinations and is regularly updated by Lonely Planet authors. *Scoop* covers news and current affairs relevant to travellers. And, lastly, the *Thorn Tree* bulletin board and *Postcards* section of the site carry unverified, but fascinating, reports from travellers.

Correspondence The process of creating new editions begins with the letters, postcards and emails received from travellers. This correspondence often includes suggestions, criticisms and comments about the current editions. Interesting excerpts are immediately passed on via newsletters and the Web site, and everything goes to our authors to be verified when they're researching on the road. We're keen to get more feedback from organisations or individuals who represent communities visited by travellers.

Lonely Planet gathers information for everyone who's curious about the planet – and especially for those who explore it first-hand. Through guidebooks, phrasebooks, activity guides, maps, literature, newsletters, image library, TV series and Web site we act as an information exchange for a worldwide community of travellers.

Research Authors aim to gather sufficient practical information to enable travellers to make informed choices and to make the mechanics of a journey run smoothly. They also research historical and cultural background to help enrich the travel experience and allow travellers to understand and respond appropriately to cultural and environmental issues.

Authors don't stay in every hotel because that would mean spending a couple of months in each medium-sized city and, no, they don't eat at every restaurant because that would mean stretching belts beyond capacity. They do visit hotels and restaurants to check standards and prices, but feedback based on readers' direct experiences can be very helpful.

Many of our authors work undercover, others aren't so secretive. None of them accept freebies in exchange for positive write-ups. And none of our guidebooks contain any advertising.

Production Authors submit their raw manuscripts and maps to offices in Australia, USA, UK or France. Editors and cartographers – all experienced travellers themselves – then begin the process of assembling the pieces. When the book finally hits the shops, some things are already out of date, we start getting feedback from readers and the process begins again...

WARNING & REQUEST

Things change – prices go up, schedules change, good places go bad and bad places go bankrupt – nothing stays the same. So, if you find things better or worse, recently opened or long since closed, please tell us and help make the next edition even more accurate and useful. We genuinely value all the feedback we receive. A well travelled team reads and acknowledges every letter, postcard and email and ensures that every morsel of information finds its way to the appropriate authors, editors and cartographers for verification.

Everyone who writes to us will find their name in the next edition of the appropriate guidebook. They will also receive the latest issue of *Planet Talk*, our quarterly printed newsletter, or *Comet*, our monthly email newsletter. Subscriptions to both newsletters are free. The very best contributions will be rewarded with a free guidebook.

Excerpts from your correspondence may appear in new editions of Lonely Planet guidebooks, the Lonely Planet Web site, *Planet Talk* or *Comet*, so please let us know if you *don't* want your letter published or your name acknowledged.

Send all correspondence to the Lonely Planet office closest to you:

Australia: Locked Bag 1, Footscray, Victoria 3011
USA: 150 Linden St, Oakland, CA 94607
UK: 10a Spring Place, London NW5 3BH
France: 1 rue du Dahomey, 75011 Paris

Or email us at: e talk2us@lonelyplanet.com.au

For news, views and updates see our Web site: w www.lonelyplanet.com

WALKING YOU THROUGH THIS GUIDEBOOK

Walking is an individual pursuit and we expect that people will use our guidebooks in individual ways. Whether you carry it in your backpack or read it as you walk along (not recommended near cliffs), a Lonely Planet walking guide can point your wandering spirit in the right direction. Never forget, however, that the finest discoveries are those you make yourself.

What We've Packed All Lonely Planet guidebooks follow roughly the same path, including the walking guides. The Facts about the Country chapter provides background information relevant to walkers, ranging from history to weather, as well as a detailed look at the plants and animals you're likely to encounter on the track. Facts for the Walker deals with the walking practicalities – the planning, red tape and resources. We also include a special Health & Safety chapter to help combat or treat those on-track nasties. The Getting There & Away and Getting Around chapters will help you make your travel plans.

The walking chapters are divided into regions, encompassing the walks in those areas. We start each walk with background, planning and how to get to/from the walk information. Each walk is detailed and highlights en route are included in the text. We also suggest where to rest your weary feet and fill your empty stomach. You will have earned it.

Maps Maps are a key element of any Lonely Planet guidebook, particularly walking guides. The maps are printed in two colours, making route-finding a snap, and show everything from town locations to the peaks around you. We strive for compatability between word and image, so what you read in the text will invariably feature on the map. A legend is printed on the back page.

Navigating the Guidebook The traditional 'map and compass' for a Lonely Planet guidebook are the contents and index lists but, in addition, the walking guides offer a comprehensive table of walks, providing thumbnail information about every described walk, as well as a table of maps.

Although inclusion in a guidebook usually implies a recommendation we cannot list all the good places. Exclusion does not necessarily imply criticism. There are a number of reasons why we might exclude a place – sometimes it is simply inappropriate to encourage an influx of travellers.

Introduction

Scotland has a wonderfully varied heritage of mountains, glens, waterways, coasts and islands where walkers of all tastes and inclinations can enjoy a wealth of walking – easy-going and accessible or rugged and remote.

The rolling 'hills' of the Southern Uplands are startlingly different from the knife-edged ridges of Skye's Black Cuillin. The bold Cairngorms with their magnificent corries contrast with the undulating, cliff-lined ridges of the Highlands. The crumpled profile of the rocky western coast contrasts with the long, sandy beaches of the Western Isles. Moorlands range from the familiar, heather-carpeted Uplands to the surreal rock- and water-scapes in the far north-west. There are tall Scots pines, birch woodlands and dense thickets of juniper; broad rivers and tumbling mountain streams; and vast Loch Lomond and Loch Ness, along with intimate lochans.

Scotland's reputation for bad weather – all mist and rain, with sunshine a rare privilege – is mythical. Some western areas do have more than their fair share of rain but, country wide, more days are fine than not. True also, Scotland isn't noted for hot summers, but it's often pleasantly warm and a Highlands' suntan is almost guaranteed. Spring, early summer and autumn are the ideal walking seasons, however, many low-level walks are possible on wonderfully clear, sparkling, cold days in midwinter.

Some of the finest walking areas will fall within Scotland's first national park when it is declared in 2002. Many more walks pass through areas of comparable scenic beauty and ecological importance – national nature reserves and national scenic areas. Some of these reserves are owned by government agencies but most are in private hands – individuals and conservation organisations – where walkers are welcome.

Scotland has four official long-distance paths and many other shorter walks, all well signposted and waymarked. The historic network of public rights of way also provides guaranteed access through remote country and many of the finest glens; these routes, and many others along coasts and to mountain summits, aren't waymarked but most are not difficult to follow.

Nearly all the walks in this book are based at a village or town where there's a choice of accommodation. You'll rarely be far from a hostel or B&B and there are camping sites near most popular walking areas. On the long-distance paths you'll find shelter at the end of each day's walk; other extended walks may take you past a bothy or two (simple huts with no facilities) but you do need to be self-sufficient with your own camping equipment.

Scotland may not have Australia's kangaroos, Africa's big cats or America's bears, but it does have superb Caledonian and birch woodlands, and prolific displays of spring and summer wild flowers. The highlight for wildlife enthusiasts will be the birds; from the magnificent golden eagle to

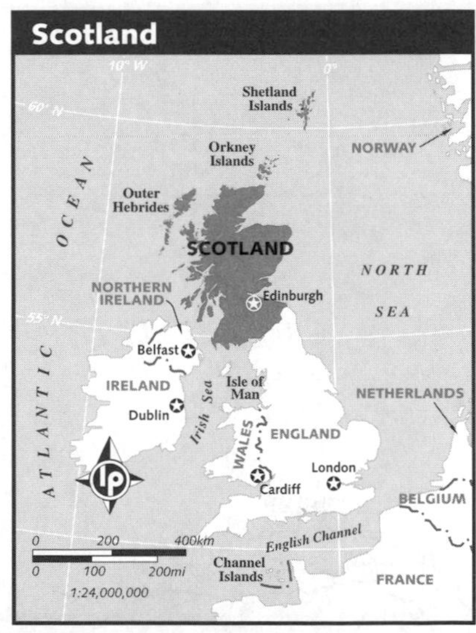

the mountain-dwelling ptarmigan, the finches and warblers of the woodlands to the internationally famous seabirds of the Northern Isles.

Whether you enjoy the company of other walkers or prefer not to see another soul, Scotland is the place for you. On fine weekends many popular walks are seriously busy, with scores of people congregating on summits and chatting amiably. In more remote areas, and especially on the islands, you're more likely to be alone – for a while.

Food and drink become more important than usual during a walking holiday. Scotland's reputation in this realm is improving all the time and it's easy to enjoy the best of the great variety of tasty fresh produce, unique real ales and fine malt whiskies available.

Within its compact boundaries, Scotland clearly has enough variety and attractions to happily occupy the most active walker for half a lifetime so, will ye no' come back again and again?

Facts about Scotland

HISTORY

Scotland's history is often portrayed by familiar images of warring clans, tragic clearances and grimy industrial cities; these and many other themes have been played out during the last 5000 years. The land has been populated by people from many countries; the nation was absorbed and eventually regained self-determination. Scots have been world leaders in numerous endeavours from philosophy to engineering. For more than a millennium religion has been a dominant influence.

The following chart of significant events frames the local events mentioned in the walk chapters and can illuminate the unique experience that is walking in Scotland.

c. 3500 BC – Neolithic times; village of Skara Brae (Orkney) built
2500-500 BC – use of metal introduced during Bronze Age
c. 500 BC-AD 200 – Iron Age; *dùns* (forts) built
AD c. 140 – Romans built Antonine Wall between Forth and Clyde; Pictish tribes well established by this time
397 – Whithorn Christian monastic centre established by St Ninian
500-600 – the Scotti (a Celtic tribe) arrived from northern Ireland (Scotia)
600-700 – Anglo-Saxons colonised south-east Scotland
790s – Viking raids on the west coast
843 – Kenneth MacAlpin, king of the Scotti of Dalriada and son of a Pictish princess, made himself king of Alba (Scotland)
1057 – Malcolm III slew Macbeth
1124-53 – rule of David I; Norman feudal system adopted
1263 – Alexander III defeated Vikings at Battle of Largs
1295 – 'Auld Alliance' forged with France; Stone of Destiny (coronation stone of Scottish kings) removed to Westminster Abbey
1297 – William Wallace's forces defeated the English at the Battle of Stirling Bridge, marking the start of the Scottish war of independence
1306 – Robert the Bruce crowned king of Scotland
1314 – English routed at Battle of Bannockburn, a turning point in Scotland's fight for independence
1410 – St Andrews University founded
1542 – Mary Queen of Scots ascended the throne
1560 – Scottish Parliament created a Protestant Church that was independent of Rome and the monarchy
1600 – 3% of population in towns of over 10,000
1603 – James VI of Scotland became James I of England, uniting the crowns
1689 – government forces routed at the Battle of Killiecrankie; Protestant William and Mary crowned the king and queen of England and Scotland
1692 – massacre of Glencoe
1707 – Act of Union between England and Scotland
1715 – the Jacobite Rebellion
1730s – beginning of Scottish Enlightenment, which produced major works in philosophy, economics, geology, sociology and history
1746 – Jacobites finally defeated at Battle of Culloden; Disarming Act prohibited the carrying of weapons and forbade anyone not in the army to wear Highland clothes, or even to use tartan or plaid in any form
1755 – population reached 1.25 million
1759 – the Industrial Revolution signalled with opening of Carron ironworks, the largest ironworks in Britain
1767 – James Craig won a competition to design Edinburgh's New Town
1782 – Disarming Act repealed
1786 – village of new Lanark established, an early experiment in creating a civilised working environment
1790 – Forth & Clyde canal, crossing Central England, opened
1792 – William Gilpin's *Observations...on...picturesque beauty* helped launch tourism in the Highlands
1801 – population reached 1.6 million, 17.3% living in towns of more than 10,000
1807-21 – notorious clearances of Highlanders from Sutherland Estate (in the north) to make way for sheep
1812-20 – sporadic civil unrest against suppression of trade unions
1820 – day trips by steamer to Loch Lomond popular
1830s – sea-going paddle steamers began operating on the west coast
1840s – overpopulation, poverty, potato famine precipitated emigration and evictions – the worst phase of the Highland Clearances
1841 – population stood at 2.6 million

1843 – Free Church established as a result of the Great Disruption
1846 – Thomas Cook's tours by steamer and rail launched
1850 – Scotland became second most-urbanised country in Europe – 32% of population in towns of over 10,000
1853 – legislation forced closing of pubs on Sundays (this remained in force for over a century)
1859 – Loch Katrine project in Trossachs gave Glasgow the first public water supply in Scotland
1867 – Scotland's first football club, Queens Park, founded
1872 – Education Act provided for compulsory education
1885 – Scottish Home Rule Association established
1886 – Crofters' Holding Act curbed landlord power and gave secure tenure and fair rent to small tenants
1888 – Scottish Labour Party established
1890 – Forth Rail Bridge, a remarkable engineering feat of the Victorian era, opened
1900 – Saturday half-holiday had become common
1901 – 4.5 million people in Scotland; International Exhibition in Glasgow; Scotland a leading international economic power
1910 – first cinema opened in Glasgow
1914 – Home Rule Bill defeated; Glasgow's population one million; Glasgow had largest area of parkland of any municipality
1918 – women given the vote
1918-21 – break-up of large estates, about 20% of the land changed hands
1919 – Forestry Commission set up; legislation passed providing for public housing
1921 – population reached 4,882,500
1922 – Labour won largest number of Scottish seats at General Election
1926 – Britain-wide general strike over pay and conditions
1931 – population count at 4,843,000, down by almost 40,000 since 1921
1932 – unemployment reached 27.7%
1934 – Scottish National Party founded
1935 – Saltire Society established to promote Scotland's cultural heritage
1939 – outbreak of WWII
1941 – Glasgow's Clydebank bombed
1944 – hydroelectric power schemes launched in the Highlands
1947 – first Edinburgh International Festival
1948 – railways nationalised
1950 – Stone of Destiny seized from Westminster Abbey
1958 – Clydebank shipbuilding in severe decline
1964 – decision to base nuclear submarine *Polaris* at Holy Loch
1966 – Dounreay nuclear power station on north coast, near Thurso, opened
1967 – Scottish National Party won its first seat in parliament
1970 – Forties oilfield opened off Aberdeen
1971 – population stood at 5,235,600
1973 – UK joined Common Market (later European Union)
1979 – Home Rule referendum failed
1980s – hi-tech centre developed in Glasgow's Silicon Glen as heavy industry declined rapidly
1988 – A Claim of Right for Scotland published to stimulate campaign for Home Rule; widely representative Constitutional Convention set up
1990 – Constitutional Convention's Blueprint for Scottish Parliament published
1992 – Scottish Natural Heritage, the government's nature conservation agency, established
1993 – parties advocating Home Rule or independence won 85% of Scottish seats at general election
1995 – Old and New Towns of Edinburgh declared World Heritage site
1997 – at referendum for establishment of Scottish Parliament, 74.3% voted yes
1998 – elections for Scotland's parliament; Labour government elected
1999 – first meeting of parliament with Donald Dewar as First Minister
2000 – World Heritage site status for prehistoric sites on Orkney
2001 – outbreak of foot-and-mouth disease among livestock in Britain (in Scotland confined to Dumfries & Galloway and The Borders), unprecedented restrictions imposed for some time on access to the countryside to prevent the disease spreading

History of Walking

People have been walking through Scotland's glens for centuries but it wasn't until well into the 19th century that walking for pleasure, rather than necessity, became possible as public transport improved, working hours were shortened and wages increased.

By then there was a substantial heritage of roads and paths, many recognised as public rights of way. Of the roads built by Roman soldiers between AD 78 and 185, Dere Street, the line from the Cheviots to Melrose, is probably the most obvious and now forms part of St Cuthbert's Way (see page 146). Several centuries passed before roads were again built but tracks, mainly for trade, developed from the passage of feet (and hooves) – across the Cheviots into England and southward across the Cairngorms from Deeside. Cattle and sheep were driven from the Highlands to southern markets for hundreds of years along two main routes: from the area north of Strathspey via Drumochter, Atholl and Crieff; and from Wester Ross and the Western Isles via Glen Coe, Black Mount and Callander. Kirk and coffin roads developed as people made their way from remote settlements to the nearest kirk (church) and as coffins were carried to clan burial grounds, sometimes for considerable distances.

In two bursts during the 18th century, 1724–34 and 1740–67, nearly 1100mi of military roads were built in the Highlands, so called because they were constructed by soldiers. They were designed to link forts built by the English government to ensure peace in the rebellious Highlands and to improve communications. The military road through Glen Coe (en route between Stirling and Fort William) now forms part of the West Highland Way, and the road linking Fort Augustus and Dalwhinnie via the Corrieyairack Pass is a popular walking route.

In the early 19th century adventurous men and women, inspired by Sir Walter Scott's Highland tales, embarked on the 'Grand Tour' of the Highlands and islands, which usually included ascents of Ben Nevis and Ben Lomond and visits to the remote Outer Hebrides.

The foundation of the Association for the Protection of Public Rights of Roadway in and around Edinburgh in 1845 marks an early recognition of walking as a form of recreation. From concern for the Edinburgh area, the association soon broadened its remit to the whole of Scotland. In 1849 it led the way in a successful court case to prevent the Duke of Atholl from closing Glen Tilt to walkers.

A threat to paths in the Pentlands in 1883 galvanised the association following an inert period. Renamed the Scottish Rights of Way & Recreation Society Limited, it set about erecting right-of-way signs in the Pentlands and was soon busy doing the same in the Cairngorms. In 1884, an Access to Mountains (Scotland) Bill was introduced to Parliament by Scottish MP James Bryce but was not passed. Not deterred, the Scottish Rights of Way & Recreation Society Limited successfully defended a right of way through Glen Doll in 1887. In the same year the independent Cairngorm Club was founded; members ventured far into the hills, built bridges across large streams and installed topographs (circular plates showing direction/bearing of landscape features) on summits.

The Scottish Mountaineering Club was founded in 1889 and several of its members laid siege to the Cuillins of Skye (see the boxed text 'Early Ascents in the Black Cuillin' on page 288). Two years later, Sir Hugh Munro's *Tables of 3000 foot Mountains* was published by the club, from which, decades later, grew the 'Munro bagging' industry (see the boxed text 'Munros & Munro Bagging' on page 52).

Attempts by landowners to keep out the growing number of walkers spurred the founding of many more walkers' organisations, one of the most prominent being the West of Scotland Ramblers Alliance in 1892. *Hill Paths in Scotland* was published by the Scottish Rights of Way & Recreation Society in 1924, effectively publicising its work in defending and signposting paths. The Scottish Youth Hostels Association (SYHA) arrived in 1931; by providing inexpensive accommodation in many remote areas, it did much to encourage and promote walking (and climbing) throughout the country. The Ramblers' Association was born in England in 1935, taking over from the Britain-wide Council of Rambling Federations, which included representatives from Glasgow and Edinburgh.

At the outbreak of WWII right-of-way signs were taken down lest an invading army used them to find its way about the countryside. The signs were restored from 1946 by the renamed Scottish Rights of Way Society (SROWS), which then published *Scottish Hill Tracks* – the definitive guide to rights of way, now in its fourth edition.

By the mid-1970s there were plenty of walking clubs, mainly based in the cities and towns of the central belt, and walking in Scotland began to be taken seriously at government level. After several years of planning and negotiation, Scotland's first long-distance path, the West Highland Way, was opened in 1980. It was followed four years later by the Southern Upland Way. Also in 1980 was the inaugural Ultimate Challenge (now the TGO Challenge), an annual cross-country, noncompetitive walk from the west to the east coast.

During the 1990s walking grew and grew, and by 2000 had become the most popular participation recreation in Scotland, boosted annually by visitors from far and wide. This growth has been cultivated on many fronts. The Ramblers' Association, which has had a Scottish presence since 1935, appointed its first full-time employee in Scotland in 1985 and has become a leading player in the many issues affecting walkers in Scotland. The inevitable wear and tear on footpaths has been tackled by many different groups and organisations with extensive path-building projects (on Goatfell, Ben Lawers, Lochnagar and many more), in the process reviving stonework skills and providing employment. The outstanding success of walking festivals in Ireland led to the introduction of walking festivals in Scotland, from the Borders to Shetland. At the end of the 1990s, SROWS completed a project to signpost every recognised right of way in Scotland. In 2000 the Speyside Way became the third official long-distance path and is expected to be followed in 2002 by the Great Glen Way.

Access to the 'hills', through glens and in more settled areas, became a major issue during the 1990s (see Conservation on page 26). The signing of the Letterewe Accord in 1993 (see the boxed text 'Wild Camping & the Letterewe Estate' on page 312) and the foundation of the Access Forum in 1996 (see Access under Responsible Walking on page 64) represented a new level of understanding between users, landowners and managers. The forum aims to promote greater understanding of countryside access issues, and improved access arrangements with minimal impact on land management and conservation. The development of the Hillphones system, a forum initiative providing a telephone answering-machine service for walkers with information on deer stalking activities on participating estates (see the boxed text 'Deer Management' on page 25), and similar arrangements elsewhere, marked a welcome openness and a spirit of cooperation, rather than mystery and confrontation. In 1998, Scottish Natural Heritage (advised by the Access Forum) recommended to the Scottish Office (Scotland's presence in the British government system) that it should legislate for public right of access to virtually all land and water, exercised responsibly, for informal recreation and passage. In February 2001 the Scottish Executive (the senior decision-making body in the Scottish parliamentary system) published a draft Scottish Outdoor Access Code and a draft Land Reform (Scotland) Bill.

GEOGRAPHY

Scotland covers 30,414 sq mi, about one-third of the area of Britain. The maximum distance north to south is 268mi (440km) and east to west is 151mi (248km). It can be divided into four areas – the Southern Uplands, the central Lowlands, the Highlands, and the islands off the north and west coasts.

South of Edinburgh and Glasgow is the Southern Uplands, including the Galloway Hills in the west and, to the east, the Cheviots, bordering England.

The central Lowlands comprises a triangular block from Edinburgh to Stonehaven in the east and across to Glasgow in the west; this is the most populous area of Scotland.

North of the Highland Boundary Fault, running north-east from Helensburgh (west of Glasgow) to Stonehaven (south of Aberdeen), lies the Highlands, occupying about two-thirds of the country. Here are the major mountain ranges, crowned by the highest mountain in Britain (Ben Nevis) at 1343m (4406ft), separated by long, deep glens. The Highlands' east-west divide is not far from the west coast; many of the east-flowing rivers wander through straths (wide valleys) to the North Sea. Fertile land is generally confined to coastal areas between Aberdeen and the Dornoch Firth (north of Inverness), and the far north-eastern corner in Caithness. The Highlands is nearly split in two by the largest of the glens – the Great Glen, stretching from Fort William to Inverness along another fault line and cradling a chain of freshwater lochs, including Loch Ness.

There are 790 islands around the coast, 130 of which are inhabited. To the north are two island groups, Orkney and Shetland. The Western Isles (or Outer Hebrides) parallel the north-west coast and comprise 550 islands, of which 10 are inhabited. The Inner Hebrides are the scattering of mainly small islands farther south including Mull, Jura and Islay, and the sub-group of the Small Isles (Canna, Rum, Muck and Eigg). The larger islands of Skye and Arran, closer to the mainland, aren't usually included in the Inner Hebrides.

The western coastline, north of the central Lowlands, is deeply indented with dozens of long, deep sea lochs separated by rugged headlands and peninsulas. The westernmost tip of Scotland is Ardnamurchan Point. The profile of the east coast is generally smoother, although three sea lochs (called firths on this side of Scotland) – Dornoch, Moray and Forth – reach well inland.

GEOLOGY

It's not difficult to grasp the essentials of Scotland's extremely ancient and diverse geology if you think of the country as being divided into two major 'regions' – Highlands and Lowlands. Each region is sub-divided into two 'districts'. The divides being geological fault lines, all following a north-east to south-west trajectory.

The Highland Boundary Fault, separating the Highlands from the Lowlands, is one of the most striking features of the landscape (see the boxed text 'The Great Divide' on page 180).

Geologically, the Highlands is subdivided by the Moine Thrust (where one layer of rock was pushed over another), stretching from Skye's Sleat peninsula to Loch Eriboll on the north coast. To its west, Lewisian gneiss predominates – the most ancient rock in Scotland, formed between 1600 and 2900 million years ago. In the same area red, pebbly Torridonian sandstone was laid down by great rivers more than 5mi deep; subsequent erosion has created the characteristic isolated, tiered peaks. The Isle of Skye is quite different, with the awesome Black Cuillins of black gabbro (a volcanic rock), and the mountains, plateaus and spectacular coastal cliffs in the north formed by great lava flows. East of the Moine Thrust, the northern and central Highlands are dominated by schist and quartzite, metamorphic rocks that were originally sediments but converted by heat and pressure around 1000 million years ago. The great granite massifs of the Cairngorms pushed up beneath these rocks and were gradually exposed by erosion of the overlying material.

Between the Highland Boundary Fault and the Southern Upland Fault are the central Lowlands. The much younger rocks here – Carboniferous coal, mudstone and limestone (formed between 280 and 350 million years ago) – are of considerable economic importance. The deep red soil around the Firth of Forth, derived from old red sandstone, is valuable for agriculture. The many remnants of volcanic activity, also dating from the Carboniferous period, include volcano-like North Berwick Law and Arthur's Seat in Edinburgh. The Southern Upland Fault extends from just north of Stranraer to Cockburnspath on the east coast. Between there and the English border, the characteristic rounded mountains consist of sedimentary rocks formed when Scotland was separated from England by the 1000mi-wide Sea of Iapetus (450 million years ago). The Eildon Hills and the Cheviots, along the border, are the most obvious representatives of volcanic activity in the area.

Two major, land-transforming events wrought great changes on the rock structure. About 500 million years ago a prolonged phase of mountain building (the Caledonian orogeny) shoved, squashed and folded the rocks, altering (metamorphosing) them and creating ridges and mountains (several times higher than Ben Nevis), which were then worn down into less regular clusters of

Signs of a Glacial Past

Many of the world's finest walks are through landscapes that have been – or are being – substantially shaped by glaciers. As a glacier flows downhill under its weight of ice and snow it creates a distinctive collection of landforms, many of which are preserved once the ice has retreated (as it is doing in most of the world's ranges today) or vanished.

The most obvious is the *U-shaped valley* (1), gouged out by the glacier as it moves downhill, often with one or more bowl-shaped *corries* (2) at its head. Corries are found along high mountain ridges or at mountain passes or *cols* (3). Where an alpine glacier – which flows off the upper slopes and ridges of a mountain range – has joined a deeper, more substantial valley glacier, a dramatic *hanging valley* (4) is often the result. Hanging valleys and cirques commonly shelter hidden alpine lakes or *tarns* (5), such as those featured in several of the walks in this book. The thin ridge that separates adjacent glacial valleys is known as an *arête* (6).

As a glacier grinds its way forward it usually leaves long, *lateral moraine* (7) ridges along its course – mounds of debris either deposited along the flanks of the glacier or left by sub-ice streams within its heart (the latter, strictly, an *esker*). At the end – or snout – of a glacier is the *terminal moraine* (8), the point where the giant conveyor belt of ice drops its load of rocks and grit. Both high up in the hanging valleys and in the surrounding valleys and plains, *moraine lakes* (9) may form behind a dam of glacial rubble.

The plains that surround a glaciated range may feature a confusing variety of moraine ridges, mounds and outwash fans – material left by rivers flowing from the glaciers. Perched here and there may be an *erratic* (10), a rock carried far from its origin by the moving ice and left stranded when it melted.

mountains and hills. At least five eras of glaciation have occurred in Scotland during the past three million years, the most recent ending about 10,000 years ago. Much of the country was covered by glaciers and ice sheets; as they melted the courses of rivers were altered, deep lochs created, corries formed, and valleys widened and deepened. After the thaw and the lifting of the great weight of ice, the land rose; the previous shoreline can be identified in many raised beaches, notably on the west coast.

CLIMATE

'Varied' accurately describes the many moods of Scotland's cool temperate climate. The weather can change within a day and from one to the next. There are also wide variations over small distances; one glen may languish under cloud and drizzle, the next may be basking in sunshine. As some locals are wont to say, 'If you don't like the weather, come back this afternoon'.

Country-wide the driest months are May and June, but rain can be expected at any time. The west coast has markedly higher annual rainfall – between 150cm and 200cm, exposed as it is to moisture-laden winds and weather fronts from the Atlantic. The east is much drier with an average rainfall around 65cm. Violent storms are rare between May and August, but fairly commonplace in the Northern and Western Isles during winter (December to February).

Considering that the country lies well to the north (Edinburgh is on the same latitude as Moscow), you'd expect a cold climate. However, the prevailing south-westerly winds, warmed by the Gulf Stream, produce a relatively mild climate. Summer (June to August) temperatures average between 16°C and 19°C in the west and in the Highlands. During prolonged spells of warm southerly airflow, the thermometer can rise well into the 20s and temperatures around 30°C aren't unknown in the glens and central Lowlands.

Daytime winter temperatures below 0°C are not common on the east coast but are more likely inland, where snow can be expected at low levels between November and March (although these became noticeably sparser and less frequent in the 1990s). Winds from the north, north-east and east can be bitingly cold, and are usually associated with clear skies.

For more detail see the climate charts on the next page and Weather Information on page 76.

ECOLOGY & ENVIRONMENT

In many ways the history of forests reflects changing attitudes towards Scotland's natural environment. For centuries Caledonian woodlands were felled to provide building material and fuel, and to make way for grazing animals. During the late 18th and 19th centuries some far-sighted landowners, who realised what had been lost, planted native woodlands on their properties. After the foundation of the Forestry Commission in 1919, geometric conifer plantations were imposed on glens and foothills, providing jobs in rural areas but with scant regard for scenic beauty. Private landowners took advantage of tax concessions to establish plantations too. From the 1970s concern about the dwindling pockets of native woodland inspired replanting projects by Forestry Commission and conservation organisations, culminating in the ambitious Millennium Forest project to help restore native woodlands on hundreds of sites across Scotland. At the same time, Forest Enterprise (part of the Forestry Commission) initiated more sensitive management of conifer plantations by avoiding, as far as possible, unnaturally straight boundaries in harvesting and replanting.

The invasion of wind farms is more problematic. Small plantations of wind-powered generators to produce electricity inevitably occupy prominent locations on ridges and headlands, and often in hitherto 'unspoiled' areas (such as Windy Standard in the Galloway Hills). This seems to be a high, but perhaps necessary, price to pay for reducing dependence on fossil fuels.

Scotland's rocky landscape, fascinating to geologists and climbers alike, and admired for its rugged beauty, also represents an economic resource. The siting of new

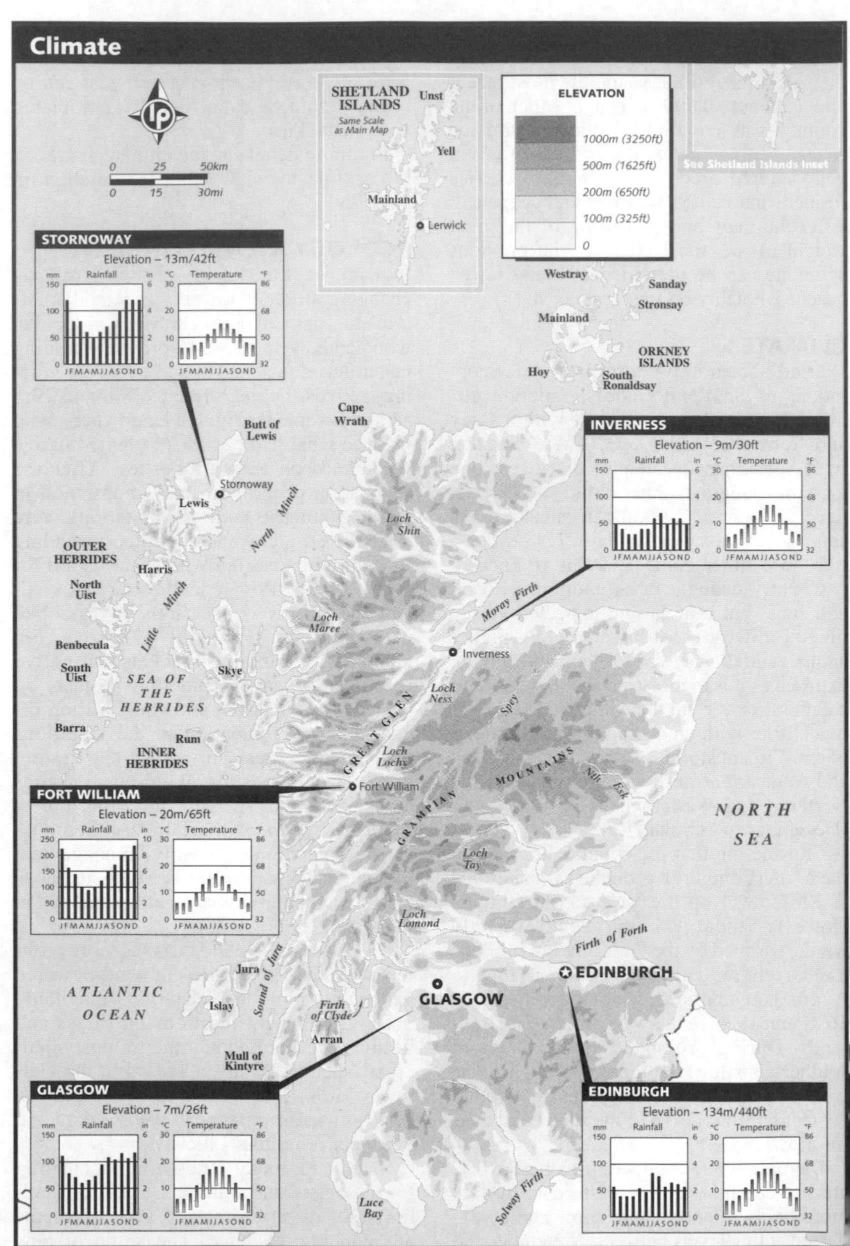
Climate
0 25 50km
0 15 30mi
SHETLAND ISLANDS
Same Scale as Main Map
Unst
Yell
Mainland
Lerwick
ELEVATION
1000m (3250ft)
500m (1625ft)
200m (650ft)
100m (325ft)
0
See Shetland Islands Inset
STORNOWAY
Elevation – 13m/42ft
mm Rainfall in
°C Temperature °F
JFMAMJJASOND
Westray
Sanday
Stronsay
Mainland
ORKNEY ISLANDS
Hoy
South Ronaldsay
Cape Wrath
Butt of Lewis
Stornoway
Lewis
North Minch
OUTER HEBRIDES
Harris
North Uist
Little Minch
Benbecula
South Uist
SEA OF THE HEBRIDES
Skye
Barra
Rum
INNER HEBRIDES
Loch Shin
Loch Maree
Moray Firth
Inverness
INVERNESS
Elevation – 9m/30ft
Loch Ness
Spey
GREAT GLEN
Loch Lochy
Fort William
GRAMPIAN MOUNTAINS
Nth Esk
FORT WILLIAM
Elevation – 20m/65ft
NORTH SEA
Loch Tay
Loch Lomond
Firth of Forth
EDINBURGH
GLASGOW
Jura
Sound of Jura
ATLANTIC OCEAN
Islay
Firth of Clyde
Arran
Mull of Kintyre
GLASGOW
Elevation – 7m/26ft
EDINBURGH
Elevation – 134m/440ft
Luce Bay
Solway Firth

quarries became much more controversial during the 1990s, and excavation companies now have to screen their activities and landscape the area when finished. An awesomely huge superquarry at Glensanda, beside lower Loch Linnhe, is less than obvious from almost anywhere except the island of Lismore. However, a proposed superquarry at Lingerbay, on the east coast of south Harris in the Western Isles, would have been visible from Skye and the mainland. This plan, involving the removal of an entire mountain, Roineabhal, divided the community. After years of investigation and inquiry, the Scottish Executive (the senior decision-making body in the Scottish parliamentary system) took a deep breath and vetoed it in 2000.

Despite massive destruction since the mid-19th century, Scotland still has more lowland raised peatland (mounds of peat sitting in basins of old lakes in lowland areas) than any other European Union (EU) country. Much of the surviving peatland is in poor condition as a result of drainage, forestry, peat extraction and other developments. Peatland is of immense importance for wildlife conservation and as an archaeological resource. Although more than 20 peatland reserves enjoyed the protection of Special Area of Conservation status by 2000, the Scottish Wildlife Trust (which manages several of the peatland reserves; see page 44) led the way in campaigning for a doubling of this number to prevent further exploitation.

For ways you can help preserve Scotland's natural environment, see Responsible Walking on page 64.

Deer Management

Management of Scotland's wild deer population is a more organised, and more ecologically and economically important undertaking than is sometimes appreciated. The 750,000-strong population comprises four species – red, roe, sika and fallow. Red deer are the biggest, most numerous and have the greatest impact. Landowners need to ensure that a balance is maintained between deer numbers and their habitat, so they have enough to eat and don't wreak havoc on vegetation by overgrazing.

The Deer Commission for Scotland (the government agency responsible for deer) has promoted the setting up of Deer Management Groups – voluntary groups of landowners covering areas with distinct deer herds – in most parts of the country. Regular deer censuses taken by each group and the commission provide the basis for the annual cull, when older and unhealthy animals are shot by skilled and experienced professional stalkers using high-velocity rifles. The sport of deer stalking, an important income-earner for estates and local communities, is integrated into the annual cull.

During the stalking season (August to October) estates request that walkers avoid areas where stalking is taking place to ensure the orderly conduct of the activity and for their own safety. Deer Management Groups provide detailed information on-site about their activities and usually specify preferred walking routes. This is also available through the Hillphones service (for details and local contact numbers, log on to the Scottish Natural Heritage Web site **W** www.snh.org.uk or pick up a leaflet at Tourist Information Centres and outdoor gear shops) or similar arrangements in the absence of Deer Management Groups. Conservation organisations such as the National Trust for Scotland and Scottish Natural Heritage may or may not carry out stalking on their land and generally take a different approach to access by walkers.

However, not all estates belong to Deer Management Groups and some are not very cooperative. It's worth remembering that access along rights of way remains open at all times, shooting isn't permitted on Sunday and statutory close seasons (when shooting is illegal) apply to all deer species in Scotland. For red deer these are 21 October to 30 June (stags) and 16 February to 20 October (hinds). For more detailed information, contact the Deer Commission (☎ 01463-231751, **W** www.dcs.gov.uk), 82 Fairfield Rd, Inverness IV3 2HZ.

Conservation

Conservation organisations in Scotland can be put into three broad groups – landowning, nonlandowning and government agencies.

Members in the first group can participate in the practical conservation work coordinated by their organisation – path repair, tree planting and so on. Throughout Scotland there are also many similar, but smaller, community organisations, giving people the chance to do something positive for nature conservation close to home.

Foremost in the second group are the Mountaineering Council of Scotland and the Ramblers' Association Scotland (see under Useful Organisations on page 67), focusing more on issues of specific concern to walkers (and climbers). The mountaineering council also has a strong commitment to education and training, especially regarding mountain safety.

In the third group, the leading conservation agency is Scottish Natural Heritage, Forest Enterprise is particularly committed to the conservation of Caledonian forests, and the Deer Commission for Scotland promotes a balanced approach to wild deer management.

When controversial issues arise, such as the construction of the Cairngorm funicular (see the boxed text 'A Cairngorm Funicular – Environmental Vandalism?' on page 218), protest by the organisations usually involves lobbying politicians and decision-makers directly or through correspondence, letters to the press, public meetings to arouse awareness and circulating petitions. Rarely do on-site demonstrations happen, although environmental activism of this nature isn't unknown in Scotland. Members of these organisations display exceptional generosity and energy in fund-raising campaigns, such as those by the John Muir Trust for the purchase of new properties, or the National Trust for Scotland's long-term 'Sole Trading' appeal to support maintenance and repair of upland footpaths.

Two historic issues – access and land ownership – will probably continue to occupy conservation organisations and concerned individuals for some time. Factors helping to reduce controversy over access to many popular walking areas include the 1996 Concordat on Access to Scotland's Hills and Mountains (see Access under Responsible Walking on page 64), coordinated deer management, increased ownership of wild lands by the National Trust for Scotland and John Muir Trust in particular, and clear definition of rights of way (see History of Walking on page 18). However, the concordat is not recognised by some uncooperative and even belligerent landowners, and access to increasingly popular urban fringe areas is not always clear-cut. At the Scottish Parliament's inception in 1999, expectations were that legislation would be passed defining rights and responsibilities of those seeking and providing access to the countryside. In February 2001 this took a small step closer to reality with the publication of a draft Land Reform Bill concerning access and draft Scottish Outdoor Access Code by the Scottish Executive (see Access under Responsible Walking on page 64).

The issue of land ownership is based on a strange anachronism. On the one hand, at the official or legal level, land is treated as a commodity to be bought and sold at will. One observer has described this as 'wild west capitalism', noting that elsewhere in Europe land is regarded as a precious resource. On the other hand, an increasing number of people in Scotland passionately oppose this view, inspired by a succession of events during the 1990s, both welcome and reviled. On the positive side, purchases by community groups have returned the land to the people, famously in Assynt (Sutherland) and the Isle of Eigg, after decades of neglect. On the negative side, estates with outstanding natural value have eluded conservation organisations, notably Glen Feshie. While the John Muir Trust did acquire Ben Nevis, questions were raised about the price paid – regarded by some as inflated. The supreme travesty was the attempt (still not successful in early 2001) to sell the Black Cuillin on the Isle of Skye. As a local lass said, 'How can someone sell a mountain?' (See also the boxed texts 'The

Continued on page 44

Fauna & Flora of Scotland

Scotland has a very diverse natural heritage, including 1117 species of native terrestrial plant, more than 50 species of mammal, amphibian and reptile, and 450 species of bird. Habitats range from the rocky coast to freshwater lochs, from pine woods to heather moors and up to the alpine-arctic mountain plateaus. It's not difficult to see many of the species when you're out walking. There are also many reserves with nature trails and interpretive signs – an enjoyable way to broaden your knowledge.

In this section, brief descriptions are provided for the species you are most likely to see on the walks described in this book. A wealth of informative books is available to help with identification; a selection is given under Books on page 74.

Title page: Captivating and elusive, the otter pauses for a portrait.
Photograph by Chris Mellor.
Title page inset: The delicate bloom of a wood anemone.
Photograph by Richard Cummins.

FAUNA

MAMMALS

Red Deer The largest land mammal in the country, the red deer *Cervus elaphus* (*fiadh* in Gaelic) stag stands to 1.3m high and can weigh up to 126kg. Antler growth is confined to the stags, which are known by the number of points carried – 14 is an Imperial. For most of the year stags and hinds live separately. During the mating season, known as the rut, the primeval roaring of the stags as they gather their harems is, perhaps, the most stirring sound to be heard in the Scottish wilds. Red deer feed on heather, berries, grass and moss. They can wreak havoc in woodlands, stripping bark and grazing on saplings. See the boxed text 'Deer Management' on page 25.

CHRISTINE COSTE

Red deer

Roe Deer The roe deer *Capreolus capreolus (earba)* is much smaller and lighter than the red, and spends much of its time grazing in woodlands. In summer its coat is reddish-brown, in winter it becomes greyish. Almost unknown on the islands, the roe is largely confined to the Highlands. It is much less sought after during the stalking season than the larger red deer.

MARTIN MOOS

Roe deer

Mountain Hare The mountain (or blue) hare *Lepus timidus (maigheach)* is one of only two mammals in Scotland that changes colour to white in winter. During summer its coat is deep brown with a bluish tinge and the ear tips are black. The white coat begins to appear from October as the brown one moults; the transformation is complete by December. The summer garb returns between March and May. The mountain hare is quite common in upland areas between 300m and 750m (and occasionally up to 1300m), and on some Hebridean islands, Hoy in Orkney and in Shetland. During winter they move up and down in tune with the weather and snowfall, always seeking the best shelter and most available food – heather, bog cotton and bark.

RICHARD MILLS

Hedgehog

Hedgehog The hedgehog *Erinaceus europaeus (cràineag)* prefers open areas, rough pastures and the edges of tall forests, in most mainland areas, on the Isle of Skye, and in Orkney and Shetland Islands. It's most active at night in search of its varied diet, ranging from mice to lizards, frogs, earthworms and even adders (although it isn't immune to their venom). The hedgehog can curl into a tight ball, making the best use of its sharp quills as a defence against its main enemies, dogs and foxes.

RICHARD MILLS

Pine marten

Pine Marten A forest dweller, the pine marten *Martes martes (taghan)* was once common throughout Scotland but disappeared from many areas as forests were felled. During the past 20 or 30 years it has made a comeback from its last stronghold in the north-west, and has been slowly spreading southward. Measuring almost 1m in overall length, it weighs up to 1.6kg. It varies in colour from chestnut to almost black and has a creamy or orange throat patch. It feeds on small rodents and birds, insects, fish and wild berries – its berry-studded droppings are a tell-tale sign of its presence in woodlands. It's most active at night, so daytime sightings are largely a matter of luck.

Otter

Otter The elusive, captivating otter *Lutra lutra (dòbhran)* is equally at home in freshwater and the sea. Although it spends most of its time in the water and feeds on fish, it does hunt on land, seeking rabbits and small rodents. The male (or dog) reaches about 1.3m in length, more than half of which is tail, and weighs around 11.25kg. With a superbly streamlined, dark brown body, it's beautifully agile in the water. The otter's strongholds are the rocky west coast and the Western Isles.

Red Squirrel Once common in most parts of Scotland, the red squirrel *Sciurus vulgaris (feòrag)* is now mainly confined to the Highlands (see Endangered Species on page 42). They're at home in coniferous forests, the source of their favourite food, which is pine cone seeds, although they will also grab the eggs and chicks of small birds. They are reddish-brown almost all over with darker, bushy tails, which they use when climbing, swimming and as blankets when sleeping. The drey, or nest, is built quite high in a tree, an oval-shaped shelter of twigs lined with moss, leaves and grass, but with no obvious entrance. The young are independent enough to leave its protection briefly after four or five weeks.

MARINE MAMMALS

Dolphins, porpoises, several species of whale and even the leatherback turtle live in or move through the waters off Scotland's coasts. Among the seals, two species are particularly easy to see during the coast walks described in this book.

Common Seal Belying its name, the common seal *Phoca vitulina* (*ròn* in Gaelic) isn't as common as its relative the grey seal. It's thought that the common seal population is around 27,000 compared with 90,000 greys. Both male and female adults have dark grey backs and light grey undersides, with black spots all over. They can be distinguished from the greys by their blunt noses and slanting eyes. Found all around the Scottish coast, common seals tend to congregate in waters off Shetland and the Western Isles during summer. The pups are born in the water or on wave-washed rocks and can swim immediately, although they are constantly shepherded by their mothers.

Grey Seal The grey seal *Halichoerus grypus (ròn)* is the largest wild animal in Scotland. The bulls are three times heavier than a decent-sized red deer stag and can measure up to 2.3m in length. They inhabit the waters off the east and west coasts, but during the summer breeding season gather on the remote islands of St Kilda, the Monach Isles off North Uist and on North Rona, north of the Western Isles. The males' pointed noses and the absence of spots on the fur are the main features distinguishing them from common seals. They also differ in coming ashore to mate and breed.

Common seal

REPTILES

Only three reptiles are native to Scotland. The common lizard and the slow worm are harmless; only the adder is poisonous.

Adder The adder *Vipera berus (nathair)* is coppery brown in colour with a dark zigzag pattern along its back. At 60cm the female is slightly longer than the male, whose colouring is more sharply defined. The adder's bite is poisonous but it's highly unlikely to be fatal. They are very excitable and more likely to escape from your presence than to attack. Adders are found throughout mainland Scotland but not in the Northern or Western Isles.

BIRDS

More than 450 species of bird have been recorded in Scotland, of which 175 are regular breeders and 19 breed in Scotland only. Several species are threatened and are the subjects of the Species Action Programme (see Endangered Species on page 42).

DAVID TIPLING

Capercaillie

Buzzard The buzzard *Buteo buteo* (*clamhan* in Gaelic) has a trade-mark call – a rather shrill, although sad-sounding mewing, frequently uttered as it soars above fields and moors with its broad wings spread in a shallow 'V' and the tail spread. It can often be seen close-up, perched on a fence post where its sandy coloured chest, light brown head and darker back and distinctive yellow feet are clearly visible. It is common throughout mainland Scotland.

Capercaillie The capercaillie *Tetrao urogallus (capall-coille)* lives in pine forests in the eastern Highlands. About the size of a turkey, the male is predominantly brownish-black, with a red band above the eye and a reddish breast. The female is quite different, speckled brown and tan, and similar to a red or black grouse. The call could be described as a 'series of accelerating clicks, ending with a cork-pulling pop'. 'Capers' come together for displays of strutting and posturing. During the breeding season males have been known to attack people and even vehicles.

Cormorant

Cormorant In coastal waters anywhere in Scotland and around estuaries, there's no mistaking the cormorant *Phalacrocorax carbo (sgarbh)* sitting on a rock or buoy with its wings bent, hung out to dry. Dark brown to black in colour, its white lower face and larger size marks it out from the smaller shag. They keep a low profile when swimming and dive frequently to satisfy their huge appetite for fish.

RICHARD MILLS
Curlew

Curlew The curlew *Numenius arquata (guilbneach)* ranges widely between farmland, foothills, moors and mud flats, in most parts of the country. Its long, curved bill and distinctive 'cur-lee' call make identification easy. It congregates in flocks in coastal areas but is usually seen in smaller groups inland. The brownish plumage is streaked with darker markings. Widespread throughout Scotland, it's particularly fond of Orkney in winter where the relatively mild climate enables it to feed easily enough on cultivated ground.

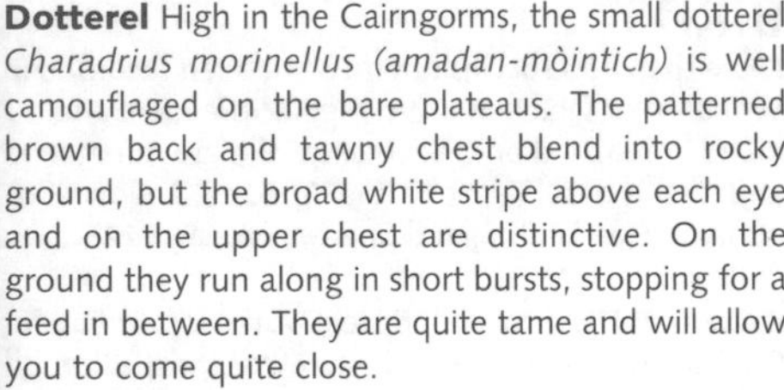

Dotterel High in the Cairngorms, the small dotterel *Charadrius morinellus (amadan-mòintich)* is well camouflaged on the bare plateaus. The patterned brown back and tawny chest blend into rocky ground, but the broad white stripe above each eye and on the upper chest are distinctive. On the ground they run along in short bursts, stopping for a feed in between. They are quite tame and will allow you to come quite close.

JOHN HAY
Golden eagle

Golden Eagle The largest resident seen in Scottish skies, the golden eagle *Aquila chrysaëtos (iolaire)* stands nearly 1m high. In flight its very broad wings, splayed at the edges and with white tapering bands, and the wedge-shaped tail are distinctive. The golden eagle's plumage is uniformly chocolate-brown. It feeds on carrion, mountain hares, grouse, ptarmigan and young deer (in season). Once persecuted and hunted nearly to extinction, the golden eagle is now a protected species and has made a comeback in the Highlands and islands.

Fulmar Stiff-winged in flight, the fulmar *Fulmarus glacialis (fulmair)* is commonly seen around coastal cliffs and skimming the sea's surface. It has distinctive tube-like nostrils, a black eye patch, grey wings, and white head and chest. At rest on the cliffs where they nest, they cackle noisily to each other.

Gannet

Gannet Diving gannets *Sula bassana (sùlaire)* are one of the more spectacular sights from coastal cliff tops. The bird folds its wings and plunges, torpedo-like, into the sea wherever it spots a shoal of fish. Otherwise, its

DAVID TIPLING

Grey heron

pure white plumage, the yellow head and nape, and black wing tips are sure identifiers. They nest on northern and western islands, and on Bass Rock (near Edinburgh) and Ailsa Craig (south of Arran).

Red Grouse This archetypical game bird is still much sought-after by hunters, especially on the 'Glorious Twelfth' in August, at the start of the hunting season. The red grouse *Lagopus lagopus (coileach-fraoich)* spends most of its time in heather moorland where its rufous, somewhat mottled plumage provides good camouflage. They can give you quite a fright as they take off with a clatter of feathers and loud 'go-bak, go-bak' squawks.

Grey Heron The grey heron *Ardea cinerea (corra-ghritheach)* is often seen standing silently (on one leg) near river banks and loch shores. Its elongated neck is usually retracted in flight, while its long legs trail behind. Predominantly grey in colour, its neck and chest are white. The sharp, dagger-like beak is well designed for spearing eels, fish and frogs.

Oystercatcher Possibly the most eye-catching of the waders, the oystercatcher *Haematopus ostralegus (gille-brighde)* has coal black upper parts, white underneath, and trademark red eye and pointed red bill. It spends most of its time on the coast, near rivers and on loch shores, and is also seen in fields and moorland edges. In groups they make a lot of noise wherever they are – their loud 'kleep' is often kept up well into the night.

Golden Plover An integral feature of walks across heather moorland is the rippling 'tlooee' calls of the golden plover *Pluvialis apricaria (feadag)*. It is well camouflaged, with golden-brown spangled upper parts and black chest. The plover's flight is fast and direct and it glides in to land; it's likely to be seen almost anywhere in the uplands.

Ptarmigan The ptarmigan *Lagopus mutus (tàrmachan)* is unique in that it changes plumage three times during each year, from the mottled brown of midsummer, through autumn greys, to winter white. It lives in the mountains year-round, perhaps moving down slightly in extreme conditions. The harsh rattling croak as they take off is unforgettable.

RAY TIPPER

Golden plover

Puffin Perhaps the most unusual-looking bird in Scotland, the puffin *Fratercula arctica (fachach)* has a vividly coloured, parrot-like beak and white cheeks. It stands bolt upright and waddles, rather than walks, about, but flies strongly and speedily. They're most numerous in the Northern Isles, where they congregate in colonies between April and July.

RICHARD MILLS

Puffin

Great Skua Notorious for dive-bombing intruders during the breeding season, the great skua *Stercorarius skua* (*fàsgadan*; bonxie in Shetland) spends the summer in the Northern Isles and moves south in late summer. It's mainly dark brown in colour with obvious white wing patches.

FLORA

Of the 11,000 plants of all groups found in Scotland and the immediately surrounding sea, 1117 species are classed as native terrestrial plants. The nine endemic species include the Scottish primrose. Scotland is particularly important botanically for its range and abundance of mountain, northern woodland and aquatic plants. Of the 76 species restricted to Scotland, 45 are mountain plants. Native pine woods are particularly important for their specialised flora and, on a European scale, Scotland's extensive springtime bluebell displays and the late summer flowering of heathers are unusual.

SHRUBS & FLOWERS

Bog Asphodel Boggy areas on the moors are enlivened in summer by clumps of the yellow-flowering bog asphodel *Narthecium ossifragum* (*bliochan*, meaning 'milk plant'). In spring the underground stems sprout narrow, stiff leaves, from which a stem grows to bear the spike of flowers.

Wood Anemone Before the woodland trees are fully in leaf in spring, the ground is carpeted with several species of wild flower, including the wood anemone *Anemone nemorosa*. Its Gaelic name *flùr na gaoithe*, meaning 'flower of the wind', has the same descriptive power as anemone, which in turn comes from the Greek word for wind, *anemos*. The frail stem rises from a cluster of three dark green, deeply notched leaves and is topped by a single white or pinkish flower, which trembles in the slightest breeze.

Wood anemone

Scotland's Useful Plants: From Beer to Midge Repellent

For thousands of years people made good use of the plants growing about them as food, fuel, medicine, building material and tools. This knowledge and the associated skills are being preserved in many ways – small industries producing beer, midge repellent, plants for cleaning polluted water, timber products from native trees and many more.

Fraoch is a superb, heather-based beer (widely available in Scotland and beyond), maintaining a tradition possibly dating back to prehistoric times. Originally barley and hops seem to have been absent, and both the *Calluna* and *Erica* genera of heather were used. The usual brewing ingredients were introduced later.

Sacrilege to some, perhaps, but various berries have been used to flavour whisky. Red rowan berries impart an acidic tang and, if you want sweetness, go for blaeberries or sloes.

Chamomile is well known as a soothing tea. Scottish alternatives include thistles and tansy, the latter traditionally recommended for 'hysterics arising from suppressions' in women. Wood sorrel makes a bitter although refreshing tea, good for relieving heat stroke, and is a tasty addition to green salads.

Maintaining another tradition, bog myrtle is used as a preservative in heather ales. The insect-repelling properties of its aromatic oils have been used in an effective midge repellent.

Based at Edinburgh's Royal Botanic Garden, Flora Celtica-Scotland 2000 (☎ 0131-552 7171, fax 248 2901) is a project aiming to record and promote the knowledge and use of native Scottish plants. Its Web site **W** www.rbge.org.uk/research/celtica is a fascinating, ever-growing source of information.

Blaeberry Beyond the limit of heather growth in moorlands, blaeberry *Vaccinium myrtilis* is the most common plant. It grows to about 60cm with twisted stems carrying small bright green leaves. From the tiny, greenish-red flowers, bluey-purple berries develop, which are edible and quite tasty – although it would take ages to gather even a cupful. The first part of the Gaelic name *caora-mhithe* means 'berry' but the meaning of *mhithe* is unknown.

Broom

Scottish Bluebell This fairly rare plant is found in machair and on rock ledges in most parts of the country. The bluebell *Campanula rotundiflora* has small leaves at the base of a longish, slender stem and the blue bell-shaped flowers appear in late summer. The Gaelic name *currac cuthaige* means 'cuckoo's cap'.

Broom A member of the pea family, broom *Cytisus scoparius* grows in dense bushes to 2m high, most commonly on sandy soils. It has small leaves on the profuse twigs and from early summer is covered with masses of golden-yellow flowers. These develop into black pods, which burst open with a surprisingly loud 'snap' when ripe. It's not known what the Gaelic name *bealaidh* originally meant.

Cotton Grass During summer many small ponds in the moorlands look as though they're holding onto the remnants of a snowfall – these white patches are the balls of white hair on the fruit of the cotton grass *Eriophorum angustifolium (canach)*, which grows in the ponds. From spreading underground stems, grass-like leaves emerge and brownish-green flowers appear at the end of long stems, developing into the cotton balls.

Cowberry Common on the moors and in woodlands of the Highlands and Borders, cowberry *Vaccinium vitis-idaea* (*lus nam braoileag*, meaning 'plant of the berries') has roughly oval, dark green leathery leaves. The pinkish-white, bell-shaped flowers produce edible but bitter red berries. It's easy to confuse the cowberry with the cranberry *Vaccinium oxycoccus*, but the latter has a more creeping habit and smaller narrower leaves; its red berries are more tasty.

Crowberry On mountain plateaus and high rocky moors, crowberry *Empetrum nigrum* forms dense mats of stems covered with small, needle-like leaves. They almost hide the tiny purplish flowers and then the round, black, bitter-tasting berry. Perhaps it's not surprising that the Gaelic name *lus na feannaig* means 'crow's plant'.

RICHARD MILLS
Gorse and heather

Gorse Better known as whin in Scotland, prickly gorse *Ulex europaeus* grows widely on rough ground and often infests derelict grazing fields. Its golden-yellow flowers appear among the long, sharp spines in almost any month, but mainly from early spring, and exude an intense almond scent. The brown pods explode loudly during dry weather. The Gaelic name *conasg* comes from the word for a quarrel or wrangle.

Cross-leaved Heath This is the heather most likely to be seen in boggy ground. Cross-leaved heath *Erica tetralix* has greyish, hairy needle-like leaves arranged in cross-shaped groups on the stems. Its slightly bell-shaped pale pink flowers are larger than those of the other two heathers. In Gaelic it's known as *fraoch frangach*, meaning 'French heather'.

NANCY FREY
Cross-leaved heath

Heather The archetypical symbol of Scotland, heather *Calluna vulgaris* (also known as ling) grows in pine woods and on moorland. The bushy shrub can grow to 1m high, if the moor isn't periodically burnt to promote new growth for grouse to feed on. Its stems have many rows of tiny, needle-like leaves and the spikes of flowers turn the moors deep pinkish-purple or mauve during August and September. It's not known where the Gaelic name *fraoch* comes from.

Bell Heather Bell heather *Erica cinerea* can be distinguished from its relations by the larger, darker reddish flowers. The leaf-covered stems are similar in appearance. Bell heather is usually the first to bloom, during July.

Wild Hyacinth Commonly called bluebell, the wild hyacinth *Hyacinthoides non-scripta* (*bròg na cuthaig*, meaning 'cuckoo's shoe') carpets woodlands in most areas during early spring. Its stalks rise from a cluster of long, glossy leaves and bear several small, violet-blue, bell-shaped flowers.

GRANT DIXON
Heather and Scots pine cones

Juniper A member of the cypress family, common juniper *Juniperus communis (aiteann)* is a slow-growing low shrub, which forms dense thickets in pine woodlands and on rocky ground. It's not unusual for juniper bushes to pass the 100-year-old mark. The needle-like leaves are usually light grey-green and, when crushed, exude an apple perfume. The fruit ripens to dark blue or black, which is crushed and used to make gin.

Bog Myrtle Bog myrtle *Myrica gale* is common throughout boglands and heaths. It creeps across the ground, the stems bearing small greyish-green leaves, which, when crushed, have a distinctly resinous aroma. Its flowers, properly called catkins (spikes of tiny flowers), actually appear before the leaves develop and are reddish-brown. (See the boxed text 'Scotland's Useful Plants' on page 35.)

Primrose Another colourful sight in woodlands everywhere, the yellow-flowering primrose *Primula vulgaris* is also found in grassy areas and even on sea cliffs. The flowers form on long furry stems, emerging from a bunch of elongated, crinkly leaves. The Scottish primrose *Primula scotica* is confined to the north coast and Orkney, and has purple, yellow-eyed flowers (see Endangered Species on page 42).

Round-leaved Sundew Sundews make a meal of insects that land on their leaves, attracted by sweet juice. The sundews trap the insects with tiny, flexible hairs and then quickly swallow them. The species you're most likely to see, in bogs and on soggy peat, is round-leaved sundew *Drosera rotundifolia*. The rounded, hairy leaves on the ends of short stalks fan out from the base of a tall stalk, on which tiny white flowers may appear. Its Gaelic name *lus na feàrnaich* means 'plant of the alder'. The great sundew *Drosera longifolia* has longer, narrower leaves.

Creeping Thistle It's not known for sure which of the thistle species is the Scottish emblem – they look much the same to the nonbotanist. Creeping thistle *Cirsium arvense* is found in fields, and beside roads and paths. The prickly leaves are dull green and lobed. The purplish flower heads sit on top of a bulbous base, which is covered with spiny bracts (leaflets). The spear thistle *Cirsium vulgare* has a spiny stem and more-pointed leaves, while the marsh thistle *Cirsium palustre* is mainly found in damp places, and has very small leaves and a spine-laden stem. The Gaelic for thistle is *fòthannan* for some species, *cluaran* for others.

RICHARD CUMMINS

Thrift

Thrift A remarkably hardy plant, thrift *Armeria maritima* is common on rocky coasts (hence its other name 'sea pink') and is also found on high plateaus far from the sea. The narrow, greyish-green leaves form a thick pad from which the stalk grows, topped with a cluster of small whitish, pink or mauve flowers. The picturesque Gaelic name *neòinean cladaich* means 'shore daisy'.

GRANT DIXON

Birch

TREES

Alder The alder *Alnus glutinosa (feàrna* in Gaelic) is one of the most common trees along the banks of watercourses. Reaching a height of about 20m, it has square-plated (arranged in square sections), grey-brown bark with egg-shaped leaves flattened across the top. The foliage is slightly shiny and very dark green, and hangs onto the tree until late autumn. It sprouts distinctive male catkins up to 5cm long.

Birch The silver birch *Betula pendula (beithe)* is one of the most widespread deciduous trees, often growing with oak and rowan. A particularly beautiful tree, its branchlets become long and drooping, bearing shiny green, triangular leaves with notched edges. The bark is white with black splotches. For successful regeneration, young birch need to be protected from hungry deer – the tree takes about 10 years to reach a safe height. The sturdy tree can then survive extremes of cold and is drought-resistant. The sap can be used to make an unusual, very dry white wine.

Hazel The common hazel *Corylus avellana (calltainn)* produces small, tasty nuts, a handy source of wild food from the woodlands if you have time to collect a handful in autumn. A comparatively small tree, it is widespread on most soils. The dark green, hairy leaves are roughly oval in shape and have a sharp point.

NICHOLAS REISS

Oak

Holly Its scarlet fruit, adorning the tree during winter and spring, make identification of the holly *Ilex aquifolium (cuileann)* easy. The leaves are distinctive too – glossy, dark green and edged with sharp spines (spikes). The fruit can be an important source of food for small birds during winter. Holly is most likely to be found in oak and beech woods throughout the country, except in the far north.

Oak Both sessile oak *Quercus petraea* and English oak *Quercus robur* are found in Scotland. The Gaelic name *darach* is quite common in place names as 'darroch'; the oak was sacred to the pagan Celts and was closely associated with *doire* (woodland) generally. The two species are similar in appearance, with the characteristic lobed leaves and grey, cracked bark. The main distinguishing feature is the acorn (fruit); it grows directly on the shoot in the sessile oak but on a stem in the English oak. The sessile oak has a more open appearance, while the English oak's foliage is more bunched. Oaks can survive for up to 800 years.

Scots Pine Once widespread throughout Scotland, the Scots pine *Pinus silvestris (giuthas)* is a superb-looking tree. Confined largely to the Highlands, it reaches a height of 35m and usually lives to about 250 years. The dark-coloured bark is deeply cracked but, on the branches, is a distinctive orange-brown or pink. The dull, grey-brown cone is roughly oval with a marked point, and the leaves are dark glossy green. (For more information see the boxed texts 'Scots Pine' on page 316 and 'Caledonian Woodland Restored' on page 257.)

GARETH McCORMACK

Scots pine

GARETH McCORMACK

Rowan

Rowan The red-berried rowan *Sorbus aucuparia (caorann)* is firmly entrenched in Gaelic folklore as a charm against witchcraft. The belief that to fell a rowan brings bad luck to the wielder of the axe is far from extinct. Rowans were traditionally grown by the front door to ensure that evil spirits did not enter the house. It's a very hardy tree – no other grows at a higher altitude than the rowan's upper limit of 1000m. Masses of white flowers appear in May or June and the fruit usually starts to colour in September, when it is raided by birds and, in the wild, by pine martens.

Yew The common yew *Taxus baccata* is often seen growing in burial grounds, as well as in the wild. These magnificent trees can survive to a great age (see the boxed text 'The Fortingall Yew' on page 165) and are the longest-living trees in the country. Up to 25m high, they are untidily conical in profile and have dark green, pointed leaves arranged around stiff shoots. There are separate male and female trees, both of which have flowers. Although of the same class of plants as pines, they aren't true pines as the seed is contained inside an aril (similar to a berry) rather than on a cone. The Gaelic name *iubhar* can be traced back to the use of yew sap to poison arrowheads.

ENDANGERED SPECIES

Many hundreds of species of plant and animal are at some degree of risk of extinction in Scotland. More than 170 species are legally protected under the Wildlife and Countryside Act 1981 but mere words on paper don't necessarily guarantee real-life achievements. In an ideal world, it would be possible to ensure the survival of all endangered species by habitat management and removal of threats such as overgrazing, but resources for such work are limited.

Scottish Natural Heritage aims to ensure survival of a good proportion of the threatened species through the Species Action Programme. This is derived from *Biodiversity: the UK Action Plan*, the UK government's means of carrying out its responsibilities under the United Nations Convention on the Conservation of Biological Diversity. Launched in 1995, the program 'provides a coordinated approach to the recovering of our priority species' and is led by Scottish Natural Heritage, in partnership with other agencies, voluntary conservation bodies and individuals. Both the United Nations and Scottish Natural Heritage's own criteria have guided selection of species to benefit from the program's action plans. The key criteria are official recognition of species as being threatened, endangered or vulnerable; that the program should take in a wide range of species, from mosses to mammals; that the threat should be significant; that the chances of recovery should be realistic; and that the species should have the potential to arouse interest and support of nonspecialists. More than 60 plans have been prepared, of which Scottish Natural Heritage is the lead partner in about 20. The target is to prepare more than 200 plans.

Among the mammals, the **red squirrel** is classed as threatened and declining. The American grey squirrel is the recognised threat, although it's not yet known exactly why. Measures to protect the red squirrel include supplementary feeding and translocation (shifting house), as well as control of the American greys.

RICHARD MILLS

Red squirrel

The **corncrake** *Crex crex* (*trèan-ri-trèan* in Gaelic) is classed as globally threatened. A brownish, hen-sized bird, best identified by its rasping call, it is resident almost exclusively in the Western Isles and its numbers have declined drastically as intensive farming

RICHARD MILLS

Corncrake

methods have replaced traditional ways. Its ideal habitat is the hayfield with nearby dense clumps of iris and reed beds. In partnership with the Royal Society for the Protection of Birds and the Scottish Crofters' Union, Scottish Natural Heritage launched the Corncrake Incentive Scheme in 1998. Crofters are paid to delay mowing hay and silage fields until at least 1 August, by when corncrakes have finished nesting, and to mow from the centre of the field outwards, thus helping to ensure the survival of the species. Early results suggest this approach can be successful.

The magnificent **red kite** *Milvus milvus (clamhan gobhlach)* is internationally threatened and was persecuted to extinction in Scotland. A reintroduction program was launched in 1989 with birds from Sweden and was immediately successful; 26 young were produced by 15 pairs in 1995. Another 20 pairs were released in 1999. Red kites live in woodland and open country and can be identified by their mewing call (similar to a buzzard), deeply forked tail, russet plumage and white wing patches.

The tiny **Scottish primrose** (see page 38) is found only on the northern coastal fringe and on some of the Orkney islands, and is endemic (found nowhere else in the world). The Scottish primrose does best in short-cropped fields, rather than among taller plants, and depends on seed dispersal for its survival. Measures to ensure its survival include identifying areas where it is relatively prolific, and encouraging field management measures to maintain suitable levels of grazing and crop height.

Other species involved in the program include the white-tailed (or sea) eagle, the European beaver (the controversial subject of a proposed reintroduction scheme), sticky catchfly (an insect-catching plant), twinflower (a fragile plant of the pine woodlands), alpine sow-thistle (confined to four sites in the eastern Cairngorms), oblong woodsia (a tiny fern of the high mountains), marine turtles and especially the leatherback turtle (a summer visitor to Scottish waters), and the northern brown argus butterfly.

Scottish Natural Heritage has produced a set of fact sheets, Species Action Programme, which, although dated by 2000, still provide good background information. The set is available via the organisation's Web site (W www.snh.org.uk) or from the publications section (☎ 01738-444177).

Continued from page 26

John Muir Trust' on page 197, 'Conservation on Skye' on page 276, 'Black Cuillin for Sale' on page 278 and 'Sale of An Teallach' on page 303.)

Following are Scotland's main nature conservation organisations:

Association for the Protection of Rural Scotland (☎ 0131-225 7012, fax 225 6592) 483 Lawnmarket, Edinburgh EH1 2NT. The association is a long-standing, low-profile champion of Scotland's countryside, and works mainly as a lobby group among local, regional and national government agencies. It is particularly concerned with the continuing loss of countryside to housing and the intrusion of wind farms.

John Muir Trust (☎ 0131-554 0114, fax 555 2112, W www.jmt.org) 41 Commercial St, Edinburgh EH6 6JD. Established in 1983 and perpetuating the memory of Scots-born US national parks pioneer John Muir, the trust acquires and sensitively manages wild areas, repairs damage, sustainably conserves the land and protects the spiritual qualities of wilderness. The trust owns Sandwood, Knoydart, Torrin & Strathaird, Schiehallion and Ben Nevis Estates. Members (numbering 6650 early in 2000) play an active part in estate management – tree planting, path repair, acorn collecting, drystone dyke building etc.

National Trust for Scotland (☎ 0131-243 9300, fax 243 9301, W www.nts.org.uk) 28 Charlotte Square, Edinburgh EH2 4ET. The trust was founded in 1931 to 'act as guardian of the nation's magnificent architectural, scenic and historic treasures'. It is now Scotland's largest conservation charity, with more than 250,000 members, and 185,000 acres of land and more than 100 buildings in its care. Its major landholdings are the Brodick (Isle of Arran), Glencoe, Kintail & West Affric, Mar Lodge and Torridon Estates. Management aims to protect the special features of these magnificent mountain areas, some of the finest in Scotland. Its 'Conservation Volunteers' participate in a wide range of activities.

Royal Society for the Protection of Birds (☎ 0131-311 6500, fax 311 6569, W www.rspb.org.uk) 25 Ravelston Terrace, Edinburgh EH4 3TP. The RSPB 'takes action for wild birds and the environment'. It's Britain's largest and one of the oldest conservation charities with numerous reserves in Scotland including Balranald (North Uist), Forsinard (Caithness), Abernethy (Cairngorms), Inversnaid (Loch Lomond) and Loch Gruinart (Islay). Its magazine *Birds* keeps members informed about conservation issues.

Scottish Natural Heritage (☎ 0131-447 4784, fax 446 2277, W www.snh.org.uk) 12 Hope Terrace, Edinburgh EH9 2AS. Set up in 1992, SNH is the government body responsible for caring for Scotland's natural heritage. It's strongly decentralised and has 11 area offices – the best points of contact locally. SNH advises the government on natural heritage issues, owns and manages numerous reserves (see National Parks & Conservation Reserves), operates many grant schemes to promote nature conservation, supports Countryside Ranger services and produces a wide range of publications.

Scottish Wildlife Trust (☎ 0131-312 7765, fax 312 8705, W www.swt.org.uk) Cramond Glebe Rd, Edinburgh EH4 6NS. Founded in 1964, the trust's mission is to protect Scotland's wildlife. It owns or manages more than 100 wildlife reserves from the Borders to Orkney and protects thousands of wildlife sites. Its 'Peat Project' has resulted in reduced use of peat-based garden fertilisers (to preserve peat bogs). Management of its reserves includes promoting the survival of endangered species. Members, especially junior members, are involved in the trust's work and its trainees gain practical qualifications on the job.

Trees for Life (☎ 01309-691292, fax 691155, W www.treesforlife.org.uk) The Park, Findhorn Bay, Forres IV36 3TZ. TFL is less well known than other organisations listed here but its achievements are extraordinary. Its principal aim is to restore Scotland's Caledonian forest and, since 1989, staff and volunteers have planted more than 227,000 native trees grown from seed they collected. Eventually it's hoped to link remnant forests into one large forested area. The major project is based in Glen Affric.

The Woodland Trust Scotland (☎ 01764-662554, fax 662553, W www.woodland-trust.org.uk) Glenruthven Mill, Abbey Rd, Auchterarder PH3 1DP. Established in England in 1972 and in Scotland in 1984, the trust's aims are to keep natural woodlands safe from development, and to enhance their diversity with new plantings and removal of exotic species. It cares for more than 80 woods including Abriachan Wood and others near Loch Ness and Ledmore and Migdale Wood (near Dornoch).

NATIONAL PARKS & CONSERVATION RESERVES

It wasn't until 2000 that Scotland legislated to create national parks – just about the last country in the world to do so (see the boxed text 'National Parks for Scotland'). However, this tardy joining of the international park community hasn't meant that statutory protection of Scotland's flora, fauna and landscapes has been ignored. Since 1949 several types of reserves have been introduced, some in recent years via the European Community. Scottish Natural Heritage is responsible for overseeing these reserves (see Conservation on page 26) and, in many cases, is directly involved in their management. The main types of reserve are outlined in this section. For more information about other reserves – Ramsar Sites (for wetlands), Biosphere Reserves, Biogenetic Reserves (for biological research) and local nature reserves – contact Scottish Natural Heritage.

Scotland has three World Heritage sites – the island of St Kilda (60mi west of Harris), the Old and New Towns of Edinburgh, and the Neolithic sites on the Orkney Islands. World Heritage sites are designated by the United National Educational, Scientific and Cultural Organization (Unesco) as natural or cultural places of world significance that would be an irreplaceable loss to the planet if they were altered. This prestigious designation places an obligation on the government to ensure that nothing is done to compromise the qualities of the sites that earned this designation.

National Nature Reserves

These are established under the 1949 National Parks and Access to the Countryside Act (passed by the UK government) or the Wildlife and Countryside Act 1981, and are administered in Scotland by Scottish Natural Heritage. Nature conservation is an important, but not the sole, concern of management; agriculture, forestry and recreation may also be involved. Scottish Natural Heritage owns or leases about half Scotland's 70-odd National Nature Reserves (NNRs); the rest are owned and managed by conservation organisations such as the Royal Society for the Protection of Birds, or are managed by Scottish Natural Heritage through agreements with the owners.

Among the NNRs owned by Scottish Natural Heritage are Beinn Eighe, the first

National Parks for Scotland

Scotland has had to wait a long time for even one national park – 128 years since the world's first and more than 50 years after they were established in England and Wales. This is despite having the finest mountain and coast landscapes in Britain, relatively large areas of undeveloped land, and many sites of national and international ecological importance.

The reasons for shunning the chance to establish national parks at the same time as England and Wales were a product of the times. The impetus to develop Scotland's and especially the Highlands' water resources for hydroelectric power was strong, owners of large estates were opposed to the idea and there wasn't much public support anyway.

By the late 1990s a host of protective designations had been heaped upon the Scottish countryside. The creation of a Scottish Parliament and Executive in 1999 provided the inspiration and opportunity to set up Scotland's own national parks. The government believed parks would enhance the long-term future of the areas concerned, local people could become more involved and more resources would become available to solve all kinds of problems. Opponents claimed national parks would spell disaster for the very land they were meant to protect, and setting up yet another type of reserve would create chaos and confusion.

After much public debate and consultation, the National Parks (Scotland) Act was passed in August 2000, giving the government the means to declare national parks. The first two parks will be Loch Lomond and the Trossachs, to be opened in 2002, and the Cairngorms in 2003 (see the respective walk chapters).

The main aims of park management will be protection and enhancement of the natural and cultural heritage, alongside social and economic development. Each park will have its own authority; the 25 members to include some directly elected, and others nominated by local authorities and by Scottish Ministers.

The best source for further information on the proposed national parks is Scottish Natural Heritage's Aberdeen office (☎ 01224-642863) or its Web site (Ⓦ www.snh.org.uk).

to be declared in Britain (see page 315), and Creag Meagaidh (see page 267); others include Hermaness (see page 384), Ben Lui and Ben Lawers (see page 167), and St Abb's Head (see page 142). Among the reserves, variety is of the essence, from the remote islands of St Kilda and Scottish Natural Heritage-owned Rum, to the vast Cairngorms plateau, by far the largest NNR (25,949ha). Most are readily accessible and the most popular have a ranger service.

Sites of Special Scientific Interest

This is the most numerous type of reserve – there are around 1450 SSSIs covering an area of nearly one million hectares. They are widely distributed, with concentrations in northern Sutherland and Caithness, on Orkney and several other islands. They represent Scotland's top nature conservation sites, with special plant communities, resident animals, habitats, rocks or landforms, or a combination of these. They are designated under the Wildlife and Countryside Act 1981

Natura 2000 Areas

Devised by the EU, the Natura 2000 network includes Special Protection Areas (SPAs) and Special Areas of Conservation (SACs). SPAs are 'classified' under the European Community Directive on the Conservation of Wild Birds. This 'Birds Directive' protects all wild birds and their habitats, and gives member states the power and responsibility to designate SPAs to protect rare or vulnerable species. SACs, derived from the European Habitats and Species Directive, cover rare, endangered or vulnerable natural habitats and species of plants or animals, other than birds. UK regulations passed in 1994 reinforce the protection provided by the two directives.

More than 100 SPAs (373,000ha) had been classified by 2000, mainly in the Caithness and Sutherland peatlands, the Cairngorms, on the Isles of Rum, Canna and Islay, and in the Solway Firth. During 1999 the UK government submitted a list of 128 Scottish sites as candidate SACs; these are to be designated within the next few years.

National Scenic Areas

These are nationally important areas of outstanding natural beauty and include some of Scotland's finest landscapes. National Scenic Areas (NSAs) are protected by a curiously informal device known as 'advice to local authorities'; Scottish Natural Heritage must be consulted on specific categories of proposed developments within NSAs. They are not widely publicised and it's next to impossible to know when you enter or leave one. There are 40 of them, covering about one million hectares. The largest are Wester Ross; Ben Nevis & Glencoe; and South Lewis, Harris & North Uist (Western Isles).

Regional & Country Parks

Regional parks are large areas where management for informal recreation is coordinated with other local land uses. All four regional parks are in southern Scotland and include Loch Lomond and Pentland Hills.

Country parks are fairly small, accessible areas of countryside managed for walking, picnicking and water-based recreation. Most of the 36 country parks are in the central belt and are owned or managed by local authorities.

POPULATION & PEOPLE

Scotland has around 5.1 million people, which amounts to 9% of the UK total; the population has generally been declining since the 1920s, mainly because of migration to better job opportunities, usually overseas.

The majority of the population lives in the central belt, between the Firths of Clyde and Forth. Glasgow is the largest city with 650,000 people, followed by Edinburgh with 450,000, Aberdeen with 212,000 and Dundee with 150,000. Highland is Britain's most sparsely populated, local government area, with an average of 20 people per sq mi, a small fraction of the British average. Inverness, which is the capital of Highland, is Britain's fastest-growing city, with a population of over 65,000.

SOCIETY & CONDUCT

Scotland's early history was replete with invasion (by the Romans, the Vikings and the English) and aggression (clan warfare). Centuries-old clan feuds are still remembered – a Colquhoun may not sit with a MacGregor because of the massacre of Colquhouns by Rob Roy and a band of MacGregors 300 years ago.

Although the influence of the churches is declining, it still affects daily life in parts of the Highlands and in the Western Isles. Although a mere shadow of the strife in Northern Ireland, sectarian tensions can surface in Glasgow, especially at football matches between the Protestant Rangers and Catholic Celtic teams.

Gaelic culture and language are strong in the Highlands, many of the Inner Hebridean isles and especially in the Western Isles. Highland society is quite different from the anglicised Lowlands – notably in the greater degree of attachment to community institutions and kinfolk.

Outside Scotland, Scots are often stereotyped as being a tight-fisted lot but most are very generous, particularly in support of 'good causes'. Scots may appear reserved in personal encounters, but they can bc passionate about politics, religion and sport, especially football. They generally treat visitors courteously and the class distinctions that still bedevil England are less prevalent, especially the farther north you go.

Traditional Culture

Traditional Scottish culture is richly diverse. The following are a few of its manifestations that are either mentioned in this book or which you're likely to encounter during your travels.

Ceilidh You'll often see posters advertising a *ceilidh* (pronounced kay-lee and meaning visit) at pubs and other venues. Originally a social gathering at people's houses after the day's work was over, when folk stories and legends were told, it also involved music and song. Nowadays a ceilidh means an evening of entertainment with music, song and dance.

Clans A clan is a group of people claiming descent from a common ancestor. The clan system evolved in the Highlands and islands between the 11th and 16th centuries, when many unrelated families united to enjoy the protection of the clan chief. After the 18th-century Jacobite rebellions the system fell apart, due to the suppression of Highland culture, but the spirit of clan loyalty is inextinguishable, especially among the 25 million Scots living abroad. Each clan still has its own chief (male or female), and its own tartan and badge.

Highland Games Highland Games or Gatherings take place during summer across the country. Originally the games were organised by clan chiefs and kings, who recruited the strongest competitors for their armies and as bodyguards. Even now the Queen, Elizabeth II, never fails to attend the Braemar Gathering in September, the best known of all.

Some events, such as tossing the caber, Scottish country dancing, Highland dancing and piping (playing the bagpipes), are peculiarly Scottish; others include athletics events and often cycling.

Dos & Don'ts

Labelling locals as British is acceptable to some Scots, but anathema to others. The Scots do not like being called English, especially in the Highlands and islands; it's extremely important to remember that Scotland is *not* part of England.

Whenever the topics of religion or Scottish nationalism crop up, it's probably best to play the role of audience, at least until you know who's on which side and some of the finer points of the subject.

For dos and don'ts on the trail, see Responsible Walking on page 64.

LANGUAGE

The ancient Picts spoke a mysterious language that hasn't survived to any significant extent in written form; the main evidence of its use is in place names prefixed by 'Pit' (eg, Pitlochry).

Between the 4th and 6th centuries, Gaelic-speaking Celts from Ireland settled here and their language became almost universal throughout what is now Scotland. Although

Anglo-Saxon largely replaced Gaelic in the lowlands from the 11th century, Gaelic remained in use in the Highlands and islands for hundreds of years, although ever on the decline. Its comeback, from the 1970s, has been strong in many communities but lacks much real government support.

Lowland Scots (Lallans) evolved from Anglo-Saxon and bears signs of Dutch, French, Gaelic, German and Scandinavian influences. It too is enjoying a modest revival. Doric, spoken mainly in the Buchan area on the east coast, is a variety of Lowland Scots, modified by contact with Gaelic and other languages.

And then there's English, which grew in influence after the union of 1707. Aye, but the several different Scottish accents can make English almost incomprehensible to the *Sassenach* (an English person or Lowland Scot) and other 'foreigners', and many Gaelic and Lallan words embellish everyday English speech. Dinnae ye ken?

The Language chapter (see page 393) provides more information on Scottish Gaelic and some useful phrases.

Facts for the Walker

HIGHLIGHTS

When it comes to walking in Scotland, the highlights are difficult to select because so much depends on your own interests and experience. The following categories should give you some ideas.

Alpine Action

Getting the adrenaline pumping on the exposed Aonach Eagach. Scrambling on the airy, knife-edged ridges of the Black Cuillin – Britain's most spectacular mountain range. Enjoying the challenge of An Teallach and Liathach's lofty, exposed ridges.

Geological Finds

Weaving through the jumble of boulders on Isle of Arran's Goatfell. Finding a sea of rose quartz on Schiehallion's summit. Exploring the weird pinnacles of the Quiraing and Storr on Skye's Trotternish.

High in the Hills

Marvelling at the bird's-eye view of the Highlands and Lowlands from Ben Lawers. Climbing to the top of Britain's highest mountain, Ben Nevis. Standing on the Cairngorms' vast alpine plateau with magnificent views to distant horizons. Traversing the Five Sisters, the slender scenic ridge above dramatic Glen Shiel. Walking on the edge of some of Scotland's highest sea cliffs on the Isle of Hoy.

Historic Footprints

Exploring picturesque castles and abbeys, relics of the Borders' turbulent history. Following centuries-old pathways through remote glens and across mountain passes. Striding along the historic Caledonian Canal on the Great Glen Way. Pondering the mysteries of Skara Brae in Orkney, Scotland's best-preserved Neolithic village.

Tranquil Walks

Exploring the hidden beauty of Nevis gorge and Steall Meadows on the Road to the Isles. Wandering through Caledonian woodland in beautiful Glen Affric. Crossing the remote and beautiful Great Wilderness in Wester Ross. Soaking up the tranquillity and peace of the Western Isles.

Urban Exploration

Gazing on the maze of streets in Edinburgh's Old and New Towns from Arthur's Seat. Visiting St Mungo's 13th-century tomb in the Gothic Glasgow Cathedral.

Wildlife Rambles

Fending off the dive-bombing skuas on Hoy and arctic terns on Westray. Searching for 'Nessie' as you pass by that famous loch on the Great Glen Way.

Waterfalls & Lochans

Standing just out of reach of the spray from the pounding Falls of Clyde. Peering into dark lochans cradled by the towering cliffs of glacier-sculpted corries in the Cairngorms. Gazing down on the Uists' extraordinary water and rock patchwork landscape.

SUGGESTED ITINERARIES

Scotland is a compact country but travelling between walking areas and individual walks within those areas can be surprisingly time-consuming, especially if you're using public transport. It would take at least six months to do all the walks described in this book, let alone all the other walks outlined plus some sightseeing. So, you have some difficult choices to make if time is limited.

The following suggestions are based on travelling by car to the walks described and include comments on the feasibility of using public transport.

One Week

Concentrate on one area and sample another within easy reach. By public transport you'd have to drop one of the walks in the first and second suggestions; in the other two, concentrate on just one area.

Edinburgh & The South Edinburgh City Walk, Pentland Hills Circuit, Peebles Circuit, Eildon Hills and Burnmouth to St Abb's Head.

Glasgow & hills Glasgow City Walk, Clyde Walkway or Greenock Cut, Ben Lomond and one or two walks in the Trossachs. The Edinburgh City Walk would provide an interesting contrast to the Glasgow walk.

Cairngorms & the Highlands From Aberdeen drive through Deeside. Climb Lochnagar and perhaps do the Linn of Dee circuit from near Braemar. Then, from Aviemore, try one of the Cairngorms walks. Continue to Fort William, visiting Creag Meagaidh on the way. Climb Ben Nevis or explore the Glen Nevis area.

Lochaber & Glen Coe Climb Ben Nevis, walk the Road to the Isles and return by train. Tackle one or two of the Glen Coe walks and then, for relaxation, sample the Great Glen Way.

Two Weeks

A fortnight allows more time on the road between areas and/or for getting to know one area really well – whether by car or public transport.

Glasgow & hills Glasgow City Walk, Isle of Arran and The Cobbler.

Edinburgh & The South Edinburgh City Walk, Pentland Hills Circuit, sample the Southern Upland Way, Grey Mare's Tail and The Merrick.

A long-distance walk West Highland Way plus side trips – Ben Lomond, a Glen Coe walk and Ben Nevis.

Another long walk A Cairngorms grand tour, starting and finishing at Blair Atholl and doing some Munro bagging along the way.

Central Scotland Hills & glens Follow Jock's Road from Glen Doll into the southern Cairngorms, then climb Ben Lawers and Schiehallion, and explore the Isle of Arran.

Highland Glens & Isle of Skye Glen Shiel or Glen Affric walks, Gleouraich and sample the Isle of Skye.

Wester Ross & The North-West Torridon walks and Slioch, Ben More Assynt, Eas a' Chùal Aluinn, Sandwood Bay & Cape Wrath and then Ben Loyal.

Island hopping Devote the whole time to either the Western or the Northern Isles.

One Month

You could combine two of the suggested fortnight-long itineraries, or experience a long-distance path and then explore another, totally different area.

The South & islands Walk the Southern Upland Way and spend another two weeks in the Western or Northern Isles – for a complete contrast.

Highlands & islands Follow the West Highland Way and continue along the Great Glen Way to Inverness. Pick up a car or jump on a bus and head for The North-West or to the Western Isles.

WHEN TO WALK

The best times for walking anywhere in Scotland are from late April to the end of June, September and, usually, most of October. By late April hours of daylight are generous and snow has receded from the glens and lower hills. Wild flowers are at their best during May and June; these are generally the driest, sunniest months and the massed onslaught of midges has yet to arrive. By September these pesky creatures are on the wane and are usually gone by October; the days still aren't too short and

Low-Flying Jets

It's a superb, sunny day, the breeze is just a whisper and you're enjoying a peaceful walk high above the Great Glen, through the Southern Uplands or almost anywhere in the Highlands. Suddenly, without warning, an ear-splitting roar destroys the tranquillity and one, two or even three sinister-looking aircraft flash past at an alarmingly low altitude – possibly even below you.

Fortunately not a constant presence, but a seemingly permanent and totally unpredictable one, these supersonic jets of the Royal Air Force (RAF) and/or the defence alliance North Atlantic Treaty Organization (NATO) are practising their low flying, mainly from Scottish bases. These skills, we are told, are put to good use overseas in 'combat zones'.

Despite protests from distressed residents and especially farmers, genuinely upset by these intrusions, and despite protests about the massive waste of fuel and the consequent pollution, the authorities insist that these activities are vital for 'national security'. Their claims that flights avoid major tourist areas and stay above 167m (500ft) are met with, what might politely be called, acute scepticism.

settled periods of mellow weather are likely. During October, displays of rich autumn woodland colours make this *the* time to be in Scotland.

July and August, the main holiday season, are the busiest months, the peak of midge season and a time when unsettled, humid weather is prevalent.

Surprising though it may seem, Scotland enjoys a year-round walking season. Even in midwinter plenty of lowland and coastal walks are accessible and safe. Only occasional bursts of bitterly cold weather, with snow down to sea level and icy paths, make walking problematic. Daylight hours are short – little more than six in the south, fewer in the north. However, frequent spells of fine weather bring incredibly clear skies, exhilarating low temperatures and light winds, especially in the north and west. Scotland is an outstanding venue for winter mountain walking or mountaineering; ice axe, crampons and complementary skills, first-class navigation, and an understanding of snow and ice conditions are all absolutely essential (see the boxed text 'Winter Walking in Scotland').

The best seasons for each walk in this book are given in the walks table on pages 4–7 and are discussed in the individual walk descriptions (see also Climate on page 23).

WHAT KIND OF WALK?

The best answer to this question is 'Whatever you wish!' You can walk independently, doing all the planning and organising of transport and accommodation yourself, or you can join a guided walk for a day or a week and have everything arranged, including the company. Alternatively you can try a combination – organised accommodation with maps and walk descriptions provided, then do the walks by yourself.

Day walks are probably the most popular style of walking, from a base at a hostel, B&B or camping site. Extended backpacking trips of a few days or more, following an official long-distance path, rights of way or a

Winter Walking in Scotland

Winter in Scotland can be severe, even at sea level. Above 900m (3000ft) conditions can become life-threatening within minutes. High winds, freezing temperatures and driving snow are complicated by short daylight hours. If the cloud comes down on a snow-covered plateau, the resulting white-out requires faultless navigation. It is not uncommon for walkers and climbers to go straight over a cliff edge in such situations. On the other hand, when anticyclones bring stable conditions to the Highlands, some of the best walking days are to be had. Firm névé (ice formed from snow) smooths out the rugged summer terrain, crystal-blue skies stretch off to infinity and, beneath the high peaks, a sea of fog cloaks the valley. For some, this is what walking in Scotland is all about. However, it is important to remember that many of the walk descriptions in this book are for summer only.

To venture safely onto the Scottish mountains in winter you need to be proficient in several areas. Navigation skills, and weather and snow condition awareness must be sound. You also need to be adequately equipped with warm and waterproof clothing and, most important of all, you should have an ice axe and crampons and know how to use them correctly. Many guides and outdoor centres run winter walking courses where you can learn essential winter skills (see Guided Walks on page 52). Glenmore Lodge (☎ 01479-861256, **W** www.glenmorelodge.org.uk) runs winter skills courses over four days (£320) and two days (£140). Also check out *Scotland's Winter Mountains* by Martin Moran (**W** www.moran-mountain.co.uk), an excellent book with both theory and personal anecdote. The author, a well-respected mountain guide, runs winter Munro courses.

Perhaps the biggest single danger for winter walkers is an avalanche, almost all of which are triggered by walkers. Throughout winter the Scottish Avalanche Information Service (SAIS; freephone ☎ 0800-960007, **W** www.sais.gov.uk) gives daily reports for five major mountain areas – Lochaber, Glen Coe, northern Cairngorms, Creag Meagaidh and the southern Cairngorms. The reports can be extrapolated to give a rough guide to the likely conditions in other ranges.

route of your own devising, are also popular. Accommodation can be in a tent, bothies, hostels, B&Bs or a combination of these.

The main, consistently waymarked routes in Scotland are the official long-distance paths and other long-distance routes such as St Cuthbert's Way. Public rights of way (see Access on page 64) are signposted at access points but not along the actual route, although most follow defined tracks or paths. Short walks in national nature reserves and in the new national parks are usually signposted and waymarked. Elsewhere, recognised routes are not waymarked. There may be cairns along the way and at crucial path junctions, but these are meaningless without a map and/or walk descriptions. Indeed, many walkers strongly oppose the use of waymarkers, even to the extent that cairns are deliberately dismantled and marker posts removed.

Munro bagging is a uniquely Scottish activity (see the boxed text) and one in which you can participate. The majority of these and other mountain walks are straightforward, and don't necessitate the use of skills such as scrambling. However, if you thrive on this kind of challenge, then Scotland is your kind of place with numerous scrambling routes in the Highlands and on some of the islands (see the boxed text 'Scrambling' on page 299).

The walks in this book provide a good cross-section of the many different types available, from scrambles along knife-edged ridges to easy-going strolls beside rivers and canals, from strenuous mountain climbs to not-too-demanding but rewarding coast walks.

GUIDED WALKS

Many reputable, experienced companies run guided walks in the major walking areas and along the long-distance paths. The Countryside Ranger Services, organised by local councils, the National Trust for Scotland and some larger private estates (such as Balmoral in Deeside), run guided day-walk programs in their areas. Including a guided walk in your visit makes a break

Munros & Munro Bagging

In 1891 Sir Hugh Munro, a member of the recently founded Scottish Mountaineering Club, published a list of more than 500 Scottish summits over 3000ft, a height at which they became 'real' mountains. Unfortunately, the modern metric equivalent of 914m loses its mystique in translation. Sir Hugh differentiated between 283 'mountains in their own right' (those with a significant drop on all sides or well clear of the next peak) and their satellites, now known as 'tops'.

In 1901 Reverend AE Robertson was the first to climb them all, initiating the pastime of what has become known as Munro bagging. This has grown to a national passion – there are books, CD-ROMs and even a Munro board game. More than 2000 people have completed the full round and their number is growing rapidly. The first person to complete a continuous round – starting with Ben Lomond and finishing on Ben Hope without a break – was writer Hamish Brown in 1974. Since then, at least one continuous round has been completed during winter, and rounds have also been completed in alphabetical and height orders. During 2000 an astounding record for the fastest round was set by a Glasgow postman who ran, cycled and swam it in 48 days 12 hours, having run 887mi (1430km), cycled 756mi (1220km) and ascended 125,000m.

Munro's original list was revised by the Scottish Mountaineering Club and in late 2000 totalled 284. List or no list, the great majority of Munros are outstanding walks with superb views; several are featured in this book.

Once you've bagged the Munros there are other collections of summits to tackle: the Corbetts – Scottish 'hills' over 2500ft (700m) with a drop of at least 500ft (150m) on all sides; and the Donalds – lowland 'hills' over 2000ft (610m). The extraordinary feat of a complete round of these 728 summits, including 722,222m of ascent, was achieved by Peter Lincoln in 1998.

from doing all the organising yourself and gives you the chance to learn more about the countryside from experienced guides, while meeting like-minded people.

Many outdoor activities companies belong to the trade association Activity Scotland (☎ 01463-244299, **W** www.activity-scotland.co.uk). This ensures they adhere to a Code of Practice, carry comprehensive insurance and follow a European Union Directive for Package Travel. The companies listed below are all members of Activity Scotland. If you're considering signing up with another operator, ensure that the leaders have a formal qualification such as the Summer Mountain Leadership Certificate from the Scottish Mountain Leadership Training Board or are certified Mountain Guides.

As well as the following selection, many companies advertise in *TGO* and *Country Walking* (see Newspapers & Magazines on page 75).

C-N-Do Scotland (☎/fax 01786-445703, **e** info@cndoscotland.com, **W** www.cndoscotland.com) Unit 32 STEP, Stirling FK7 7RP. Established in the mid-1980s, C-N-Do operates a wide-ranging program covering the Western Isles and other islands, long-distance paths, backpacking trips in the Highlands, Munro bagging, day walks, scrambling and rock climbing. They are well organised and informal without being slapdash.

North-West Frontiers (☎/fax 01854-612628, **e** NWF@compuserve.com, **W** www.nwfrontiers.com) 18A Braes, Ullapool IV26 2SZ. This company, established in 1986, specialises in the Western Isles and the north-west, ranging as far south as Knoydart and the Cairngorms. Walks are graded and accommodation is in comfortable hotels and guesthouses.

Scottish Youth Hostels Association (SYHA; ☎ 01786-891400, fax 891333, **e** syha@syha.org.uk, **W** www.syha.org.uk) 7 Glebe Crescent, Stirling FK8 2JA. SYHA operates Breakaway Holidays based at youth hostels. Graded walks cover long-distance paths, Munros (including the Skye Cuillin), scrambling and navigation instruction courses.

Scotwalk (☎ 01896-830515, fax 830889, **e** info@scotwalk.co.uk, **W** www.scotwalk.co.uk) Traquair Mill House, Innerleithen EH44 6PT. Scotwalk specialises in providing extremely well-informed guides and high-quality accommodation. The company takes small groups to the Trossachs, Argyll and the Borders, along St Cuthbert's and the Southern Upland Ways, and on a 'John Muir in Scotland' trip.

WALKING FESTIVALS

During the late 1990s, that distinctively Irish event, a walking festival, caught on in Scotland, with the Borders Festival of Walking leading the way in 1995. Not quite a contradiction in terms, because walking can be a very serious business for some, a festival involves at least one, but usually several, organised walks spread over several days, illustrated talks and, of course, *ceilidhs* (social gathering) in the evenings. Does it cost anything? Yes and no – some organisers charge participants, some don't.

Walking festivals are held each year (mainly between April and October) in many parts of Scotland. Regular venues include the Borders, Langholm and Moffat (Dumfries & Galloway), Royal Deeside (Braemar-Ballater area), Pitlochry, Loch Ness (Drumnadrochit) and Shetland. Contact local Tourist Information Centres (TICs) for details.

ACCOMMODATION

Regional tourist boards publish free, illustrated guides for the full range of accommodation types, from camping sites to luxury hotels. These guides are largely reproduced on their Web sites. However, the guides are confined to places registered with and graded by the Scottish Tourist Board (STB). This grading system uses stars to indicate the level of facilities and hospitality, from one to five, but some accommodation providers feel that the grading system focuses on less-than-important details. Gold taps, for example, can elevate a place from a three- to four-star level. Many providers do not belong to the STB and operate very successfully through their own or group Web sites, so it is worth searching under your chosen destinations.

TICs have local and country-wide booking services, usually costing £1 and £3 respectively, which can be handy during the peak season. Most TICs display local accommodation lists in the window – handy if you arrive late without a booking.

In Cities, Towns & Villages

Camping There are plenty of camping and caravan sites in most parts of the country, except in the Northern and Western Isles where they're very scarce. For many, caravans and camper vans are the main business, and tents are allocated only limited space. However, in and near major walking destinations you will find sites with spacious, usually well-grassed areas for tents. Tariffs vary widely from £4 per night to £10; some places charge separately for each person plus the tent, others simply charge for the site occupied. Hot showers are free in some, in others you'll have to pay as much as 50p. Campers kitchens, where you can cook and wash up under cover, are fairly rare; most do have laundries, where a wash and spin-dry could cost around £2. On-site shops and cafes are quite common, especially at sites well away from a town or village. Many camping sites participate in the STB's grading scheme (see introduction to this section). The STB publishes a handy *Caravan & Camping Parks Map* available from TICs.

Youth Hostels Scottish Youth Hostels Association (SYHA; ☎ 01786-891400, fax 891333, ⓔ info@syha.org.uk, Ⓦ www.syha.org.uk), 7 Glebe Crescent, Stirling FK7 2JA, produces a handbook (£1.50) giving details of more than 70 hostels from Shetland to the Borders. Costs range from £6.50 for the simple hostels to £12.75 for the large, city ones. The tariff includes hire of a sleeping sheet and, in several places, a continental breakfast. Tariffs are slightly lower for junior members (under 18). SYHA hostels are covered by the STB's grading scheme for hostels (one to three stars). However, in more remote areas, where companionship and the setting are all-important, this seems somewhat irrelevant.

All hostels have a kitchen where you can cook your own meals and some provide an evening meal for around £5. Virtually gone are the days when even a single can of beer was prohibited; alcohol with meals is now OK, provided you don't become drunk and disorderly! Sleeping accommodation is in dormitories of varying sizes, from four to 12 beds; self-contained rooms are available at some hostels. Nearly 20 hostels have Internet kiosks for members' use; the hourly rate is £5.

Some hostels are closed between 10am and 5pm, and some close their doors at 11pm; these details are given in the handbook. Hostels in more remote areas usually close during winter.

Membership of SYHA (£6 for adults) entitles you to a host of discounts on travel, car hire, various tourist attractions and even on the purchase of Lonely Planet guides through the Web.

Independent Hostels Independent hostels fill in geographical gaps in the SYHA's map, but lack the SYHA's overall control of quality and standards. Some independent hostels are registered with the STB, but the board's insistence on what are seen as irrelevant requirements (eg, matching crockery) has prompted many proprietors to consider going it alone.

Nevertheless, you can expect clean rooms and facilities, a relaxed, friendly atmosphere, and few, if any, restrictions on opening hours. Most hostels have the same range of facilities as SYHA hostels, apart from evening meals. Many have at least a couple of en suite rooms. Tariffs vary widely but generally start at £9 for a space in a small dorm.

The annual *Independent Hostel Guide* is available from Croft Bunkhouse & Bothies, Portnalong, Isle of Skye IV47 8SL (please send an A5 stamped, self-addressed envelope or international reply coupon) or through Ⓦ www.hostel-scotland.co.uk.

B&Bs & Guesthouses B&Bs provide the cheapest private accommodation. Rates start at around £14 per person, which entitles you to a bedroom in a private house, a shared bathroom (usually with a shower rather than a bath) and a substantial cooked breakfast – if you want it. Light breakfasts are always available. By paying from £17 (and up to £30) you can have a room with its own shower and toilet – en suite accommodation. Probably the majority of B&Bs

registered with the STB have at least one en suite room. Many B&Bs in popular walking areas have additional facilities such as a drying room, pick-up and drop-off service, and will provide a packed lunch – look for the 'Walkers Welcome' symbol in accommodation guides. Some remote B&Bs offer an evening meal, usually three courses and excellent value, from £10 to £15.

Guesthouses differ from B&Bs mainly in size, having more than three bedrooms. They can be more impersonal and more expensive, starting at £15 and going way beyond £30. Pubs may also offer relatively inexpensive B&B, which can be convenient, room and meals under one roof, but they may be less peaceful than a private home.

Single rooms are scarce and many hosts are reluctant to let a twin room to one person, even in the off-season, without charging a supplement of as much as £5.

Hotels At the luxury end of the accommodation scale, hotels range from the impersonal, international-style hotels in the cities and near airports, to magnificent castles and mansions in spectacularly scenic locations. Expect to pay at least £35 per person, for every imaginable creature comfort and fine food and wine.

On the Walk

Camping Wild camping in remote areas without facilities is, strictly speaking, only possible with the landowner's consent but, provided you observe the Country Code, few owners will object (see Responsible Walking on page 64). The scope for wild camping is infinite – in the hills, glens and on the coast. However, keeping in mind the changeable climate and the favourite haunts of midges, you need to choose your site carefully (see the boxed text 'Megabites from Midges' on page 85).

Bothies These are privately owned, simple shelters, usually in remote areas. They're not locked, they're free and you can't book a space. You'll need your own cooking equipment, sleeping bag and mat, lighting and food. They're not meant for extended stays – one or two nights at the most. Many are maintained by the Mountain Bothies Association (see Bothies on page 65 and Walkers' Organisations on page 68).

FOOD

Scotland produces an excellent range of fresh meat, seafood, cheeses and vegetables, which can make eating out a delight and self-catering a pleasure.

Locally grown steak is much sought after and venison, a leaner meat from red deer, is popular. Haggis, the national dish, is much maligned but, properly prepared and cooked, can be very enjoyable. Comprising chopped offal mixed with oatmeal and boiled in a sheep's stomach (or artificial substitute), it should be eaten with 'tatties and neeps' (mashed potatoes and turnips), a generous dollop of butter and plenty of black pepper.

Scottish salmon is famous, but there's a big difference between farmed salmon and the more expensive wild version. The same applies for the almost equally good brown trout. Smoked fish – kippers (herrings) and Arbroath smokies (haddock) – can be eaten cold; shellfish are widely available.

Many of the best cheeses come from the islands, particularly Arran, Bute, Mull and Orkney. Blue varieties are superior to English Stilton, the several soft cheeses are delectable, and the best cheddar styles are very sharp and tasty.

Where to Eat

The quality of cooking in pubs, hotel restaurants, B&Bs and hostels is variable. In villages and small towns, alternatives may be scarce. Almost every town has either or both an Indian and Chinese restaurant, and at least one takeaway place, which may be a 'chippie' (fish and chip shop). Look out for places displaying the 'Taste of Scotland' logo, a scheme promoted by the STB to encourage the use of Scottish produce and good cooking.

If you are re a vegetarian, it helps to have a taste for pasta, pizza and curry. It's rare not to find at least a token vegetarian dish on any menu, although vegans will have problems.

The cheapest way to eat is to do your own cooking. Good-quality precooked meals are available in abundance from supermarkets if you're lacking in skills and time.

On the Walk

If you're camping, lightweight, easily prepared and sustaining meals are all-important. Freeze-dried packet meals are available in outdoor equipment shops, although they aren't cheap (from £3) and have a sameness about them. After fresh food on the first night, it's worth experimenting with rice or couscous, pasta and the great variety of packet sauces, the many varieties of sausage, and dried vegetables from health food shops or supermarkets. For breakfast, stewed dried fruit and muesli get you off to a good start; the choice for snacks and lunch is vast.

DRINKS

Alcoholic

Takeaway alcoholic drinks are sold in off-licences (liquor shops) and in supermarkets, rather than in pubs. Opening hours vary from normal shop hours to closing as late as 10pm. Alcohol can only be sold between noon and 4pm on Sunday.

Most restaurants are licensed to sell alcoholic drinks but prices represent a premium of at least 100% on shop prices. There are a few BYO (Bring Your Own) restaurants but most charge extortionately just to remove the cork or bottle top.

Beer Scotland is blessed with a thriving brewing industry, which has two distinct components – the mass-produced beers and the small, individually brewed real ales.

Beer is now the generic name for all liquors brewed with malt and flavoured with hops – lagers and ales; there are also stouts and porter. Many Scottish brews are graded in shillings (from the days when excise was charged in this currency) and the higher the number of shillings, the stronger the beer, from 60 to 90 shillings (written 90/-). Alcoholic content averages between 3% and 5%. The country's mass market is dominated by Youngers, McEwens, Scottish & Newcastle and Tennent's.

Real ale is free of hangover-inducing preservatives and served in pubs by hand-pump from the cask, uncarbonated, drawn under pressure and at cellar temperature. Many real ales are also available in bottles, some using centuries-old recipes (see the boxed text 'A Real Ale Guide' on pages 58 and 59). The very effective lobby group, Campaign for Real Ale (CAMRA; ☎ 01727-867201, fax 867670, ⓔ camra@camra.org.uk, Ⓦ www.camra.org.uk), has done much to promote and sustain the revival of traditional brewing. The group produces an annual *Good Beer Guide* for the whole of Britain and offers many other publications.

Whisky Always spelt without an 'e' if it's Scottish, whisky is Scotland's best-known product and probably still the biggest export. The spirit was first distilled in Scotland in the 15th century and many hundreds of brands are still produced, despite a severe decline in the number of working distilleries throughout the country. The survivors are concentrated in Strathspey and on the Isle of Islay; others are found on the Isle of Skye (see the boxed text 'The Talisker Distillery' on page 291), in Easter Ross near Inverness and on Orkney.

There are two kinds of whisky: rarer and more expensive single malts made from malted barley; and blended whisky, which is distilled from unmalted grain (maize) and blended with selected single malts.

As well as these two, there are several whisky-based liqueurs, such as Drambuie, Glayva and Wallace.

If you must mix your whisky with anything other than water, try a whisky mac (whisky with a potent ginger wine). Scots drinkers may order a 'nip' or 'dram' of whisky as a chaser to a pint of beer. The standard measure is 50mL. Locals will offer you 'a dram'; only tourists call it 'Scotch'.

Wine For centuries people in Scotland made wine from wild flowers, fruit and tree saps. This tradition is continued, most successfully at Moniack Winery near Beauly in the Highlands with silver birch, elderflower and raspberry wine, among others.

Wines from all over the world are widely available and reasonably priced. In supermarkets a good, drinkable wine from the 'new world' costs around £4.

Nonalcoholic

Tea is probably still more widely drunk than coffee, despite the growing popularity of cafe bars and the like where you can get a really good coffee in its many guises, which doesn't taste like tepid dishwater. Herbal teas have become something of a cult drink and many varieties are available in supermarkets and health food shops. Mineral water bottled in Scotland can be found among the rows of plastic bottles on supermarket shelves. Scotland's very own soft drink, Irn-Bru, is popular but definitely an acquired taste; it's a ghastly orange colour, sickly sweet and has a taste impossible to describe.

On the Walk

The routes of most walks cross at least one burn from which you could, in theory, drink long and deep. However, sheep graze extensive areas of the uplands, lowlands and the coast (in fact, almost everywhere) and deer are numerous in many parts. Consequently, the chances of burns being contaminated by animals, alive or dead, are quite high. While many walkers do drink from burns in remote areas, it's probably better to play it safe and either carry your own drinks on a day walk or boil water if camping. (For purification methods see Water on page 80.)

WHAT TO BRING

Clothing

The boxed text 'Equipment Check List' on page 61 lists the essential items to bring. Remember that all your protective gear, a warm jacket, spare socks and gloves, emergency food, a torch (flashlight) and a whistle should be carried on all walks of more than a few hours.

Your waterproof jacket should be a proven performer in wet weather. The ideal specifications are a breathable, waterproof fabric, a hood, which is roomy enough to cover headwear but still affords peripheral vision, capacious map pocket, good-quality, heavy gauge zips and a minimum of fiddly draw cords. Make sure the sleeves are long enough to cover warm clothes underneath and the overall length of the garment allows you to sit down on it.

Overpants may be restrictive, but they're essential for protection in wet and windy conditions (not uncommon in Scotland); choose a model with slits for pocket access and long zips so you can pull them on and off over your boots. Gaiters go a long way towards keeping your feet dry and provide better protection against mud than overpants. The best are made of strong, synthetic fabric, with a robust zip protected by a flap and with an easy-to-undo method of securing around the foot.

Protection against the wind – such as a wind-proof fleece or polycotton jacket – is essential anywhere in Scotland but particularly in the islands. For warmth, wear fleece or wool garments. Closer to the skin it's more a matter of personal preference. A cotton garment will take longer to dry, and isn't necessarily cooler in warm weather, than one made of a synthetic or synthetic-natural fibre mix. Consider a long-sleeved shirt if you're fair-skinned. One or two thin layers of thermal underwear may be more versatile than a single thick layer.

Shorts are widely worn during summer but long trousers are handy for cooler conditions, and for protection against the sun and biting insects. Polycotton is a suitable material; the garment should be of a looser fit than you might normally wear to allow freedom of movement and to minimise the risk of chafing.

A hat with a decent, all-round brim and sunglasses with UV lenses are virtually essential in the summer, even in Scotland.

Footwear

For easier walks on level, firm surfaces, runners (training shoes), hi-tech walking sandals or walking shoes are ideal. For walks on paths and over rough ground, boots are preferable, unless your feet and ankles are used to lightweight footwear.

Continued on page 60

A Real Ale Guide

Here is a guide to some of Scotland's real ale brewers, of which there are more than 50 – small, individually owned enterprises, fortuitously located in or near some of the best walking areas. Quality is generally high, inferior products are few. This selective, geographically organised guide is based on some very pleasurable first-hand experience.

Southern Scotland

After an energetic day walking the Southern Upland Way, almost any of the beers from **Broughton Brewery** (W www.broughtonales.co.uk), near Biggar, go down well. *Merlin's Ale* is hard, flinty and thirst-quenching; *Greenmantle* is a full-flavoured bitter-sweet ale; deep honey-coloured, *The Ghillie* has plenty of spice and hops; while *Old Jock* is one to keep for later (at 6.7% alcohol), its rich fruitcake flavour resembling a port.

The same must be said for the rather exclusive (and expensive) products of the historic **Traquair House Brewery** (W www.traquair.co.uk/beer.html), situated close to the Way, especially the dark, spicy *Jacobite Ale*, which can knock you sideways at 8%. The deeply and enduringly flavoursome *Bear Ale* is slightly less powerful.

In Edinburgh, after tramping around the city and over the hills, there could be nothing better than **Caledonian Brewery's** (W www.caledonian-brewery.co.uk) organic *Golden Promise*, very refreshing with a good hop flavour and hints of honey emerging after a while. The *Flying Scotsman*, a must for steam-train enthusiasts, resembles a good red wine with its ruby colouring and fullness of flavour, while *Edinburgh Strong Ale* has lots of tangy hops.

From the town of Dunbar, which is just east of Edinburgh, **Belhaven** (W www.belhaven.co.uk) brings you several beers including *Robert Burns Ale*, a beautifully rich, dark golden coloured and slightly sweet beer, along with the refreshing *Scottish Lager*, in which you can almost taste the sea breezes.

Central Scotland

The **Isle of Arran Brewery** (W www.arranbrewery.co.uk) is right on the Goatfell walk and its three beers are worth looking forward to at the end. *Arran Blonde* and *Arran Light* have plenty of colour and aroma and a fresh sharp tang, whereas *Arran Dark* is smooth and, well, dark, one to savour after you've quenched your thirst.

The names given to several real ales are reason enough to try them. *Old Engine Oil* from **Harviestoun Brewery** (W www.beers-scotland.co.uk) near Stirling certainly is unusual. Resembling engine oil only in colour, it has a distinctive honeyed-fruit aroma and strong hops aftertaste. At 6% it's definitely an after-dinner drink. From the same company, prize-winning *Schiehallion* is labelled a 'lager beer' but loads of hops set it apart from the rest. The brewery's *Champion Ale* uses different hops to produce a complex, full-flavoured ale with a markedly floral aroma.

A Real Ale Guide

Inveralmond Brewery (**W** www.inveralmond-brewery.co.uk) in Perth (the first in the city for many years) uses evocative historic names. *Ossian's Ale* recalls a legendary Celtic bard; it's a very bitter and refreshing golden ale. *Lia Fail* (Stone of Destiny) is completely different – deep copper-hued, full of malt and orange flavours.

Maclay Thistle Brewery (**W** www.maclay.com) at Alloa produces several excellent beers, among which *Honey Weizen* yields a kaleidoscope of flavours from the honey, myrtle and hops used in its production. *Wallace* is a copper-coloured India Pale Ale (originally brewed for export in the 19th century) full of hops, contrasting with the smooth *Gold Scotch Ale* in which malt and nut flavours dominate. If you like stout, the *Oat Malt Stout* is a revelation, very smooth and completely lacking in bitterness. And once you've tried the *Export Ale* with its full hops and nut flavour, you won't want to go back to mass-produced export-style beers.

Perhaps the most innovative of all Scotland's small breweries is **Heather Ale** (**W** www.heatherale.co.uk) at Strathaven in Lanarkshire. The brewery uses purely Scottish ingredients and traditional recipes to make a unique collection of superb ales. *Fraoch*, the best known ale, uses fresh heather flowers and has a superb dry, herbal, earthy flavour. *Grozet* is an amazingly refreshing drink, light and crisp, thanks to the use of gooseberries, bog myrtle and meadowsweet (a flower). *Kelpie* is an organic ale featuring seaweed to yield a rich and tangy ale in which you can almost detect the sand grains. *Ebulum* is black, rich and deliciously full-flavoured, thanks mainly to ripe elderberries and herbs. *Alba*, based on Scots pine and spruce shoots, has a distinct pine aroma and flavour with a touch of honey, and at 7.5% makes a good after-dinner drink.

Highlands & Islands

An exhilarating day on the Black Cuillin can be topped off with one of the brews from the local **Isle of Skye Brewery** (**W** www.skyebrewery.demon.co.uk), based at Uig. Aptly named *Hebridean Gold* it is extremely smooth under a tall head, although not particularly strong-flavoured. *Blaven* is distinctively bitter and dry, as is *Red Cuillin*.

Over near Inverness, the best of the **Black Isle Brewery's** (**W** www.blackislebrewery.com) several ales are *Golden Eye Organic Ale*, with a full hops flavour that develops and intensifies as you go; *Red Kite*, slightly spicy and lemony with a superb balance between hops and malt; and *Thornbush Porter*, not unlike bottled Christmas pudding.

Perhaps the Cairngorms deserve a little more than the unco (special) Highland ales from the **Aviemore Brewery** (**e** aviemore.brewery@dial.pipex) – *Red Murdoch*, *Cairngorm Brew* and *Ruthven Brew* are all refreshing enough but rather thin. **Tomintoul Brewery** (**W** www.tomintoul-brewery.com), in the village of that name on the Speyside Way, produces colourfully named brews, including *Nessie's Monster Mash* (even though 'she' lives elsewhere) full of malt and mystery, and *Stag*, dark and peaty like its namesake's habitat.

When you're exploring the Orkney isles, don't miss *Red MacGregor* from the **Orkney Brewery** (**W** www.orkneybrewery.co.uk), another smoothy dominated by malt, and *Dark Island*, darker and even more malt-flavoured, sweetish at first then bitter.

Sandra Bardwell

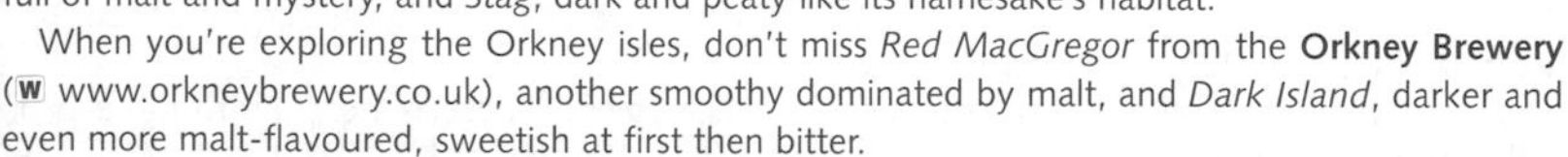

Continued from page 57

If you've never bought a pair of walking boots before, go for a walk before you visit your chosen shop so your feet can expand slightly, as they would do on the trail. Buy the best you can afford that suits your style of walking. Some rigidity in the sole is helpful on rough ground. Gore-Tex lined boots are more expensive; worn with gaiters, they're effective in keeping out water when they're new but, once the uppers start to crack, the lining is less effective. Make a point of wearing new boots a few times before you embark on your first serious walk.

Good brands of walkers' socks are made of hard-wearing, wool-synthetic mixes, free of ridged seams in the wrong places.

Equipment

See the boxed text 'Equipment Check List' for a guide to the gear you will need for walking and camping.

Backpack Your backpack must be hard-wearing and waterproof. Make sure it sits comfortably on your back when loaded and that you know how to adjust the harness. Even if the manufacturer claims it's waterproof, use heavy-duty liners (garden refuse bags are ideal, custom-made sacks are available); external pack covers can easily catch the wind and fly away. Take a small pack for day walks or use spare liners to store unwanted gear during the day.

Tent When choosing a tent, ease of pitching is an important consideration – you need to be able to put it up quickly in bad weather. Adequate headroom is invaluable if you're tent-bound in bad weather, as is space to stow your gear. An impregnable inner tent for protection against midges is essential for your comfort and sanity during summer.

Sleeping Mat & Bag A sleeping mat ensures a good night's rest and puts a layer of insulation between you and the cold and/or wet ground. Compact, self-inflating mats are far better than bulky rolls of foam, although they're more expensive.

Sleeping bags filled with synthetic materials are generally bulkier than down-filled bags but are less expensive. Your choice will depend on when you plan to use the bag (midsummer only or from early spring), your personal tolerance of cold and your budget. Gear shop staff can help demystify the wide range of fillings and designs. An inner sheet for your sleeping bag keeps it clean and adds an insulating layer. Subzero overnight temperatures are quite likely during spring and autumn.

Stove & Fuel The stove you choose needs to be stable when sitting on the ground and to have a good wind shield. Make sure you take the instructions for use and a small repair kit. Stoves that use methylated spirit (Trangia is a well-known brand) are very popular, safe and need little maintenance; the fuel is widely available in supermarkets, hardware and outdoor shops, and costs around £2 for a 500mL bottle. Some stoves run on petrol (gasoline) and the unleaded variety can be bought from any filling station. Super-refined petrol for stoves, known as Coleman fuel (Shellite or white gas in some countries) is available from outdoor shops; Coleman fuel costs from £3 for 500mL. You'll need a clearly labelled aluminium or purpose-designed plastic bottle to carry liquid fuel – the plastic containers it's sold in are too flimsy for safety. Gas stoves are clean and reliable although the gas canisters are a potential litter problem and more wasteful of resources than liquid fuel. As a guide to prices, a 250mL canister costs around £3.75 and a 500mL one £6.

Neither liquid fuel nor gas canisters can be carried when you're travelling by air. Some airlines will allow liquid fuel stoves to be carried in the hold if they're correctly labelled as dangerous goods and packaged in a specific container – contact your airline beforehand to check its requirements.

Compass There is no such thing as a universal compass. The attraction of magnetic north varies in different parts of the world, so compasses have to be calibrated accordingly. There are five calibrations – northern

Equipment Check List

This list is a general guide to the things you might take on a walk. Your list will vary depending on the kind of walking you do – camping, staying in a bothy, hostel or B&B, and on the terrain, weather conditions and season.

Equipment
- ☐ **backpack** with **waterproof liner**
- ☐ **camera**, **spare film** and **batteries**
- ☐ **emergency food** (high-energy)
- ☐ **gaiters**
- ☐ **map**, **compass** and **guidebook**
- ☐ **medical kit***, **toiletries** and **insect repellent**
- ☐ **pocket knife** (with tools & corkscrew)
- ☐ **repair kit**
- ☐ **small towel** and **soap**
- ☐ **sunglasses** and **sunscreen**
- ☐ **survival bag** or **space blanket**
- ☐ **toilet paper** and **toilet trowel**
- ☐ **torch** (flashlight), **spare batteries** and **globe**
- ☐ **water containers**
- ☐ **whistle** (for emergencies)

Clothing
- ☐ **runners** (training shoes) or **sandals**
- ☐ **shorts** and **trousers**
- ☐ **socks** and **underwear**
- ☐ **sunhat**
- ☐ **sweater**, **fleece** or **windproof jacket**
- ☐ **thermal underwear**
- ☐ **T-shirt** and **long-sleeved shirt** with collar
- ☐ **walking boots** and **spare laces**
- ☐ **warm hat**, **scarf** and **gloves**
- ☐ **waterproof jacket**
- ☐ **waterproof overpants**

Camping
- ☐ **cooking**, **eating** and **drinking utensils**
- ☐ **dishwashing items**
- ☐ **matches** or **lighter** and **candle**
- ☐ **portable stove** and **fuel**
- ☐ **sleeping bag**
- ☐ **sleeping mat**
- ☐ **sleeping sheet**
- ☐ **spare cord**
- ☐ **tent** (check pegs, poles and guy-ropes)
- ☐ **water purification tablets**, **iodine** or **filter**

Optional Items
- ☐ **altimeter**
- ☐ **backpack cover** (waterproof)
- ☐ **binoculars**
- ☐ **day-pack**
- ☐ **GPS receiver** **
- ☐ **lightweight groundsheet**
- ☐ **midge net** (for headwear and/or tent)
- ☐ **mobile phone** **
- ☐ **notebook** and **pen/pencil**
- ☐ **swimming costume**
- ☐ **walking poles**

* see the Medical Kit Check List on page 80
** see Safety on the Walk on page 86

northern tropical, equatorial, southern tropical and southern. You need the northern species for Scotland so, if you're coming from another region, you will need to buy a compass when you arrive. Good-quality models cost from £15.

For a discussion on the pros and cons of carrying a mobile phone or GPS navigation system, see Safety on the Walk on page 86.

Buying & Hiring Locally

Outdoor equipment shops are prominent in the cities, larger towns and many smaller ones too. Major national chains include Blacks, Nevisport and Scottish-owned Tisos; there are many individual proprietors as well, no less competitive and with equally expert and helpful staff. Check the outdoor magazines (see Newspapers & Magazines on page 75) and the specialist gear Web site (see Digital Resources on page 73) for more information.

The ruling exchange rate with your home currency will govern whether or not it's worth buying equipment locally, although prices are generally competitive. The individual walk chapters include details on local outdoor shops.

Hiring gear locally is virtually unknown; some branches of Tisos may hire boots for £5 per weekend or £8 weekly. Tisos also offers an extensive repair service – much cheaper than buying new items.

MAPS & NAVIGATION

Small-Scale Maps

Britain's official map maker, the Ordnance Survey (OS), publishes 1:250,000 maps in the Travelmaster series, three of which cover Scotland (including the Northern and Western Isles). They are contoured and are well suited to navigating your way around the country. You may prefer the more convenient format of a road atlas; the *OS Road Atlas (2001)* has maps at a scale of 1:190,000 (1 inch to 3mi) and costs £6.99.

There are many varieties of regional maps, usually available at TICs, which may be the best bet of all – although you could end up with a backpack full of maps.

Large-Scale Maps

For the majority of walks in this book the recommended maps are in the OS Landranger (1:50,000) series. With a contour interval of 10m, these superb maps contain an enormous amount of tourism-related information (such as the location of TICs and car parks). Around 80 maps cover Scotland. The OS also produces an Outdoor Leisure (1:25,000) series, which covers seven areas in Scotland. These double-sided maps have more information, but are rather large and need to be severely folded when in use. The OS Pathfinder (1:25,000) series is being phased out and replaced by the improved Explorer series in single- and double-sided formats. This series will largely take over as the best series for walkers, especially in less-visited areas.

Harvey, an independent map publisher, produces an excellent range of walkers' maps in its Superwalker (1:25,000) and Walker's (1:40,000) series. These works of cartographic art (with 10m contours) are printed on waterproof paper and have loads of useful information. Areas covered include Torridon, Skye: The Cuillin, Lochnagar, Cairn Gorm, Ben Nevis, Arran, Pentland Hills and Galloway Hills. Harvey has also mapped the West Highland, Speyside and St Cuthbert's Ways.

Buying Maps

The OS Travelmaster (£4.25), Landranger (£5.25), Outdoor Leisure (£6.50) and Pathfinder/Explorer (£6.50) maps are widely available from outdoor shops, newsagents, bookshops, TICs and through the OS Web site (W www.ordsvy.gov.uk).

Harvey maps can be purchased through the Web site (W www.harveymaps.co.uk), and from outdoor shops and TICs in the areas the maps cover. The Superwalkers sell for £7.45, the Walker's maps for £5.75 and the long-distance path maps for £7.95.

WALKS IN THIS BOOK

All the walks described are summarised in the Walks Table on pages 4–7, including duration, standard, best time and features.

Route Descriptions

Each walk description is organised in day-long stages. At the end of each stage on a multi-day walk, there is somewhere to spend the night, be it a camping site (near a water supply), bothy, hostel or B&B. Places passed during the day where you could stop overnight are also mentioned, giving you the scope to extend or shorten the daily stages. Features of interest are highlighted in bold in the walk description. Side trips to worthwhile places are outlined at the end of each day.

Each walk is prefaced with a short discussion of its main features, track conditions, any escape routes and opportunities for variations, such as doing the walk in the opposite direction to that described. The Planning section for each walk includes the best time to do the walk, access details during the deer stalking season, any special equipment needed and contacts for general information.

Level of Difficulty

The walks are graded according to a five-tier scheme – easy, easy-medium, medium, medium-hard and hard. These are based on daily distance, the amount of ascent and descent, the quality of the paths (rough, well formed, clear, vague), the type of ground where paths are absent (rocky, heathery, sandy), navigation difficulty, and any other factors such as rock scrambling. The grades are for people of average ability – neither rank beginners nor extremely fit and experienced types.

Easy Routes on paved surfaces or good, well-signposted paths, strictly walking only (no scrambling), with minimal ascent, and comfortably within the abilities of a family with children aged over 10.

Medium Walks accessible to anyone of average fitness, with a little effort. The upgrade from easy reflects one or more factors – ascent, greater distances, rougher or less clear paths, unbridged stream crossings, or the need for route finding using a map and compass.

Hard Walks physically challenging in terms of their length and/or duration, terrain, need for scrambling and navigation.

Times & Distances

The times given for walks in this book are the actual times taken to complete the described routes and do not include any rest stops. In most cases a range is given (eg, 5½–6 hours) to allow for different walking speeds. The authors have provided an average time, irrespective of how long they took to do the walk. Allowance has been made for rocky, sandy or boggy ground. Those walks involving long ascents (more than 500m) assume a climbing rate of roughly 300m per hour.

The walk descriptions also include intermediate times, for example from the start to the first landmark, from there to a lunch spot and so on. Distances between significant points, especially short ones between track junctions, are also given (in metres). These can be crucial in areas where there is a web of paths, and where waymarkers can disappear overnight and may not be replaced immediately.

Overall distances for walks are either those given by the responsible agencies or have been carefully measured by the authors.

Maps in This Book

The maps in this book are intended to show the general route of the walks described. They are drawn to a metric scale with varying contour intervals. They are not detailed enough for route finding or navigation. You will need a properly surveyed map at an adequate scale, showing important relief features (recommended in the Planning section for each walk).

A solid green line shows the main route covered by the text; alternative routes are marked with a dashed green line and side trips are shown with a dotted green line. Start and finish points, camping sites, view points, roads, tracks, reserve boundaries and nearby accommodation – the features mentioned in the walk descriptions – are indicated. The coverage of any adjoining or overlapping maps is shown with their page numbers.

Each chapter has a regional map showing the gateway towns or cities, nearest towns or settlements, principal transport routes and the borders of the walk areas mapped in greater detail.

A map legend appears at the back of this book on page 408.

Altitude Measurements

Heights of mountains, hills and cliffs are taken from the official OS maps. Where an amount of ascent or descent is quoted, it has been derived by counting contours on the OS maps.

Place Names & Terminology

Scottish place names are a fascinating blend of Gaelic, Lowland Scots, Norse, English and other words, reflecting the country's diverse history. The spellings used by OS are generally adopted. Gaelic names are widely used in areas where the language is spoken and wherever Gaelic names have traditionally been used. At the time of writing, the OS was reviewing its Gaelic terminology, so some changes to Gaelic spelling could be made to new editions of maps published during the life of this book.

Path is used in Scotland to describe formed ways for walkers (although there are also cycle paths); trail is also used for the same purpose but less commonly. Track usually refers to a formed way, without a hard surface, for vehicles.

Describing which side of a watercourse you should be on can be confusing. A compass direction is used in this book where there's no risk of ambiguity (eg, northern side of the stream). Alternatively, the 'true' right or left bank means the right/left side as you face downstream.

Within Scotland, mountains are popularly called hills, irrespective of height (Ben Nevis is just as much a hill as Arthur's Seat in Edinburgh), and walkers who go there are called hillwalkers. To avoid confusion, the term mountain is generally used in this book.

Other common Scottish terms are explained in the Glossary on page 396.

RESPONSIBLE WALKING

Scotland's mountains and glens have been altered by the impact of many different human activities for thousands of years. However, the invasion by walkers (and other outdoor enthusiasts) during the past 30 years is probably unprecedented in scale.

The Mountaineering Council of Scotland's *Wild Camping: A Guide to Good Practice* (see also the boxed text 'Wild Camping & the Letterewe Estate' on page 312) and the *Country Code* (see the boxed text 'Country Code' on page 66), promoted by Scottish Natural Heritage, provide guidelines for 'minimal impact' camping and walking. Some of the main points are elaborated in the accompanying paragraphs.

Access

Access is a complex issue and a full discussion would occupy a small book. The following summarises the most important points relating to access. For more detailed information contact Scotways (☎/fax 0131-558 1222, e srws@scotways.demon.co.uk, w www.scotways.demon.co.uk), 24 Annandale St, Edinburgh EH7 4AN, or Scottish Natural Heritage (see page 44 for contact details).

Contrary to popular belief, Scotland has a law of trespass. No-one has the right to enter anyone else's property without consent, except along an established public footpath or right of way, and anyone who does so is actually trespassing. However, Scotland's common law provides no penalty for the mere act of trespass; damage or nuisance must first be proved by the owner or occupier. Trespassers can be asked to leave and can be removed if they refuse to do so voluntarily. Under the Trespass (Scotland) Act 1865, it's a criminal offence to camp or light fires without permission on private property. However, many owners allow walkers to camp in remote areas, although they appreciate the courtesy of being asked permission if practicable.

Scotland has a long tradition of mutual tolerance between landowners and walkers about access to the hills and moors, provided walkers observe the Country Code. Local restrictions may apply during the lambing, deer stalking and grouse shooting seasons, when alternative routes are usually provided, via the Hillphones system and other contacts (see the boxed text 'Deer Management' on page 25). On the whole, this informal arrangement continues to work well, although there are still renegades among owners and walkers alike.

Access through farmland, in the absence of public footpaths or rights of way, is more contentious; by following the Country Code faithfully and you can't go wrong.

Public footpaths, many of which are signposted, can be those where an owner or tenant tolerates public use, without conceding that a right of way exists. Other public footpaths have been created by law and are the subject of a formal agreement between the owner and a government agency.

A right of way is a right of public passage over private property by a more or less defined route, which has been used continuously for 20 years in recent times. Rights of way must connect two public places; use is a matter of right rather than tolerance by the landowner.

During the 1990s, the number of people taking to the mountains soared and demand for access to lowland walking areas grew. In 1996 the Access Forum was set up, bringing together representatives of land managers (including the Scottish Landowners' Federation), recreation groups (the Mountaineering Council of Scotland and others) and public agencies (such as Scottish Natural Heritage). The forum promotes greater understanding of access issues and better access arrangements. The forum's Concordat on Access to Scotland's Hills and Mountains was an important step in this direction; it endorses:

- Freedom of access exercised responsibly and subject to reasonable constraints for management and conservation.
- Acceptance by visitors of the needs of land management, and understanding how this sustains those who live and work in the hills.
- Acceptance by land managers of the public's expectation of access to the hills.
- Acknowledgment of a common interest in Scotland's hills, and the need to work together for their protection and enhancement.

It was expected that the new Scottish Parliament would move quickly to change the law to provide greater freedom for people to enjoy the countryside. In the late 1990s the Access Forum participated in a review of access provisions, initiating a long, slow haul to legislation and a Scottish Outdoor Access Code. In February 2001 the Scottish Executive published a draft Scottish Outdoor Access Code and a draft Land Reform (Scotland) Bill. After three months of consultation, the Bill was due to be debated in the Scottish Parliament in September 2001.

Hill folk were outraged at some of the provisions of the Bill, which would make trespass a criminal offence, enable land managers to close access if they felt it was compromising their activities and would empower councils to restrict access to 'particular land'. These provisions were thought to undermined the progress made by the Access Forum towards cooperation and consultation between land managers and visitors to the countryside. The saga is documented on the Mountaineering Council of Scotland's Web site at **W** www.mountaineering-scotland.org.uk.

Bothies

- Don't depend on bothies – always carry a tent.
- Space is available on a first-come, first-served basis and for short stays only. Some bothies in remote areas are not available for public use.
- Some are used by their owners (usually the local estate) during the lambing and stalking seasons, when walkers may be asked not to stay overnight.
- Keep fires small and within existing fireplaces.
- If there's a logbook, fill in details of your trip and party – this may help with mountain rescue.
- When you leave, tidy up, ensure the fire is out, replace kindling if possible, and close windows and door(s) properly. Take all your rubbish away with you and don't leave any food behind as it encourages rats and mice.

Camping

- If camping near a farm or house, seek permission first.
- In remote areas use a recognised site rather than creating a new one. Keep at least 30m from lochs, watercourses and tracks. Make sure you move on after a night or two.
- If the tent is carefully sited away from hollows where water is likely to accumulate, it won't be necessary to dig damaging trenches if it rains heavily.
- Leave your site as you found it – with minimal or no trace of your use.

Dogs

- A dog is an indispensable companion for many walkers. While some dogs are trained not to annoy other people or harass farm animals or wildlife, the rest of the world doesn't necessarily realise this.
- Even if your dog is normally well behaved, you should *always* keep it on a lead in farming country and along any trafficable road. Elsewhere, keep the dog in sight, as far as possible, to ensure it doesn't chase wildlife or pester other people, some of whom may be genuinely afraid of dogs.
- During the lambing season (April and May) it's best not to take your dog through farming country, including hill grazing ground, even on a lead. Farmers' lives are difficult enough without the unwanted intrusion of barking canines. The same applies to wildlife breeding seasons, particularly birds; notices requesting thoughtful behaviour are often displayed at access points to sensitive areas.

Fires & Low-Impact Cooking

- Don't depend on open fires for cooking (any wood may be too wet anyway). Use a lightweight liquid fuel stove rather than one powered by disposable gas containers.
- A driftwood fire might be possible near a beach but in wooded areas fallen timber is a precious natural habitat. If you do light a fire, keep it small and use the bare minimum of fallen timber. Extinguish it thoroughly, scatter the charcoal and cover the fire site with soil and leaves.

Human Waste Disposal

- At the few bothies that have an established toilet, please use it.
- Otherwise, bury your waste. Dig a small hole 15cm deep and at least 30m from any stream, 50m from paths, and 200m from bothies or camping sites. Take a lightweight trowel or large tent peg for the purpose. Cover the waste with a good layer of soil and leaf mould. Ideally, use biodegradable toilet paper; it should be burnt, but this is not recommended in a forest or on dry grassland. Otherwise, carry it out – burying is a last resort.
- Contamination of water sources by human faeces can lead to the transmission of Giardia, a human bacterial parasite; gastroenteritis is probably caused by exposed human faecal waste.

Country Code

- Respect those who live and work in the countryside.
- Guard against all risk of fire.
- Leave all gates as you find them – open or closed.
- Keep your dog under close control.
- Keep to paths through farmland; walk around the edge of fields with crops.
- Use gates and stiles to cross fences and walls; if necessary, climb a gate at the hinged end.
- Leave livestock, crops and machinery alone.
- Take your rubbish home or to the nearest disposal point.
- Avoid polluting water sources.
- Leave all natural places and creatures as you find them.
- Drive and park considerately on country roads.

Always check the surrounding area for contamination before you collect water and do this above your camping site.

- Get hold of a copy of the Mountaineering Council of Scotland's leaflet *Where To 'Go' in the Great Outdoors* (see under Walkers' Organisations on page 68 for contact details) and make sure all your friends are familiar with its advice.

Rubbish

- If you've carried it in, you carry it back out – wrappers, citrus peel, cigarette butts and empty packaging, everything, stowed in a dedicated rubbish bag. Make an effort to pick up rubbish left by others.
- Sanitary napkins, tampons and condoms don't burn or decompose readily, so carry them out, whatever the inconvenience.
- Burying rubbish disturbs soil and ground cover, and encourages erosion and weed growth. Buried rubbish takes years to decompose and will probably be dug up by wild animals, which may be injured or poisoned by it.
- If you're camping, before setting out remove all surplus food packaging and put small-portion packages in a single container.

Washing

- Don't use detergents or toothpaste in or near streams or lochs; even if they are biodegradable they can harm fish and wildlife.
- To wash yourself, use biodegradable soap and a water container at least 50m from the watercourse. Disperse the waste water widely so it filters through the soil before returning to the burn.
- Wash cooking utensils 50m from streams using a scourer instead of detergent.
- Strain food scraps from dishwashing water and carry them out in your rubbish bag.

WOMEN WALKERS

Scotland is generally a safe place for women travellers, including women walkers. As a walker, you'll most likely be accepted as a walker first and a woman second. Women are prominent among those who have completed the round of the Munros and when you meet solo walkers in the mountains, they're more likely to be women than men. Virtually all walking clubs in Scotland are open to women and men alike. Nevertheless, it is worth remembering that, historically, walking has been regarded as a predominantly, but certainly not exclusively, male activity.

Sexual harassment still occurs, more likely in cities than in country areas. Female hitchers should take care at all times (see Hitching on page 98).

Shorts are widely worn these days in the countryside and elsewhere, so you won't encounter any censorious looks when you wear them; exercise discretion in the Western Isles on Sunday.

Please remember the advice given under Rubbish in the Responsible Walking section earlier about disposal of sanitary items.

WALKING WITH CHILDREN

Walking certainly isn't an adults-only activity; introducing children to walking at a fairly early age can set them on the path to a lifetime's enjoyment. However, you do need to put a lot of thought into planning walks with kids.

The distance and duration have to be well within their demonstrated capabilities. As a guide, 10-year-olds should be able to cover 3mi to 5mi (5km to 8km) on good paths with no more than 200m ascent in a comfortable day's outing. It's important to have a set plan so you can tell them what's coming next. Be aware of the point of no return (beyond which the end is nearer than the start) and, ideally, have an escape route for emergencies.

Trees and flowers may have little appeal but wildlife – such as squirrels, deer, seals – should. Panoramic views may be largely lost on young people; they'll be more interested in unusual rock formations to scramble around and small caves to explore. Incorporate plenty of stops (for exploration and rest) into the estimated walk time and consider organising an activity at lunchtime, perhaps related to the wildlife they have seen.

Suitable clothing and good equipment are extremely important – children will feel the cold sooner and more keenly than you will, and their tolerance of sore feet, for example, will probably be pretty low. Getting children to carry a small pack isn't a bad idea, especially to encourage a sense of participation, but not one that upsets their balance or normal gait.

Carry plenty of food and drinks, including as many of their favourites as possible. Having friends along could be a good idea, if they're of much the same ability and suitably equipped.

Of the walks described and outlined in this book, those suitable for children include:

Edinburgh & Glasgow Edinburgh City Walk, Glasgow City Walk, Greenock Cut, Clyde Walkway, Campsie Fells
The South Peebles Circuit, Eildon Hills, Burnmouth to St Abb's Head, Borders Abbeys Way, parts of St Cuthbert's Way
Central Scotland Ben A'an, Cock of Arran, Islay walks, West Lomond (Lomond Hills)
Lochaber & Glencoe Glen Nevis Circuit, Glencoe Lochan Trail, Beinn Chlaonleud & Gleann Dubh
Cairngorms Linn of Dee to Derry Lodge, Loch Einich, Glenmore to Bynack Stable, Glen Feshie, Loch Muick Circuit, Upper Glen Doll, Loch Callater, Speyside Way
Highland Glens Aberarder to Lochan a' Choire (Creag Meagaidh), Loch Affric circuit, Drumnadrochit & Glen Urquhart
Isle of Skye Quiraing
Wester Ross Beinn Eighe National Nature Reserve, Coire Mhic Fhearchair
The North-West Sandwood Bay, Point of Stoer, Stac Pollaidh
Western Isles Tolsta to Ness, Rhenigidale Path, Scalpay, Huishinish, Eoligarry
Northern Isles Skara Brae, West Westray Way, Hermaness, Muckle Roe, Eshaness Coastal Circuit, Odin Bay – Stronsay, The Sanday Trail, Ness of Hillswick, St Ninian's Isle

As far as travelling is concerned, child concessions for accommodation and transport are often available. Discounts may be up to 50% of the adult rate, although the definition of 'child' varies from under 12 to under 16 years. Lonely Planet's *Travel with Children* contains plenty of useful information.

USEFUL ORGANISATIONS

Government Departments

In addition to Scottish Natural Heritage (listed under Conservation on page 44), the Deer Commission (see the boxed text 'Deer Management' on page 25) and Forest Enterprise (discussed on page 23 and in some walk chapters), Historic Scotland is another government organisation that crops up on some walks in this book (and other walks elsewhere in Scotland):

Historic Scotland (☎ 0131-668 8600, W www.historic-scotland.gov.uk) Longmore House, Salisbury Place, Edinburgh EH9 1HS. This group safeguards the nation's built heritage – everything from prehistoric burial cairns to WWII fortifications, and is best known as the custodian of Edinburgh, Stirling and Urquhart Castles.

Walkers' Organisations

As well as the conservation organisations listed on page 44, the following bodies are concerned with walkers' interests and activities in various ways. There are dozens of walking clubs in the cities and towns; the Ramblers' Association Scotland has many active walking groups and many clubs are members of the Mountaineering Council of Scotland – a good first port of call if you're interested in joining a club.

Mountain Bothies Association (W www.mountainbothies.org.uk), founded in 1965, maintains about 100 bothies in remote country throughout Scotland (and in England and Wales). The association does not own any bothies itself but undertakes maintenance work with the owners' consent. Informal and friendly work parties are organised at individual bothies, and there's usually some time for workers to explore the surrounding countryside. Details of bothy locations are published only for the purposes of organising work parties.

Mountaineering Council of Scotland (☎ 01738-638227, e info@mountaineering-scotland.org.uk, W www.mountaineering-scotland.org.uk) The Old Granary, West Mill St, Perth PH1 5QP. This organisation represents the interests of walkers, climbers and mountaineers. It has at least 130 affiliated clubs and hundreds of individual members. It strongly promotes safe practice in the hills through publications and courses on navigation, winter walking and climbing, and leadership. It operates an information service and keeps members informed about access and conservation issues.

Ramblers' Association Scotland (☎ 01577-861222, fax 861333, e enquiries@scotland.ramblers.org.uk, W www.ramblers.org.uk) Kingfisher House, Auld Mart Business Park, Milnathort, Kinross KY13 9DA. Originally established in England, the association now has more than 40 local groups in Scotland. It works to protect the countryside and to promote walkers' enjoyment, and is particularly concerned with national parks and access issues.

Scottish Mountaineering Club (SMC; e smc@smc.org.uk, W www.smc.org.uk), founded in 1889, is open to anyone who can meet the technical standards for membership and who is nominated and seconded by club members. The club's offshoot, the Scottish Mountaineering Trust, publishes an extensive and authoritative selection of guidebooks, walking and climbing guides, and supports several projects related to mountaineering in Scotland.

TOURIST OFFICES

Local Tourist Offices

VisitScotland (☎ 0131-332 2433, fax 343 1513, W www.visitscotland.com) has its headquarters at 23 Ravelston Terrace (PO Box 705), Edinburgh EH4 3EU. In London contact VisitScotland at ☎ 020-7321 5732, 19 Cockspur St, SW1Y 5BL.

Most towns have TICs that open from 9am to 5pm or later Monday to Friday and on summer weekends. In many of the small towns, TICs may only be open from Easter to the end of September. They are invaluable sources of information about accommodation and transport. They stock books and maps, and the larger ones have a *bureau de change* and their own Web sites. TICs relevant to the walks described in this book are listed in the respective walk chapters.

Tourist Offices Abroad

Overseas, VisitScotland is represented by the British Tourist Authority (BTA, W www.visitbritain.com), which provides heaps of interesting information, much of it free.

The BTA is a useful source of advice about travel reservations that need to be made overseas to earn a discount. For a complete list of overseas offices, see the BTA Web site.

Australia (☎ 02-9377 4400, fax 9377 4499) Level 16, The Gateway, 1 Macquarie Place, Sydney, NSW 2000

Canada (☎ 905-405 1840, fax 405 1835) 5915 Airport Rd, Suite 120, Mississauga, Ontario L4V 1T1

France (☎ 01 44 51 56 20, fax 01 44 51 56 21) Maison de la Grande Bretagne, 19 rue des Mathurins, 75009 Paris

Germany (☎ 069-97 1123, fax 97 112 444) Westendstr 16–22, 60325 Frankfurt
Ireland (☎ 01-670 8000, fax 670 8244) 18–19 College Green, Dublin 2
Italy (☎ 06-462 0221, fax 474 2054) Via Nazionale 230, 00184 Roma
Netherlands (☎ 020-689 0002, fax 689 0003) Stadhouderskade 2 (5e), 1054 ES Amsterdam
New Zealand (☎ 09-303 1446, fax 377 6965) 17th Floor, 151 Queen St, Auckland 1
Sweden (☎ 08-4401 700, fax 213129) Klara Norra Kyrkogata 29, S111 33 Stockholm (Box 3102, 103 62 Stockholm)
USA (☎ 1 800-462 2748) 625 N Michigan Ave, Suite 1001, IL 60611; (☎ 1 800 GO 2 BRITAIN) 7th Floor, 551 Fifth Ave, New York, NY 10176-0799

VISAS & DOCUMENTS

Visas

Visa regulations are subject to change, so it's essential to check requirements and any restrictions with your local British embassy, high commission or consulate before you leave home.

Currently, if you are a citizen of Australia, Canada, New Zealand, South Africa or the USA, you are given 'leave to enter' Britain at your place of arrival. You do not need to have an onward ticket. Visitors from these countries are generally allowed to stay for up to six months but not to work. For a longer stay you need an entry clearance certificate, available on application from the British High Commission. If you arrive in Scotland from England, Wales or Northern Ireland, you do not need a visa.

Citizens of the European Union (EU) don't need a visa to live and work in Britain.

Visa Extensions To obtain an extension, contact the Immigration and Nationality Directorate (☎ 0870-606 7766), Block C, Whitgift Centre, Wellesley Rd, Croydon, London CR9 1AT, *before* your existing permit expires. You'll need to send your passport or ID card with your application.

Travel Insurance

This not only covers you for medical expenses, theft or loss, but also for cancellation of or delays to any of your travel arrangements. Your travel agent should be able to recommend the best type of policy for your needs. If you're planning on doing any walks involving scrambling or climbing, make sure that your policy covers such activities. Mountain rescue is free in Scotland, although many people who are rescued make a donation to the mountain rescue team that extricated them. Go for the most comprehensive and generous policy you can afford, and ensure that it includes health care and medication, especially if you're planning to visit other countries where the cost of medical treatment is high. Make sure it also covers emergency flights home. See Medical Cover on page 79 for details on cover in Britain.

Other Documents

Your normal driving licence is valid for 12 months from the date of your most recent arrival in Britain; after that, you can apply for a British licence at a post office.

Inquire at your home automobile association before leaving about documentation needed to obtain reciprocal services from a British organisation.

If you're travelling on a budget membership of the Scottish Youth Hostel Association/Hostelling International (SYHA/HI) is a must and a good investment anyway – it is, essentially, a passport to meeting other walkers and travellers (see Accommodation on page 53).

An International Student Identity Card (ISIC), which displays your photograph, can trigger discounts on many forms of transport. If you're under 26 but not a student, you can apply for a Federation of International Youth Travel Organisations card or a Euro26 Card, which should give similar discounts. These cards are issued by student unions, hostelling organisations and student travel agencies.

EMBASSIES & CONSULATES

Don't expect much from your embassy in Britain (or in any other country for that matter)!

It will probably only worry about you if you get into trouble with the police or depart this life while on holiday. It will help you to replace a lost passport and offer advice on other emergencies. It won't hold mail for travellers but will help someone in your home country contact you in an emergency.

British Embassies & Consulates

Although Scotland now has its own parliament, it is still represented abroad by the UK government. Contacts for embassies or consulates are available from the Foreign and Commonwealth Office (☎ 020-7270 1500, W www.fco.gov.uk).

Australia (☎ 02-6270 6666) Commonwealth Ave, Yarralumla, Canberra, ACT 2600
Canada (☎ 613-237 1530) 80 Elgin St, Ottawa K1P 5K7
France (☎ 01 44 51 31 00) 35 rue du Faubourg St Honoré, 75383 Paris Cedex 08
Germany (☎ 30 20457-0) Wilhelmstrasse 70, 10117 Berlin
Ireland (☎ 01-205 3700) 29 Merrion Rd, Ballsbridge, Dublin 4
Italy (☎ 06-4220 0001) Via XX Settembre 80a, 1-00187 Roma RM
Netherlands (☎ 070-427 0427) Lange Voorhout 10, 2514 ED, The Hague
New Zealand (☎ 04-472 6049) 44 Hill St, Wellington 1
Sweden (☎ 08-671 3000) Skarpögatan 6–8, Box 27819, Stockholm
USA (☎ 202-588 6500) 3100 Massachusetts Ave NW, Washington, DC 20008

Consulates & High Commissions in Scotland

Most foreign diplomatic missions are in London, but several also have consulates or high commissions in Edinburgh. These are listed in the Yellow Pages, in print or online (W www.yell.com).

Canada (☎ 0131-220 4333) 30 Lothian Rd, Edinburgh EH1 2DH
France (☎ 0131-225 7954) 11 Randolph Crescent, Edinburgh EH3 7TT
Germany (☎ 0131-337 2323) 16 Eglinton Crescent, Edinburgh EH12 5DG
Ireland (☎ 0131-226 7711) 16 Randolph Crescent, Edinburgh EH3 7TT
Italy (☎ 0131-226 3631) 32 Melville St, Edinburgh EH3 7PG
Netherlands (☎ 0131-220 3226) 53 George St, Edinburgh EH2 2HT
Sweden (☎ 0131-220 6050) 22 Hanover St, Edinburgh EH2 2EP
USA (☎ 0131-556 8315) 3 Regent Terrace, Edinburgh EH7 5BW

CUSTOMS

When you enter Britain, go through the green channel if you have nothing to declare. If you do have something to declare, the red channel is your route. There's a two-tier system for imported goods – those bought duty-free, and goods purchased in an EU country where tax and duty have been paid.

If you patronise a duty-free shop, you can import 200 cigarettes or 250g of tobacco, 2L of still wine plus 1L of spirits or another 2L of wine (sparkling or still), 60mL of perfume, 250mL of toilet water and any other duty-free goods (eg, cider and beer) to the value of £145.

You can import goods purchased at a normal retail outlet elsewhere in the EU, provided they're for your own consumption. Alcohol is much cheaper in many continental European countries than in Britain, so it's well worth taking advantage of the allowances – 10L of spirits, 90L of wine (maximum 60L sparkling) and 110L of beer – if you have a car!

MONEY

Currency

The British, and therefore Scottish, currency is the pound sterling (£), which comprises 100 pence (p). One and 2p coins are bronze; 5p, 10p, 20p and 50p coins are silver; the £1 coin is gold-coloured; and the £2 coin is gold- and silver-coloured. The word pence is usually abbreviated and pronounced 'pee'.

Notes (bills) come in £5, £10, £20, £50 and £100 denominations. The three Scottish banks – the Clydesdale, Royal Bank of Scotland and Bank of Scotland – issue their own notes, including the slowly disappearing (but popularly treasured) £1 note. The Scottish notes are legal tender throughout the UK, despite what people in England may tell you. You shouldn't have trouble changing them immediately south of the border with England but, beyond there, a bank is your best bet.

Exchange Rates

country	unit		sterling
Australia	A$1	=	£0.36
Canada	C$1	=	£0.46
euro	€1	=	£0.62
Japan	¥100	=	£0.57
New Zealand	NZ$1	=	£0.30
South Africa	R1	=	£0.09
USA	US$1	=	£0.70

Exchanging Money

The best *bureaux de change* are those at international airports. They charge less than most banks and cash sterling travellers cheques for free. They also guarantee that you can buy up to £500 worth of most major currencies. Bureaux de change in TICs charge a minimum of £2.50 and 4% for sums over £100. Try to avoid small bureaux de change elsewhere; the exchange rates may look attractive, but fees and commission can be extortionate.

If you're planning to spend some time in Scotland, it may be useful to open an account with a Scottish bank. The staff will explain the facilities available with their particular credit, credit/debit, debit and charge cards – these differ from bank to bank.

Cash This is convenient and essential, but relatively risky – once lost, there's no replacement. Banks rarely accept foreign coins but some airport exchanges will.

Travellers Cheques For a short stay in Scotland, travellers cheques are the most straightforward method of carrying money and generally enjoy a better exchange rate than foreign cash. American Express and Thomas Cook are widely used. A passport is usually adequate for identification, but a driver's licence or other form of identification may also be useful.

The fees for cashing travellers cheques vary from bank to bank. As a guide, the Bank of Scotland charges £2 per person to cash sterling cheques and £3 minimum for foreign-currency cheques. The best idea is to bring sterling cheques. Travellers cheques are rarely accepted outside banks and are not used for everyday transactions.

Credit/Debit Cards & ATMs Most overseas credit cards can be used in Scotland for retail purchases, car hire, some accommodation and to obtain cash advances – they are accepted by most automatic telling machines (ATMs, sometimes called cashpoints). Most ATMs also accept debit cards issued by your own bank. Most banks do not charge for transactions on cards issued by other banks. ATMs aren't fail-safe, however, especially if your card was issued outside Europe. If an ATM swallows your card, replacing it can be infuriatingly time-consuming. Generally it's safer (although possibly less convenient) to go to a real-live teller in a bank.

American Express and Diners Club cards may not be accepted in small establishments or off the beaten track, but Visa and MasterCard (also known as Access) are widely accepted, although some places charge for accepting them.

International Transfers You can instruct your bank at home to send you a draft. Specify the city, the bank and the branch to which you want your money directed, or ask your home bank to suggest any suitable locations. This will be much easier if you've authorised someone at home to access your account.

Money sent by telegraphic transfer, usually at a cost of £6 in Scotland, should reach you within a week; by mail, allow at least two weeks. You can also transfer money through American Express or Thomas Cook. American travellers can also use Western Union (freephone ☎ 0800-833833).

On the Walk

If you're doing day walks from a town or village base, then all you're likely to need is some small change for telephone calls (or a charge card, see Telephone on page 72). On long-distance walks, make sure you have plenty of cash (in relation to the expected costs of accommodation and meals – see the relevant walk chapters). B&Bs and smaller youth hostels don't usually take credit cards; cheques drawn on local accounts are OK if backed by a guarantee card; this is a debit card given to you when you open a cheque account, and guarantees that cheques up to a specified amount will be accepted for cash or purchases.

Security

Never leave anything of value in a parked car or, if you must, make sure it is well hidden.

Costs

Although Scotland isn't among the cheapest countries for visitors (or residents), there are ways of economising without sacrificing quality or enjoyment, especially by taking advantage of travel discounts (see the Getting Around chapter for details). Average costs for some basic items are as follows:

item/service	cost
camping ground (tent & person)	£7
night at SYHA hostel	£9.25
B&B (per person sharing)	£16
bar supper (main course)	£6.50
pint of beer	£1.75
loaf of bread (800g)	82p
500mL of milk	38p
litre of unleaded petrol	85p
Edinburgh-Inverness, return bus fare	£22.50
Edinburgh-Inverness, return rail fare	£32
local phone call from public phone	20p + 4p/minute
national newspaper	48p

Tipping & Bargaining

Tipping is becoming less common now that all workers must be paid at least the fixed national minimum wage. It's still expected in restaurants (around 10% unless the service was abysmal) but less so in pubs. Check the bill before you leave something – if it includes a service charge (up to 15%), a tip isn't necessary. Taxi drivers expect to be tipped around 10%.

Bargaining is virtually unknown, even at markets, although don't hesitate to ask for student, youth or hostel member discounts.

Taxes & Refunds

Value-Added Tax (VAT) of 17.5% is levied on all goods and services, except food and books. Restaurant prices must, by law, include VAT.

You may be able to claim a refund of VAT if you've lived in Britain for *less* than 365 days out of the two years before making the purchase and you're leaving the EU within three months of making the purchase. The minimum purchase requirement varies between shops, usually around £40. On request participating shops will give you a special form/invoice; you'll need to show your passport. The form must be presented to customs with the goods and receipts when you depart. Once customs has certified the form, return it to the shop in the envelope provided for a refund; an administrative fee will be deducted.

POST & COMMUNICATIONS

Post

Most post offices open weekdays from 9am to 5.30pm, and Saturday 9am to 12.30pm.

Royal Mail claims that 1st-class mail will be delivered the following day; it's more expensive (26p per letter) than 2nd-class (19p per letter), which is also slower. Airmail letters to EU countries cost 36p, and to the Americas and Australasia 45/65p (up to 10/20g). An airmail letter generally takes less than a week to reach the USA, Canada, Australia or New Zealand.

If you don't have a permanent address, mail can be sent to poste restante in the town or city where you're staying or passing through. American Express offices hold card-holders' mail free.

Telephone

British Telecom (BT) is the largest telephone operator, with most of the public phone booths.

The most common type of phone booth is a glass cubicle; those with a green band below the roof take phonecards and, in some cases, debit and credit cards and coins; those with a maroon band take coins only. The latter can be found even in quite remote areas, but card phones are confined to the cities and larger towns. The minimum fee is 20p. BT phonecards might not offer the cheapest calls but they are convenient, especially if you need to make international calls. With values of £3, £5 and £10, they're available from post offices, newsagents and many other retailers.

Two dialling codes worth remembering are ☎ 0800 (call is free to caller) and ☎ 0845 (call is charged at local rate irrespective of distance).

Local & National Calls Local and national calls are charged by duration, time of day and the location of the number you're calling. Daytime rates apply from 8am to 6pm weekdays; a cheaper rate applies from 6pm to 8am weekdays; and there is an even cheaper weekend rate from midnight Friday to midnight Sunday.

For local and national directory inquiries call ☎ 192 (this service is free from a public phone only). For help in making a call, ring ☎ 100 (this service is free).

International Calls Dial ☎ 153 for directory inquiries and ☎ 155 for help with making calls. To make an international call direct, dial ☎ 00 then the country code, area code (drop the first zero if there is one) and number. Direct dialling is cheaper but it may be more convenient to make an operator connected, reverse-charge (collect) call.

The Home Country Direct service enables you to make a reverse charge or credit card call through an operator in your home country.

For all international numbers it's cheaper to call between 6pm and 8am Monday to Friday and at weekends.

Emergency Dial ☎ 999 or ☎ 112 (free calls) for fire, police or ambulance. However, see Search & Rescue Organisations on page 88 for details on mountain rescue.

Fax

Fax can be useful for booking accommodation, in the absence of an email address. Weather forecasts (see Weather Information on page 76) are available by fax, which can be very handy if you want to be sure of the fine detail. However, the difficulty is to find somewhere to send and receive messages; Internet cafes and some general shops may offer this service.

Email

You'll find Internet cafes in the cities and some larger towns. A good alternative, but with limitations on opening hours, are public libraries in the cities and many larger towns. Costs vary, of course, but expect to pay around £3 per hour at a public library, where it's usually necessary to book a slot in advance. Nearly 20 SYHA hostels have Internet kiosks for members' use; the hourly rate is £5.

Email can be very useful to reserve accommodation, through major sites such as STB and SYHA, and through individual proprietors' sites.

The cheapest way to have email access while you're travelling is to get a free, Web-based email account such as Lonely Planet's eKno (W www.ekno.lonelyplanet.com), Hotmail (W www.hotmail.com) or Yahoo! (W www.yahoo.com). These enable you to access your mail from Internet cafes anywhere in the world, using a net-connected machine running a standard Web browser such as Explorer or Netscape.

DIGITAL RESOURCES

For walkers, useful Web sites are maintained by the Mountaineering Council of Scotland (W www.mountaineering-scotland.org.uk), Ramblers' Association (W www.ramblers.org.uk) and the Scottish Mountaineering Club (W www.smc.org.uk) – all of which have good links. Another site is TrailWalk (W www.trailwalk.com), a gear fanatic's paradise with masses of information about the latest gear.

For a host of ideas about day-long and extended walks, check W www.walkscotland.com, which also has links to other online walk sites. VisitScotland (W www.visit.scotland.net/outdoor) has some interesting pages for walkers.

One of the *Scotsman* newspaper's Web sites W www.leisure.scotsman.com/cfm/outdoors has an extensive database of walk descriptions from all over Scotland.

CitySync *Edinburgh* is Lonely Planet's digital city guide for Palm OS handheld devices. With CitySync you can quickly search, sort and bookmark hundreds of Edinburgh restaurants, hotels, attractions, clubs and more – all pinpointed on scrollable street maps. Sections on activities, transport and local events mean you get the big picture plus all the little details. Purchase or demo City-Sync *Edinburgh* at **W** www.citysync.com.

BOOKS

This book cannot cover every aspect of walking in Scotland but there are numerous books available covering more specific information. This section will guide you between the shelves. Detailed guidebooks to routes and areas are listed in the relevant sections.

Lonely Planet

For general travel around the country, Lonely Planet's *Scotland* is an excellent companion to this book. For more detail there is a separate guide to *Edinburgh*. Those who want to get to grips with local forms of the English language should pick up a copy of Lonely Planet's *British phrasebook*. Also helpful, particularly if you are planning to visit neighbouring England or Wales, are *Britain* and *Walking in Britain*. If you would like to try some other activities take a look at *Diving & Snorkeling Scotland* and *Cycling in Britain*, the latter covering several rides in Scotland.

Walking Guidebooks

The shelves of bookshops are groaning with walking guides to virtually all parts of Scotland and lavishly illustrated guides to the Munros.

The six volumes of the Scottish Mountaineering Club's District Guides cover the whole country, including the islands, and are the most authoritative, detailed and best-written guides on the market. They're not cheap (between £17 and £20) but are excellent investments for serious walking. The club's Hillwalkers Guides, one for *The Munros* edited by Donald Bennet, and one for *The Corbetts & Other Scottish Hills* edited by Johnstone et al, are hard to beat. Exploiting the Munro phenomenon to the limit, there's also *The Munroist's Companion* by Robin N Campbell, which has a wealth of background information. *Munro's Tables* by DA Bearhop is a book of lists, including the Corbetts, Donalds and Grahams (hills between 2000ft and 2500ft), plus a Gaelic guide. *Scotland's Mountains* by WH Murray has been reissued by the Scottish Mountaineering Club and is a classic in mountain literature by one of the best-known Scottish mountaineers and writers (even if the discussion of access and conservation is now dated).

Of the other guides to the Munros and Corbetts, two by Cameron McNeish (editor of *TGO*) are of considerable practical value – *The Munro Almanac* and *The Corbett Almanac* are in pocket-size format with all the basic information needed for a major bagging campaign. Hamish Brown's account of his historic first continuous round, *Hamish's Mountain Walk*, and *Climbing the Corbetts* aren't so much guidebooks as sources of inspiration.

Exploring Scottish Hill Tracks by Ralph Storer is a good guide to low-level walks and complements the more exhaustive *Scottish Hill Tracks*, published by the Scottish Rights of Way Society, with succinct track notes for more than 300 cross-country walks.

Cicerone Press (**W** www.cicerone.co.uk) has a list of about 25 titles for Scotland from the Hebrides to the Borders, several of which are recommended in this book. Any of the several volumes in the 25 Walks series, originally published by The Stationery Office, can be recommended, as can the equally extensive Pathfinder series, all covering day walks for a range of abilities and priced under £10.

Lastly, but not of least importance, food. *The Backpacker's Cookbook: A Practical Guide to Dining in Style* by Dave Coustick has many easy recipes although with a strong reliance on fresh ingredients, which may be less than practical for a trip of more than three days.

Natural History

Wild Scotland by James McCarthy is just what the cover blurb says, 'The essential guide to the best of natural Scotland', with brief overviews of plants and animals, places to see them and details of conservation reserves. Taking a step further towards specialist guides, *Scottish Wild Flowers* by Michael Scott (in the Collins' Field Guide series) is the best on the subject, with clear drawings and adequate identification information. In the same series, *Scottish Birds* by Valerie Thom is of more practical value than the more comprehensive *Field Guide: Birds of Britain & Europe* by Peterson et al. The *Wild Guide: Wild Animals of Britain & Europe* by John A Burton has good photos. For tree identification, the *Mitchell Beazley Pocket Guide to Trees* by Keith Rushforth has plenty of illustrations. All these guides are priced under £10. The Lomond natural history guides to trees and wild flowers are inexpensive (£2) but less detailed than the Collins guides.

History

Modern writing about Scotland's colourful and turbulent past, distant and very recent, is light years away from stodgy recitations of dates of battles, and the doings of kings and other powerful people. The focus is more on ordinary people and how the goings-on in high places influenced their lives. *Scotland: A New History* by Michael Lynch covers the near-millennium from around 400 BC to the 1990s. TM Devine's *The Scottish Nation 1700–2000* (in paperback) is very readable and looks at a wide range of themes, from industrial decline to football. Tom Nairn's *After Britain – New Labour and the Return of Scotland* discusses the decline of the British state and the rise of Scotland. Both sides of the still-emotive subject are presented in Eric Richards' *The Highland Clearances*. *Scotland's Mountains before the Mountaineers* by Ian Mitchell achieves the feat of being highly informative and entertaining, and is much more than a story of first ascents.

Buying Books

Most outdoor-gear shops stock a range of guides and general books on climbing and walking in Scotland. TICs, National Trust for Scotland and other organisations' visitor centres carry a similar range, plus natural history and history references. You'll find at least one bookshop in every town; James Thin in Edinburgh, Glasgow and Inverness is particularly good for Scottish titles.

Apart from normal retail outlets, Scottish Mountaineering Club publications can also be purchased online through its Web site at W www.smc.org.uk.

CD-ROMS

The Scottish Mountaineering Club has produced an interactive CD *The Munros*. It has descriptions and routes for all 284 of them, route and area maps, safety advice and several other innovative features. It costs £40, requires 20Mb of hard drive space and is available at W www.smc.org.uk or by calling ☎ 01389-756994.

ISYS Direct's CD-ROM *The Corbetts* (£39.99) includes descriptions of 204 walks, and lists hundreds of Scottish hills as well as the Corbetts. It has plenty of photos and includes a walker's logbook. It's available from ISYS at e sales@hillwalker.org.uk or through W www.hillwalker.org.

The Art of Outdoor Navigation (£19.95) is a fully interactive course for beginners and experts alike, including tutorials on contours and bearings, and interactive navigational challenges. You can preview it on W www.outdoornav.com or order it by calling ☎ 0808-107 1020 (free call).

NEWSPAPERS & MAGAZINES

Of the several outdoor magazines published in Britain, *TGO* (The Great Outdoors, monthly, £2.60) consistently has the best coverage of Scottish walks and news about Scotland. The equipment reviews are a highlight and the magazine generally takes a strong stand on environmental issues. *Trail* (monthly, £2.95) covers walking, including regular walk descriptions for Scotland, plus mountain biking, climbing and ski touring.

The Angry Corrie (W www.bubl.ac.uk/org/tacit/tac) is an iconoclastic, idiosyncratic magazine (or 'fanzine'), giving what may be a mystifying insight into the preoccupations of many Scottish hillwalkers. It costs 50p and can be found only in gear shops. *Country Walking* (monthly, £2.70) always features at least one walk in Scotland and is perhaps a more informal magazine than *TGO*.

The *Sunday Herald* (70p) has an outdoor section in which the editor of *TGO* has a regular column, usually in the shape of a walk description. The *Scotsman on Sunday* (70p) also has an outdoor section, which features walks from time to time.

WEATHER INFORMATION

It's not only a deluge of rain you may encounter but torrents of weather information – the Scots share the English obsession with weather. Several telephone/fax and online forecasting services tailored for walkers are available.

The most detailed service comes direct from the Met Office (the government's meteorological agency) in its daily mountain area forecasts by phone and fax; these include cloud base, visibility, wind and temperature at 900m. Call ☎ 09068-500441 for the western Highlands (Trossachs, Argyll, Lochaber, north-west Highlands and Skye) and ☎ 09068-500442 for the eastern Highlands (Cairngorms and the area east of Rannoch Moor). The cost is 60p/minute. The fax numbers are 09060-100405 for the western Highlands and 09060-100406 for the eastern Highlands, and the cost for these is £1/minute. The Met Office's Web site **W** www.met-office.gov.uk leads to everything you will ever need to know about weather and climate anywhere.

An online weather information service (**W** www.onlineweather.com) divides Scotland into five areas and gives details of wind, cloud base, freezing level, visibility, temperature at 914m (3000ft) and a weather index.

Forecasts in newspapers are of little use, having been issued the previous afternoon or evening.

BBC's Radio 4 (94.6-96.1FM) broadcasts a detailed hillwalkers' forecast at 6pm on Saturday; Radio Scotland's (92.7-94.5FM) forecasts are probably the most useful. Forecasts on television show the movement of pressure systems but lack detailed information about conditions in the mountains.

During 2001 a new index will be introduced to replace the wind chill factor, which has been used to adjust winter temperature forecasts. The thermal comfort index (TCI), on a scale from -10 to +10, will take into account a wider range of factors and will be quoted separately from the air temperature figure.

PHOTOGRAPHY

Film & Equipment

Since landscapes will feature prominently in your photographs of Scotland, 35mm transparency (slide) film will give the best results. Kodak Elite and Fuji Sensia (from £7.50 process-paid) are good, readily available films. For serious photography, Kodak Ektachrome E100 or Fuji Velvia will help to compensate for dull and overcast conditions. Slide film is generally difficult to find, so stock up wherever you can. Boots, the chemist chain, is a reliable source in larger towns.

Print film is widely available. Fuji or Kodak ISO 200 or 400 is suitable for Scottish conditions. Thirty-six exposure print films cost from £5.50. Processing can be done overnight for around £6 or in up to six days for £4.

A compact, lightweight camera with a mini zoom lens (35–70mm) is ideal for walking, rather than a heavier and more cumbersome SLR (single lens reflex) camera, especially if you use a zoom lens (eg, 28–110mm). A polarising filter will deepen colours in sunny conditions and cut out any haze. An 81a filter will help lighten cloudy days, and a graduated, neutral density filter will work wonders in unevenly lit landscapes. A padded camera carry bag with shoulder strap is essential to protect the camera from the elements. At the very least, pack your camera in a waterproof bag.

Airport Security

You'll have to put your camera and film through the X-ray machine at all British airports. The machines are supposed to be film safe but it may be worth putting exposed films in a lead-lined bag for protection. Luggage carried in the hold may be subjected to super-powerful scrutiny, which will ruin unprocessed film, so it's best to carry all film in your hand baggage.

TIME

Anywhere in the world, the time on your watch is measured in relation to Greenwich Mean Time (GMT) – the time at Greenwich, England.

Summer Time (daylight savings time) has been used in Britain since WWI; the clocks are put forward one hour during the last weekend in March and put back one hour the last weekend in October. This means, during Summer Time, Britain is ahead of GMT by one hour. As a standard, New York is five hours behind GMT and Sydney is 10 hours ahead. Phone the international operator (☎ 155) for other differences or look in the telephone directory under International Codes.

Most public transport timetables in Britain use the 24-hour clock but in everyday conversation it is rarely used; instead people refer to 9am or 9pm etc.

ELECTRICITY

The standard voltage in Scotland is 240V AC, 50Hz. Plugs have three square pins and adaptors are widely available.

WEIGHTS & MEASURES

With a marked absence of enthusiasm, Britain is edging towards full-scale adoption of metric weights and measures, although imperial measurements are still widely used. This has resulted in an odd mix of metric and imperial.

Since January 2000, goods in shops have to be advertised in kilograms (kg) although most British people still think and talk in pounds (lb) and ounces (oz). When it comes to volume, things are even worse. Most liquids are sold in litres (L) or half-litres. Petrol stations sell petrol priced in pence per litre, but measure car performance in miles per gallon. (A British gallon is equivalent to 1.2 US gallons or 4.55L.)

For length, most British people still use the old units of inches (in), feet (ft) and yards (yd), but on maps the heights of mountains are now given in metres (m) only. So walkers, more than any other section of the population, have become familiar with the 'new' metre measure.

However, all distances on road signs are in miles and some distances on footpath signs are given in miles too, although kilometre equivalents are becoming more and more common. One annoying aspect of this intransigence is that on signposts 'mile' is often abbreviated to 'm', which to everybody in the world except the sign-makers means 'metre'.

In this book we have reflected this rather wacky British system of mixed measurements. In the route descriptions, daily distances along footpaths are given in miles (mi) with some kilometre (km) equivalents, shorter distances are given in metres and heights of mountains are given in metres with some feet equivalents. That's the way things are in Britain, and who are we to swim against the tide?

In weather forecasts, Celsius temperatures are used in Britain (with Fahrenheit occasionally as a concession to conservative locals).

For conversion tables, see the inside back cover of this book.

BUSINESS HOURS

Offices generally open from 9am to 5pm on weekdays. Most post offices are open from 9am to 5.30pm weekdays and from 9am to 12.30pm Saturday. Shops and petrol stations may also open longer hours weekdays and from 9am to 5pm on Saturday. Sunday trading is fairly common, from 10am to 4pm, except in the Western Isles. Alcohol cannot be purchased in supermarkets or off-licences (liquor shops/stores) until noon on Sunday. In country towns, shops and post offices may have an early closing or half holiday, most likely Wednesday or Thursday afternoon. Late-night shopping, until 9pm, is usually on Thursday or Friday. Supermarkets and petrol stations in cities and larger towns open long hours most days and some never close (except on public holidays).

Bank hours vary but you can expect to find them open on weekdays from 9.30am to

4.30pm. Some banks in the cities open on Saturday, generally from 9.30am to noon. Banks in small towns and large villages may only open two or three days per week.

PUBLIC HOLIDAYS & SPECIAL EVENTS

Bank holidays in Scotland are just that – days when banks (and perhaps commercial offices) are closed, but everything else is (usually) open.

To confuse the issue, some commercial organisations with headquarters in England observe English bank holidays! General public holidays are also held on New Year's Day, the 2 January bank holiday and on Christmas Day, and some organisations may observe a holiday on Good Friday, the Friday before Easter. Annual holidays are:

New Year's Day 1 January
Bank Holiday 2 January
Bank Holiday first Monday in March
May Day Bank Holiday first Monday in May
Spring Bank Holiday last Monday in May
Summer Bank Holiday first Monday in August
Christmas Day 25 December
Boxing Day 26 December

At Hogmanay (New Year's Eve), public and private celebrations welcome in the new year, including street parties in Edinburgh and other major centres. All TICs have lists of special events in their areas, some of which perpetuate very old traditions.

Health & Safety

Keeping healthy during your walks and travels depends on your predeparture preparations, your daily health care while travelling and how you handle any medical problem that does develop. The potential problems can seem quite frightening but few travellers actually experience anything more than an upset stomach. The sections that follow aren't intended to alarm but are highly recommended reading before you go.

PREDEPARTURE PLANNING

Medical Cover

Citizens of European Union (EU) countries outside Britain are covered for emergency medical care upon presentation of an E111 form, which you need to get before you travel; obtain information from your doctor or local health service.

In Scotland the form entitles you to free treatment in government (National Health Service) clinics and hospitals, but you will have to pay for dental treatment, any medicines bought from pharmacies (even if a doctor has prescribed them) and possibly tests. Once home, you may be able to recover some or all of these costs from your national health service.

Health Insurance

Make sure you have adequate health insurance. See Travel Insurance on page 69.

Immunisations

No immunisations are required for Scotland but, before your trip, it's a good idea to make sure you are up to date with routine vaccinations. Those for diphtheria, tetanus and polio are usually given in childhood and boosters are necessary every 10 years.

First Aid

It's always a good idea to know what to do in the event of a major accident or illness. Consider doing a recognised basic first aid course before you go and/or including a first aid manual with your medical kit (and reading it). Although detailed first aid instruction is outside the scope of this book, some basic points are given under Medical Problems & Treatment on page 81. Prevention of accidents is also important (see Safety on the Walk on page 86 for more advice). You should also know how to summon help should a major accident or illness befall you or someone with you (see Rescue & Evacuation on page 87).

Physical Preparation

Some of the walks in this book are physically demanding and most require a reasonable level of fitness. Even if you're tackling the easy or easy-medium walks, it pays to be moderately fit at the start of your trip, rather than launch straight into them after months of fairly sedentary living. If you're aiming for the medium or hard walks, then fitness is essential.

Unless you're a regular walker, start your get-fit campaign about a month before your visit. Take a vigorous walk of about an hour, two or three times per week and gradually extend the duration of your outings as the departure date nears. If you plan to carry a full backpack on any walk, carry a loaded pack on some of your training jaunts. Walkers over the age of 55 with little previous experience should have a medical checkup beforehand.

Other Preparations

If you have any ongoing medical problems or are concerned about your health in any way, it's wise to have a full checkup before you go. It's far better to have any problems identified and treated at home than to find out about them halfway up a mountain. It's also sensible to have a dental checkup since toothache on the trail, with solace a couple of days away, can be a miserable experience. If you wear glasses, take a spare pair and your prescription. If you need a particular medicine, pack enough with you to last the trip. Take part of the packaging showing

Medical Kit Check List

This is a list of items to consider including in your medical kit – consult your pharmacist for brands available in your country.

First-Aid Supplies

- ☐ **adhesive tape**
- ☐ **bandages** and **safety pins**
- ☐ **elasticised support bandage** – for knees, ankles etc
- ☐ **gauze swabs**
- ☐ **nonadhesive dressings**
- ☐ **small pair of scissors**
- ☐ **sterile alcohol wipes**
- ☐ **sticking plasters** (eg, Band-Aids, blister plasters)
- ☐ **paper stitches**
- ☐ **thermometer** (note that mercury thermometers are prohibited by airlines)
- ☐ **tweezers**

Medications

- ☐ **anti-diarrhoea** and **anti-nausea** drugs
- ☐ **antifungal cream** or **powder** – for fungal skin infections and thrush
- ☐ **antihistamines** – for allergies (eg, hay fever), to ease the itch from insect bites or stings, and to prevent motion sickness
- ☐ **antiseptic** (eg, povidone-iodine) – for cuts and grazes
- ☐ **calamine lotion, sting relief spray** or **aloe vera** – to ease irritation from sunburn and insect bites or stings
- ☐ **cold and flu tablets**, **throat lozenges** and **nasal decongestant**
- ☐ **painkillers** (eg, aspirin or paracetamol, acetaminophen in the USA) – for pain and fever
- ☐ **rehydration mixture** – to prevent dehydration (eg, due to severe diarrhoea); particularly important for children

Miscellaneous

- ☐ **antibacterial preparation** – for hand washing
- ☐ **eye drops**
- ☐ **insect repellent**
- ☐ **sunscreen** and **lip balm**
- ☐ **water purification tablets** or **iodine**

the generic name, rather than the brand, as this will make getting replacements easier. It's also a good idea to have a legible prescription or letter from your doctor to prove that you legally use the medication, to avoid any problems at customs.

Health Guides

Lonely Planet's Healthy Travel guides are compact and useful, while *Travel with Children* includes advice on travel health for younger children. *Travellers' Health* by Dr Richard Dawood is comprehensive, easy to read, authoritative and highly recommended.

Online Resources

There are a number of excellent travel health sites on the Internet. From the Lonely Planet home page there are links at **W** www.lonelyplanet.com/weblinks to the World Health Organization plus many other useful sites.

STAYING HEALTHY

Hygiene

Make a point of washing your hands, especially before preparing food and eating. In areas where detergents cannot be used, teatree oil is a useful substitute.

Take particular care to dispose carefully of all toilet waste when you are on a walk (see Human Waste Disposal on page 66).

Food

Strict food hygiene regulations are in force in Scotland so you should feel confident that the food you eat in cafes and such places is safe.

Although instances of Creutzfeldt-Jakob Disease (CJD, the human form of mad cow disease) received a great deal of publicity at the end of the 1990s, the likelihood of contracting the disease now through local beef consumption is quite remote.

Water

Tap water in Scotland is safe to drink. Always beware of natural water sources; a bubbling stream in the mountains may look clear but the risk of infection, from human or animal contamination, is real.

Water Purification The simplest way of purifying water is to boil it vigorously and thoroughly. If you cannot boil water you can use a chemical purifying agent. Chlorine and iodine in powder, tablet or liquid form are usually used, and are available from outdoor equipment suppliers and pharmacies. Follow the recommended dosages and allow the water to stand for the correct length of time. Chlorine tablets will kill many pathogens, but not some parasites including Giardia and amoebic cysts. Iodine is a more effective purifier; follow the directions carefully and remember that too much iodine can be harmful.

You could also consider purchasing a water filter. There are two main kinds – total filters take out all parasites, bacteria and viruses, and simple filters (which can be a nylon mesh bag) take out dirt and larger foreign bodies so that chemical solutions work more effectively.

Nutrition

Nutrition should not be a problem in Scotland. Nevertheless, once you've been walking for a week or more, you'll find your appetite increases; boosting your intake of energy-giving carbohydrates (pasta, bread) with the evening meal isn't a bad idea. The range of readily available fruit and vegetables should ensure a balanced diet.

Common Ailments

Blisters This problem can be avoided. Make sure your walking boots or shoes are well worn in before your visit. At the very least, wear them on a few short walks before tackling longer outings. Your boots should fit comfortably with enough room to move your toes; boots that are too big or too small will cause blisters. Similarly for socks – be sure they fit properly and wear socks specifically made for walkers; even then, check to make sure that there are no seams across the widest part of your foot. Wet and muddy socks can also cause blisters, so even on a day walk pack a spare pair. Keep your toenails clipped but not too short. If you do feel a blister coming on, treat it sooner rather than later. Apply a simple sticking plaster or, preferably, one of the special blister plasters, which act as a second skin, and follow the maker's instructions for replacement.

Fatigue A simple statistic – more injuries of whatever nature happen towards the end of the day rather than earlier, when you're fresher. Although tiredness can simply be a nuisance on an easy walk, it can be life-threatening on narrow, exposed ridges or in bad weather. You should never set out on a walk that is beyond your capabilities on that day. If you feel below par, have a day off and relax. To reduce the risk, don't push yourself too hard – take rests every hour or two and build in a good half-hour's lunch break. Towards the end of the day, moderate the pace and increase your concentration. You should also eat and drink sensibly throughout the day, to replace the energy used and fluids expended. Nuts, dried fruit and chocolate are all good, energy-giving snack foods.

Knee Pain Many walkers feel the strain in their knees on long, steep descents. To reduce the stress on knee joints (you can't avoid it entirely) try taking shorter steps, keeping your legs slightly bent, and ensure that your heel hits the ground before the rest of your foot. Some walkers find tubular bandages help, while others use strap-on supports. A pair of walking poles effectively takes some of the weight off the knees.

MEDICAL PROBLEMS & TREATMENT

Environmental Hazards

There's no doubt that walkers are at risk from environmental hazards. The risk, however, can be significantly reduced by using common sense and reading the following sections.

Asthma & Hay Fever Among air-borne allergens, pollen is a widespread hazard for asthma and hay fever sufferers. The main danger period in Scotland is from May to August. Inhalers (or puffers) are available without prescription at pharmacies.

Warning

Self-diagnosis and treatment can be risky, so you should always seek medical help. Tourist Information Centres (TICs), B&B hosts or hostel staff should be able to direct you to the nearest doctor. Correct diagnosis is vital.

Generic rather than brand names for drugs are used in this section; check with a pharmacist for locally available brands.

Sun Even in Scotland, protection against the sun should always be taken seriously. Particularly in the deceptive coolness of the mountains, sunburn occurs rapidly. Slap on the sunscreen and a barrier cream for your nose and lips, wear a broad-brimmed hat whenever the sun appears and protect your eyes by wearing good-quality sunglasses with UV lenses, particularly when walking near water, sand or snow. If, despite these precautions, you are burnt, calamine lotion, aloe vera or other commercial sunburn relief preparations will soothe.

Heat Hot weather isn't unknown in Scotland. Take time to acclimatise to high temperatures, drink sufficient liquids and do not do anything too physically demanding until you are acclimatised.

Dehydration & Heat Exhaustion Potentially dangerous and generally preventable, dehydration is precipitated by excessive fluid loss. Sweating and inadequate fluid intake are the most common causes among walkers. Other important causes are diarrhoea, vomiting and high fever (see Diarrhoea under Infectious Diseases on page 83 for appropriate treatment). The first symptoms are weakness, thirst and passing small amounts of very concentrated urine. This may progress to drowsiness, dizziness or fainting on standing up and, finally, coma.

It's easy to forget how much fluid is lost via perspiration while you are walking, particularly if a strong breeze is drying your skin quickly. You should always maintain a good fluid intake – a minimum of 3L a day is recommended.

Dehydration and salt deficiency can cause heat exhaustion. Salt deficiency is characterised by fatigue, lethargy, headaches, giddiness and muscle cramps; adding extra salt to your food should be sufficient – taking salt tablets isn't necessary.

Cold Too much cold can be just as dangerous as too much heat.

Hypothermia When the body loses heat faster than it can produce it and the core temperature of the body falls, hypothermia occurs. It is a real and ever-present threat for walkers – people do die from it. In the mountains, always be prepared for the onset of cold, wet and windy conditions, no matter how warm and clear the weather when you set out. Always carry basic supplies (see What to Bring on page 57) and some high-energy food such as nuts, dried fruit and chocolate.

The progression from very cold to dangerously cold can happen with frightening speed if wet clothing, fatigue and hunger are combined with windy conditions. If the weather deteriorates take precautions immediately; put on extra layers of warm clothing, a wind and/or waterproof jacket, plus wool or fleece hat and gloves. Have something to eat and make sure everyone in your group is fit, feeling well and alert.

Symptoms of hypothermia, in the approximate order of appearance, are lethargy, exhaustion, shivering, cold extremities, stumbling, dizzy spells, slurred speech, irrational or violent behaviour (such as trying to take off protective clothes), violent bursts of energy, and numb fingers and toes.

To treat mild hypothermia, first get the victim to the best available shelter from the wind and/or rain, remove their clothing if it's wet and replace it with dry, warm garments. Wrap the person in a sleeping bag, space blanket or large bivouac bag; failing this, have other members of your group sit or lie as close to the sufferer as possible. Do not rub victims; instead, allow them to slowly warm themselves. Give them warm, sweet fluids (*never* alcohol), and some high-energy, easily digestible food. Early

Everyday Health

Normal body temperature is up to 37°C (98.6°F); more than 2°C (4°F) higher indicates a high fever. The normal adult pulse rate is 60 to 100 per minute (children 80 to 100). As a general rule the pulse increases about 20 beats per minute for each 1°C (2°F) rise in fever.

Respiration (breathing) rate is also an indicator of illness. Count the number of breaths per minute; between 12 and 20 is normal for adults and older children (up to 30 for younger children). People with a high fever or serious respiratory illness breathe more quickly than normal. More than 40 shallow breaths per minute may indicate pneumonia.

recognition and treatment of mild hypothermia is the only way to prevent severe hypothermia, which is a life-threatening condition.

Infectious Diseases

Diarrhoea Simply a change of water, food or climate can cause a mild bout of diarrhoea, but a few rushed toilet trips with no other symptoms is not indicative of a major problem. More serious diarrhoea is caused by infectious agents transmitted by faecal contamination of food or water, using contaminated utensils or directly from one person's hand to another. Paying particular attention to personal hygiene is the most important precaution to take to avoid getting diarrhoea on your travels.

Dehydration is the main danger, particularly in children or the elderly as it can occur quite quickly. *Fluid replacement*, at least equal to the volume being lost, is the most important thing to remember. Weak black tea with a little sugar, soda water, or soft drinks allowed to go flat and diluted 50% with clean water are all good. For severe diarrhoea a rehydrating solution, to replace minerals and salts lost, is preferable. Commercially available oral rehydration salts (ORS) are very useful; add them to boiled or bottled water. In an emergency you can make up a solution of six teaspoons of sugar and a half teaspoon of salt to 1L of boiled or bottled water. You need to drink at least the same volume of fluid that you are losing in bowel movements and vomiting. Urine is the best guide to the adequacy of replacement – if you pass small amounts of concentrated urine, you need to drink more. Keep drinking small amounts often and stick to a bland diet as you recover.

Tetanus This disease is caused by a germ, which lives in soil and in the faeces of horses and other animals, and enters the body via breaks in the skin. The first symptom may be discomfort in swallowing, or stiffening of the jaw and neck; this is followed by painful convulsions of the jaw and body. The disease, which can be fatal, can be prevented by immunisation, so make sure your vaccination is up to date before you leave.

Lyme Disease This is a tick-transmitted infection which may be acquired through contact with bracken and merely walking in areas inhabited by red deer. The illness usually begins with a spreading rash at the site of the tick bite, and is accompanied by fever, headache, extreme fatigue, aching joints and muscles, and mild neck stiffness. If untreated, these symptoms usually resolve over several weeks but disorders of the nervous system, heart and joints may develop later. Medical help should be sought as treatment works best at an early stage.

Traumatic Injuries

Sprains Ankle and knee sprains are common, particularly among walkers crossing rough ground. To help prevent ankle sprains you should wear boots that have adequate ankle support. If you do suffer a sprain, immobilise the joint with a firm bandage, and relieve pain and swelling by keeping it elevated for the first 24 hours and, where possible, by applying ice or cold water to the swollen joint. Take simple painkillers to ease the discomfort. If the sprain is mild, you may be able to continue your walk after a couple of days. For more severe sprains, seek medical attention as an x-ray may be needed to show whether a bone has been broken.

Major Accidents Falling or having something fall on you, resulting in head injuries or fractures, is always possible, especially if you're crossing steep slopes or unstable terrain. Here is some basic advice about what to do if a major accident happens; detailed first aid instruction is outside the scope of this book. If someone suffers a bad fall:

- Make sure you and other people with you are not in danger.
- Assess the injured person's condition.
- Stabilise any injuries, such as bleeding wounds or broken bones.
- Seek medical attention – see Rescue & Evacuation on page 87.

If the person is unconscious, immediately check the breathing (clear the airway if it is blocked) and check the pulse by feeling the side of the neck rather than the wrist. If there is a pulse but no breathing, start mouth-to-mouth resuscitation immediately. In these circumstances the patient should be moved as little as possible in case the neck or back is broken. Keep them warm by covering with a space blanket, sleeping bag or dry clothing; insulate from the ground if possible.

Check for wounds and broken bones; if the victim is conscious ask where pain is felt. Otherwise, gently inspect them all over (including their back and back of the head), moving them as little as possible. Control any bleeding by applying firm pressure to the wound. Bleeding from the nose or ear may indicate a fractured skull. Don't give the person anything by mouth, especially if they are unconscious. Anyone who has been knocked unconscious should be watched closely. Note any signs of deterioration (eg, change in breathing patterns), to report to the rescuers/doctor.

Indications of a fracture (broken bone) are pain, swelling and discolouration, loss of function or deformity of a limb. Unless you know exactly what you're doing, don't try to straighten an obviously displaced broken bone. To protect from further injury, immobilise a nondisplaced fracture by splinting it; if the thigh bone is broken, strap it to the good leg to hold it in place. Check the splinted limb frequently to ensure the splint hasn't cut off circulation to the hand or foot. Broken ribs are painful but usually heal by themselves and do not need splinting. If breathing becomes difficult, or the person coughs up blood, a lung may be punctured, so medical attention should be sought urgently.

Fractures associated with open wounds (compound fractures) require more urgent treatment than simple fractures as there is a risk of infection.

Dislocations – where the bone has come out of the joint – are very painful, and should be set as soon as possible.

Internal injuries are more difficult to detect and cannot usually be treated on site. Watch the patient closely for the onset of shock, a specific medical condition associated with failure to maintain circulating blood volume. Signs include a rapid pulse and cold, clammy extremities. A person in shock requires urgent medical attention.

Cuts, Scratches & Grazes

Even small cuts, scratches and grazes should be washed well and treated with an antiseptic such as povidone-iodine. Dry wounds heal more quickly, so where possible avoid bandages and Band-Aids, which can keep wounds wet. Infection in a wound is indicated by the skin margins becoming red, painful and swollen. More serious infection can cause swelling of the whole limb and of the lymph glands. The patient may develop a fever and will need medical attention.

Burns

Immerse the burnt area in cold water as soon as possible, then cover it with a clean, dry sterile dressing. Keep this in place by plasters for a day or so in the case of a small, mild burn, but longer for more extensive injuries. Medical help should be sought for severe and extensive burns.

Bites & Stings

Bees & Wasps These are usually painful rather than dangerous. However, people who are allergic may suffer severe breathing difficulties and need urgent medical

Megabites from Midges

The tourist literature promoting Scotland, and the western Highlands and islands in particular, is still coy about mentioning an unavoidable and less than delightful fact of life during summer – midges.

The midge is a pin-head size, black insect, which gathers in dense, dark clouds and swarms on humans (and animals), making life a misery. The insect can detect its prey from up to 100m by scent and shape, and can also let other midges know about the 'find'. Of the 37 species of midge found in Scotland, six inflict bites.

Midges usually appear in early June and blight the countryside until the first chilly weather of autumn. They congregate wherever there's damp or wet ground, in rushes and sphagnum moss. They're most active in early morning and evening, and on overcast days. Fortunately they don't like wind, dry ground, bright sunshine or a scent emitted by some lucky people, who remain untouched while their companions are being attacked.

The bite causes an itchy reaction in most people, which can last from several minutes to several hours. Scratching the bite only prolongs the itch. It is best to brush rather than slap them away so as not to spread the saliva.

Stories abound about the desperate measures taken to escape the biting hordes – immersion in the sea, and donning gloves and balaclava to eat a meal outdoors. Some people swear by swallowing heaps of vitamin C, others add liberal amounts of garlic to their meals.

The best protection is to cover your arms and legs, and wear a hat with a fine netting veil, available at outdoor equipment shops. Insect repellents, containing DEET (di-ethyl toluamide), DMP (dimethyl phthalate) or natural oils (including bog myrtle), should keep your skin midge-free for a few hours. Burning coils impregnated with repellent are an effective weapon, especially at camping grounds. It's best to avoid sheltered, windless sites when you stop for lunch or to pitch a tent. Midges rarely venture indoors – your last refuge.

The creatures have a place in the scheme of natural things as food for some species of birds, bats and worms, and insectivorous plants such as sundews love them. Midge larvae in turn feed on other organisms in the soil (where they live for about 10 months after the eggs hatch).

Attempts to eradicate midges from their natural habitat have adversely affected other wildlife, and research into harmless and 100% effective methods of protection continues. If you really want to find out more, George Hendry's book *Midges in Scotland* (£4.95) has the answers.

care. Calamine lotion or a commercial sting relief spray will ease discomfort, and ice packs will reduce the pain and swelling.

Snakes The adder is the only poisonous snake you're likely to encounter and its venom is rarely fatal; an antivenin is usually available.

Immediately wrap the bitten limb tightly, as you would for a sprained ankle, and then attach a splint to immobilise it. Keep the victim still and seek medical help. Tourniquets and sucking out the poison are now comprehensively discredited.

Ticks You should always check all over your body if you have been walking through a potentially tick-infested area (mainly overhanging bracken), as ticks can cause skin infections and other more serious diseases. If you find a tick attached to your skin press down around its head with tweezers, grab the head and gently pull upwards. Avoid pulling the rear of the body as this may squeeze the tick's gut contents through the attached mouth parts into the skin, increasing the risk of infection and disease. Smearing chemicals on the tick will not make it let go and is not recommended.

Women's Health

Walking can promote good health, although some care is needed in coping with specific women's health matters when you're out walking, especially on an extended trip. Maintaining good personal hygiene is vital but is not always easy when wild camping and if water is scarce. Make sure you regularly change your underwear (cotton is best) and try to at least sponge wash daily. For more information on women's health while travelling, see Women Travellers in one of Lonely Planet's Healthy Travel guides.

Menstruation A change in diet, routine or environment, as well as intensive exercise can all lead to irregularities in the menstrual cycle. This, in itself, is not a huge issue and your cycle should get back to normal when you return to your usual lifestyle. It is particularly important during the menstrual cycle to maintain good personal hygiene, and regularly change sanitary napkins or tampons. (For disposal options see Rubbish on page 66.) Anti-bacterial hand gel or premoistened wipes can be useful if you don't have access to soap and water. You can also use applicator tampons to minimise the risk of contamination, although these are quite bulky. Because of hygiene concerns and for ease while on an extended trip, some women prefer to temporarily stop menstruation. You should discuss your options with a doctor before you go. It is also important to note that failure to menstruate could indicate pregnancy! If concerned about irregularities seek medical advice.

Pregnancy If you are pregnant, see your doctor before you travel. Even normal pregnancies can make a woman feel nauseated and tired, making long-distance walking difficult or uncomfortable.

Thrush (Vaginal Candidiasis) Antibiotic use, synthetic underwear, tight trousers, sweating, contraceptive pills and unprotected sex can each lead to fungal vaginal infections. The most common is thrush (vaginal candidiasis). Symptoms include itching and discomfort in the genital area, often in association with a thick white discharge. The best prevention is to keep the vaginal area cool and dry, and to wear cotton, rather than synthetic, underwear and loose clothes. Thrush can be treated by clotrimazole pessaries or vaginal cream. If these are not available, a vinegar or lemon-juice douche, or yoghurt can also help. If prone to thrush, you may wish to carry medication to deal with a possible infection.

Urinary Tract Infection Dehydration and 'hanging on' can result in urinary tract infection and the symptoms of cystitis, which can be particularly distressing and an inconvenient problem when out walking. Symptoms include burning when urinating, and having to urinate frequently and urgently. Blood can sometimes be passed in the urine. Drink plenty of fluids and empty your bladder at regular intervals. If symptoms persist, seek medical attention because a simple infection can spread to the kidneys, causing a more severe illness.

SAFETY ON THE WALK

Although Scotland's mountains aren't high by continental European standards, conditions can become hazardous very quickly at any time of the year. By taking a few simple precautions you'll significantly reduce the odds of getting into difficulties. See the boxed text 'Walk Safety – Basic Rules' for a list of simple precautions.

For information on the clothes and equipment you should take with you when walking, consult What to Bring on page 57. There are various ways of learning and improving the essential skills, especially navigation – see under Walkers' Organisations on page 68.

Crossing Streams

Sudden downpours can turn a small burn into a raging torrent very quickly. If you're in any doubt about the safety of a crossing, look for a safer passage or wait; if the rain is short-lived it may subside quickly.

If you decide it's essential to cross (late in the day, for example), try to find a wide shallow stretch of the stream. Keep boots on – your feet could easily be injured on the stream bed. Put dry, warm clothes and a towel near the top of your pack. Undo the chest strap and hip belt and secure them out

Walk Safety – Basic Rules

- Allow plenty of time to complete a walk before dark, particularly when daylight hours are short.
- Don't overestimate your capabilities. Study the route carefully, noting the point of no return (where it's quicker to continue than to turn back). Monitor your progress against the time estimated for the walk and keep an eye on the weather.
- Unless you're very experienced, it's wise not to walk alone. Always leave details of your intended route, number of people in your group and expected return time with someone responsible before you set off; let them know when you return. Use route cards, available from TICs, outdoor shops and hostels.
- Before setting off, make sure you have the relevant map, compass, whistle, some spare clothing, adequate food and water, and that you know the local weather forecast for the next 24 hours.

of the way, making it quick and easy to offload the pack if you lose your balance and get swept downstream. Use a walking pole as a third leg or you can link hands with a companion, holding at the wrist for a firmer grip, and cross side-on to the flow, taking short steps.

Lightning

If a storm brews, avoid exposed areas. Lightning has a penchant for crests, lone trees, small depressions, gullies, caves and cabin entrances, as well as wet ground. If you are caught out in the open, try to curl up as tightly as possible with your feet together and keep a layer of insulation between you and the ground. Place metal objects such as metal-framed backpacks and walking poles away from you.

Communications Equipment

Modern technology has its uses, but in the end is *no* substitute for skills and experience. It does not, by itself, make walking any safer.

Mobile Phones Although coverage of walking areas in Scotland is improving all the time, it's very unlikely to extend to gullies, glens and corries. Reception may be good on high points but the strength of transmission can't be guaranteed. Mobiles can reduce the waiting time for rescue but should *only* be used to summon assistance when immediate help is a matter of life or death.

GPS Receivers Global Positioning System receivers use microwave signals from satellites to fix the user's position on the ground to within 10m – nearly all the time. However, they are fallible, expensive, easy enough to lose, and inadequate substitutes for map and compass and the ability to find your way between two points. Dense vegetation and nearby high ground can render the less sophisticated models almost useless. You need to monitor the batteries' life, although more expensive models do have back-up batteries. They cost from £145 to beyond £200.

Rescue & Evacuation

If someone in your group is injured or falls ill and can't move, leave somebody with him or her while another one or more goes for help, taking a written description of the location of the victim (as a six- or eight-figure grid reference) and of the terrain should a helicopter be needed. If there are only two of you, leave the injured person with as much warm clothing, food and water as it's sensible to spare, plus a whistle and torch. Mark the position with something conspicuous – an orange bivvy bag or perhaps a large stone cross on the ground.

If you need to call for help, use these internationally recognised emergency signals. Give six short signals, such as a whistle, a yell or the flash of a light, at 10-second intervals, followed by a minute's rest. Repeat the sequence until you get a response. If the responder knows the signals, this will be three signals at 20-second intervals, followed by a minute's pause and a repetition of the sequence.

Be ready to give information on where the accident occurred, how many people are injured and the injuries sustained.

Search & Rescue Organisations In Scotland, search and rescue operations for walkers are coordinated by the police, and involve the local volunteer mountain rescue team, and possibly a search and rescue dog team and an RAF helicopter. Although you can be connected to a police station by ringing ☎ 999, the operator may not have a good knowledge of Scottish geography. It's better to call the nearest full-time police station; these numbers are given under Information Sources in the walk chapters.

Helicopter Rescue & Evacuation If a helicopter arrives on the scene, there are a couple of conventions you should know. Standing face on to the chopper:

- Arms up in the shape of a letter 'V' means 'I/We need help'.
- Arms in a straight diagonal line (like one line of a letter X) means 'All OK'.

For the helicopter to land, there must be a cleared space of 25m x 25m, with a flat landing pad area of 6m x 6m. The helicopter will fly into the wind when landing. In cases of extreme emergency, where no landing area is available, a person or harness might be lowered. Take extreme care to avoid the rotors when approaching a landed helicopter.

Getting There & Away

However you choose to arrive in Scotland, make sure you take out travel insurance (see Visas & Documents on page 69).

For travel to/from Europe or other parts of the UK, buses are both the cheapest and most exhausting type of transport, although discount rail tickets are competitive and budget flights can be good value. Bear in mind that a small saving on the fare may not make up for time spent travelling and being exhausted when you arrive.

If you fly into London, it's probably best to take the bus or train north. Flying time from London to Edinburgh or Glasgow is about one hour. However, when you consider the time taken to go from one London airport to another and then to the city centre at the other end, plus boarding/unloading time, the 3½- to four-hour centre-to-centre rail journey may be more attractive.

When you're weighing up the pros and cons, don't forget the hidden costs – getting to/from airports, departure taxes, and food and drink consumed en route.

Warning

The information in this chapter is particularly vulnerable to change – prices for international travel are volatile, routes are introduced and cancelled, schedules change, special deals come and go, and rules are amended. Airlines and governments seem to take a perverse delight in making price structures and regulations as complicated as possible. Check directly with the airline or a travel agent to make sure you understand how a fare (and the ticket you may buy) works.

The upshot is you should gather opinions, quotes and advice from as many airlines and travel agents as possible before parting with your cash. The travel industry is highly competitive and there are many lurks and perks. The details given in this chapter should be regarded as pointers and are not a substitute for your own careful, up-to-date research.

AIR

Airports & Airlines

The three main international airports are Glasgow (☎ 0141-887 1111), Edinburgh (☎ 0131-333 1000) and Aberdeen (☎ 01224-722331). Other airports include Inverness (☎ 01667-464000), Stornoway (☎ 01851-702256), Kirkwall (☎ 01856-872421) and Sumburgh (☎ 01950-460654). Frequent direct flights arrive from England, Wales, Ireland, Scandinavia and continental Europe; flights from North America land at Glasgow.

The main operators to Scotland are Air France (☎ 0845-7581393), Aer Lingus (☎ 0845-973 7747), British Airways (☎ 0845-773 3377, W www.british-airways.com), British Midland (☎ 0870-607 0555), Continental (☎ 0800-776464), easyJet (☎ 0870-600 0000, W www.easyjet.com), KLM uk (☎ 0870-507 4074) and Scotairways (☎ 0870-606 0707, fax 01223-292160, W www.scotairways.co.uk).

Buying Tickets

An air ticket can make a big dent in anyone's budget but you can reduce the cost with discounted fares. Stiff competition has resulted in widespread discounting but you need to buy carefully.

Plenty of discount tickets for long-term travel are available, which are valid for 12 months and allow multiple stopovers. For short-term travel, it's usually cheaper to travel midweek, staying away at least one Saturday night or taking advantage of the many short-lived promotional offers. Return tickets usually work out cheaper than two one-ways or sometimes even less than a single ticket.

When you're looking for discounted air fares, go to a travel agent rather than directly to the airline (unless it's one of the low-cost carriers like easyJet). Airlines do have promotional fares and special offers, and their student and senior citizens' fares can be competitive, but generally they only sell fares at the official listed price.

Another way to save money is to book on the Internet, where many airlines offer some excellent fares. Travel Web sites can make it quick and easy to compare prices before you visit a travel agent. Online ticket sales are fine for a simple one-way or return trip on specified dates, but are no substitute for a travel agent who knows all about special deals and can offer all kinds of advice.

The days when some travel agents would routinely fleece travellers by disappearing with their money are almost over. Paying by credit card generally offers protection, as most card issuers provide refunds if you can prove you didn't get what you paid for. Similar protection can be obtained by buying a ticket from a bonded agent, such as one covered by the Air Transport Operators Licence (ATOL) scheme in the UK.

You may decide to pay more than the rock-bottom fare by opting for the safety of a better-known travel agent. Firms such as STA Travel (W www.statravel.com), which has offices around the world, Council Travel (W www.counciltravel.com) in the USA and Trailfinders (W www.trailfinder.com) in the UK are firmly established and offer good prices to most destinations.

The fares quoted in this book are a guide only. They'll almost certainly have changed by the time you read this.

Travellers with Special Needs

If you require a special diet, are taking a baby or small child, or have other special needs, let the airline know from the outset. Remind them when you reconfirm your booking and again when you check in at the airport.

Children aged under two travel free or for 10% of the standard fare if they don't occupy a seat. Children aged between two and 12 usually get a seat for half to two-thirds of the full fare, and do merit a baggage allowance.

Departure Tax

All domestic flights and those to destinations within the European Union (EU) from Britain carry a £10 departure tax. For flights to other cities abroad you pay £20. This is usually built into the price of your ticket.

England & Wales

Trailfinders (☎ 020-7938 3939), 194 Kensington High St, London W8 6FT, produces a brochure that includes air fares.

STA Travel (☎ 020-7361 6262), 86 Old Brompton Rd, London SW7, has several branches in the UK.

British Airways flies from London's Heathrow, Gatwick and Stansted, and from Birmingham, Manchester and Cardiff. British Midland flies from Heathrow, Manchester, the East Midlands and Leeds. EasyJet flies from London's Luton airport. Scotairways flies from London City airport.

Prices vary hugely. The standard economy return ticket from London to Edinburgh on British Airways costs £271.50; British Airways' lowest return fare is £130.50 but there are restrictions. EasyJet offers no-frills flights for £50 return between London and Edinburgh, Glasgow, Aberdeen or Inverness. Scotairways offers London to Edinburgh or Glasgow flights for around £91.

Ireland

Competition on air routes between Scotland (and Britain generally) and Ireland means you can usually get a discount ticket for as little as £50. Besides the main Dublin to London route, regional services link Glasgow and Edinburgh with Northern Ireland and the Republic.

Continental Europe

There isn't much variation in prices to/from the main European cities. All the major airlines usually offer some sort of deal and travel agents generally have a number of special deals, so shop around.

Expect to pay the equivalent of between £50 and £200 on major airlines for discounted return tickets to Scotland. The low-cost carriers charge about £50 to £150 to their Scottish destinations, usually the most competitive markets.

Across Europe many travel agencies have ties with STA Travel, where cheap tickets can be purchased and STA-issued tickets can be altered (usually for a fee of US$25). Major outlets include Voyages

Wasteels (☎ 08 03 88 70 04 from within France, fax 01 43 25 46 25), 11 rue Dupuytren, 756006 Paris; STA Travel (☎ 030-311 0950, fax 313 0948), Goethestrasse 73, 10625 Berlin; and Passaggi (☎ 06-474 0923, fax 482 7436), Stazione Termini FS, Galleria Di Tesla, Rome.

A Paris agent with some of the best services and deals is Nouvelles Frontières (☎ 08 03 33 33 33, **W** www.nouvelles-frontieres.com), 5 ave de l'Opéra (1er). In the Netherlands, a recommended travel agent in Amsterdam is Malibu Travel (☎ 020-626 32 30) at Prinsengracht 230.

The USA

There's a long-running fare war on flights between the US and London, the busiest intercontinental route in the world. The major airlines have all had fares between eastern USA and London as low as US$300 in winter, US$400 in spring and autumn, and US$600 in summer. From the west coast, fares have been about US$100 higher. These haven't changed for several years. With these low advertised fares you may not need a travel agent, just check with the airlines or Web sites.

If you do need an agent, Council Travel (☎ 800-226-8624, **W** www.counciltravel.com), 205 E 42 St, New York, NY 10017, is the USA's largest student travel organisation and has around 60 offices. STA Travel (☎ 800-777-0112, **W** www.statravel.com) has offices in Boston, Chicago, Miami, New York, Philadelphia, San Francisco and other major cities.

Canada

Canada has also enjoyed discount fares to Britain but, as Canadian Airways International has been taken over by Air Canada, things may change.

Canadian discount air ticket sellers are also known as consolidators and their air fares tend to be about 10% higher than those sold in the USA. The *Globe & Mail*, the *Toronto Star*, the *Montreal Gazette* and the *Vancouver Sun* carry travel agents' advertisements and are good places to look for cheap fares.

Travel CUTS (☎ 800-667-2887, **W** www.travelcuts.com) is Canada's national student travel agency and has offices in all major cities.

Australia

Several airlines compete on the routes from Australia to Britain and a wide variety of fares is available. Round-the-World (RTW) tickets are often real bargains. It may be cheaper to go right round the world on a RTW ticket than to do a U-turn on a return ticket. Expect to pay from A$1800 in the low season to A$3000 in the high season for return tickets between Australia and Britain. A RTW ticket might take you to Edinburgh or Glasgow directly, or as a side trip from London.

Some travel agents, particularly smaller ones, advertise cheap air fares in the travel sections of weekend newspapers, such as *The Age* in Melbourne and the *Sydney Morning Herald*. Two well-known agents for cheap fares are STA Travel and Flight Centre. STA Travel (☎ 03-9349 2411, ☎ 131 776 Australia wide, **W** www.statravel.com.au), 224 Faraday St, Carlton, VIC 3053, has offices in all major cities and on many university campuses. Flight Centre (☎ 131 600 Australia wide, **W** www.flightcentre.com.au), 82 Elizabeth St, Sydney, NSW 2000, has dozens of offices throughout Australia.

New Zealand

RTW tickets for travel from New Zealand are usually the best value, often cheaper than a return ticket. Depending on the airline, you may fly across Asia or the USA. Prices are similar to those from Australia but the trip is even longer; about two 12-hour flights minimum.

The *New Zealand Herald* has a travel section where agents advertise fares. Flight Centre (☎ 09-309 6171) has a large central office in Auckland at the National Bank Towers (corner Queen and Darby Sts) and many branches throughout the country. STA Travel (☎ 09-309 0458, **W** www.statravel.com.au) has its main office at 10 High St in Auckland and has branch offices in the larger towns.

LAND

Bus

Long-distance buses (coaches) are usually the cheapest way to reach Scotland.

The main operator is National Express (☎ 0870-580 8080, W www.gobycoach.com), which has numerous services from London, and from other cities in England and Wales.

The standard single/return fares from London to Glasgow and to Edinburgh are the same – £22/33. The journey to Glasgow takes about eight hours and to Edinburgh slightly less.

Discount cards, including Advantage 50 (for anyone aged 50 and over), Student Coachcard (for full-time students) and Young Persons Coachcard (for people aged 16 to 25), offer savings of 20% to 30% on many National Express fares.

All three discount cards cost £9 for one year and are available from National Express or from a National Express agent – call ☎ 0870-501 0014 to find the nearest one to you.

The main operator within Scotland, Scottish Citylink (☎ 0870-550 5050, W www.citylink.co.uk), provides services between Belfast in Northern Ireland (including a ferry crossing) and Edinburgh, Glasgow and other centres.

Silver Choice Travel (☎ 01355-249499, W www.silverchoicetravel.co.uk) operates a nightly service from London to Glasgow and to Edinburgh; the single/open return fare is £20/35 for both destinations.

Backpackers Buses The Stray Travel Network is an excellent service (☎ 020-7373 7737, W www.straytravel.com), which is designed especially for those staying in hostels but is also very useful for all budget travellers.

Buses call at hostels on a regular circuit – London, the Lake District, Glasgow, Stirling, Edinburgh, York and London. You can get on and off the bus wherever you like and catch another one when it comes along. Ticket options include three days' travel in two months for £79 and six days in four months for £129.

Train

Services on the privatised British network are provided by 25 train companies. ScotRail (☎ 0845-755 0033, W www.scotrail.co.uk), the major operator within Scotland, also runs the Caledonian Sleeper service from London Euston to Inverness, Fort William and Aberdeen. Great North Eastern Railway (GNER; ☎ 0845-722 5225, W www.gner.co.uk) and Virgin Trains (☎ 0845-722 2333, W www.virgintrains.co.uk) operate services to Scotland from many stations in England, while Virgin Trains also operates services from Wales.

Overnight trains between London and Scotland have sleeping compartments, with one berth in 1st class and two in standard, as well as standard seating. A range of fares is available; they may be better value than a night in a B&B. Advance reservations are essential. Bicycles are carried on the Caledonian Sleeper, provided a reservation is made in advance.

High-speed services can whisk you from London Kings Cross to Edinburgh in less than four hours; from London Euston to Glasgow takes a little longer.

Standard single/return fares from London are: to Edinburgh £91/81, to Glasgow £96/108.80, to Perth £93.50/187 and to Inverness £96.50/193. Apex (a cheap return fare, which must be booked at least seven days in advance) and Super Apex (a very cheap return fare for journeys on certain lines, which must be booked at least 14 days in advance) tickets are good value but only limited seats are available. A first-class seat costs 30% to 50% more than one in standard class and, except on very crowded trains, is not really worth the extra money.

You can get information or buy tickets at any train station or from authorised travel agents, although travel agents are not able to sell the full range of tickets. Alternatively, for timetables you can check the Railtrack Web site (W www.railtrack.co.uk) or the UK Public Transport Information service (☎ 0870-608 2608, W www.pti.org.uk). For tickets try a commercial site such as Train line (W www.thetrainline.co.uk). Or you can call the National Rail Enquiry Service

(☎ 0845-748 4950, W www.nationalrail.co.uk); a helpful human voice will tell you all the times you want, then give you the number you can phone to buy your ticket.

Car & Motorcycle

Bringing a vehicle registered in any other EU country to Scotland is a fairly straightforward process. The car must have registration papers and a nationality plate, and the driver must have insurance.

Motorways from all the main ferry ports and the Channel Tunnel converge on the M25 motorway around London. You can use this often clogged artery to skirt (inch past) the city and continue north to Scotland.

The main roads into Scotland are busy and fast. Edinburgh is 373mi (604km) north of London, and Glasgow 392mi (635km); allow eight hours. From Carlisle in north-west England, the main road to western Scotland is the A74 (M) via Moffat to Glasgow, and for the east follow the A7 via Galashiels to Edinburgh. From Newcastle upon Tyne in England's north-east, the A1 follows the east coast and the Firth of Forth to Edinburgh; take the A696 and A68 to reach Edinburgh via Jedburgh.

See Car & Motorcycle on page 96 for details of road rules, driving conditions and information on renting and buying vehicles.

SEA

Ferry companies may offer a host of different prices for the same route, depending on the time of day or year, the validity of the ticket and the size of a vehicle. A return ticket may be much cheaper than two single fares, and vehicle tickets may also cover a driver and passenger. It's worth booking ahead as there may be special reductions on off-peak sailings, for which a limited number of tickets is available.

Northern Ireland

Ferries arrive from Larne at Stranraer and Cairnryan, and catamarans ply the Belfast to Troon route; all three ports are south-west of Glasgow. On some routes the cost for a car includes up to four or five passengers. If you can hitch a ride in a less-than-full car, the driver doesn't have to pay extra. Figures quoted are return fares for one adult and for one adult with a car, both in the high season.

Belfast to Stranraer Stena Line (☎ 0870-570 7070, W www.stenaline.com) has several daily slow ferries (three hours) that cost £40/189. The frequent fast ferry service takes 1¾ hours and costs slightly more than the regular ferry.

Larne to Cairnryan P&O Irish Sea (☎ 0870-242 4777, W www.poirishsea.com) has at least two daily slow ferries (2¼ hours) that cost £42/238. Frequent fast ferries (one hour) cost £50/290.

Belfast to Troon Sea Containers Ferries (☎ 0870-552 3523, W www.steam-packet.com) has several daily catamarans (2½ hours) that cost £50/249.

WALKING HOLIDAYS

This is a small selection of companies abroad that run or organise guided walking holidays in Scotland.

Continental Europe

Active Tours (☎ 8374-5899 525, fax 5899 530, e info@activetours.de, W www.activetours.de) Alpenrosenweg 20, 87463 Dietmannsried. A German company that runs week-long tours, which include several day walks, such as Northern Highlights to Orkney and Shetland (DM2120), and Islands & Highlands to Mull, Iona and Skye (DM2000).

USA

Backroads (☎ 510-527-1555, fax 527-1444, W www.backroads.com) 801 Cedar St, Berkeley, California 94710-1800. Backroads operates a six-day trip, graded moderately easy to moderate, visiting Torridon and Skye, staying in grand country houses. The cost is US$2698.

Cross Country International (☎ 800-828 8768, fax 914-677-6077, e XCINTL@aol.com) PO Box 1170, Millbrook, NY 12545. The company offers The Scottish Borders Walk, a week-long tour with six easy day walks near Melrose and Peebles, along part of St Cuthbert's Way and on the coast. The cost is US$1890.

Great Outdoors Recreation Pages (GORP; ☎ 1877-440 4677, fax 303-444 3999, e info@gorptravel.com, W www.gorp.com) PO Box 1486, Boulder, Colorado 80306. GORP offers several walking trips of varying duration, including 'Inn to Inn' in the western Highlands and on Skye (12 days, US$2500), and an easy 'Inn to Inn' trip in the southern Highlands (seven days, US$2000).

Getting Around

Public transport in Scotland is generally of a high standard; it can be expensive but there are many discounts and passes available for travel by air, bus, train and ferry. Services can be infrequent to more distant areas and nonexistent on Sunday. Most of the walks in this book can be reached by public transport – if you have plenty of time.

AIR

It might be worth flying to Barra in the Western Isles to experience landing on a beach; otherwise flying is a pricey way to cover relatively short distances. Unless you're going to the islands, planes are only marginally quicker than trains and buses if you include the time it takes to get to/from the airports.

The British Airports Authority (☎ 0141-848 4441) publishes a free *Scheduled Flight Guide* for Scotland with information on schedules, airlines, and Aberdeen, Edinburgh and Glasgow airports. The main carrier is British Airways/British Airways Express/ Loganair (☎ 0845-773 3377, W www.british-airways.com). Full fare is the most expensive way to fly; you need to book at least 14 days ahead to purchase a cheaper Apex ticket. Details of fares to the Northern and Western Isles are given in the respective walk chapters.

Air Passes

If you're flying into the UK with British Airways you could look into its oneworld Visit Europe airpass. The cost is calculated on a mileage and zone basis; at least two journeys must be completed. It costs from US$60 and must be purchased outside the UK.

There's also British Airways' Highland Rover ticket, which provides five separate flights on routes within Scotland (and between Glasgow and Northern Ireland) with British Regional Airlines. The price is £169, plus any airport taxes. Extra sectors cost £40 each and the duration of the ticket is three months. You have to book all flights at the same time and at least seven days before you start travelling. This ticket is not available within Scotland.

Domestic Departure Tax

A standard £10 tax is charged on all flights within the UK, plus a passenger service charge that varies between airports but is around £10. This is added to the cost of your ticket.

BUS

Scotland's bus network is dominated by Scottish Citylink (☎ 0870-550 5050, W www.citylink.co.uk). The numerous regional companies include Stagecoach (☎ 0870-608 2608, W www.stagecoachgroup.com) and Rapson's (☎ 01463-710555, W www.rapsons.co.uk) in the Highlands. Altogether, the network fills in most of the gaps that are not covered by trains.

Some regions have telephone inquiry lines, which try to explain the frequently changing transport timetables (see Getting There & Away and Getting Around in the walk chapters); area-wide timetables are available from Tourist Information Centres (TICs). For the Highlands and islands (except Shetland) an excellent series of *Public Transport Guides*, covering all forms of transport, is available from TICs for only £1 each. Another handy source of general travel information for the Highlands is the Web site W www.hi-ways.org.

Passes & Discounts

Scottish Citylink offers an Explorer Pass for unlimited travel on its network within Scotland, plus a 50% reduction on Caledonian MacBrayne (CalMac) ferry services (see Boat on page 98). It costs £30 for three consecutive days, £65 for five days out of 10 consecutive days, and £95 for eight out of 16 days. Scottish Citylink also has a range of discount cards available for travel on all Scottish Citylink and National Express services within Scotland.

Hop On, Hop Off Buses

Operating a year-round service on a circuit from Edinburgh, Haggis Backpackers (☎ 0131-557 9393, W www.haggisadventures.com), 60 High St, The Royal Mile, Edinburgh EH1 1TB, departs Monday, Wednesday, Friday and Saturday. The service stops (usually at hostels) in numerous places close to walks in this book, including Fort William, Inverness, Ullapool and the Isle of Skye. A flexitour (a flexible, guided trip) ticket costs £79, requires a minimum of three days to complete the circuit and is valid for up to three months. You can get on and off, and back on again wherever you fancy.

A daily service, MacBackpackers (☎ 0131-558 9900, e enquiries@macbackpackers.com, W www.macbackpackers.com), 105 High St, Edinburgh EH1 1SG, operates through the Highlands via Pitlochry, Inverness, Kyle of Lochalsh/Kyleakin (Isle of Skye), Fort William and Oban. A ticket costs £55; you can explore at your own pace and accommodation can be arranged in good-quality hostels.

Postbus

Many small and remote places can only be reached by using Royal Mail Postbuses – minibuses that follow postal delivery routes. There's usually only one run daily along any route, so planning a walk around it can be difficult; postbuses don't run on Sunday or public holidays. Postbuses will stop and pick up passengers anywhere along the route, provided it's safe to do so. Fares are struck by the local council and are based on local bus fares. Royal Mail publishes a free *Postbus Timetable* for Scotland, usually available at TICs and post offices. For more information contact Royal Mail's Postbus Helpline on ☎ 01246-546329 or the Web site at W www.royalmail.co.uk (under At Home). Timetables are also available from Royal Mail Customer Service Centre, Freepost, Guild Hall, 57 Queen St, Glasgow G1 3AT.

TRAIN

ScotRail (☎ 0845-755 0033, W www.scotrail.co.uk) operates most of the services on Scotland's very scenic train routes, and is generally regarded as the best of Britain's 25 privatised train operating companies.

Virgin Trains (☎ 0845-722 2333, W www.virgintrains.co.uk) and Great North Eastern Railway (GNER; ☎ 0845-722 5225, W www.gner.co.uk) services from London and other English cities to Edinburgh, Glasgow and a few other Scottish centres are also available for limited travel within Scotland. The National Rail Enquiry Service (☎ 0845-748 4950, W www.nationalrail.co.uk) has full timetable, fare and ticket information, and links to the individual companies.

Passes

Eurail passes are not recognised in Britain and the local equivalents aren't recognised in the rest of Europe. The BritRail pass, which includes travel in Scotland, must be bought outside Britain. For details and other options see W www.britrail.com.

ScotRail's Freedom of Scotland travelpass covers an enormous range of public transport services. It can be used on all scheduled ScotRail and Strathclyde Passenger Transport services, GNER and Virgin Trains (only within Scotland), selected long-distance Scottish Citylink bus services (such as Inverness-Ullapool) and all CalMac ferry services. In addition, discounts are available on P&O Ferries to the Northern Isles and ScotRail's Caledonian Sleeper service from London Euston.

It costs £79 for four days travel out of eight, £109 for eight days out of 15 and £119 for 12 days in 20. Discounts are available for Senior Citizen and Young Person Railcard holders and children up to 15 years. And on top of all that, travelpass holders are entitled to discounts at 70 SYHA hostels.

The Highland Rover ticket covers train travel between Glasgow and Oban; Fort William and Mallaig; and Inverness and Wick, Thurso, Kyle of Lochalsh, Aviemore and Aberdeen (and intermediate stations). It is also valid for Scottish Citylink bus travel between Oban/Fort William and Inverness. Ticket holders are entitled to reduced fares on some CalMac ferry services, including

Mallaig and Skye. The cost is £49 for any four out of eight consecutive days in the peak season (£39 at other times).

The Central Scotland Rover ticket covers train travel between Edinburgh, Glasgow Queen Street, North Berwick and Stirling, and on the Glasgow Underground. It costs £29 for travel on three out of seven consecutive days.

The Freedom of Scotland and Rover tickets, along with other ScotRail passes, can be purchased at staffed railway stations, rail-appointed travel agents and from ScotRail telesales (☎ 0845-755 0033, W www.scotrail.co.uk).

Railcards

The Young Person's Railcard costs £18 and gives you 33% off most tickets and some ferry services; you must be aged 16 to 25, or a student of any age studying full-time in the UK. You need proof of age or proof of student status, and a passport-size photo. The Senior Citizen's Railcard, available to anyone over 60, costs £18 and gives a 33% discount. You need to have proof of age. There is also a railcard for families.

All railcards are valid for one year and are available from major stations. For more information contact the National Rail Enquiry Service (☎ 0845-748 4950, W www.nationalrail.co.uk).

Sheep May Safely Roam

Driving to the starting points of many of the walks in this book takes you through areas where sheep, and occasionally cattle, graze unconfined, particularly in the Western Isles.

Sheep are particularly fond of the roads on wet or cool days, when the bitumen surface is the driest and/or warmest place for miles around. During April and May, beware of very young lambs – they have absolutely no road sense.

In more settled and fenced farming country, cattle and sheep are often moved along public roads on the way from one field to another. If you do encounter a herd on the move, it's best to stop and wait for them to pass around you or until the farmer waves you on.

With long hours of daylight during summer, it's easy to see stock on the roads if you're driving in the evening. As the days close in from late September, wandering stock can be a hazard – especially dark-coated animals. A Western Isles farmer, concerned for the safety of a prized black sheep, painted its horns luminous orange to warn drivers of its presence!

CAR & MOTORCYCLE

Travelling by private car or motorcycle enables you to get to remote places, moving quickly, independently and flexibly. Unfortunately, the independence you enjoy does tend to isolate you and cars are nearly always inconvenient in city centres.

A motorcycle is cheaper to run than a car and a great way of getting from one walk to another. Just make sure your wet-weather gear is up to scratch. Crash helmets are compulsory. The Auto-Cycle Union (☎ 01788-566400, fax 573585), ACU House, Wood St, Rugby, Warwickshire CV21 2YX, publishes a useful booklet about motorcycle touring.

At around 85p per litre (equivalent to about US$2.50 for a US gallon), petrol is expensive by overseas standards; and diesel is a only a few pence cheaper. Distances, however, aren't great. Prices rise unbelievably the farther you get from the larger towns, and petrol stations are few and far between (and sometimes closed on Sunday).

The major roads (trunk routes) are toll-free in Scotland but you do have to pay a toll to cross the Forth Road bridge north-west of Edinburgh (it costs 80p for cars, motorcycles free), the Erskine bridge west of Glasgow (80p for cars, motorcycles free) and the Skye bridge at Kyle of Lochalsh (£5.70 for cars, £2.90 for motorcycles).

Road Rules

For information on British, and particularly Scottish, road rules you should read *The Highway Code* or *Driving in Scotland* (available in many TICs). A foreign driving licence is valid in Britain for up to 12 months from the time of your most recent entry into the country. If you're bringing a

Edinburgh is a 'pleasing juxtaposition' of old and new – historic buildings inside the Edinburgh Castle, which overlooks the city and nearby hills; the distinctive clock tower (inset) of the Canongate Tolbooth on the Royal Mile. *Main photo: Bethune Carmichael. Inset: Paul Bigland.*

Glasgow offers an abundance of architectural delights – Kelvingrove Art Gallery & Museum is an elaborate Victorian masterpiece of jumbled styles; Glasgow Cathedral's stained-glass window (inset) depicts the Creation. *Main photo: Neil Setchfield. Inset: Paul Bigland.*

car from Europe, you must make sure you are adequately insured.

Briefly, vehicles drive on the left-hand side of the road; front seat belts are compulsory and if belts are fitted in the back they must be worn; in built-up areas the speed limit is up to 30mi/h (48km/h), on single carriageways it is generally 60mi/h (96km/h), and on dual or triple carriageways 70mi/h (112km/h). You give way to your right at roundabouts; traffic already in the roundabout has the right of way.

Although drinking and driving do not mix (and have become socially unacceptable in Scotland), you are permitted to have a maximum blood-alcohol level of 35mg/100mL when driving. For the 'average' person, this roughly equates to two glasses of wine, a measure of spirits or two pints of beer spread over a 'normal' evening at the pub – but it also depends on when, how much and what type of food is consumed.

Parking

In virtually all towns you'll find off-street parking areas, which use a pay-and-display system, usually costing around 60p for 30 minutes. In major centres, there are also long-stay car parks; handy if you need to leave the car for more than a couple of hours.

In the countryside, at the starting and finishing points of popular walks, there's usually a formal free car park. Only in remote areas are you likely to have to park beside the road (making sure you are clear of gateways).

Rental

Car rental is expensive in Scotland so you might do better to arrange a package deal in your home country. The big international rental companies charge from around £120 a week for a small car (Ford Fiesta, Fiat Punto). The main companies include Avis (☎ 0870-606 0100), Budget (☎ 0541-565656), Europcar (☎ 0870-607 5000), Hertz (☎ 0870-844 8844), National (☎ 0870-400 4502) and Thrifty (☎ 01494-751600). TICs usually have lists of local companies, which may offer better deals.

When you're heading for the Northern or Western Isles, it may be cheaper to rent a car locally rather than pay to bring one over on the ferry.

Motorbike rental is also expensive and unusual. A relatively big company in Inverness, Pro-Bike (☎ 01463-714515, fax 714525, **e** sales@probikeuk.com, **w** www.probikeuk.com), 42 Millburn Rd, Inverness IV2 3QX, has a wide selection of machines from 50cc to 1000cc. A 600cc to 749cc bike costs £75 per day, £175 for a weekend or £350 for a week, including VAT and insurance; a mileage limit applies. Prospective hirers must be at least 23 years of age and have been fully licensed for a year.

Motoring Organisations

The two largest motoring organisations in the UK, both of which offer 24-hour breakdown assistance, are the Automobile Association (AA; ☎ 0800-444999) and the Royal Automobile Club (RAC; ☎ 0800-550550). One year's membership starts at £44 for the AA and £39 for the RAC. Your motoring organisation at home may have a reciprocal arrangement with the AA or RAC.

BICYCLE

Travelling by bicycle is a popular way to explore Scotland. Bikes aren't allowed on motorways but you can cycle on all other roads (on the left!), unless the road is marked private. A-roads are busy and best avoided. B-roads are generally quieter but the best roads are the unclassified ones linking villages. They're not numbered, you simply follow the signs, guided by your trusty OS Landranger or Travelmaster maps (see Maps & Navigation on page 62). The Scottish National Cycle Network, developed by civil-engineering charity Sustrans (☎ 020-7929 0888, **w** www.sustrans.org.uk), links Carlisle in northern England to Inverness, a distance of 425mi (689km) and much of it on specially built cycle paths or quiet country roads. There is also a route from Edinburgh to John o'Groats via Inverness, and on to Orkney and Shetland.

Lonely Planet's *Cycling Britain* covers four tours through Scotland, all you need to know about cycling in Britain and tips on travelling with bikes.

Bike hire operators can be found in most towns; expect to pay from £10 per day or less by the week. Helmets are not compulsory in Britain but it's always wise to wear one.

Ferries transport bicycles for a small fee and airlines usually accept them as part of your 44lb/20kg luggage allowance. Bicycles can be transported on buses provided there's space in the luggage compartment and they're partly dismantled. Bikes are carried free on all ScotRail services but tandems are not accepted.

HITCHING

Hitching is never entirely safe in any country and we don't recommend it. If you decide to hitch, bear in mind that you're taking a small but potentially serious risk. It's safer to travel in pairs and let someone know where you're planning to go. If you don't like the look of someone who stops for you, don't get in the car. Likewise, if you're a driver, take care about who you pick up.

It's against the law to hitch on motorways or the immediate slip roads; make a sign showing your destination and use approach roads, nearby roundabouts or the service stations.

Hitching isn't uncommon in rural areas and out on the islands where public transport is less frequent; in fact hitching is so much a part of getting around that local drivers may stop and offer you lifts without you even asking. But remember, you won't get far if you try hitching on a Sunday in the Western Isles.

BOAT

Caledonian MacBrayne (CalMac; ☎ 01475-650100, W www.calmac.co.uk) is the major ferry operator on the west coast, with services from Ullapool to Stornoway (Lewis), from Uig (Skye) to Tarbert (Harris) and Lochmaddy (North Uist), from Mallaig to Armadale (Skye) and, infrequently, to Lochboisdale (South Uist) and Castlebay (Barra). Oban is the busiest port, with ferries to several islands including Barra and South Uist. CalMac ferries to Islay and Jura go from Kennacraig, south of Oban, and to Arran from Ardrossan.

A simple return fare is the most expensive way of travelling; it pays to plan your complete island trip in advance as CalMac's 'Island Hopscotch' tickets offer a good deal with a choice of ferry combinations on 15 set routes. CalMac also offers 'Island Rover' tickets for unlimited travel for eight and 15 days (£42/61 per passenger for eight/15 days plus £204/307 for a car).

P&O Ferries (☎ 01856-850655, W www.poscottishferries.co.uk) is the main operator to the Northern Isles. On the service from Scrabster on the north coast to Stromness in Orkney a high-season return costs £32 plus £81 for a car. P&O also has services between Stromness and Lerwick in Shetland, from Aberdeen to Stromness and to Lerwick. A return ticket on the Aberdeen-Lerwick service costs £116. A company called Northlink will take over from P&O as the main shipping service provider in October 2002; timetables and fares may change as a result.

For short visits taking a car on the ferries is expensive, so it may be worth hiring one when you get there.

LOCAL TRANSPORT

All the cities and major towns have comprehensive local bus networks. Relevant numbers are in the walk descriptions or you can contact the UK Public Transport Information inquiry line (☎ 0870-608 2608), which will automatically connect you to an operator in the area you are phoning from (who can also help with other areas). You can also check the associated Web site W www.pti.org.uk, which is very comprehensive in some areas, although patchy in others.

Glasgow also has an extensive suburban rail network and a handy underground service. See Getting Around under Glasgow on page 108.

Taxis aren't too expensive and are particularly useful in the evenings when bus services are less frequent. You'll always be able to find a local taxi service in rural areas to take you to the start of a walk if need be.

Edinburgh & Glasgow

Scotland's two major cities, Edinburgh and Glasgow, make ideal gateways for day trips and longer jaunts to the north and south. The many artistic and natural assets of both cities also make for interesting walking within the city limits and nearby mountains. This chapter introduces each city, provides respective city walking tours and then presents several convenient walk options. Excellent public transport makes it easy to enjoy the Pentland Hills in Edinburgh's backyard, Inverclyde to the west of Glasgow, the winding Clyde Walkway south of Glasgow and, in between, locals' favourite big little hill, Tinto.

INFORMATION

Maps & Books

For general orientation purposes, OS Travelmaster 1:250,000 map No 4 *(Southern Scotland)* will suffice. Large-scale maps (1:50,000) are given in each walk description. Local Tourist Information Centres (TICs) carry OS maps and walking guides.

For 'meat and potato' details on the area's geology and geography, use the Scottish Mountaineering Club's guide *Southern Uplands* by KM Andrew.

Highlights

TOM SMALLMAN

Distinctive Salisbury Craigs and Arthur's Seat – a landmark in Edinburgh's heart.

- Gazing on Edinburgh from the heights of Arthur's Seat and Allermuir Hill
- St Mungo's 13th-century tomb in the Gothic Glasgow Cathedral
- Standing below the pounding Falls of Clyde
- The 5mi-long, sweeping balcony of the Greenock Cut

Edinburgh

In Edinburgh, geography and history have conspired to create a delightfully chaotic urban plan. The city won World Heritage site status in 1995 for the 'pleasing juxtaposition of the chaotic medieval fortress' area of the Old Town and the 'grandiose neo-classical New Town'. The curious and attractive layout of winding narrow streets, lush gardens, 19th-century Grecian-style temples and fairy-tale castle wouldn't be the same without the city centre's high cliffs and valleys.

It started with the castle or, more precisely, with the lava rock underneath it. Lava flowed, it layered and the most violent attempts by erosion and ice age melt to wear its cooled form (basalt rock) into sand were resisted. In Edinburgh proper, three volcanic outcrops – Castle Rock (131m), Calton Hill (100m) and Arthur's Seat (251m) – survived these natural forces, becoming emblematic landmarks on the sloping plain between the Pentland Hills to the south of the city and the Firth of Forth to the north. The Water of Leith, Edinburgh's only river, travels this same plain, skirting the city's hills to the north.

Dramatic Castle Rock was the obvious choice for settlement; it could be easily defended with sheer cliffs on three of its sides and a long, gentle eastern slope (glacial moraine), leading to a triangular bowl within the three hills. Popular thought holds that an invading 6th-century Northumberland king, Edward, had a stronghold here (Din Eidyn – providing the origin of the city's name), although clear records only report an 11th-century castle.

In any case, the city grew eastward and downward, creating what is known as the Royal Mile. The former royal hunting ground, 650-acre Holyrood (Holy Cross) Park, complete with moor, marsh, loch, crag and valley, stands at the foot of this singular street. With a radius of 5mi, the park is easily accessed by Queen's Drive.

Arthur's Seat, a natural watchtower providing 360-degree views, dominates the park. Archaeological digs have found four prehistoric forts, cultivation terraces and hut circles (the foundations of simple, ancient dwellings) on Arthur's Seat, which has been inhabited since 5000 BC. Duddingston Loch, the largest and only naturally occurring of the Holyrood Park waters, is also the Bowsinch Reserve Bird Sanctuary.

CLIMATE

In (and around) Edinburgh, July and August are the warmest (average 18°C) and wettest months. The driest months are March and April. Winter temperatures rarely fall below freezing, but wind chill (from the North Sea) is significant. Radio Forth (FM 97.3) gives road and weather reports.

PLANNING

Maps

Collins *Illustrated Edinburgh Map Millennium Edition* provides useful illustrations of monuments and transport links. Harvey's 1:25,000 *Edinburgh Seven Hills* map is recommended.

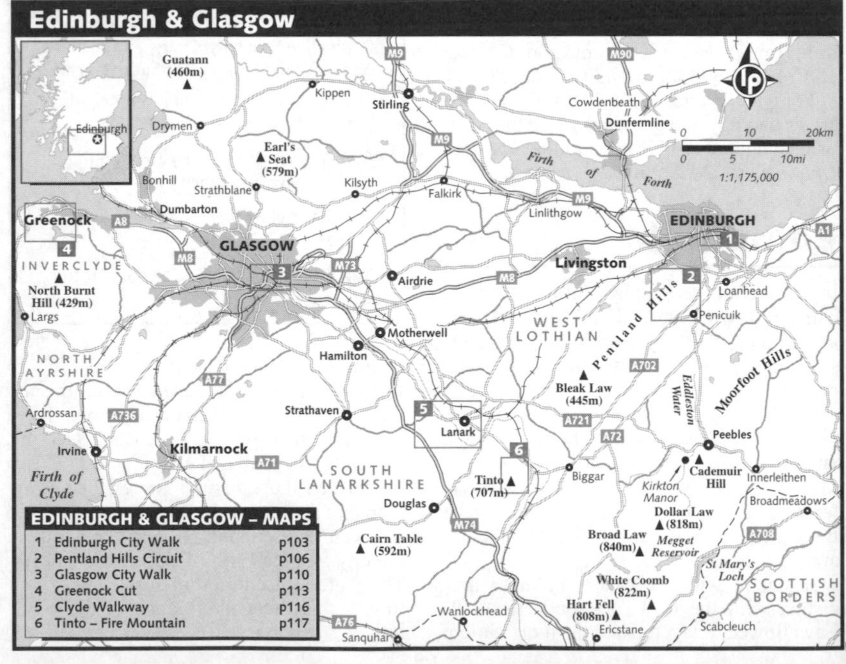

Books

For greater Edinburgh, *25 Walks – Edinburgh and Lothians* covers the Pentland Hills, the city and the Lothians. The weighty *100 Countryside Walks Around Edinburgh* by Derek Storey and *100 Hill Walks Around Edinburgh* by John Chalmers certainly cover the territory.

Lonely Planet's *Edinburgh* is an essential companion with information on accommodation, places to eat and getting around, as well as descriptions of two city walks. Designed for the foot traveller, both *Edinburgh Step by Step*, a well-illustrated slim volume packed with useful history, and *Edinburgh On Foot*, a handy booklet that includes nine rough itineraries, are recommended. *A Guide to Holyrood Park and Arthur's Seat* by Gordon Wright et al offers in-depth information.

Waterstone's Booksellers, 13–14 Princes St, and James Thin's, 53–59 South Bridge St, have decent selections of walking maps and books.

Information Sources

Expect some waiting at Edinburgh's main TIC (☎ 0131-473 3800, e esic@eltb.org, w www.edinburgh.org), Waverley Market, 3 Princes St. Ask for the free *Walks In and Around Edinburgh* sheet for rough walk outlines. For the morbid, Edinburgh's gory history is explored on walking tours; details are posted outside the TIC.

In an emergency (in the Lothian and Borders area), contact Edinburgh police station on ☎ 0131-311 3131.

Supplies & Equipment

The Camping and Outdoor Centre, 77 South Bridge St, closed Sunday, can handle any last-minute needs. Other sport stores are on Rose St in the New Town.

PLACES TO STAY & EAT

Consult Lonely Planet's *Edinburgh* guide or the free *Edinburgh & Lothians Accommodation Guide* available at the TIC. Centrally located backpacker and youth hostels charge from £7.50 in bunks. ***Edinburgh Mortonhall Caravan Park*** *(☎ 0131-664 1533, 38 Mortonhall Gate, Frogston Rd East)*, located on the southern fringe of the city and minutes from the Pentland Hills, charges £8.25 for a car and tent.

Edinburgh's Seven Hills

Edinburgh, like Rome, has seven hills giving character to its horizon. In addition to the three included on the city walk are Corstorphine (150m), Craiglockhart (175m), Blackford (164m) and Braid (208m). Corstorphine, west of the city, has a wooded nature reserve and the Edinburgh Zoo. The other three are between Edinburgh and the Pentland Hills to the south. They all have walking trails and on Blackford is the Royal Observatory and the City of Edinburgh Ranger Service (☎ 0131-447 7145), which offers guided walks. Each June the chaotic 15mi Seven Hills Race has runners linking all seven summits by a course of their own choosing.

GETTING THERE & AWAY

Flights from continental Europe, Ireland and elsewhere in the UK land at the Edinburgh international airport, 8mi west of the city. There are frequent bus services to the city centre.

National Express (☎ 0870-580 8080) and Silver Choice Travel (☎ 01355-249499) both run coaches from London Victoria to/from Edinburgh's St Andrew Square. National Express runs four times a day and there is one Silver Choice night service per day in each direction.

Trains to Edinburgh's Waverley station (off Princes St) from London are operated by GNER (☎ 0845-722 5225) from Kings Cross station, and by Virgin Trains (☎ 0845-722 2333) and ScotRail (☎ 0845-755 0033) from Euston station. ScotRail trains run every 15 minutes between Glasgow Queen St and Edinburgh from 7am to 7pm Monday to Saturday for £15 return.

GETTING AROUND

The free and useful *Edinburgh Travelmap* provides extensive information on bus and train services in and around Edinburgh. For local bus or rail inquiries call Traveline (☎ 0800-232323) Monday to Friday from 8.30am to 8pm. Edinburgh's main train station is Waverley, although most trains also pass through the west-end Haymarket station. St Andrew Square bus station is Edinburgh's main hub for coach services.

Edinburgh City Walk

Duration	4–4½ hours
Distance	6.3mi (10.1km)
Standard	easy-medium
Start & Finish	Waverley Market TIC
Public Transport	yes

Summary A circuit taking in the city's three volcanic hills and the spectacular Old Town that lies between them.

Walking the city's three hills permits you to see Edinburgh from its best angles and get a taste of its countless highlights. The walk starts at the Waverley Market TIC, climbs up to the castle, descends along the Royal Mile, takes in Arthur's Seat (almost 3mi round trip) and then curves up to Calton Hill, before returning to the TIC. Sturdy, multi-use footwear is recommended for the combination of city streets and the potentially muddy Arthur's Seat section. While it's possible to do this walk in four hours, the city lends itself to a slow meander through its interminable nooks and crannies. The Arthur's Seat section is particularly fine at sunset overlooking Edinburgh's skyline.

THE WALK

From the Waverley Market TIC, head west down Princes St towards the castle. Past Waverley Bridge is the **East Princes Street Garden**, replete with benches, promenade and bronze statues of the city's prodigal sons. Literary great Sir Walter Scott (1771–1832) sits within the eye-catching **Scott Monument**. After passing the gardens turn left up the pedestrian Playfair Steps, past the 19th-century Greek-revival Royal Scottish Academy and the National Gallery of Scotland buildings. Cross diagonally over the intersection to, and ascend, Mound Place, curving left up cobbled Ramsay Lane. At the top, Ramsay Lane joins the **Royal Mile** (a series of streets extending from the castle to the Palace of Holyroodhouse) at the Castlehill section, near its highest point of Castle Rock. **Edinburgh Castle's** large esplanade is a few steps to the right and the historic fortification is open daily from 9.30am to 5pm.

Descend the Royal Mile past Outlook Tower and Camera Obscura (both left) and the Scotch Whisky Heritage Centre (right). At the roundabout veer right down Johnstone Terrace. Edinburgh's festival centre, The Hub, once the neo-Gothic Tolbooth Church, dominates the corner (right). With terrific views of the castle's imposing backside, head left down the Patrick Geddes Steps at Castle Wynd South to Grassmarket. Originally a 15th-century hay and corn market, it has many colourful pubs and cafes.

Turn left and cross the road to Cowgatehead. Veer right down Candlemaker Row past Greyfriars Kirk (right) and ascend to the busy corner. Pert, bronzed Bobby, a remarkably loyal Skye terrier, greets you at the **Greyfriars Bobby** fountain. The national Museum of Scotland is across the street. Turn hard left and walk north along the George IV Bridge. About a quarter of the way along the bridge affords views of bustling Merchant St below. The Central Library (left) and the National Library of Scotland (right) dominate the rest of the bridge. Reaching the Royal Mile turn right onto High St and a few steps away (right) is **St Giles Cathedral**. Although its facade appears medieval, only its tower and spire predate 19th-century renovations.

You soon reach Hunter Square, dominated by the 17th-century Tron Kirk, which houses the Old Town Information Centre Cross Bridge St and continue down High St to the **Museum of Childhood** (right), which harbours an enormous doll collection, and the picturesque **John Knox House** (left) named for the ardent Protestant reformer.

The last section of the Royal Mile is known as Canongate, originally a burgh outside the medieval walls, which has suffered

Edinburgh City Walk

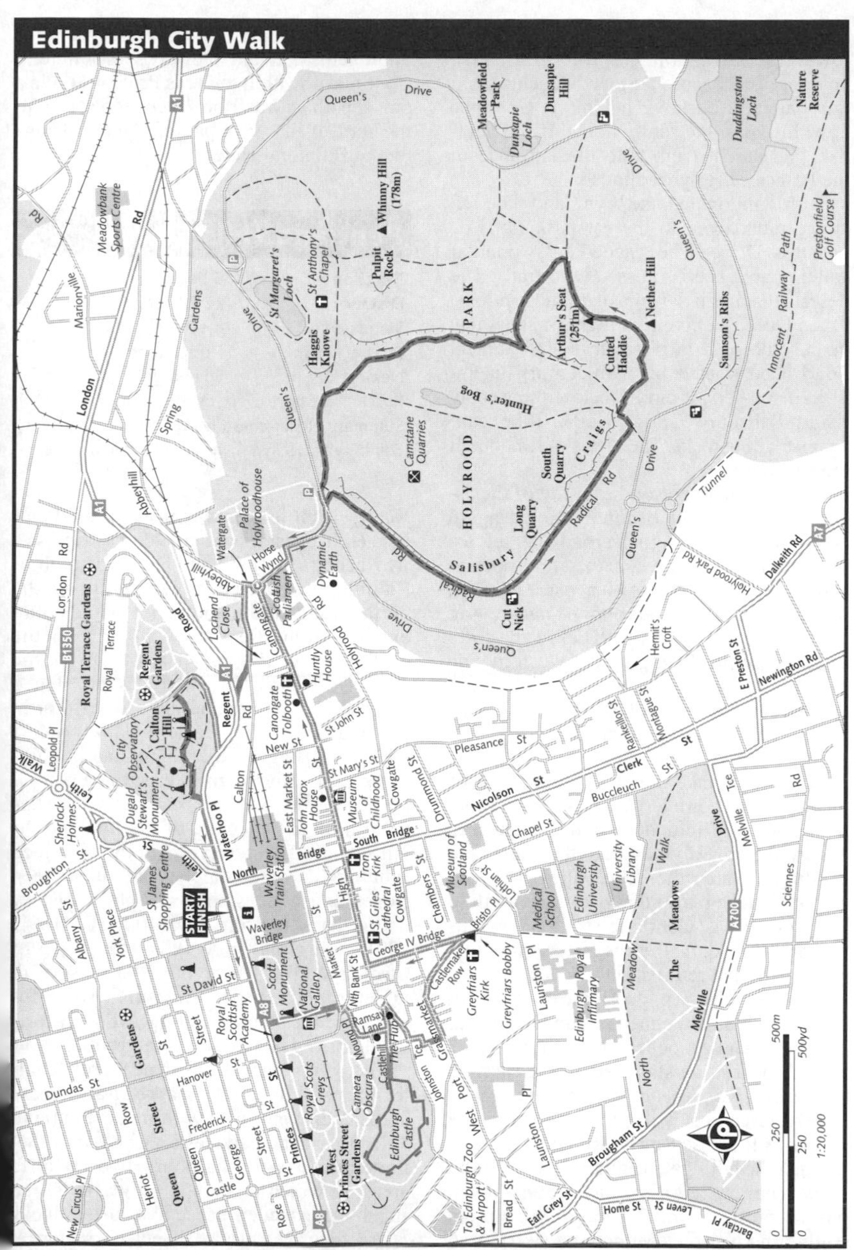

countless renovations. The distinctive **clock tower** of the Canongate Tolbooth (left), housing The People's Story Museum, is a familiar and well-loved landmark. Continue downhill, past the future home of the Scottish Parliament (right), to the entrance of the **Palace of Holyroodhouse**.

Turn right onto Horse Wynd and then left at the roundabout to the car park (left) on Queen's Drive. The exceedingly popular walking area is crisscrossed with trails. The described circuit is one of many options. Cross Queen's Drive to a flight of stairs that quickly becomes a dirt path called **Radical Road**. Constructed by 19th-century unemployed weavers, it circles below the steeply rising Salisbury Craigs (left). Take care against falling rocks. The views of Edinburgh are superlative.

As you round the southern side of the escarpment, the trail becomes paved again and descends almost to the road. Cut left towards Arthur's Seat where the crags open at a narrow pass leading to a natural bowl. Make a quick right and follow a narrow, yet well-trodden, steep dirt path below the cliffs of Nether Hill. Zigzag up the western side of the hill to a flattish outcrop that leads to the clear summit trail of **Arthur's Seat**. Enjoy the views of Edinburgh's hills; Calton Hill is north-west.

To descend take the stairs to the base of the north side. Turn left along a wide, grassy path and keep left, descending westward. Where the crag divides, take the stairs descending towards the deep valley. Leaving the stairs, take a trail that bee-lines north to Holyrood Park. Continue straight towards the grassy field. At the base veer left onto a small path that returns to the car park.

Retrace your steps to Horse Wynd, turn right onto Watergate then left up Calton Rd. Before reaching Lochend Close (left), take a small pedestrian staircase on the right up to Regent Rd. Ahead William Playfair's stately Greek-revival buildings dominate **Calton Hill**. Cross Regent Rd and turn right through the hill's gated entrance. After 300m make a hairpin left turn onto a footpath that passes between the National Monument (right) and Nelson's Monument (left). Also of interest are the City Observatory and the photogenic Dugald Stewart's Monument. Continue downhill towards Princes St, via a paved path to Waterloo Place, and return to the start of the walk passing North Bridge St and Balmoral Hotel.

Pentland Hills Circuit

Duration	6 hours
Distance	12.2mi (19.6km)
Standard	medium
Start & Finish	Flotterstone
Nearest Town	Edinburgh
Public Transport	yes

Summary Roller-coasting regional park circuit in Edinburgh's backyard, including 775m of ascent.

Nearly 16mi long and 6mi wide, the Pentland Hills boast more than 90mi of rights of way access. Only 7.6mi (12.5km) south of Edinburgh, the fine range, lying on the northern side of the Southern Upland Fault, extends from Bleak Law (445m) in the south-west to Allermuir Hill (493m) at the north-west end. The latter has privileged views of Edinburgh and the Firth of Forth. Its long and bumpy eastern flank borders the A702 (Biggar Rd), which largely coincides with a Roman road, creating a natural barrier to the long, deep Logan Glen running through the centre of the hills' northern section. Two reservoirs in the glen feed Edinburgh's water supply. The quiet, steep slopes and valleys shelter a noisy history dating back to Iron Age (400 BC to AD 200) settlements, preserved on the slopes of Castlelaw Hill. Apparently the preserved, underground earthen structures were for storage rather than dwelling; wooden forts would have been built above ground.

Today it's easy to find peaceful, challenging walking on the marked trails (some are old drove ways) within the Pentland Hills Regional Park, established in 1986. Flotterstone Glen harbours two wildlife areas, in which dippers, grey wagtails, redshanks, goosander, geese and tufted ducks take refuge. Red grouse, winchat, ring ouzel and golden plover can also be seen. Sadly, an August 2000 report revealed that poachers had driven the peregrine falcon out of the park. It's believed that the chicks were targeted by falconers (who sell them on the black market), pigeon fanciers (who blame falcons for eating birds) and gamekeepers (who discourage their presence). There are also believed to be 80 species of micromoths and 120 species of spiders in the park.

PLANNING

Keep in mind that this is active sheep farming country, the critical time being April and May, and grouse shoots take place from mid-August to November. Bring water, wear sturdy walking shoes and enjoy the highs and lows year-round. Wind on the ridge can be very brisk.

Maps

OS Landranger 1:50,000 map No 66 *(Edinburgh)* covers the walk and most of Pentland Hills Regional Park. OS Landranger 1:50,000 map No 65 *(Falkirk & Linlithgow)* covers the rest of the park. The Harvey 1:25,000 *Pentland Hills* map is also suitable.

Information Sources

Pentland Hills Ranger Service (☎ 0131-445 3383), Boghall Farm, maintains the Pentland Hills Ranger Centre (☎ 01968-677879) at Flotterstone, near the trailhead. The centre is open daily from 9am to 4.30pm and has restrooms, weather and wind speed information, and free visitor guides, which have an area map showing the marked trails and danger zone.

GETTING TO/FROM THE WALK

MacEwan's Coach Services (☎ 01387-256533) and Western Buses (☎ 0870-608 2608) leave from Edinburgh's St Andrew Square and stop at Flotterstone near the inn. The 25-minute trip goes each way 13 times per day Monday to Friday, 10 times on Saturday and five times on Sunday. Walk 300m to the Pentland Hills Ranger Centre and the start of the walk. For the return trip, bus schedules are posted outside the ranger centre.

> **Warning**
>
> A military live-firing range is located on the south side of Castlelaw Hill. The circuit skirts the area on recognised park trails. When red flags are flying on Castlelaw's summit and flanks, do not walk in the vicinity. You may opt out of the walk at the base of Glencorse Reservoir to avoid the danger zone. Call the ranger service (☎ 0131-445 3383) for details.

By car, take the A702 (Biggar Rd) from Edinburgh to Flotterstone. Turn right at the inn by the poorly marked 'Pentland Hills Regional Park' sign. The car park is usually full on Sunday.

THE WALK

From the Pentland Hills Ranger Centre car park, head west on a path through the woods past a reconstructed sheep stell (once a common structure, like a small corral). Cross the sealed road 300m farther on. Pass through a wooden gate following the metal 'Scottish Rights of Way' signs towards Scald Law. Soon cross a wooden bridge and then ford another stream. Steeply ascend Turnhouse Hill's long spine for 1.2mi to the ridge, passing a pleasant sycamore grove en route The rewards are great and the superlative views constantly improve. In 10 minutes reach **Turnhouse Hill's** rocky-summit (506m) cairn.

Now the roller coaster begins its downward rush. After another small hill descend to the col, divided by a stone wall (with a handy stile), and ascend a breathtaking half a mile or so to **Carnethy Hill** (573m). A Bronze Age summit cairn, formed into semicircular windbreaks, adorns the top. The next and highest hill is Scald Law, which is reached by a long, gradual descent and steep, winding ascent. The once busy **Old Kirk Road** bisects the pass, formerly providing Bavelaw and Loganlea churchgoers with a convenient passage to Penicuik. Visible below is The Howe settlement. Once on **Scald Law** (579m) enjoy the views from the Pentland's rooftop.

Descend to the col at East Kip's base and head right (north), following the contour of

East Kip's flank in a wide, sweeping U-curve to the valley below. At the valley floor, turn right (east) towards the sycamore-flanked shepherd's house and parallel to Logan Burn (left). Cross the wooden bridge at The Howe and continue about 2.2mi along the sealed access road running the length of the Loganlea Reservoir and beside the boomerang-shaped Glencorse Reservoir. At the second reservoir's extreme northern end you can return directly (avoiding Castlelaw Hill and the danger zone) to the ranger centre, about 1.4mi along the road, or continue left (north-west) through a kissing gate and onto the trail marked 'To Collington by Bonaly'.

Soon after the gate turn right (north) on the trail towards Collington, ascend for 15 minutes and, 100m before reaching a wire fence, descend right (east), crossing a burn. Continue on a poorly marked trail that follows Capelaw Hill's southern, then eastern flank. Castlelaw Hill is on your right (east) and Allermuir Hill can be clearly seen ahead (north-east). Leaving a wire fence off to the left, cross the open rolling moorland past a kissing gate and parallel to a stone wall. Ascending to another wall head-on,

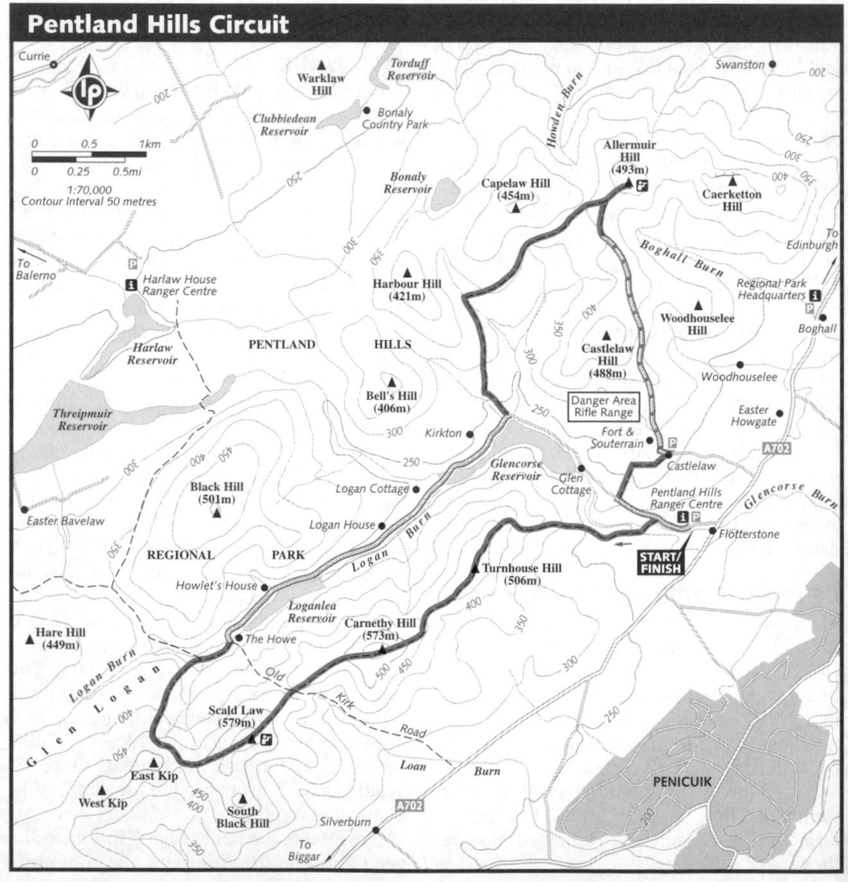

cross over it and a dirt road, then follow the waymarks north-east. The ascent of **Allermuir** (493m) steepens considerably and the trail to the top is straightforward. Edinburgh, its suburbs and the Firth of Forth sweep out in waves below.

Return the same way, following the wire fence used to ascend but, instead of turning right where two paths meet, maintain a straight (south) path towards Castlelaw. Reaching a kissing gate, take the dirt road left (south) and descend for 1.25mi, leaving Castlelaw Hill on the right, to **Castlelaw Fort** (right) and its curious cellars. A kissing gate marks the dirt road's end. Cross the car park to a trail marked Flotterstone. Skirt (right) round the farm to another Flotterstone waymark. Descend left (at first cross-country) to a sealed road and head left for 800m to the ranger centre.

For a convenient post-walk coffee, lunch or evening meal, the ***Flotterstone Inn***, just off Biggar Rd, serves from noon to 9.30pm. The extensive menu offers lunch for about £5 and evening main courses for double that.

Glasgow

Considering Glasgow's past as an industrial superpower, this 'dear green place', as its name implies, harbours a broad range of attractive green spaces among its contours. Many of the finest parks, sprinkled throughout the city, are associated with the area's waterways.

The great River Clyde (see the boxed text 'The River Clyde' on page 114) provides the backdrop for Glasgow Green, the city's oldest park (c. 1450) and centre of working-class activism, and the Clyde Walkway, described later in this chapter. The river also hosts the Clyde Bridges Heritage Trail, which uses the 18 bridges spanning the Clyde River within the city to tell Glasgow's colourful history.

Two tributaries of the Clyde also provide escape from the hubbub. The (River) Kelvin Walkway meanders north-south through Glasgow's West End, boasting the excellent Botanic Gardens and the spacious, wooded Kelvingrove Park. South of the Clyde, the White Cart Water marks the southern boundary of the expansive Pollock Country Park, which supports a myriad of birds (sparrowhawks, great-spotted woodpeckers, grey herons) and mammals (grey squirrels, foxes, brown long-eared bats), and is home to the 8000-piece Burrell (art) Collection. Farther upstream the White Cart flows through the centre of Cathcart and peaceful, 212-acre Linn Park, which has a surprising number of wild flowers, broad-leaved trees, enjoyable footpaths and even a waterfall.

Birders will also be interested in the paved towpath bordering the Forth and Clyde Canal, which since 1790 has divided Scotland in half and provided an aquatic link between the Firths of Forth and Clyde, and Edinburgh and Glasgow. The east and oldest end of Glasgow, dominated by the cathedral, offers the best views of the city from the spectacular hill-top graveyard, the Glasgow Necropolis.

CLIMATE

In (and around) Glasgow nearly 100mm of rain falls monthly from July to January, making it much wetter than Edinburgh. April and May are the driest months. Glasgow has similar temperatures to Edinburgh, averaging 18°C during summer (July and August). Radio Clyde (FM 102.5) gives road and weather reports.

PLANNING

Maps & Books

The Collins 1:10,000 *Glasgow Streetfinder Colour Map* is the best map to carry.

The best-known local walks are covered in *25 Walks In and Around Glasgow* by Alan Forbes, while *100 Hill Walks Around Glasgow* by John Chalmers provides skeletal information but is useful for orientation. The Pathfinder series guide *Glasgow, the Clyde Valley and Ayrshire & Arran* is also good. David Williams' *The Glasgow Guide* is an artfully crafted work offering walking itineraries and abundant reference information.

To purchase maps and books, try either Waterstone's, 153–157 Sauchiehall St, or Borders, 98 Buchanan St.

Information Sources

Glasgow's attentive TIC (☎ 0141-204 4400, e enquiries@seeglasgow.com, w www.seeglasgow.com), 11 George Square, sells books and maps, arranges accommodation (£2 fee) and has an exchange bureau. Printed leaflets on walking routes are scant. Ask for information on the Merchant City Trail, the Clyde Bridges Heritage Trail, the Burrell Walkway and the Kelvin Walkway. Worthwhile Walkman Walkabout tours are available for £5 a day. Themed city walks, from the gruesome to scientific, are also available.

In an emergency, you should contact Strathclyde Police on ☎ 0141-532 2000.

Supplies & Equipment

Tiso's Outdoor Experience, Couper St, Townhead, is a revolutionary gear shop and is open seven days a week. There are also outdoor gear shops in Sauchiehall St.

Left Luggage

Of the city's three transport hubs the Queen St train station has the best deal, charging £2/3 for small/large bags for 24 hours.

PLACES TO STAY & EAT

See Lonely Planet's *Scotland* for excellent suggestions on Glasgow accommodation and dining. Cheap options (from £8) include the ***Berkeley Globetrotters*** *(☎ 0141-221 7880, 63 Berkeley St)* and ***Glasgow Backpackers Hostel*** *(☎ 0141-332 9099, 8 Park Terrace)*. The closest camping site is ***Craigendmuir Park*** *(☎ 0141-779 4159)* at Stepps, 4mi north of the city centre in North Lanarkshire.

GETTING THERE & AWAY

Glasgow's international airport is 8mi west of the city centre. Flights from North America, continental Europe, Ireland and elsewhere in Britain land here. Frequent bus services link the airport with the city centre.

National Express (☎ 0870-580 8080) and Silver Choice Travel (☎ 01355-249499) both run coaches to/from London Victoria to Glasgow's Buchanan St bus station four times and once daily respectively.

Trains to Glasgow's Central Station from London are operated by Virgin Trains (☎ 0845-722 2333) and ScotRail (☎ 0845-755 0033) from Euston station. ScotRail trains also run every 15 minutes between Edinburgh's Waverley St station and Glasgow Queen St from 7am to 7pm Monday to Saturday for £15 return.

GETTING AROUND

Glasgow's major transport hubs are the Buchanan St bus station and the Central (southbound services) and Queen St (northbound services) train stations. Underground rail services ring the city in both directions with trains reaching stations nearly every eight minutes Monday to Saturday from 6.30am to 11.10pm and on Sunday from 11am to 5.35pm. First Glasgow (☎ 0141-636 3124) runs an extensive network of bus services across the city. Strathclyde Passenger Transport publishes handy rail timetables (including rail-connected ferry services and bus interlinks) for travel in and around Glasgow; available from all transport hubs. For public transport inquiries in Strathclyde (in and around Glasgow) call ☎ 0141-332 7133 Monday to Saturday from 7am to 9.30pm and Sunday from 9am to 9.30pm. Ask for maps and transport guides at the TIC.

Glasgow City Walk

Duration	4 hours
Distance	6.2mi (10km)
Standard	easy
Start & Finish	George Square
Public Transport	yes

Summary A circuit exploring Glasgow's most important districts and monuments from the West End's Kelvingrove Art Gallery to Glasgow Cathedral in the Cathedral Precinct.

Until the 19th century Glasgow's most important monuments were located on the eastern uplands of the Cathedral Precinct. Unbridled industrial success produced a rapid westward expansion, clearly visible today. The prominent Victorian architecture favours red Dumfriesshire sandstone and makes numerous references to classical

Greece and Rome, conjuring the sense of glory the rich, middle-class Glaswegians enjoyed as the British Empire's 'Second City'. Literally filthy rich, the ecological price was a polluted Clyde and a skyline curtained in black smoke, which monuments still wear as a veil and reminder. Now, thankfully, the situation is much improved. While the walk is easy, Glasgow has some gentle rises that give contour. The walking surface is entirely paved.

THE WALK

Impeccably maintained **George Square** is watched over by 12 statues; Queen Victoria is the only female representative. With your back to the TIC turn left and left again down Queen St. Cross the street to the forest of Corinthian pillars that shelter the **Gallery of Modern Art**; a mounted Wellington often sports a traffic cone. Take the pedestrian street (right), passing under the Royal Exchange Square archway to **Buchanan St**, Glasgow's most important pedestrian and shopping thoroughfare. Walk left, noting the commercial centres – peacock-festooned Princes Square and Argyll Arcade.

At Argyle St bear right, passing under **Central Station's** enclosed glass and cast-iron walkway. Turn right onto Hope St and take a peek into the expansive and highly attractive, wood-panelled Central Station. On St Vincent St turn left and gently ascend, aiming for a dark tower. The three-storey houses contrast with the previous high, sandstone buildings. Particularly noteworthy here is the fascinating 19th-century, imitation Greek temple of the **Free Church of Scotland** (left), showing aesthetic elements from Egypt, India and Assyria. Descend to the 60m tower of the **Eaglais Chalium Church**, St Columba's Gaelic Church, which stands out among the surrounding unsightly office buildings.

Continue to Elmbank St and bear right. At Bath St turn left past the red **King's Theatre**, complete with dome and sculpted human and lion heads. Keep on Bath St, over the roaring M8, and stately **Mitchell Library**, Europe's largest public reference library, is immediately left. At Granville St look left to the **Mitchell Theatre and Moir Hall's** dramatic entrance personifying the arts. Entering the West End, at Elderslie St turn right and then left onto tree-lined Sauchiehall St. Continue past the Henry Wood Hall (left), the Royal Scottish National Orchestra's home, through quiet streets, finally veering right onto Argyle St. You soon reach one of Glasgow's gems, the **Kelvingrove Art Gallery & Museum**, a symphony of towers, domes and turrets. A true highlight, this popular museum contains superb collections of civic arts, Scottish history, natural history and culture.

Continue along Argyle St, passing the Kelvin Hall International Sports Arena (left), to Patrick Bridge. Instead of crossing here, bear right and cross on the footbridge spanning the River Kelvin. Bear right uphill on a wide, sealed road, which passes below the 17,000-student Glasgow University (left). Just before reaching Kelvin Way turn left, up the stairs, towards the university. When you reach the top head left and pass below the 85m neo-Gothic University Tower. Exit the university, taking the first right to the visitor centre and the main gate. You are now halfway.

Two nearby noteworthy attractions are **Hunterian Museum**, Scotland's oldest public museum with impressive anthropology, geology and coin collections, and **Mackintosh House**, a reconstruction of the Glasgow home of Charles Rennie Mackintosh. The museum is located inside the university's main gate and Mackintosh House, along with the Hunterian Gallery, lies just outside the main gate up the hill. At the gate bear right and descend University Ave to Kelvin Way. Turn right and immediately veer left, along a pedestrian path into deeply wooded Kelvingrove Park. Continue left over the bridge, walk straight uphill along a paved trail and fork left once to reach the top of Woodlands Hill, presided over by **Lord Roberts Statue**, honouring primarily his key role in the 1857–8 Indian Mutiny.

Cross the oval-shaped Park Circus to Park Circus Place. Reaching **Park Church**, a brilliant white neo-Gothic tower, bear right onto

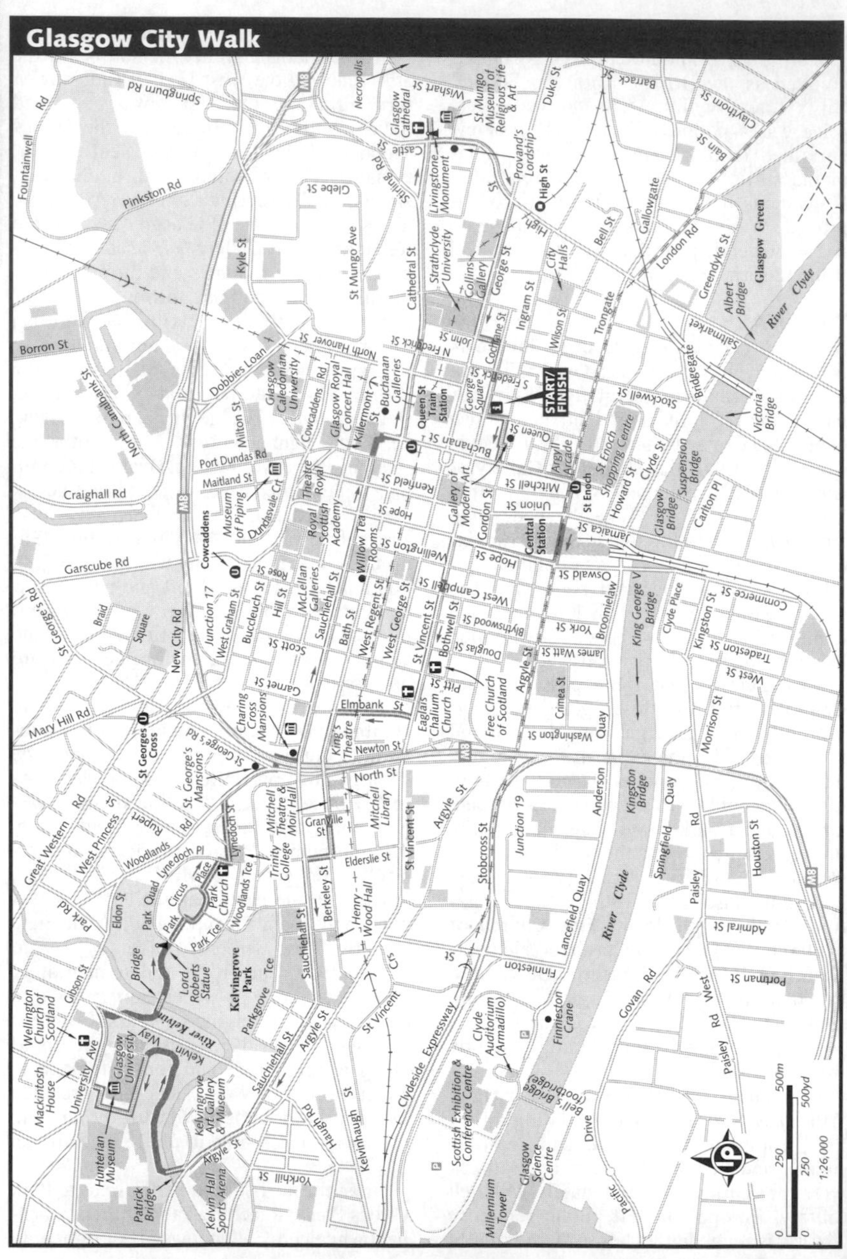
Glasgow City Walk
START/FINISH
George Square
Queen St Train Station
Buchanan Galleries
Glasgow Royal Concert Hall
Glasgow Caledonian University
Gallery of Modern Art
Argyll Arcade
St Enoch Shopping Centre
St Enoch
Central Station
Royal Scottish Academy
Theatre Royal
Museum of Piping
Cowcaddens
Willow Tea Rooms
McLellan Galleries
Free Church of Scotland
Eaglais Chalium Church
Charing Cross Mansions
King's Theatre
St George's Mansions
St Georges Cross
Mitchell Theatre & Moir Hall
Mitchell Library
Trinity College
Park Church
Henry Wood Hall
Lord Roberts Statue
Kelvingrove Park
River Kelvin
Glasgow University
Hunterian Museum
Mackintosh House
Wellington Church of Scotland
Kelvingrove Art Gallery & Museum
Kelvin Hall Sports Arena
Patrick Bridge
Scottish Exhibition & Conference Centre
Clyde Auditorium (Armadillo)
Finnieston Crane
Bell's Bridge (footbridge)
Glasgow Science Centre
Millennium Tower
River Clyde
Kingston Bridge
King George V Bridge
Glasgow Bridge
Suspension Bridge
Victoria Bridge
Albert Bridge
Glasgow Green
City Halls
Collins Gallery
Strathclyde University
Livingstone Monument
Provand's Lordship
High St
Glasgow Cathedral
St Mungo Museum of Religious Life & Art
Necropolis
Clydeside Expressway
M8
Junction 17
Junction 19
500m
500yd
1:26,000

St Mungo & His Cathedral

Popping up all over Glasgow's buildings is the endearing coat-of-arms depicting St Mungo (St Kentigern), the city's patron, and five symbols (following in bold) associated with him. Born in Fife, c. 530, the bastard son of the Lothian king's daughter grew up under St Serf's tutelage and demonstrated his saintly qualities early on, bringing a **bird** back to life and relighting a dead flame with a hazel **tree** branch. Once independent he journeyed westward, coming upon holy Fergus who soon died. He accompanied Fergus to a cemetery consecrated by St Ninian in the village of Glesgu (ie, Glasgow). Convinced by the king to remain, he became bishop, constructing the first church where the present cathedral now stands. During his long reign he managed to get embroiled in a royal love triangle, helping out the adulteress queen by catching a salmon **fish** who'd eaten a damning **ring**, and curried enough favour with the Pope to be gifted a **bell**.

Dating from the 13th century, the Gothic cathedral we see today is divided horizontally into the upper church (with the high open nave and the enclosed, intimate quire or chapel) and, the real highlight, the lower church. The impressive underbelly is accessed by a twin staircase leading to a forest of columns, four of which surround the stone tomb of St Mungo. During the medieval period St Mungo's tomb attracted many pilgrims (and many rich donors), allowing Glasgow to become a powerful ecclesiastic seat.

Open Monday to Saturday from 9.30am to 4pm (longer in summer) and Sunday from 2pm to 4pm, an information desk sells guides including the informative *A Walk Through Glasgow Cathedral*.

Lynedoch Place and then down cobbled Lynedoch St. Distinctive **Trinity College**, noted for its soaring Italian Renaissance-style towers, stands on the right. At the end of the street turn right onto Woodlands Rd and then continue heading right to cross the M8 footbridge. The bridge affords great views of two 19th-century tenements – St George's Mansions (left) and Charing Cross Mansions (right). Curve right, down the bridge to Sauchiehall St, a corruption of the Gaelic *sauchie haugh* (meaning 'willow hollow').

Head left, passing the Royal Highland Fusiliers Museum (left), the McLellan Galleries (left) and the area's most famous willow, the Mackintosh-designed **Willow Tea Rooms** (right). The street becomes a tree-lined pedestrian way at Rose St. At Hope St a you can take a brief detour to the left, leading to the Theatre Royal, the Museum of Piping and the Royal Scottish Academy of Music and Drama.

Back on Sauchiehall St, Glasgow Royal Concert Hall and the massive Buchanan Galleries form the corner with Buchanan St. Note Glasgow's coat-of-arms (see the boxed text 'St Mungo & His Cathedral') gracing the concert hall while veering right down Buchanan. Head left onto Cathedral St (where Bath St ends), passing under the Buchanan Galleries.

The walk then transits into Glasgow's oldest quarter, the Cathedral Precinct, via Cathedral St and passes Strathclyde University (right) to Castle St. Cross over Castle St to **Livingstone Monument**, dedicated to the great African explorer, and **Glasgow Cathedral**, another highlight of the walk. **St Mungo's Museum of Religious Life and Art** is an exceptional museum located on the same square. The hill-top Cathedral Precinct dominated the skyline of Glasgow until the 1750s. When the city expanded westward many of the medieval structures were lost in the building fervour, including the Bishop's Palace.

Descend Castle and High Sts, past Glasgow's oldest house **Provand's Lordship** (right), and head right onto George St. Turn left at John St and then enter into **Merchant City**, named for the tobacco lords and cotton magnates who constructed warehouses there. Finally, head right on Cochrane St, to be greeted by the Thomas Graham statue in George Square.

Greenock Cut

Duration	4 hours
Distance	8.2mi (13.2km)
Standard	easy
Start & Finish	Cornalees Bridge
Nearest Town	Inverkip
Public Transport	no

Summary Excellent family walk in the low hills west of Glasgow, offering superb views of the Firth of Clyde, the southern Highlands and the Isle of Bute.

Serving as the western gateway to Glasgow, the district of Inverclyde includes the major port and industrial towns of Port Glasgow, Greenock and Gourock, as well as the coastal villages of Inverkip and Wemyss Bay, located farther south and west. Inland the region boasts two large reservoirs, Loch Thom and the Gryfe, and an extensive, protected area of rolling moorland, forming part of the 30,000-acre Clyde Muirshiel Regional Park. The popular park runs north to south along the Renfrewshire hills, and the Hill of Stake (522m) is the area's high point.

The Greenock Cut walk sweeps above these maritime centres offering unbeatable views of the Firth of Clyde and beyond. Five miles of the walk follow the now-disused Greenock Cut (aqueduct), built between 1825 and 1827 to carry water from the Great Reservoir (later renamed Loch Thom) to a booming Greenock. Robert Thom headed the engineering feat, subcontracting the work to teams who excavated countless tons of dirt and built 23 bridges. The walk's last section – the People's Trail – passes through Shielhill Glen, a Site of Special Scientific Interest, and the area's only regenerating broad-leaved forest of deciduous oak, ash, rowan, hawthorn and silver birch.

PLANNING

Accessible year-round, the route is easy to follow despite scant waymarking. Going anticlockwise gives the best views and allows you to end with the glen as a final highlight. Be prepared for some muddy and wet sections, and bring water or get it at the visitor centre, if open. Glasgow's proximity allows for a comfortable day trip although Inverkip is an attractive stopover.

Maps

The OS Pathfinder 1:25,000 map No 402 *(Greenock & Port Glasgow)* covers the route.

Information Sources

At Glasgow TIC ask for the free *Discover Inverclyde* visitor guide. It includes a map showing the route and Cornalees Bridge Visitor Centre (☎ 01475-521458, **e** enquiries@muirshiel.sol.co.uk, **w** www.scottishpark.com). The visitor centre opens from noon to 7pm at weekends from April to October and daily in July and August. Confirm opening hours in advance. The centre has free leaflets for two marked trails – the Greenock Cut and the Cornalees Bridge Trail (the People's Trail).

NEAREST TOWN

Inverkip

Once a whisky smuggler's stopover on runs from Argyll and the Islands, Inverkip, 2.8mi from the Cornalees Bridge Visitor Centre, is a quiet, charming alternative to bustling Greenock.

Places to Stay & Eat In Station Rd, ***Foresters House B&B*** *(☎ 01475-521433, **e** forestershouse@msn.com)* has en suite rooms and two exterior cottages with bunks from £17 to £27. ***Inverkip Hotel*** (☎ 01475-522065, **e** enquiries@inverkip.co.uk) has spacious en suite rooms from £35 per person and serves Scottish mains (duck, venison, haggis, salmon) from £6.50 to £10. Open daily, the ***Village Store*** *(☎ 01475-521270 to advance order)*, in the main street, has general supplies and sandwiches. At the ***Chartroom*** at Kip Marina, across the main road, enjoy evening music, good meals and the sailboats.

Getting There & Away From Glasgow (Central Station) daily morning and afternoon ScotRail (☎ 0845-755 0033) Glasgow–Wemyss Bay and Gourock trains stop and pick up at the tiny Inverkip station. It is a

40-minute trip by car; take the M8 (A8) west to Greenock. Continue on the A78 towards Inverkip and Wemyss Bay.

GETTING TO/FROM THE WALK

No public transport reaches the trailhead nor links to/from Inverkip. From Inverkip train station it's a 3.5mi walk along rural roads. Walk down Station Rd to the main street. Turn right and right again after 200m up Langhouse Rd. Veer left at the top with the road, then bear right onto Millhouse Rd and fork right at the crossroads. Cornalees Bridge and the visitor centre are 1.7mi farther along this road.

By car, 4.2mi on the A78 from Greenock (north of Inverkip) turn left into the Clyde-Muirshiel Park. Drive 2.5mi farther to the Cornalees Bridge Visitor Centre.

THE WALK

From the Cornalees Bridge Visitor Centre head left (north-east) on the sealed road, over the cow grid. The flat access road, in Hillside Hill's (297m) shadow, follows the shore of Compensation Reservoir (stocked with rainbow trout) to an iron gate and winds uphill to Loch Thom Cottage. Pass a kissing gate, continuing on a dirt and gravel road. To the left a small **fountain** (drinkable), built by the WWI Gallipoli-bound 5th Battalion Argyll and Southern Highlanders who trained here, sits at McNoble Hill's (245m) base. Continue gently climbing for about 20 minutes. Loch Thom slips from view as the trail summits between 274m White Hill (left) and 250m Jock's Hill (right).

Spectacular views begin as the path descends north-east towards two small reservoirs; Greenock's busy port with towering cranes, the Firth of Clyde, Helensburgh and the southern Highlands beyond. Continue towards Greenock to the whitewashed waterkeeper's cottage, the trail's lowest point. Turn left (west) onto Greenock's famous aqueduct. You then keep to the serpentine

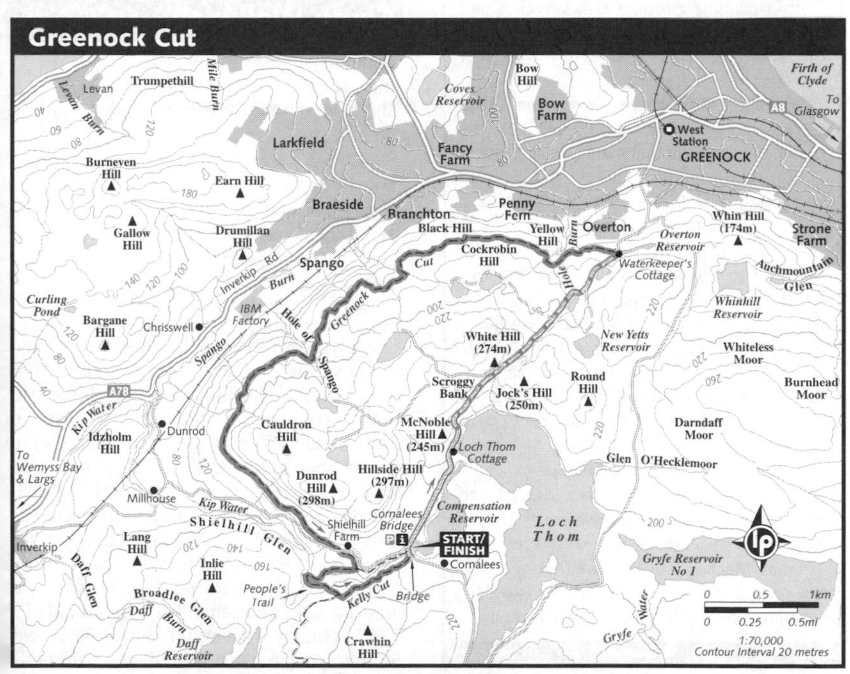

footpath for the next 5mi, lined with ferns, heather, rushes, rowan, broom and gorse. In 10 minutes pass a kissing gate to reach Hole Burn and the first sluice hut. In 200m pass the first of Greenock Cut's bridges, which gives access to the now fallow pastures.

After 30 minutes views of Greenock diminish and you reach the halfway mark as the huge IBM factory begins to dominate the panorama below. Twenty minutes later the **Hole of Spango**, a deep and lush valley, descends the hillside. A bit farther, the spacious inland pastures and the large energy tower of coastal Inverkip appear. The oil-powered chimney, a 30-year-old eyesore, has, disgracefully, only worked once when a four-day coal miner's strike coincided with a cargo of oil sitting in the harbour. Now it serves as a lighthouse; its red illumination lights guide late-night carousers home.

A brief, heavily forested section leads to **Shielhill Farm**, which raises blackface sheep and Friesian dairy cows. Cross the road and continue along the aqueduct. At the next bridge, 200m farther, either continue 600m to the visitor centre or turn right downhill along the People's Trail (about 1.5mi to the visitor centre). Cross the stile and enter the dense woods. A brook lined with red sandstone accompanies the trail's left side to a boardwalk. After the last bridge (look for wild thyme growing), the boardwalk climbs 500m from forest to open moorland. Where the boardwalk ends, turn left and follow the Kelly Cut for 15 minutes to the sealed road. Turn left to reach the visitor centre.

The River Clyde

A popular local saying claims: Glasgow made the Clyde, and the Clyde made Glasgow. Glesgu (ie, Glasgow) would have remained a rural backwater had it not been for the cathedral, which during the medieval period attracted pilgrims, prestige and power. Then, during the Industrial Revolution, the River Clyde allowed the city to turn into a great port and industrial city.

Scotland's third-longest river, the Clyde journeys some 105mi from its source in the Lowther Hills catchment area, falling some 2000ft, as it wends through the Clyde Valley and Lanarkshire to the centre of Glasgow. It flows 28mi out to sea forming the Firth of Clyde. More than half of Scotland's population lives just a short distance from its flow, which drains a 4000-sq-km area.

Looking at the Clyde from Glasgow's docks and knowing that some 35,000 boats were launched from its once productive shipyards, it's hard to believe that in the 1700s it was too shallow (less than 1m in some places) to navigate. In the 1690s the city's harbour was located 20mi downstream at Port Glasgow. Late 18th-century efforts to narrow, dredge and shore up the river and its banks permitted the docking of steamboats in the 19th century.

Innes MacLeod & Margaret Gilroy's *Discovering the River Clyde* offers excellent background information.

Clyde Walkway

Duration	4 hours
Distance	8.5mi (13.7km)
Standard	easy
Start	Crossford
Finish	Falls of Clyde
Nearest Town	Lanark
Public Transport	yes

Summary Densely wooded upstream river walk with a dazzling grand finale, the three plummeting Falls of Clyde.

The Clyde Walkway is an ambitious project to transform the banks of this beloved river into a 40mi (65km) footpath stretching from Glasgow's centre to the Falls of Clyde in New Lanark. The most spectacular section that is open connects the villages of Crossford and New Lanark through heavily wooded gorges where herons and kingfishers thrive. The clearly waymarked trail winds upstream past the once great Stonebyres Linn (21m high), now harnessed for its power, to New Lanark, a cotton mill village founded in 1785. Hugely successful, by 1799 it was Scotland's largest mill village. Utopianist

Robert Owen brought revolutionary ideas regarding labour management and workers' conditions to New Lanark in what he called his Millennium Experiment. Nominated a World Heritage site, New Lanark has extensive visitor facilities and a history museum.

The walkway culminates along an 18th-century trail that ascends past Dundaff Linn (3m high), Corra Linn (28m) and, finally, three-stage Bonnington Linn (11m). Ice melt created the gorges and falls 10,000 years ago, artfully carving up the 400 million-year-old red sandstone base. Romantic painters (Turner, Nasmyth, More) and poets (Scott) were enthralled by the falls, especially with Corra Linn (Corra being, according to legend, a princess who catapulted over the falls on horseback), which became the subject of numerous works. Since the 1920s the Bonnington Power Station has captured the falls' collective force.

PLANNING

Accessible year-round, the falls are best seen after heavy rains. For five widely advertised days, between April and October, the power station halts and the falls return to their original fury.

Maps & Books

The OS Landranger 1:50,000 map No 72 *(Upper Clyde Valley)* covers the area but is superfluous.

Information Sources

The South Lanarkshire River Valleys Project (☎ 01698-455396) and the Clyde & Avon Valleys Project (☎ 01555-665244) promote and publish free leaflets on the Clyde Walkway – *Welcome to the Clyde Walkway* and *The Clyde Walkway: Crossford to the Falls of Clyde*, which include local maps and history. The Lanark TIC (see Lanark under Nearest Towns) supplies both.

For transport information in the Lanark area, call the local travel helpline (☎ 0141-332 7133). For train services and times see the Strathclyde Passenger Transport's *South East Rail Timetable* and for local bus services pick up a copy of the *Lanark Area Transport Guide*.

NEAREST TOWNS

Lanark

Lanark TIC (☎ 01555-661661, ⓔ lanark@seeglasgow.com), in Horsemarket, close to the train and bus stations, is open daily, year-round. Ask for the free *Lanark Heritage Trail*, a self-guided walk through this historic market town with strong links to William Wallace. Fraser's, at South Vennel and Bannayne St, sells outdoor gear. All basic services are located on High St.

Places to Stay & Eat At ***Westport Guest House*** *(☎ 01555-660263, 35–37 Westport)* plush single/double rooms with and without bathroom cost from £20; it also caters for vegetarians. Open April to October, ***Clyde Valley Caravan Park*** *(☎ 01555-663951)*, Kirkfieldbank, 1.5mi from Lanark on the A72, charges £8 per tent.

In Lanark, self-caterers should look for ***Iceland*** supermarket on High St. Find reasonably priced pub meals at the ***Crown Tavern*** *(17 Hope St)*. ***Armando's*** *(90 High St)* does tasty pizzas, and fish and chips.

Getting There & Away Frequent ScotRail (☎ 0845-755 0033) trains connect Lanark and Glasgow Central. The roughly 45-minute trip runs nearly every hour each day.

New Lanark

Scottish Wildlife Trust manages the Falls of Clyde Visitor Centre (☎ 01555-665262, ⓦ www.newlanark.org) in New Lanark and the Falls of Clyde Wildlife Reserve that extends 1.25mi upstream from the village. The centre is open daily (except 25 December and 1 January) from 11am to 5pm.

Places to Stay & Eat Popular ***New Lanark SYHA Hostel*** *(☎ 01555-666710)*, Wee Row, set in a former mill building, charges £11.25 for B&B and closes from November to March. Warm and welcoming ***Bankhead B&B*** *(☎ 01555-663855)*, on Braxfield Rd, is a beautiful working farm just up the road from New Lanark with a £16 tariff.

New Lanark Mill Hotel does pricey evening meals, and also serves soups and sandwiches in its coffee shop.

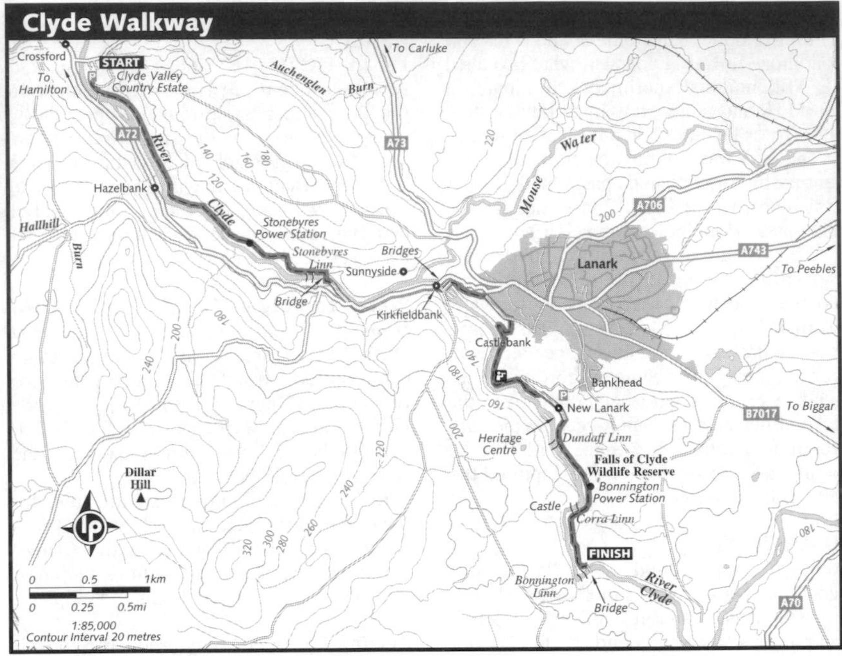

Getting There & Away On weekdays and Saturday, Stuart's Coaches (☎ 01555-773533) operates a service between Lanark and New Lanark. On Sunday there is a bus service (No 335) between Lanark and New Lanark (listed in Strathclyde Passenger Transport's South East timetable), which connects with the ScotRail trains from Glasgow (see Getting There & Away for Lanark on page 115). A 20-minute walk also connects Lanark and New Lanark; follow the ample signs for the New Lanark World Heritage Village. Keep in mind there is a steep ascent from riverside New Lanark up to Lanark.

GETTING TO/FROM THE WALK

Crossford, at the start of the walk, is roughly 4mi north of Lanark. To reach Crossford take the hourly ScotRail (☎ 0845-755 0033) Glasgow-Lanark train to Hamilton and then transfer to the hourly (except Sunday when there are five services in each direction) Hamilton-Lanark bus service No 317, getting off at Crossford. Once in tiny Crossford walk over the bridge at Braidwood Rd (B7056) and follow the directions to the Garden Centre within the Clyde Valley Country Estate.

By car from Glasgow take the M74 then the A72 south to the B7056 (Braidwood Rd). Turn left over the bridge and then right at the 'Narrow Gauge Railway & Country Walks' sign. Bear left into the Clyde Valley Country Estate car park. From Edinburgh take the A71 then the A72 south to Crossford and the B7056.

THE WALK

Clyde Valley Country Estate (☎ 01555-860691) is a tranquil complex set in 20ha of woodland and gardens, which includes the Garden Centre and the ***Conservatory Coffee Shop*** *(☎ 01555-860203)*; the latter is open daily from 9.30am to 5pm for a pre-walk aperitif.

From the Clyde Valley Country Estate car park head towards the river and turn left onto the marked Clyde Walkway. Continue upstream along the 1m-wide dirt trail that winds through lush, broad-leaved woodland. A section of tumbling rapids coincides with the first houses of Hazelbank on the river's far side. Progressively ascend above the river. When the Stonebyres Power Station appears below, curve right downhill to **Stonebyres Linn**, which once thwarted salmon and trout on their uphill runs. The walkway crosses the river via the station's weir bridge.

Continue along the narrow asphalt road to the main road. Bear left onto the path and in 10 minutes reach Kirkfieldbank. Coffee or a snack are available at ***Shiloh Coffeehouse*** (left) or ***The Tavern*** (right). At the end of the village, on the right side of the road, search for and cross the old bridge. An iron gate gives access to the river's true right bank. Islets enliven the Clyde here. Reaching Lanark's water-purifying station, the trail twists steeply up and away from the river to a sealed road. Continue five minutes to the Castlebank Park mansion's stone doorway (right). Pass through, as indicated. You soon leave the asphalt for a descending dirt path laden with red pebbles. You're now halfway.

Zigzag downhill through a beech wood to the Clyde's banks. Traverse a thick spruce and birch woodland and ascend to a magnificent lookout and New Lanark. Continue to the roadway and bear right, descending 100m to a right-hand staircase, which drops down to the first row of houses closest to the river. After passing New Lanark Visitor Centre, take a right-hand trail parallel to the canal, which supplies water to the mill. The trail crosses over the canal on top of the tunnel at the point where the canal enters the hillside. Follow the well-marked trail 1.25mi through the Falls of Clyde Wildlife Reserve and up past the impressive series of waterfalls – Dundaff Linn (3m high), Corra Linn (28m) and, finally, three-stage Bonnington Linn (11m). To reach the nearest public transport links, retrace your steps to New Lanark.

Tinto – Fire Mountain

Duration	2½ hours
Distance	4.9mi (7.9km)
Standard	easy-medium
Start & Finish	Thankerton
Nearest Towns	Lanark, Thankerton
Public Transport	yes

Summary A quick, although heart-thumping, jaunt up Lanarkshire's favourite landmark.

Tinto (707m), coming from the Gaelic for fire, ranks high among locals' favourites, explaining its inclusion despite being relatively low, short and straightforward. This distinctive conical and elongated hill stands alone, separated from higher Southern Upland mountains by the River Clyde, a silver stream pulsing along Tinto's eastern flank. Its prominence and relative isolation have attracted humans for thousands of years; a natural watchtower, it retains one of Scotland's largest Bronze Age summit cairns, measuring 6m by 45m. Pre-Roman inhabitants may have used Tinto as a sun altar, lighting fires on the summit to honour their gods. The hill also gives off a reddish glow

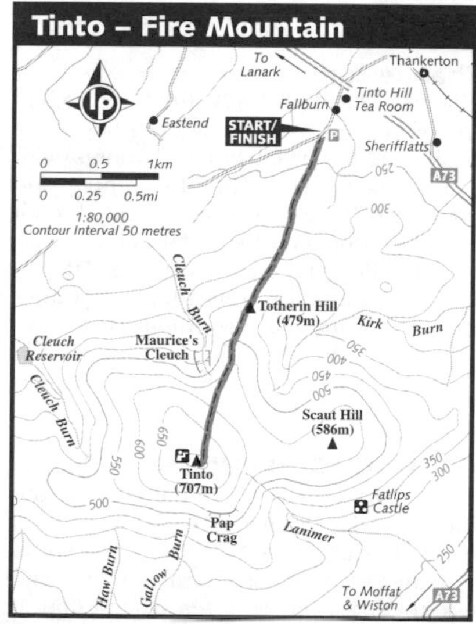

as the setting sun hits the red felsite littering its slopes. Modern-day folk have their own rituals; stalwarts climb up with torches (flashlights) on New Year's Eve, religious faithful carry crosses up the first Sunday in May, and kids race up and down in an annual cross-country meet. The distinctive calls of game birds and black-faced sheep accompany the journey.

With so much traffic the hill is being loved to death, a situation not helped by a landowner who owns much of the mountain (raises grouse and pheasant) and is unsympathetic to walkers' rights of way issues. As a consequence, the only path is a wide, eroded track. Initially a gentle incline, then several steep and boggy sections follow. Brace yourself for stiff winds at the summit. There are no public restrooms at or near the trailhead.

PLANNING

Maps & Books

The OS Landranger 1:50,000 map No 72 *(Upper Clyde Valley)* covers the walk but it's virtually impossible to get lost.

NEAREST TOWNS

Lanark

See under Nearest Towns on page 115.

Thankerton

Elmwood B&B** (☎ 01899-308740, 32 Sheriflats Rd)* in tiny Thankerton village, opposite the trailhead, has £17 rooms with shared bathroom. A ***YMCA Camping Site *(☎ 01899-850228)* at Wiston, located south of Thankerton on the A73, takes backpackers and offers spectacular views of Tinto.

Ideal for a snack or meal before or after the walk, ***Tinto Hill Tea Room*** *(☎ 01899-308346)*, near the trailhead, serves daily from 9.30am to 4pm; the menu includes venison burgers for £1.90.

GETTING TO/FROM THE WALK

From Lanark, take one of the hourly (four buses Sunday) Irvine's (☎ 01698-372452) or HAD Coaches (☎ 01501-820598) No 191 buses, which run to/from Biggar, and ask for the Tinto Hill Tea Room stop at Thankerton. It's a 15-minute trip. From Edinburgh, take the hourly MacEwan's Coach Services (☎ 01387-256533) Edinburgh-Biggar bus No 100 to Biggar and transfer to the Biggar-Lanark No 191 bus.

By car it is a 30-minute drive from Glasgow (take the A73 from Lanark to Thankerton) and 45 minutes from Edinburgh (take the A702 to Biggar then the A73 to Thankerton). Turn towards the hill at the Tinto Hill Tea Room and continue 200m to the car park.

THE WALK

From the car park, the summit cairn (left) and nearly the entire route (a wide gash stretching up the mountain) are visible. Heading south pass through a kissing gate to begin the gentle ascent. After a second kissing gate, etched 'Tinto Hill', continue on a wide path lined with barbed wire to another doorless gate.

Thirty minutes later the trail briefly levels at Totherin Hill (479m) and then steeply ascends again south along a wide, red 'highway'. Another 500m climb leaves you at a fork (either direction is OK). Continue until the paths rejoin 15 minutes later. The 'highway' begins to parallel a right-hand wire fence. In 500m scoot up to the huge cairn on the **summit** (707m) and enjoy this ancient lookout. There is a view indicator on the summit that is very helpful. Descend the same way.

Other Walks

CAMPSIE FELLS

Nine miles north-east of Glasgow, the Campsie Fells run 9.9mi from east to west between the Kilpatrick Hills in the west (the West Highland Way's corridor) and the Fintry and Gargunnock Hills in the east. All volcanic in origin, ice age melt scrubbed them clean leaving behind generally flat, grassy tops with often steep escarpments, falls and lush glens. The Crow Rd (B822) bisects the Campsie Fells. Horned Dumgoyne (427m) dominates the west end and Meikle Bin (570m) reigns in the east. Trails are unmarked yet offer good, accessible practice for young hillwalkers. The Harvey 1:25,000 map *Glasgow Popular Hills* covers the Campsies.

Meikle Bin

Afforested with spruce, Meikle Bin (570m) offers good views of Glasgow, the Carron Valley Reservoir and the southern Highlands. Four ways to attack it are: 1) On the Crow Rd, 2.2mi from Lennoxtown and 200m above unmarked Alnwick Bridge, ascend east to Lecket Hill. Descend, crossing Boyd's Burn, to a firebreak. Follow it and a burn up to the summit. It's an 8.1mi (13.1km) return; 2) From Corrie, north of Queenzieburn, ascend north via Birkenburn Resevoir then north-west to Black Hill and the summit; 3) The shortest and easiest leaves from Crow Rd via Waterhead Farm and ascends Bin Burn; 4) From Carron Valley Reservoir's west end, follow the forestry road up (south-west) past Little Bin. Either the OS Landranger 1:50,000 map No 64 *(Glasgow)* or OS Pathfinder 1:25,000 map No 392 *(Fintry & Carron Bridge)* would suffice.

NORTH BERWICK COAST

With superlative views of the Firth of Forth, an easy coast walk just 15.5mi from Edinburgh begins from the Gullane Bents car park off the A198 at Gullane and ends 5.6mi farther north along the coast at beautiful Dirleton village, known for its castle. A frequent bus service connects Gullane and Dirleton. The walk is not well marked. From the car park follow the gravel road to the coastal track that makes its way to the fence edging the Muirfield golf course. Follow the fence and continue towards the dunes, bordering the wood. Walk along the shore by tiny Eyebroughty Island. Fidra Island is just offshore. At the end of the cliffs and beach ascend to Marine Villa and continue close to the shore. At the Yellowlees car park turn right and walk approximately 1mi to Dirleton along the road. OS Landranger 1:50,000 map No 66 *(Edinburgh)* covers the walk.

The South

Clearly discernible on a topographical map of southern Scotland is a nearly continuous range of mountains (and underlying fault) running coast to coast from Ballantrae (south-west) to Dunbar (north-east). These rolling Southern Uplands, plus the extensive network of hidden beaches, verdant glens, desolate lochs and winding rivers, packed in between the east and west coasts and the Cheviot Hills to the south-east constitute the South. In lieu of Munros, here walkers tick off seven Corbetts (2500–2999ft) and 82 Donalds (2000–2499ft). Although not Scotland's highest mountains, they nonetheless offer endless opportunity for challenge and exploration. This chapter is broken into three sections. The Southern Uplands covers the Southern Upland Way (SUW), a long-distance, coast-to-coast path linking the two other sections: Dumfries & Galloway and The Borders. The described walks are conveniently located near the SUW, allowing easy coordination of day or multi-day trips.

Highlights

Maxton village church on St Cuthbert's Way, which links Melrose and Lindisfarne.

- Catching sight of the east coast for the first time on the Southern Upland Way
- Ascending the Grey Mare's Tail to lonely Loch Skeen
- Cliffs and Coldingham Bay on the Berwickshire coast
- Dense woodland, tumbling burns and views from the Merrick
- Tramping around ruins of prehistoric and Roman forts
- Picturesque castles and abbeys, relics of the region's bloody history

INFORMATION

When to Walk

The most sensitive periods for stock are during lambing (April to June) and calving. Walkers should also take care during bird nesting and grouse shooting (12 August to 10 December). You must keep to the paths, leave gates as found and keep dogs on leads. See the walk descriptions for details.

Maps & Books

For general orientation, OS Travelmaster 1:250,000 map No 4 *(Southern Scotland)* is adequate. The Scottish Mountaineering Club's guide, *The Southern Uplands* by KM Andrew, gives an excellent overview of the area's geology and geography, as well as walk ideas.

Information Sources

The main Tourist Information Centre (TIC) in Dumfries & Galloway is in Dumfries (☎ 01387-253862, **e** info@dgtb.ossian.net, **w** www.dumfriesandgalloway.co.uk). In the Borders the main TICs are Jedburgh (☎ 01835-863435/863688, **e** info@scot-borders.co.uk, **w** www.scot-borders.co.uk), Peebles (☎ 01721-720138, **e** peebles@scot-borders.co.uk) and Hawick (☎ 01450-372547, **e** hawick@scot-borders.co.uk).

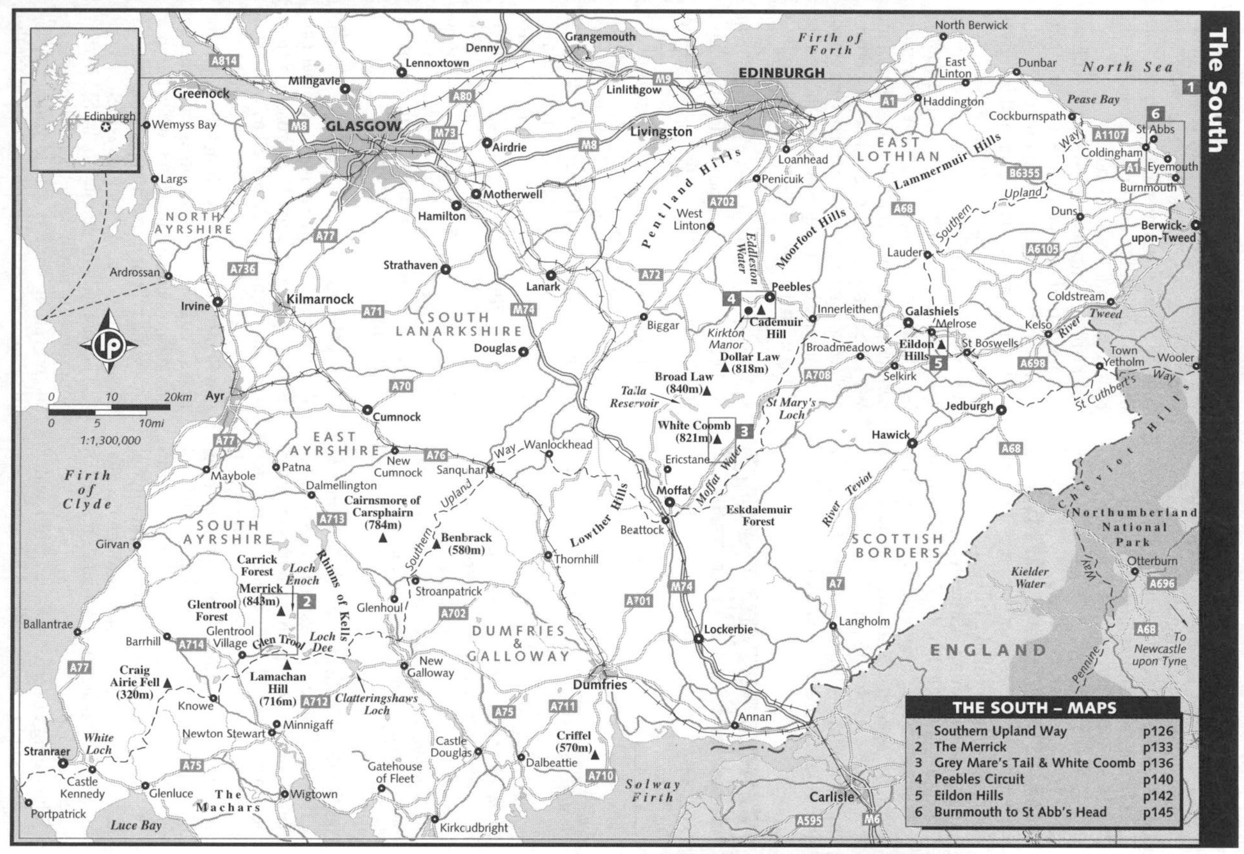
The South
THE SOUTH – MAPS
1 Southern Upland Way p126
2 The Merrick p133
3 Grey Mare's Tail & White Coomb p136
4 Peebles Circuit p140
5 Eildon Hills p142
6 Burnmouth to St Abb's Head p145
North Sea
Firth of Forth
EDINBURGH
GLASGOW
EAST LOTHIAN
SCOTTISH BORDERS
SOUTH LANARKSHIRE
EAST AYRSHIRE
SOUTH AYRSHIRE
NORTH AYRSHIRE
DUMFRIES & GALLOWAY
ENGLAND
Northumberland National Park
Kielder Water
Cheviot Hills
Pennine Way
St Cuthbert's Way
Southern Upland Way
Lammermuir Hills
Moorfoot Hills
Pentland Hills
Lowther Hills
Rhinns of Kells
The Machars
Solway Firth
Firth of Clyde
Luce Bay
Pease Bay
White Loch
St Mary's Loch
Talla Reservoir
Eddleston Water
Moffat Water
Loch Enoch
Loch Dee
Clatteringshaws Loch
River Tweed
River Teviot
Eskdalemuir Forest
Carrick Forest
Glentrool Forest
Broad Law (840m)
Dollar Law (818m)
White Coomb (821m)
Cademuir Hill
Eildon Hills
Merrick (843m)
Lamachan Hill (716m)
Cairnsmore of Carsphairn (784m)
Benbrack (580m)
Criffel (570m)
Craig Airie Fell (320m)
St Abbs
Eyemouth
Burnmouth
Coldingham
Berwick-upon-Tweed
Dunbar
North Berwick
East Linton
Haddington
Cockburnspath
Duns
Coldstream
Kelso
Town Yetholm
Wooler
St Boswells
Melrose
Galashiels
Selkirk
Lauder
Jedburgh
Hawick
Innerleithen
Peebles
Broadmeadows
Kirkton Manor
Loanhead
Penicuik
West Linton
Biggar
Ericstane
Moffat
Beattock
Lockerbie
Annan
Langholm
Carlisle
Otterburn
To Newcastle upon Tyne
Grangemouth
Linlithgow
Livingston
Denny
Lennoxtown
Milngavie
Airdrie
Motherwell
Hamilton
Lanark
Strathaven
Douglas
Kilmarnock
Cumnock
New Cumnock
Sanquhar
Wanlockhead
Thornhill
Dumfries
Dalbeattie
Castle Douglas
Kirkcudbright
Stroanpatrick
Glenhoul
New Galloway
Gatehouse of Fleet
Dalmellington
Patna
Maybole
Ayr
Irvine
Ardrossan
Largs
Wemyss Bay
Greenock
Girvan
Barrhill
Glentrool Village
Glen Trool
Knowe
Newton Stewart
Minnigaff
Wigtown
Glenluce
Castle Kennedy
Stranraer
Portpatrick
Ballantrae
Edinburgh
1:1,300,000
0 10 20km
0 5 10mi
A1 A1107 B6355 A6105 A698 A68 A696 A7 A708 A72 A702 M8 M9 A80 M73 M74 A76 A70 A71 A77 A736 A814 A713 A714 A712 A75 A711 A710 A701 A595 M6

THE SOUTH

Southern Scotland weather forecast is available on W www.met-office.gov.uk.

In an emergency contact either the Dumfries & Galloway constabulary (☎ 01387-252112) or the Lothian and Borders police (☎ 01450-375051).

Southern Uplands

Taking in virtually all the hill country across southernmost Scotland through Dumfries & Galloway and the Borders, the Southern Uplands is an area of great diversity and interest for walkers. Although none of the mountains reach the much sought-after Munro height of 3000ft (914m), they offer fine, often challenging, walking.

Southern Upland Way

Duration	9 days
Distance	212mi (341km)
Standard	medium-hard
Start	Portpatrick
Finish	Cockburnspath
Nearest Towns	Portpatrick, Cockburnspath
Public Transport	yes

Summary An extremely challenging, very long route passing through remote country in the west and more settled areas in the east, crossing high ground (up to 700m) and following minor roads, farm and forest tracks, and paths.

The Southern Upland Way (SUW), opened in 1984 and Britain's first official coast-to-coast, long-distance path, provides an introduction to the Southern Uplands, traversing one of the broadest parts of the country. It cuts across the grain of the countryside, roller-coasting over hills and moorland and through conifer plantations, descending to cross rivers and streams, then climbing out the other side. It also passes through deciduous woods and agricultural land, mainly in the eastern half.

The going underfoot ranges from sealed roads to muddy forest paths. Unfortunately, there are some long (over 2mi) stretches of bitumen (although not on busy roads), which some walkers feel have no place on official routes. There's some comfort in the fact they do link some very fine paths across the hills and through woodlands.

The route is not very well served with accommodation, so you have to anticipate some long days to get from one roof to the next. Camping or staying in bothies gives more flexibility, but all the necessary gear can weigh heavily after several hours. These factors, combined with the route's length and remoteness, make it a far more serious proposition than the West Highland Way. Nevertheless, the rewards are considerable: you get a real sense of moving across the country, becoming attuned to the gradual changes in the landscape, meeting fellow walkers and the satisfaction of sighting the North Sea on the last day. It's essential to be fit before you start and preferably have some experience of long-distance walking.

Alternatives If you like the sound of the SUW but don't have time to go the whole way, two two-day walks can be recommended. In the west, the section between St John's Town of Dalry and Overfingland includes the highest point on the Way and some fine upland walking, with a minimum of tedious pine plantations and road walking. Farther east, two easy days would account for the section from St Mary's Loch to Melrose (or Galashiels) with plenty of variety and minimal drawbacks.

PLANNING

You can expect a wide range of weather conditions during a complete crossing; thick mist and strong winds, as well as warm sunshine, are likely at any time between April and September, the best, if not the only time to walk the SUW. Snowfalls over the higher ground are standard in winter, when the short hours of daylight make it impossible to complete the necessarily long days before dark.

The majority of people do the SUW from south-west to north-east. Usually this means the prevailing wind is behind you but, when the Way was walked in this direction for this book, the persistent north wind was coming either from the side or head-on. There is much to be said for finishing in the east, with more open and settled countryside where shorter days are possible, than in the west, with monotonous conifer plantations and some unavoidably big daily distances.

The full walk of 212mi (341km) may take as few as nine days or as many as 14 (although people do spread the journey over a number of years, doing a bit at a time), depending on your best walking speed and the number of rest days. We have described the route in nine daily stages; these are within the reach of fit walkers but should be used mainly as a guide to what's involved. It's as well to have some flexibility in your plans as bad weather, likely at any time, may slow you down.

Daily stages between accommodation can be as short as 8mi (13km) or as long as 30mi (48km); the amount of ascent is a significant factor when you're planning an itinerary, especially in the central section between Sanquhar and Beattock. You also need to anticipate that you'll often have to carry all the food and drink you'll need for the day – there are precious few watering places en route.

Another factor to reckon with is transport. Many hosts along the Way provide a vehicle back-up service, picking you up from an agreed spot and returning you there the next day. Some people may do this gratis, others may charge – so check first. The Way crosses several main roads with bus services and one railway line with a convenient station. These enable you to reach the SUW from many major centres and to walk parts of it.

The route is well waymarked with a thistle hexagon logo and signposts, but you should still carry maps and a compass in case visibility deteriorates on the exposed stretches. Distances between waymarkers vary widely, from line of sight across moorland, to miles apart along minor roads. Sections of the route are changed (often for the better) from time to time, so waymarkers should always be more reliable than the mapped route.

Maps & Books

The Southern Upland Way Official Guide by Roger Smith is invaluable. It comes in a pack with strip maps of the Way, extracted from the seven OS Landranger 1:50,000 maps covering the full length of the Way. The pack costs £17.50 but this is less than half the cost of buying the maps individually. The only catch is, at the time of writing, the current edition is dated 1996, so some of the route details are outdated.

Anthony Burton's guide *The Southern Upland Way* has a more up-to-date and livelier description but its OS Pathfinder 1:25,000 maps are antiquated.

For really in-depth study of the area, you can't go past the Scottish Mountaineering Club's guide *The Southern Uplands*.

Information Sources

TICs on or near the route include Stranraer (☎ 01776-702595), Sanquhar (☎ 01659-50185), Moffat (☎ 01683-220620), Galashiels (☎ 01896-755551) and Melrose (☎ 01896-822555); Moffat, Galashiels and Melrose are open from April to the end of October.

Two free leaflets *Southern Upland Way* and *Accommodation List* (updated annually) are useful for preliminary planning. They are available from the ranger services at Dumfries (☎ 01387-260000) and Jedburgh (☎ 01835-830281). The Dumfries service also produces leaflets on the wildlife, history, archaeology and place names of the area, and a booklet describing short circular walks based on the SUW. *Southern Upland Way: Access by Public Transport* is available from Scottish Borders Council (☎ 01835-824000).

For more information you can also take a look at a special Southern Upland Way Web site (W www.southernuplandway.com).

Guided Walks

Locally based Scotwalk Ltd (☎ 01896-830515), Traquair Mill House, Innerleithen EH44 6PT, conducts guided tours of the Way and can organise self-guided walks. Also covering this popular route is C-N-Do Scotland (☎/fax 01786-445703, e info@cndoscotland.com, W www.cndoscotland.com), Unit 32 STEP, Stirling FK7 7RP.

NEAREST TOWNS

Portpatrick & Around

The peaceful harbour in the village of Portpatrick was once the port for ferries from Ireland. These days it quietly looks after anglers, sailors and walkers.

Places to Stay & Eat On the seafront, ***Carlton Guest House*** *(☎ 01776-810253)* is recommended; the tariff is £17. At nearby ***Harbour House Hotel*** *(☎ 01776-810456)* you can, with luck, sit outside and enjoy a meal of suitable proportions for the miles ahead, washed down with real ale.

There's a small ***shop***, which has a good range of the sorts of things you will need during the first day.

Stranraer, which is 8mi north-east of Portpatrick, is a large town with plenty more accommodation. Contact Stranraer TIC (☎ 01776-702595) in Harbour St for more information.

Getting There & Away Stranraer can be reached by Western Buses (☎ 0870-608 2608) or ScotRail (☎ 0845-755 0033) train from Glasgow or Carlisle, and Stena Line (☎ 0870-570 7070) ferry from Belfast.

McCulloch's Coaches (☎ 01776-830236) operates a bus service from Stranraer to Portpatrick about six times per day.

By car, from Glasgow follow the M77 and then the A77 to Stranraer, which then links to Portpatrick .

THE SOUTH

Laws, Cleuchs & Rigs

As you pore over the maps at home, the names of the hills, rivers and other natural features can help give a clearer picture of what the landscape looks like, and can also reveal something of the local history.

While Gaelic place names are commonplace in the Highlands and islands to the north, in the Southern Uplands they're largely confined to the south-west, even though Gaelic is now little spoken in these parts. In the Borders, however, the names are mainly from Lowland Scots (Lallans), a distinct language (still in use) with origins in the languages of settlers from the east, rather than the Celtic-Gaelic influences from the west.

Starting at the beginning of the Way, Portpatrick's origin is obvious, given the Irish connection, although it was originally called Portree, from the Gaelic *port righ* meaning 'harbour of the king'. Killantringan, the location of the fine lighthouse, includes the anglicised version of the common Gaelic prefix *cill*, meaning 'church', in this case of St Ringan or Ninian. Balmurrie, the farm near New Luce, has another widespread Gaelic element *bal*, meaning 'farm' or 'small township', in this case of the Murray family.

Laggangairn, the site of the two prehistoric cairns beyond Balmurrie, means hollow of the cairns (*lag* meaning 'hollow'). A bit farther on you climb over Craig Airie Fell – a hybrid of Gaelic and Norse. Craig is derived from *creag*, which is Gaelic for 'cliff' or 'crag'; *àiridh* is Gaelic for 'shieling' (a temporary dwelling); and fell, once a Norse term, is commonly used in the English Lake District to mean 'mountain'. Dalry is from the Gaelic *dail righ* or 'meadow of the king'. Benbrack, the hill between that town and Sanquhar, is the speckled *breac* or 'hill', while Fingland comes from the Gaelic *fionn gleann*, meaning 'white glen'.

In the east, the Lammermuir Hills feature prominently in the latter stages; the name comes from Old English for lamb – still appropriate today.

Among the most common names for geographical features are cleuch, which comes directly from the Lowland Scots for ravine; the similar-sounding heugh is a cliff. The name law pops up all over the Borders and is the equivalent of the Gaelic *beinn*, meaning 'mountain' or 'hill', often isolated and conical in shape. A knowe is also a high sort of place (a small hillock), while a dod is a bare round hill.

Scottish Hill and Mountain Names by Peter Drummond, the Scottish place names guru, should answer almost any query you come up with.

Cockburnspath

Places to Stay & Eat There are a couple of B&Bs on nearby farms, including ***Mrs Hood*** *(☎ 01368-830499)* who charges around £20. The excellent ***Chesterfield Caravan & Camping Site*** *(☎ 01368-830459)* is a couple of miles away; the tariff is £6. Unfortunately the nearest pub is at Grantshouse, a few miles south along the A1, but the small shop in Cockburnspath is licensed!

Getting There & Away Both First Edinburgh (☎ 0131-663 9233) and Perryman's (☎ 01890-781533) buses on services to/from Edinburgh and Berwick-upon-Tweed (on the main east coast railway line) stop here. The village, just off the A1 between Edinburgh and Berwick-upon-Tweed, is 35mi from Edinburgh and 20mi from Berwick.

THE WALK

Day 1: Portpatrick to New Luce

8–8½ hours, 23mi (37km), 370m ascent

In Portpatrick the Way starts at the foot of a flight of stairs at the north-western end of the small harbour. From here it heads northwest above impressive cliffs (take care, especially in poor visibility) and around scenic coves. The route ahead isn't always obvious but trust the thistle waymarkers to show the way from the shore back up to the cliff top. Killantringan lighthouse comes dramatically into view and the SUW joins the minor road leading inland.

Minor roads and farm tracks lead to a high point with fine views on a clear day. From here more minor roads, farm tracks and short, sometimes muddy paths take you down past the outskirts of Stranraer to Castle Kennedy. The village has a small ***shop*** and ***Eynhallow Hotel*** *(☎ 01581-400256)*, where you can choose a comfortable room or camping nearby; B&B costs £30 and camping is free if you eat at the hotel.

From Castle Kennedy a sealed drive takes you through the pleasant, wooded grounds of the ruined castle to a minor road. You soon leave this to follow farm tracks to another minor road, then right round the edge of a cleared conifer plantation. The route descends to a footbridge over a railway line, then goes down to a suspension bridge over the Water of Luce. New Luce is off the Way, 1mi north along a nearby road. If you feel like covering a few more miles before stopping at New Luce, continue across open moorland, past deserted Kilhern and down to a minor road about 1mi east of New Luce.

New Luce

Here you'll find the fine old ***Kenmuir Arms Hotel*** *(☎ 01581-600218)*, which charges £25, and its adjacent camping and caravan site. There's a small ***shop*** in the village. A limited bus service operated by A&F Irvine (☎ 01581-300345) links the village with Stranraer (one bus each way on Tuesday, Wednesday and Friday).

Day 2: New Luce to Bargrennan

6¾–7¼ hours, 17mi (27km), 340m ascent

Follow very quiet roads to Balmurrie farm, from where the route rises across moorland then follows a wide, heathery ride (a path specially made for riding on horseback) through a plantation. A short stretch of forest road leads to an open area with a timber, beehive-shaped ***bothy***, which only has sleeping platforms; there is a fresh water supply nearby. Also nearby are the 4000-year-old **Laggangairn standing stones**, with information about their history. Beyond a large cairn the Way follows a different route from that on the official map as it climbs over **Craig Airie Fell** (320m) for an excellent view all round. The Way then descends past Derry Farm and follows minor roads past Knowe and Glenruther Lodge, over Glenvernoch Fell and down to Bargrennan.

Bargrennan

Here ***House O'Hill Hotel*** *(☎ 01671-840243)* provides accommodation (£20 for B&B) and serves excellent bar meals. At ***Glentrool Holiday Park*** *(☎ 01671-840 280)*, about half a mile north along the road, it costs around £7 to pitch a tent. There are also B&Bs in Glentrool Village, a mile north and off the Way. Western Buses (☎ 0870-608 2608) runs several services a day (only twice on Sunday) between Bargrennan and Girvan, on the coast.

Day 3: Bargrennan to St John's Town of Dalry

9–9½ hours, 24mi (38.5km), 500m ascent

Day 3 starts along mossy, partly overgrown paths through conifers. Having crossed a minor road, the Way passes through pleasant woodlands and follows the Water of Trool to the spacious ***Caldons Campsite*** *(☎ 01671-840218)*, which has a small shop; the fee for pitching a tent is about £6. The Way then traverses above Loch Trool, with some good views towards Merrick (843m), the highest point in the Galloway Hills, before dropping down to cross Glenhead Burn. Follow the burn briefly then diverge from the mapped route and head south-east across country to meet a forest road about 1mi west of Loch Dee. ***White Laggan Bothy*** is about 350m off the route to the south.

Past Loch Dee Angling Club's hut, the Way crosses the River Dee then there's almost no respite from the conifers for about 4mi, until you reach the road to Mid Garrary, which you follow west for a short distance.

The Way leaves the road on a good path north through wide clearings between more plantations, rises across moorland and descends to Clenrie Farm. Farther on and well

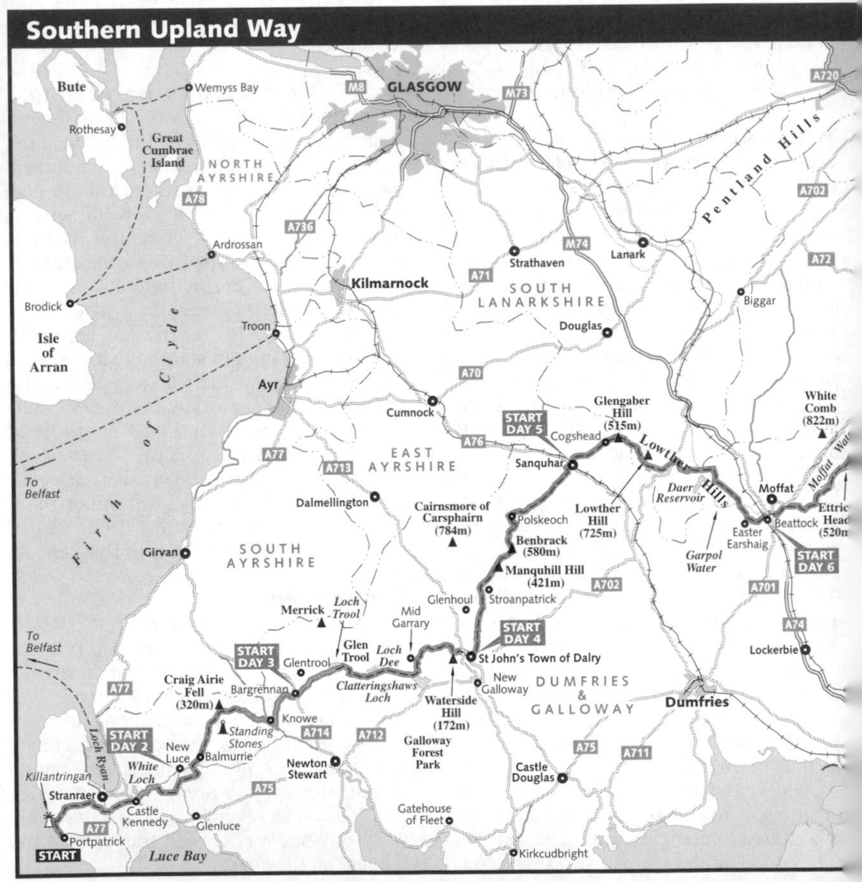

down the valley of Coom Burn, the Way cuts east across Waterside Hill and follows the Water of Ken to a fine suspension bridge leading to St John's Town of Dalry.

St John's Town of Dalry

Often shortened to Dalry, this large village has two hotels including ***Clachan Inn*** *(☎ 01644-430241)*, in Main St, where the tariff is £20, and a couple of B&Bs including ***Mrs Findlay*** *(☎ 01644-430420)*, in Main St, costing £15. There is an excellent licensed grocer and another small shop. From Dalry, MacEwan's (☎ 01387-256533) operates bus services to Ayr, on the coast, and nearby Dumfries.

Day 4: St John's Town of Dalry to Sanquhar

9¾–10¼ hours, 27mi (43km), 900m ascent

From Dalry the Way crosses rough grazing land, past Ardoch Farm, to Butterhole Bridge. Friendly ***Kendoon SYHA Hostel*** *(☎ 01644-460680)* is about 1.5mi farther west, off the SUW at Glenhoul (the warden may be able to help with transport from the hostel). The route continues across rough grazing ground to Stroanpatrick, then climbs

Southern Upland Way

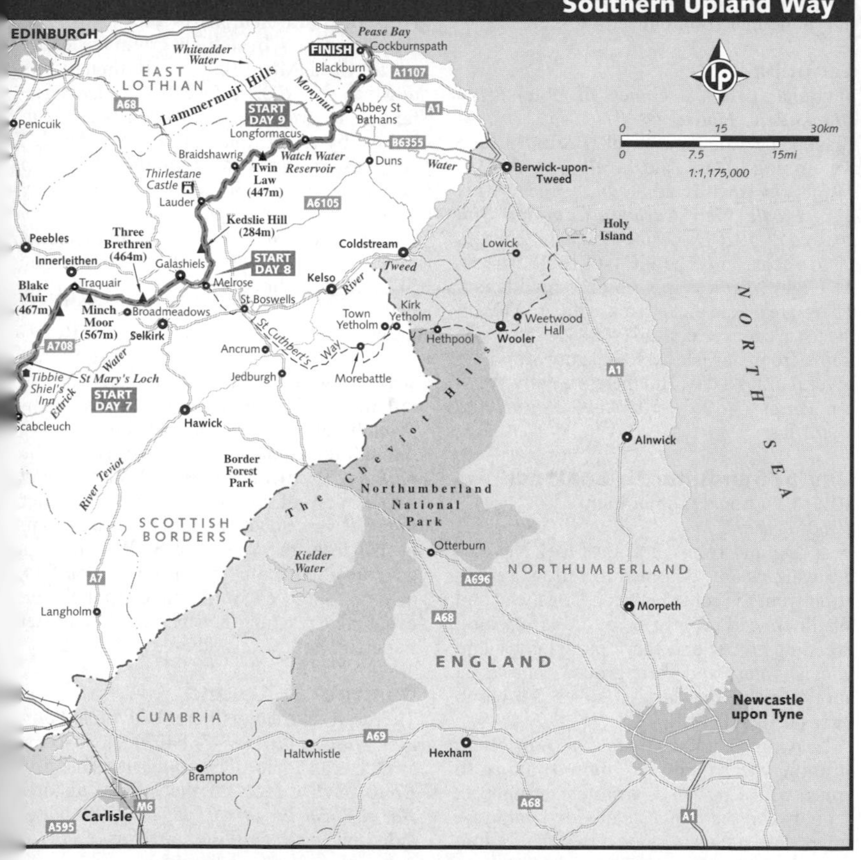

a wide ride through plantations and skirts the summit of Manquhill Hill (421m). Continue past the track to ***Manquhill Bothy*** and up to **Benbrack** (580m) for excellent panoramic views. You descend over a couple of lesser tops, through a plantation, past Allan's Cairn and along a forest road, passing the rather spartan ***Polskeoch Bothy*** to the scattering of buildings at Polskeoch.

After about 2mi along a minor sealed road, the Way sets off across the ridge to the north along rough tracks. Sanquhar comes into view from the top but there's a long descent into the valley of the River Nith (Nithsdale) before you finally reach the bridge over the river and the path leading into Sanquhar (pronounced san-ker).

Sanquhar

Sanquhar offers a choice of hotels. Try ***Blackaddie House*** *(☎ 01659-50270)*, in Blackaddie Rd, for a meal. B&Bs include welcoming ***Mrs McDowall*** *(☎ 01659-50751)*, in Town Head St, where the tariff is £15. ***Castle View Caravan/Camping Site*** *(☎ 01659-50291)*, beside the Way, charges £3 to pitch a tent. The TIC (☎ 01659-50185), 41 High St, can help with accommodation. There are shops and a bank with an ATM in the town centre. ScotRail (☎ 0845-755 0033) trains from Carlisle and Glasgow stop here several times a day, and there's a daily Western Buses (☎ 0870-608 2608) service to Dumfries.

Day 5: Sanquhar to Beattock

10¼–10¾ hours, 28mi (45km),
1550m ascent

In spring and from 12 August to 1 November walkers are requested to follow a deviation from the route between Cogshead and Wanlockhead, firstly to avoid disturbing breeding grouse and very young lambs, and later shooters and their grouse. This adds about 2mi to the day but saves the climb over Glengaber Hill.

Leaving Sanquhar there's a short climb straightaway, then two more bumps to cross, with Cogshead, a ruined farmhouse, set between them in a steep-sided valley. A steep descent on a good track leads into **Wanlockhead**, the highest village in Scotland. It is an old lead mining village with plenty of industrial archaeology, and a striking contrast to the bare, lonely moorland. There's a ***SYHA Hostel*** *(☎ 01659-74252)*, Lotus Lodge, which charges £8.25, several B&Bs and a small ***shop***. Wanlockhead's Museum of Lead Mining and its ***tearoom*** are worth a visit.

From here the Way climbs to **Lowther Hill**, crossing and recrossing the sealed road to the surreal golf ball domes (containing radar equipment) in a fenced enclosure on the summit (725m). Here, on the highest point on the Southern Upland Way and on a good day, it's possible to see the Pentland Hills (near Edinburgh) to the north. The Way continues over high ground, steeply up to Cold Moss (628m). It then drops down to the A702 at Overfingland, a large farm. Dumfries and Edinburgh buses, run jointly by MacEwan's (☎ 01387-256533) and Western Buses (☎ 0870-608 2608), stop here three times daily Monday to Saturday (only once on Sunday).

Just beyond the A702, in Watermeetings Forest, you reach the halfway point of the SUW as you climb through a wide clearing in the conifers. Then it's down to a road near the cottages beside the extensive Daer Reservoir. Here a long climb begins over Sweetshaw Brae, Hods Hill and Beld Knowe (507m), overlooking the reservoir. This is inevitably followed by an equally long descent through the plantation to Cloffin Burn. The ***bothy*** at Brattleburn is out of sight, about 400m west of the Way. There's another ***bothy***, Rivox, about 1mi farther on, and signposted from the Way. The SUW continues generally downhill, still in dense conifers, across a large clearing and Garpol Water, eventually reaching a minor road at Easter Earshaig. Follow this down to Beattock.

Beattock & Around

There are two hotels here, of which ***Beattock House*** (☎ 01683-300403), close to the Way, has an adjacent camping site, charging £7 to pitch a tent. Of the B&Bs, historic ***Barnhill Springs*** *(☎ 01683-220580)* is beside the Way and the tariff is £21. A

Quaint fishing villages, coastal cliffs and rolling uplands provide variety in **The South** – historic Eyemouth Harbour; St Abb's Head lighthouse (left inset) on the Burnmouth to St Abb's Head path; walking the Grey Mare's Tail & White Coomb circuit with Lochcraig Head (801m) in the background (right inset). *Main photo: Nancy Frey. Left Inset: Jose Placer. Right Inset: Nancy Frey.*

Central Scotland is an intensely beautiful dividing line between the lowlands and highlands – walking the Glen Rosa path with Cir Mhòr (798m) ahead on the Isle of Arran; a sea of rose quar (inset) from Schiehallion's summit (1083m). *Main photo: Sandra Bardwell. Inset: Jose Placer.*

Craigielands, about 1mi south of the Way, there's a ***shop*** and ***Craigielands Country Park*** (☎ *01683-300591*), where the tariff for one camper is £4.

Moffat, just over 1mi north, has more accommodation and places to eat (and banks with ATMs), but the A701 is very busy, so try for a place that provides vehicle back-up. See Moffat on page 135 for deatils.

Day 6: Beattock to St Mary's Loch

8–8½ hours, 21mi (34km), 1200m ascent

From Beattock go under the A74(M), across the River Annan, up and over a small hill, then beside Moffat Water. The Way then winds up through a plantation on a forest road and on to a path up a deep valley. This leads to the gorge carved by **Selcloth Burn**; the path traverses this dramatic cleft then climbs to **Ettrick Head** (520m), the boundary between Dumfries & Galloway and the Borders. Beyond here you soon meet a forest road, which leads down to ***Over Phawhope Bothy*** and a minor road beside Ettrick Water. Follow this for 6mi down the valley, its natural beauty somewhat compromised by blankets of conifers.

Turn off at Scabcleuch along a signposted public path, which climbs up a narrow glen then crosses Pikestone Rig and goes down to Riskinhope Hope, a once-solid stone house now a bramble-covered ruin. The route then turns around Earl's Hill and picks up a forest track for the descent to historic ***Tibbie Shiel's Inn*** (☎ *01750-42231*) at St Mary's Loch, scene of the Way's opening in 1984. The inn offers relatively luxurious accommodation (the tariff starts at £24) and excellent bar meals. There's also a camping site nearby, run by the inn; the tariff is £2. A limited bus service run by McCall's (for timetable details phone the transport information service on ☎ 0845-709 0510) links the nearby Glen Cafe with Galashiels and Moffat.

Day 7: St Mary's Loch to Melrose

11½–12 hours, 30mi (48km), 1120m ascent

This ultra-long day could be split into two, with an overnight stop at Traquair, 12mi (20km) from St Mary's Loch. Of the total climb, 800m comes between Traquair and Melrose.

From the inn pass in front of the St Mary's Loch Sailing Club building and follow a path, then a vehicle track, beside the loch; farther on cross Yarrow Water to the A708. The Way crosses the road and returns to open country. Good paths and tracks climb over a spur to Douglas Burn, then it's up again, across heathery Blake Muir and down to the hamlet of Traquair in the valley of the River Tweed, at the junction of the B709 and B7062. First Edinburgh (☎ 0131-663 9233) buses link Traquair with Peebles and Selkirk, and there are daily services from these towns to Edinburgh.

Traquair Mill Bothy (☎ *01896-830515*) is a commodious bunkhouse, which provides vehicle back-up; the tariff is £13. There's more accommodation in Innerleithen, about 1mi north along the B709 (and a bus service to Edinburgh).

Turning your back on Traquair, follow a lane (which can be muddy) climbing steadily into a plantation. **Minch Moor** (567m) rises on the right and the short detour is well worth the effort for the panoramic view, including the Eildon Hills near Melrose to the east. The SUW continues along a wide ride through a plantation and rises to **Brown Knowe** (523m), which also provides good views. The next tops are skirted on the right and left. The turn-off to ***Broadmeadows SYHA Hostel*** (☎ *01750-76262*), Scotland's first youth hostel, is signposted and is a mile to the south. If you're considering staying here, remember that the nearest shops are in Selkirk, 5mi away. The route continues up to the three massive cairns known as the **Three Brethren**. Then it's down to Yair and a bridge over the River Tweed.

You then climb over a fairly broad ridge and go down across fields, crossing numerous stiles, to woodland on the outskirts of Galashiels. The Way follows a rather devious route through parklands and along suburban streets, skirting Gala Hill. Cross the busy A7 and follow riverside paths and a sealed bicycle path to Melrose. See Melrose on page 141 for details.

THE SOUTH

Day 8: Melrose to Longformacus

9–9½ hours, 25mi (40km), 750m ascent

From Melrose cross the River Tweed, this time by a 19th-century chain suspension bridge for pedestrians and 'light carriages' only. The Way goes back up beside the river then heads north, steadily gaining height. There are fine views on a good day from the highest point around flat-topped **Kedslie Hill**. The route passes through several fields occupied by grazing cows – they're very inquisitive but not aggressive. The steep descent into Lauder skirts the local golf course.

Lauder has three pubs and several B&Bs in and near the town, of which ***Thirlestane Farm*** (☎ *01578-722216)*, about 1.5mi east of the Way beside the A697 (a pick-up service may be available), is particularly recommended; the tariff is £23. At ***Thirlestane Castle Caravan & Camp Site*** *(☎ 01578-722254)*, near splendid Thirlestane Castle, the charge is £4. In the main street you'll find an excellent ***baker***, small supermarkets, a ***coffee shop*** and a bank with an ATM. All of which is just as well – Lauder is the last place where you can stock up on chocolate and other daytime staples before Cockburnspath at the end of the Way. First Edinburgh (☎ 0131-663 9233) buses from Galashiels and Edinburgh stop here.

From Lauder the Way weaves through the grounds of **Thirlestane Castle** (open to visitors). Cross the A697 and follow a lane up through the curiously named Wanton Walls Farm and steeply up to a small plantation. The Way then wanders up and down across open grassland, then crosses Blythe Water on a substantial bridge. Continue on to Braidshawrig, part of the Burncastle Estate grouse moor. It's essential to keep to the track, especially during the grouse shooting season, which always starts on 12 August. The track climbs across the vast empty moors, dotted with shooting butts and old tin sheds providing shelter for stock, to the ridge crest. It then turns right to the high point of **Twin Law** (447m), topped with two giant cylindrical cairns, each with a sheltered seat facing south-east. From there the Tweed valley is spread out before you and the sea is in sight at last. The descent towards Watch Water Reservoir is easy – a good track leads to Scarlaw and a sealed road. Continue down to the small village of Longformacus (pronounced long-for-may-cus).

The excellent ***Eildon Cottage B&B*** *(☎ 01361-890230)*, where you'll undoubtedly appreciate Mrs Amos' magnificent four-course evening meal, charges from £16.

Day 9: Longformacus to Cockburnspath

6¾–7¼ hours, 17mi (27km), 450m ascent

After about 1mi along a minor road east of Longformacus, the Way branches off to climb over moorland, past some small plantations and down to the B6355. From here the route follows steep-sided Whiteadder Valley through mixed woodland to the hamlet of Abbey St Bathan. Cross Whiteadder Water, just below where it joins Monynut Water. In a change from the officially mapped route, the Way follows the Whiteadder for a while then turns north (the ***Riverside restaurant*** is just across the river here) to follow paths and lanes, crossing some fields in the process. From a minor road at Blackburn you can catch a last glimpse back to the hills. Then it's down to the busy A1 (cross with care) to follow an old road between the A1 and the railway to a pleasant green track into Penmanshiel Wood. It seems cruel at this stage but the route climbs through the wood, fortunately to a very rewarding view of the North Sea and the Firth of Forth. A long flight of steps takes you down to the A1107, beyond which is Pease Dean Wildlife Reserve, where the native woodland is being regenerated.

Skirt the serried ranks of vans in ***Pease Bay Caravan & Camp Site*** *(☎ 01368-830206)*, where tent pitches cost around £5, and walk up the road above the bay. The final cliff-top walk – mirroring the start – is blessed with impressive coastal scenery, along to colourful Cove Harbour tucked below. To officially finish the Way turn inland, under the A1 and the railway line, to the mercat (market) cross at Cockburnspath (pronounced co-burns-path or just co-path). It takes a while to sink in that you really have walked 212mi from Portpatrick.

Dumfries & Galloway

Touted as Scotland's hidden gem, this area's low population density, mild climate, varied wildlife, 200mi of coastline, extensive forests and numerous monuments make for fascinating walking on often desolate trails. The dramatic coast includes the Mull of Galloway, Scotland's southernmost point and a haven for seabirds, the Machars, a peninsula noted for its links to early Scottish Christianity, and Solway, known for its impressionist-style landscapes.

One of Scotland's most densely forested regions, the 290-sq-mi Galloway Forest Park contains the highest, most challenging mountains in the south. Other noted regions for walking are Nithsdale (between the Galloway and Lowther Hills), with its tranquil glens around Moniaive, and the Moffat Hills, on the north-western fringe of Dumfries.

Keep in mind that some of the fences are electrified, up to 5000 volts. Feral goats abound, as do red squirrels, roe deer, badgers, foxes, numerous small mammals, and woodland and seabirds. The unusual natterjack toads are also a noted inhabitant. For the non-British visitor, belted Galloway cattle (known locally as belties), with thick white belts wrapped around their otherwise black midriffs, will be particularly eye-catching. The area is also known for its flourishing gardens and nurseries.

CLIMATE

The Gulf Stream's arrival from the west gives Dumfries & Galloway Scotland's driest and warmest climate. The mountains near the western coast are wettest. Snow falls from November to March and varies considerably year to year.

PLANNING

Books

Innes MacLeod & John Donald's *Discovering Galloway* is a good general reference. The Pathfinder Guide *Dumfries & Galloway* gives good walk descriptions. The very readable booklet *Walking in Dumfries and Galloway* is good for orientation purposes. Birdwatchers will enjoy the pamphlet *Birdwatching: Dumfries & Galloway*. The latter two are available from local TICs.

Information Sources

The Dumfries & Galloway Council Countryside Ranger Service (☎ 01387-260184, W www.dumgal.gov.uk) sponsors guided walks and activities. Ask for the booklet *Dumfries & Galloway: Ranger Led Walks & Events* at TICs and libraries. In an emergency contact the Dumfries & Galloway constabulary (☎ 01387-252112).

GETTING THERE & AWAY

Virgin (☎ 0845-722 2333) and ScotRail (☎ 0845-755 0033) trains run between London Euston and Glasgow, stopping in Dumfries approximately eight times per day.

National Express (☎ 0870-580 8080) buses serve Dumfries & Galloway from London, and Western Buses (☎ 0870-608 2608) runs the convenient express Nos X73/74 Kirkcudbright-Dumfries-Glasgow/Ediburgh.

The Dumfries & Galloway area is a six- to seven-hour drive from London, a three-hour drive from Manchester and a two-hour drive from Glasgow or Edinburgh.

GETTING AROUND

Fourteen miles west of Lockerbie, which is on the A74(M), Dumfries is the area's major gateway. Dumfries & Galloway Council's Travel Information Line (☎ 0845-709 0510), which operates Monday to Friday from 9am to 5pm, covers local services. Five area timetables, giving bus routes and times as well as connecting rail services, are available from TICs. Particularly relevant for the walks in this section are *Bus Times Annandale and Eskdale Area* and *Bus Times Stewartry and Wigtownshire Area*. The former includes the useful route No 114 between Dumfries and Moffat, operated by MacEwan's Coach Services (☎ 01387-256533) and Western Buses (☎ 0870-608 2608), and the latter includes route No 500/X75 between Dumfries and Stranraer via Newton Stewart, operated by MacEwan's, Western Buses and, on Sunday, King of Kirkcowan (☎ 01671-830284).

The Merrick

Duration	4–4½ hours
Distance	8mi (12.9km)
Standard	medium-hard
Start & Finish	Bruce's Stone car park
Nearest Town	Newton Stewart
Public Transport	no

Summary Classic walk to the Southern Uplands' highest peak along a very scenic trail of lochs, valleys, dense forest and tumbling burns.

Of the 40 summits over 2000ft in the Galloway Hills, the most popular is south-west Scotland's highest, the Merrick (843m or 2766ft). Part of the Range of the Awful Hand, this impressive mountain offers great visual rewards along a very scenic and steep trail. The gnarled hand starts south with Benyellary (Hill of Eagles) as the thumb and continues north to the Merrick (derived from the Gaelic *meurach* meaning 'branched finger') as the index finger. Kirriereoch, Tarfessoch and the Shalloch complete the hand northward. Rife with gory local history, around Loch Trool (at Caldons Wood) there is a memorial stone for three murdered Convenanters and, near the trailhead, the Bruce's Stone commemorates a 1307 victory. The well-worn trail of the Merrick, quite steep at times, is easy to follow during the 750m ascent from Loch Trool. An alternative, looping return is provided but the trail from Loch Enoch to Loch Neldricken is heavily eroded, boggy and difficult to find. Forest Enterprise hopes to repair the trail with European Union (EU) funding. Ask at the visitor centre for an updated.

PLANNING

Be prepared for strong winds and rapid weather changes; the area requires considerable respect when the weather is poor, especially in winter. Midges are particularly grim in August. Bring water for the whole walk and pack your map and compass.

Maps

The OS Landranger 1:50,000 map No 77 *(Dalmellington & New Galloway)* covers the Merrick. More specific is OS Outdoor Leisure 1:25,000 map No 32 *(Galloway Forest Park)*.

Books

Locally popular, *The Galloway Hills: A Walker's Paradise* by George Brittain (£3) describes 90 distinct walks. The romantic thriller, *The Raiders* by SR Crockett, uses the Merrick Hills as a backdrop.

Information Sources

Forest Enterprise's Glen Trool Visitor Centre (☎ 01671-840302), 1.8mi from the A714 and Glen Trool village (where the bus stops), is open April to October from 10.30am to 5.30pm (to 4.30pm in October). There is a small cafe, as well as area books, maps and gifts for sale. Free leaflets on short walks are provided. Call for local bus schedules.

NEAREST TOWN
Newton Stewart & Around

An old-fashioned market town, Newton Stewart is joined at the hip with Minnigaff by the Cree Bridge, both towns sharing the same local services. The Newton Stewart TIC (☎ 01671-402431, e newtonstewart@dgtb.ossian.net), Dashwood Square, opens from April to October and sells books and maps. Newton Stewart's busy main street (the A714 in disguise) changes names three times – Arthur, Victoria and Albert. Very basic outdoor gear is available at DG Guns & Tackle, 19–21 Albert St.

Places to Stay & Eat Five minutes down Millcroft Rd, ***Minnigaff SYHA Hostel*** *(☎ 01671-402211)* has knowledgeable staff,

> **Warning**
>
> In summertime, adders are occasionally spotted in Galloway Forest. Adders have a distinctive, dark zigzag stripe down their grey-green backs and usually reach a length of about 60cm. While poisonous the venom is rarely fatal. They usually only become aggressive when disturbed. If bitten, seek medical assistance and advise a park ranger immediately.

a self-catering kitchen and charges from £7.25 to £9.25. Riverside 300-year-old ***Ivy Bank Cottage*** *(☎ 01671-403139)*, Millcroft Rd, charges £19.50 with shared bathrooms. Forest Enterprise runs the ***Caldons Campsite*** *(☎ 01671-840218)*, about 1mi from the trailhead, from before Easter to October; backpackers with tent pay from £3.50 and it has a small shop that sells fresh bread and dairy products.

In Newton Stewart, the ***Brig End Pantry*** *(78 Victoria St)* has the best-value meal in town; open Monday to Friday from noon to 2.30pm, soup, main course and dessert cost £3.99. The ***Galloway Arms Hotel***, on the main street, serves good pub grub from £5.75 to £10 and caters to vegetarians. Self-caterers will find ***Costcutters*** market along the main street.

Getting There & Away Bus No 500/X75 (Dumfries-Stranraer), run by MacEwan's Coach Services (☎ 01387-256533), Western Buses (☎ 0870-608 2608) and, on Sunday, King of Kirkcowan (☎ 01671-830284), stops at Dashwood Square in Newton Stewart. The service runs six times a day Monday to Saturday and three times on Sunday. By train, take the ScotRail (☎ 0845-755 0033) Glasgow Central-Stranraer line, getting off at Barrhill or Stranraer. From Barrhill Western Buses No 359 (Whithorn-Girvan via Newton Stewart) goes to/from Newton Stewart in 40 minutes. Newton Stewart is 50mi west of Dumfries on the A75.

GETTING TO/FROM THE WALK

Western Buses (☎ 0870-608 2608) No 359 stops along the A714 at Glen Trool. From the road, walk a flat 1.8mi to the Glen Trool Visitor Centre and then 3.25mi to Bruce's Stone and the trailhead. By car, from Newton Stewart take the A714 (towards Girvan) for 8.7mi and turn right to Glentrool Village. Continue to the visitor centre and the trailhead. There are public restrooms and two small car parks on the left.

THE WALK

At the east end of the Bruce's Stone car park look left for a Merrick sign (4mi to top). Take the rocky trail ascending north-east. After 500m of moorland, birch and hawthorn trees, pass through a kissing gate. The trail borders Buchan Burn's west side. A bit farther take the recommended high path, which heads left, slightly above the burn. Another kissing gate and a 'forest trail' sign mark the entrance to the woods.

After just over half a mile of easy going the path emerges from the forest and passes the abandoned bothy at Culsharg, which shelters walkers. The path becomes rocky and the ascent more difficult. Reaching a forestry road turn right, cross a bridge over a Buchan Burn tributary, and then bear left onto an ascending path through trees marked 'Merrick Climb'. After 800m of very steep going, the trail leaves the forest and continues north-north-west along the open Benyellary slopes. Continue past a kissing gate and a boggy zone to a dry-stone dyke and follow it north-east up to Benyellary (719m). Follow the wall for just under 1mi towards the

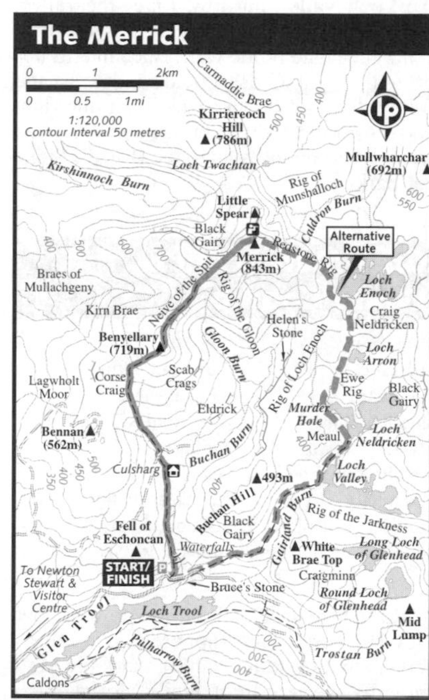

THE SOUTH

Merrick summit, along the **Neive of the Spit** ridge crest. Enjoy the outstanding views.

Where the wall separates from the trail, head north-east to the **summit** (843m), marked with a view indicator. Northern Ireland, Ben Lomond and the Lake District are visible in the distance, but don't miss nearby Mullwharchar (north-east), Craignaw (south-east) and Muldonoch and Lamachan Hills (south). Retrace your steps to Bruce's Stone.

Alternative Route: via Loch Enoch

3 hours, 5mi (8km)

From the Merrick summit, descend steeply along Redstone Rig to Loch Enoch's south-west corner. Head south-east along a col above Loch Arron and then descend to the lake. Follow the western slopes of Ewe Rig along a wall heading south to Murder Hole. According to Crockett's book (see Books on page 132), the Raiders used this lagoon as an ambush hideout. Cross a wall then follow the outflow of Loch Neldricken to the Loch Valley outflow. Enter the valley, through which Gairland Burn runs, and descend via a gate in the wall. Buchan Hill lies off to the right. Cross a field south-west and follow the trail down to a stile on the right and cross over. Cross a bridge and then head west (right) on the road to the Bruce's Stone car park.

Grey Mare's Tail & White Coomb

Duration	5 hours
Distance	8.3mi (13.4km)
Standard	medium-hard
Start & Finish	Grey Mare's Tail car park
Nearest Town	Moffat
Public Transport	yes

Summary An initial spectacular waterfall leads to a steep climb up White Coomb and becomes an ambling ridge walk above Loch Skeen.

A Roman road and the great cow hollow, Devil's Beef Tub (apparently used by reivers to hide stolen cattle), mark the Moffat Hills' western limit, while Moffat Water cuts through the highly scenic, steep-sided Moffat Valley, creating the eastern edge. Two summits in this triangular sector stand out for their height and peculiar history; the 808m Hart Fell (see Other Walks on page 146) and White Coomb (821m), meaning 'white corrie'.

White Coomb's most scenic approach is the 570m ascent via the Grey Mare's Tail waterfall. Initially the trail is obvious and then it follows a dry-stone wall roughly marking the National Trust for Scotland property line. The land was purchased by the Trust in 1962 and 1972 for conservation and public access. From Firthhope Rig the wall also corresponds with the regional border separating Dumfries & Galloway from the Borders. While navigation is easy, the uphill pull to White Coomb is hard work. Be prepared for very wet and boggy sections, and steep parts around the falls; fatalities have occurred.

Moffat Literary Notes

The base of White Coomb is bathed by the leaping Grey Mare's Tail, a 200ft waterfall named for the grey mare in Robert Burns' poem *Tam O'Shanter*. Sir Walter Scott also eulogised the falls in *Marmion*: 'Then, issuing forth one foaming wave, And wheeling round the Giant's Grave, White as the snowy charger's tail, Drives down the pass of Moffatdale.'

The Moffat Hills are also rich in Arthurian legends. The great wizard Merlin was said to inhabit these hills, even becoming a hart, a deer linked with royalty. Nicolai Tolstoy utilised Hart Fell as Merlin's secluded refuge in *The Quest for Merlin*.

NATURAL HISTORY

The Grey Mare's Tail is a 'hanging valley', meaning that during the thaw after the last ice age the Tail Burn and adjacent valley were left hanging above the more deeply cut Moffat Water valley. Glacial moraine (debris) dams Loch Skeen and fascinating fossilised remains of graptolites (warm water oceanic organisms alive 400 million years ago) can be found here. National Trust for Scotland naturalists lead 2mi 'fossil forays' and meet at the Grey Mare's Tail trailhead; to book call ☎ 01750-42288. Common birds include peregrine falcon, red grouse, common sandpiper and dipper. Delicate globe flowers intermix with lady's mantle, and mountain sorrel sprays the hillsides with colour, while purple saxifrage scales the vertiginous slopes.

PLANNING

Enjoy the walk year-round although expect icy winter conditions and difficulty crossing Tail Burn after heavy rains. The first section is busy but you'll find solitude in the heights. Bring enough water for the whole route.

Maps & Books

The OS Landranger 1:50,000 map No 79 *(Hawick & Eskdale)* is sufficient. *Walks in the Moffat Hills and the Lowthers* by Jim Manson provides good background information on 33 walks.

Information Sources

The trailhead National Trust for Scotland visitor centre (☎ 01556-502575 – office in Castle Douglas) opens from April to October.

NEAREST TOWN

Moffat

Famous for its mouth-watering toffee and woollen-mill products, Moffat is also close to the Southern Upland Way. Moffat's TIC (☎ 01683-220620, ⓔ moffat@dgtb.ossian.net), near the town entrance from the A74(M), has varying hours from April to November. The centre has OS maps and a wide selection of regional books. There are no outdoor gear shops; the closest are in either Dumfries (21mi) or Lockerbie (16mi). Banks, markets, public toilets and eateries are found along High St and nearby streets.

Places to Stay & Eat A stone's throw from the TIC, ***Hammerland's Camping and Caravan Club*** *(☎ 01683-220436)* is open from March to November and charges backpackers £6.25 in high season. ***Marvig Guest House*** *(☎ 01683-220628, ⓔ marvig.moffat@tesco.net)*, Academy Rd, charges £17 to £22.50 per person. ***Kirkland House*** *(☎ 01683-221133)*, Well Rd, enveloped by exotic trees and gardens, has three B&B en suite rooms from £17 to £19 per person.

The ***Co-op*** supermarket, opposite the TIC, is open daily. For delicious baked goods, sweets and filled rolls or sandwiches (from 95p to £1.40), head to ***Alex Hupburn & Son's Bakery*** *(25 Well St)*. For a reliably good evening meal in the 'narrowest detached hotel', according to the Guinness Book of World Records, head for the ***Star Hotel*** *(44 High St)*.

Getting There & Away Located just north of the A74(M) on the A701, Moffat is a convenient gateway to the Borders to the east (on the A708 to Selkirk), Glasgow 30mi to the north-west A74(M), Edinburgh 52mi to the north-east (A701) and Dumfries 21mi to the south-west (A701).

From either Edinburgh or Glasgow take the Western Buses (☎ 0870-608 2608) Nos X73 and X74 to Moffat. On the express, Moffat is 40 minutes from Dumfries, 1½ hours from Glasgow and two hours from Edinburgh. The closest train stations are at Lockerbie and Dumfries, with services from/to the south on Virgin Trains (☎ 0845-722 2333) and ScotRail (☎ 0845-755 0033).

GETTING TO/FROM THE WALK

Public transport is complicated. Harrier operates a scenic bus from early July to late September on Tuesday between Hawick and Moffat return, and on Thursday between Melrose and Moffat return; both routes stop at Grey Mare's Tail. The contact for the service is First Borders Busses (☎ 01896-752237). McCall's (☎ 01576-204309) runs a Saturday-only service (No 130) between Moffat and Galashiels with a stop at Grey Mare's Tail; there are two buses in each direction but at odd hours. Contact Moffat TIC to confirm the irregular timetables. By car take the A708 towards Selkirk for 9mi to the trailhead. Look for the Grey Mare's Tail trailhead sign and the National Trust for Scotland visitor centre on the left (north).

THE WALK

From the car park take the refurbished path, which quickly and steeply ascends the slopes of Bran Law (north-west). Rewards come fast; after 10 minutes it's possible to view the **Grey Mare's Tail** in its full glory. Ascend along the clear trail to the top of the falls and continue along the burn as the trail levels out. Look left for a stone wall, which paints a straight line up White Coomb's broad backside. Cross the burn to the wall. Keep the wall on the left and follow it all the way to the top, past Upper Tarnbery (546m) to a col where a tough, steep ascent past the Rough Craigs begins and the wall briefly disappears. Continue climbing until White Coomb's rounded summit is visible off to the left. Leave the wall and in 150m reach the **summit cairn**.

Return to the wall and follow it just over half a mile west to Firthhope Rig (800m). Make a 90 degree right turn, pleasantly rolling along Donald's Cleuch Head ridge for about 1mi. Where the wall makes another right-angle turn at Firthybrig Head (763m), the halfway point, roller-coast downhill to the col (701m) and back up again to the summit of **Lochcraig Head** (801m). The views continue to impress; White Coomb lies south, the three Eildon Hills are clearly visible to the east and Loch Skeen shimmers below. Descend along the wall just over 1mi towards the loch. The wall ends but follow a wire fence through increasingly boggy conditions. After 10 minutes the path separates from the wire and it's necessary to search for the best option. Aim (right) for the lake's outflow. The easy descent follows the course of the burn back to the ascent trail.

Grey Mare's Tail & White Coomb

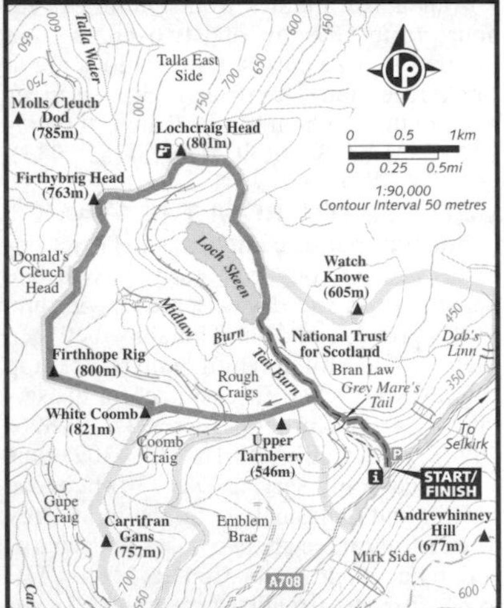

Deciphering Place Names

Place names tell us a tremendous amount about an area's history. Traces of ancient languages and the cultures of those who spoke them are encoded in curious strings of vowels and consonants, revealing the link that ancient peoples had to the land and the sacred qualities they attributed to inanimate life forces such as trees and waterways.

It's curious to note that the 18 letters of the old Gaelic alphabet are taken from tree and plant names: A – *ailm* (elm), B – *beith* (birch), C – *coll* (hazel), D – *dair* (oak), E – *eadha* (aspen), F – *féarn* (alder), G – *gort* (ivy), H – *uath* (hawthorn), I – *iogh* (yew), L – *luis* (quicken, rowan), M – *muin* (vine), N – *nuin* (ash), O – *onn* (gorse), P - *beith* (birch), R – *ruis* (elder), S -*suil* (willow), T – *teine* (furze), U - *ur* (yew).

The following place names, from south-west Scotland, reveal these connections. The root darr, as in Bardarroch, Craigdarroch, Glendarroch or Kildarroch, refers to oak; that is oak steading, -rock, -glen and -corner. Birch is encrypted in the root bei: such as Auchenvey (birch field), Beoch (birch wood), Craigenbay (birch rock) and Stronbae (birch point). The places Barwhillanty and Drumwhill reveal a past connection to hazel, and in Darsalloch and Knocksallie are remnants of the willow tree's importance.

The Borders

The Borders refers to the area of south-east Scotland laid out in rolls between the Moorfoot and Lammermuir Hills in the north and the Cheviot Hills, which are shared with England, in the south. The western fringe reaches 840m at Broad Law, the highest of the Tweedsmuir Hills, back-to-back with the Moffat Hills (in Dumfries & Galloway). The craggy eastern Berwickshire coast reaches out in impressive swoops and jags to the North Sea. Through the centre runs the Tweed River, a silver thread travelling 96mi steadily eastward through the major Borders towns of Peebles, Galashiels, Melrose and Coldstream, before meeting the sea in England at Berwick-upon-Tweed.

Roughly 1800 sq mi of gently rolling, heather-clad moorland are sparsely populated by 102,000 people and 1.4 million sheep. Not surprisingly, woollen products, including cashmere, are a major local industry. An integral part of the Borders landscape is the abbeys and strongholds, silent witnesses to the region's grizzly past (13th to 17th centuries) when the reivers (rustlers, robbers) terrorised the countryside with their bloody feuds, and English/Scottish border disputes were the order of the day. The 16 species of fish found in the Tweed River have made it a Site of Special Scientific Interest. Common waterway birds include the dipper (see the boxed text 'Dipper: Scotland's Ubiquitous Bird-Fish' on page 139), heron and goosander.

The day walks presented here explore the lush Tweed Valley – its river and nearby hills – and a 10.4mi section of the Borders' 32mi of coast that stretches from Lamberton to Cockburnspath (the eastern terminus of the SUW). Melrose, the base for the second walk, is also traversed by the SUW and is the starting point for St Cuthbert's Way (see Other Walks on page 146).

CLIMATE

The driest months are March, April, June and July, with the wettest being August. Prevailing winds come from the south-west. Winter walking is feasible even on the higher hills, where snow falls but doesn't usually stick too long. All TICs either display or have the local forecast available. Forecasts are also available on Radio Borders 96.8/97.5/103.1/103.4 FM.

PLANNING

Books

The Scottish Borders: 25 Walks by Peter Jackson concentrates on circular walks in the Tweedsmuir, Moorfoot and Lammermuir Hills. *The Border Country: A Walker's Guide* by Alan Hall describes 50 walks including the Cheviot Hills. *The Borders Book*, edited by Donald Omand, treats everything from the Romans to rugby.

Information Sources

The Borders' TICs are particularly solicitous and well stocked with information for walkers, including the useful booklet *Walking in the Scottish Borders*. Also ask for the Scottish Borders Council Ranger Service's (☎ 01835-830281) *Out & About in the Scottish Borders* describing ranger-led walks and activities. The ranger service also produces useful *Borders Countryside Walks* pamphlets. The free Borders *Town Trail Guide* series includes 2.5mi walks covering the most important monuments.

In an emergency contact the Lothian and Borders police (☎ 01450-375051).

GETTING THERE & AWAY

The Borders has no train stations; towns are linked by buses from the closest train stations at Carlisle, Berwick-upon-Tweed, Dunbar and Edinburgh. The western Borders and Peebles is most easily accessed from the A74(M) via the A701 or A702 to the east/west A72. The A708 (Moffat-Selkirk) takes you to the heart of the Borders while the A7 and the A68 bisect the region into eastern and western halves as they beeline north to Edinburgh. The A1 gives access to the eastern and coastal areas of the region.

Most of the Borders' major towns are within an hour's drive of Edinburgh and 1½ hours from Glasgow.

GETTING AROUND

Free public transport timetable booklets called *Travel Guides* are distributed by TICs, bus offices and libraries, or write to Scottish Borders Council, Technical Services, Newtown St Boswells, Melrose TD6 OSA. The guides cover Central Borders, Duns and Merse, Eyemouth, Hawick, Jedburgh, Kelso and Coldstream, and Peeblesshire. For general rail link service information call ☎ 01835-825200.

Peebles Circuit

Duration	5 hours
Distance	10mi (16.1km)
Standard	easy-medium
Start & Finish	Tweed Bridge car park
Nearest Town	Peebles
Public Transport	yes

Summary Circuit above picturesque Peebles to several Iron Age forts, ending with a meander along the River Tweed past Neidpath Castle.

Most likely a derivation of the ancient Cumbric word *pebyl* meaning 'tent pitch', Peebles lies at the confluence of the River Tweed and Eddleston Water. Dominated by the high tower of its late-19th-century parish church, the Borders' third-largest town makes an attractive launch point for day walks. Climbing some 250m, this walk uses a combination of minor roads, old railway line, forest paths and rural lanes, partially coinciding with the Tweed Walk. Look for the dipper bird waymarkers where the walk overlaps with the Tweed Walk (see the boxed text 'Dipper: Scotland's Ubiquitous Bird-Fish').

PLANNING

Maps & Books

The OS Landranger 1:50,000 map No 44 *(Tweed Valley)* covers the route. Local publications *Walks Around Peebles: Innerleithen & Walkerburn* and *Tweed Walk* cover parts of the route, providing historical and scientific information. Both publications are available at area TICs.

NEAREST TOWN

Peebles

Peebles TIC (☎ 01721-720138, ⓔ peebles@scot-borders.co.uk) in High St is open year-round. Also on High St you will find ATMs and most general supplies. The outdoor shop Out and About, 2 Elcho St Brae, is open Monday to Saturday from 9am to 5.30pm.

Places to Stay & Eat On Edinburgh Rd, ***Crossburn Caravan Park*** *(☎ 01721-720501, ⓔ enquiries@crossburncaravans.co.uk)* charges £8 for two people, car and tent. Beautiful gardens welcome at two comfortable B&Bs: ***Viewfield*** *(☎ 01721-721232, 1 Rosetta Rd)* where doubles/singles with shared bathroom cost £17.50/18.50 per person and ***Rowanbrae*** *(☎ 01721-721630, 103 Northgate)* where rooms with and without bathroom cost £17.50 to £19.50 per person.

Somerfield Grocery *(38 Northgate)* is the most convenient, although Peebles also has a large ***Safeway***. The best local bakery is ***WTS Forsyth & Sons*** *(21 Eastgate)* with outstanding pies and sausage rolls. The local's favourite fish and chip shop is ***Big Eb's*** *(16 Northgate)*; fish supper costs £2.95. Award-winning ***Sunflower Restaurant*** *(4 Bridgegate)* serves hot and cold lunches and dinner entrees, such as sea bass with basil, from £7.95 to £14.50.

Getting There & Away To reach Peebles from Glasgow, take a ScotRail (☎ 0845-755 0033) train to Lanark. The roughly 45-minute trip runs nearly hourly each day. Transfer to the No 191 bus (Hamilton-Lanark-Biggar), operated by HAD Coaches (☎ 01501-820598), Irvine's (☎ 01698-372 452) and WM Stokes & Sons (☎ 01555-870344), with hourly services from Monday to Saturday and four each way on Sunday with HAD. In Biggar transfer to the First Edinburgh (☎ 0131-663 9233) No 291 bus (Biggar-Broughton-Peebles). To/from Edinburgh take one of the hourly First Edinburgh No 62 buses (Edinburgh-Peebles-Melrose). The trip to Peebles takes just under an hour. If coming from the south, take either the Dumfries-Biggar-Edinburgh No 100 bus, operated by MacEwan's (☎ 01387-256533) and Western

Dipper: Scotland's Ubiquitous Bird-Fish

The common, small black or brown, white-breasted dipper *Cinclus cinclus*, also known as the water craw/ouzel or bessy dooker, is a bird that thinks it's a fish. The name dipper comes from the habit of bobbing its head up and down in the water as it feeds from its favourite riverside perch. Usually seen walking in streams, short tail ever erect, the bird will exhale and swiftly plunge headlong into the water and swim after tasty insects, molluscs, small fish, fry, crustaceans and tadpoles. Its thick, rounded body and downy feathers keep the dipper warm and buoyant, while its heavy bones and wings (which use the current to submerge) assist the underwater escapades. The bird's warbling song occasionally breaks into sharp squawks from its moss-lined nest built under bridges, waterfalls or overlooking streams.

RICHRAD MILLS

Buses (☎ 0870-608 2608), or the latter company's express X73 service (Annan-Moffat-Biggar-Edinburgh) and transfer in Biggar to the First Edinburgh No 291 bus.

GETTING TO/FROM THE WALK

The walk begins and ends from the car park below the Tweed Bridge, south of the A72 and a two-minute walk from the TIC.

THE WALK

From the car park on the River Tweed's true right bank, cross the road and turn right onto Caledonian Rd. Continue 500m and head left onto Edderston Rd. Near the end of the street look for the 'Public Footpath to Manor Water' sign and exit via an iron gate to a field. Follow the Tantah House stone wall, passing through a wooden gate to a fork where you head south-west (right). Make an undulating ascent for 30 minutes to the base of a lumpy hill, which hides an ancient settlement. Continue on the trail to a summit (407m) and the ruins of the first fort.

Continue south-west along the ridge crest for 15 minutes to the second and most interesting **fort**, which retains evidence of its defences. The buried, partially protruding stones were invisible until attackers neared the walls, slowing their progress. Head west along the ridge to the third fort. Return to the base of the second fort and look for a path that descends north-west, passing close to a stone sheepfold. Reaching a dirt lane bear left, parallel to a wire fence, and continue to a paved road. Turn right and cross the Manor Water. Continue along the road and bear right entering Kirkton Manor. Once past the 1874 church make a hard left onto a private dirt road, flanked by broad-leaved trees. In just over half a mile the route joins the Tweed Walk. You're now halfway.

Pass the well-preserved **Barns Tower** or peel, a typical stronghold built in the 15th century and owned by William Burnet, nicknamed Howlet or Hoolet (meaning owl), (in)famous for his wee-hour raids. In 15 minutes, where the road turns hard left, continue straight on the Tweed Walk along a descending track through forest. Fork left, as indicated, and continue parallel to the River Tweed to the bridge. Cross and pick up a paved road. When you reach a bridge climb its stairs, cross and begin an almost 2mi stretch along the Caledonian Railway tracks, closed to passengers in the 1950s when car culture took over. Before the train line crosses the Tweed via Queen's Bridge (the viaduct) to South Park Wood, take the descending stairs that lead to the river bank. Meander along the river's left bank, passing the intimidating, medieval **Neidpath Castle**,

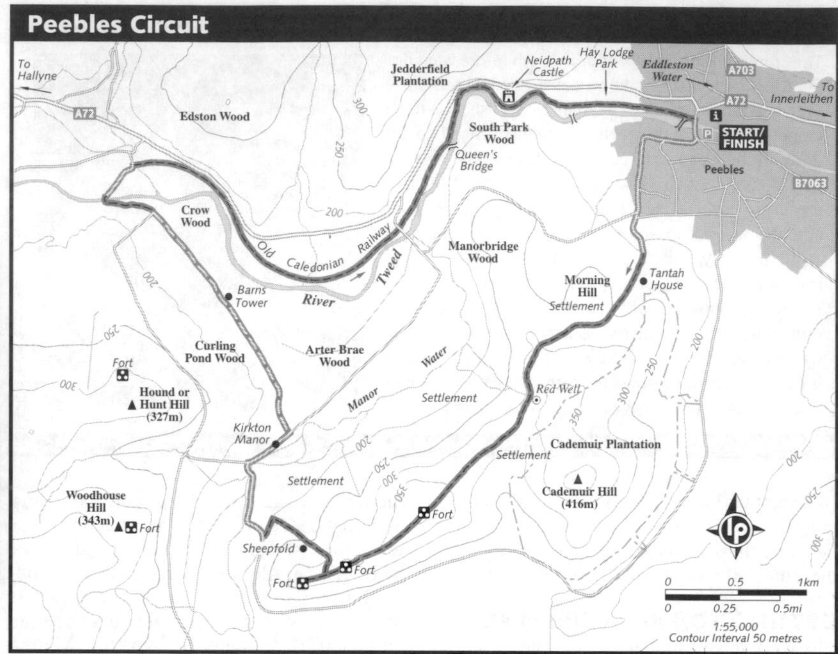

built in the 14th century, enlarged in the 17th century and typical of the reivers period. After 500m reach Hay Lodge Park. Soon Peebles' first houses, a footbridge, the pool and, finally, Tweed Bridge appear.

Eildon Hills

Duration 4 hours
Distance 7.9mi (12.7km)
Standard easy-medium
Start & Finish Melrose Abbey
Nearest Town Melrose
Public Transport yes
Summary Circuit taking in Melrose Abbey, the three distinctive Eildon Hills, the ancient Roman settlement of Trimontium and the River Tweed.

Forming the backdrop to historical Melrose (from the Cumbric for promontory) and its beautiful Cistercian abbey (the purported final resting place of Robert the Bruce's heart), the distinctive Eildon Hills are three sandstone-clothed volcanic mountains visible throughout southern Scotland. The Romans recognised their strategic value and established a huge settlement, Trimontium, nearby (see the boxed text 'All Roads Led From Trimontium'). Melrose's 19th-century claims to fame include the invention of 'seven-a-side' rugby and calling Sir Walter Scott, who moved into riverside Abbotsford in 1812, neighbour. He died there in 1832. The Eildon Hills trail (mostly dirt tracks with two short bits on the road) coincides with the fascinating St Cuthbert's Way (see Other Walks on page 146) to the saddle between the Eildon Hills and then goes its separate way.

PLANNING

Maps

The OS Landranger 1:50,000 map No 44 *(Tweed Valley)* covers the route.

NEAREST TOWN
Melrose

Melrose TIC (☎ 01896-822555, e melrose@scot-borders.co.uk), in Abbey House on Abbey St, is opposite the abbey and next to a car park. It is open from April to the end of October. Market Square has a pharmacy, market, bookshop and ATM. Galashiels has the closest outdoor gear shop.

Places to Stay & Eat Open year-round, ***Gibson's Park Caravan and Camp Site*** *(☎ 01896-822969)*, High St, has limited tent sites although excellent facilities; it costs around £6.20 to pitch a tent. Set in a Georgian mansion, the ***Melrose SYHA Hostel*** *(☎ 01896-822521)*, Priorwood, has a self-catering kitchen and charges from £10 to £11.25. Both ***Braidwood*** *(☎ 01896-822488)* and ***Dunfermline House*** *(☎ 01896-822148, e bestaccom@dunmel.freeserve.co.uk)*, opposite each other in Buccleuch St, offer friendly B&B service. The former caters to vegetarians and has en suite and private bathrooms from £20 to £23. Dunfermline has en suite rooms, coordinates luggage transfer for St Cuthbert's Way and charges £25 per person.

Abbey Coffee Shop, Buccleuch St, serves soup and sandwiches in a cosy atmosphere. The more upmarket ***Russell's*** in Market Square does delicious lunch and tea. The warm, wood-panelled ***King's Arms Hotel***, High St, does the town's best evening meal from 6.30pm to 9.30pm including roast leg of lamb (£6.95) and Indian curry (£6.50), as well as scampi, venison and haddock.

Getting There & Away Consult the *Central Borders Travel Guide* timetable for Melrose bus connections and rail links. From London Kings Cross via Berwick-upon-Tweed on GNER (☎ 0845-722 5225), connect with the First Edinburgh (☎ 0131-663 9233) No 60 bus (Berwick–Scottish Border Towns). Or, from London Euston via Carlisle on Virgin Trains (☎ 0845-722 2333), connect with MacEwan's (☎ 01387-256533) No 195 bus (Carlisle–Scottish Border Towns). Alternatively, from Edinburgh or Glasgow make your way to Melrose via Peebles (see Getting There & Away for Peebles on page 138).

By car from Edinburgh take the A7 south to Galashiels and then head east on the A72 to Melrose.

THE SOUTH

All Roads Led From Trimontium

Around AD 80 the Romans, under Julius Agricola, established what would become one of the largest Roman forts in Scotland, Trimontium, meaning 'place of the three hills', just 1.5mi east of Melrose. The Selgovae tribe, who lived on top of Eildon Hill North, were displaced by the Romans, who took advantage of their base and set up a signalling station or shrine on the top of this same mount. Named on Ptolemy's AD 145 map, the fort was a strategic base and supply centre in the Roman campaigns to subdue Highland Scotland.

It was also used as zero point to measure distances. Of the 500mi of Roman road in Scotland, only one milestone has been found. Engraved upon it is '*MP Trimontio*', the MP standing for *milia passum*, meaning 'thousands of Roman paces' from Trimontium. Digs have revealed metalwork, ditches and additional settlements on the Eildon hillsides. Open from April to November, 10.30am to 4.30pm, Melrose's Trimontium Museum, Market Square, exhibits daily life on the Roman frontier. On Thursdays, from 1.30pm to 5pm, local guides run the Trimontium Walk.

MARTIN HARRIS

THE WALK

Facing Melrose Abbey turn right up Abbey St to Market Square, then head up Dingleton Rd, following St Cuthbert's Way markers (Celtic cross). Pass under the A6091 and in 150m turn left between houses, following an 'Eildon Walk' sign. Cross a stream and ascend wooden stairs to a path, flanked with wire, that opens to a field and the Eildon Hills' base. Continue to the saddle between the north and centre hills. Even though the Eildon Way sign directs left, take a heather-lined path south-west to **Eildon Mid Hill** (422m). The 700m ascent meets two forks and at both veer right. At the summit is a view indicator. Descend the same way to the col and then make the 700m, straightforward ascent of **Eildon Hill North** (404m). Return again to the col.

To reach the third summit, **Eildon Wester Hill** (371m), descend south along St Cuthbert's Way. After 300m, before reaching a visible gate, leave the Way and turn right (south-west) keeping a lush forest on the left. Where the forest ends, the trail ascends to open moor. At a fork head left along a firebreak to a rocky, and at first steep, path that winds to the summit. You're now halfway.

Return to the last St Cuthbert's Way waymarker and take a narrow, descending eastbound trail hedged in by thick vegetation. Continue for 10 minutes and then pass through a gate (right) that leads to a narrow sealed road in the forest. Turn left and continue for just over half a mile to a stile (left) that you cross, leaving the woods for an open area. Follow the wire fence north, first cross-country and then on a path canopied by oaks. About 400m from the stile, reach and take a trail that descends right. Turn right onto the sealed road and immediately pick up a path to the left that passes under the A6091 and a train bridge to descend to Newstead village.

Turn right along the main street. After 200m bear left onto Eddy Rd. (To visit Trimontium continue on the main street for 200m.) Reaching the Tweed's banks in five minutes, head left along the river to **Battery Wall**, a 350m elevated walkway. The banks of the battery were built by monks to protect their crops from flood. Arriving at an iron gate, turn hard left and soon reach a sealed road. Turn left to the main road, veer right and, 350m later, reach the abbey.

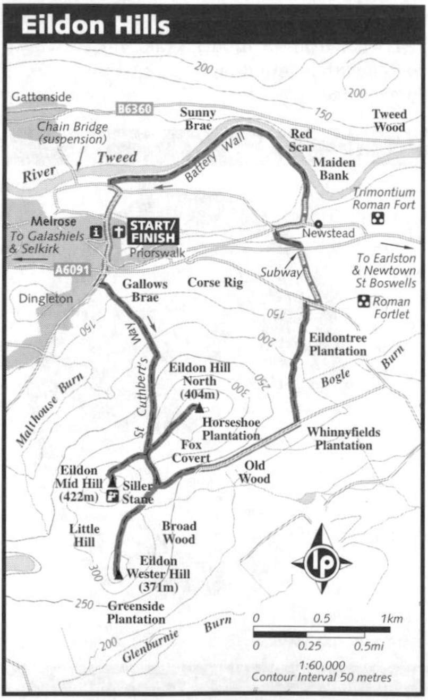

Eildon Hills

Burnmouth to St Abb's Head

Duration	6 hours
Distance	11.9mi (19.2km)
Standard	easy
Start	Burnmouth
Finish	St Abb's Head Visitor Centre
Nearest Town	Eyemouth
Public Transport	yes

Summary Riveting cliff and beach walk, passing fishing villages, and areas rich in geological curiosities and marine flora and fauna.

'Coastal Footpath' signs waymark this easy walk connecting Burnmouth, Eyemouth, Coldingham and St Abbs, and reach as far

St Abb's Head National Nature Reserve

The National Trust for Scotland owns the 192 acres of coastal habitat that constitute the gorgeous St Abb's Head National Nature Reserve. A wide variety of marine birds find sanctuary off the rocky coast of St Abb's Head; some 20 pairs of puffins can be seen nesting in the cliffs from May to July. More common species include guillemots, razorbills, kittiwakes and herring gulls, shags and fulmars. With the water's great visibility and the interesting combination of Arctic and Atlantic marine animals and plants, it's a scuba diver's paradise. Especially appreciated are the wolf fish and dahlia anemone, which are normally found in colder waters to the north. Large mammals such as grey seals, harbour porpoises and occasionally dolphins are also sighted. Contact the ranger (☎ 01890-771443), Ranger's Cottage, St Abbs, for guided reserve walks.

as the lighthouse at St Abb's Head National Nature Reserve (see the boxed text). The trail goes perilously close to the cliffs in several sections.

NATURAL HISTORY

In Burnmouth, sedimentary Silurian mudstone (greywacke) and siltstone, laid down on the seabed 440 million years ago, are visible in dramatic, swirling layers along the cliffs of Fancove. Burnmouth's harbour shows the same rock transformed by the action of the waves, where the neatly packed layers rise vertically from the sea floor at low tide. You'll find them folded and faulted at Linkim Kip and Coldingham Bay. Contrasting rusty red sandstone sedimentary rocks were laid down in river beds 380 million years ago – as you can see in the cliffs to the north of Eyemouth. Between these two periods harder igneous rocks, produced from lava flows, created the steep, slow to erode St Abb's Head headland.

PLANNING

The walk is described south to north, although it's possible to do it in reverse. Excellent public transport connections make it easy to pick and choose start/end points. June and July are best for wild flowers, and July and August for butterflies. May and July are the best months for seeing nesting seabirds, and May and September to mid-October are best for spotting migratory seabirds. The area is very popular in summer. Be prepared for winter nor-easters unleashing bone-chilling winds.

Maps

The OS Pathfinder 1:25,000 map No 423 *(Eyemouth & Granthouse)* covers the walk.

Information Sources

St Abb's Head Visitor Centre, at the end of the walk, is open year round. For further information on the reserve, contact the National Trust for Scotland head ranger at the Ranger's Cottage (☎ 01890-771443); ranger-led walks are available by appointment.

The free pamphlet *The Berwickshire Coastal Path* is a miniguide to a longer version of the described walk; 24km starting from Berwick-upon-Tweed. The National Trust for Scotland's booklet *St Abb's Head National Nature Reserve* is a valuable resource (available at the visitor centre). Two pertinent and interesting pamphlets, *A Cliff Top Walk from Burnmouth to Eyemouth* and *A Coastal Walk from Eyemouth to Coldingham*, are available from TICs.

NEAREST TOWNS

Burnmouth

Burnmouth is a tiny village divided into Upper Burnmouth, Partanhall (a string of cottages at the foot of the cliff), Cowdrait and Ross (just south, nearer the harbour). If you are looking for a bite to eat before you set out, try ***The Flemington Inn*** *(☎ 01890-781277)*; bar meals are available and it is open from 12.30pm to 9pm.

Getting There & Away GNER (☎ 0845-722 5225) Glasgow via Edinburgh to/from London trains stop in Berwick-upon-Tweed, the closest train station to the walk. Perryman's Buses (☎ 01890-781533) operates two convenient services – route No 253 runs six times daily (three on Sunday) between Edinburgh and Berwick-upon-Tweed, stopping in Coldingham, St Abbs, Eyemouth and Burnmouth, and route No 235, which operates every half-hour daily (every hour on Saturday and Sunday) between Berwick-upon-Tweed and St Abbs, stops in Eyemouth and Coldingham. First Edinburgh (☎ 0131-663 9233) buses No 34, 35 and 36 run every 15 minutes between Berwick and Eyemouth, stopping in Burnmouth.

By car take the A1 either north from Berwick-upon-Tweed or south from Edinburgh to the A1107 – this road links (from south to north) Burnmouth, Eyemouth and Coldingham.

Eyemouth

Eyemouth is the only town on the described route and has an active fishing port, attractive town centre and local history museum. Eyemouth TIC (☎ 01890-750678), Auld Kirk in Manse Rd, is open from April to the end of October.

Convenient ***Hillcrest*** *(☎ 01890-750463)*, Coldingham Rd, offers comfortable rooms with shared bathrooms for £17. The harbourside ***Whale Hotel*** *(☎ 01890-752142)* has basic but clean B&B rooms with shared bathrooms from £17 to £20. ***Old Bakehouse***, Manse Rd, open daily from 9am to 5pm serves mouth-watering home-made sweets and has £3 lunch specials (soup and sandwich). Self-caterers look for the ***Co-op*** supermarket in High St.

See Getting There & Away under Burnmouth for transport options.

Coldingham

Picturesque Coldingham has several pubs, a small market and post office.

Scotscroft Holiday Centre *(☎ 0800-169 7386)*, in the village centre, accepts tents and cars year-round and charges from £4.50/6 for one/two-person tents. Overlooking the ocean, ***Coldingham Youth Hostel*** *(☎ 01890-771298)* is open from April to October, has a self-catering kitchen, provides information on walks and charges from £7.25. For a meal, try the ***New Inn*** on the main road in the centre of the village.

See Getting There & Away under Burnmouth for transport options.

St Abbs

St Abbs (named for the 7th-century monastery founded here by Ebba or Abb) has a village market and heritage museum. The west entrance to the nature reserve, at Northfield Farm, has public toilets, an artists' gallery and the ***Head Start Coffee Shop***, open daily from 10.30am to 5pm from April to October and convenient for a post-walk snack. At Murrayfield on the trail just before St Abbs, ***Castle Rock*** *(☎ 01890-771715, ⓔ boowood@compuserve.com)* must be the most spectacular B&B locale on the coast. Open mid-February to mid-November, attractive en suite rooms cost £24. Evening meals are available by prior arrangement.

See Getting There & Away under Burnmouth for transport options.

GETTING TO/FROM THE WALK

There are car parks at Burnmouth harbour (space is limited) and in the village, in the centre of Eyemouth, and at the walk's end near the visitor centre. Once in Burnmouth, walk to the north-west edge of the village where the main and harbour roads meet. On the ocean side of the main road you will see the primary school and to the right a sealed road descends steeply to the harbour. Locate the 'Coastal Footpath' waymarker.

The walk ends at the St Abb's Head Visitor Centre. To reach the bus stop in St Abbs walk down the B6438 Coldingham-St Abbs road or take the visible rural path into the tiny centre of St Abbs village.

THE WALK

Depart east along the signed coastal path and reach the cliffs in five minutes. Looking south see Burnmouth's harbour and curious combed rock. Once on the cliffs the way ambles north 1.4mi past cultivated fields to the cliffs' highest point, **Fancove Head**. In 10 minutes the trail reaches the golf course. Ignore a trail that heads off left and continue just over half a mile along the cliffs, reaching a sign that indicates two options; turn left towards the clubhouse and then right onto the sealed road to Eyemouth or continue along the cliffs. If following the second option, at the seventh tee sign keep an eye out for wayward balls in the drop zone. Cross the course and exit through an opening in the wall. Turn right onto the sealed road to Eyemouth, joining those following the first option.

After a hairpin turn you reach Eyemouth's fish market. Keep the Lifeboat Station and **Gunsgreen House**, a renowned 18th-century smuggler's house, off to the left and continue quayside to a car bridge. Turn right towards Eyemouth and in 200m you reach Manse Rd (left) and the TIC a few steps away. Continue along the harbour road and turn left onto the maritime walkway bordering the half-moon beach. Turn left past the swimming pool and right onto the sealed road to the caravan park. Before reaching the park, veer right past a gate and onto a marked grassy trail. Reaching a fork, head right towards the coast. Two rusting cannons at Eyemouth Fort are reminders of Eyemouth's importance as a military centre in Borders conflicts.

Follow the contour of the red sandstone cliffs west. The trail rejoins the path bordering the caravan park. Cross a grassy clearing and continue along the cliff edge for 500m, passing above Killiedraught Bay and cultivated fields to the left. At the end of the bay avoid the temptation to veer right along the coast, instead continue straight across the field on the path to a gate. In another 500m (about an hour from Eyemouth and the halfway point of the walk) pass a second gate. A head-level red sandstone wall separates the trail from the cliff edge. Weave along the long, rolling wall 600m to another stile. Cross and just beyond descend a set of stairs through a gully to **Linkim Shore**. Walk along the beach and at the other end hike back up to the cliffs. In 15 minutes descend more stairs to a pebble beach, which you cross before climbing out at the other end. Descend again and cross the sandy beach of Coldingham Bay, exiting via its northern extreme to rejoin the obvious trail, which is paved to St Abbs.

Entering the village, a sign directs left but continue straight on the road fronting the cliffside homes. Reaching a phone box, turn right and then left past the Heritage Museum and church (both left), walking parallel to a high stone wall (right). At the wall's corner turn right and continue towards the sea and a kissing gate, which marks the **St Abb's Head National Nature Reserve** entrance. The cliffs soon commence again, gently rising and offering splendid views of St Abbs village behind you. Where the rise ends, Mire Loch appears (left). During the next 20 minutes the path undulates along the cliffs passing the stone beaches of Burnmouth Harbour and Horsecastle Bay, before reaching a summit and, finally, the lighthouse appears. Skirt left round the houses near the lighthouse to a sealed road. Turn left and in about 2mi reach the reserve car park and the visitor centre.

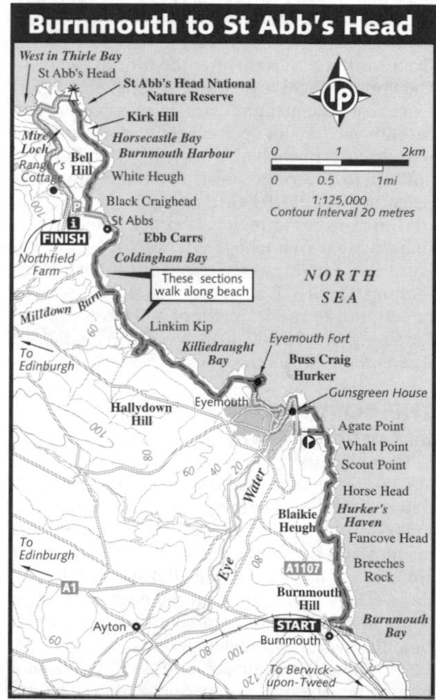

Other Walks

DUMFRIES & GALLOWAY

Criffel & Sweetheart Abbey

Close to Dumfries (south on the A710 to Sweetheart Abbey and almost 2mi farther to Ardwall Farm), a good, easy 'hill' walk ascends Criffel (569m). Rising swiftly out of the Solway Firth, Criffel gives excellent views of the coast. To ascend, pass through the gate to the obvious path and head up (south-east) to the forest, passing another gate. Follow the Craigrockhall Burn up to the open hillside and bear left to the summit. To loop back head north-west then north to Knockendoch. Descend south-east to the open hillside junction and then follow the same burn back to Ardwall. The abbey's 'sweetheart' refers to devoted Devorgilla de Balliol (d. 1290) who carried the embalmed heart of her beloved husband with her. She founded the Cistercian abbey in 1273. Use OS Landranger 1:50,000 map No 84 *(Dumfries & Castle Douglas)*. Expect boggy conditions.

Arthur's Seat & Hart Fell

A classic Moffat Hills walk is the double ascent of Arthur's Seat (731m) and Hart Fell (808m), returning above the Devil's Beef Tub, a steep-walled, enclosed valley. Taking the A701 (north) from Moffat turn right after the Moffat Academy and continue 3mi to a 'Hart Fell Spa' sign before Ericstane. The medium-hard 7.2mi circular route ascends steeply along Auchencat Burn, past the purportedly medicinal waters of Hart Fell Spa and up to the ridge crest. Continue north-east reaching first Hart Fell then Arthur's Seat. The trail then uses the regional border fence to continue west to Whitehope Knowe (614m), Chalk Rig Edge (499m) and Great Hill (466m). Overlooking Devil's Beef Tub, look for the south-bound trail to reach Corehead and Ericstane. OS Landranger 1:50,000 map No 78 *(Nithsdale & Annandale)* covers this walk.

THE BORDERS

St Cuthbert's Way

St Cuthbert was a 7th-century Celtic saint whose vocation with the church began at Melrose in AD 650 and where he later became prior of the local monastery. He explored the Borders countryside on foot and was particularly drawn to the coast. He was eventually appointed Bishop of Lindisfarne (Holy Island), just off the Northumberland coast in England. For Cuthbert, walking was a time for peaceful contemplation.

St Cuthbert's Way links Melrose and Lindisfarne in a route of great variety and interest, passing through places associated with Cuthbert's life and ministry. It crosses the Eildon Hills, and the Cheviot Hills in Northumberland National Park, follows sections of the beautiful Tweed and Teviot Rivers, and part of the ancient Roman road Dere Street, and traverses fertile farmland. It follows footpaths, vehicle and forest tracks, and quiet country roads. At low tide you can cross to Lindisfarne by the causeway or by the Pilgrims' Route across the sands. The route is well waymarked throughout, most prominently with the Way's own Celtic cross logo.

By starting at Melrose you'll follow Cuthbert's lifetime journey and finish with the inspirational experience of crossing the sands to Lindisfarne. The distance of 62.5mi (100.5km) includes 1200m of ascent; this could be walked in four days but you'll probably need to allow five or six to fit in with safe crossing times to Lindisfarne to spend time exploring the island. The Way links with the Pennine Way at Kirk Yetholm and the Southern Upland Way at Melrose (see page 122), thus making possible a grand long-distance walk.

There's no shortage of B&Bs and pubs along the Way. There are also hostels and camping sites, although probably too widely spaced to be able to use either type of accommodation exclusively.

The official trail guide *St Cuthbert's Way* by Roger Smith & Ron Shaw comprises a detailed guidebook and a 1:40,000 Harvey map. The OS Landranger 1:50,000 maps are No 73 *(Peebles & Galashiels)*, No 74 *(Kelso & Coldstream, Jedburgh & Duns)* and No 75 *(Berwick-upon-Tweed)*.

The free, annual St Cuthbert's Way *Accommodation & Facilities Guide* is invaluable; it is available from regional TICs including Jedburgh (☎ 01835-863435) and Berwick-upon-Tweed (☎ 01289-330733). Vital information about safe crossing times to Lindisfarne is available on a fortnightly basis from Wooler TIC (☎ 01668-282123) and is displayed there out of hours.

Borders Abbeys Way

Still being developed, once complete this 65mi (105km) circular route will connect the towns of Kelso, Jedburgh, Melrose and Dryburgh, and their abbeys. This is not the same as the Four Abbeys Cycleway and is specifically designed for walkers, complete with its own waymarkers; AW for Abbeys Way. The only section open in mid-2001 was the 12mi (18km) connecting the majestic abbeys of Kelso and Jedburgh. Initially closely following the River Teviot, the walk is flat and then climbs before descending into Jedburgh. Kelso TIC (☎ 01573-223464, e kelso@scot-borders.co.uk) opens April to October. All Borders TICs should carry *The Borders Abbeys Way* pamphlet.

Central Scotland

Dull-sounding 'Central Scotland' fails to evoke the grandeur of this intensely beautiful dividing line between lowland and highland Scotland. From the rugged and isolated Isles of Jura and Arran in the far west to the highly scenic Loch Lomond/Trossachs area (made Scotland's first national park in 2002) and, finally, to the dramatic high mountains of south-western Perthshire, the area offers a wide range of challenging Corbetts and Munros; and some of Scotland's finest walks within a compact area, easily accessed from either Edinburgh or Glasgow. Offering a selection of these walks, this chapter is divided into three parts: Isle of Arran; Arrochar, Lomond & Trossachs; and Around Loch Tay.

Highlights

SANDRA BARDWELL

A' Chir's soaring cliffs on the rugged ridge along Glen Rosa's west, Isle of Arran.

- Last scramble to The Cobbler's unusual summit
- Lush Stank Glen on Ben Ledi
- Sea of rose quartz on Schiehallion's summit
- Bird's eye-view of the Highlands and Lowlands from Ben Lawers
- Jumble of boulders on the ridges of Arran's Goatfell

NATURAL HISTORY

The Highland Boundary Fault extends from Stonehaven, on the east coast, in an unwavering line south-westward to Helensburgh, west of Glasgow on the shore of Gare Loch. In geological terms, it's a fault line or a weakness in the earth's crust where, about 600 million years ago, the tough, ancient rocks (crystalline schist) of the Highlands collided with the younger, softer sedimentary rocks (sandstone) of the central belt lowlands. If you climb to the top of Conic Hill (on the West Highland Way) you can see this line marching across the landscape.

The Central Scotland habitats of loch and sea shore, broad-leaved and conifer woodlands, and mountain and moorland all roughly sustain the same variety of flora and fauna. The boundaries of Forest Enterprise forest parks closely overlap with the areas described in this chapter: Argyll (Cowal and Ardgoil Peninsulas and Arrochar Alps); Queen Elizabeth (extensions in the Trossachs and along Loch Lomond); and Tay (sections of Highland Perthshire around Loch Rannoch).

Conifer woodlands support red and roe deer, and voles, as well as some foxes, wild cats and red squirrels. These forests also support coal tits, goldcrests, woodpeckers, short-eared owls, siskins and crossbills. The relics of once great broad-leaved forests (oak, ash, hazel, birch and, in wet zones, willow) provide shelter for redstarts, wood warblers, jays, cuckoos, tree pipits and the capercaillie. Flowers such as primrose, bluebell, sorrel and wood anemone also thrive. On the moorland and mountain slopes ptarmigan (above 600m) and red grouse roam, peregrine and golden eagles nest on the crags, ravens and hoodie crow scavenge,

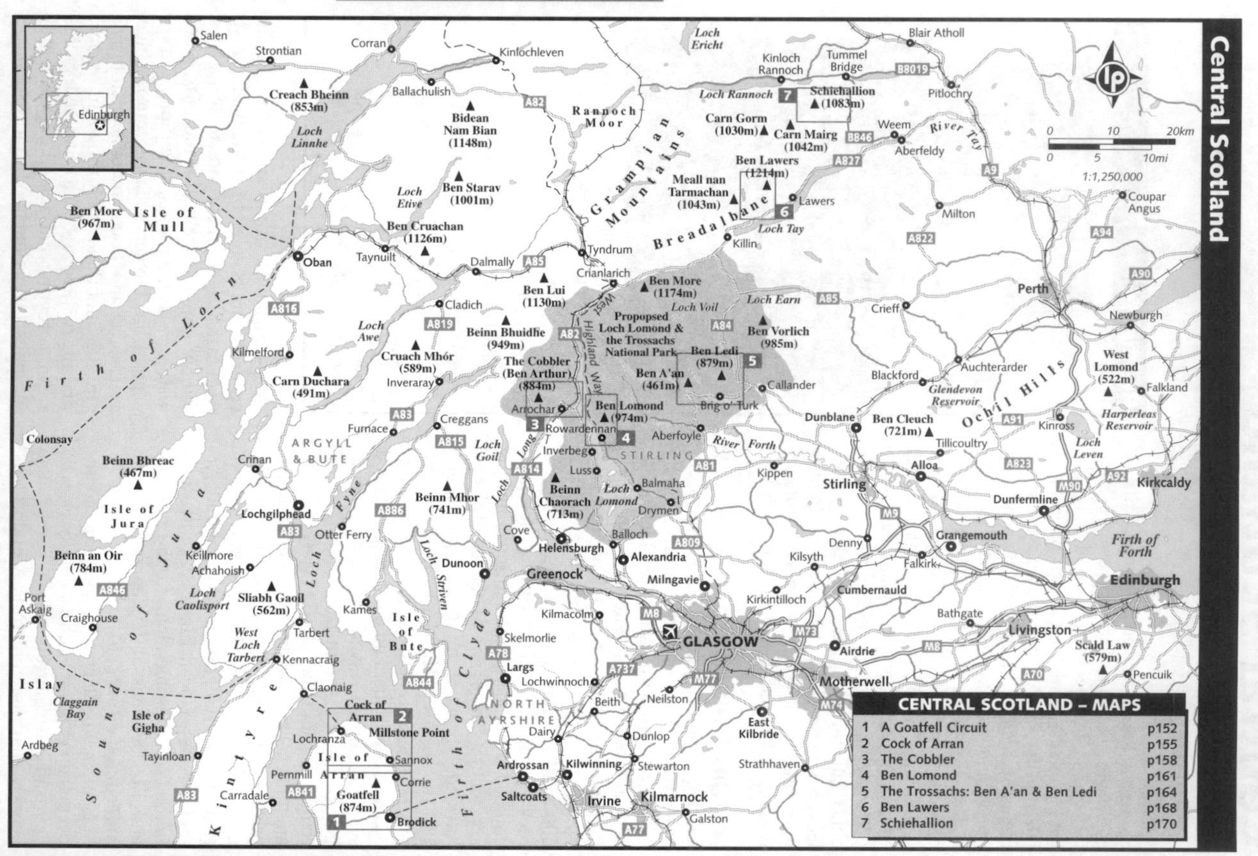

Central Scotland
CENTRAL SCOTLAND – MAPS
1 A Goatfell Circuit p152
2 Cock of Arran p155
3 The Cobbler p158
4 Ben Lomond p161
5 The Trossachs: Ben A'an & Ben Ledi p164
6 Ben Lawers p168
7 Schiehallion p170
0 10 20km
0 5 10mi
1:1,250,000
Edinburgh
Edinburgh
Glasgow
Perth
Stirling
Dunblane
Callander
Aberfoyle
Killin
Crianlarich
Tyndrum
Oban
Inveraray
Arrochar
Helensburgh
Greenock
Dunoon
Largs
Ardrossan
Saltcoats
Kilmarnock
Irvine
Kirkcaldy
Dunfermline
Livingston
Falkirk
Grangemouth
Alloa
Motherwell
Airdrie
Cumbernauld
Milngavie
Alexandria
Balloch
Drymen
Balmaha
Luss
Inverbeg
Rowardennan
Lochgilphead
Tarbert
Brodick
Lochranza
Schiehallion (1083m)
Carn Mairg (1042m)
Carn Gorm (1030m)
Ben Lawers (1214m)
Meall nan Tarmachan (1043m)
Ben More (1174m)
Ben Vorlich (985m)
Ben Ledi (879m)
Ben A'an (461m)
Ben Lomond (974m)
Ben Lui (1130m)
Beinn Bhuidhe (949m)
The Cobbler (Ben Arthur) (884m)
Beinn Chaorach (713m)
Ben Cleuch (721m)
West Lomond (522m)
Scald Law (579m)
Bidean Nam Bian (1148m)
Ben Starav (1001m)
Ben Cruachan (1126m)
Cruach Mhór (589m)
Carn Duchara (491m)
Creach Bheinn (853m)
Beinn Mhor (741m)
Sliabh Gaoil (562m)
Goatfell (874m)
Ben More (967m)
Beinn Bhreac (467m)
Beinn an Oir (784m)
Propopsed Loch Lomond & the Trossachs National Park
West Highland Way
Grampian Mountains
Breadalbane
Ochil Hills
Rannoch Moor
Loch Rannoch
Loch Tay
Loch Earn
Loch Voil
Loch Lomond
Loch Long
Loch Fyne
Loch Awe
Loch Etive
Loch Linnhe
Loch Leven
Firth of Forth
Firth of Clyde
Firth of Lorn
Sound of Jura
Kintyre
Isle of Mull
Isle of Jura
Isle of Arran
Isle of Bute
Isle of Gigha
Islay
Colonsay
ARGYLL & BUTE
STIRLING
NORTH AYRSHIRE

while dippers, grey wagtails and sandpipers hang out around the burns. Butterwort, purple saxifrage, alpine lady's mantle and bog asphodel are all common flowers. Finally, loch side, look for waders (curlew, turnstone, oystercatcher), as well as herons, goosanders and eider ducks.

INFORMATION

Maps & Books

OS Travelmaster 1:250,000 map *Southern Scotland* covers all of the described walks.

An excellent general reference is DJ Bennet's *The Southern Highlands*, giving information on geology, geography and routes. For a good historical read, try David Craig's *On the Crofters' Trail: In Search of the Clearance Highlanders*.

Isle of Arran

Arran is often called 'Scotland in miniature'; the steep hills and long deep glens in the north of the island are reminiscent of the Highlands, while the rolling moorland and the scattered farms of the south are similar to southern Scotland. There's even a long straight valley dividing the north from the south, a minor version of the mainland's Great Glen.

The island, little more than 20mi (32km) from north to south, is only an hour's ferry ride across the Firth of Clyde from the mainland and is easily accessible from Glasgow and its hinterland. Consequently, it's a very popular place, especially with walkers, irresistibly drawn to the rugged hills. The highest peak, Goatfell (874m), overlooks Brodick, Arran's largest town.

This section covers routes up Goatfell and an easy-going outing along the scenic north coast. A challenging traverse of the northern spine of the island is outlined in Other Walks at the end of this chapter.

NATURAL HISTORY

Arran's geology is amazingly varied – you will find all kinds of rock types and evidence of different geological processes, which have taken place over countless millennia. In fact, a trip to Arran is virtually compulsory for geology students from all over the world; one of the most famous features is Hutton's Unconformity, named after its discoverer Dr James Hutton. An unconformity is the occurrence, side by side, of rocks from different geological era at a discordant or unexpected angle. On the north coast, about 1mi north-east of Newton Point, Hutton identified one of these areas, where ancient metamorphic rock (schist, altered from its original form) was overlain by less ancient sandstone.

The northern rocky peaks and ridges and the deep glens consist of granite, sculpted by glaciers during the last ice age. This granite mass is almost surrounded by very much older schist and slate and some river sediment. Sedimentary rock – limestone and sandstone – monopolise the north coast. The southern half of the island has a more mixed array: granite (most prominently on Holy Island in Lamlash Bay), extensive outcrops of ancient lava and shale, and widespread sedimentary rock originating from times when the climate was much drier.

To demystify the complexities of Arran's geology, two readable publications are available locally – a brochure *Isle of Arran Trails: Geology* and the more detailed *Arran & the Clyde Islands: A Landscape Fashioned by Geology* published by Scottish Natural Heritage.

PLANNING

Please remember that wild camping is not permitted anywhere on Arran without the landowner's permission.

When to Walk

Snow is not very common on Arran, but the best times to visit the island are May–June and September–October; July and August are very busy.

Stalking Generally walkers are free to roam throughout Arran. However, deer control measures (stalking) are carried out from mid-August to mid-October in the north of the island. Call the Hillphones (☎ 01770-302363) service for daily updates on where stalking is to take place and which paths should be used or avoided. Access to National Trust for Scotland property – Glen Rosa, Goatfell and Brodick Country Park – is unrestricted at all times.

Maps

Arran is covered by two OS maps – Landranger 1:50,000 No 69 *(Isle of Arran)* and Outdoor Leisure 1:25,000 No 37 *(Isle of Arran)*. Harvey's *Arran* map comprises the whole island at 1:40,000 and the northern half at 1:25,000. It has lots of useful information and is highly recommended; it's more versatile than the separate Harvey 1:25,000 maps *North Arran* and *South Arran*.

Books

Paddy Dillon's *Walking in the Isle of Arran* describes 41 day walks on the island and is invaluable for an extended visit. *Forty-four Walks on the Isle of Arran* by Mary Welsh is useful for its flora and fauna notes, but the walk descriptions are vague and practical information sparse. Forest Enterprise's brochure *Guide to Forest Walks on the Isle of Arran* concentrates on southern Arran and is available from the Tourist Information Centre (TIC) in Brodick. To find out more about local history and heritage, Alastair Gemmell's *Discovering Arran* is the book to have; *Birds of Arran* by John Rhead & Philip Snow is particularly strong on where to see the bird life. Both books are available locally.

Information Sources

For general information about Arran, contact Brodick TIC (☎ 01770-302140, ⓔ arran@ayrshire-arran.com). Useful Web sites are ⓦ www.arran.uk.com and ⓦ www.scotland-info.co.uk/arran.htm. In an emergency, ring ☎ 999 and ask for mountain rescue.

GETTING THERE & AWAY

Western Buses (☎ 0870-608 2608) runs from Edinburgh and Glasgow to Ardrossan, the ferry terminal on the Ayrshire coast. Several ScotRail (☎ 0845-755 0033) trains reach Ardrossan daily from Glasgow; make sure you catch one that goes to the harbour, otherwise you'll have to walk or take a taxi from Ardrossan South Beach. Caledonian MacBrayne (☎ 01475-650100) operates the car ferry between Ardrossan and Brodick with at least four sailings daily in each direction. The return fare for foot passengers is £7.20 and the return for a standard car is £43. You can leave your car at Ardrossan in a secure place for £3.40. Ardrossan is about 25mi south-west of Glasgow.

GETTING AROUND

On Arran, Stagecoach (☎ 0870-608 2608) buses circle the island several times daily in both directions. A Rural Day Card (£3) is a good investment, allowing an unlimited number of trips. There are also handy postbus (☎ 01246-546329) services; all these are detailed in the *Area Transport Guide* available from the Brodick TIC. Hendry's (☎ 01770-02274) in Brodick operates a taxi service. Roads on Arran are generally narrow and rather rough.

ACCESS TOWN

Brodick

This surprisingly large town is the best base; it's the ferry port and the hub of the island's bus services. The well-organised TIC (☎ 01770-302140), on the pier, has an array of leaflets, accommodation lists, menus of the several places to eat, maps and guidebooks. The local weather forecast is displayed daily, and it also provides a fax and photocopying service.

Brodick has a post office and two banks, both with ATMs. Next to the Co-op supermarket, Arran Active (☎ 01770-302416) is the one place where you can purchase the full range of fuel for camping stoves.

Places to Stay & Eat The nearest ***SYHA hostel*** *(☎ 01770-700339)* is at Whiting Bay, about 6mi to the south; the tariff starts at £7.25. It's not ideal for Goatfell but the island's bus service enables you to get around fairly easily (see Getting Around earlier). The beautifully situated ***Glen Rosa Farm*** *(☎ 01770-302380)*, about 2.5mi north-west of Brodick Pier, is well placed for Goatfell. Facilities are limited to a basic toilet block and taps; the fee is £2.50. The owner hopes to install showers in 2002. There are more than 20 B&Bs in Brodick – the TIC has a detailed list. In particular, ***Tigh na Mara*** *(☎ 01770-302538)*, on Shore Rd, is conveniently located and charges from £18.

For places to eat in Brodick, ***Stalkers Restaurant*** *(☎ 01770-302579)* offers good-value meals from a basic menu with main courses from £6; it's licensed and open daily. Several pubs do bar meals, including the ***Douglas Hotel*** *(☎ 01770-302155)*, opposite the pier, which provides a cosmopolitan range of menus including an Indian set meal for £14. At Duncans Bar in the ***Kingsley Hotel*** *(☎* 01770-302531) you can sample one of Arran's very own beers (Arran Blonde, Light and Dark) with a standard bar supper.

For self-catering and picnic lunches, there are two supermarkets (open daily). ***Collins Good Food Shop***, on the Auchrannie House access road just north of Brodick, sells health foods and excellent bread and cakes, which you can also sample in its tearoom. ***Arran Brewery*** *(☎ 01770-302061)*, very conveniently located beside the Goatfell path at Cladach, is open daily.

Getting There & Away For details on getting to Brodick, see Getting There & Away for Arran on page 150.

A Goatfell Circuit

Duration	6–7½ hours
Distance	11mi (18km)
Standard	medium-hard
Start & Finish	Brodick
Nearest Towns	Brodick, Corrie
Public Transport	yes

Summary A demanding walk through scenic Glen Rosa and along steep, rocky ridges to outstanding views from the island's highest point.

The most popular routes to the summit of Goatfell are from the east – Brodick, Cladach (Arran Craft Centre) or Brodick Castle. There's also a good route from the settlement of Corrie up to North Goatfell. A quieter and more pleasing approach is from the west, via Glen Rosa to The Saddle, then up the steep, narrow west ridge to North Goatfell and along Stacach Ridge to the summit. The return to Brodick is via the steep, rocky eastern face, moorland and the grounds of Brodick Castle.

Paths are clear, deeply eroded in places and easy to follow. Maintenance and repair of the main paths is an ongoing task for the landowner, the National Trust for Scotland. The path just below the summit to the east was being rerouted and improved when this walk was being researched. There are steep cliffs on both sides of the west ridge and Stacach Ridge, where extra care is needed.

This route can be done in either direction but clockwise is recommended. The overall ascent is more gentle, with some steep bits, and the summit comes in the latter part of the route. There are signposts where paths leave the road but not on Goatfell itself. The distance of 11mi (18km) includes at least 800m of ascent and some minor scrambling.

Alternatives Of the alternative approaches to Goatfell, Corrie Burn is preferable to Glen Sannox, which is a boggy sort of a glen with a hair-raising climb to The Saddle. At the southern end of Corrie, a sign 'Public Footpath to Goatfell' points along a narrow road. After a few hundred metres, leave the road at a sharp bend, just before the settlement of High Corrie, and follow a track, then a path, up Corrie Burn's glen to a saddle below North Goatfell. It's a steep climb most of the way and the ground can be wet.

NATURAL HISTORY

Goatfell marks the high point of the eastern arm of the magnificent horseshoe-shaped ridge around Glen Rosa. This eastern branch has an extension northward, above the eastern side of Glen Sannox, and it all rises steeply from Arran's forested east coast. Glen Rosa is truly magnificent and also the site of reforestation work by the National Trust for Scotland – native rowans and oaks are returning to exclosures on the south-western slopes.

PLANNING

It can turn very cold, wet and windy on Goatfell very quickly, at any time of the year, and the mountain creates its own weather – Brodick can be basking in hot sunshine while Goatfell is mist-bound.

Guided Walks

The Countryside Rangers at Brodick Country Park (☎ 01770-302462), about 2mi (3km) north of Brodick, lead walks during summer, ranging from afternoon wildlife strolls through the low-level forests to days out on Goatfell and other peaks.

NEAREST TOWN

Corrie

A spread-out village on the east coast, Corrie is about 5.5mi (9km) north of Brodick and well served by local buses (see Getting Around on page 150). The village is near the start of the alternative route to Goatfell. At ***Blackrock Guest House*** *(☎ 01770-810282)*, which has an excellent outlook, tariffs start at £17. The ***Corrie Hotel*** *(☎ 01770-810273)* serves snacks and bar meals.

THE WALK

From Brodick TIC walk north beside the main road (A841) for about 1.5mi to a major junction and turn left along the B880 towards Blackwaterfoot. About 100m along this road turn right down the narrow 'Glen Rosa Cart Track'. Follow this to the camping site, above which the sealed section ends, and continue along a clear vehicle track into **Glen Rosa** itself. There are superb views of the precipitous peaks on the western side of the glen, culminating in Cir Mhòr (799m) at its head.

The track becomes a path at the crossing of Garbh Allt, the boundary of the National Trust for Scotland property. Aiming unerringly for The Saddle, the low point between Cir Mhòr and the massive, rock-encrusted bulk of Goatfell, the path climbs gently then

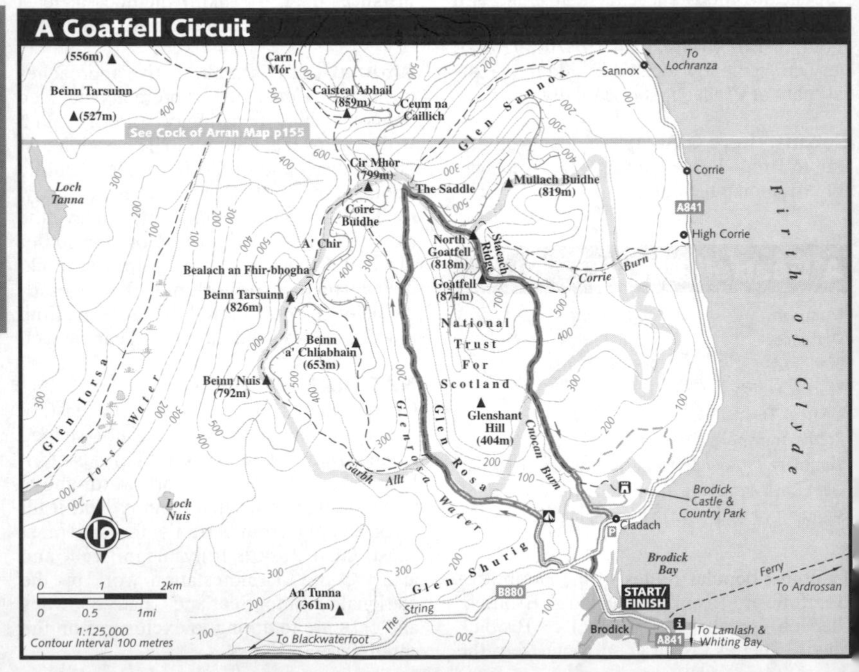

National Trust for Scotland on Arran

The Trust has been a big landowner on the island since 1958 when Brodick Estate was placed in its care after centuries of the Hamilton family's stewardship. Today the 2833ha estate takes in the Goatfell massif, Glen Rosa and its western slopes, and Brodick Castle and its grounds – these last two being the nucleus of Brodick Country Park. The park has extensive paths, fine formal gardens, a visitor centre, National Trust for Scotland shop, a restaurant and, of course, the castle. The grounds and facilities are open daily from April to October (see also Guided Walks on page 152).

Elsewhere the Trust is encouraging the regeneration of native woodland with exclosures (fenced areas to keep out red deer) where oaks, rowans and other species are making a comeback.

Footpath maintenance and repair is another big commitment, especially around Goatfell – a battle against the elements and the impact of thousands of walkers' feet.

quite steeply. From **The Saddle** (2½ to three hours from the start), there's a fine view among the granite boulders down Glen Sannox to the sea. Cir Mhòr's alarmingly steep crags rise immediately to the left. To the north are the castellated ridge of Caisteal Abhail (859m), Arran's second-highest peak, and the notorious cleft, Ceum na Caillich (Witch's Step). To the right the features of the next section of the walk are clearly visible: the bouldery west ridge, leading steeply up to North Goatfell; and Stacach Ridge, which is crowned by four small, rocky peaks.

From The Saddle, a braided and deeply eroded string of paths leads up the ridge towards North Goatfell. There are some narrow, exposed sections and a few near-vertical 'steps' where you'll need to use your hands. More tricky, though, are the patches of loose granite gravel. After about an hour from The Saddle the route nears the summit of **North Goatfell** (818m). The final section is a scramble but, if this is too intimidating, pass below the top, keeping it on your left, then return to the ridge. Turn back to gain the summit from the east over large slabs and boulders.

From North Goatfell you can keep to the crest of the ridge, scrambling over the rocky knobs. Alternatively, drop down to the less exposed eastern side of the ridge and follow paths below the knobs. The final section involves hopping over giant boulders to the summit of **Goatfell** (874m), about 30 minutes to an hour from North Goatfell. The summit is topped by a trig point and a large topograph, from which you can identify features in the panoramic view. On a good day Ben Lomond (see the Ben Lomond walk on page 159) and the coast of Northern Ireland can be seen. The whole of Arran is spread out below, with the conical mass of Holy Island rearing up from the sea in Lamlash Bay.

From the summit a path winds down the steep eastern face, then straightens out as the ridge takes shape. At a path junction with a large cairn, turn right and follow the all-too-clear path south-east then south across moorland, down the valley of Cnocan Burn and into scattered woodland. At a junction in a pine plantation continue straight, turning right at a T-junction. Go down through pines and the grounds of Brodick Castle, across a sealed road and past Arran Brewery to the main road at Cladach. The route into Brodick involves walking south along the road for a few hundred metres to a public footpath sign on the left. Follow the path down to a footbridge over Glen Rosa Water and back to the road on the edge of the town (two to 2½ hours from the top).

To reach **Brodick Castle and Country Park** (see the boxed text 'National Trust for Scotland on Arran'), turn left 30m after the T-junction in the pine plantation mentioned above. Walk through rhododendron-infested grounds and woodland to the ranger office, and on to the car park and nearby National Trust for Scotland shop.

Cock of Arran

Duration	3½–4 hours
Distance	8mi (13km)
Standard	easy-medium
Start	North Sannox
Finish	Lochranza
Nearest Towns	Sannox, Lochranza
Public Transport	yes

Summary A fairly easy-going walk around Arran's north coast with superb scenery and interesting historical features, mostly following good paths and with some rock-hopping.

For a change of scene or if the cloud is too low for a mountain jaunt, the north coast provides fine walking between North Sannox and Lochranza. There are some impressive cliffs, the site of a landslip, isolated cottages, remains of early coal mining and salt harvesting, and the Cock of Arran itself – a prominent block of sandstone, not named after a rooster but probably from the Lowland Scots word meaning 'cap' or 'headwear'. On a good day the views across the Sound of Bute to the mainland, the Isle of Bute and part of the Kintyre peninsula are excellent. There's also a good chance of seeing common seals near the shore.

The walk is described from North Sannox to Lochranza, but can be done in the opposite direction, depending on the time of day and wind direction. The rise and fall of the tide isn't particularly great, so high tide shouldn't complicate things. The distance of 8mi includes only 60m of ascent, from the coast to North Newton. The boulder-hopping sections and some potentially wet stretches of path could easily increase the time taken. If need be, you can catch a bus back towards Sannox and alight at the North Sannox turn, from where it's about 300m to the North Sannox picnic area.

Alternatives Shorter versions of this walk are possible, including out and back from either end of the walk described. The distance from North Sannox to Millstone Point and back is 5mi (8km), for which you should allow 2½ to three hours. At the other end follow the minor road on the north side of Loch Ranza then the path round Newton Point and on to the cottage near Fairy Dell; return to Lochranza by the route described for the main walk. The distance for this walk is 4mi (6.4km), which should take about two hours.

Yet another possibility is to leave the main walk at Laggan cottage, climb over the ridge rising from the coast and follow a path (which could be partly overgrown with bracken in summer) up the hillside. It reaches a height of 261m on the moorland ridge, then descends across some boggy ground to a minor road at Narachan. Follow this to a junction and turn left to reach Lochranza. The distance is 9mi (12.9km); allow about four hours.

NEAREST TOWNS

Sannox

Places to Stay & Eat In the village of Sannox, 7mi from Brodick and Lochranza, ***Gowanlea*** *(☎ 01770-810253)*, on the seafront, offers B&B for £16 or DB&B for £25; a self-catering cottage is also available. ***Ingledene Hotel*** *(☎ 01770-810225)* has bar meals or you can dine in the Sannox Bay Restaurant; rooms with en suite are also available. See Getting Around on page 150 for transport options to Sannox.

Lochranza

Places to Stay & Eat The handsome ***SYHA Hostel*** *(☎ 01770-830761)* is beside the main road overlooking Loch Ranza; the tariff starts at £8. ***Lochranza Golf Caravan & Camp Site*** *(☎ 01770-830273)* has plenty of grassy pitches, for which you'll pay £6. There are also two hotels, of which the ***Lochranza Hotel*** *(☎ 01770-830223)* is the least expensive at £20 per person sharing. ***Apple Lodge*** *(☎ 01770-830229)* is an award-winning guesthouse with en suite rooms from £30.

Lochranza Hotel is one of two places to go for a meal; the other is the ***Pier Tearoom & Restaurant*** *(☎ 01770-830217)*, which looks out across the sea. The Pier Tearoom is also the only place on Arran where you can access the Internet, although you'll have to pay £3 for just 15 minutes. There's a small, off-licence ***shop*** in the village.

Getting There & Away There's a small, summer-only car ferry from Claonaig on the Kintyre peninsula to Lochranza, which has several sailings daily. The return passenger fare is £6.65 and the return journey for a standard car costs £30. See also Getting Around on page 150.

GETTING TO/FROM THE WALK

The walk starts at a picnic area (with toilets) at the end of a minor road, which branches from the A841 about 800m north-west of Sannox. See Getting Around on page 150 for transport options to the A841/minor road turn-off.

The walk ends in Lochranza village. It's possible to park beside the road at the north-west corner of Lochranza golf course or, farther on, at the end of this road beside Loch Ranza.

THE WALK

The forest track leading north from the picnic area gives good views across the Firth of Clyde, a theme sustained for the whole walk. After nearly 2mi the track gives way to a footpath along the shore. At the far end of a shingle beach, **Fallen Rocks**, a jumble of massive conglomerate boulders resting at the foot of a steep, bracken-covered hillside, are easily bypassed. The mainly grassy path keeps close to the high tide mark to **Millstone Point** where white-painted **Laggan cottage** comes into view, about 20 minutes further on and about 1½ hours from North Sannox.

Less than 1mi from the cottage, the local scene changes with birch-oak woodland on the lower slopes. In summer, tall bracken hides the remains of cottages and the coal pits and salt pans that were excavated here to support local fishing in the 18th century. Ignore paths climbing into the trees and stick to the rocky shore, where you might find scraps of blackish coal. Farther on, although

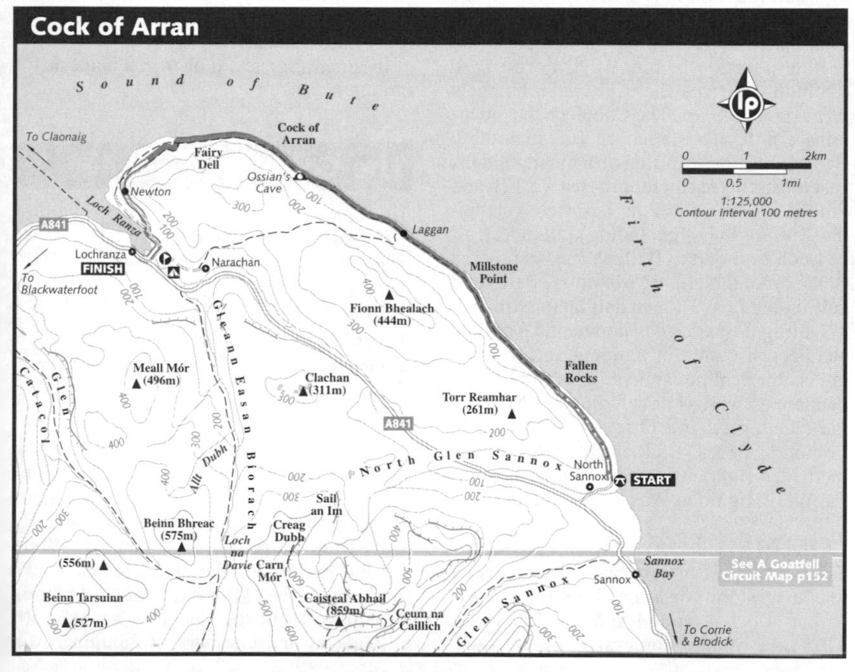

Ossian's Cave is marked on the map, it's invisible from the shore. The pinkish-red sandstone cliffs then start to close in. Around the **Cock of Arran** flat red slabs of sandstone line the shore. Below Fairy Dell Cave you have to clamber over and around rough conglomerate boulders, which arrived here in a landslip centuries ago; soon you're back on grass. From the two cottages at **Fairy Dell**, follow a path from the corner of a dyke in the trees, up through bracken to moorland. Then it's down to a gravel road near two cottages, soon with good views of Loch Ranza. Continue down to the minor road along the loch shore and turn left to reach Lochranza village (two hours from Laggan).

Arrochar, Lomond & Trossachs

All of the walks in this section will be part of Scotland's first national park – Loch Lomond & the Trossachs. Expected to be established in 2002, the park will cover the northern section of the Argyll Forest Park (including the Arrochar Alps and robbing its *pièce de résistance*, The Cobbler), the mountains south of Crianlarich (most notably Ben More and Stob Binnein), the mountains east of Strathyre (including Ben Vorlich and Stuc a' Chroin), all of the Trossachs (including Aberfoyle but excluding Callander), all of Loch Lomond to Balloch (respecting the Ben Lomond National Memorial Park) and cutting the Luss Hills in half up to Arrochar.

During the park's development, £6 million has been invested in building and improving visitor facilities at Inveruglas and Rowardennan, as well as developing the National Park Gateway and Orientation Centre at Lomond Shores, Balloch, a public launch facility at Balloch Pierhead, and improving the West Highland Way within the park.

CLIMATE

The warm Gulf Stream brings wet weather to the western coast and hills around Arrochar, Loch Lomond and the Trossachs. TICs post weather forecasts.

PLANNING

Maps & Books

Harvey's Superwalker 1:25,000 *Glasgow Popular Hills* covers the Dumgoyne (Campsie Fells) and several mountains presented in this chapter: The Cobbler, Ben Ledi, Ben Lomond and Ben A'an. The fully mapped Collins' *Walk Loch Lomond & the Trossachs* presents a good array of area walks.

Information Sources

During the national park's development, interim information centres are located at Balloch Castle Country Park (☎ 01389-722600), the Loch Lomond Park Centre at Luss (☎ 01301-702785) and Balmaha (☎ 01360-870470). For current information and updates, contact the Loch Lomond (☎ 01389-757295) and Trossachs (☎ 01877-382034) ranger services and the Argyll, the Isles, Loch Lomond, Stirling & Trossachs Tourist Board (☎ 01786-445222, e info@scottish.heartlands.org, W www.scottish.heartlands.org). Additionally, the national park's Web site (W www.lochlomond-trossachs.org) reports the latest news.

In an emergency, dial ☎ 999 and ask for mountain rescue.

The Cobbler

Duration	5 hours
Distance	8mi (13km)
Standard	medium-hard
Start & Finish	Succoth
Nearest Town	Arrochar
Public Transport	yes

Summary Ascent of one of Scotland's most famous and unusually shaped peaks, only an hour from Glasgow.

Ben Arthur, fondly referred to as The Cobbler (884m), with its distinctive three-pronged rooster crown, stands majestically apart from its rounded neighbours. While not the highest of the six Arrochar peaks (including four Munros), The Cobbler is without a doubt the favourite among both hillwalkers and climbers. It dominates the southernmost section of the Arrochar Alps, delimited by Glen Loin, the head of Loch Long and Glen Croe (along the A83) in the south, Loch Lomond in the east and Glen Kinglas in the west. The popular story of the mountain's name identifies a cobbler hunched over (north and centre peaks) listening to his wife, Jean (south peak). Instrumental in the development of Scottish rock climbing, especially among young, working-class Glaswegians, The Cobbler Club (1866) was Scotland's first climbing group. Composed of schistose grit and mica-schist, the last ice age littered the mountain sides with moraine, leaving behind the notable Narnain Boulders below The Cobbler's peaks.

Following a well-traversed path, the unmarked trail gains 850m. It ends with a steep and rocky section from the corrie at the peaks' base and then a short, exhilarating scramble. Seen from the corrie, the south peak's (left) steep sides make it the dominion of climbers. The north peak is easily reached along its northern face. The centre's ascent is dramatic: a huge, box-shaped rock with a body-sized hole that must be squeezed through to reach the top via a narrow shelf (and steep drops!). People hang out around the centre peak gathering nerve just before the last shoot to the top or observing others 'threading the needle'.

PLANNING

Enjoy The Cobbler year-round, although when wet (which is often – 2500mm rainfall yearly) the mica-schist tends to be very slippery. Be prepared for snow and ice in winter. Spring and early summer are the warmest and driest. Expect boggy sections all year and bring enough water for the whole walk.

Maps & Books

The OS Landranger 1:50,000 map No 56 *(Loch Lomond & Inverary)* covers the area. Two Harvey maps are recommended: Superwalker 1:25,000 and Walker's 1:50,000, both titled *Arrochar Alps*. Forest Enterprise's *Argyll Forest Park: Guide Book* is an excellent local resource.

Information Sources

While the national park develops, general information is available from the Argyll Forest Visitor Centre (☎ 01369-840666) at Ardgartan. For the local mountain weather forecast, phone MetCall (☎ 0906-850 0441). For travel information pick up the *Argyll and Bute Travel Map* or call the Helpline (☎ 01546-604695). If coming via Glasgow and Helensburgh call ☎ 0141-332 7133.

NEAREST TOWNS

Arrochar & Around

Places to Stay & Eat ***Lochside Guest House*** *(☎ 01301-702467, ⓔ LochsideGH@aol.com)*, Main St, offers B&B, spectacular views of The Cobbler and caters to vegetarians. Prices range from £18 to £25. Evening meals (£10) can also be arranged. ***Hotel Loch Long*** has five-course meals for £6.95. ***Greenbank Guest House***, Main St, prepares lunch (soup and sandwich) for £3.50 and evening entrees (salmon, trout) from £6.95. Self-caterers can find basic supplies at the ***Post Office shop*** in Main St.

Two miles west of Arrochar on the A83 is Ardgartan, an old forestry village, and the Forest Enterprise's ***Ardgartan Caravan & Camping Site*** *(☎ 01301-702293)*. Open from late March to mid-October the tariff is £3 to £4 per person including tent and/or car. Nearby, ***Loch Long SYHA Hostel*** *(☎ 01301-702362)* has an unbeatable position on Loch Long, does B&B for £12.25 and opens from late January to late November.

Getting There & Away Take the Scottish Citylink (☎ 0870-550 5050) Glasgow-Oban No 976 bus to Arrochar. In addition, Garelochhead Minibuses (☎ 01436-810200) No 301 (Helensburgh-Carrick Castle via Arrochar) and No 318 (Succoth-Helensburgh via Arrochar) are useful links. ScotRail (☎ 0845-755 0033) trains stop at Arrochar & Tarbet station (a 20-minute walk from Arrochar) on the Edinburgh-Mallaig and London Euston-Fort William lines.

If driving, from Glasgow take the M8 (Greenock) towards Loch Lomond and then the highly scenic A82; continue on the A83 to Arrochar.

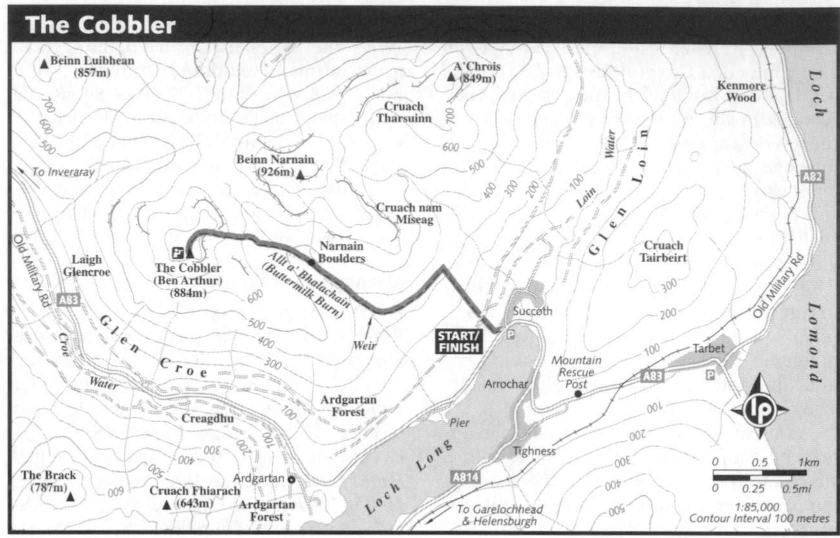

GETTING TO/FROM THE WALK

The most straightforward route up The Cobbler, and with the best views, leaves from the Succoth car park, which is just north of Arrochar village on the A83. It is a five-minute walk from the village to the car park, walking around the head of Loch Long in a horseshoe.

THE WALK

From the Succoth car park cross the A83 and follow the woodland trail heading southwest, near the 'Argyll Forest Park' sign. The trail soon narrows and abruptly turns northwest, steeply ascending first through a conifer plantation and then an open hillside of ferns and juvenile spruce. Huge blocks of cement, the anchors for the 'pipetrack' that once fed a hydroelectric plant below, mark the trail. Upon reaching a wide, forestry road, cross it and continue with the steep, straight ascent.

Thirty minutes later, when the trail reaches a rocky outcrop (left) topped with two rowans make a 90 degree turn southwest (left) onto a well-worn path. For a pleasant 20 minutes the trail follows the hill's contour and provides superlative views of Arrochar and Loch Long, a deep glacial valley with depths from 26m off Arrochar to 91m near Loch Goil. Royal Navy submarines still occasionally glide up the waters, also popular with scuba divers and anglers.

Reaching the gurgling **Allt a' Bhalachain**, also known as the Buttermilk Burn, and weir, The Cobbler's famous peaks come into magnificent view (right). You are now halfway. Continue about 1mi, following the obvious path upstream and crossing numerous tributaries to the distinctive **Narnain Boulders**.

Over the next half-mile or so cross the burn, wade through a very boggy, heavily eroded area and ascend to the rocky corrie below the three peaks. Head towards the saddle between the central and north peaks marked with a cairn. The steepness and erosion require a scramble.

The centre and highest peak lies to the left, while the more easily accessed north peak is to the right – your choice! Enjoy the superlative views of Ben Lomond and the Firth of Clyde, as well as the nearby Luss Hills behind Arrochar. Return the same way to the Succoth car park.

Ben Lomond

Duration	4½–5 hours
Distance	6.5mi (10.5km)
Standard	medium
Start & Finish	Rowardennan
Nearest Towns	Rowardennan, Balmaha, Drymen
Public Transport	no

Summary A circular route over one of the most popular 'hills' in Central Scotland; the paths are clear and there are magnificent views of famous Loch Lomond.

Loch Lomond is Scotland's largest freshwater loch, nearly 22mi long and up to 4.5mi wide. Standing guard over the loch is Ben Lomond (974m), the most southerly Munro. Until officially being declared part of Scotland's first national park in 2002, Ben Lomond and the loch are within the smaller Loch Lomond Regional Park, a reserve not unlike a national park. It's thought that the name Lomond comes from an old Lowland Scots word *llumon* or the Gaelic *laom* meaning a 'beacon' or 'light'. Loch Lomond is a very popular venue for water sports and on fine weekends the droning of power boats and jet skis is all too audible, right up on the summit.

Ben Lomond is the most popular of all Scotland's mountains – more than 30,000 people do the walk each year. Most follow the 'tourist route' up and down, which starts at Rowardennan car park. It's a straightforward climb on a well-used and maintained path; on the day this walk was researched, more than 130 walkers (and several dogs) passed by. However, the scenic Ptarmigan Route, described here, is less crowded and follows a narrower but still clear path up the western flank of Ben Lomond, directly overlooking the loch, to a curving ridge leading to the summit. You can then descend via the tourist route, making a satisfying circuit.

The distance is about 6.5mi and the ascent is 950m, for which the walking time should be around five hours, for both the circular walk described and the there-and-back route on the tourist path. There are no easy alternative routes; Ben Lomond slopes very steeply down to the loch and tracks through the forest on the eastern side aren't particularly attractive. The West Highland Way (see the West Highland Way on page 173) passes between the loch and the Ben, and many Way walkers take a day off to do the climb.

NATURAL HISTORY

Loch Lomond is a relic of the last ice age, gouged out by south-flowing glaciers. To

Ben Lomond National Memorial Park

Well within the compass of the future national park, Ben Lomond National Memorial Park is already managed along the lines of a national park.

The park was dedicated in 1996 as a memorial to those who served their country in WWII. A fitting sculpture stands close to the shore, just north of the Rowardennan car park. The dedication document is on display at Rowardennan youth hostel.

Extending along 8mi of Loch Lomond's shore, the park takes in Ben Lomond and its approaches (virtually all the area of the accompanying walk map). It will be incorporated in the national park, retaining its identity.

The park is jointly owned and managed by the National Trust for Scotland and Forest Enterprise to enhance nature conservation values and to provide access for peaceful recreation in harmony with the social and economic needs of the area's residents.

The Trust's most visible work is in footpath repair – the average width of the main path on Ben Lomond has been reduced from 9m to 1.75m. Over the years, Forest Enterprise is replacing the spruce plantations with native woodlands, and the Trust is encouraging the growth of woodland on its ground – Ben Lomond will undoubtedly look quite different by the mid-21st century.

the north it is narrow, steep-sided and deep, while to the south it is much wider and shallower, and dotted with wooded islets – there are 38 islands in the loch.

Climbing Ben Lomond takes you from the relatively luxuriant woodlands of birch, beech, oak and chestnut along the loch shore and on the lower slopes, to the bare windswept moorlands. The National Trust for Scotland has established at least one exclosure – a large fenced area within which native trees are thriving, safe from grazing sheep and deer.

Bird life is plentiful in the woodlands, including restarts and pied flycatchers. Much higher up, on open rocky ground you might see the ptarmigan, a chook-sized bird, which blends beautifully with its surroundings. It has a wardrobe of two sets of plumage, white in winter and mottled brown to speckled grey in summer. Sightings of golden eagles are not uncommon, although buzzards are more common.

PLANNING

When Ben Lomond is snow-covered during winter the final stages of the climb could be quite difficult, requiring ice axe and crampons. Without snow, possibly April to late October, it's relatively straightforward. However, like all Scottish mountains, Ben Lomond can create its own weather, so be prepared for much cooler and windier conditions up the top than down by the loch. Carry plenty of drinking water; sheep graze the upper slopes and the very few streams may not be safe to drink from.

National Trust for Scotland policy is to maintain open access to its ground at all times, including the stalking season.

Maps & Books

Harvey's 1:25,000 map *Glasgow Popular Hills* includes Ben Lomond but isn't much help for identifying surrounding features. For this purpose, either the OS Landranger 1:50,000 map No 56 *(Loch Lomond & Inveraray)* or OS Outdoor Leisure 1:25,000 map No 39 *(Loch Lomond)* is preferable.

Walk Loch Lomond & The Trossachs by Gilbert Summers includes several walks around the loch; *Loch Lomond & Trossachs Walks* by John Brooks covers a wider area. For general background information *Loch Lomond & The Trossachs* by Rennie McOwan is recommended.

NEAREST TOWNS

Rowardennan & Around

A new visitor centre (☎ 01360-870429) has opened at the end of the sealed road in Rowardennan. It has interpretive displays covering the proposed Loch Lomond & the Trossachs National Park and a park ranger is based here. Facilities include toilets and luggage lockers for walkers wishing to ditch large packs and make the climb up Ben Lomond. National Trust for Scotland rangers (☎ 01360-870224) lead guided walks on Ben Lomond.

Places to Stay & Eat Located in Rowardennan Lodge, ***Rowardennan SYHA Hostel*** *(☎ 01360-870259)* is very convenient but also very popular so it pays to book ahead – the tariff is £9.25 and meals are available. Nearby, ***Rowardennan Hotel*** *(☎ 01360-870273)* has rooms from £35 and reasonably priced bar meals in the lively Rob Roy Bar. ***Ben Lomond Cottage B&B*** *(☎ 01360-870411)* is right beside the walk and has well-appointed facilities for £25; evening meals are available.

The Forest Enterprise's ***Cashel Camping and Caravan Site*** *(☎ 01360-870234)* is also very popular; the average tariff per 'unit' (person and tent) is £4.40.

Across the loch at Inverbeg there's the ***Inverbeg Inn*** *(☎ 01436-860678)* for B&B from £38; the nearest SYHA hostel is ***Loch Lomond*** *(☎ 01389-850226)*, about 10mi south of Inverbeg.

Getting There & Away The only public transport to Rowardennan is the small ferry (operated by the Rowardennan Hotel), which plies the loch to and from Inverbeg during summer. Use the regular Scottish Citylink (☎ 0870-550 5050) bus service between Glasgow and Fort William to Inverbeg, then catch the passenger ferry (☎ 01360-870273) to Rowardennan, leaving at 10.30am, 2.30pm and 6pm, and returning at 10am, 2pm and 5.30pm.

Balmaha

Balmaha is a small village 6mi (10km) south of Rowardennan, usually thronged with people messing about in boats. The Loch Lomond Park Centre (☎ 01360-870470) has displays about the park's natural and cultural history. Loch Lomond Park Rangers (01389-757295) occasionally lead walks during the summer. The village has a very small ***shop***, ***coffee shop***, a couple of B&Bs and the ***Highland Way Hotel*** *(☎ 01360-870225)*, which has a bunkhouse where the tariff is £12.50.

Getting There & Away McColl's Coaches (☎ 01389-754321) opeates a bus service to Balmaha from Balloch via Drymen but there are no buses on to Rowardennan, a distance of 6mi. Balloch is the terminus of a ScotRail (☎ 0845-755 0033) service from Glasgow.

Drymen

Drymen has the nearest shops of any size to the start of this walk and a good selection of pubs and places to stay. There's a ***Spar*** off-licence and at ***It's Great Outdoors*** you can buy small gas canisters for camping stoves (but not liquid fuel). There's an ATM on the Glasgow road. The TIC is in the public library (☎ 01360-660068); it's open daily from late May to late September. At other times, the library staff can help with information about local accommodation, and sales of maps and books. You can check emails at the library, the charge being £1.25 per half-hour; it's closed on Wednesday and Sunday.

Places to Stay & Eat ***Green Shadows*** *(☎ 01360-660289)* is a walker-friendly B&B in a peaceful setting overlooking the nearby Buchanan golf course; the tariff is £24.

Drymen Tandoori *(☎ 01360-660099)* has a huge menu and offers a rare chance to escape from standard bar menus. Of the pubs, ***The Clachan Inn*** *(☎ 01360-660824)*, the oldest licensed pub in Scotland, has plenty of atmosphere. Alternatively try ***Drymen Pottery*** *(☎ 01360-660458)*, which specialises in pies and traditional Scottish dishes.

Getting There & Away Drymen is on the bus route from Balloch to Balmaha. See Getting There & Away under Balmaha.

GETTING TO/FROM THE WALK

The walk starts and finishes at the Rowardennan car park, at the end of the public road from Drymen (6mi), which can be reached from Glasgow via the A809 or from the east via the A811.

THE WALK

From the car park walk north along the dirt road, past the side road on the left to the youth hostel/lodge. Pass a gate and bear left at a fork, following the West Highland Way. Beyond Ardess Lodge National Trust for Scotland Ranger Centre and Ben Lomond Cottage, which are on the right, cross a burn

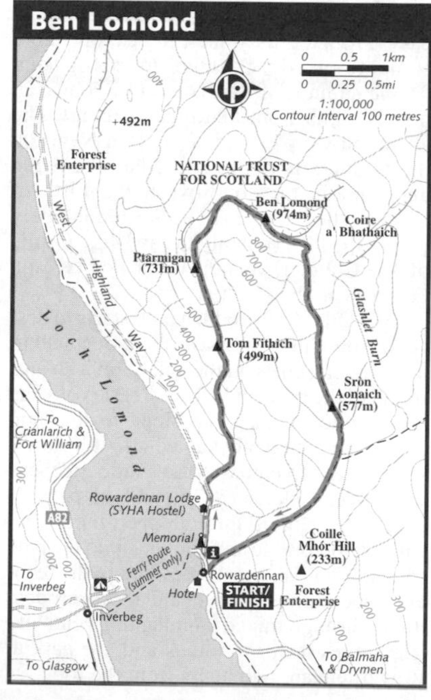

and immediately turn right along a path through the trees. It climbs beside the burn for a short distance then goes steeply up the bracken-covered hillside. Straightaway you're treated to views of the loch and the hills on its western side. The path passes a fenced exclosure on the right, climbs steadily across the steep slope and traverses just below a small cliff, with Ptarmigan summit in view. Farther up, above another low cliff, go through a small gate. The path gains more height on an open spur then zigzags steeply up a grassy bluff to the ridge, and on to **Ptarmigan** summit (731m), near a small pond, between 1½ to two hours from Rowardennan. The fine views include virtually the full length of the loch and its cluster of islands, and the Arrochar hills to the west.

The path leads on along the bumpy ridge, through a chain of grassy, rocky knobs, to a narrow gap where stepping stones keep you out of the mud. The final, steep climb starts through formidable crags, but natural rock steps and the well-used path make it quite easy. From a grassy shelf there's one more straightforward rocky climb to the trig point on the summit of **Ben Lomond** (974m), an hour's climb from Ptarmigan summit. The all-round view extends from Ben Nevis on the northern horizon, to the Isles of Arran and Jura in the south-west, the Firth of Clyde, the Arrochar hills immediately across the loch (notably the awl-like profile of The Cobbler), and the Campsie Fells and Glasgow to the south.

The wide, well-trodden path starts to descend immediately, past the spectacular, north-facing cliffs on the left. Soon it swings round to the right and makes a series of wide zigzags down the steep slope to the long ridge stretching ahead, which it follows southward. Eventually the grade steepens over Sròn Aonaich (577m) and the path resumes zigzagging through open moorland. Cross a footbridge and continue into the pine forest, along an open ride. The path steepens, becoming rockier and more eroded, down through mixed woodland. Eventually it emerges near the toilets and car park at Rowardennan, two hours from the top.

Ben A'an

Duration	2½ hours
Distance	3.7mi (6km)
Standard	easy
Start & Finish	Ben A'an car park
Nearest Town	Callander
Public Transport	yes

Summary Classic Trossachs walk offering superlative visual rewards.

The Trossachs, the enchanting network of lochs, woodlands, deep glens and rugged mountains between the Highlands and the River Forth valley, are, in a word, captivating. Eulogised by 19th-century Romantic poets, Sir Walter Scott definitively immortalised them in his two works the *Lady of the Lake* and *Rob Roy*. The Trossachs heartland lies between Loch Katrine (Glasgow's water source) and Loch Achray. The area's classic walk ascends to diminutive 454m Ben A'an (or A'n). Originally called Am Binnein, meaning 'rocky peak', Sir Walter Scott is responsible for changing the name. This low peak offers excellent visual rewards – Bens Venue, Lomond and Ledi. Some beautiful birch and oak stands particularly enhance the aesthetic value of autumn, crowd-free walks. While unmarked, the trail is easy to follow. Bring enough water for the short outing.

PLANNING

Maps & Books

Use the OS Landranger 1:50,000 map No 57 *(Stirling & The Trossachs)*. Ben A'an's summit is marked farther east than it really is. Harvey's Superwalker 1:25,000 map *Ben Ledi: Hills around Callander* includes Ben A'an. Louis Scott's *The Ring of Words: Literary Loch Lomond* is a good read.

Information Sources

Much of the Trossachs forms part of the Queen Elizabeth Forest Park and the park's visitor centre (☎ 01877-382383) in Aberfoyle sells maps and guides. Callander also has a well-stocked TIC (☎ 01877-330342) see Callander & Around for details.

NEAREST TOWN
Callander & Around

Callander's proximity to Glasgow and Edinburgh via Stirling make it an ideal gateway to the Trossachs. The TIC doubles as the Rob Roy and Trossachs Visitor Centre (☎ 01877-330342), in Ancaster Square, and opens daily from March to December and at weekends in January and February. It has information panels and a video program on 17th-century outlaw Rob Roy. The town's main street has ATMs, a book and map shop, and a sporting goods store.

Places to Stay & Eat Mrs McAlpine at ***Craigburn House*** *(☎ 01877-330322)*, North Church St, offers B&B charm in town. Shared bath and en suite singles/doubles cost £17 and £18 per person. ***Scotch Bakery & Tearoom*** *(8 Main St)* has delicious loaves and scones. Charming ***Dun Whinny's Coffee House*** *(9 Bridge St)* serves home-made soup and open sandwiches from £1.80. For an evening meal, ***Sherry's Restaurant*** *(114 Main St)* has entrees from £5.50 to £9.

Keltie Bridge Caravan Park *(☎ 01877-330606)*, east of the town on the A84 and within walking distance, charges £8 for tents and with car £9.50. ***Trossachs Backpackers hostel*** *(☎ 01877-331200)*, 1.25mi from Callander on the Invertrossachs Rd off the A81, charges from £12.50 for B&B.

Getting There & Away Citylink (☎ 0870-550 5050) bus No 974 Edinburgh-Fort William stops in Callander. Citylink buses Nos 963, 965, 995 and 538 connect Glasgow and Stirling. From here transfer to the First Edinburgh (☎ 0131-663 9233) No 59 Stirling-Killin service. ScotRail (☎ 0845-755 0033) trains frequently service Stirling from Glasgow and Edinburgh. By car from Glasgow (on the M80) or Edinburgh (M9) head to Stirling and then Callander (A84).

GETTING TO/FROM THE WALK

Infrequent postbus (☎ 01246-546329) No 24 services Callander and the Trossachs Hotel near the start of the walk Monday to Saturday. By car from Callander, continue north towards Killin (A84) and turn left onto the A821 at Kilmahog. Beyond Brig o' Turk, turn left into the Forest Enterprise's Ben A'an car park, after the Trossachs Hotel.

THE WALK

See map page 164

From the Ben A'an car park cross the A821 to the obvious, northbound forest track. Initially steep, keep left to the left side of the track. You then reach a burn and falls, and maintain them on the right in constant ascent. Cross the burn at a wooden bridge and continue up through the forest. One third of the way, after about 20 minutes, a quick detour to a left-hand hillock reveals majestic Ben A'an (right). The forest track continues to a level clearing with cone-shaped Ben A'an visible ahead. You're now halfway. Continue along the stream and then cross it, walking up its true right side. At a second clearing take the 'stairs' straight up towards Ben A'an's south-east base, along another stream. Near the top cross to the stream's true right bank leaving the stairs. Continue along the burn's bank, scrambling up a rocky section.

At the top circle north around Ben A'an's east face and then pick among the trails on the mountain's boggy north backside to the rocky summit; aim for the middle to get the splendid views all at once. Of Loch Katrine (right) Scott wrote: 'So won'drous wild, the whole might seem, The scenery of a fairy dream'. Retrace your steps to the car park.

Ben Ledi

Duration	4 hours
Distance	7.4mi (12km)
Standard	medium-hard
Start & Finish	Ben Ledi car park
Nearest Town	Callander
Public Transport	yes

Summary A circular walk through lush woodland, including enchanting Stank Glen, past rushing cascades and across a spectacular ridge.

The Trossachs have come to signify the wild region bounded by some of its 12 lochs: Loch Ard and Lake of Menteith in the south,

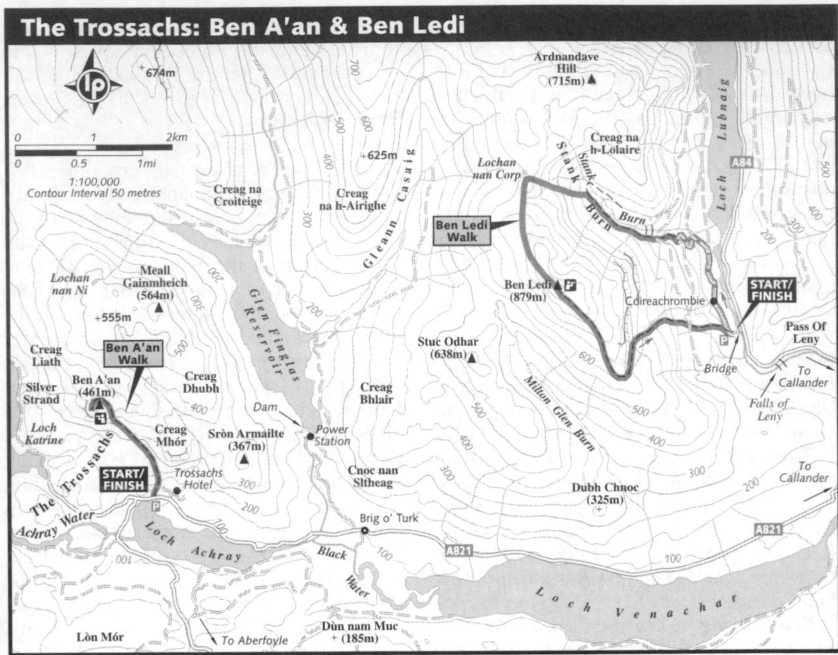

the north end of Loch Katrine marks the west, Loch Doine and Loch Voil hem in the north and Loch Lubnaig rounds out the east. To the west of Loch Lubnaig, the Trossachs' highest mountain, Ben Ledi (879m), makes a formidable back-drop to Callander and Loch Venachar, and is deserving of its name God's Hill (a 1791 account links it to an annual summer solstice celebration). A less dramatic definition, 'hill of the gentle slope', perhaps refers to the broad grassy ridge running north from the summit down to Lochan nan Corp – the wee loch of the dead bodies! Local legend suggests an ill-fortuned funeral party fell through the ice as they crossed the apparently frozen surface.

While fairly straightforward in good conditions, Ben Ledi should be taken very seriously when it is inclement. The circular walk, which gains some 740m in altitude, makes a steep descent. Only initially waymarked, the trail is well worn and generally easy to follow.

PLANNING

See Planning under Ben A'an on page 162.

NEAREST TOWN
Callander

See Nearest Town on page 163.

GETTING TO/FROM THE WALK

From Callander it is 3mi to the trailhead, off the A84 (Killin) at the Forestry Enterprise's Ben Ledi car park by the bridge to Strathyre Forest Cabins. You can easily walk this distance (which passes the Falls of Leny) along the cycle route connecting Callander and Killin.

The First Edinburgh (☎ 0131-663 9233) Stirling-Killin bus service passes the trailhead; ask for drop possibility near the bridge. Postbus (☎ 01246-546329) No 27 drops at Kilmahog from Callander.

A taxi (☎ 01877-330496/331240) service from Callander to the trailhead will cost you around £5.

THE WALK

See map page 164

From the car park return to the bridge and continue straight (north) on the sealed road marked with green posts, parallel to the Garbh Uisge river, for just over half a mile. Turn left onto a forestry road that makes a curving ascent to a fork. Head left here through a broad-leaved forest. After five minutes abandon the forestry road at a sharp curve and turn right (west) onto a footpath through a magical beech wood that ascends alongside the rushing Stank Burn (right). In 200m spruce dominate, and the trail reaches and crosses another forestry road to continue its north-west course through the forest. Five minutes later a natural balcony (right) overlooks a leaping cascade.

Reaching another forestry road turn right for 30m and then head left again onto another, narrow road that ascends west. After a tough, steep stretch, the trail enters breathtaking **Stank Glen**. Stank Burn's source, at the end of the valley, tumbles down in a series of spectacular falls. Ignore a left-hand ascending road and continue west along the valley's floor, which is studded with stumps. After crossing another road, take a footpath that approaches the burn's winding course and ford it. A white post indicates the end of the modern green posts. From here the waymarking is irregular and clearly antiquated. The footpath heads to the valley's left side through a boggy, heather-lined section. Reaching a wire fence, continue along its right side to a gate. The real, back-breaking work, an approximately half-mile stretch to reach the ridge crest, begins. Once on the crest, iron fence posts run along the ridge marking old boundary estates. A five-minute detour right (north) leads to eerie Lochan nan Corp. To reach the **Ben Ledi** summit, follow the posts just over 1mi south (left); the sweeping views are just reward after the long uphill pull.

To descend, follow the posts south-east along a heavily eroded trail for almost 1.5mi, where the trail swings sharply left (north-east). Descend towards the forest along Ben Ledi's abrupt east face. At the base use the stile to cross another wire fence and then cross a stream and follow its right bank into the forest. When this walk was researched in late 2000, the trees were being harvested. Continue 1mi down a steep path to the start.

Around Loch Tay

A Munro bagger's delight, the area bounded by Loch Tay (south), Lochs Rannoch and Tummel (north), Pitlochry (east) and Loch Lyon (western extreme) packs in a vast amount of incredible scenery and ancient, fascinating history. Bisected east to west by Glen Lyon, this valley, arguably Scotland's most magnificent, lies between the two largest massifs in the southern Highlands: Carn Mairg to the north and the seven-peak

The Fortingall Yew

Near Scotland's geographical centre an amazing relic survives in enchanting Glen Lyon: the Fortingall yew. Europe's oldest tree, it's dated between 3000 and 5000 years old. The Celts who populated the Highlands treated the yew *(Taxus baccata)* as a sacred tree, symbolising eternal life. This may explain the tree's presence next to Fortingall's church and the practice, common in much of Europe, of planting yews in churchyards. The etymology of nearby Coshieville confirms this; *cas a bhile* comes from the Gaelic meaning 'at the foot of the sacred tree'.

In 1769 the traveller Thomas Pennant measured the yew's girth at 54ft. Disgracefully, this great tree, having lived through eons of invasions and history stretching from the earliest settlement of the Isles to the Romans to crises with the English, nearly succumbed to total destruction when thoughtless 18th- and 19th-century treasure hunters whacked off souvenir-size chunks. Fires were also lit underneath and later funeral processions marched through the gaping hole. Finally a wall was erected to protect the tree and markers were sunk to show the 1769 size. Two trunks remain and, remarkably, still sprout lovely green needles.

(all over 900m), 7.5mi ridge of the Ben Lawers group to the south. The Tarmachans, another noted range topped by Meall nan Tarmachan (1043m), lies to the west of the Lawers group, separated by the Lochan na Lairige pass. An excellent full-day walk traverses the Ben Lawers group. The described walks focus on the area's two signature peaks: Ben Lawers (1214m) and Schiehallion (1083m). Killin, at the west end of Loch Tay, and Aberfeldy, to the east of the loch along the River Tay, are recommended as good launching points for exploration of this rich area. Also consider Kinloch Rannoch, located on the B846 to the north of Schiehallion for this peak and Rannoch Moor.

CLIMATE

Loch Tay gets hit by weather brewing from both the east and the west, producing very unpredictable conditions. April, May and June tend to be the driest months and July and August the warmest (averaging 17°C). If prepared for winter walking, it's possible to walk these mountains year-round.

PLANNING

When to Walk

Stalking The West Rannoch Deer Management Group stalks and culls stags from August to 20 October and hinds from 21 October to 15 February (except Sundays) in the area from Bridge of Orchy, Crianlarich, Glen Dochart, Ben Lawers and upper Glen Lyon. Most activity occurs in November and December. Special care should be taken during this period to keep to trails, burns and ridges. Hillphones inform walkers about areas to be stalked and recorded messages (from August to October) are updated daily by 8am. West of Killin (Glen Dochart/Glen Lochay) call ☎ 01567-820886 and around Ben Lawers call ☎ 01567-820553.

Maps & Books

The OS Landranger 1:50,000 map No 51 *(Loch Tay & Glen Dochart)* covers both Ben Lawers and Schiehallion. Harvey's 1:25,000 map *Ben Lawers: From Loch Tay and Loch Rannoch* includes both peaks, the important massifs and a visitor guide. Felicity Martin's useful *Walks: North Perthshire* succinctly covers 26 walks on Loch Tay's east end.

Information Sources

A useful Web site for information on the Loch Tay area is W www.perthshire.co.uk. In an emergency, dial ☎ 999 and ask for mountain rescue.

GETTING THERE & AWAY

See under Access Towns & Facilities following for details on how to get to Killin and Aberfeldy.

GETTING AROUND

Public transport around Loch Tay and to trailheads is limited. With careful, advance planning it's possible to make infrequent connections between Aberfeldy and Killin, a distance of 23mi along the A827. Postbuses (☎ 01246-546329) Nos 212 and 213 make a couple of runs Monday to Saturday. Caber Coaches' (☎ 01887-820090) No 893 has an infrequent school-day service as well. For taxi service call (from Killin) ☎ 01567-820777/820386 and (from Aberfeldy) ☎ 01887-820433/820090/820219. The Perthshire transport helpline is ☎ 0845-301 1130. Ask for the *Highland Perthshire and Stanley Area* public transport guide at local TICs.

ACCESS TOWNS & FACILITIES

Killin

Open March to October from 10am to 5pm (weekends February), the TIC (☎ 01567-820254, e info@scottish.heartlands.org), Breadalbane Folklore Centre, lies over the bridge spanning the Falls of Dochart and has a slew of books and maps. For local weather contact W www.killin.co.uk. Main St has ATMs, a laundrette, post office and Killin Outdoor Centre, open daily for last-minute gear needs.

Places to Stay & Eat *Cruachan Farm Caravan & Camping Park (☎ 01567-820302)* opens from mid-March to October and charges from £5 for a person and tent.

Killin Youth Hostel *(☎ 01567-820546)*, Aberfeldy Rd, opens year-round (only weekends in winter), charges £7.75 to £9.75 and provides linen, self-catering kitchen and walking information. ***Fairview House*** *(☎ 01567-820667, e info@fairview-killin.co.uk)*, in Main St, warmly welcomes walkers in seven comfortable rooms and charges from £22 to £26. Book evening meals (£15) in advance.

Also on Main St find ***Costcutter*** and ***Co-op*** supermarkets, and ***Tarmarchan Tea Shop*** for coffee, lunch and afternoon tea. For an evening meal or drink with spectacular views, try Killin Hotel's ***Riverview Bistro*** where entrees cost around £8.95.

Getting There & Away First Edinburgh (☎ 0131-663 9233) buses Nos 59, 569 and 359 connect Stirling and Killin via Callander. Citylink (☎ 0870-550 5050) buses Nos 916 (Glasgow) and 974 (Edinburgh) go to Crianlarich. ScotRail's (☎ 0845-755 0033) Edinburgh/Glasgow (Queen St)-Fort William line stops at Crainlarich after Arrochar & Tarbet. Infrequent postbus (☎ 01246-546329) services link both Crianlarich (No 025) and Callander (Nos 025 and 027) to Killin. By car, from Edinburgh/Glasgow take the A84 via Stirling and Callander. If coming by car from Arrochar take the A82 to Crianlarich then the A85.

Aberfeldy

Quiet, riverside Aberfeldy came into the spotlight with Robert Burns' 1787 poem *The Birks O' Aberfeldy*, a paean to the nearby Falls of Moness and birch wood (birk). All shops and services are conveniently located around The Square including the TIC (☎ 01887-820276, e info@ptb.ossian.net), which is open year-round and sells guidebooks and maps. Call to confirm reduced winter hours. Munros, 1 Bridgend, has outdoor equipment and helpful, knowledgeable staff.

Places to Stay & Eat ***Aberfeldy Caravan Park*** *(☎ 01887-820662)*, on Dunkeld Rd just east of town, charges per car (£1.10), tent (£2.20) and person (£2.40). ***Claremont*** *(☎ 01887-829370, e slorance@aberfeldy.fsbusiness.co.uk)*, Taybridge Rd, has friendly B&B from £18 to £22. Self-caterers should look for the ***Co-op*** in The Square. ***Country Fare***, next to the TIC, has outstanding dessert and lunch offerings. ***Ailean Chraggan Hotel*** *(☎ 01887-820346)*, on the B846 after Wades Bridge, serves the best evening meals. ***The Bunk House*** *(☎ 01887-820265, e llinosrob@aol.com)*, at Glassie Farm, is located 1.3mi off the B846 (towards Schiehallion) and has great views, a self-catering kitchen and outdoor activities for £8.

Getting There & Away ScotRail (☎ 0845-755 0033) and GNER (☎ 0845-722 5225) Glasgow/Edinburgh-Inverness lines drop at Pitlochry. Scottish Citylink (☎ 0870-550 5050) also connects Glasgow (No 995) and Edinburgh (No 957) to Pitlochry. From Pitlochry to Aberfeldy, Stagecoach Perth (☎ 0870-608 2608) No 27 makes Monday to Saturday runs and Sundays are covered by Caber Coaches' (☎ 01887-820090) No 83. By car take the A9 out of Stirling and Perth connecting to the A822 (then A826) or the A827 to Aberfeldy.

Ben Lawers

Duration	5 hours
Distance	8.2mi (13km)
Standard	medium-hard
Start & Finish	Ben Lawers Visitor Centre
Nearest Town	Killin
Public Transport	no

Summary Direct ascent to Scotland's 10th-highest mountain known for its alpine flora.

Reigning mightily over Loch Tay's north shore, handsome Ben Lawers (1214m) is Perthshire's highest Munro. Some 3374ha of its southern slopes (and 1348ha of the Tarmachans to the west) are under the care of the National Trust for Scotland. Of particular interest is the recovery of willow, marsh hawk's beard and golden rod on the mountain. Using a well-worn trail, the walk makes a 940m elevation gain to reach the rocky summit, a remnant of an 1878, 30-man attempt to elevate Ben Lawers 7m to reach Scotland's elite 4000ft club.

PLANNING

Popular not only with hillwalkers in summer, the Lawers group's smooth, grassy slopes also attract winter skiers. Bring enough water for the excursion.

Information Sources

The National Trust for Scotland maintains the Ben Lawers Visitor Centre up on the mountain with displays on geology and fauna. The centre opens daily from 1 April to 30 September, from 10am to 5pm. The *Ben Lawers Nature Trail* booklet describes the flora and fauna. The ranger service (through the visitor centre) offers guided walks in July and August.

GETTING TO/FROM THE WALK

Ben Lawers Visitor Centre, at the start of the walk, is located 9.5mi east of Killin. At Edramucky on the A827, turn up Ben Lawers Rd for 1.5mi to the car park. Postbus services Nos 212 and 213 drop at Edramucky (see Getting Around on page 166).

THE WALK

From the Ben Lawers Visitor Centre take the Nature Trail that heads north-east. Clearly visible in the distance is the footpath that ascends the open hillside of Beinn Ghlas. After the boardwalk protecting the bog, cross an elevated, double-staired stile (and fence, which keeps the hungry sheep and deer out of the lush protected area). Fork left (north-east) and ascend along a burn (right). At the next rise fork right and cross the burn.

A few minutes later ignore the Nature Trail's right turn and continue ascending parallel to the burn's true left bank for just over half a mile. Leave the protected zone by another double stile and steeply ascend Beinn Ghlas' shoulder. Reaching a couple of large rocks, ignore a northbound footpath and continue zigzagging uphill. The rest of the 1.5mi ascent is a straightforward succession of three false summits. The last and steepest section alternates between erosion-sculpted rock and a meticulously crafted cobbled trail. A cairn marks the **Beinn Ghlas** summit (1103m). Enjoy the great view of Ben Lawers ahead.

Descend north-east along the ridge crest for 20 minutes to the base of Ben Lawers. The initial segment of the half-mile ascent is made easier by the cobbled sections reminiscent of ancient Roman highways. After a brief plateau, the ascent continues along a heavily eroded trail up to the rocky **Ben Lawers'** summit (1214m).

Return the same way, or take one or both of two straightforward detours. Instead of continuing along the ridge crest and climbing Beinn Ghlas again, from the base of Ben Lawers take a dirt trail that heads south-west and gently descends along the contour of Beinn Ghlas' north face. After about 1mi, old iron fence posts appear and soon you see Loch Tay and the visitor centre. In just over 1mi the alternative rejoins the main trail. Another worthwhile option is to finish up along the eastern segment of the Nature Trail, near the start of the route. At the 'To Car Park' sign, turn left and you will soon reach the double stile.

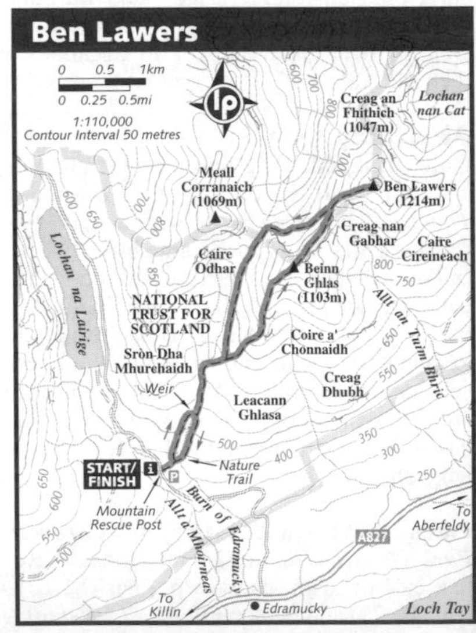

Ben Lawers

Schiehallion

Duration	4 hours
Distance	7.6mi (12km)
Standard	medium
Start & Finish	Braes of Floss car park
Nearest Town	Aberfeldy
Public Transport	no

Summary Walk the famous landmark and 'hill' responsible for the development of cartographers' contour lines.

Famed for its symmetrical conic appearance, especially when viewed from Loch Rannoch's birch-lined north shore, Schiehallion (1083m), 'the fairy hill of the Caledonians', is an isolated, huge whale of a mountain. A distinctive landmark from many viewpoints, even the great Roman chronicler Ptolemy marked it on his AD 145 map. Named a Site of Special Scientific Interest, look for the limestone pavements, ptarmigans and the yellow saxifrage and wild thyme scenting the hillsides.

The John Muir Trust owns and manages the summit, path and eastern slopes (915ha) and is attempting to restore the heavily eroded, described trail. The Trust plans to establish a new path using the eastern ridge, described as more interesting and with better vistas in ascent, allowing restoration work along the lower half of the present trail. From the car park at Braes of Foss, the planned route will go south, to the left of a small forestry block, past a cup-marked stone, and lead to a sheepfank at about 380m as on the present track from Braes of Foss to Gleann Mor. Uphill from the fank, the route follows the line of an existing narrow track, up to where it joins the present main track at 720m. On this section a narrow stalker-style path will be sensitively created to blend into the terrain. At the time of writing no date had been set for this work. For the latest information see the John Muir Trust Web site at W www.jmt.org.

The current (described) trail is initially boggy and grassy, and then gives way to an uneven sea of quartzite rocks, progressively more awkward to cross on the long upper slope. The large cairns are helpful on the descent and when foggy. The all-encompassing views are especially fine in summer when the setting sun makes the Highlands glow in the west.

PLANNING

Be prepared for snowy winter conditions. Winter walking is feasible and possibly more pleasant when the boggy and rocky trail is snow-covered. Schiehallion's isolated position attracts bad weather quickly and strong winds on the upper ridge are common. Bring water for the entire outing.

Information Sources

The John Muir Trust has installed toilets and information panels at the trailhead. The Tay Forest Park runs the Queen's View Centre (☎ 01796-473123) – the magnificent 'view' is of Schiehallion – located on the east end of Loch Tummel, 7mi from Pitlochry on the B8019.

Birth of Contour Maps

Contour lines, the bread and butter of map-crafting, were indirectly born due to Schiehallion, its famous symmetry and a 1774 attempt to calculate the earth's mass. Applying Isaac Newton's theory of the universal gravitational constant, Astronomer Royal Nevil Maskelyne set up observatories on the north and south sides of the mountain 'to measure by how much plumblines would be pulled out of the vertical and towards the mountain by gravitational force due to its mass'. At the time this was known as attraction of mountains. (Now attraction of mountains isn't measured by gravitational pull but by eroded trails!) Apparently the project took a huge effort over two years, moving a 10ft telescope around the mountain in order to take highly accurate sightings off stars. The apparent and true differences in latitude were then compared. While analysing the results, mathematician Charles Hutton began to connect similar heights on the mountain with lines, developing the first concept of contours.

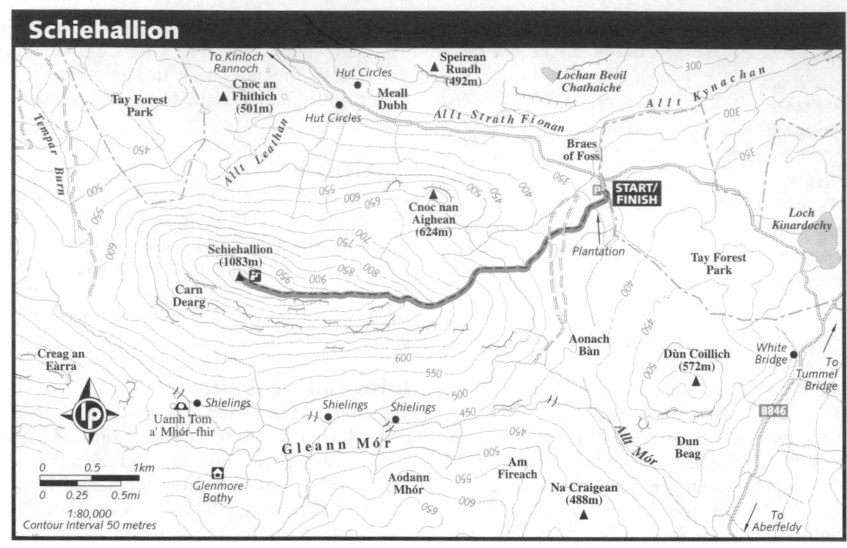

GETTING TO/FROM THE WALK

To reach the trailhead take the B846 and turn down the Braes of Foss Rd between Coshieville and Tummel Bridge. Continue 2mi on Braes of Foss Rd and turn left into the well-marked Schiehallion car park. The only feasible public transport option leaves from Kinloch Rannoch. On school days Elizabeth Yule's (☎ 01796-472290) No 895 service to Aberfeldy leaves Kinloch Rannoch Square at 7.35am and drops at the B846/Braes of Foss Rd junction at 8am. Walk 2mi to the trailhead. The return leaves Aberfeldy at 3.40pm and stops at the B846/Braes of Foss junction at 4.20pm, reaching Kinloch Rannoch at 4.45pm.

THE WALK

The straightforward ascent to the summit is clear from the beginning, largely due to unfortunate, heavy erosion. At the car park's south end, the footpath heads west, passes through a kissing gate and then edges a spruce plantation. After another kissing gate the way flattens towards the base of Schiehallion. Ignore two dirt tracks running perpendicular to the original trail and take a left-hand (south-west) wider trail. Cairns begin to mark the way. In 10 minutes, after a particularly boggy zone, the major uphill section begins along a wide dirt and stone trail that runs wet after rain. Continue ascending 1mi to a three-pronged fork, which is halfway up; the left is very boggy and eroded, the centre (best option) rocky and least eroded, and the right first gently ascends and then turns steep. Once on the ridge crest you'll notice an abundance of rose and white quartz. Ascend continuously and awkwardly, about 1.5mi to the pointed summit. The trail disappears below the rocks but cairns guide the way. Enjoy the 360 degree view from the numerous windbreaks. Return the same way.

Other Walks

ISLE OF ARRAN

Glen Rosa to Lochranza

The extremely rugged ridge on the western side of Glen Rosa and its extension from Cir Mhòr via Caisteal Abhail towards the north coast offers as fine a ridge walk as you'll find anywhere in Britain. Although it looks impossible from below, there are miraculous ways around those crags and peaks, which only experienced rock climbers can traverse. The views all along are tremendous, especially westward. The 11mi (18km) walk includes 1360m of climbing, much of which is precipitous and rocky; allow at least seven hours. The recommended map is Harvey's 1:40,000 *Arran*, which includes coverage of this walk at 1:25,000.

The approach to Glen Rosa is described under the Goatfell walk on page 151. Walk up Glen Rosa to the bridge over Garbh Allt; turn left from the main path and follow clear paths up through two exclosures to the foot of the ridge. The climb to the first summit, Beinn Nuis (792m), is steep and unrelenting. Descending from there, keep west of large bluffs down to a grassy ridge. On the way up to Beinn Tarsuinn (826m) look out for the striking rock formation known as the Old Man of Tarsuinn. On the next steep descent, keep to the left, on grass as much as possible, and continue to Bealach an Fhir-bhogha. Here you leave the ridge to traverse below A' Chir's soaring cliffs on its western side; return to the ridge about 150m above the gap overlooking Coire Buidhe. Cir Mhòr (799m) can easily be bypassed, but is worth the effort for an eagle's-eye view of Goatfell. Next, Caisteal Abhail (859m) is easy, up grass and small rocks. The more northerly of two summit tors is the higher, and accessible from the north. A path continues northwest from here down a ridge but soon fades. Where the ridge turns northward then broadens, head north-north-west and down into Gleann Easain Biorach. The path on the western side of the burn is very boggy between Allt Dubh and the next unnamed stream northward, but the last stretch, through a small gorge to the main road on the edge of Lochranza, is much drier.

ISLE OF JURA

Jura is a magnificently wild and lonely island, the wildness of its uplands only matched on the Isle of Rum and on Harris in the Western Isles. Fewer than 200 people live here, most in the southern corner – the rest of the island, 27.5mi (44km) by about 8mi (12km), is uninhabited and unspoiled.

In Craighouse you'll find the excellent ***Jura Hotel*** *(☎ 01496-820243)*. To reach Jura catch the CalMac (☎ 01475-650100) ferry from Kennacraig to Port Askaig on the Isle of Islay then the small Western Ferries (☎ 01496-840681) boat to Feolin. From there a bus goes to Craighouse and north to Inverlussa twice daily, Monday to Saturday.

The OS Landranger 1:50,000 map No 61 *(Jura & Colonsay)* is the one to have. Scottish Mountaineering Club's guide *The Islands of Scotland including Skye* by DJ Fabian, GE Little & DN Williams covers the mountains with a short section on path walks. Much of the island is managed for deer stalking, so the best time for a visit would be from early May to early July.

The Paps of Jura

These three conical peaks – Beinn a' Chaolais (734m), Beinn an Oir (784m) and Beinn Shiantaich (755m) – dominate the island. A circuit of their summits provides a fairly energetic and outstandingly scenic day; the distance is 11.6mi (18.5km) with about 1500m of ascent. Allow eight hours – the going is generally rough, the hills are very steep and paths generally less well beaten than on mainland mountains. A convenient place to start is by the bridge over the Corran River, about 3mi (5km) north of Craighouse.

The West Coast

Along Jura's west coast, all 39mi (63km) of it, you'll find raised beaches, caves, rocky headlands and natural arches. To explore the full length would take a couple of weeks of rugged, self-contained walking, as isolated as any in Britain. Feolin makes a convenient starting point; the track to Glenbatrick from the east coast road (4mi north of Craighouse) is another possibility.

ISLE OF ISLAY

Although separated from Jura by the narrow Sound of Islay, this isle is remarkably different. Together, Jura and Islay can provide an extremely varied two-island walking holiday.

Larger and more settled, although much less rugged, Islay (pronounced i-lay) has opportunities for plenty of easy and medium walks – and some more demanding. The west coast has fine beaches, especially Machir and Lossit Bays, and there are numerous historic and prehistoric sites to visit, notably Finlaggan, the ancient seat of the Lords of the Isles. The highest peak, Beinn Bheigeir (491m), can be climbed via its long south-eastern ridge from near the hamlet of Ardtalla. In the far south is The Oa, a bumpy area with some fine sea cliffs. One longer walk on the east coast follows an old track to the deserted settlement of Proaig, then crosses the mountains above the Sound of Jura to Storakaig and a minor road to Ballygrant.

For further information contact the TIC at Bowmore (☎ 01496-810254, ⓔ info@isle-of-islay.com). A locally produced *Walks Booklet* describes a dozen varied walks. OS Landranger 1:50,000 map No 60 *(Islay)* is the one to take. Details of ferry services are given under Isle of Jura; the ferry also calls at Port Ellen.

ISLE OF BUTE

West Island Way

Opened in September 2000, this 'long-distance' path – the first on a Scottish island – encompasses some of the best walking the Isle of Bute has to offer. As well as a changing landscape, including coast, moors, farmland and forest, the Way showcases the island's natural attractions, geography, geology and history. It is 30mi long, the walking is easy and can be easily split into two days. The Way is signposted and navigation is straightforward using a brochure with map available locally. For more information contact the Rothesay TIC (☎ 01700-502151) or the Countryside Ranger Service (☎ 01700-503858).

AROUND LOCH TAY

Ben Vorlich & Stuc a' Chroin

South of Killin on the A84 between Lochearnhead and Callander are popular Ben Vorlich (985m) and Stuc a' Chroin (975m). Usually hiked together the easiest route leaves from Callander (north) along the road to Braelany Farm. Continue on the old right of way access between Callander and Ardvorlich to Arivurichardich. Ascend along the trail to west of Meall na h-lolaire. Head north-west, following the border fence, up the grassy ridge to Stuc a' Chroin. Continue 700m along the fence north-east to Ben Vorlich. Descend via Ben Vorlich's south-east flank to Dubh Choirein. Continue south-west then south and rejoin the ascent trail. OS Landranger 1:50,000 map No 57 *(Stirling & The Trossachs)* suffices.

Ben More & Stob Binnein

The fraternal twins Ben More (1174m) and Stob Binnein (1165m) rise off the south side of the A85 (Crianlarich-Killin), and make a great outing. From Benmore Farm, east of Crianlarich, follow the Benmore Burn south and continue to the rocky outcrop of Cragan Liatha. Climb to the south-south-east ridge of Stob Binnein, north-west of Stob Coire an Lochain (1066m), to the summit. Descend the ridge to Ben More. Taking care with Ben More's north-west corrie, descend north-west to Benmore Farm. Use OS Landranger 1:50,000 map No 51 *(Loch Tay & Glen Dochart)*.

CENTRAL SCOTLAND

OCHIL & LOMOND HILLS

The Lomond and Ochil groups rise up between the Forth and Tay valleys. The compact Lomond Hills in Fife top out at West Lomond (522m) and include East Lomond (424m) and Bishop Hill (460m). The Ochil Hills measure 18.5mi from east to west and 8mi from north to south. The highest and steepest hills are west of the A823 (Dunfermline-Crieff). OS Landranger 1:50,000 maps No 57 *(Stirling & The Trossachs)*, No 58 *(Perth & Alloa)* and No 59 *(St Andrews)* cover these hills. The A91 (Stirling-Kinross) gives access to the south side of the Ochils and the A91, A911 and the A912 encircle the Lomond Hills.

West Lomond

A easy 6mi walk leaves from the Craigmead car park on the Falkland-Leslie minor road dividing West and East Lomond. Head west on the obvious path to the summit around the mountain's right side. Loop back descending south-south-east and turn left at lovely Glen Vale towards the Harperleas Reservoir. Continue north-east to Ballo Castle and east past East Ballo Farm to the minor road. Turn left and return to the car park.

Ochil Traverse

A 9.5mi north-south traverse starts in Blackford (on the A9) and climbs up Glen of Kinpuach and down Glen Bee to Upper Glendevon Reservoir. Skirt around its west end and ascend to the saddle between Skythorn Hill and Andrew Gannel Hill. Continue south-east then south-west down Gannel Burn to Tillicoutry.

FIFE

Fife Coastal Path

Fife isn't a major walking area, however, it does have a scenic and varied coastline, much of it accessible via long-established paths. Fife Coastal Path (FCP), when completed, will incorporate these paths in a route linking the Firth of Forth in the south with the Firth of Tay in the north, a distance of 78mi (126.4km). By late 2000, the FCP had reached Crail, more than halfway to the Tay from North Queensferry on the Forth.

Fife's coastal landscape bears the imprints of its industrial and maritime heritage. Consequently, a few stretches of the FCP are better seen from the window of a bus. However, the constantly changing vistas are the highlight of the FCP – across the Firth of Forth and along the subtly indented coast. The fishing villages on the east coast – Elie, Pittenweem and Crail – are fascinating. Bird life is plentiful, common seals bask on rocks and the route passes through many fine woodlands.

With the most walker-friendly section in the north-east, North Queensferry is the place to start – saving the best to last. The distance to Crail, 44.25mi (71.3km), can be split into three days of reasonably easy walking, especially if you drive through the black spots. These are Burntisland to Kinghorn (2.5mi beside a busy road) and Buckhaven to Leven Links (4mi in industrial towns).

Contact Kirkcaldy TIC (☎ 01592-267775) for an accommodation guide and information about the FCP. It may have some or all five leaflets, each with a map and outline description, for the sections from North Queensferry to Leven Links. OS Landranger 1:50,000 maps No 59 *(St Andrews)*, No 65 *(Falkirk & Linlithgow)* and No 66 *(Edinburgh)* cover the walk.

West Highland Way

Title page: Rapidly dwindling peat bogs on isolated Rannoch Moor – crossed by the West Highland Way. Photo by Grant Dixon.

West Highland Way extends 95mi from the outskirts of Scotland's largest city to the base of its highest mountain. The route is walked by approximately 50,000 people every year, and is officially the most popular long-distance path in Scotland (and Britain). It starts in the lowlands, but the greater part is among the mountains, lochs and fast-flowing rivers of the Highlands. The route is signposted with the thistle and hexagon motif, and uses a combination of ancient ways: drove roads, along which cattle were herded; military roads, built by troops to help control the Jacobites in the 18th century; and disused railway lines.

West Highland Way

Duration	7 days
Distance	95mi (153km)
Standard	medium
Start	Milngavie
Finish	Fort William
Nearest Towns	Glasgow, Milngavie, Fort William
Public Transport	yes

Summary Scotland's most popular long-distance path, passing through a tremendous variety of landscapes. It is easy to follow but covers some rough and exposed terrain in the northern sections.

The first section of the walk is fairly easy-going as far as Rowardennan. After that, and particularly north of Bridge of Orchy, it's quite strenuous and remote; you need to be properly equipped with good boots, maps, a compass, and food and drink. There's no shelter on Rannoch Moor if the weather turns bad, which it's quite likely to do.

Most people do the walk in six or seven days, although you will need to add extra days for any diversions off the route, such as an ascent of Ben Lomond or Ben Nevis. Since the northern section is more challenging, it is generally advised to start at Milngavie. This also gives the advantage of having the sun and the prevailing wind behind you. This way you'll arrive in Fort William fit and ready to start the Great Glen Way, Scotland's fourth official long-distance path, linking Fort William and Inverness (see page 248).

If your time is limited and you just want to walk a day or two of the West Highland Way, see the Route Highlights box on page 188 for the best day walks along the route. For a seven-day walk, as described here, the most convenient places to start and end each day are:

day	from	to	distance
1	Milngavie	Drymen	12mi (19km)
2	Drymen	Rowardennan	14mi (22.5km)
3	Rowardennan	Inverarnan	14mi (22.5km)
4	Inverarnan	Tyndrum	13mi (21km)
5	Tyndrum	Kings House Hotel	19mi (30.5km)
6	Kings House Hotel	Kinlochleven	9mi (14.5km)
7	Kinlochleven	Fort William	14mi (22.5km)

PLANNING

When to Walk

The route can be walked at any time of the year. May is the most popular month, as many people try to avoid the midges, and spring and autumn can be particularly beautiful. The Conic Hill section is closed for lambing during the last two weeks in April and the first two weeks in May, and the section between the Bridge of Orchy and Fort William is often used for the annual Scottish motorcycle trials around the same time. Diversions are set up, but contact the ranger service (see Information Sources on page 176) for further details. The Way itself is unaffected by deer stalking, but detours from the track should be avoided from August to October.

What to Bring

Although the route is fully waymarked, a map and compass and the ability to use them is still recommended. You should also wear good boots and carry a full range of warm and waterproof clothing. If you plan to camp at any stage you'll also need to bring all the necessary gear. Use a good pack-liner to keep spare clothing dry.

Maps

Four OS Landranger 1:50,000 maps, No 41 *(Ben Nevis)*, No 50 *(Glen Orchy & Loch Etive)*, No 56 *(Loch Lomond & Inveraray)* and No 64 *(Glasgow)*, cover the Way, although most people find the best option is to take a purpose-designed, all-in-one route map. The excellent Harvey's *West Highland Way Map* and the cheap and cheerful Footprint *West Highland Way* are more than adequate, and also include lots of additional practical information for walkers.

Books

There are numerous guides to this famous path. Probably the best is the new and innovative *West Highland Way* from Rucksack Readers (W www.rucsacs.com). The official guide is the more expensive *West Highland Way* by Bob Aitken & Roger Smith, which comes with its own 1:50,000 OS route map.

For details of side trips from the track or as an alternative challenge for mountain-lovers, *The Highland High Way* by Heather Cannon & Paul Roper details a high-level route from Loch Lomond to Fort William. Walks suggested broadly stick to the traditional West Highland Way route and take in 23 Munros along the way.

Information Sources

For a free leaflet listing accommodation on the West Highland Way, contact the Loch Lomond Park Ranger Service (☎ 01360-870470), the Glen Nevis Countryside Ranger Service (☎ 01397-705922) or the Scottish Tourist Board (☎ 0131-332 2433). The West Highland Way Web site (W www.west-highland-way.co.uk) is also useful, offering practical information, accommodation listings and links to the ranger's email site for further queries. Copies of the free *West Highland Wayfarer* newspaper can be found at Milngavie Station or at TICs in the area.

In case of an emergency, in the Glasgow area contact Strathclyde Police on ☎ 0141-532 2000 and along the northern section of the West Highland Way call Fort William police on ☎ 01397-702361.

Permits & Regulations

Camping is only permitted on the West Highland Way in designated areas. There are several free, one-night only backpacker sites without facilities along the route, with a strict policy of no open fires. There are also restrictions on walking with dogs in certain areas – contact the information services listed for details.

Guided Walks & Baggage Services

Several companies organise walking holidays on the Way with vehicle support. C-N-Do (☎ 01786-445703, e info@cndoscotland.com) and Lomond Walking Holidays (☎ 01786-447752, e paul@milligan.force9.co.uk) are two of the larger companies.

Rather than taking a full tour, you can make the going easier for yourself by using a pack-carrying service. Travel-Lite (☎ 0141-956 6810) charges £32 to pick up your bag each morning and deliver it to your next B&B or hostel (a total of up to eight collections and deliveries).

The West Highland Way is well signposted with the thistle and hexagon motif.

Other Information

The location of accommodation towards the north of the walk means you will either have some very long or rather short days in this section. Accommodation should not be too difficult to find, although between Bridge of Orchy and Kinlochleven it's quite limited. There are numerous B&Bs and hotels along the rest of the route, as well as three SYHA hostels, several bunkhouses and some camping sites, so walking on a budget is possible. Some B&Bs, particularly those not right on the route, will send someone to meet you and drive you back next morning for a small charge. During the peak period, from May to August, you must book all accommodation in advance. A company called Easyways (☎ 01324-714132, W www.easyways.com) offers an accommodation booking service.

Banks are intermittently located along the route, although many B&Bs and hotels accept credit cards if you run out of cash.

If you only want to do part of the walk, Crianlarich, Upper Tyndrum (on the Fort William line), Lower Tyndrum (on the Oban line) and Bridge of Orchy are all well served by trains. For details contact the National Rail Enquiry Service (☎ 0845-748 4950) or ScotRail (☎ 0845-755 0033). Scottish Citylink (☎ 0870-550 5050) coaches on the Glasgow-Fort William route also stop at Crianlarich, Tyndrum and Bridge of Orchy.

In summer there are ferry services across Loch Lomond between Rowardennan and Inverbeg (☎ 01360-870273), Inversnaid and Inveruglas (☎ 01877-386223), and Ardleish and Ardlui (☎ 01301-704243). It's not necessary to use a ferry on the actual walk, but they can be useful for reaching accommodation options and transport links on the western shore of the loch.

NEAREST TOWNS

Glasgow

Many walkers will arrive in Milngavie via Glasgow. The TIC (☎ 0141-204 4400) is on George Square. See the Edinburgh & Glasgow chapter for details of facilities and accommodation in Glasgow.

Milngavie

Milngavie (pronounced mullguy) is the official start point for the walk. The town has several banks and numerous shops, although for specialist outdoor gear you're better off shopping in Glasgow.

Places to Stay & Eat Milngavie has no hostels but plenty of B&Bs, including ***Barloch Guest House*** *(☎ 0141-9561432)*, on Strathblane Rd, and ***West View Guest House*** *(☎ 0141-9565973, 1 Douglaston Gardens)*, both charge around £20. Camping is available for £2.50 at ***Bankell Farm*** *(☎ 0141-9561733)*, about 1mi from the start of the walk. The pick of places to eat in Milngavie is ***Toscana***, it is Italian-run and good for just a coffee or a full pasta meal from £5.

Getting There & Away Milngavie is 7mi north of Glasgow on the A82/A809 (exit 17 off the M8). Glasgow has excellent rail links with the rest of the country – 20 trains a day from London Euston to Glasgow Central (five hours). From Glasgow Central it's a 10-minute walk to Glasgow Queen St for trains to Milngavie (departures every half-hour). There are also frequent buses from Glasgow bus station to Milngavie, but they take twice as long as the train.

Fort William

Fort William marks the end of the West Highland Way. For details on transport connections, facilities and accommodation, see under Gateway in the Lochaber & Glen Coe chapter (page 192).

GETTING TO/FROM THE WALK

The official start of the West Highland Way is a granite obelisk (unveiled in 1992) beside the bridge over the Allander Water on Douglas St, Milngavie. However, many walkers begin their journey at Milngavie train station; bus stops are also located here and for those with their own transport the station, just off Station Rd, makes a convenient place to leave a car. To reach the obelisk from the train station, go through the underpass and up a flight of steps to the pedestrianised centre of Milngavie. Bear left at the exit of the underpass to join Douglas St, passing through a shopping precinct before reaching the Allander Water and the official start point.

THE WALK

Day 1: Milngavie to Drymen

4½–5½ hours, 12mi (19km)

From the obelisk at the official start of the route, a small sign on a nearby building indicates a turn upstream. Follow a walkway over the river and continue alongside the Allander Water, through the trees, to join good paths through Mugdock Wood. At the end of the wood you meet a road; turn left then almost immediately turn right onto a path again. The path soon becomes a vehicle track and there's a good view to your right over Craigallian Loch.

Pass a collection of holiday homes and you soon arrive at the B821. Turn left along the road and follow it for about 300m until a style leads onto another path to the right. The route skirts Dumgoyach Hill (watch out for Bronze Age standing stones to your right just before the hill) and after Dumgoyach Bridge joins a disused railway track. After about 800m you pass Glengoyne Distillery, which can be visited from April to October. Another 800m farther on you reach the ***Beech Tree Inn*** at Dumgoyne, a pub that serves food all day. The village of Killearn is 1.5mi off the route to the right – it has accommodation, shops, pubs and a post office.

The West Highland Way continues along the old railway track to Gartness. Here you join a minor road, turn left, and cross the village's attractive bridge and weir. The Way follows the road all the way to Drymen. A mile after Gartness is ***Easter Drumquhassle Farm*** *(☎ 01360-660893)*, which has B&B for £18.50. There are also places in wigwams for £7 and camping costs £4. You get your first view of Loch Lomond from here.

Pass an ugly quarry and continue along the road to a sharp left turn. Just before the bend, there's B&B at ***Gateside Lodge*** *(☎ 01360-660215)* from £17. Just after the bend, the West Highland Way leaves the road and follows a path to the right. If you're going to Drymen, continue along the road and cross the A811 to enter the village.

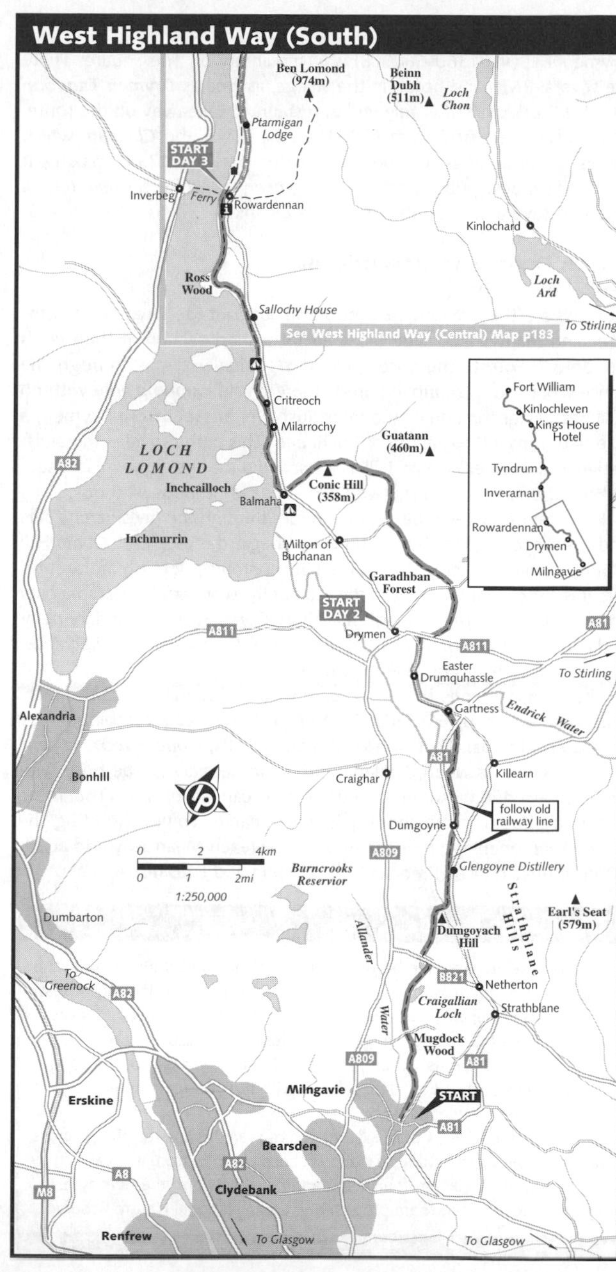
West Highland Way (South)
Ben Lomond (974m)
Beinn Dubh (511m)
Loch Chon
Ptarmigan Lodge
START DAY 3
Inverbeg
Ferry
Rowardennan
Kinlochard
Ross Wood
Loch Ard
Sallochy House
To Stirling
See West Highland Way (Central) Map p183
Critreoch
Milarrochy
Guatann (460m)
LOCH LOMOND
A82
Inchcailloch
Conic Hill (358m)
Balmaha
Inchmurrin
Milton of Buchanan
Garadhban Forest
START DAY 2
Drymen
A811
A81
Easter Drumquhassle
To Stirling
Alexandria
Gartness
Endrick Water
Bonhill
Craighar
Killearn
follow old railway line
Dumgoyne
A809
Glengoyne Distillery
Burncrooks Reservior
1:250,000
Strathblane Hills
Earl's Seat (579m)
Dumbarton
Dumgoyach Hill
Allander Water
To Greenock
B821
Netherton
Craigallian Loch
Strathblane
Mugdock Wood
Milngavie
START
Erskine
Bearsden
A8
M8
Clydebank
Renfrew
To Glasgow
To Glasgow
Fort William
Kinlochleven
Kings House Hotel
Tyndrum
Inverarnan
Rowardennan
Drymen
Milngavie

Drymen

Drymen TIC (☎ 01360-660068) is in the library on The Square. There are several B&Bs and hotels in the village, as well as ***Drymen Tandoori*** *(☎ 01360-660099)*, the only Indian restaurant/takeaway on the route, which also offers B&B from £20. The best pub is the ***Clachan***, which serves a good range of food and dates back to 1734, making it Scotland's oldest pub. There's also a ***grocery shop*** for self-caterers, a ***cafe*** and several more pubs, as well as a bank.

Day 2: Drymen to Rowardennan

5–6½ hours, 14mi (22.5km)

From where the Way crosses the A811 just outside Drymen, it turns right and follows alongside the road for a short section. It then veers left onto a Forest Enterprise track and gradually climbs through the dense woods to Garadhban Forest (there is wild ***camping*** here with no facilities). Near the end of the trees, just over an hour from Drymen, a side path runs left to Milton of Buchanan. This path provides the alternative route when Conic Hill is closed during the lambing season. Milton of Buchanan boasts two B&Bs, but has no pubs or shops.

For most of the year the Way continues through the trees, over a stile and onto open moor. Cross a burn and begin the ascent of **Conic Hill** (358m), a climb of about 200m. The path contours just north of the summit. It is a short detour to reach the top but the wonderful panorama over Loch Lomond is certainly worth the effort. Conic Hill is a boundary point and a landmark for walkers; from here onwards you're in the Highlands, see the boxed text 'The Great Divide'.

The path descends through a pine wood to Balmaha and the loch. ***Oak Tree Inn*** *(☎ 01360-870357)* offers B&B from £20, camping for £5 and food in the bar. There are several other B&Bs, a ***pub***, ***shop*** and ***cafe***.

The section between Balmaha and Rowardennan can be busy with day-trippers during summer and solitude can be elusive. The route begins by hugging the shore, passing a marker commemorating the Way's 1980 opening. In under an hour you reach Milarrochy and about 800m farther on is Critreoch, with camping and B&B respectively.

Loch Lomond, the largest body of fresh water in Britain and an area of grea beauty, accompanies the West Highland Way on Da 2 and 3.

The Great Divide

The obvious dividing line between the Highlands and the lowlands, the Highland Boundary Fault extends from Stonehaven, on the east coast, in an unwavering line south-westward to Helensburgh, west of Glasgow on the shore of Gare Loch. In geological terms it is a fault line or a weakness in the earth's crust where, about 600 million years ago, the tough, ancient rocks of the Highlands collided with the younger, softer rocks of the central belt lowlands.

Climb to the top of Conic Hill and you can see this line marching across the landscape via the string of islands in Loch Lomond from Inchcailloch to Inchmurrin. Inchcailloch, four neighbouring islands and the nearby estuary of the River Endrick are protected within a National Nature Reserve.

CHRIS MELLOR

Loch Lomond

Loch Lomond is the largest body of fresh water in Britain, covering 27 sq mi. It is also an area of great beauty (and a large number of visitors during the summer). Loch Lomond and the nearby Trossachs are scheduled to become Scotland's first national park in 2002 (see Arrochar, Lomond & Trossachs in the Central Scotland chapter).

The loch is believed to have been gouged by a glacier flowing from the expanse of ice that covered Rannoch Moor during the last ice age. At its deepest, just south of Inversnaid, the water is 190m deep. The loch lies across the boundary between the lowlands and the Highlands, and two distinct environments can be seen along its shores.

The southern part of the loch is bordered by relatively flat, arable land, and is wide, shallow and dotted with islands, some of which host early Christian sites. This part of the loch freezes over during severe winters, and islanders have managed to access the mainland by foot on several occasions over the last 50 years.

The northern end of the loch is deeper, generally less than 1mi wide, and is enclosed by steep hillsides. It is unknown for this part of the loch to freeze. The slopes at the loch shore are covered by Scotland's largest remnant of oak forest mixed with newer conifer plantations. The plantations are currently in the process of being felled, to be replaced by native broad-leaved trees as part of a forestry regeneration program.

The West Highland Way follows the eastern shores of the loch for 19mi. Botanical studies have found that a quarter of all known British flowering plants and ferns can be found in this area, and this section is undeniably a highlight of the walk.

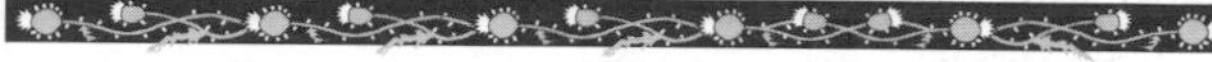

The path now dives into a dark forest, before emerging to follow the road for about 1mi. Just after you join the road is the popular Forest Enterprise's ***Cashel Camping and Caravan Site*** *(☎ 01360-870234)*; the average cost per 'unit' (person and tent) is £4.40. After Sallochy House the Way returns to the trees and climbs through **Ross Wood** to Rowardennan. This oak forest is some of the finest remaining natural woodland in Scotland.

Rowardennan

Rowardennan is really just the ***Rowardennan Hotel*** *(☎ 01360-870273)*, which serves bar meals and does B&B from £35. A few hundred metres farther on, near a large car park, a path leads up to the summit of Ben Lomond (974m), a 7mi return trip. See Ben Lomond on page 159.

A new visitor centre (☎ 01360-870429) has opened at the end of the sealed road in Rowardennan. It has interpretive displays covering the proposed Loch Lomond & the Trossachs National Park and a park ranger is based here. Facilities include toilets and luggage lockers for walkers wishing to ditch large packs and make the climb up Ben Lomond.

Rowardennan SYHA Hostel *(☎ 01360-870259)* is 20 minutes beyond the hotel and beds cost £9.25. Two hundred metres to the right of the hostel entrance is a wild ***camping site*** (no facilities).

Day 3: Rowardennan to Inverarnan

6–7½ hours, 14mi (22.5km)

From Rowardennan follow the unsurfaced road that runs parallel to the loch shore. After private Ptarmigan Lodge an alternative path branches left and takes a low route through the trees, but this path is eroded and heavy going. The official route offers much easier walking and follows the track higher up the hillside. From both routes you can reach ***Rowchoish Bothy***, a stone shelter with a fireplace, a sleeping platform and a dirt floor. It's free and always open.

About 400m after the bothy the low route meets the high route, and soon afterwards the forestry track becomes a path again. The path now dives down to the loch side and there's some difficult walking along to Inversnaid. Shortly before the hotel the path crosses Snaid Burn just above the impressive **Inversnaid Falls**. ***Inversnaid Hotel*** *(☎ 01877-386223)* has 109 rooms at £30 per person. Four hundred metres farther north is the Inversnaid Boathouse, where wild ***camping*** is permitted.

From Inversnaid to the foot of Glen Falloch is one of the most difficult parts of the route, although recent work on the path has improved things greatly. The path goes up and down through wooded slopes (oak and birch) and can involve some scrambling. The loch is now much narrower and the valley deeper. The path passes the outlaw Rob Roy's cave (see the boxed text 'Rob Roy'), although there's little to see. There's basic accommodation at ***Doune Bothy*** (with the same facilities as Rowchoish Bothy). Almost 1mi beyond the bothy, at Ardleish, there's a landing stage

Rob Roy

Robert MacGregor (1671–1734) was given the nickname Roy from the Gaelic *ruadh*, meaning 'red', thanks to his shock of red hair. Born into the MacGregor clan, already notorious for violent lawlessness and rebellion, he was a cattle trader who made occasional raids to the lowlands to rustle cattle. He owned much of the land around Inversnaid and had effectively become head of the clan soon after the age of 30.

He went bankrupt in 1711 when his head drover absconded with his annual profits, and he was subsequently betrayed and outlawed by the Duke of Montrose, a former ally. His home was burnt and his family evicted, and he took to the hills to begin a campaign of revenge against the Duke. Tales of his generosity to the poor and daring escapes from the clutches of the law earned him a reputation as a Scottish Robin Hood, and legends and romantic stories have since ensured him a place among the characters of popular Scottish history. The Hollywood film *Rob Roy* (largely shot in Glen Nevis) is a contemporary addition to the legend.

A natural rock cell in a crag about 1.5mi north of Ptarmigan Lodge is given the distinction of being Rob Roy's Prison, where he is said to have kept kidnap victims. The cave where he is supposed to have hidden from the Duke's men is north of Inversnaid. Both sites can be visited from the West Highland Way, but there is little of real interest to see, and tales of his use of them can be attributed more to mythology than to hard fact.

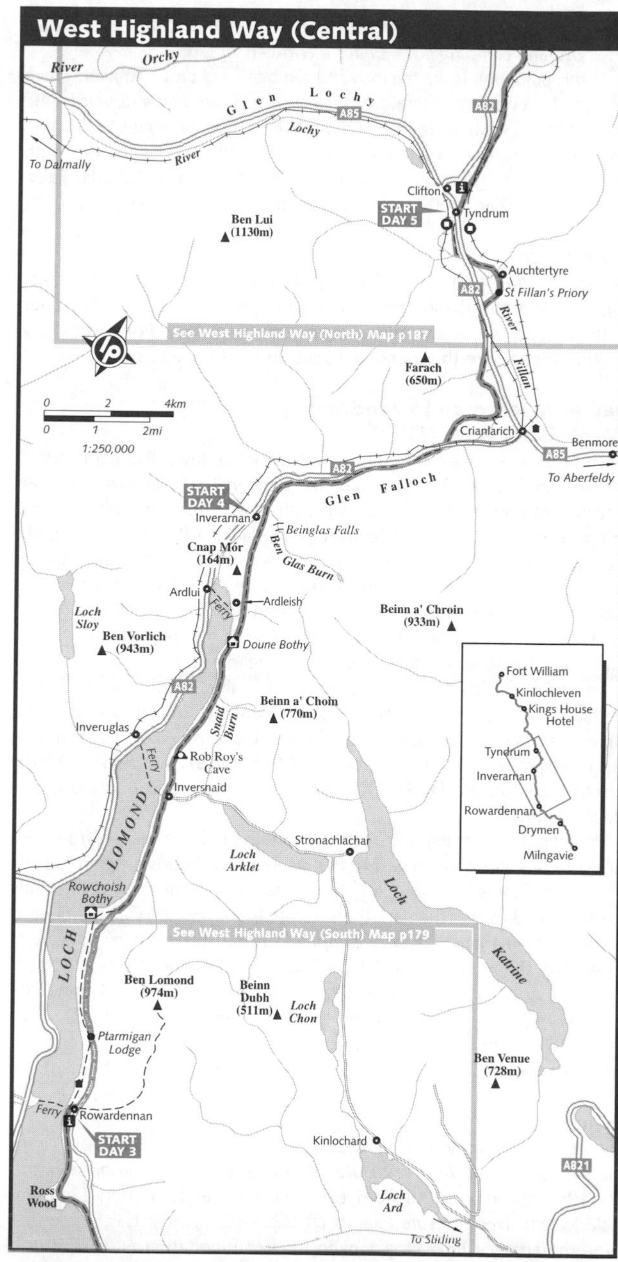
West Highland Way (Central)
River Orchy
Glen Lochy
A85
A82
Lochy
River
To Dalmally
Clifton
START DAY 5
Tyndrum
Ben Lui (1130m)
Auchtertyre
A82
St Fillan's Priory
River Fillan
See West Highland Way (North) Map p187
Farach (650m)
0 2 4km
0 1 2mi
1:250,000
Crianlarich
Benmore
A85
To Aberfeldy
A82
Glen Falloch
START DAY 4
Inverarnan
Beinglas Falls
Ben Glas Burn
Cnap Mór (164m)
Ardlui
Ferry
Ardleish
Beinn a' Chroin (933m)
Loch Sloy
Ben Vorlich (943m)
Doune Bothy
A82
Beinn a' Choin (770m)
Snaid Burn
Inveruglas
Ferry
Rob Roy's Cave
Inversnaid
Fort William
Kinlochleven
Kings House Hotel
Tyndrum
Inverarnan
Rowardennan
Drymen
Milngavie
LOMOND
Stronachlachar
Loch Arklet
Loch Katrine
Rowchoish Bothy
See West Highland Way (South) Map p179
LOCH
Ben Lomond (974m)
Beinn Dubh (511m)
Loch Chon
Ptarmigan Lodge
Ben Venue (728m)
Ferry
Rowardennan
START DAY 3
Kinlochard
A821
Ross Wood
Loch Ard
To Stirling

used by the ferry across to ***Ardlui Hotel*** *(☎ 01301-704243)*, where B&B costs £30 and camping costs £7 for a two-person tent.

At this point you leave the loch and climb to a col on **Cnap Mór**. There are good views from here on a clear day, both north towards the Highlands and south over Loch Lomond. The path now begins to descend towards Inverarnan. Shortly before arriving at the village, the path crosses the Ben Glas Burn. Just upstream is the spectacular **Beinglas Falls**, a cascade of 300m (1000ft) that is very impressive after heavy rain.

Inverarnan

Beinglas Farm *(☎ 01301-704281)*, just north of Ben Glas Burn, offers wigwam accommodation for £8 and camping for £4. Across the river in the village, there are several places offering B&B. For a meal try ***Stagger Inn***, where the traditional Scottish food is excellent.

Day 4: Inverarnan to Tyndrum

4½–5½ hours, 13mi (21km)

From Inverarnan the route follows the attractive River Falloch most of the way to Crianlarich. At the beginning the valley is narrow, the river is turbulent and the banks are lined with trees. Soon the valley begins to open out and the river becomes more placid. After 3.5mi the path crosses the river and continues along the west bank. Half a mile farther on it leaves the river and climbs through a small tunnel under the railway line, and then crosses under the A82 to join an old military road.

This track climbs out of Glen Falloch towards the trees ahead. At the stile into the forest there's a side path leading down to the right towards Crianlarich; this is the approximate halfway point on the West Highland Way. There's no need to go to Crianlarich but the village does have a railway station, post office, shops, a bank (no ATM) and numerous places to stay and eat. Crianlarich ***SYHA Hostel*** *(☎ 01838-300260)* costs £9.25. The ***Rod & Reel*** has a good restaurant and is also a great place to drink.

Back on the West Highland Way, the route climbs to the left from the stile, offering good views east to Ben More. It continues on good paths through the trees for about 2mi then crosses under the railway line and over the road again. The path then crosses the River Fillan via a wooden bridge, where there is a wild ***camping site*** (no facilities) on the west bank. Pass the remains of St Fillan's Priory, turn left and follow the track to reach ***Auchtertyre Farm*** *(☎ 01838-400251)* in about 20 minutes. There's wigwam accommodation from £9 and camping for £3. The route crosses the A82 once more, passes several minor roads and, in under an hour, reaches Tyndrum, formerly a lead-mining settlement.

Tyndrum

This village is strung out along the A82. The TIC (☎ 01838-400246) is in the car park of the ***Invervey Hotel*** *(☎ 01838-400219)*. The hotel has a good bar and offers B&B from £25. Other places to stay in Tyndrum include ***Pine Trees Leisure Park*** *(☎ 01838-400243)*, which is beside the river and charges £8.50 for bunkhouse accommodation and £3.50 for

Cattle Droving

Tyndrum, meaning 'the house of the ridge', was a major stop-off point for the cattle droving trade during the 18th and 19th centuries. Herds of small, black, Highland cattle were traditionally driven past this point on their way to the 'trysts' (cattle markets) at Crieff or Falkirk, north-east of Glasgow. The animals and their drovers had often trekked hundreds of difficult miles to this point, sometimes swimming across tidal narrows to get to the mainland in the first place (as from the Isle of Skye), and then crossing mountain passes and traversing remote glens. The Road to the Isles (see the Lochaber & Glen Coe chapter) is one famous route used by the drovers on their way from the north to Tyndrum.

Tyndrum itself was something of a marker post and a service station for the cattle trains. It represented the point where the soft, open ground of the uplands was left behind, to be replaced by the gravel roads and tracks of the lowlands. In later years a smithy shod the beasts at this point, to protect their feet from the change of terrain. An inn also offered respite for the drovers and there are many tales of drunken celebrations that emanate from this time.

For both the cattle and the men, the trysts were far from the end of the journey. Cattle often continued on foot with their new owners to cross the border into England and the drovers were faced with the long, return journey home. It is no wonder that the annual drives were the basis of whole lifestyles, and the cattle rustling, thieving and celebrations that accompanied the marches are still notorious today.

camping. In the village there's also a train station, an outdoor equipment shop, a ***coffee shop*** and a taxi/pack-carrying service (☎ 01838-400279).

Day 5: Tyndrum to Kings House Hotel

6½–8 hours, 19mi (30.5km)

From Tyndrum the path runs parallel to the A82 and the railway line, crossing the train tracks twice before rejoining the old military road. This is easy, clear walking with lovely views. Three miles from Tyndrum, you cross a burn at the foot of Beinn Dòrain (1074m), the 'hill' that dominates this section of the path. Just before the bridge there's B&B on the left at ***Auch Farm*** *(☎ 01838-400233)* for £14.

From here it's just under 3mi to Bridge of Orchy. The path climbs gradually to pass the entrance to Glen Orchy, crossing the railway again. This is the beginning of the really mountainous scenery. Bridge of Orchy is not much more than a railway station, a post office and a church. The ***Bridge of Orchy Hotel*** *(☎ 01838-400208)* is the village's dominant feature. B&B costs from £49 and there's bunkhouse accommodation for £9. There are no cooking facilities but the bar serves good food. A self-catering bunkhouse, the ***West Highland Way Sleeper*** *(☎ 01855-831381)*, in the old station building, charges around £8. There is a free ***camping site*** (no facilities) just over the bridge on the right.

Cross the old bridge (built in 1750) and climb through the trees onto moorland, from where there are superb views across to Rannoch Moor.

Rannoch Moor

Barren, bleak, desolate and inhospitable: all describe the wild expanse of Rannoch Moor. This is the largest moor in Britain and stretches for over 50 sq mi. The West Highland Way merely skirts the perimeter of the moor but is enough to offer an impression of the powerful atmosphere of the place.

The moor is a triangular plateau of blanket bog framed by mountains. It has a base of grey granite about 400 million years old and owes its present form to the last glacial period, when it served as a gathering area for ice. Since then the area's exposure and high rainfall have ensured that the poorly drained ground has become covered in bog and lochans. The moor holds so much water that it has been said it is possible to swim from one side to the other during summer and to skate across in winter!

The impression that the walker receives when skirting the moor is highly dependent on the season and weather conditions. On a calm day, with the blue sky reflected in the lochans, and curlew, golden plover and snipe darting among the tussocks, the sense of open space is inspiring. In poor weather, especially if low cloud, driving wind and rain conspire, the less endearing descriptions of the moor can be appreciated!

The path here has been upgraded and is now very good. It winds down to the secluded ***Inveroran Hotel*** *(☎ 01838-400220)*, where there's B&B for £29. Another free ***camping site*** (no facilities) can be found beside a stone bridge 400m west of the hotel.

The Way follows the road around a bend before the sealed road turns into a track. It then climbs gently past three tree plantations and out onto **Rannoch Moor** (see the boxed text 'Rannoch Moor'). There's no shelter for about 7mi, and Bà Bridge, about 3mi after the tree plantations, is the only real marker point. It can be very wild and windy up here, and there's a real sense of isolation. A cairn marks the summit at 445m and from here there's a wonderful view down into Glen Coe.

As the path descends from the moor to join the road again, you can see the chairlift of the Glen Coe Ski Centre to the left. There's a ***cafe*** and skiing museum at the base station, about 500m off the West Highland Way. ***Kings House Hotel*** *(☎ 01855-851259)* is just over 1mi ahead across the A82. Dating from the 17th century, the building was used as barracks for George III's troops – hence the name. There's accommodation from £24, but breakfast costs an extra £7. There's a restaurant and popular climbers' bar at the back. Free ***camping*** (no facilities) is available just behind the hotel.

If you can't get a bed here you may want to consider taking a bus to Glencoe (11mi west) where there's a wider selection of accommodation. See Glencoe on page 205 for details.

Isolation – West Highlan
Way on Rannoch Moor.

Day 6: Kings House Hotel to Kinlochleven

3–4 hours, 9mi (14.5km)

From Kings House Hotel the route goes along an old military road and then follows alongside the A82 to a parking area at Altnafeadh. This is a

West Highland Way (North)
To Mallaig
To Inverness
A830
West Highland Railway
Spean Bridge
A861
FINISH
Fort William
Loch Linnhe
A82
Glen Nevis
River Nevis
Dùn Deardail
Ben Nevis (1344m)
Aonach Mór (1221m)
Beinn na Gucaig (617m)
Blàr a' Chaorainn
Aonach Beag (1234m)
Stob Choire Easain (1116m)
Ballachulish
Sgurr a' Mhaim (1097m)
Tigh-na-sleubhaich
Allt Nathrach
Binnein Mór (1127m)
Loch Leven
START DAY 7
Ballachulish
Glencoe
Kinlochleven
Pap of Glencoe (740m)
Glas Bheinn (788m)
River Leven
Glen Coe
Bidean nam Bian (1148m)
Blackwater Reservoir
Devil's Staircase
Buachaille Etive Beag
Altnafeadh
START DAY 6
Buachaille Etive Mór
Meall nan Ruadhag (646m)
Glen Etive
River Etive
Kings House Hotel
Stob Dubh (884m)
Loch Etive
Loch Laidon
Rannoch Moor
Stob Ghabhar (1086m)
River Bà
Bà Bridge
Loch Bà
Loch Dochard
0 3 6km
0 2 4mi
1:350,000
Loch Tulla
Water of Tulla
Inveroran Hotel
A82
Beinn Achaladair (1038m)
Bridge of Orchy
Glen Orchy
River Orchy
Beinn Dòrain (1074m)
See West Highland Way (Central) Map p183
Auch
Loch Lyon
River Orchy
Glen Lochy
A85
River Lochy
Ben Lui (1130m)
Clifton
Tyndrum
START DAY 5
Auchtertyre
A82
Fort William
Kinlochleven
Kings House Hotel
Tyndrum
Inverarnan
Rowardennan
Drymen
Milngavie

BRYN THOMAS

Route Highlights

If you want to get a taste of the West Highland Way without attempting the entire path, one of the best sections is between the Kings House Hotel and Glen Nevis. It is possible to complete these two sections in a single day, although the distance adds up to a fairly lengthy 19mi (30.5km). Paths are good all the way and you should allow about nine hours for the walk.

Start at the Altnafeadh car park on the A82, 3mi south of Kings House Hotel. Citylink (☎ 0870-550 5050) buses from Glasgow and Fort William both pass the car park, and the driver will stop if you request it in advance. At the end of the day you can either stay at Glen Nevis, or catch one of the frequent buses to Fort William. This service is run by Highland Country Buses (☎ 01463-222244) and there are 11 services a day (except Sunday).

One of the other highlights of the route is walking along the wooded shores of Loch Lomond, passing several spectacular waterfalls along the way. The section from Inversnaid to Inverarnan covers 7mi (11km) and can be easily completed as a day walk. A passenger ferry from Inveruglas on the western side of the loch (☎ 01877-386223) will take you across the water to the start of the section. Both Inveruglas and Inverarnan, at the end of this section, are request stops on the Glasgow–Fort William bus service run by Citylink.

wonderful vantage point from which to appreciate the mountainous scenery of Glen Coe. The conical mountain to your left is Buachaille Etive Mór – see page 206 for details of the ascent.

From here the Way turns right, leaving the road to begin a steep, zigzagging climb up **Devil's Staircase**. The cairn at the top is at 548m and marks the highest point of the Way. The views are stunning, especially on a clear day, and you may be able to see Ben Nevis. The path now winds slowly down towards Kinlochleven, hidden below in the glen. As you descend you join the Blackwater Reservoir access track, and meet the pipes that pump water from there down to the town's hydroelectric power station. It's not a particularly pretty sight but was essential for the now defunct aluminium smelter, the original reason for the town's existence.

Kinlochleven

Kinlochleven offers a return to 'civilisation': with a bank (open Thursday only, no ATM), shops, pubs, restaurants and plenty of accommodation. Stay on the west bank of the river as you enter the town and the first accommodation you reach is the ***Blackwater Hostel*** *(☎ 01855-831253)*. Beds cost from £10 and camping is £4. The ***Tailrace Inn*** *(☎ 01855-831777)*, on Riverside Rd, offers B&B for £23 and there's good pub grub served all day. At the north end of the village, just where the path leaves the road again, is ***Macdonald Hotel and Lochside Campsite*** *(☎ 01855-831539)*, charging from £24 for B&B and £4 for camping.

An isolated farmhouse dwarfed by the 'hills' of Glen Coe.

GRANT DIXON

Day 7: Kinlochleven to Fort William

5½–7 hours, 14mi (22.5km)

From Kinlochleven follow the road north out of town. The route leaves the road to the right, just opposite the school. The path climbs through woodland, crosses over a lane and emerges onto an old military road. At an altitude of about 250m you can see far down the wide glen ahead, which is enclosed on both sides by mountains. The track that you are following runs right up through the middle of the valley. The highest point is at 335m, which comes shortly before you reach the ruins of several old farm buildings at Tigh-na-sleubhaich. From here the path continues gently downhill to enter Forest Enterprise plantations 2mi farther on.

Walk through the plantation for 1mi to emerge at Blàr a' Chaorainn, which is nothing more than a bench, but the information panel with Fort William bus and train timetables could be useful. The path then goes through some more plantations and there are several steep descents to cross streams. Occasionally there are breaks in the trees with fine views of Ben Nevis. At the end of the forest a sign directs you to **Dùn Deardail**, an Iron Age fort with walls that have been partly vitrified (turned to glass) by fire. The fort is a short detour from the path.

Shortly after the fort cross another stile and follow the Forest Enterprise track down towards Glen Nevis. Across the valley the huge bulk of Ben Nevis fills your vision. A side track leads down to the village of Glen Nevis. There are several accommodation options here and this would be a good base if you wanted to finish your walk with an ascent of 'The Ben'. See the Ben Nevis walk descriptions on pages 192 and 195.

Continue along the path if you're heading for Fort William, passing a small graveyard just before you meet the road running through Glen Nevis. Turn left here and, soon after, there's a large visitor centre on the right. Continue along the roadside down into Fort William. The West Highland Way ends, like many other long-distance paths, with a bit of an anticlimax; just a sign by the busy but rather anonymous road junction on the edge of town. Thankfully Fort William has enough restaurants and bars for you to go on and celebrate your arrival in style. See Gateway on page 192 for details.

A Scottish Odyssey

Combine Scotland's most popular long-distance path with the country's newest long-distance walk, throw in Britain's highest mountain, a famous glen and an infamous loch, along with some magnificent scenery, a slice of history and a touch of mystery, and you have a Scottish odyssey.

The West Highland Way links Scotland's largest city, Glasgow, with Fort William at the base of Ben Nevis, a distance of 95mi, while the Great Glen Way links Fort William, via the Great Glen, with Inverness on the shores of the Moray Firth, a 70mi walk – together they offer the walker a unique opportunity to experience Scotland.

See the Great Glen Way description, from Inverness to Fort William, on page 248.

Lochaber & Glen Coe

Lochaber stretches from the eastern end of the Ben Nevis range as far as Ardnamurchan on the west coast. Its northern extent is marked by Fort Augustus and the southern boundary by Lochaline. Although Lochaber includes Glen Coe, this famous glen has been given a separate section within this chapter to reflect the concentration of classic walks there. Together, Lochaber and Glen Coe offer walkers some of the most spectacular mountain scenery in Scotland. If there is a Mecca for walkers visiting Scotland, this is probably it. The region also boasts a certain convenience and accessibility not found in many of the country's other mountain areas. This, coupled with the quality of the landscape, has led to the region becoming incredibly popular with outdoor enthusiasts. It is rare to have the mountains to yourself for the day so, if you're searching for a wilderness experience, you would be better off heading farther north. Nonetheless, this region is one of superlatives and a visit is a must for any walker, if only to climb Ben Nevis – Britain's highest mountain.

Highlights

GARETH McCORMACK

Looking across The Mamores from the top of Scotland (and Britain), Ben Nevis.

- Standing on top of Ben Nevis, Britain's highest mountain
- Getting the adrenaline pumping on the exposed scramble along the Aonach Eagach ridge
- Exploring the hidden beauty of Nevis gorge and Steall Meadows on The Mamores and Road to the Isles walks
- Passing through the Lost Valley on the way to the lofty ridge of Bidean nam Bian

NATURAL HISTORY

The 'hills' of Lochaber and Glen Coe are the worn-down roots of a great mountain chain that once included the Appalachian mountains of North America. The rocks that made up the chain were created some 600 million years ago; it was only 60 million years ago that the ancient land mass split apart and moved across the planet.

Today the region's mountains are home to a wide variety of plants and animals. The old Caledonian forest, which once covered much of the area, has largely disappeared, except for a few isolated pockets. Moorland grasses, heather and ling are now dominant up to around 600m. Towards the summits, a wide variety of flora more commonly associated with arctic and alpine regions can be found. Ravens and buzzards are the most commonly sighted birds.

CLIMATE

The Lochaber and Glen Coe region is one of the wettest areas in Scotland, with an average rainfall of 200cm in Fort William. This figure increases to more than 400cm on the summit of Ben Nevis. Down low, the climate can be mild due to the proximity of the sea but conditions become increasingly severe with altitude; high winds and low cloud are common on the summits. Some years patches of snow survive on the region's higher peaks until late into the summer. The steepness of the glens can cause frequent temperature inversions, with fog and hard frosts affecting the valley floors.

December and January are the wettest and coldest months (with average daily maximums of 5°C or 6°C), while May is the driest and July the warmest month (average daily maximum of 16°C). Surprisingly, August can see as much rainfall as February!

> **Warning**
>
> Police have reported an alarming increase in the number of thefts from parking areas in the Lochaber and Glen Coe area. Police notices are posted at several of the most popular access spots, but the general advice if you are leaving a car is to ensure that all belongings are hidden and you take valuables such as cameras and wallets with you.

INFORMATION

Maps & Books

OS Travelmaster 1:250,000 map No 3 *(Western Scotland)* provides an overview of the region. The OS Pathfinder guide *Fort William and Glen Coe* details a range of walks in the area, with several easier options. *Ben Nevis and Glen Coe* by Chris Townsend also has a good selection of routes. Alternatively, for mountain enthusiast there's *20 Hill Walks; Glen Coe and Lochaber* by Ruaridh Pringle.

Information Sources

The Highlands of Scotland Tourist Board (☎ 01997-421160, W www.host.co.uk) can help with accommodation and planning.

The mountain weather forecast for the western Highlands is available on ☎ 09068-500441 or fax 09060-100405.

Highland Council publishes a set of four comprehensive transport guides, of which *South Highland* covers the area in this chapter; available from local TICs.

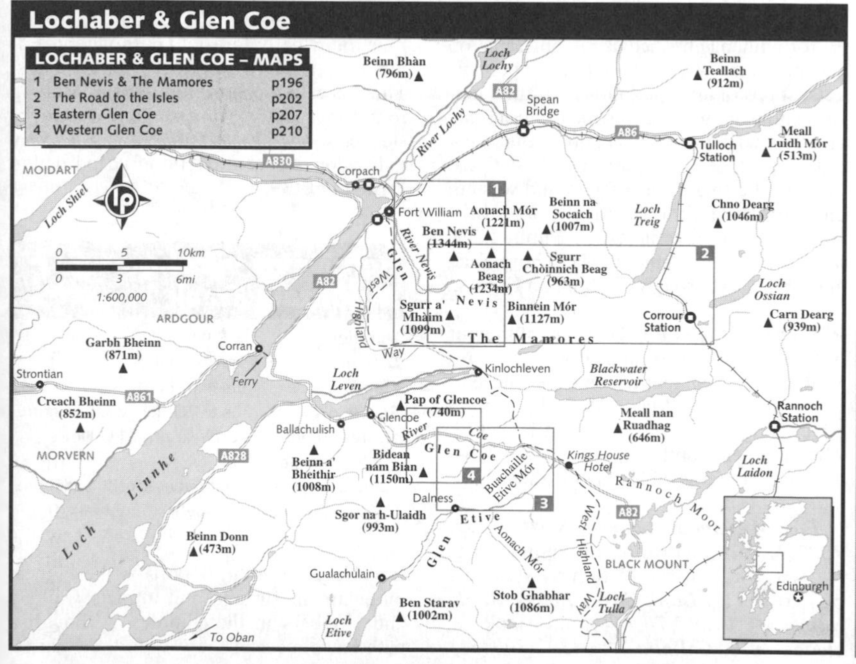

Don't forget about the 'Let Someone Know Before You Go' form, available from **W** www.northern.police.uk. In case of an emergency, call Fort William police station on ☎ 01397-702361.

Guided Walks

Mountain Craft (☎ 01397-722213), Alan Kimber (☎ 01397-700451, **e** mountain@guide.u-net.com) and Glencoe Mountain Sport (☎ 01855-811472, **W** www.glencoe-mountain-sport.co.uk) all offer professional mountain guide services for the Lochaber and Glen Coe area.

GATEWAY
Fort William

Fort William, the town at the heart of Lochaber, was originally established as a garrison for the king's troops during the 17th century. Separated from Loch Linnhe by a bypass, it has lost any charm it may once have had to modern development.

Information The TIC (☎ 01397-703781, **e** fortwilliam@host.co.uk) is on Cameron Square, in the centre of High St. Supermarkets, shops of all descriptions, leisure facilities and mainline train and bus stations can all be found in the town. Outdoor equipment outlets include Nevisport and West Coast Outdoor Leisure at the eastern and western ends of High St respectively, and Ellis Brigham near the train station. Public Internet access is available at The Thing King and The Maryborough Inn, both on High St.

Places to Stay & Eat There are numerous hotels, guesthouses and B&Bs in Fort William, and competition means that bargains can be had. Many B&Bs have signs advertising their rooms for as little as £13. The summer months are very busy, however, and it is advisable to book ahead to be sure of a bed.

Fort William Backpacker's *(☎ 01397-700711)*, on Alma Rd, is very popular and is a short walk from the railway station; a bed costs £11. ***Bank Street Lodge Bunkhouse*** *(☎ 01397-700070)*, on Bank St, charges £10. ***Calluna*** *(☎ 01397-700451)*, five minutes from the centre of town in a residential area (head uphill from West End Hotel roundabout, then take the third road on the left), is run by mountain guide Alan Kimber and his wife, and offers homely accommodation for £9.

For a big meal to celebrate climbing Ben Nevis, the best place in town is also the best located; ***Crannog Seafood Restaurant*** is on the pier, and offers an uninterrupted view over the loch and excellent food. For cheaper meals, ***Nevisport*** has both a cafe and a bar with good-value food. There are also many takeaway food outlets.

Getting There & Away Fort William is a major stop on both the national bus and rail networks. Citylink (☎ 0870-550 5050) has six buses daily to/from Glasgow and Inverness. There are also three buses daily to and from Kyle of Lochalsh and the Isle of Skye, as well as connections to Edinburgh and most other parts of Scotland.

ScotRail (☎ 0845-755 0033) links Fort William to the rest of Scotland. There are four trains daily to/from Glasgow and Edinburgh, with two or three on Sundays. There is also a connection to/from Mallaig four times daily. An excellent overnight sleeper service links Fort William directly to London. A standard return fare to London Euston is £139.

Ben Nevis via the Mountain Track

Duration	6–8 hours
Distance	9mi (14.5km)
Standard	medium-hard
Start/Finish	Ionad Nibheis Visitor Centre
Nearest Town	Fort William, Glen Nevis
Public Transport	yes

Summary A steep, continuous ascent leading to the summit of Britain's highest mountain.

Ben Nevis (1344m, 4406ft) is the highest mountain in Britain, and attracts walkers and climbers in their hordes. Although a path leads most of the way to the summit,

Ben Nevis – An Extreme Climate

As might be expected, the weather on Britain's highest mountain can be the most extreme in the country. The temperature on the summit is typically 9°C colder than at the base of the mountain, and this figure does not allow for wind chill – there are an average of 261 gales per year at the summit and wind speeds well in excess of 100mph have been recorded on numerous occasions. Even if skies are clear when you set out, caution is still necessary because the weather can turn arctic at any time. The mean annual summit temperature is below 0°C and snow often lies until early summer – the summit is only a couple of hundred feet below the permanent snow line. Furthermore, if the views are superb, the chances of seeing them are not – the summit, on average, is cloud-covered six days out of seven.

GRAEME CORNWALLIS

Looking towards Ben Nevis (1344m) from An Garbhanach (975m) on a rare clear day.

the mountain is also the scene of frequent mountain rescue call-outs and an average of eight fatalities every year. The mountain's name tempts tourists with barely any walking experience up its slopes, and many discover they have taken on more than they expected.

The climb starts almost at sea level and the ascent is continuous all the way to the summit. Conditions near the top can be extreme and navigating off the top in poor visibility is notoriously dangerous (sheer gullies cut into the plateau very near to the line of the path). The old bridle path up Ben Nevis is now known as the Mountain Track. The path is very well maintained at the bottom (including a £50,000 upgrade around the Red Burn gully area in 2001) but becomes rougher, crossing steep rocky slopes, towards the top. The distance is about 4.5mi each way, but the ascent (and descent) of over 1300m and inevitable stops along the way mean up to eight hours should be allowed for the round trip.

HISTORY

The Gaelic name Nibheis can be traced back to words meaning 'dread' and 'terrible'. The mountain first appeared on a map in 1654, then named Bion Novesh, and by the early 1700s ascents were being alluded to in literary records.

Gradually the scientists at the Scottish Meteorological Society began to take an interest in the mountain. During the summers of 1881 and 1882 a member of the society, one Clement Wragge (soon nicknamed 'the inclement rag'), climbed to the summit every day to take weather measurements. In 1883 a summit observatory was built and maintained until its closure in 1904. A bridle path (the origins of today's Mountain Track) was also constructed to supply the observatory, and a small 'hotel' was annexed to its side. The hotel was run by two local women, and B&B was provided there for 10 shillings (50p) a head until its closure in 1918.

The idea of a race up the mountain was originally intended as a distraction from the daily routine of life at the observatory. The first timed and recorded ascent took place in October 1895, when William Swan, a local tobacconist, recorded a time of two hours 41 minutes for the return trip from Fort William. The challenge took hold and today up to 500 people enter the 'Ben Race', which is held on the first Saturday of September every year. The current record stands at one hour and 25 minutes.

Warning

The most dangerous part of a walk on 'The Ben' is the descent from the summit plateau. Particular care is needed if there is snow on the ground or if visibility is poor. To reach the head of the Mountain Track in safety, use the following bearings:

From the trig point, walk for 150m (count your paces – probably about 200 paces) on a grid bearing of 231 degrees. Then follow a grid bearing of 281 degrees. This should take you safely off the plateau and onto the path. Remember to allow for magnetic variation – this is given on the recommended maps, and must be *added* to the grid bearing.

The first motor car to reach the summit was a model T Ford in 1911, during an ascent that took five days. The fastest car to the summit was an Austin 7 in 1928, in seven hours 23 minutes. The descent took two hours and then the car was driven back to Edinburgh!

PLANNING

When to Walk

The best month for an ascent is August, by which time the summit plateau is normally free of snow, although it should be safe enough from June until late September.

What to Bring

Bring plenty of warm and waterproof clothing in addition to all the normal gear needed on a high mountain ascent. Also make sure you have a note of the bearings needed to descend from the summit plateau in safety; bearing cards can be purchased from local outdoor shops or can be copied from the warning box.

Maps & Books

The walk is covered by OS Landranger 1:50,000 map No 41 *(Ben Nevis)*, OS Outdoor Leisure 1:25,000 map No 38 *(Ben Nevis & Glen Coe)*, and Harvey's 1:25,000 Superwalker map *Glen Coe*. Local leaflets covering this route include *Ben Nevis – walking the path from June to September* produced by the ranger service, and *Great Walks No 2* by Fort William & Lochaber Tourism.

NEAREST TOWN

Glen Nevis

The village of Glen Nevis is really a collection of amenities at the entrance to the glen itself, and is just 2mi from Fort William. It can be extremely busy in summer.

Information Ionad Nibheis Visitor Centre (☎ 01397-705922) is situated 1.5mi up the glen from Fort William, and is open from 9am to 6pm from Easter to the end of October. Exhibits include displays and videos about the geology and history of Ben Nevis and the surrounding area, as well as information about the John Muir Trust, which recently bought the estate (see the boxed text 'John Muir Trust' on page 197). Up-to-date mountain weather forecasts are displayed at the centre and at the SYHA Hostel in Glen Nevis. The Highland Countryside Ranger Service leads low-level guided walks from the visitor centre during summer. The Glen Nevis Centre (next to the SYHA Hostel) hires boots and backpacks.

Places to Stay & Eat To reach ***Achintee House*** *(☎ 01397-702240)* walk across the footbridge over the river from the visitor centre, or drive along the northern banks of the River Nevis from Fort William. B&B costs from £20 and beds in the bunkhouse are £9.50. There are plans for an inn and restaurant.

Glen Nevis Caravan & Camping Park *(☎ 01397-702191)* is open from March to October. It is a large, family-oriented site with its own grocery/outdoor shop and chip van, and costs £8.90 for two in a tent or £10.50 with a car. Glen Nevis ***SYHA Hostel*** *(☎ 01397-702336)* costs £12.25 for a dorm bed, plus £1 extra in July and August.

For food in Glen Nevis, ***Cafe Beag*** offers main courses from £6 and ***Glen Nevis Restaurant & Bar*** has bar meals and a small shop – all open during summer months only.

Getting There & Away Highland Country Buses (☎ 01463-222244) operates 11 services a day (except Sunday) between Fort William and Glen Nevis. Alternatively, it doesn't take long to walk the 2mi.

GETTING TO/FROM THE WALK

Some variation is possible at the start/finish of the walks up Ben Nevis. Ionad Nibheis Visitor Centre, 1.5mi from Fort William and 500m from the village of Glen Nevis, makes a good starting point. There is a large (although often busy) parking area. Alternatively, it is possible to join the path via a side track that begins opposite the SYHA Hostel in Glen Nevis – the two paths meet at a small plantation above the hostel. If you have your own transport and are coming from Fort William, access is also possible from the road to Achintee House, where there is adequate space for parking.

THE WALK

See map page 196

From the Ionad Nibheis Visitor Centre take the path signed 'Achintee and Ben Path' and cross the suspension bridge. Follow the river bank upstream and then turn left, following a stone wall to reach the Ben Nevis Path (the Mountain Track), where the climb begins in earnest. Continue up, crossing a couple of footbridges, and then follow a gully, which the Red Burn flows down on your right. As the ground begins to level off a little, the path turns sharp left. Keep on the path and don't take the short cut, avoiding further erosion. Your route will soon turn right again and then level out as Lochan Meall an t-Suidhe (also known as Halfway Lochan) comes into view.

Just east of Lochan Meall an t-Suidhe the path turns right to reach Red Burn Ford. The ruins of Halfway House, used in association with the summit observatory, are nearby. In days gone by, walkers were charged one shilling (5p) for walking to the summit, the proceeds being used for path maintenance. This is a good place to take stock. Is the weather fit to continue? Are you? From here to the top and back is a good three to five hours. If in any doubt, enjoy the view and go back down.

If you decide to continue, start zigzagging steeply up across stony slopes. The angle of ascent eases at around 1200m and the path forks beside a large, circular stone shelter. The right-hand path is easier, but either will take you across the plateau to the summit cairn and trig point. Take care on this final section as the last bit of the path goes very close to the edge of the cliffs and gullies on the north face of the mountain. Keep particularly well clear of any patches of snow. In poor visibility, once you've reached the summit cairn don't lose sight of it until you are ready to descend.

The summit is a bit of a wasteland, with the remains of the substantial walls of the observatory, several cairns and an emergency shelter as well as the trig point – all set in a boulder-strewn moonscape. However, the views are exceptional, with the islands of Mull, Rum and Skye to the west, and a myriad of mountain peaks all around, as far as the eye can see.

To return, you must retrace your steps. Remember to watch out for the dangerous summit gullies that cut into the mountain near the path and, in poor visibility, use the bearings listed in the warning box on page 194 to reach the top of the path. Once on the path continue carefully – most accidents occur during the descent.

Ben Nevis via Carn Mór Dearg Arête

Duration	8–9 hours
Distance	9.5mi (15km)
Standard	hard
Start/Finish	Ionad Nibheis Visitor Centre
Nearest Towns	Fort William, Glen Nevis
Public Transport	yes

Summary The connoisseur's route up Ben Nevis. A tough and potentially serious walk involving a thrilling rock ridge and superb views throughout.

This second route up the Ben makes a horseshoe circuit of the Ben Nevis massif, approaching from the satellite peak of Carn Mór Dearg to the north east. The two peaks are linked by a wonderfully narrow rock-ridge

Ben Nevis & The Mamores

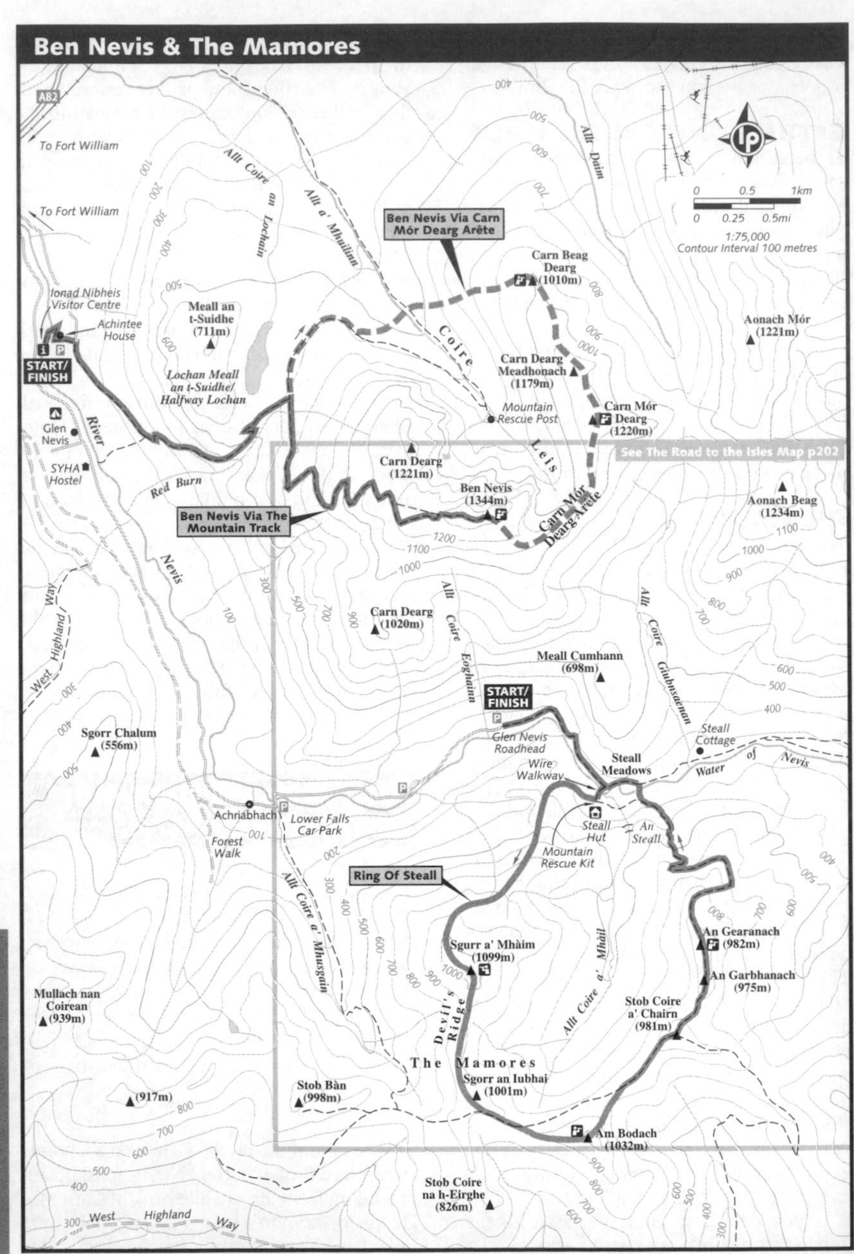

John Muir Trust

Ownership of Ben Nevis, Britain's highest mountain, changed recently. The Ben Nevis Estate was put on the market in 1999, and the John Muir Trust conservation charity launched an appeal and snapped up the property for approximately £500,000.

The area purchased extends east into the Grey Corries and west past the upper Glen Nevis gorge. The intention of the Trust in buying the land is to safeguard the mountain environment, and manage it in such a way as to preserve and enhance the natural heritage of the area. An integral part of this remit is to guarantee the right to roam, and to improve and manage paths for walkers.

Ben Nevis is the most recent addition to an already impressive portfolio held by the John Muir Trust in Scotland. Six other properties totalling some 19,000ha have been purchased by the trust since 1987. All the areas encompass wilderness environments, and almost all include significant mountain peaks. Over 12,000ha are on Skye, including many of the Red Cuillin peaks, as well as one or two of the Black Cuillin summits (see the boxed text 'Conservation on Skye' on page 276).

The history of the Trust is an interesting story in itself. John Muir was born in the fishing port of Dunbar, on the east coast of Scotland, in 1838. His family emigrated to Wisconsin in the USA when he was 11 years old. He arrived in California at the age of 30, and there he became well known as a pioneer of botanical and geological conservation and the father of US national parks. Two hundred sites in the USA are named after him, including the John Muir Trail through the High Sierra mountains. Muir's ethos of conservation was formally established in the UK in 1983 with the foundation of the John Muir Trust.

In recent years a number of Scottish estates incorporating valuable mountain areas have come up for sale (see the boxed text 'Black Cuillin for Sale' on page 278). This has both ensured the future role of the Trust in Scotland, and exposed its financial limits as a charitable organisation. The purchase of Ben Nevis (even at a generous discount) stretched the Trust considerably, and funds to maintain the estate on a year to year basis still have to be fully secured. The Trust does not have the financial clout to compete with developers or wealthy individuals who may have less ecologically sensitive plans. Eyes are turning now to the Scottish Executive to examine its responsibility in preserving one of Scotland's most valuable resources – its wild and beautiful mountain landscapes.

HUGE D'ANDRADE

For more information about the John Muir Trust, visit the Ionad Nibheis Visitor Centre in Glen Nevis or contact the Trust (☎ 0131-554 0114, e jmt_admin@compuserve.com, w www.jmt.org).

(Carn Mór Dearg Arête), the traverse of which provides the highlight of the day. The route follows the Mountain Track to Lochan Meall an t-Suidhe and then drops down into Coire Leis before climbing again to the summit of Carn Mór Dearg (1220m). The ridge is then traversed to reach Ben Nevis and a descent made on the Mountain Track.

With a total ascent of 1660m, this is a strenuous day and is significantly more challenging than the ascent via the Mountain Track. However, it is a classic among Scottish mountain walks, and the sense of achievement is immense.

PLANNING

For more information on when to walk, what to bring, maps and books, see Planning under Ben Nevis via the Mountain Track on page 194.

When to Walk

A calm, dry day in midsummer makes for the safest conditions to cross the rocky arête. In wet weather the rock and steep grassy slopes can become very slippery.

What to Bring

Bring all the normal gear needed for a high mountain ascent. Also make sure you have a note of the bearings needed to descend from Ben Nevis in safety; see the 'Warning' box on page 194.

Maps

The walk is covered by OS Landranger 1:50,000 map No 41 *(Ben Nevis)*, OS Outdoor Leisure 1:25,000 map No 38 *(Ben Nevis & Glen Coe)* and Harvey's 1:25,000 Superwalker map *Glen Coe*.

NEAREST TOWN

Glen Nevis

See Nearest Town on page 194.

GETTING TO/FROM THE WALK

See Getting To/From the Walk under Ben Nevis via the Mountain Track on page 195.

THE WALK

See map page 196

Follow the Ben Nevis via the Mountain Track description on page 195 as far as Lochan Meall an t-Suidhe. The Mountain Track takes a sharp right turn here but you should continue straight over a boggy but obvious path leading across to Coire Leis. Leave the path and make a rough and steep descent directly into Coire Leis. Cross Allt a' Mhuilinn and climb onto the flanks of Carn Beag Dearg. Either climb directly to the summit of Carn Beag Dearg (1010m) or aim to join the ridge somewhere between it and Carn Dearg Meadhonach. The ascent is steep and relentless, but the view of the gullies on the north face of Ben Nevis offers a distraction. Once you reach the **ridge**, the views across the Aonachs and the Grey Corries to the north-east are ample reward.

Follow the ridge to the south, still ascending but over easier ground, to Carn Dearg Meadhonach (1179m). A slight dip is crossed to the summit of **Carn Mór Dearg** where fabulous views of The Mamores are revealed. From here the ridge narrows and descends slightly to the beginning of the **Carn Mór Dearg Arête**. The drop to either side is steep, and the fairly easy scramble over the boulders on the airy crest is thrilling. An easier path, mostly on the left, avoids some of the exposure.

The terrain becomes slightly easier after a subsidiary top, and the ridge then rises to join the eastern flanks of **Ben Nevis** (1344m). A foot-worn path then zigzags for 300m up the steep, rocky slope to the rounded summit plateau. The sense of achievement is immense.

The descent from the summit is the same as for the Ben Nevis via the Mountain Track, see the description on page 195.

Ring of Steall

Duration	7–8 hours
Distance	8.5mi (13.5km)
Standard	medium-hard
Start/Finish	Glen Nevis roadhead
Nearest Towns	Fort William, Glen Nevis
Public Transport	no

Summary A challenging mountain circuit taking in no less than seven Munros and one knife-edged ridge. Views include Ben Nevis and several of Scotland's other highest mountains.

The Mamores is a shapely mountain range in an incredible location. Often overlooked in favour of the more famous peaks of Glen Coe and Ben Nevis, this is good news for serious walkers who may be able to escape some of the 'hill' traffic.

The route makes for a strenuous day and there is a total ascent of some 1500m. It is arguably the best mountain circuit The Mamores has to offer, featuring several Munros, a crossing of the Devil's Ridge, and an approach through the beautiful, mini-Himalayan Nevis gorge. Such variety of scenery and situations in the space of a single day is very special, and a sense of satisfaction at the end of the day is guaranteed.

Alternatives Although terrain is steep, there are several escape routes into Coire a' Mhàil, in the centre of the circuit, after passing Sgorr an Iubhai. The Glen Nevis Circuit, a much shorter, less demanding walk, provides an introduction to the area for those who don't want to attempt the longer route described here. The Glen Nevis Circuit is outlined on page 212.

PLANNING

This walk is generally accessible throughout summer, although if the Water of Nevis is high the only way to cross will be on a wire walkway (which comprises three wire ropes). High winds will make the crossing of Devil's Ridge dangerous. The access path through the Water of Nevis gorge also crosses rocky ground and can be treacherous when icy. Bring all the normal gear for a high mountain walk, as well as plenty of water as there is little on the circuit.

Maps

The walk is covered by OS Landranger 1:50,000 map No 41 *(Ben Nevis)*, OS Outdoor Leisure 1:25,000 map No 38 *(Ben Nevis & Glen Coe)* and Harvey's 1:25,000 Superwalker map *Glen Coe.*

NEAREST TOWN

Glen Nevis

See Nearest Town on page 194.

GETTING TO/FROM THE WALK

Highland Country Buses (☎ 01463-222244), which runs the service between Fort William and Glen Nevis village, extends five daily services as far up Glen Nevis as the Lower Falls parking area. This brings walkers to within 1.5mi (2.5km) of the roadhead where this walk starts and finishes. Unfortunately the times of the service are not convenient for a long walk – the first bus arrives at 9.30am and the last one leaves at 4.30pm.

If you don't make the last bus, then it is still 4mi to Glen Nevis village and 6mi to Fort William. Glen Nevis and Steall Falls are popular destinations with day-trippers, so it might be possible to catch a lift. If you prefer to walk, there is a track through the forest starting at Achriabhach, about 250m west of where the road crosses to the other side of the river. Alternatively, you can leave the road in parts to follow the river bank along informal paths. It should take about 1½ hours to reach Glen Nevis and 2½ hours to reach Fort William by foot.

THE WALK

See map page 196

Leave the parking area at the roadhead and follow the obvious path winding through the trees high above the turbulent Water of Nevis. Higher up the path runs along the edge of the river, and the huge boulders and swirling rock features carved by the water are very impressive. This section has some steep drops and can be treacherous if icy (there have been fatal accidents).

The path exits the gorge and the ground opens up to reveal another wonderful sight – the flat plateau of Steall Meadows. Steall means 'waterfall' and the area takes its name from An Steall, the 100m-high cascade that pours down slabs in the south-east corner of the plateau. Steall Hut (private) can be seen on the opposite bank. The river needs to be crossed at this point, which can be achieved by either balancing on the wire walkway or by wading (in low levels only) where the water is shallower slightly upstream. If the river is in spate and you doubt your ability on the bridge, do not continue.

From Steall Hut pick your way through long grass to the west, skirting around a thicket of trees. Gain the north-east shoulder of Sgurr a' Mhàim and veer to the south, climbing between craggy outcrops on the ridge. You will soon pick up a faint path that leads up the shoulder to a scree-filled corrie, where a well-worn path leads onto the north-west ridge and the summit of **Sgurr a' Mhàim** (1099m), 3½ to four hours from the start. The view across to Ben Nevis is hard to beat, and ahead the horseshoe of peaks you are about to cross should be visible.

From Sgurr a' Mhàim the path drops down to a saddle, and meets the fearsomely named **Devil's Ridge**. The ridge is narrow and airy, but easily negotiable with just a little handwork, and is very enjoyable. It leads up to Stob Coire a' Mhàil, where the ridge becomes broader. Drop down to a saddle and then climb once again to reach the flat summit of **Sgorr an Iubhai** (1001m); the Gaelic name means 'peak of the yew tree', which grow wild in the area.

Easier ground now leads east to Am Bodach. From Sgorr an Iubhai descend to a col, ignoring a path that contours around Am Bodach's north-western slopes, and climb the rocky slope to the **summit** (1032m). There are fine views to the south over Loch Leven and most of The Mamores should be visible. A steep path now heads down the north-east ridge, weaving its way between boulders and stones. The path is well worn for the rest of the route. Pass over Stob Choire a' Chairn (where the main spine of The Mamores range heads east), make a short descent and then the sharp ascent to An Garbhanach (975m). You may need to use your hands just before the top. Between An Garbhanach and the final summit of An Gearanach (982m), the ridge narrows briefly to a knife-edge. After savouring the airy views from An Gearanach, follow the path steeply down to Steall Meadows.

At the bottom swing round to the west, passing the tumbling cascade of An Steall on your left. Recross the Water of Nevis and follow the path back to Glen Nevis roadhead.

The Road to the Isles

Duration	6–8 hours
Distance	14.5mi (23km)
Standard	medium
Start	Corrour Station
Finish	Glen Nevis roadhead
Nearest Towns	Fort William, Glen Nevis, Corrour
Public Transport	yes

Summary A long and remote low-level walk starting on the wild expanses of Rannoch Moor and following a historical route to finish in the spectacular Nevis gorge.

The Road to the Isles is an ancient route through the western Highlands that links central Scotland to the Isle of Skye via Fort William. It was much used by cattle drovers heading for the cattle trysts (fairs) at Crieff and Falkirk. Armies, their quarries and refugees have also marched and fled along the route. (Today the 'Road to the Isles' handle is also used by the scenic A82, which runs to the south of its original namesake.)

The walk starts at Corrour Station, 11mi from the nearest public road in the heart of Rannoch Moor. The route then follows a right of way to Fort William, passing beneath some of Scotland's highest mountains. Ben Nevis, the Aonachs and the Grey Corries are on one side, The Mamores on the other. The terrain is largely wild and remote, although there are basic bothies at Staoineag and Meanach, about halfway along the route. These offer shelter or, if you've got suitable overnight gear, they would allow you to split the walk into two days. Both bothies are open and free to hillwalkers all year round, but are simply damp shells of old cottages and are not particularly alluring. Of the two, Staoineag is the more attractively situated.

The route can be done in either direction, although the majority of your progress is downhill and the views are better in the direction described. The route should only be attempted by experienced hillwalkers and in suitable weather conditions.

PLANNING
When to Walk

This route crosses low-lying ground that can be rather boggy, so is best avoided in wet weather. It is generally passable during the winter, although navigational skills need to be solid when paths are obliterated by snow. The final section along the Nevis gorge crosses rocky ground that can be treacherous when icy.

Stalking This route passes through the Grey Corries-Mamore Estate, where stalking usually takes place between mid-August and the end of October. If you're planning on walking around this time, phone ☎ 01855-831511 for route advice.

The West Highland Railway

The West Highland Railway runs between Glasgow and Fort William, passing through some of Scotland's most wild and spectacular mountain scenery. Stations such as Arrochar & Tarbet, Crianlarich, Bridge of Orchy and Spean Bridge allow you to set off on a seemingly endless range of wonderful mountain walks direct from the platform. There are several opportunities for circular walks, or you can get off at one station, have a good walk, then catch the train from another station up or down the line.

Possibly the most intriguing place to get off is at Corrour which, at 408m above sea level, is the highest and most remote station in Britain. Work on the line began in 1889 and in total 5000 men were employed to build it, laying foundations of brushwood and earth across miles of bog to support the tracks. It's a tribute to the railway's Victorian engineers that the line has remained in place for over a century. From Corrour you can reach lonely peaks or wind your way through remote valleys.

As you go north on the West Highland Railway, the magic continues. Beyond Fort William the train runs to Mallaig, from where it's a short ferry ride to the Isle of Skye, and there is a branch line to Oban, a gateway port for the Outer Hebrides.

From May to September there are four trains per day (two or three on Sunday) in each direction. There's also a standard passenger coach attached to the sleeper train, which travels between London and Fort William; very handy for getting to walks early in the morning.

For more information phone the National Rail Enquiry Service (☎ 0845-748 4950) or ScotRail (☎ 0845-755 0033). For more ideas on where to go, pick up a copy of *Walks from the West Highland Railway* by Chris & John Harvey. It covers 40 walking routes ranging from fairly gentle strolls to the ascents of 18 Munros.

What to Bring

Bring all of the normal equipment required for a remote mountain route. This includes plenty of food and water, a map and compass, and warm, waterproof clothing. Walking poles could be useful for burn crossings.

Maps

The whole route is covered by OS Landranger 1:50,000 map No 41 *(Ben Nevis)*.

NEAREST TOWNS

Glen Nevis

See Nearest Town on page 194.

Corrour

Labelling Corrour a 'town' is not strictly accurate. In fact the place consists of a single building: the train station! However, as far as train stations go, this one is pretty special. The station house sells basic provisions, but it is wise to bring important items with you.

Places to Stay & Eat An intriguing place to spend the night, ***Corrour Station House and Bunkhouse*** *(☎ 01397-732236)* is open for most of the year, except March and November. It offers a real impression of the isolation of Rannoch Moor. Bunkhouse accommodation is in a former station building (the old signal box is the common room) and costs £6.50. The station cafe offers excellent snacks and meals from 9am to 9pm.

Alternatively, the simple but popular ***Loch Ossian SYHA Hostel*** *(☎ 01397-732207)* charges £6.75 and is a 1mi walk east of Corrour Station. You'll need to bring your own sleeping bag.

Getting There & Away The only way to get to Corrour – besides walking in – is by train. The station is on the main Glasgow-Fort William line. ScotRail (☎ 0845-755 0033) runs four services in each direction from Monday to Saturday, with two or three services on Sunday. The overnight sleeper service from London will also stop here on request. The platform at Corrour is so small that only one door of the train can be opened to let passengers off; check with the conductor where you should sit to be near the right door.

The Road to the Isles

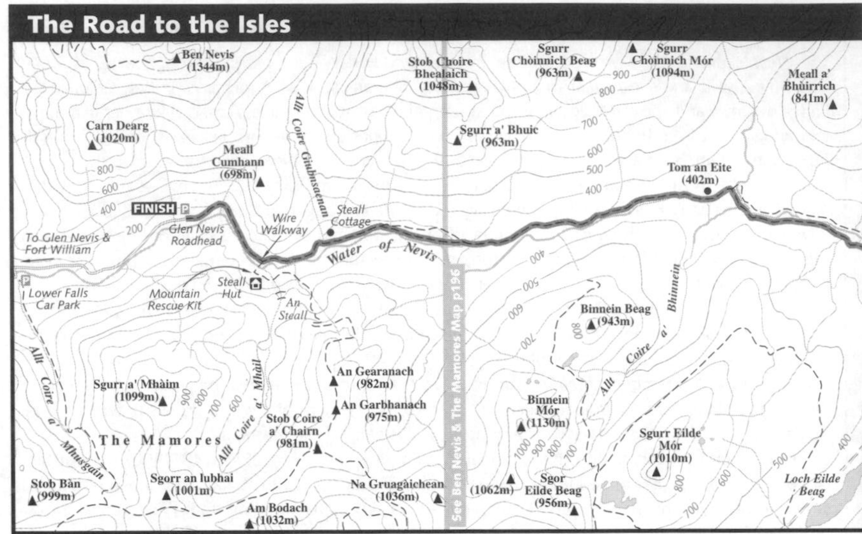

GETTING TO/FROM THE WALK

To get to the start, see Getting There & Away for Corrour on page 201. From the finish, see Getting to/from the Walk under Ring of Steall on page 199.

THE WALK

From Corrour Station on a clear day you get a view of Ben Nevis and nearby mountains. Cross to the west of the railway line and follow the track to the north-west, walking alongside the line. Old railway sleepers have been helpfully placed across wet patches and several small burns.

After about 1mi you reach a point where the Allt Lùib Ruairidh runs through an underpass below the railway line. A track from the Loch Ossian SYHA Hostel also comes under here and you join it after crossing the bridge over this stream. Continue ahead on the much better track below the railway line down to a bridge across Allt a' Chamabhreac; here you cross the burn just before it empties into Loch Treig. There are excellent views of The Mamores and shapely Binnein Beag ahead.

Walking round **Loch Treig**, you may well feel it lives up to its name, which means 'forsaken', so it's something of a surprise to see Creaguaineach Lodge ahead. A private house, the lodge just survived the raising of the water level in the 1930s, when the loch was dammed as part of the hydroelectric scheme for the aluminium works at Fort William. Immediately before the lodge there is a major bridge over the Abhainn Rath, which flows down a small gorge into Loch Treig. At the south end of this is a junction marked by a signpost. Although the original right of way to Glen Nevis and the path shown on the OS map both follow the north side of the Abhainn Rath, the preferred route (and that indicated by the signpost) keeps to the south. This avoids the river crossing that is otherwise necessary at Lùibeilt, which can prove a major difficulty after wet weather.

The signposted route follows a rough path alongside the river, swinging left to cross two small tributaries and then right where it climbs a narrow section of the valley to a wide level area near Staoineag Bothy. The path continues along the valley floor, crossing a substantial tributary, to another step in the valley, down which the river tumbles. Above this the valley becomes wide and flat again, although the

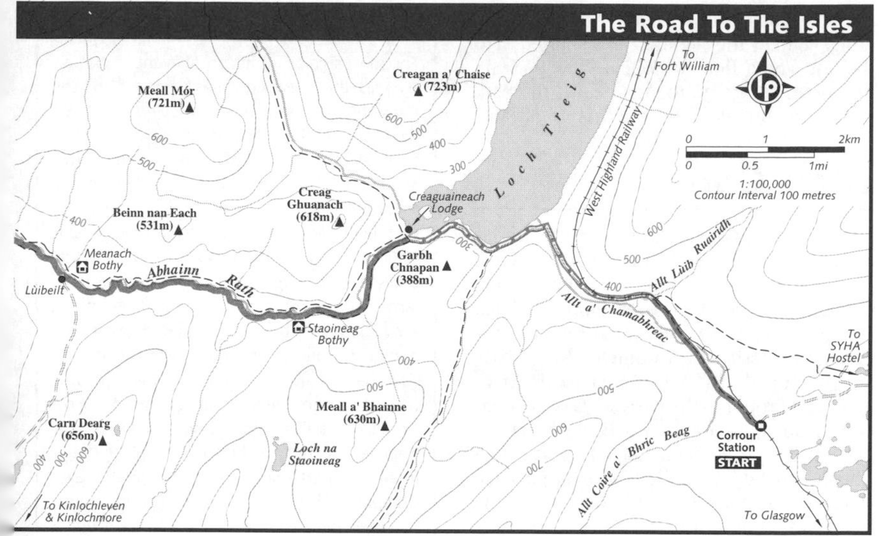

buildings at Lùibeilt and Meanach Bothy are visible ahead. The river meanders here, and there are stepping stones across another major tributary. The marshy ground makes for slow walking but the ground is firm immediately alongside the river.

Lùibeilt itself is a ruin but if you need shelter Meanach Bothy is just across the river (although this is the very crossing you have avoided by following the south side of the river!). A rough track leads south from Lùibeilt to Kinlochleven, about 7mi away.

Continue north-west, following a track that winds between stony knolls and then becomes grassy and re-enters wilder country. About 1mi after Lùibeilt the path ascends a stony slope on the left and then traverses along the side of glacial deposits towards a small metal hut on the far side of the Allt Coire a' Bhinnein. This hut is known as 'The Water Shed' and marks the approximate point where the waters begin to flow their different ways, west towards Loch Linnhe and east towards Loch Treig. Cross the river to the hut, which is in a poor state but offers limited shelter.

From the hut follow the usually dry river bed to the north for about 200m and join the path on the north side of the infant Water of Nevis (just below the hillock of Tom an Eite), where the path turns west. The ground ahead is often boggy. Alternative paths are numerous but the highest is often best. Where the peat is exposed, the remains of ancient trees are sometimes apparent – relics of the very different vegetation that was once present.

As you descend towards Glen Nevis, many more fine peaks of The Mamores come into sight and there's a dramatic view of Ben Nevis' north-east profile. Eventually you reach a substantial bridge over a burn, beside the ruins of Steall Cottage. You'll soon discover the reason for the cottage's name; **An Steall** cascades down more than 100m of rock slabs on the other side of the river. Steall Hut, just west of the falls, is private and reached by a bridge comprising just three wire ropes – cross if you dare! The area will probably be quite crowded as this is a popular strolling zone. (See also the Ring of Steall walk on page 198.)

The way out of this sanctuary now becomes apparent. The river takes an abrupt turn to the right and tumbles down a steep rocky gorge, the bed of which is filled with massive boulders. A well-constructed path clings to the valley side. After a sharp turn to the left (and a final, excellent view back up this dramatic gorge to An Steall), the path brings you out at the Glen Nevis roadhead.

Glen Coe

Glen Coe is among the most popular destinations for walkers and climbers in Scotland. It is one of the most dramatic valleys in the country, and most visitors approach Glen Coe from the east on the A82. From that direction you descend off Rannoch Moor, pass the pyramidal sentinel of Buachaille Etive Mór, and drop into the narrow Pass of Glencoe, a notch between Am Bodach (at the eastern end of Aonach Eagach) and Beinn Fhada. Ahead, the valley floor is pancake flat and no more than 500m wide. To the north, sweeping up from sea level to more than 900m, the ramparts of the Aonach Eagach ridge are so steep that you must crane your neck to see the top. To the south the massive jutting buttresses known as the Three Sisters throw shadows across the valley. Partially hidden behind them are the tantalising peaks of Bidean nam Bian and Stob Coire nan Lochan. The view is one of the most arresting in Scotland – and that's just from the car!

Glen Coe was one of the first major tracts of land to be acquired by the National Trust for Scotland. In 1935 Aonach Eagach and Signal Rock were purchased, and two years later the mountains on the south side of the valley were donated to the Trust. The estate now covers some 22 sq mi. The Trust's mandate is simple: to protect the natural and cultural heritage of the area and to ensure open access for hillwalkers.

NATURAL HISTORY

The event that makes Glen Coe significant in geological terms occurred towards the end of a period of volcanic activity 60 million years ago. A circle of the land's surface, roughly 6mi in diameter, fractured and sank into the hot magma below. This phenomenon is known as cauldron subsidence, and the discovery of the cauldron at Glen Coe marked an important development in geological understanding. A small quarry near Clachaig Inn exposes the fault line of the cauldron, which then follows the prominent gully west of Achnambeithach Cottage.

Some 25,000 years ago, the ice age further shaped Glen Coe. The Lost Valley between Gearr Aonach and Beinn Fhada (see Bidean nam Bian on page 209) is a good example

Glen Coe Massacre

The most significant historical event in the valley was the Glen Coe massacre – Glen Coe translates as 'the glen of weeping'. In 1691 King William III demanded that all Scottish clan chiefs sign an oath of allegiance to the crown and the date for compliance was 1 January the following year. The price of failing to comply was death. Maclain, chief of the MacDonalds of Glencoe, went to Fort William to sign, only to discover that signatures were being collected farther south in Inveraray. This mistake meant it was 6 January before he signed the oath, but nonetheless he left Inveraray with the impression that his allegiance had been accepted. A few weeks later the Secretary of State for Scotland, Sir John Dalrymple, despatched the Argyll Regiment. Led by Robert Campbell, the regiment included many soldiers from the Clan Campbell, who had a long-held grudge against the MacDonalds. The Campbells were under orders to exterminate all MacDonald men under the age of 70. As was the tradition in the Highlands, the men were offered hospitality and entertained for more than 10 days. However early in the morning of 13 February, the Campbells rose and turned on their hosts, killing around 40 people and forcing many more to flee to the hills where they perished of hunger and exposure.

Signal Rock, where the order was given to begin the massacre, is on the north bank of the River Coe, 200m west of the Clachaig Inn. There is a monument to the MacDonalds in Glencoe village, and an exhibition about the massacre at the National Trust for Scotland visitor centre.

of a hanging valley – formed when a higher glacier is cut off in its downhill journey by a larger glacier in the valley below. The Lairig Gartain and Lairig Eilde valleys (see the Glen Coe & Glen Etive Circuit on page 208) are classic U-shaped glacial valleys.

PLANNING

When to Walk

All the walks described here, perhaps with the exception of the Glen Coe & Glen Etive Circuit, are not recommended if the cloud is down or if winds are strong. The traverse of the Aonach Eagach, in particular, should be avoided if the rock is likely to be wet.

What to Bring

Bring all the normal equipment for a remote mountain walk, including plenty of warm clothing, food and water. You might also be glad of walking poles for balance when negotiating stream crossings on the Glen Coe & Glen Etive Circuit, while a walking rope, used correctly, may add security on sections of the Aonach Eagach ridge.

Maps & Books

All the walks in the Glen Coe valley are covered by OS Landranger 1:50,000 map No 41 *(Ben Nevis)*, OS Outdoor Leisure 1:25,000 map No 38 *(Ben Nevis & Glen Coe)* and Harvey's 1:25,000 Superwalker map *Glen Coe* (which also includes a useful little visitor guide).

Information Sources

For some good background information, plus transport and accommodation details, try **W** www.glencoe-scotland.co.uk.

Guided Walks

Glencoe Ranger Service (☎ 01463-232034) organises guided walks from June to August and Glencoe Outdoor Centre (☎ 01855-811350) provides activity holidays and courses.

ACCESS TOWN

Glencoe

Glencoe is a picturesque village situated at the bottom of Glen Coe (the valley). Most of the village is now bypassed by the A82, so although it is easily accessible it retains a quiet atmosphere. There is a reasonable-sized ***shop*** (open 8am to 9pm daily), a petrol station, and several coffee and craft shops. Mountain Sports Equipment, on the A82, stocks outdoor gear and maps, and hires equipment.

Information The TIC (☎ 01855-811296) at Ballachulish, 1mi west of Glencoe, is open from April to October. The National Trust for Scotland Visitor Centre (☎ 01855-811307) is 2.5mi south of the village along the A82, and is open daily from April to October. Presentations cover the area's natural heritage and exhibits include a video on the Glen Coe massacre; entry costs 50p. The Trust plans to build a new, £3 million visitor centre closer to Glencoe village at the Inverigan camping site; it is expected to open in 2002. There is public Internet access at Clachaig Inn, near the visitor centre. Glencoe Ski Centre, at the eastern end of the glen, has a Museum of Scottish Skiing and Mountaineering.

Places to Stay & Eat There are numerous B&Bs and hotels in the village of Glencoe, but many of the traditional walker's haunts are spread out along the old Glencoe road leading east from the village. ***Glencoe SYHA Hostel*** *(☎ 01855-811219)*, about 1.5mi from the village, charges £9.25.

Leacantium Farm Bunkhouse *(☎ 01855-811256)*, next along the road, charges £6.50 in a large room with triple-tiered sleeping platforms or £7.50 in a farmhouse hostel. The fairly basic but popular ***Red Squirrel Campsite***, run by the same people, is slightly farther along; the charge is £4.

Clachaig Inn *(☎ 01855-811252)*, at the end of the road and 2.5mi from the village, offers B&B from £23. The inn also has a selection of self-catering mountain lodges available. Clachaig Inn really comes into its own during the evening, when most outdoor people in the area congregate in the climbers' bar. The food is hearty, the selection of real ales has won awards and there is regular live music.

Getting There & Away The A82, from Glasgow to Fort William, runs down the centre of Glen Coe. It bypasses the village, which is still one of the stops on the main Glasgow-Fort William bus route. Scottish Citylink (☎ 0870-550 5050) offers six services daily in each direction. Highland Country Buses (☎ 01463-222244) also provides a service between Fort William and Glencoe, with seven buses daily except Sunday.

Buachaille Etive Mór

Duration	5–6 hours
Distance	6.5mi (10.5km)
Standard	medium-hard
Start/Finish	Altnafeadh
Nearest Town	Glencoe
Public Transport	yes

Summary An excellent walk on the ridges and summits of one of Scotland's most distinctive mountains, suitable for reasonably fit and well-equipped walkers.

Standing sentinel at the head of Glen Coe is Buachaille Etive Mór (meaning 'great shepherd of the glen'), one of the most distinctive landmarks in the Scottish landscape. The initial appearance of the mountain, when viewed from the east on the A82 or from the start at Altnafeadh, is one of an impregnable pyramid of buttresses and chasm-like gullies. But looks are often deceiving and a steep but reasonably straightforward ascent can be made via Coire na Tulaich. An ascent can also be made from Glen Etive to the south.

The summit, commonly referred to as Buachaille Etive Mór, is actually Stob Dearg (1022m). Behind Stob Dearg the mountain continues to the south-west with a high-level ridge connecting a further three summits. The name Buachaille Etive Mór properly refers to this entire massif. With such deep valleys on either side the views and feeling of space from the ridge and summits is exceptional. Once the ridge is gained from Coire na Tulaich, the walking is quite easy with only a few short ascents to reach the various summits. The route described here continues along the ridge across Stob na Doire and then descends into Lairig Gartain via Coire Altruim. This gives a total ascent of 1080m.

Alternatives As a shorter option you can simply return down Coire na Tulaich after visiting the summit of Stob Dearg, a walk which will need about three to four hours to complete.

For those who want to maximise distance and effort, Stob na Broige can be a side trip towards the end of the route described. Add an extra hour or more for this option; the distance is 1.5mi, involving just over 200m ascent on fairly easy ground.

GETTING TO/FROM THE WALK

The walk starts and finishes at the parking area at Altnafeadh on the A82. Bus services operating along the A82 should stop here if requested in advance – see Getting There & Away on this page.

THE WALK

See map page 207

From Altnafeadh car park, follow the wide 4WD track to a large footbridge and then walk along a good path past Lagangarbh Cottage. Continue gently upwards into Coire na Tulaich and ignore a path going off to the left (this is used to reach the many scrambles and rock climbs on the buttresses farther east). Follow the path along the right bank of the Allt Coire na Tulaich, which will probably be dry in summer.

Higher up the ground on both sides becomes steeper and the stream bed becomes choked with boulders. The path climbs up to the right onto easier ground heading for the scree slopes above. Once on the scree slopes it is easiest to stick to the right, where by following the sides of small outcrops you can find firmer footing. Just below the rim of Coire na Tulaich you may need your hands for balance to scramble over rocky ground, emerging suddenly onto the ridge between Stob Dearg and Stob na Doire (1½ hours from the start).

Eastern Glen Coe

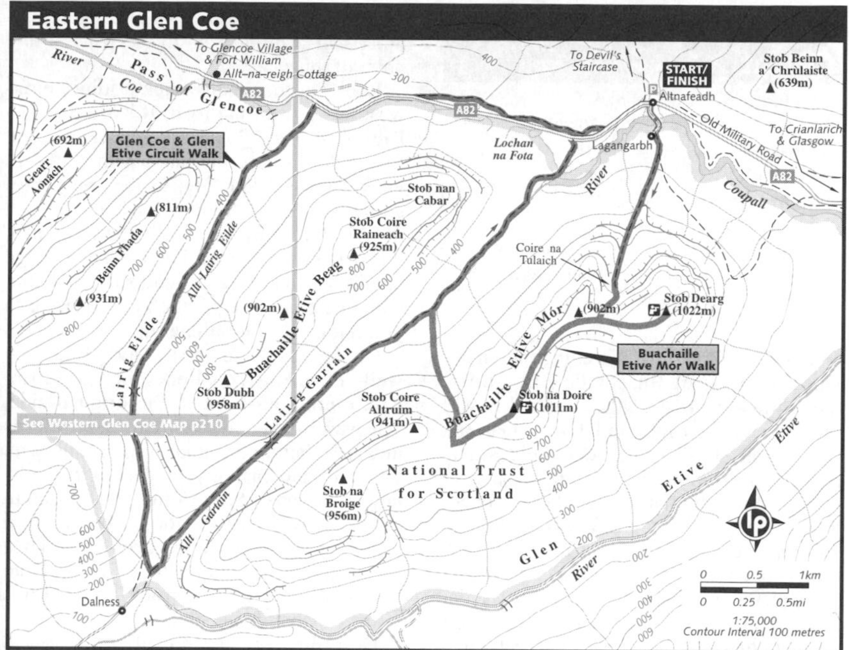

Turn east and climb steadily for about 20 minutes over stony, frost-shattered ground to the summit of **Stob Dearg** (1022m). There are fine views to the east across exposed Rannoch Moor, and to the north and north-west across the shapely summits of The Mamores as far as the unmistakable, whale-backed profile of Ben Nevis. Closer to home, the eye is drawn to the steep, north-east face of Stob na Doire, which is next on the agenda.

Descend back to the top of Coire na Tulaich and head west and then south-west across a lovely, broad ridge with many small lochans filling the depressions between the grassy hummocks. Ten or 15 minutes of walking on this ridge should see you at the base of the short, steep haul to **Stob na Doire** (1011m). A well-defined path shows the way to the small summit cairn. The views to the west across Bidean nam Bian now dominate and there are also excellent views south into Glen Etive.

The ridge of Buachaille Etive Mór continues to Stob na Broige to the south-west, while immediately below in a col you can make out the red erosion scar of a path heading down into Coire Altruim. Descend steeply to reach the col; from here you can do the side trip to Stob na Broige for good views of Loch Etive.

From the col, the descent into Coire Altruim is steep but straightforward, except for a few wet, rocky steps towards the bottom where a little care is needed. Most parties will take an hour to reach the River Coupall, which may be difficult to ford if it is in spate.

If in doubt about fording here, simply follow the river back to Altnafeadh and cross it on the footbridge that you used at the start of the walk. If the river is low, cross over and follow the well-defined but boggy path that takes you to the A82 just a few hundred metres west of Altnafeadh (one hour from the river crossing).

Glen Coe & Glen Etive Circuit

Duration	5 hours
Distance	10mi (16km)
Standard	medium
Start/Finish	Altnafeadh
Nearest Town	Glencoe
Public Transport	yes

Summary A rough and quite demanding walk passing through remote terrain and crossing two mountain passes.

Glen Coe & Glen Etive Circuit circumnavigates the base of Buachaille Etive Beag, the 'little shepherd of the glen'. It passes through Lairig Eilde and Lairig Gartain, two classic, U-shaped glacial valleys, and serves up a sample of the wilder parts of Glen Coe's dramatic mountain scenery without tackling any really serious terrain. However, the paths are, for the most part, either rough and rocky or (beside the River Coupall) very muddy. The route is described in an anticlockwise direction for aesthetic reasons, however, there is no reason why it can't be walked in the opposite direction. The walk includes more than 600m ascent, but five hours should see it completed. Allow longer for stops or if you know you're slow over rough paths.

GETTING TO/FROM THE WALK

The walk starts and finishes at the parking area at Altnafeadh on the A82. Bus services operating along the A82 should stop here if requested in advance – see Getting There & Away for Glencoe on page 206.

THE WALK

See map page 207

From Altnafeadh, walk west on the A82, almost to the AA telephone, before escaping right on an old road. This provides some relief from the traffic, but not from the noise, as it leads you west, overlooked by the steep, north end of Buachaille Etive Beag. Ahead you can see the Three Sisters on the south side of Glen Coe. The old road rejoins the A82 about 1mi west of the AA telephone, and the traffic must now be endured for another half a mile or so to the real starting point of this walk.

Look out for a stony track leading southwest away from the road. It has a Scottish Rights of Way Society signpost to Loch Etiveside. Follow the path, with excellent views across Glen Coe, to the spiky, precipitous ridge of Aonach Eagach, to reach the Allt Lairig Eilde. If the river is in spate it is dangerous to cross but, even in average conditions, it can be difficult so, if in doubt, continue along the pathless east bank until you rejoin the path higher up.

On the other side of Allt Lairig Eilde, the well-defined path continues for around 1mi before crossing back to the original side. The way, marked by a few cairns, now leads upwards, bending round to the south, with views of increasingly wild country – the jagged ridges of Stob Coire Sgreamhach to the west with rocky gorges below. You might be lucky to see red deer here. When you eventually reach the top of **Lairig Eilde** (489m) the views open up across Glen Etive to the mountains beyond.

Descend from the top of the pass and cross a small stream. The path continues steeply down to Dalness in Glen Etive. You can avoid about 100m of this descent (and the subsequent 100m ascent) by taking a path that leads to the left when a fenced enclosure is reached, about 1mi from the top of Lairig Eilde. This path traverses around the lower slopes of Stob Dubh to reach the Allt Gartain, where you join a small path coming up from the right.

Now heading north-east, go up the steep and fairly narrow valley, with the Allt Gartain tumbling down it in a series of small waterfalls. The route up involves some easy scrambling in places and on a fine day there are many opportunities to stop beside the waterfalls and enjoy the views back down to Loch Etive.

Eventually you reach **Lairig Gartain** (489m) with extensive views ahead to the mountains around Loch Treig and a final opportunity to look back to Loch Etive. The remainder of the walk back to Altnafeadh can now be seen. This classic, U-shaped valley (resulting from glacial erosion) is very wet, and the path that follows along the north-west bank of the River Coupall has many muddy and eroded sections. Follow the path down the glen, between Buachaille Etive Beag on the left and Buachaille Etive Mór on the right, to the A82 and the finish at Altnafeadh.

Bidean nam Bian

Duration	6–7 hours
Distance	6mi (9.5km)
Standard	medium-hard
Start/Finish	parking area west of Allt-na-reigh Cottage
Nearest Town	Glencoe
Public Transport	yes

Summary This is a stunning circuit on a rugged and beautiful mountain massif. The approach through the Lost Valley is particularly beautiful.

The ascent of Bidean nam Bian, the highest mountain in Argyll at 1150m (3772ft), is one of the classic walks in Glen Coe. The route squeezes up and down the steep-sided valleys that divide the Three Sisters, the towering buttresses that enclose Glen Coe on its southern side. It then ascends the massif of Bidean nam Bian, which rears up at the head of the valleys. The walking on the massif itself is on fine, rocky ridges, which are narrow enough to feel airy without being dangerous or difficult. The route largely follows maintained paths, although faint footworn trails rather than purpose-built paths mark the way along the high, rocky ridges. The total ascent on the route is 1150m.

The approach includes a crossing of the Lost Valley, a bowl-like hanging valley that was created during the last ice age (see Natural History under Glen Coe on page 204). In more recent years this mountain sanctuary was used as a hiding place for cattle stolen by the MacDonald clan from the Campbells (see the boxed text 'Glen Coe Massacre' on page 204). A walk to the Lost Valley is worthy in its own right for those who don't fancy the full circuit described; allow three hours for the return trip.

GETTING TO/FROM THE WALK

The walk begins and ends at the large parking area on the south side of the A82, a short distance west of the cottage at Allt-na-reigh. Buses operating along the A82 should stop here if requested in advance – see Getting There & Away for Glencoe on page 206.

THE WALK

See map page 210

From the parking area drop down the grassy slope south of the road and join a track that follows the banks of the River Coe upstream. Cross the river on a wooden footbridge and join a well-maintained path. This path leads up the rocky gorge that cuts between the towering crags of Beinn Fhada and Gearr Aonach, and hands are needed in several places to help mount easy rock steps. The path soon crosses onto the east bank of the Allt Coire Gabhail, and a short climb brings you over a rise and into the **Lost Valley**.

The floor of the valley is a jumble of rocks and boulders – pick your way diagonally across the muddle to join a more distinct path to the right. At the head of the valley a steep rock wall seems to rise almost vertically – the route ascends directly up this wall, although the terrain is not as steep as it first seems. The path continues up the valley, contouring above a gorge that has been chiselled out by the burn. Care is needed here in wet or icy weather.

The terrain steepens as you reach the headwall of the valley, and the ground becomes less stable underfoot. The climb itself is less than easy-going as a mixture of mud, scree and boulders rises sharply up to the ridge. Hands may be needed for balance in one or two places. Once on top of the ridge, however, the views suddenly open out in all directions.

The summit of Bidean nam Bian is now about three-quarters of a mile away, along the ridge to the west. Stick to the crest of the ridge and climb over the boulders of several rises and subsidiary peaks, passing one narrow section, before making a final ascent to the large cairn on the **Bidean nam Bian** summit (1150m), about four hours from the start. The views are exceptional, and on a clear day the panorama includes the Western Isles, Ben Nevis and many of the peaks and ranges of the western Highlands.

Descend from Bidean nam Bian in a north-easterly direction, following a narrow and rocky spur down to a col between Bidean nam Bian and Stob Coire nan Lochan (care is needed here in poor visibility). Climb back up to the summit of **Stob Coire nan Lochan** (1115m), where the view is dominated by the Aonach Eagach ridge on the other side of Glen Coe.

To descend from Stob Coire nan Lochan it is necessary to walk north-west for a few hundred metres and then north for about the same distance again, following the rim of some impressive cliffs. At a col turn east, descending into Coire nan Lochan. Cut across the grassy hollow and pick up faint paths running alongside the many small streams flowing towards the River Coe below. The streams soon converge and the path becomes well established, descending steeply on the eastern banks of the burn. At the bottom of the descent another wooden footbridge crosses the River Coe. From here it's a few hundred metres up the grassy slopes to the parking areas.

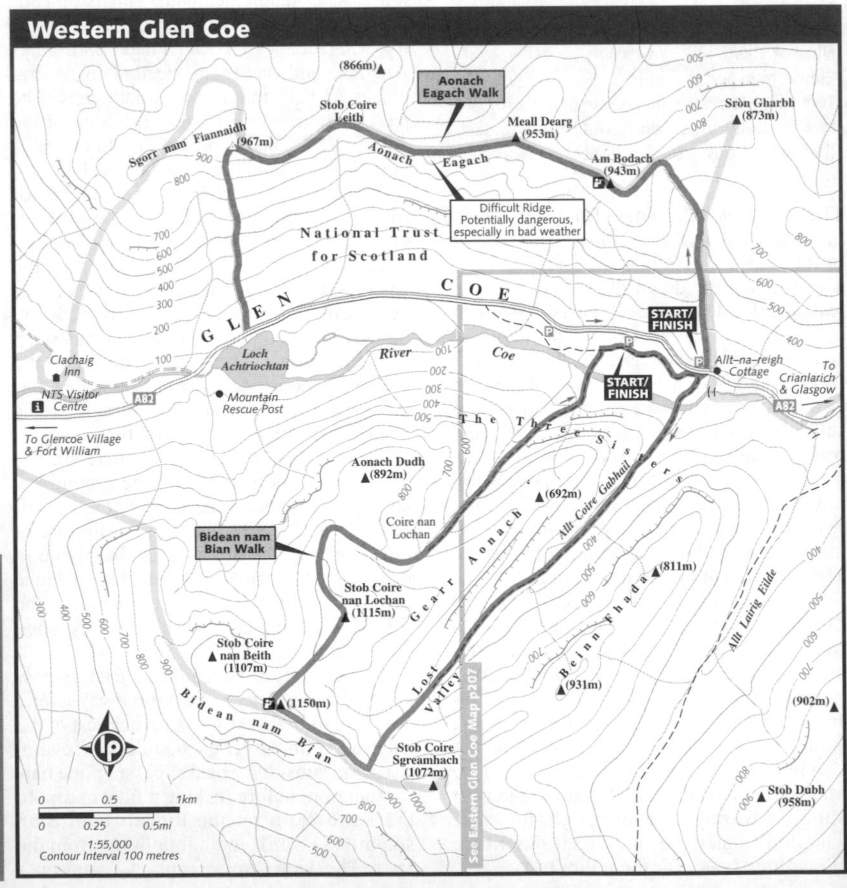

Aonach Eagach

Duration	7–8 hours
Distance	6mi (9.5km)
Standard	hard
Start/Finish	parking area just west of Allt-na-reigh cottage
Nearest Town	Glencoe
Public Transport	yes

Summary Probably the most thrilling ridge-line scramble on the Scottish mainland, demanding confidence and commitment in a spectacular situation. For experienced walkers only.

Aonach Eagach forms a precipitous wall on the northern side of Glen Coe. Its slopes sweep upwards directly from the main road, becoming steeper and more broken with crags and gullies, to the crest some 900m higher up. On the other side, the mountain also falls away precipitously, forming a knife-edge ridge about 1.5mi long. Aonach Eagach translates as 'the notched ridge' and provides one of the most aspired-to 'walks' in Scotland. Walkers attempting it should be fit and experienced, with a good head for heights and a reasonable aptitude for rock scrambling. The positions encountered in two or three short sections are either sensational or terrifying, depending on your vertigo tolerance.

The ridge is reached via a steady ascent through the corrie south-east of Am Bodach, and is left at Sgorr nam Fiannaidh, from where a steep and unrelenting descent takes you back to the main road close to Loch Achtriochtan, about 1.5mi west of the start. The total ascent of the route is 1000m. Once on the ridge there is no easy way to bypass difficulties at the crest and no simple escape routes into the valleys on either side. The route is generally walked from east to west because rock steps are less problematic in this direction.

GETTING TO/FROM THE WALK

The route starts and finishes at the parking area just west of Allt-na-reigh Cottage, on the north side of the A82. Bus services operating along the A82 should stop here, or close by, if requested in advance – see Getting There & Away for Glencoe on page 206.

THE WALK

See map page 210

From the parking area pick up a good path climbing steeply onto the south-east ridge of Am Bodach. After about 15 minutes the path flattens out beneath some crags and then turns to the east, skirting the base of these cliffs to reach the Allt Ruigh, which flows down from the basin between Am Bodach and Sròn Gharbh. Follow the stream on either side and continue to gain altitude, reaching the ridge between Am Bodach and Sròn Gharbh 1½ hours from the start. In clear weather the ridge gives wonderful views north across the mountains of Lochaber. The sweeping ridges of The Mamores partly obscure the Aonachs, Grey Corries and Ben Nevis.

Turn to the south-west and clamber up a broad, rocky ridge to reach the summit of **Am Bodach** (943m) in another 10 minutes. The views from here include those previously mentioned to the north, but there are also sweeping views to the south across Glen Coe and Bidean nam Bian. Am Bodach marks the beginning of the ridge, and from here you can only see along as far as Meall Dearg. Difficulties are encountered immediately as you descend a rock step with one slightly awkward manoeuvre that is exposed on the right. If you find this section particularly stressful don't attempt to continue as there are harder sections to come. Once down off this rock step the ridge is narrow but not technical, and provides superb walking as far as **Meall Dearg** (953m), 30 minutes from Am Bodach.

Once you've had a breather and admired the view from Meall Dearg, descend onto the ridge again, which narrows considerably and frequently calls for the use of hands. Edge across an exposed notch and then tackle the crux of the whole walk – a gendarmed section of the ridge with vertical exposure on both sides. Tackle this on the right (north) side and use a ledge to bypass a block before regaining the crest of the ridge and easier ground. As long as you keep a calm head and pay attention to your hands and feet, it is quite straightforward. Descend steeply into a notch where another difficult section begins – you must scramble up an obvious ramp on the left (south) side of the ridge, again in an exposed position. Descend again into another notch and scramble steeply but easily up a prominent gully to escape the final difficulties. Most people will need an hour for this section and perhaps longer if you are roping-up at difficult sections.

Climb a rocky ridge to the summit of Stob Coire Leith (940m) from where there is a fine view east, back along the length of the Aonach Eagach. Onwards from Stob Coire Leith a broad ridge descends gently and then sweeps around for the final climb of the day to the highest summit on the ridge, **Sgorr nam Fiannaidh** (967m). Descend steeply to the south from the summit, picking up a faint path in the scree and working around outcrops. The descent is steep and unrelenting, and if the grass on the lower half is wet you should be extra careful.

Once back at the A82 (one to 1½ hours from the top of Sgorr nam Fiannaidh), turn left and walk east along the road for 1.5mi to return to the parking area. It is possible to avoid some of the road by following an obvious track to the right.

Other Walks

LOCHABER

The Aonachs

The Aonachs are a dominant feature of the view from Ben Nevis, and Aonach Beag, at 1234m (4048ft), is the sixth-highest mountain in Scotland. The flatness of the summit plateau contrasts with the savage crags that drop away into the eastern corries. Conditions on this mountain can be severe and navigation challenging. The connoisseur's route begins at the Nevis Range car park, 6.5mi north-east of Fort William along the A82. This is a commercial ski centre during the winter and is well signed. The route approaches Aonach Mór along a fine northern spur. Aonach Beag can then be visited before traversing back along the summit plateau and descending across the ski fields. The distance is 11mi (18km) and requires at least eight hours. Of course you could take advantage of the cable car (open all year), which will take you approximately halfway to the top of Aonach Mór. Consult OS Outdoor Leisure 1:25,000 map No 38 *(Ben Nevis & Glen Coe)*.

The Grey Corries

The Grey Corries lie at the eastern end of the massif that includes Ben Nevis and the Aonachs. A string of graceful, conical summits is linked by a high-level ridge that provides one of the best ridge walks in Scotland. The approach is quite long, however, and you'll need around eight or nine hours for the traverse as far as Beinn na Socaich, or 10 hours if you go all the way to Sgurr Chòinnich Beag. Start and finish at Corriechoille, down a minor road 2.5mi east of Spean Bridge. Unfortunately public transport will only take you as far as Spean Bridge. Nearest facilities are in Spean Bridge and Fort William (see Gateway on page 192). For the truly heroic, how about the Lochaber Traverse, beginning at Corriechoille and traversing the Grey Corries, Aonachs and Carn Mór Dearg, before finishing with an ascent of Ben Nevis. All in one day of course! Consult OS Outdoor Leisure 1:25,000 map No 38 *(Ben Nevis & Glen Coe)*; the walk is also described in *100 Best Routes on Scottish Mountains* by Ralph Storer and *20 Hill Walks: Glen Coe and Lochaber* by Ruaridh Pringle.

Glen Nevis Circuit

The short walk through the Nevis gorge to Steall Meadows (see the Ring of Steall walk on page 198) is one of the finest low-level walks in Scotland. It can be made into a short but interesting circuit by climbing the southern side of Glen Nevis to reach Steall Hut, before returning down through the gorge. It could be done in the other direction, but the route finding would be much more difficult. The terrain above Glen Nevis is rugged but affords brilliant views of Ben Nevis and Aonach Beag. Start and finish at the parking area on a sharp left-hand bend three-quarters of a mile south of the Glen Nevis roadhead. There is a footbridge across the Water of Nevis very close by. Cross the bridge and climb the obvious spur to the left. By picking your way up this spur you'll reach the lower slopes of Sgurr a' Mhàim. Contour along these and then descend to Steall Hut. Use the wire walkway to recross the Water of Nevis and then follow the path down through Nevis gorge. The total distance is only 3.5mi but you'll probably need three hours. Nearest facilities are in Glen Nevis (see page 194) and Fort William (see page 192). See Ring of Steall for details of the bus service operating in Glen Nevis (see page 199). Use OS Outdoor Leisure 1:25,000 map No 38 *(Ben Nevis & Glen Coe)*.

GLEN COE

Beinn a' Bheithir

Beinn a' Bheithir offers a route every bit the equal of Bidean nam Bian or Buachaille Etive Mór, but is normally overlooked. The walk starts in Ballachulish, 1mi west of Glencoe village on the A82, and follows a good track south to gain the north-east ridge of Sgòrr Bhan. After an exhilarating scramble to this summit, the route continues along a fine, airy ridge across Sgòrr Dearg (1024m) and Sgòrr Dhonuill, with fine views across Morvern and Ardgour, before descending back to the A82 via Gleann a' Chaolais. You'll need seven or eight hours for the 10mi (16km) circuit, and as there is more than 1300m of ascent you'll need to be reasonably fit. Consult OS Outdoor Leisure 1:25,000 map No 38 *(Ben Nevis & Glen Coe)*.

Glencoe Lochan Trail

This is a very short, waymarked forest trail close to Glencoe village. The centrepiece is the lochan, which has fine views (and sometimes reflections) of the surrounding mountains. You'll only need an hour or two and you can start in Glencoe itself.

MORVERN, ARDGOUR & MOIDART

These rugged and unfrequented districts are separated from Lochaber by Loch Linnhe. Morvern and Ardgour can be reached most easily on the Corran Ferry, otherwise you need to make a circuitous detour via Fort William. Moidart and the Rois-bheinn Ridge are most easily reached via Fort William. These areas do not receive many visitors and they have a quiet, wild charm, which will suit those put off by the crowds in Glen Coe. Although the peaks are not particularly high, the terrain can be serious and the added remoteness means that getting into difficulties can have grave consequences. Although they are not described here, there are numerous possibilities for beautiful low-level walks, both among the long, lonely glens and along stretches of the Atlantic coastline.

If you have your own transport, all of the walks mentioned below can be walked as a day trip from Fort William or Glencoe. It is also possible (theoretically) to reach the starts of all of these walks via postbus (☎ 01246-546329) and Shiel Buses (☎ 01967-431272), but the schedules may be less than convenient. Accommodation is mostly limited to hotels and B&Bs, although there are camping sites in Salen and Strontian.

The Scottish Mountaineering Club's guide *North-West Highlands* focuses on Ardgour and Moidart, and the Garbh Bheinn and Rois-bheinn routes are described in *100 Best Routes on Scottish Mountains* by Ralph Storer.

Beinn Chlaonleud & Gleann Dubh

In the wild heart of Morvern, various circuits and linear walks can be devised from a start at Acharn on the A884. There are great views of the Isle of Mull from the summit of Beinn Chlaonleud, and the Gleann Dubh valley running to the north-west offers scenic, low-level walking. Also nearby is the John Raven Wildlife Reserve. For details on the reserve call into the Ardtornish Estate Office, 2mi south of Acharn on the A884. Use OS Landranger 1:50,000 map No 49 *(Oban & East Mull)*.

Garbh Bheinn

Garbh Bheinn (885m) is the fine, distant peak viewed so compellingly from Glencoe. Located in the south-western corner of Ardgour, it is only 30m shy of being a Munro, and is quite neglected by walkers. This is a bonus for those who can ignore such arbitrary judgements of worth, because Garbh Bheinn is a superb mountain with some demanding terrain and great views. A good circuit starts on the A861, just west of Inversanda, not far from the Corran Ferry. A long ridge is climbed to reach Sgòrr Mhic Eacharna, from where there are excellent views of the buttresses and gullies on Garbh Bheinn's east face. Once across the next top, Bheinn Bheag, a steep descent is made into the Bealach Feith an Amean before ascending to the summit of Garbh Bheinn. With over 1000m of ascent, the 9mi should take seven to eight hours. Navigation can be difficult, so this route is best avoided in poor weather. Consult OS Pathfinder 1:25,000 map No 289 *(Strontian & Ardgour)*.

Rois-bheinn Ridge

Rois-bheinn (882m) is the highest point on a ridge that includes several summits over 800m. This massif dominates Moidart, and a long and strenuous circuit of the rocky ridge can be made from Inverailort on the A861. The climbs add up to over 1500m of ascent. The terrain is complex and navigation in poor weather may be difficult. Consult OS Landranger 1:50,000 map No 40 *(Mallaig & Glenfinnan)*.

Beinn Resipol

Strictly speaking Beinn Resipol (845m) is in Sunart, just west of Ardgour. It is a shapely mountain with broad, rugged ridges descending from a conspicuous, conical summit. A fine there-and-back walk from Resipol Farm, 2.5mi east of Salen on the A861, will take around six or seven hours. Climb along the Allt Mhic Chiarain, on a path at first and then over open ground to reach Lochan Bac an Lochain. From there climb steeply to the summit of Beinn Resipol. Consult OS Landranger 1:50,000 map No 40 *(Mallaig & Glenfinnan)*.

The Cairngorms

The Cairngorms is the wildest and most extensive area of uplands in Scotland and embraces the largest tracts of land over 1200m, 900m and 600m. For this chapter 'Cairngorms' is interpreted very broadly – from Strathspey in the north, to Braemar and central Deeside in the east and south, and around the edge of the uplands to Blair Atholl in Glen Garry, following the authoritative Scottish Mountaineering Club guide. Originally the Cairngorms was called Am Monadh Ruadh, meaning 'red rounded mountains' (referring to the big outcrops of pinkish-red granite) but the name of the summit most visible from Strathspey was adopted for the entire area in the 19th century. Oddly, the name of this summit – Cairn Gorm – means 'blue rocky mountain'. The Grampians label is spread across the Cairngorms on many maps, but the name isn't much used by outdoor people nor in conservation issues.

Whatever the name, with the central plateau generally above 1000m, the Cairngorms is a place to be taken seriously and not where you'd go for a casual stroll. The area offers some of Scotland's finest opportunities for long-distance walks, using its network of public paths, and for magnificent treks across rolling mountains and plateaus. In winter it's one of Scotland's two main mountaineering and ice climbing venues, and a Mecca for cross-country and downhill skiers. It's also an area of outstanding ecological importance – the Cairngorms will become Scotland's second national park in 2003 (see the boxed text 'Cairngorms National Park' on page 216).

The Cairngorms can seem intimidatingly bleak and featureless. However, once you have spent some time there, you may understand what Henry Alexander, an early Scottish Mountaineering Club guidebook author, meant by: 'the greatness and dignity and calm of the Cairngorms cast their spell over the spirit'.

This chapter is divided into two sections; the northern section focuses on the central Cairngorms plateau and the southern section covers the big, long-distance routes and introduces the 'hills' and glens of Deeside.

Highlights

GRAEME CORNWALLIS

Linn of Dee – the picturesque start of a superbly scenic, low-level walk.

- A vast alpine plateau, seemingly on top of the world, with magnificent panoramic views to distant horizons
- Impressive Caledonian pine woodlands, with purple carpets of heather in late summer
- Centuries-old pathways through remote glens and across mountain passes
- Mysterious, darkly beautiful lochans cradled by the towering cliffs of glacier-sculpted corries

NATURAL HISTORY

Granite and schist predominate in the Cairngorms, giving rise to two basic types of landscape. The plateau and the big, rounded mountains with smooth, contoured slopes consist principally of granite, which commonly weathers into vast sheets of scree and fine gravel. Crags, bluffs and generally more broken slopes and cliffs indicate the presence of schist (and gneiss and diorite).

The landforms have glaciation and the ice age written all over them; long, deep U-shaped glens, great cliff-lined trenches, scores of stunning corries gouged out of the mountain slopes, and curiously shaped mounds of moraine in the glens.

The Caledonian woodlands, which include birch and juniper, in Rothiemurchus, Glen Derry and Glen Feshie in particular, are but remnants of the once extensive tree cover. The arctic-alpine vegetation of the Cairngorms is outstanding in its variety and extent. Tiny flowering plants, mosses and liverworts survive in areas where snow lingers into summer and on the crags and the gritty plateaus. Heather moorland is widespread below 750m (higher in some areas, lower elsewhere); the heather species are mixed with grasses and sedges.

Only a few birds and mammals live on the high ground; long-legged mountain hare, introduced reindeer on the Cairngorm plateau, golden plover, dotterel, snow

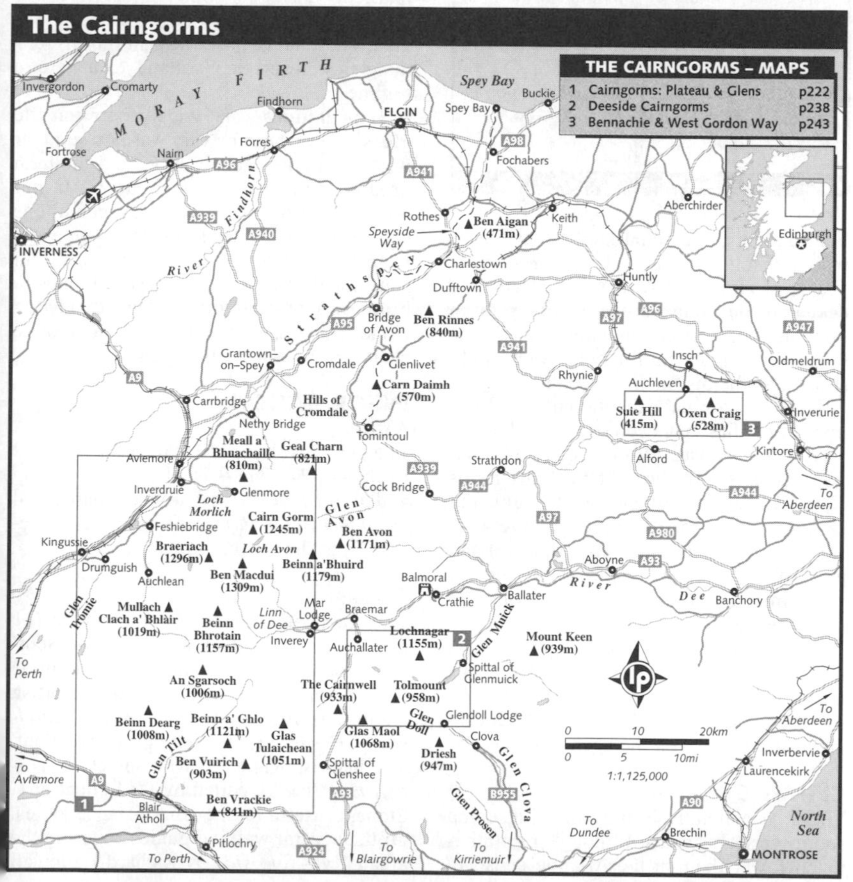

Cairngorms National Park

After lengthy public consultations, mainly conducted by Scottish Natural Heritage, Cairngorms National Park will finally be declared during 2003. Its boundaries look set to be drawn very generously, probably taking in the watersheds of the Rivers Spey and Dee, and extending south-eastward through the Angus glens to Kirriemuir. If this happens, the high plateaus that for many people are the essence of the Cairngorms could constitute but a small part of a large (by Scottish standards) and diverse park, including several towns and villages.

The park should be operational in April 2003, with its own staff, offices, logos and all the modern paraphernalia for conservation reserves.

The best source for further information is Scottish Natural Heritage (☎ 01224-642863, **W** www.snh.org.uk).

bunting, and the remarkable ptarmigan, which changes plumage three times a year and is a permanent resident. Red and roe deer and red grouse are most likely to be seen on the moors and in woodlands. In the trees, bird life is plentiful, notably crossbill, siskin and the big black capercaillie.

The Cairngorms' exceptional ecological importance has long been recognised in scientific and conservation circles. The national park (see the boxed text 'Cairngorms National Park') will take in the existing Cairngorms National Nature Reserve, several Sites of Special Scientific Interest and parts of two National Scenic Areas. The UK government will consider nominating the core mountain area (25% of which is owned by conservation and public organisations) as a World Heritage site, principally for its geological features; Special Area of Conservation and Special Protection Area designations are also on the agenda.

CLIMATE

The area generally is prey to mild, damp south-westerly winds, although rainfall is much lower than on the Atlantic coast. In the glens the annual total is around 80cm and on high ground it exceeds 200cm.

The mountains stand exposed to the coldest winds, from Arctic regions to the north, and from the continental European landmass to the east and south-east. From any direction, the wind can be ferociously strong; speeds exceeding 150 mi/h have been recorded at the Cairn Gorm summit weather station. As the mountains are well inland, snow accumulates to greater depths and lasts much longer than elsewhere in Scotland, from late November until May, although the cover waxes and wanes markedly during that time. In fact snow can fall in any month, although rarely in August. These facts make the Cairngorms' climate the closest in Scotland to an arctic regime.

Temperatures vary widely between the glens, where it can be very warm in summer with maximums above 20°C, and the high ground, with a drop of about 2.2°C per 300m elevation. On any one day, conditions can vary dramatically from glen to glen and from ridge to ridge – thick cloud here, bright sunshine there. The central plateau tends to be a law unto itself, quite often shrouded in cloud and rain, at other times rising into the clear air above fog-filled glens.

INFORMATION

Maps

The OS Travelmaster 1:250,000 map No 2 *(Northern Scotland)* is ideal for planning and finding your way around; map No 4 *(Southern Scotland)* would be useful for access from the south.

Books

The most comprehensive guidebook is *The Cairngorms* by Adam Watson in the Scottish Mountaineering Club's District Guide series. For in-depth information, Scottish Natural Heritage's *Cairngorms: A Landscape Fashioned by Geology* is excellent. The Scottish Rights of Way Society's *Scottish Hill Tracks*, edited by DJ Bennet & C Stone, is useful for the long-distance routes. Of the several walking guides covering the area, *Walks Speyside* by Richard Hallewell

Spectacular mountain scenery in **Lochaber & Glen Coe** – descending into famous Glen Coe; approaching Stob Dearg (1022m) on the magnificent Buachaille Etive Mór massif (inset). *Photos: Gareth McCormack.*

Known for its spectacular vistas and ecological importance, **The Cairngorms** will be Scotland's second national park – walkers enjoy a summer outing on the vast plateau; a climber atop Beinn Mheadhoin's (1182m) summit tor (inset). *Main photo: David Tipling. Inset: Graeme Cornwallis.*

is very compact and describes a good range of walks; John Brooks' *Cairngorms Walks* has better maps and more generous descriptions. Jim Crumley's *The Heart of the Cairngorms* is a passionate statement of the 'need for wildness' to be recognised in conservation and development proposals.

Information Sources

For information about natural history and conservation issues, Scottish Natural Heritage, the government agency responsible for such matters, is the best source. Its local office is at Achantoul (☎ 01479-810477), about 1mi north of Aviemore, open Monday to Friday. The web site W www.snh.org.uk is loaded with information about issues and activities, and has an inquiry service.

For weather forecasts, the area covered in this chapter is within the eastern Highlands region on ☎ 0891-500442, fax 0336-500442.

Northern Cairngorms

The focus is mainly on the vast, central Cairn Gorm-Macdui plateau, crowned by Ben Macdui (1309m, 4294ft), Scotland's second-highest mountain, rising to the south of Cairn Gorm (1245m, 4084ft) itself. The plateau is separated from neighbouring mountain massifs by the deep gash of Lairig Ghru in the west and Lairig an Laoigh in the east, and is pitted with spectacular, cliff-lined corries on its northern and southern faces. The weather on the plateau is notoriously fickle, with low cloud, mist, strong winds and sleet likely at any time. Visibility can quickly deteriorate to zero and, although the paths are well worn, prominent landmarks are scarce so finding the way can be difficult. Navigation skills, using a map and compass, are therefore essential.

Don't be put off if you're not keen on climbing mountains. On the northern slopes of the plateau, in Rothiemurchus Estate (privately owned) and Glenmore Forest Park (managed by Forest Enterprise), there are many low-level walks suitable for all and ideal for days when the mountains are shrouded in cloud.

Two walks, a high-level circuit over the summit of Cairn Gorm with an optional extension to Ben Macdui and a medium-level route deep into the range through Lairig Ghru, give a good introduction to the scale and wildness of the Cairngorms. The Other Walks section on page 241 includes outlines of the ascent of nearby Braeriach, third only to Ben Nevis and Ben Macdui and a truly magnificent peak; a much shorter climb over Meall a' Bhuachaille with fine views of the plateau; a long, low-level walk to beautiful Loch Avon; and an outline of the Speyside Way – a long-distance path linking Aviemore and Buckie on the North Sea coast.

PLANNING

When to Walk

Extensive snow cover can persist on the high plateau until well into May and start to build up again in November, so the best months for the area are May to September. Bad weather, with minimal visibility, is likely at any time, so it's vital to be aware of the local weather forecast before setting out.

What to Bring

The terrain is relatively featureless, so map and compass – and the ability to use them – are essential. There isn't much fresh water on the plateau, so carry all you'll need for the day.

Maps

Harvey's 1:25,000 *Cairn Gorm* map covers both walks very well. The OS Outdoor Leisure 1:25,000 map No 3 *(The Cairngorms – Aviemore & Glen Avon)* is a big, unwieldy double-sided sheet but excellent for fine detail. The OS Landranger 1:50,000 map No 36 *(Grantown & Aviemore)* would do as an alternative.

Information Sources

At the Cairngorm funicular's base station at Coire Cas, the Cairngorms Countryside Ranger Service (☎ 01479-861261) can give expert advice about walks on the plateau;

the local weather forecast is posted there daily. The service runs a program of guided walks during summer.

In an emergency, the mountain rescue contact for the area is the Aviemore police station on ☎ 01479-810222.

ACCESS TOWNS

Aviemore

Open all year, Aviemore TIC (☎ 01479-810363, e aviemoretic@host.co.uk), on Grampian Rd, has a good range of maps and guides, accommodation listings, weather

A Cairngorm Funicular – Environmental Vandalism?

At the beginning of the 1960s the northern slopes of the Cairngorms were opened up for downhill skiing with the building of a road from Glenmore into Coire Cas. From there chair lifts ascended to an intermediate station and on to Ptarmigan, the top station and restaurant at 1080m. Other later lifts and tows gave access to the eastern slopes, and a road snaked up from Coire Cas to Ptarmigan.

However, because the plateau is buffeted by winds stronger than 35 mph for more than 50% of the year, the chair lift often had to be closed.

In 1994 the Cairngorm Chairlift Company (CCC; now called the Cairngorm Mountain Company) proposed a more reliable and comfortable replacement for the chair lift – a funicular railway similar to those operating in continental European alpine resorts.

It was claimed it would attract a huge number of visitors – up to 200,000 annually was the late 1990s guesstimate, compared with about 50,000. Consequently, many jobs would be created and the local economy soundly underpinned.

The proposal ignited fierce opposition from walkers, mountaineers and conservation groups, led by the Cairngorms Campaign. They protested that the environmental impact of the development would be disastrous in an area of supreme ecological and scenic importance, that it couldn't possibly be economically viable and would probably drive visitors away rather than draw them in. What's more, snowfalls seem to be on the decline.

The European Regional Development Fund and the Bank of Scotland were eventually persuaded to back the project, anticipated to cost £14.7 million. Scottish Natural Heritage, the statutory environmental agency, sanctioned the proposal (confined to the Cairngorm Ski Area of 598ha), subject to mandatory access restrictions to protect adjacent European Union-designated conservation areas. The Scottish Executive finally approved the proposal and construction began in August 1999. To minimise the visual impact of the funicular and its support columns, the top 250m of the track to the Ptarmigan Visitor Centre will go through a shallow tunnel, blasted out of the hillside.

The funicular will take off in winter 2001–02, the new base station will open in December 2001 and the new Ptarmigan Visitor Centre and restaurant in spring 2002. The Daylodge, next to the base station, is being refurbished and will be open in December 2001. The Coire Cas car park will be upgraded. The operating company will plough profits back into facilities within the ski area, including footpath repair and construction.

The European money was provided on condition that the funicular operated as a closed system during summer, to ensure the increased number of visitors didn't cause severe damage to the fragile mountain environment. According to the official Visitor Management Plan, this means that between 1 May and 30 November funicular riders will not be allowed out onto the mountain – their experience will be confined to displays in the Ptarmigan Visitor Centre and what they can (with luck) see from the viewing platform and the funicular carriage. Whereas in the past people have been able to take the chair lift up to Ptarmigan and then walk up to the summit, this is no longer possible. Access on foot is now from Coire Cas only.

For more information on the project, contact Cairngorm Ski Area (☎ 01479-861261, fax 861207, e info@cairngorm.sol.co.uk). The informative Web site w www.cairngormmountain.com includes a link to local weather forecasts.

information and an exchange bureau. Contact the TIC for details of the numerous B&Bs in Aviemore.

If you are looking for something to eat, the ***Old Bridge Inn*** *(☎ 01479-811137)*, in Dalfaber Rd, is a largely unspoiled, traditional pub specialising in Scottish fare, including venison and salmon, and doesn't ignore vegetarians; prices represent good value and there's local ale on tap.

If you need some supplies, there is a good range of shops, including a ***Tesco*** supermarket. Aviemore Photographic (☎ 01479-810371), opposite the supermarket, provides Internet access for £3.50 per hour, Monday to Saturday.

Getting There & Away Aviemore is easily reached from Inverness, Glasgow and Edinburgh by frequent daily Scottish Citylink (☎ 0870-550 5050) bus services, which stop at the train station; the TIC handles bookings and inquiries. From late May to late September, Highland Country Buses (☎ 01463-222244) runs a twice-daily service between Fort William and Coire Cas car park via Aviemore. ScotRail (☎ 0845-755 0033) services linking Inverness with Edinburgh and Glasgow stop at Aviemore daily (at least nine trains) as does the GNER (☎ 0845-722 5225) midday service from London Kings Cross to Inverness via Edinburgh. If driving, turn off the A9 between Kingussie and Daviot to reach Aviemore.

Glenmore

Glenmore (7mi from Aviemore), beside the Ski Road up to Coire Cas, is the closest settlement to the start of the walks. Forest Enterprise's Glenmore Forest Park Visitor Centre (☎ 01479-861220), open daily, concentrates on the surrounding forest park. *Guide to Glenmore & Inshriach Forests*, available from the centre, includes maps and notes for waymarked walks in the park.

Places to Stay & Eat Forest Enterprise runs the large and well-maintained ***Glenmore Camping & Caravan Site*** *(☎ 01479-861271)*; the tariffs vary according to season, up to £9 per pitch. Opposite is ***Loch Morlich SYHA Hostel*** *(☎ 01479-861238)*, a spacious former lodge; the tariff is £9.25 and meals are available – only £4.95 for a three-course evening meal and £3.50 for a cooked breakfast.

Friendly Mrs Ferguson's ***Cairn Eilrig*** B&B *(☎ 01479-861223)* charges £17 for B&B. ***Glenmore Lodge*** *(☎ 01479-861256)*, about 1mi east of Glenmore, houses the National Sports Training Centre; the B&B tariff starts at £17.50. The lodge's ***Lochain Bar*** has a marvellous view of the Cairngorm plateau and – when you can't see the view – stunning posters of more distant mountains. It specialises in whiskies and serves reasonably priced bar meals, including a vegetarian option.

Glenmore ***shop***, next to the camping site, has a small range of supplies and liquid fuel and gas; the local forecast is posted outside. The adjacent ***cafe*** does light meals and snacks and is open during summer evenings.

Getting There & Away Highland Country Buses (☎ 01463-222244) operates services to Glenmore from late May to late September; see Getting to/from the Walk under Cairn Gorm High Circuit on page 220 for details.

Inverdruie & Coylumbridge

Rothiemurchus Visitor Centre (☎ 01479-812345, e rothie@enterprise.net) at Inverdruie is open daily all year. It's run by Rothiemurchus Estate and provides information about the estate, including guided walks led by the estate's own rangers; there's a ***farm shop*** (selling farm produce) next door. For all walking gear try Cairngorm Mountain Sports (☎ 01479-810729) in Inverdruie.

Junipers B&B *(☎ 01479-810405)* at Inverdruie is welcoming and comfortable; the tariff is £17. The small ***Rothiemurchus Camp & Caravan Park*** *(☎ 01479-812800)*, in pine woodland beside the Lairig Ghru path at Coylumbridge, charges £3.50.

For public transport options to Inverdruie and Coylumbridge, see Getting to/from the Walk under Cairn Gorm High Circuit on page 220.

Cairn Gorm High Circuit

Duration 4½–5 hours
Distance 7mi (11km)
Standard medium-hard
Start & Finish Coire Cas car park
Nearest Town Glenmore
Public Transport yes (seasonal)
Summary An outstanding mountain walk across a sprawling plateau, with magnificent wide-ranging views and an optional extension to Ben Macdui.

This is the most popular high walk in the Cairngorms, the highlights being the summit of Cairn Gorm, the dramatic peaks of Stob Coire an t-Sneachda and Cairn Lochan, and the awesome corries. It can't be stressed too strongly that this walk is not a doddle. The vast plateau drops precipitously in almost all directions and severe weather is possible at any time; conditions may be fine at Glenmore but up on top it can be completely different. Inexperienced walkers should only tackle this walk in seasoned company. Ben Macdui provides even wider views and a greater sensation of remoteness, out of sight of the developments on the northern slopes. The extra distance involved is 5mi (8km), for which you should allow at least two hours.

Although this walk can be done in either direction, it is described clockwise, going up to Cairn Gorm from the north-east, around the rim of Coire an t-Sneachda, over Cairn Lochan then down the ridge and back to the start. The path to Ben Macdui diverges from Cairn Lochan south-westward across a gap and up to the undulating plateau studded with cairns.

The ascent to Cairn Gorm's summit is about 645m and there's an additional climb of about 155m over Cairn Lochan; for Ben Macdui add another 200m of climbing. Realistically, the only escape route is down Fiacaill a' Choire Chais, the ridge between Coire Cas an Coire an t-Sneachda. The main Cairn Gorm walk isn't a particularly long day, allowing plenty of time for enjoying the views; adding Ben Macdui makes for a full day but well within the scope of fit walkers.

GETTING TO/FROM THE WALK

From late May to late September Highland Country Buses (☎ 01463-222244) puts on a daily service between Aviemore railway station and Coire Cas, providing at least three runs in each direction. The first bus leaves Aviemore at 9.30am and the last departs Coire Cas at 7.05pm; the single/return fares are £2.50/4. In addition, Highland Country Buses' Munro Bagger service from late May to late September between Fort William and Coire Cas goes via Aviemore railway station twice daily; the single/day return fares are £6/10.50.

By road from Aviemore take the B970 via Inverdruie to Coylumbridge, then continue along the Ski Road to Glenmore and the Coire Cas car park.

THE WALK

See map pages 222–3

Start by walking back (north) down the road, away from the car park, to a road junction and take the road to the right for about 90m to a stonework drain on the right. A small cairn in the heather marks the start of a narrow path on the other side of the ditch, parallel to the road. Follow this entrenched old track for about 200m and you'll find that it becomes wider and clearer, up the heather-clad slope. After a while cairns mark the route, which continues steadily upwards, with views unfolding of the corries and spurs of the Cairngorm plateau. The path goes beneath a ski lift, past the top of another, weaving in and out of the picket fences lining the routes of the lifts. Having left the heather behind, the path then crosses gravelly ground. Until the new Ptarmigan Visitor Centre opens in spring 2002, you need to follow path diversion signs around the construction site. Beyond the centre, a stone-paved path leads fairly steeply up to a boulder field where cairns and poles clearly mark the route across this minor obstacle course and up to the large cairn on the summit of **Cairn Gorm** (1245m), with a weather station nearby.

Among the multitude of features in the panoramic view are the long, flat plateau of Ben Wyvis (just west of Inverness) to the north, the sprawling bulk of Ben Macdui nearby, beyond it the sharper profile of Braeriach and, to the south-east, flat-topped Ben Avon, dotted with granite tors.

Descend sharply westward over a jumble of big boulders – initially there's no clear path – towards a wide path on clearer ground below. Then, on a broad saddle, diverge a little to the right to a prominent cairn (1141m) at the head of Fiacaill a' Choire Chais (the escape route mentioned earlier) for a great view of the crags on the eastern side of Cairn Lochan.

To continue, follow the broad path around the rim of Coire an t-Sneachda, which is lined with cliffs. Its flat floor is decorated with swampy lochans. A cairned route, rather than a path, leads up to **Stob Coire an t-Sneachda** (1176m) and more great views. Drop down westward to a small gap. The path to Ben Macdui leads south from here (see Side Trip). Otherwise, climb steeply to **Cairn Lochan** (1215m) with its sprawling cairn close to the rim of the plunging cliffs. The beautiful green patchwork of broad Strathspey dominates the outlook north-west and westward.

Continue generally south-west following a cairned route, then descend the steep, mostly rocky slope to the clearly defined path along the north-south ridge rimming the western side of Coire an Lochain. The path loses height fairly quickly down the heathery slope as it bends north-eastward and crosses a small stream. A well-made path takes over – you may be grateful for the huge stepping stones planted across a very boggy stretch. The excellent path leads on, making it much easier to enjoy the superb views of the northern corries, then across Allt Coire an t-Sneachda and on to the car park at Coire Cas.

Side Trip: Ben Macdui

2½ hours, 5mi (8km), 200m ascent

From the small gap between Stob Coire an t-Sneachda and Cairn Lochan, follow the clear, narrow path leading south then south-west above the shallow valley of Féith Buidhe and down to a wide saddle cradling Lochan Buidhe. Snow can linger on the north-facing slope, just east of the lochan, into late summer. Beyond Lochan Buidhe you can see the dramatic cliffs of Carn Etchachan, while in the opposite direction, across the depths of the Lairig Ghru, Braeriach's magnificent corries look as if some giant hand had scooped them out of the plateau. Follow a cairned route south-east across boulders then climb the steep slope, past a minor peak, and on to the summit of **Ben Macdui** (1309m), marked by a lonely survey pillar, near which is a low stone shelter and a topograph, erected by the Cairngorm Club (Aberdeen) in 1925. It helps identify the features in the extraordinarily wide view – from Ben Nevis and Creag Meagaidh (west-south-west), to Lochnagar (east-south-east) and Ben More Assynt (north-north-west).

To return to the Cairn Gorm High Circuit route, retrace your steps to the saddle of the anonymous lochan. From there keep to the left or westerly path over the broad spur, then it's down – with an awesome view straight into the Lairig Ghru, overlooked by rugged Lurchers Crag. Follow this path back to Coire Cas as described above.

Chalamain Gap & the Lairig Ghru

Duration	6–6½ hours
Distance	14mi (22.5km)
Standard	medium-hard
Start	Sugar Bowl car park
Finish	Coylumbridge
Nearest Towns	Coylumbridge, Inverdruie, Aviemore, Glenmore
Public Transport	yes (seasonal)

Summary An energetic walk into the finest mountain pass in Scotland, following rocky paths and crossing boulder fields, with a choice of return routes.

Far from any road, the Lairig Ghru is widely regarded as the finest mountain pass in Scotland. Cut by a massive glacier slicing right through the mountain mass, it provides a natural route from Strathspey to upper Deeside. Lairig Ghru means 'pass of

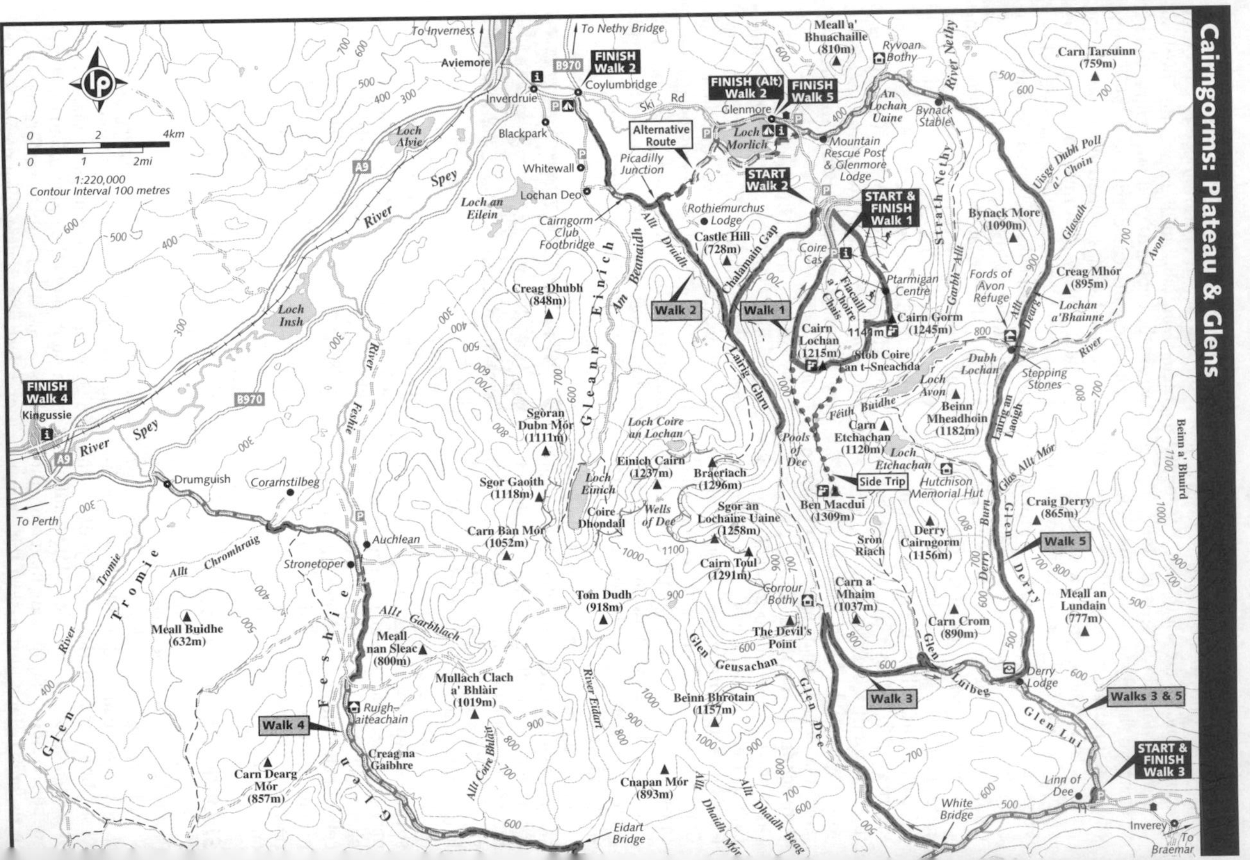
Cairngorms: Plateau & Glens
To Inverness
Aviemore
To Nethy Bridge
B970
FINISH Walk 2
Coylumbridge
Inverdruie
Blackpark
Whitewall
Lochan Deo
Loch an Eilein
Loch Alvie
Spey
River
A9
Loch Insh
0 2 4km
0 1 2mi
1:220,000
Contour Interval 100 metres
Meall a' Bhuachaille (810m)
Ryvoan Bothy
FINISH (Alt) Walk 2
FINISH Walk 5
Glenmore
Ski Rd
Loch Morlich
An Lochan Uaine
Bynack Stable
River Nethy
Mountain Rescue Post & Glenmore Lodge
Alternative Route
Picadilly Junction
START Walk 2
START & FINISH Walk 1
Rothiemurchus Lodge
Castle Hill (728m)
Chalamain Gap
Cairngorm Club Footbridge
Allt Druidh
Am Beanaidh
Gleann Einich
Walk 2
Walk 1
Coire Cas
Fiacaill a' Choire Chais
Ptarmigan Centre
Cairn Gorm (1245m)
Cairn Lochan (1215m)
1141m
Stob Coire an t-Sneachda
Strath Nethy
Garbh Allt
Carn Tarsuinn (759m)
Uisge Dubh Poll a' Choin
Glasath
Bynack More (1090m)
Avon
Creag Mhór (895m)
Fords of Avon Refuge
Allt Dearg
Lochan a'Bhainne
River
Dubh Lochan
Stepping Stones
Loch Avon
Beinn Mheadhoin (1182m)
Lairig an Laoigh
Féith Buidhe
Carn Etchachan (1120m)
Loch Etchachan
Hutchison Memorial Hut
Glas Allt Mór
Beinn a' Bhuird
Lairig Ghru
Pools of Dee
Side Trip
Ben Macdui (1309m)
Craig Derry (865m)
Walk 5
Glen Derry
Derry Burn
Derry Cairngorm (1156m)
Sron Riach
Meall an Lundain (777m)
Creag Dhubh (848m)
Sgòran Dubh Mór (1111m)
Loch Coire an Lochan
Einich Cairn (1237m)
Braeriach (1296m)
Sgor Gaoith (1118m)
Loch Einich
Coire Dhondail
Wells of Dee
Sgor an Lochaine Uaine (1258m)
Carn Bàn Mór (1052m)
Cairn Toul (1291m)
Corrour Bothy
Carn a' Mhaim (1037m)
Carn Crom (890m)
Tom Dudh (918m)
The Devil's Point
Glen Geusachan
Glen Luibeg
Derry Lodge
Walk 3
Walks 3 & 5
Glen Lui
START & FINISH Walk 3
Linn of Dee
White Bridge
Inverey
To Braemar
Glen Dee
Beinn Bhrotain (1157m)
River Eidart
Mullach Clach a' Bhlàir (1019m)
Allt Coire Bhlàir
Cnapan Mór (893m)
Allt Dhaidh Mór
Allt Dhaidh Beag
Eidart Bridge
FINISH Walk 4
Kingussie
River Spey
B970
Drumguish
Corarnstilbeg
To Perth
River Feshie
Auchlean
Stronetoper
Allt Chromhraig
Glen Tromie
River Tromie
Meall Buidhe (632m)
Allt Garbhlach
Meall nan Sleac (800m)
Ruigh-aiteachain
Walk 4
Creag na Gaibhre
Glen Feshie
Carn Dearg Mór (857m)

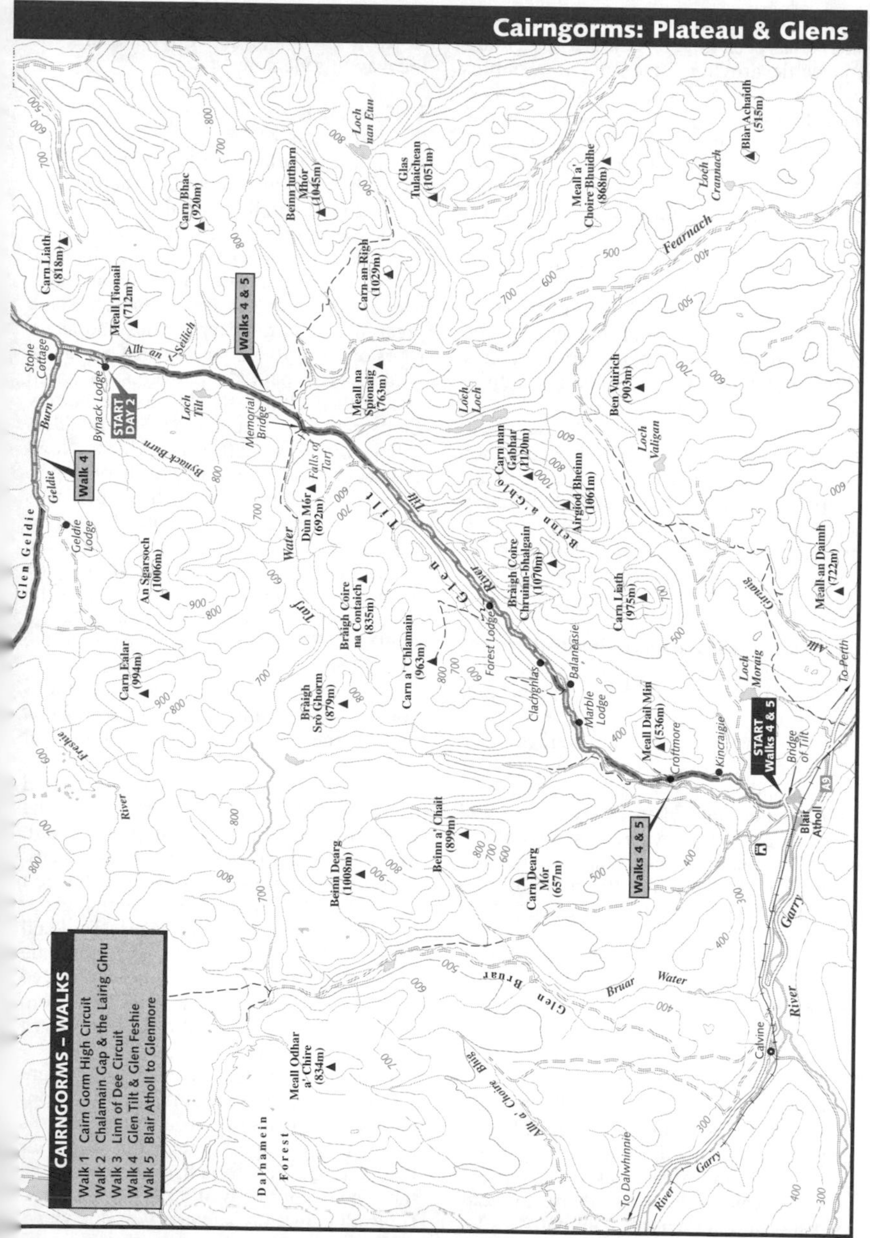
Cairngorms: Plateau & Glens
CAIRNGORMS – WALKS
Walk 1 Cairn Gorm High Circuit
Walk 2 Chalamain Gap & the Lairig Ghru
Walk 3 Linn of Dee Circuit
Walk 4 Glen Tilt & Glen Feshie
Walk 5 Blair Atholl to Glenmore
Walks 4 & 5
Walk 4
START DAY 2
START Walks 4 & 5
Stone Cottage
Bynack Lodge
Geldie Lodge
Glen Geldie
Geldie Burn
Bynack Burn
Allt an t-Seilich
Loch Tilt
Memorial Bridge
Falls of Tarf
Tarf Water
Glen Tilt
River Tilt
Forest Lodge
Clachghlas
Balaneasie
Marble Lodge
Croftmore
Kincraigie
Bridge of Tilt
Blair Atholl
Loch Moraig
Calvine
River Garry
Bruar Water
Glen Bruar
Allt a' Choire Bhig
River Feshie
Dalnamein Forest
Fearnach
Allt Girnaig
Loch Valigan
Loch Loch
Loch nan Eun
Loch Crannach
To Perth
To Dalwhinnie
Carn Liath (818m)
Meall Tionail (712m)
Carn Bhac (920m)
Beinn Iutharn Mhór (1045m)
Glas Tulaichean (1051m)
Carn an Righ (1029m)
Meall na Spionaig (763m)
Meall a' Choire Bhuidhe (868m)
Blàr Achaidh (515m)
Ben Vuirich (903m)
Carn nan Gabhar (1120m)
Beinn a' Ghlo
Airgiod Bheinn (1061m)
Bràigh Coire Chruinn-bhalgain (1070m)
Carn Liath (975m)
Meall an Daimh (722m)
Meall Dail Min (536m)
Dùn Mór (692m)
An Sgarsoch (1006m)
Bràigh Coire na Contaich (835m)
Carn a' Chlamain (963m)
Carn Ealar (994m)
Bràigh Sròn Ghorm (879m)
Beinn a' Chait (899m)
Beinn Dearg (1008m)
Carn Dearg Mór (657m)
Meall Odhar a' Chire (834m)
A9

Druie' – the stream that drains its northern side. It has been used for centuries as a trade and cattle droving route, and is a public right of way. Traditionally, people walked the full distance from Aviemore to Braemar (28mi/45km), but these days many start from Coylumbridge or Glenmore. The walk described here is a day's outing from just south of Glenmore, through dramatic Chalamain Gap and up to the top of Lairig Ghru then back to Coylumbridge through Rothiemurchus pine woodlands.

The best way to do the walk is as described, starting at a point higher than the finish. Crossing Chalamain Gap involves a climb of 240m and it's another 225m up to the top of Lairig Ghru.

Alternatives One possible alternative for the return is to walk back to Herons Field car park on the Ski Road near Glenmore, a distance of 14.8mi (23.5km); Forest Enterprise charges £1 for the use of this car park. Or, you can reach the Ski Road near the western end of Loch Morlich via the Rothiemurchus Estate road, although car parking there is less satisfactory. The distance for this version is 12.8mi (20.5km). An outline of these alternatives follows the main walk description.

If you have plenty of time, there are several interesting possibilities to consider. You could continue down Lairig Ghru to the Luibeg path, and on to Derry Lodge and Linn of Dee, from where it's possible to reach Braemar, or keep going southward, right through Glen Tilt to Blair Atholl (see Glen Tilt & Glen Feshie on page 229).

GETTING TO/FROM THE WALK

The walk starts at Sugar Bowl car park, on the north-eastern side of the Ski Road 1.75mi south of Glenmore. You could use the seasonal Highland Country Buses (☎ 01463-222244) service from Aviemore to Coire Cas (see Getting to/from the Walk under Cairn Gorm High Circuit on page 220), although the driver will probably stop below the car park, for safety's sake.

At the end of the walk, there's a small roadside car park nearby. Alternatively, the same bus service to the start of the walk stops in Glenmore and Coylumbridge on the way to Aviemore.

THE WALK

See map pages 222–3

From the car park cross the road and follow the path down to a footbridge across Allt Mór. Climb up to the right then, on the rim of the bank, veer left along a stone-paved path and continue past a sign warning that you're entering a wild mountainous area, across moorland. The views along here are great, taking in the deep corries and sharp spurs of the northern face of the Cairngorm plateau. The path dips to cross a small stream then climbs steadily to the narrow **Chalamain Gap**. Clamber over the boulders filling its narrow cleft, keeping to the lowest level to avoid the peaty, heathery slopes. It's an eerily quiet place, where rock falls seem to happen fairly frequently. On the far side there are magnificent views across the Lairig Ghru to mighty Braeriach and the cairn-topped Sgòran Dubh Mór beyond. The wide, rocky, occasionally wet path crosses a shallow valley then descends steeply to the **Lairig Ghru** path beside Allt Druidh.

The path crosses the stream on enormous boulders and climbs the heathery slope, then emerges onto more open ground but still with the steep slopes towering above. Elongated mounds of moraine, left behind by the retreating glaciers, partly block the valley as you climb towards the summit. The path is marked by occasional cairns; follow these carefully, keeping to the left (east) for the final stretch to the crest. Ahead, the rugged peaks of Cairn Toul and The Devil's Point come into view. Continue for another 500m or so to the **Pools of Dee** – the headwaters of the River Dee – from where you can look far down the southern side of Lairig Ghru.

Retrace your steps to the point where you joined the Lairig Ghru path and continue downstream. The rough path crosses steep, rocky slopes with Allt Druidh far below in a deep trench cut through the moraine. Continue past a path to the right (to Rothiemurchus Lodge), with fine views of the Monadhliath Mountains on the western side of Strathspey and Meall a' Bhuachaille above Loch Morlich. After about 1.25mi you meet some beautiful Scots pines, the outliers of the Caledonian woodland and a precious remnant of the great forests that once covered much of the Highlands. The path junction, known unofficially as Piccadilly, has direction signs to Aviemore (to the left/west) and Loch Morlich (to the right/east).

Follow the track to Aviemore, beside Allt Druidh, past a stream junction and down to the **footbridge**, built in 1912 by the Cairngorm Club over Allt na Beinne Moire (mapped as Am Beanaidh). A short distance farther on, bear right along a path to Coylumbridge. This leads through dense pines then more open pine woodland (where the displays of purple heather in August are magnificent), across small burns and through gates. Pass a path to the left (to Glen Einich) and continue along the broad track, past the Rothiemurchus camping site, to the road at Coylumbridge. There is a small roadside car park to the left.

Alternative Finish: Piccadilly to Glenmore

1¼ hours, 3mi (5km)

Turn right at Piccadilly along the wide path towards Loch Morlich. This leads through pine woodland to a high deer fence, just beyond which you meet the wide gravel road to Rothiemurchus Lodge. Bear left and continue along the gravel road for nearly 1mi to an unsigned junction.

To reach the Ski Road near the western end of Loch Morlich directly from here, just continue ahead for 300m. There is some roadside car parking here and there's a Forest Enterprise car park 200m to the right, where the fee is £1. Glenmore is 1.25mi along the Ski Road.

For Herons Field, follow the path from the unsigned junction to a footbridge across a small burn then go through a tall gate (where you leave Rothiemurchus Estate and enter Glenmore Forest Park) and go left along a wide forest track, skirting the shore of Loch Morlich. Near its eastern end turn left along a path marked with a red-banded post. Follow the route, marked with these posts, north and east through cleared land and pines to the car park just south of Glenmore. Sugar Bowl car park is 1.25mi farther south along the Ski Road.

Southern Cairngorms

The highlights of this area, south of an east-west line roughly through Ben Macdui, are the lengthy public footpaths through the glens, which serve to unify the entire Cairngorms area. For walkers, these pedestrian 'highways' offer outstanding opportunities for extended walks in remote, uninhabited country, and easy access to scores of mountains. Many of the walks pass through the large Mar Lodge Estate, owned by the National Trust for Scotland (see the boxed text 'Restoring Mar Lodge Estate' on page 226). The estate is rich in archaeological evidence of past settlement and many hundreds of sites have been identified. Examples of these are quite common through Glen Dee – the foundations of stone cottages and stone-walled enclosures.

This section features walks along some of the public footpaths and a mountain walk to beautiful Lochnagar in Deeside, the area centred on the River Dee and its broad strath. The Other Walks section on page 241 includes notes about a walk around Loch Muick (near Lochnagar) and another up Morrone, a fine mountain above Braemar.

PLANNING

Information Sources

For mountain rescue, contact the Aberdeen headquarters (☎ 01224-386000) of the Grampian police force; the stations in Ballater and Braemar aren't full-time.

ACCESS TOWN

Braemar

Braemar, internationally famous for its annual September Highland Gathering, is a compact village deep in the mountains, just off the A93. The TIC (☎ 01339-741600) is open daily year-round and carries a good range of guidebooks; the local weather forecast is usually on display. The one bank does not have an ATM – the nearest is in Ballater (see Nearest Town on page 240). Braemar Mountain Sports (☎ 01339-741242) is open daily and has a comprehensive stock, including cooking fuels. The National Trust for Scotland Mar Lodge Estate Rangers (☎ 01339-741669) lead guided walks during summer.

Places to Stay & Eat Beside the A93 just south of the village, ***Braemar SYHA Hostel*** *(☎ 01339-741659, e braemar@ syha.org .uk)* has smallish dorms (the tariff is £9.25), an excellent drying room and a large kitchen; the hostel is open throughout the day. The mountain weather forecast is displayed daily. ***Invercauld Caravan Club Site*** *(☎ 01339-741373)*, near the hostel, is open to non-members. It's well laid out with plenty of trees and grass, and costs £3.50 for a tent and £4 per adult; facilities include a drying room.

If you'd prefer a bit of luxury, then you can't go wrong with ***Schiehallion*** B&B *(☎ 01339-741679)*, on the main road, run by keen walkers Julie and Steve Heyes; the tariff in the strikingly decorated rooms is from £18.

For a meal, of the substantial hotels in Braemar, ***Invercauld Arms*** *(☎ 01339-741428)* deservedly has the best reputation. Servings are generous and the menu includes pasta (£6) and venison casserole (£6.50), provided in the tartan-clad, whisky carton-lined cocktail bar.

For self-caterers there's an ***Alldays*** supermarket, ***Strachan's*** grocery for Scottish delicacies, and a good butcher where you can also buy fresh bread.

Getting There & Away Stagecoach (☎ 0870-608 2608) provides regular daily buses between Aberdeen and Braemar, via Ballater; the single/return fare is £6/9.50. Stagecoach's summer-only Heather Hopper service between Aberdeen and Perth calls at Braemar once daily; it costs £6 per journey, wherever you get on and off.

Braemar is on the A93, 59mi (95.6km) from Aberdeen and 17mi (27.5km) west of Ballater.

Restoring Mar Lodge Estate

The National Trust for Scotland's purchase of the vast Mar Lodge Estate (29,500ha) in 1995 was hailed by many conservationists as a victory for the protection and better management of natural areas. All too frequently estates had been acquired by wealthy people with no real understanding of the natural values of the land. In the mid-1990s, the estate's red deer population (3300 of them) was too high to allow the precious Caledonian woodlands to regenerate naturally (a problem for the past 250 years), magnificently wild and lonely glens were blighted with exotic conifer plantations (although not on a large scale) and bulldozed tracks scarred some hillsides.

The Trust set out to restore Mar Lodge, to conserve its landscape, archaeology, buildings and wildlife, and to cater for visitors by providing compatible access. This was an immense undertaking; the estate embraces the watershed of the upper River Dee, east to Glen Ey on the south side of the river and to the Beinn a' Bhuird ridge to the north.

This policy directly affects walkers in two ways. Firstly, access is based on the principle of maintaining the long walk-in. In other words, unlike areas such as Glen Coe where the mountains are within sight of a busy road, you have to cover several miles on foot from a car park before you reach the start of a climb. So you really earn the 15 Munros within the estate! Secondly, footpaths are being repaired using local materials – as you'll find in Glen Derry and Glen Luibeg. In keeping with the wilderness spirit of the estate, signposting is limited to those installed by the Scottish Rights of Way Society at key locations along public footpaths. A logical extension of the long walk-in principle is that the Trust permits wild camping, although open fires are strictly prohibited.

Linn of Dee Circuit

Duration	6½–7 hours
Distance	16mi (26km)
Standard	medium
Start & Finish	Linn of Dee
Nearest Towns	Braemar, Inverey
Public Transport	yes

Summary A varied day exploring the southern reaches of two long-distance routes with superb views of the Braeriach massif above Lairig Ghru.

This is a superbly scenic, comparatively low-level walk, exploring Glen Dee and Glen Lui, west of Braemar. It's a good way of familiarising yourself with the area and its special feeling of remoteness and isolation. With a high point of 610m (only 250m of ascent), it is ideal for a misty day. A clockwise direction is recommended so you walk up the ever narrowing Glen Dee towards spectacular Lairig Ghru and the best of the going underfoot is concentrated in the second half of the walk. The walk can be extended farther up Lairig Ghru as far as the Pools of Dee; this involves an extra 7mi (11km) return.

National Trust for Scotland has a policy of encouraging the long walk-in to the mountains in the estate – the reason for the car park being at Linn of Dee rather than Derry Lodge (see the boxed text 'Restoring Mar Lodge Estate').

This walk is the key to several mountain climbs (or Munro bagging excursions): massive Beinn Bhrotain (1157m) rising from the western side of Glen Dee, The Devil's Point (1004m) towering over Corrour Bothy, Carn a' Mhaim (1037m) opposite the bothy, Ben Macdui (1309m) via Glen Luibeg and Sròn Riach, and Derry Cairngorm (1156m) on its own or coupled with Ben Macdui. All are very fine walks, although adding any to the route described here makes for a long day, best kept for good midsummer weather. Spreading these walks over a couple of days would be better; Corrour Bothy (resembling a remote rubbish tip in late summer 2000) can't be recommended, but there's plenty of tent space nearby. Being in National Trust for Scotland territory there's no problem with wild camping for a night or two, although open fires are strictly prohibited.

NATURAL HISTORY

This walk is essentially a tour around the River Dee and its tributaries, crossing the foothills of Derry Cairngorm and Ben Macdui and a low divide between the River Dee and Luibeg Burn.

During the walk you see plenty of evidence of the National Trust for Scotland's work to restore the magnificent pine woodlands, with fenced areas (exclosures) in Glen Luibeg where the native woodland, safe from hungry deer, is slowly making a comeback. In Glen Derry and Glen Dee, conifer plantations and their enclosing fences are being removed, to make way for native species and to give capercaillie and black grouse a better chance of thriving without the hazard of lethal fencing. Less obviously, the number of red deer has been greatly reduced, to about half the 1995 population.

PLANNING

When to Walk

The best season here is from May to September, although the walk could be undertaken as early as March and as late as November, when there may be some snow beyond Glen Derry.

Stalking The walk is entirely within the National Trust for Scotland's Mar Lodge Estate where estate staff do the stalking, but never on weekends; walkers' access is not affected by stalking activities.

Maps & Books

The OS Landranger 1:50,000 map No 43 *(Braemar & Blair Atholl)* covers this walk. The Harvey Superwalker 1:25,000 *Cairn Gorm* map excludes the area north-west from Linn of Dee, between Glen Luibeg and the River Dee.

The Scottish Mountaineering Club's guide *The Cairngorms* contains some relevant information. The National Trust for Scotland has a booklet about Mar Lodge

Estate, which is available from the rangers' office at Mar Lodge or, more conveniently, from the TICs in Braemar and Ballater.

NEAREST TOWN

Inverey

Small ***Inverey SYHA Hostel (☎ 01339-741969)***, about 5mi west of Braemar and just west of the village on the Linn of Dee road, is off the beaten track; there's always plenty of hot water on tap to compensate for the lack of a shower. A bed in a small dorm costs £6.50. The weather forecast is available daily. The postbus service from Braemar (see Getting to/from the Walk) passes Inverey on the way to Linn of Dee; ask the driver to drop you at the hostel.

GETTING TO/FROM THE WALK

The walk starts at the free National Trust for Scotland Linn of Dee car park, 6.4mi (10.5km) west of Braemar, just north of the River Dee bridge. A postbus (☎ 01246-546329) service from Braemar calls at Linn of Dee Monday to Saturday, but the timing (1.40pm) isn't very convenient.

THE WALK

See map pages 222–3

From the car park head west along the road and continue past a barrier, along a vehicular track. You soon leave a pine plantation behind, entering wide, steep-sided Glen Dee. Follow the road, past many former settlements and scattered Scots pines, to White Bridge (about 1¼ hours from the start). Continue west beside the River Dee for about 200m then turn away from the river, following a narrow path up a steepish heather-clad bank. The path, generally pretty rough but easy enough to follow, leads up Glen Dee, well above the river at first. After a couple of miles it drops down to the river bank where the glen narrows; views of the mighty cliffs of The Devil's Point, the gateway to Lairig Ghru, and Cairn Toul beyond begin to unfold. As the glen widens again, near cliff-lined Glen Geusachan to the west, the path rises across the heathery-peaty slope and leads to a junction, spectacularly overlooked by The Devil's Point and just about opposite **Corrour Bothy** (2½ hours from White Bridge).

To reach the bothy go down a narrow path on the left to a bridge across the river. Pick your way through the peat hags up to the bothy standing more or less high and dry above the peaty morass. The bothy, built in 1877 and renovated in 1950 by the Cairngorm Club, is rather small; the outlook to Ben Macdui is truly awesome.

From the path junction it takes a good three hours to continue up through the magnificent depths of Lairig Ghru to the Pools of Dee and to return – well worth the effort if time is on your side (see the Chalamain Gap & the Lairig Ghru walk on page 221).

The route back to Linn of Dee heads south from the path junction. The path rises steadily up the lowermost slopes of Carn a' Mhaim to the divide between the Dee and Luibeg Burn. Around here the quality of the path improves dramatically, with sections of stone paving and beautifully built culverts. The path descends into Glen Luibeg to an exclosure – go through the gate. There's a choice to be made here; the dry feet option is to turn left (north), cross 300m of muddy ground to Luibeg Bridge, then go back downstream through an exclosure, past a path junction (to Ben Macdui) on the left (1½ hours from Corrour Bothy). The alternative, when Luibeg Burn is low, is to go straight ahead and cross the stream on widely spaced stepping stones, then rejoin the main path.

Shortly a vehicular track diverges to the right; continue on it (for easier going) down Glen Luibeg – the scattered pine woodlands are a dramatic change from the moors and crags earlier. After about 1mi you reach the edge of a flat stretch of grassland. Follow a rough path east from here to a bridge over Derry Burn, near boarded-up **Derry Lodge** (an hour from Luibeg Bridge). There is a telephone for public and emergency use in a red box on the side of a brown timber building near the lodge. It's coin-operated and maintained (at a loss) by the volunteer Braemar Mountain Rescue Team.

The last hour or so's walking is easy, down Glen Lui along a vehicular track, past exclosures, areas cleared of exotic conifers and the scattered remains of former settlements. Don't miss the turn-off to the right, following a path through a plantation to the car park.

Glen Tilt & Glen Feshie

Duration	2 days
Distance	38.7mi (62km)
Standard	medium
Start	Blair Atholl
Finish	Kingussie
Nearest Towns	Blair Atholl, Kingussie, Braemar
Public Transport	yes

Summary A magnificent, long walk following historic rights of way through remote glens bordering the Cairngorms uplands, with opportunities for climbing several peaks en route.

This walk follows two of the Cairngorms' finest public footpaths through remote glens. By following the direction chosen for this description, you have a more prolonged experience of being in the mountains and, even when you finish at Kingussie, the Cairngorms aren't far away. The going is good nearly all the way, along vehicular tracks and footpaths; just a few miles in upper Glen Geldie could be described as rough, although still on a path. Only 500m of ascent is involved, mostly on the first day.

The recommended place to camp, near the ruins of Bynack Lodge, is within the National Trust for Scotland's Mar Lodge Estate (see the boxed text 'Restoring Mar Lodge Estate' on page 226). For a second night out, Ruigh-aiteachain Bothy in Glen Feshie offers simple but comfortable shelter.

Among the mountains (Munros) that can easily be climbed along the way are the mighty Beinn a' Ghlo (1120m), which comprises three Munros and can be approached from the north along the ridge rising from the junction of the River Tilt and An Lochain. On the western side of Glen Tilt is Carn a' Chlamain (963m), easily climbed by a path from near Forest Lodge. Huge Beinn Bhrotain (1157m), between Geldie Burn and the upper River Dee, is another possibility, and Mullach Clach a' Bhlair (1019m) and Carn Bàn Mór (1052m) rise steeply from Glen Feshie.

Alternatives The walk up Glen Tilt, say as far as Forest Lodge, would make a good day out from Blair Atholl, the distance being 16mi (26km). At the other end, from the car park in Glen Feshie near Auchlean Farm, a fine day's walk would take you up through the glen to the River Eidart and back, a distance of about 18.3mi (29.5km).

From Blair Atholl to Geldie Burn is also part of the Blair Atholl to Glenmore walk description later, and links with the Linn of Dee walk (see page 227).

HISTORY

Glen Tilt provided a natural, low-level route between Blair Atholl and Braemar for centuries; the Duke of Atholl tried to frustrate this tradition by closing the glen in the 1840s but lost his court case, ensuring the right of way's integrity.

Forest Lodge is a long-standing centre for hunting; Queen Victoria was a visitor in 1844, and she and Prince Albert drove through Glen Tilt to Braemar in 1861.

During the 1990s controversy surrounded Glen Feshie when the estate was put up for sale. A coalition of Scottish conservation groups tried, but failed, to win government backing for the purchase, to revitalise the Caledonian woodland. The estate has since changed hands at least once and conservationists remain sceptical about promises to restore the woodland.

NATURAL HISTORY

The unswerving south-west to north-east trend of Glen Tilt reflects its location on a major geological fault line. The rocks here, predominantly schist and limestone, have produced relatively fertile ground so the glen looks much greener than others in the Cairngorms. You can never get away from the ice age in the Cairngorms; the unusual evidence in Glen Tilt is the sharp bend in the course of Tarf Water – where a bank of moraine rerouted its original flow into the River Dee. Glen Feshie also lies on schist and its broad river flows through skeins of shingle banks on its way to join the River Spey. Caledonian woodlands here have suffered grievously from abundant red deer; attempts to reduce the number may be too late to save the forests.

PLANNING

When to Walk

This walk could be undertaken any time from April to October; at other times there could be some snow in the glens and some stream crossings could be hazardous. The southern part of the walk is through Atholl Estates; during lambing season (April and May) walkers should check with the estate office (☎ 01796-481646) about access.

Stalking In Atholl Estates the most sensitive period for stalking is from mid-August to mid-October; while it's fine to follow the path through Glen Tilt, for walks elsewhere you should check with the estate office (☎ 01796-481646) about daily activities.

The central part of the walk is in the National Trust for Scotland's Mar Lodge Estate where access is open at all times.

At the Glen Feshie end, the stalking season is from mid-August to the end of January the following year; the contact number is ☎ 01540-845939 if you're looking at the mountains east of the glen.

Maps

You'll need OS Landranger 1:50,000 maps No 43 *(Braemar & Blair Atholl)* and No 35 *(Kingussie & Monadhliath Mountains)*.

Information Sources

Pitlochry TIC (☎ 01796-472215), about 6mi (10km) south of Blair Atholl along the A9, is open all year.

NEAREST TOWNS

Blair Atholl & Around

Blair Atholl is a large village on the southern fringe of the Cairngorm uplands, close to the A9 trunk road, and ideally placed for exploring the area.

Atholl Estates, the major local landowner, has a Countryside Ranger Service (☎ 01796-481646), based in a building next to the large car park near the Bridge of Tilt. The rangers can provide details of guided walks and waymarked routes on the estate. The office is open daily from Easter to October.

At the western end of the village, Atholl Browse is an excellent little bookshop. It's open from April to October.

The local bank is only open on Monday, Thursday and Friday mornings; there's an ATM at Atholl Stores, just off the main road and next to the Atholl Arms Hotel.

Places to Stay & Eat The spacious ***Blair Castle Caravan Park*** *(☎ 01796-481263)* is extremely well set-up and maintained. The tariff for two people and a tent is £8.50, with a car it is £10. There are a coffee shop and small shop on site.

Of the several B&Bs in the village, ***The Firs*** *(☎ 01796-481256)*, in a quiet side street, has beautifully furnished rooms in a fine old house from £20; Mrs Crerar's breakfast is first-rate.

The nearest hostel is the ***SYHA hostel*** *(☎ 01796-472308)* at Pitlochry, about 6mi (10km) south on the A9.

For a meal in Blair Atholl, it would be hard to beat ***The Loft Bistro*** *(☎ 01796-481377)*, which has excellent meals, including the house speciality, Aberdeen Angus steaks from £11, although vegetarian choices are limited. The bistro is open daily.

There's also the ***Atholl Arms Hotel*** *(☎ 01796-481205)*, which serves superior-quality bar meals and offers an excellent deal with DB&B for £80 per room.

For self-caterers, ***Atholl Stores***, a smallish off-licence supermarket, is open daily, as is ***Tilt Stores*** on the main road towards the eastern end of the village.

Getting There & Away At least six ScotRail (☎ 0845-755 0033) services between London and Inverness, via Edinburgh and Glasgow, stop at Blair Atholl daily.

Buses on Scottish Citylink's (☎ 0870-550 5050) run between Edinburgh and Inverness bypass Blair Atholl; the nearest stop is about 4mi west at Calvine. Stagecoach (☎ 0870-608 2608) operates a once-daily bus service between Blair Atholl and Perth (which is served by Citylink).

Blair Atholl is on the B8079, directly accessible from the A9 trunk road, 32mi (51.8km) north of Perth and 33mi (53.5km) south of Kingussie.

Kingussie

This sizable town is spread out along a fairly busy road in a great location looking towards the western side of the Cairngorms. There's a helpful TIC (☎ 01540-661297) at the end of Duke St, off the south side of High St; it's open daily from Easter to October. The Bank of Scotland, in High St, has an ATM.

Places to Stay & Eat Friendly ***Greystones B&B*** *(☎ 01540-661052)*, north of High St, has superbly decorated rooms in a substantial stone-built home from £19. ***The Laird's Bothy*** *(☎ 01540-661334)* is a lively hostel in the centre of town with a range of rooms from £8; most importantly, there's a drying room and an adjacent restaurant.

In quieter surroundings, the ***Scot House Hotel*** *(☎ 01540-661351)* offers superior bar meals from £7 for main courses. Real ale fans shouldn't miss the ***Royal Hotel***, in High St, which has its own wee brewery producing delectable Iris Rose beers; the Creag Bheag lager is truly memorable.

In High St, three supermarkets are open daily; ***Service Sports*** sells camping gas and liquid fuel.

Getting There & Away Most ScotRail (☎ 0845-755 0033) services between London Euston and Inverness stop daily at Kingussie, as does GNER's (☎ 0845-722 5225) London Kings Cross to Inverness service.

Scottish Citylink (☎ 0870-550 5050) buses on the Edinburgh to Inverness service stop at Kingussie at least three times daily. The single/return fare Kingussie to Inverness is £6.10/10.20. Between late May and September, Highland Country Buses' (☎ 01463-222244) Munro Bagger service between Fort William and Cairngorm stops at Kingussie twice daily.

Kingussie is on the A86, close to the A9 trunk road, 15mi (24.3km) south-west of Aviemore and the same distance north of Dalwhinnie.

THE WALK

See map pages 222–3

Day 1: Blair Atholl to Bynack Lodge

6½–7 hours, 19mi (30.5km)

The walk starts at the Bridge of Tilt on the main road (B8079) through Blair Atholl. Cross the bridge, to the eastern side of the River Tilt, and go left down some steps to a riverside path through mature woodland. The path follows the river for just over half a mile then leads up to the road; follow the road for 100m then turn right as the Scottish Rights of Way Society sign suggests, towards 'Deeside by Glen Tilt'. There's another of these signs at the next road junction; turn left then, shortly, cross a bridge and go steeply up to the final turn, left towards Kincraigie Farm. From here there's a fine view of white Blair Castle amid trees to the south-west. Follow the gravel road and soon, at a bend, cross a stile and follow a grassy track to a gate. This leads through woodland and across open ground; just past Croftmore (a stone house with well-tended gardens) ignore a track going up to the right and continue gently down to a gravel road (1½ hours from Blair Atholl).

Soon, a grassy track offers a short cut from the road. A few hundred metres farther on is solitary Marble Lodge, a stone cottage. The steep, scree-strewn slopes of Beinn a' Ghlo are starting to dominate the view ahead. The road crosses the River Tilt and leads along the bank. Almost opposite deserted Balaneasie cottage, bear left along a grassy track to cut off another bend in the road, with Glen Tilt opening up invitingly ahead. The startling sound of roosters crowing leaves you in no doubt that Clachghlas is lived in. A good mile farther on you reach the imposing entrance to **Forest Lodge** (a map shows preferred walking routes during the stalking season). Walk past the lodge, along the edge of a small conifer plantation and into the ever-narrowing glen. The road becomes a vehicular track, which eventually ends about 6mi from Forest Lodge. The **Falls of Tarf** and **Tarf Water Bridge** are about 200m farther north along a path (2¾ hours since joining the road). The bridge was originally built in 1886 by the Scottish Rights of Way Society to commemorate a drowning there in 1878. Just beyond the bridge a stone in the ground bears the figure '13' – the miles from Blair Atholl.

A good path continues up the glen, more of a narrow defile, for about 1mi. It widens suddenly around the source of the River Tilt where the new outlook is towards big, sprawling mountains. About an hour's walk from Tarf Water brings you to the start of a rough vehicular track and another 20 minutes to the rather forlorn remains of Bynack Lodge, with a few windswept larches.

Day 2: Bynack Lodge to Kingussie

7–7½ hours, 19.7mi (31.5km)

Return to the vehicular track between Bynack Burn and Allt an t-Seilich; it soon fords the latter stream and leads on to Bynack Burn and nearby Geldie Burn (30 minutes from Bynack Lodge), where stepping stones make for straightforward crossings unless the burns are in spate. The stone cottage nearby has become a 'dangerous building' with wide cracks splitting its stonework.

A vehicular track affords easy going west up **Glen Geldie**, a lonely, almost desolate glen, enlivened by glimpses of Beinn Bhrotain to the north and big mountains to the south. A bridge crosses **Allt Dhaidh Beag** but it's stepping stones for the larger **Allt Dhaidh Mór**. Where the vehicular track starts to lose height, turning towards Geldie Burn and the ruins of Geldie Lodge on the far side, turn right along a rougher track. This soon becomes a fairly clear path; ignore a track leading uphill to the right (an hour from the Geldie Burn crossing). Farther on some of the minor stream crossings could be boggy but generally the going isn't too bad, with long westward views and glimpses of Beinn Bhrotain's pinkish scree mantles. After about 3mi the path crosses the divide between Geldie Burn and the River Feshie, revealing the satisfying prospect of Glen Feshie ahead as you start to descend to the River Eidart. Keep watch for a small finger post sign 'Bridge', indicating a diversion from the path's line to cross the surging river. About 1¼ hours from Geldie Lodge junction you reach **Eidart Bridge**, built in 1957; a Scottish Rights of Way Society sign tells you Kingussie is only 15mi away.

Continue along the path (almost immediately there's a good view of the waterfall just below the bridge) and down to a decrepit shed on the bank of the River Feshie. About 200m on from the shed, a vehicular track leads off through the heather but the path persists with its own, preferable route closer to the river. About 1mi farther on, the path crosses **Allt Coire Bhlàir**, at the bottom of a dramatically narrow gorge, and leads down to the vehicular track. The views of the crags below Creag na Gaibhre ahead are magnificent; the steep hillsides are covered with scree, heather and scattered Scots pine. The track has been washed away just above a right-angle bend in the river; the safest way round this is low down, along a narrow path across the slope. However, the unstable ground dictates caution, whichever way you negotiate it. Rejoin the track through pine woodland, with many magnificent old trees, across the river flats. Another wash-away where the cliffs rise directly from the track should be easier to negotiate. With a stone building in sight, follow a grassy track to the right to ***Ruigh-aiteachain Bothy***, which has a toilet (2½ hours from Eidart Bridge).

The track leads on downstream and into a conifer plantation; keep to the left at a track junction. Emerging from the pines, turn very sharp right and follow a path along the western edge of the plantation, descending to cross Allt Garbhlach. On the other side, walk along the edge of a high, heathery bank for about 200m, then drop down to the broad grassy river flats. You'll shortly come to a footbridge across the river.

If you're finishing the walk at the end of the Glen Feshie road near Auchlean Farm, continue downstream, cross a burn, then a decrepit stile. Beyond another boggy stream crossing go up a heathery slope to skirt the fenced Auchlean Farm and reach the end of the sealed road – the car park is about half a mile farther on (1½ hours from Ruigh-aiteachain Bothy).

To continue to Kingussie, cross the foot-bridge and go up to and cross a gravel road, following another path to a sealed road. Walk north along the road, past Stronetoper Cottage, to a junction in a pine plantation and turn left along a forest road signposted to Kingussie. A few hundred metres along, at a crossroads, go straight ahead and on to a gate into open moorland. Keep straight on, ignoring tracks to the left. Cross a small burn then a (probably) dry channel to a rick-ety bridge over a burn. Cross the bridge then bear left for about 50m to stepping stones across Allt Chomhraig and go up the bank to a vehicular track and turn left. A bit farther on, pass the entrance of Corarnstil-beg Farm and follow the forest road west into a plantation. The road soon begins to lose height, with a good view of the ex-panses of Strathspey. At a crossroads con-tinue ahead to signposted 'Drumguish. Walk' through Drumguish (1¾ hours from Auchlean) and, at a T-junction, turn left. Follow this minor road across the River Tromie, under the A9, immediately over the River Spey and on into the centre of Kingussie (1¼ hours from Drumguish).

Blair Atholl to Glenmore

Duration	2 days
Distance	44mi (71km)
Standard	medium-hard
Start	Blair Atholl
Finish	Glenmore
Nearest Towns	Blair Atholl, Glenmore, Braemar
Public Transport	yes

Summary An outstanding extended walk across the length of the Cairngorms, skirting the east-ern slopes of the plateau through isolated glens and beautiful Caledonian woodlands.

The first part of this walk, to the Geldie Burn crossing, follows the same Day 1 route described in the Glen Tilt & Glen Feshie walk on page 231. From the crossing it's on to Linn of Dee, then through Glen Lui and Glen Derry along vehicular tracks. A foot-path, boggy in places, then leads over Lairig an Laoigh, down across the Fords of Avon and around the eastern side of Bynack More. From Bynack Stable, a vehicular track makes for an easy walk into Glen-more. The amount of ascent involved is about 820m, the greater part of which is in the stretch north from Linn of Dee.

Alternatives Some of the finest camping sites in the Cairngorms are in Glen Derry beneath the Scots pines, not far from de-serted Derry Lodge. This is in the heart of the National Trust for Scotland's Mar Lodge Estate, where wild camping is perfectly OK – provided you follow the Country Code and leave the area as you find it (see Re-sponsible Walking on page 64). However, Derry Lodge is 27mi (43.5km) from Blair Atholl – on the long side for a day's walk. If you're tempted by the Munros within easy reach of Glen Derry – Derry Cairngorm (1156m) and Carn a' Mhaim (1037m), or even Ben Macdui (1309m) – then a short day to Glen Derry from Bynack Lodge makes sense. As you walk through Glen Derry and over Lairig an Laoigh, you'll also pass Beinn Mheadhoin (1182m) and Bynack More (1090m) to the west, not to mention the magnificent mountains to the east, fore-most among which is Beinn a' Bhuird (1196m). For these, it would be worth con-sidering making a base at the Hutchison Memorial Hut on upper Derry Burn.

Another possibility is to stay at Inverey SYHA Hostel (see Inverey under Nearest Town on page 228), just over 1mi east of Linn of Dee (23mi/37.3km from Blair Atholl). And lastly, if you have five or six days to spare, there's a grand Cairngorms tour worth contemplating. From Glenmore, it's easy to reach the path through Lairig Ghru (see Chalamain Gap & The Lairig Ghru on page 221), which can be followed all the way down to White Bridge, where you pick up the path followed earlier from Blair Atholl.

NATURAL HISTORY

This walk takes you across three major watersheds – between the River Garry and the River Dee north of Glen Tilt, between the Dee and the River Avon over Lairig an Laoigh, and between the Avon and Strathspey north of the Fords of Avon. Typical of the Cairngorms, there is clear evidence of glaciation in the wide, flat-bottomed glens and the great mounds of moraine in upper Glen Derry.

Glen Derry pine woods are one of the outstanding features of this walk – the National Trust for Scotland's work to restore their vigour is outlined in the boxed text 'Restoring Mar Lodge Estate' on page 226.

PLANNING

When to Walk

You could expect to find snow over Lairig an Laoigh and on the slopes of Bynack More, and the Fords of Avon crossing could be difficult between November and March, so the best time for this walk is between May and September.

Stalking For the Glen Tilt section, see Stalking under Planning on page 230. Most of the remainder of the walk is through the National Trust for Scotland's Mar Lodge Estate, where access is open at all times.

Maps

The OS Landranger 1:50,000 maps to carry are Nos 43 *(Braemar & Blair Atholl)* and 36 *(Grantown & Aviemore)*. The eastern boundary of Harvey's Superwalker 1:25,000 *Cairn Gorm* map coincides with the path followed northward from Glen Derry, so it's worth having this map if you are planning to climb any of the mountains west of the route that is described here.

NEAREST TOWNS

Blair Atholl

See Nearest Towns under Glen Tilt & Glen Feshie on page 230.

Glenmore

See Access Towns under Northern Cairngorms on page 219.

THE WALK

See map pages 222–3

Day 1: Blair Atholl to Bynack Lodge

6½–7 hours, 19mi (30.5km)

This section is described under Day 1 in the Glen Tilt & Glen Feshie walk on page 231.

Day 2: Bynack Lodge to Glenmore

10 hours, 25mi (40km)

The first stage of this long day is comparatively easy along the path on the eastern side of Bynack Burn, shortly crossing Allt an t-Seilich. A vehicular track continues to the Geldie Burn crossing, which shouldn't present any problems unless the burn is in spate. Continue north along the track, past a conifer plantation, to White Bridge and the River Dee. After crossing the bridge head east down broad Glen Dee to the sealed road near Linn of Dee (1¾ hours from Bynack Lodge).

Continue east along the road to the car park and, from its northern edge, continue along a signposted path to Glen Lui. This leads through the conifer plantation to a vehicular track in Glen Lui and another straightforward stretch up the broad glen, dominated by the bulk of Derry Cairngorm ahead. After about an hour, you reach Derry Lodge, standing silently with boarded-up windows in the open pine woodland. There is a telephone for public and emergency use in a red box on the side of a brown timber building near the lodge. It's coin-operated and maintained (at a loss) by the volunteer Braemar Mountain Rescue Team.

Cross the bridge over Derry Burn and follow a path leading north away from the burn (rather than along the faint and discontinuous path beside the burn). Go through the woodland, past an exclosure, over a low, heathery hillock and then down to a footbridge over Derry Burn. The path meets a vehicular track about 200m farther on. The glen soon starts to close in. There are inspirational views ahead to the tors on the broad summit plateau of Beinn Mheadhoin, rising impressively above Stob Coire Etchachan's cliffs.

The vehicular track ends beside an exclosure and a wide track continues through another one, but follow the path leading on and starting to climb. Soon, large stepping stones provide an easy crossing of Glas Allt Mór and a good path leads on to the junction with the path to Hutchison Memorial Hut below Stob Coire Etchachan (1½ hours to the junction from Derry Lodge).

From the path junction continue heading north. A steepening climb on a rougher path, across a few muddy patches, takes you up to **Lairig an Laoigh** (30 minutes from the path junction). A new outlook unfolds down a wide glen, with boulder-strewn slopes cradling Dubh Lochan, and across the Fords of Avon to the great bulk of Bynack More. Follow the path down, past the well-named Dubh Lochan (small dark lake) to the Fords of Avon (45 minutes from the Lairig). Boulders, rather than stepping stones, should enable you to keep your feet dry on the two crossings, separated by a tiny grassed island. The nearby refuge is small, dark and windowless, and could only be inviting in foul weather.

The path leads on up the glen of Allt Dearg, past Lochan a' Bhainne and across the low divide between the allt and a stream called Glasath, which you soon cross on good stepping stones. The path rises rather muddily from the crossing, around the broad shoulder of Bynack More, wanders around a bit and then drops down to cross Uisge Dubh Poll a' Choin on treacherous, mossy stones. Then it's a short, steep pull up to the broad northern spur of Bynack More – a bleak, windswept place in poor weather, but on a good day with the classic Cairngorms feel of openness and space. To the south-east Ben Avon's great, tor-studded summit plateau and Beinn a' Bhuird's crag-lined top dominate the view. The path, muddy and badly eroded in places, soon sets out on the long descent to the bridge over the River Nethy, with Bynack Stable nearby – a doorless tin shed with an earthen floor (about 1½ hours from Fords of Avon).

A stony vehicular track leads on from here and, about 1mi from the stable, joins a track from the right at the base of the steep scree- and heather-clad slopes of Meall a' Bhuachaille. The rest is easy – south-west down the vehicular track or forest road, past beautiful An Lochan Uaine, through pine woodlands and some conifers. Glenmore Lodge, just over 1mi from the lochan, seems large and incongruous after the emptiness of the moors and glens – but it does have a good bar! Glenmore village is another mile along the sealed road (1½ hours from Bynack Stable).

Jock's Road

Duration	6–6½ hours
Distance	14mi (22.5km)
Standard	medium
Start	Auchallater
Finish	Glen Clova car park
Nearest Towns	Braemar, Glen Clova
Public Transport	finish only

Summary A historic path crossing a high pass between Glen Callater and remote Glen Doll, passing beautiful Loch Callater and going through Caenlochan National Nature Reserve.

Jock's Road is an old route crossing the high ground south-east of Braemar and linking upper Deeside with the lowlands of Angus. The walk is described here from north to south, but it can just as well be done in the opposite direction. The climb from both ends is steep and route finding on the high plateau in poor visibility could be difficult either way. The ability to navigate using map and compass is essential. Starting from the Braemar end at Auchallater does have the advantage of involving a little less ascent, 545m compared with 650m from Glen Doll. Vehicle tracks to Loch Callater and down through the Glen Doll pine plantation make for easy walking. The path beyond Loch Callater is rocky and tends to spread out around the many muddy patches as it ventures into the deepening, narrowing glen; the path in upper Glen Doll is generally in good condition. On the broad plateau the going is variable across the moorland; cairns mark the line of the path.

If the practicalities of transport for this one-way walk seem daunting, it's worth considering one or two there-and-back walks from Auchallater and/or from Glen Doll, up to the highest and roughly midway point at Crow Craigies (920m).

HISTORY

Jock's Road was long used by drovers taking sheep from Braemar to near Kirriemuir. It was for this reason that in 1887 the Court of Session (Scotland's highest court), in a case brought by the Scottish Rights of Way & Recreation Society, thwarted an attempt by the owner of Glen Doll to close the road. The road's name is thought to be that of a local man, John Winters.

On New Year's Day 1959, five members of Glasgow's Universal Hiking Club died in a snowstorm above Glen Doll near Davy's Bourach; in March 1976, two people died near Loch Esk, below Jock's Road to the north, having walked from Glen Doll.

NATURAL HISTORY

The main local rock type is schist in a distinctive glaciated landscape with Glen Callater cradling Loch Callater. The well-named White Water foams and cascades through magnificent, cliff-lined Glen Doll.

In the north, Callater Burn reaches the River Dee via Clunie Water. White Water is a tributary of the River South Esk, which flows into the North Sea at far-away Montrose.

Caenlochan National Nature Reserve, in upper Glen Doll, protects a remarkably varied collection of alpine-arctic plants, including many rare species.

PLANNING

When to Walk

The ideal time to walk Jock's Road is between May and September. The high ground is usually snow-covered in winter, and is subject to mist and strong winds at any time, so it's vital to check the local weather forecast before setting out (available at TICs and SYHA hostels).

Stalking Being a public footpath, access along Jock's Road is unaffected by stalking activities. However, if you're thinking of climbing any of the mountains accessible from this route from August to October, you should find out what's going on beforehand. The northern half of the walk passes through the Callater & Clunie Estate where stalking usually takes place from 1 September to 20 October; contact ☎ 01339-741997 for daily information. The southern half is mostly through the Glen Clova Estate where the season extends from early August to 20 October; ring ☎ 01575-550335 for more information. A map showing the location of daily activities is displayed at the information shelter in the Glen Clova car park.

Maps & Books

The best map for this walk is Harvey's Superwalker 1:25,000 *Lochnagar*, rather than two OS Landranger 1:50,000 maps – No 43 *(Braemar & Blair Atholl)* and No 44 *(Ballater & Glen Clova)*.

The Scottish Rights of Way Society's *Scottish Hill Tracks* has an outline of the route and some historical background. Robert Smith's *25 Walks – Deeside* includes an informative description of a walk to Loch Callater with a side trip to overlook remote Loch Kander. *Walks: Deeside* by Richard Hallewell also covers Jock's Road and offers an interesting variation for a round walk.

Information Sources

The TIC in Kirriemuir (☎ 01575-574097) is open from Easter to October. The nearest full-time TIC is in Forfar (☎ 01307-467876), 21mi (33.6km) from Glen Clova.

NEAREST TOWN

Glen Clova

This is actually a long glen, deep and cliff-lined in its upper reaches, extending far into the south-eastern Cairngorm uplands. It's fairly sparsely settled and although there's no shortage of accommodation, the nearest shops (and ATM) are in Kirriemuir down in the lowlands, 18mi (29.2km) from the Glendoll SYHA Hostel. There is an emergency telephone at the Glen Clova car park and a public telephone at Clova.

Places to Stay & Eat A substantial former hunting lodge, ***Glendoll SYHA Hostel*** *(☎ 01575-550236)* is 0.75mi beyond the end of the public road in a very secluded setting. Accommodation in one of the spacious dorms costs £9.75; facilities are excellent and some basic supplies are stocked in a small shop.

Glen Clova Camping Ground, a spacious grassy area across the road from the car park and beside the River South Esk, is run by Forest Enterprise. Toilets and wash basins are provided; pay the £3 fee into a machine in the car park.

Glen Clova Hotel *(☎ 01575-550350)*, 4mi down the road from the hostel at Clova, dates from the mid-19th century and has very comfortable rooms from £22 for B&B. Alternatively, there's the adjacent bunkhouse for £7 per night. You can dine in the hotel's restaurant or in the atmospheric Climbers Bar, where standard bar fare starts at around £6.

Getting There & Away The car park at the end of the mostly single track public road through Glen Clova is 18mi (29.2km) from Kirriemuir on the A926.

A postbus (☎ 01246-546329) leaves Glendoll SYHA Hostel for Kirriemuir at 10.55am Monday to Saturday. This connects with a bus operated by Meffans Coaches (☎ 01575-572130) to Alyth, from where Strathtay Scottish (☎ 01382-228345) bus services will take you to Perth or Dundee. The postbus departs Kirriemuir for Glendoll SYHA Hostel at 8.30am; as there are no connections from the outside world you'd have to stay in Kirriemuir the previous night to catch this service.

GETTING TO/FROM THE WALK

Auchallater car park is beside the A93, 2mi (3km) south of Braemar. From the end of the walk at Glen Clova car park, see Getting There & Away for Glen Clova.

THE WALK

See map page 238

From Auchallater car park set out along the vehicular track signposted as a public path to Clova. It winds up steep-sided Glen Callater beside a tumbling burn, overlooked by the broken crags of Creag na Dearcaige. After 2mi the track crosses the burn on a solid bridge and a new vista of much more rugged hillsides opens up ahead. With the roof of Lochcallater Lodge in sight, bear right at a fork and cross the grass in front of the lodge, joining a narrow path along the edge of beautiful **Loch Callater** (about 1¼ hours from the start). Nearby, ***The Stables Bothy***, maintained by the Mountain Bothies Association, provides simple accommodation in a solid stone building.

The narrow, clear path generally hugs the loch shore to the small beach at its head. The path then fades beyond crossings of two small burns; the easiest going is along the grassy, occasionally boggy, true right (eastern) bank of Allt an Loch. The view ahead is wildly beautiful – a massive bluff separates the corrie sheltering Loch Kander and the steep-sided head of the glen. The flat ground ends abruptly at a low, heathery spur (45 minutes from the lodge) and a clearer path leads along or just below the edge of a high bank above the burn. Once past a point opposite the junction of Allt Loch Kander, the often muddy path trends away from the burn. Here, too, you turn towards the dramatic head of the glen, almost enclosed by precipitous cliffs. There's a public footpath sign close to the junction of Allt an Loch and Allt an Droighnean, although not beside the main route. Climb beside the latter stream, switching from one side to the other as you gain height up the extremely steep slope, crossing several minor burns and gradually moving away from the allt. When you find the first of a line of old metal fence posts a cairned, rather faint, path materialises. Follow this up to the broad divide between Tolmount to the south and Fafernie to the north, and on to the cairn on top of **Crow Craigies** (two hours from the start of the climb). Lochnagar dominates the view to the north, while Braeriach, Ben Macdui and the Cairngorm plateau can be made out to the north-west.

To continue to Glen Doll drop down from Crow Craigies and follow the intermittently

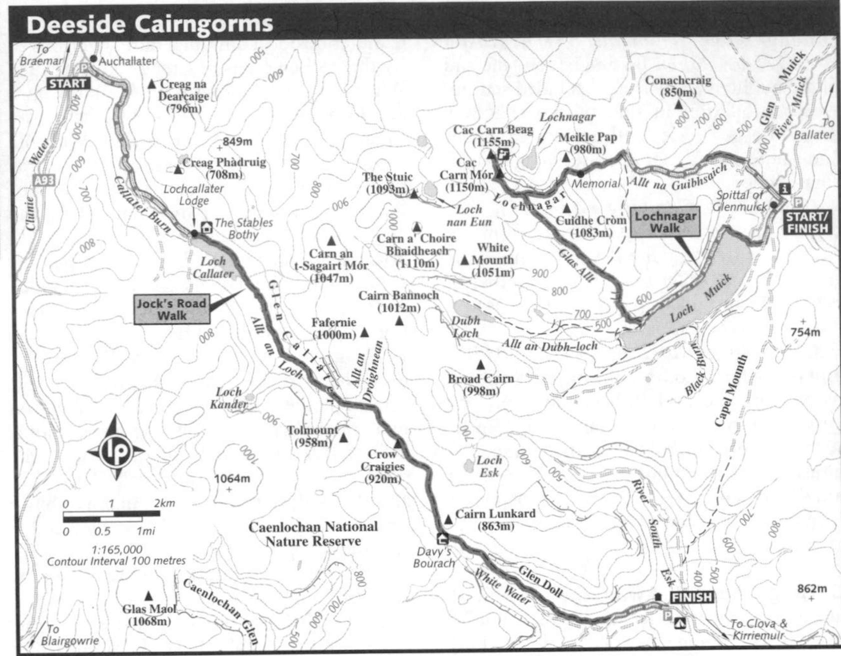

cairned path across the grassy moor and around the western side of an amorphous bump (874m). The path becomes ever more peaty and rocky as it descends the steepish flank of Cairn Lùnkard to a pair of prominent cairns. From here the mighty cliffs and corries of upper Glen Doll, crowned by rugged Dreish (947m) to the south-east, are in full view. A few hundred metres farther on, **Davy's Bourach** is a curious, stone-walled shelter with earth and heather covering its iron roof; it's dark and windowless but would provide more or less dry shelter. Nearby is a plaque erected to the memory of the walkers who died here in 1959 (see History on page 236). A good path continues across the precipitous, rugged north side of the glen, high above aptly named **White Water** and down to a gate at the entrance to the pine plantation (1½ hours from Crow Craigies). The forest road provides an easy, if somewhat enclosed walk down to a minor path on the left leading to the youth hostel. Bypass this turn-off to reach the car park half a mile farther on along the forest road (nearly an hour from the forest gate).

Lochnagar

Duration	6–6½ hours
Distance	14mi (22.7km)
Standard	medium
Start & Finish	Spittal of Glenmuick
Nearest Town	Ballater, Braemar
Public Transport	no

Summary The best-known peak in the Deeside Cairngorms, with spectacular panoramic views and a descent beside a dramatic waterfall to Loch Muick, in the heart of an important nature reserve.

Lochnagar (1155m, 3788ft) is the highest of the peaks to the south of Deeside, a magnificent mountain with huge corries scooped out of its northern face. It provides a dramatic backdrop to the town of Ballater and is the feature of a huge, roughly horseshoe-shaped ridge embracing Loch Muick. The name Lochnagar can be confusing – it refers to the twin peaks of Cac Carn Beag and Cac Carn Mòr, as well as the lochan in one of the northern corries.

The walk described here follows a vehicular track, then a well-used and maintained path, with long sections of stone paving and steps, steeply up to the gap between Lochnagar and its outlier, Meikle Pap (980m). Another steep, rocky climb leads to the spectacular rim of the corrie cradling Lochnagar; the summit (Cac Carn Beag) stands on a spur between Lochnagar and Loch nan Eun to the west. To make an excellent circular walk, the return is down a steep, stone-built path beside Glas Allt to the shore of Loch Muick, where a vehicular track leads back to the start at Spittal of Glenmuick. The total ascent for the walk is 800m; it's graded medium on account of the extent of relatively easy going on well-made tracks and paths.

Alternatives For fit and experienced walkers, there's the temptation to 'do the round' of Loch Muick – and to bag another four Munros. To do this, continue from Lochnagar's secondary summit (1150m) south-west and west over The Stuic (1093m) above Loch nan Eun (and/or Carn a' Choire Bhaidheach at 1110m, if you're bagging the Munros), to Carn an t-Sagairt Mór (1047m), then south-east to Cairn Bannoch (1012m) and on to Broad Cairn (998m).

From there it's a long descent to a boggy saddle; then you can either follow a path down to Loch Muick or the vehicular track, which keeps to high ground for another 2mi then drops down across Black Burn to the loch, and back to the start. This superb walk of around 16.5mi (26.5km) involves at least 1130m of ascent and would take a good nine hours.

HISTORY

Lochnagar means 'loch of noise' or 'laughter', or perhaps 'noisy' or 'laughing loch' – possibly describing the sound of falling scree on the cliffs.

Glen Muick (pronounced mick) once supported many crofting families and the Spittal of Glenmuick (a resting-place) was used by drovers taking cattle along the Capel Mount route over the mountains to Glen Clova. The famous Romantic poet George Lord Byron, a native of Aberdeenshire, fondly remembered Lochnagar with the lines:

England! Thy beauties are tame and domestic
To one who has roved o'er the mountains afar:
Oh for the crags that are wild and majestic!
The steep frowning glories of dark Lochnagar!

The nucleus of the Balmoral Estate, which extends from the River Dee south-eastward to well beyond Loch Muick, was purchased by Queen Victoria in 1878. She acquired the Ballochbuie Forest and saved it from imminent felling. Glen Muick was one of her favourite places in this area, of which she was very fond, and she had Glas-allt-Shiel Lodge built beside the loch soon after her husband Prince Albert died. The estate has remained the property of the Royal family, who are regular summer visitors to nearby Balmoral Castle.

Loch Muick and Lochnagar Wildlife Reserve was established in 1974 by the estate, in partnership with the Scottish Wildlife Trust; the reserve is now managed by the estate in cooperation with Scottish Natural Heritage.

NATURAL HISTORY

Lochnagar is essentially a granite mountain, the originally grey-pink rock taking on darker tones as lichen accumulates on exposed surfaces. Evidence of the work of glaciers during the last ice age is clearly seen in Loch Muick's U-shaped valley and in the corries where, even now, snow lies well into spring.

Mountain hares are occasionally seen bounding about on the higher ground and you'd be unlucky not to see ptarmigan, which are not at all shy and easily identifiable by their croaking call.

PLANNING

When to Walk

Lochnagar is usually snow-covered from November to April, making the ideal walking season between May and September.

Stalking Within Balmoral Estate the stalking season is from mid-August to mid-October. Although access to Lochnagar is maintained throughout the season, stalking takes place around the other mountains in the area. Very detailed information is available daily from the estate on ☎ 01339-755532 and at the Spittal of Glenmuick Visitor Centre (see Information Sources).

What to Bring

Bad weather and poor visibility are likely at any time, so check the local weather forecast beforehand, and ensure you take a map and compass. The paths are well used, but the summit plateau is fairly featureless and the flanking cliffs very steep so you need to know just where you are.

Maps & Books

Harvey's Superwalker 1:25,000 *Lochnagar* map is the one to use for this walk and its possible extensions. The relevant OS Landranger 1:50,000 map is No 44 *(Ballater & Glen Clova)*.

Naturally, Lochnagar features in all the Munros guides (see Books in the Facts for the Walker chapter on page 74); the Scottish Mountaineering Club's guide *The Cairngorms* (see Books on page 216) devotes a chapter to 'Dark Lochnagar'. Balmoral Estate's guidebook *Loch Muick and Lochnagar* provides a solid introduction to the area.

Information Sources

At Spittal of Glenmuick, the starting point for the walk, Balmoral Estate has a small, information-packed visitor centre, where you'll often find one of the Countryside Rangers (☎ 01339-755059). It's open daily between Easter and October and on winter weekends; information about stalking activities is displayed there. The rangers run guided walks in and around the glen during spring, summer and autumn.

NEAREST TOWN

Ballater

Very much aware of being in 'Royal Deeside', Ballater is a small town sitting on a wide bend in the River Dee. The very friendly TIC (☎ 01339-755306), in the renovated train station building, is open daily. Internet access, and many other services, are available here. Lochnagar Leisure, opposite the TIC, has a good range of outdoor gear including fuel. There are two banks, both with an ATM.

Places to Stay & Eat Beside the river, ***Anderson Road Caravan Park*** *(☎ 01339-755727)* is well set up and can be very busy; it costs £9 for a tent. Of the several B&Bs, ***Netherley Guest House*** *(☎ 01339-755792)* is central and has striking blue shutters; the tariff starts at £18 in en suite rooms.

La Mangiatoia *(☎ 01339-755999)*, off the A93 on the eastern side of town, has an Italian-inspired menu, including pizzas for £6 (although the pasta is a better bet) and some Scottish dishes; the wine list includes Australian and Italian vintages. ***The Highlander*** *(☎ 01339-755509)* licensed restaurant has a large and varied menu (but not much for vegetarians) with prices ranging from £6 to £13.50.

For self-catering, there are two supermarkets open daily, ***Strachan's*** (a superior grocery shop), an excellent baker and a fruit and vegetable shop.

Getting There & Away Stagecoach (☎ 0870-608 2608) operates regular daily bus services between Aberdeen and Ballater from around 7am to 7pm; the single/return fare is £6/9.50. During summer Stagecoach also puts on the Heather Hopper, a handy daily run between Aberdeen and Perth via Ballater, Braemar and Pitlochry, with a morning and an afternoon service; it costs £6 per journey, wherever you get on and off.

By road, Ballater is on the A93, 42mi (67.5km) west of Aberdeen and 17mi (27km) east of Braemar.

GETTING TO/FROM THE WALK

The walk starts at the Spittal of Glenmuick, at the end of the public road through the glen. From Ballater, cross the River Dee bridge and turn right. About 0.75mi along bear left at a junction to Glen Muick (as signposted). The car park is 8mi (12km) farther on. A pay and display system operates here, and the charge for parking is £2 per day; the proceeds are channelled to mountain path repair work.

Ballater Taxis (☎ 01339-755548) will take you up the glen, and come and pick you up for £20 for the round trip.

THE WALK

See map page 238

From the car park, walk across to the visitor centre and, a short distance farther on, turn right along the path signposted to Lochnagar. Ahead, the scree-encrusted Meikle Pap, the cliffs on Lochnagar's north face and the broad plateau of Cuidhe Crom are framed in the V formed by nearer heathery mountains. Follow the track across River Muick in its flat-bottomed glen and, where the track bends right, continue straight ahead across a road and to the left of a stone cottage, along a signposted path. This passes a plantation on the left and goes through pine woodland, merging with a wider track from the left; soon you're out in heather moorland. The wide track rises beside Allt na Giubhsaich, crosses it on stepping stones, and continues to gain height steadily in the rather bleak heather moorland. About an hour from the start you reach a fairly broad col between Conachcraig to the north-east and Lochnagar.

Leave the track and drop down a well-made stone path, which then climbs the slope of Meikle Pap, strewn with granite boulders. Well up, a short path to the left leads to a memorial to a man who died here in 1953. The steep path ends close to the col south of Meikle Pap, from where there are spectacular views of the cliff-girt corrie sheltering Lochnagar's loch. Now, follow a line of ascent south-westward on the steep rocky slope, well to the left of the corrie rim, up to the spacious plateau. Skirt the corrie rim and cross a shallow gap; a line of cairns marks the route, which then swings away from the edge to mount the slope leading to Cac Carn Mòr. Despite its name, it's not Lochnagar's highest point – this honour goes to **Cac Carn Beag**, 450m north, topped by a massive cairn (about two hours from the Conachcraig col). A direction finder installed in 1924 and, remarkably, still in fair condition helps identify the features of the amazing panorama of mountains and glens; among the more distant are the Pentland Hills (near Edinburgh), Ben Lomond, Creag Meagaidh and Ben Nevis (all featured elsewhere in this book).

Retrace your steps over Cac Carn Mòr and down its south-eastern flank to a prominent path junction; descend steeply into the deep glen of Glas Allt. Extensive path repairs have made this descent into a particularly peaty and heathery place relatively easy. Ptarmigan are common hereabouts – a group of eight were flushed when this walk was being surveyed. The path follows the stream closely, crossing on a good bridge after nearly 1mi. Here a track leads away north-east across the hillside but continue in a south-easterly direction. Glas Allt plunges into a dramatic gorge and the path clings miraculously to the steep, rocky slope as it descends towards the deep trench of Loch Muick. The **Falls of Glasallt** aren't particularly high but attractive nonetheless, pouring down grey blocky cliffs with long cascades below. The path descends to a pine woodland; go past the end of a dyke beside the stream, cross a footbridge and continue down to the loch-side vehicular track (two hours from Cac Carn Beag). Follow this north-east to the end of Loch Muick and turn right onto the path along its northern shore. Cross River Muick and follow the vehicular track north, which takes you back to the start (1¼ hours from where you met the loch-side vehicular track).

Other Walks

NORTHERN CAIRNGORMS

Braeriach

Braeriach (1296m, 4251ft), meaning 'the brindled upland', is the second-highest peak in the Cairngorms and the third-highest in Scotland. It's the culmination of a great, undulating plateau with Lairig Ghru on its precipitous eastern side and its western flank rising almost as steeply from lonely

Glen Einich. This magnificent massif, with dark mysterious corries scooped out of its northern and eastern slopes, is unspoiled by any alien developments. For Munro enthusiasts it also boasts Sgòr an Lochain Uaine (1258m) and Cairn Toul (1293m), perched on the rim above Lairig Ghru.

The climb to Braeriach starts only after a fairly long walk in, so you'll need a fine, midsummer day. The distance is 18.75mi (30km) and the ascent is 1000m; allow about nine hours. The best map is either Harvey's 1:25,000 *Cairn Gorm* map or the OS Outdoor Leisure 1:25,000 map No 3 *(The Cairngorms – Aviemore & Glen Avon)*. The Scottish Mountaineering Club's guide *The Cairngorms* is an invaluable reference.

The most popular approach is from the Lairig Ghru path by Allt Druidh to a minor track junction about 150m south of the Chalamain Gap path junction (see Chalamain Gap & the Lairig Ghru on page 221). Rather than return the same way, a descent west into Glen Einich and return down that valley makes a much more interesting walk. Extending the walk to Sgòr an Lochain Uaine and Cairn Toul would add 4mi (6.5km), 300m ascent and about two hours to the walk. The route described is preferred by Rothiemurchus Estate during stalking season (September and October); for more information contact the estate's visitor centre (☎ 01479-812345).

The walk starts and finishes at Whitewell car park at the end of the Inverdruie-Blackpark road. It is also possible to start from Coylumbridge. A short path leads to a north-south vehicular track. Follow this to Lochan Deo and head east to reach the Lairig Ghru path near the Cairngorm Club footbridge. The first part of the climb, south-west from Allt Druidh, scales the steep heathery slope. Once you gain the ridge, the direction changes to south-east then south up to a broad plateau topped by Sròn na Lairige (1184m). Cross a small saddle then climb to the summit, spectacularly overlooking Lairig Ghru. Continue along the rim for a few hundred metres then head south-west to cross a burn, the headwaters of the River Dee, the highest spring in Scotland at 1190m. Go on to Carn na Criche (1265m).

To reach the other two Munros keep to the rim all the way; then retrace your steps towards Carn na Criche. About 600m north-west of the saddle west of Sgòr an Lochain Uaine, set a compass course westward, unless you find a faint path, to the top of the pass into Glen Einich beside Allt Coire Dhondail. To go direct to Glen Einich from Carn na Criche, head generally south-westward down an indeterminate path. The start of the descent is marked with a large cairn beside Allt Coire Dhondail. The path leads to a precarious traverse of a small cliff then descends to the vehicular track near Loch Einich. Follow this back to Whitewell or Coylumbridge. Keep in mind, for a misty overcast day, that the walk into Loch Einich and back is well worth doing by itself.

Meall a' Bhuachaille

This shapely mountain (the name means 'shepherd's hill') overlooks Glenmore and Loch Morlich and gives superb views of the Cairngorm plateau and Braeriach from its summit (810m). A path waymarked with orange banded posts leads north from behind the Glenmore Forest Visitor Centre and climbs steeply through the pines to open moorland. From here a clear path leads up to a broad saddle between Creagan Gorm (782m) to the west and the Meall, then on to the summit. To make a circuit, continue east down the broad spur to Ryvoan Bothy and follow a vehicular track down, past beautiful An Lochan Uaine (green lake), Glenmore Lodge and back to the village. Allow three hours for this 6mi (9.5km) walk, which includes 480m climbing. Use Harvey's 1:25,000 *Cairn Gorm* or the OS Landranger 1:50,000 No 36 *(Grantown & Aviemore)* maps.

Loch Avon

Dramatically beautiful Loch Avon is almost surrounded by cliffs – the precipitous slopes of the Cairngorm plateau to the north, Carn Etchachan (1120m) and Beinn Mheadhoin (1182m) to the south. The loch is the very scenic centrepiece of this long, generally low-level walk around the eastern side of an outlier of the plateau. The approach to Loch Avon and the lower reaches of Strath Nethy can be very wet so keep this walk for a dry spell. The distance is 21mi (34km), with 470m of ascent, for which you should allow at least 8½ hours. The walk could be spread over two days – a tent could be pitched near the tiny Fords of Avon refuge, a windowless stone hut. This would allow time for climbing some of the mountains nearby – Bynack More (1090m) and Beinn Mheadhoin. Use the Harvey 1:25,000 *Cairn Gorm* map or the OS Landranger 1:50,000 map No 36 *(Grantown & Aviemore)*.

From Glenmore walk up the road past the lodge and An Lochan Uaine and on to Bynack Stable – a small tin shed. A muddy path continues south-east up a broad hillside, over the shoulder of Bynack More, down slightly and on across its eastern slopes to the Fords of Avon. Turn west from the refuge; the path of sorts is faint until the flanking slopes close in. Keep close to the youthful River Avon up to Loch Avon and continue along its northern shore for nearly 0.6mi to a path diverging uphill. Follow this to The Saddle then down Strath Nethy (the path varies from good to invisible) to Bynack Stable and Glenmore.

Bennachie – The Cairngorms' Eastern Sentinel

Bennachie is the name given to the Cairngorm uplands' easternmost outlier, a range of lowish mountains overlooking the coastal plain north-west of Aberdeen. The highest point is Oxen Craig (528m) and there are five satellites or tops over 450m, including the best known, Mither Tap (518m), much loved by the people of the north-east. The view from Mither Tap on a good day is incredibly far-ranging, from Morven (a mountain in eastern Sutherland) in the north to the Cairngorm plateau and around to Aberdeen.

Heather moorland covers the higher ground of this granite ridge; its scattering of tors give rise to its Gaelic name Beinn na Ciche – mountain of the breast. Farmland and plantations of Scots pine, larch and spruce occupy the lower ground. People have lived on and around Bennachie for thousands of years. There's an Iron Age fort on Mither Tap; settlers were evicted from crofts on the eastern slopes in the 19th century.

The Forestry Commission (Forest Enterprise) arrived in the 1930s and is now a major landowner. In 1995 the Bennachie Centre, at the eastern foot of the mountain, was opened – the product of a partnership between Forest Enterprise, the local council, Scottish Natural Heritage and the Bailies of Bennachie (see later).

Forest Enterprise has developed a web of waymarked walks across Bennachie, from short woodland strolls to the scenic, 12mi-long West Gordon Way. Using forest tracks and footpaths, these walks spread out from the centre and from three car parks on the northern and southern sides of Bennachie.

The West Gordon Way partly follows the old peat extraction route on Bennachie. It crosses the ridge to the B992, then traverses another, slightly lower ridge to the Suie car park, which is on a minor road between Rhynie and Alford. The West Gordon Way is shown on OS Landranger 1:50,000 map No 37 *(Strathdon & Alford)*; it extends onto OS Landranger 1:50,000 map No 38 *(Aberdeen)* but isn't highlighted.

The award-winning Bennachie Centre (☎ 01467-681470) is open daily (9.30am to 4pm in winter and 10.30am to 5pm in summer) except Monday and has excellent displays about the natural and social history of the area. Several inexpensive leaflets on these themes, and one for the waymarked walks, are available. At the centre you can also learn about the Bailies of Bennachie, a conservation group founded in 1973 to preserve the mountain, its history and folklore.

The centre is a few miles west of Inverurie; access from there, via Burnhervie, is signposted. Alternatively you can reach the centre from Chapel of Garioch to the north. For information about accommodation and facilities in Inverurie and Alford (the nearest towns) contact the Inverurie TIC (☎ 01467-625800) – it's open all year.

West Gordon Way

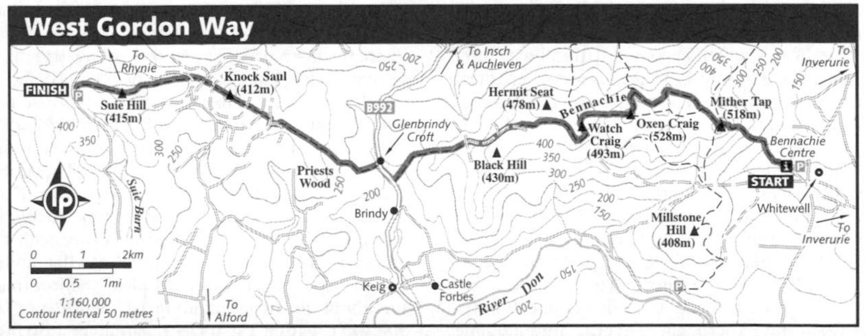

Speyside Way

This long-distance path links Aviemore in Strathspey and Buckie on the North Sea coast, and generally follows the course of the River Spey – Scotland's second-longest river and one of its most scenic. Rising in the Monadhliath Mountains west of Kingussie, the river flows generally east and north to enter the North Sea at Spey Bay. Overlooked by the Cairngorm mountains at its Strathspey end, the Way passes through Boat of Garten, Nethy Bridge, Grantown-on-Spey, Cromdale, Aberlour, Craigellachie, Fochabers and Spey Bay to reach its other end at Buckie. Two spur routes, from Bridge of Avon to Tomintoul (the highest village in the Highlands) and from Craigellachie to Dufftown, provide attractive walks in their own right and are well worthwhile. The Way is well signposted and waymarked with the official thistle hexagon logo.

The Way, which can be followed in either direction, is 65mi (104.5km) long; the Tomintoul Spur is 14.3mi (23km) one way and the Dufftown Spur 4.3mi (7km) one way. It is possible to do the whole lot in five days, but six or seven allows time for visiting whisky distilleries, the famous Strathspey Steam Railway and the reopened scenic Dufftown to Keith railway.

The Speyside Way Ranger Service (☎ 01340-881266) publishes a free, annual *Accommodation and General Information* brochure with a map, facilities and places to stay. The service also produces a public transport guide and maintains an good Web site **W** www.moray.org/area/speyway.

The 1:40,000 Harvey map *Speyside Way*, the official map for the route, shows facilities and some features of interest. *The Speyside Way* guide published by Rucksack Readers has easy to use 1:100,000 strip maps and helpful information. For coverage of the surrounding area you'll need OS Landranger 1:50,000 maps No 28 *(Elgin & Dufftown)* and No 36 *(Grantown & Aviemore)*, which also show the route of the Way.

The official brochure is invaluable for planning, as it indicates which accommodation hosts offer a pick-up and drop-off service, useful where there are long gaps between shelter of any type (particularly between Cromdale and Aberlour). Camping sites are spaced so you could camp each night.

Aviemore is well served by ScotRail (☎ 0845-755 0033) and GNER (☎ 0845-722 5225) trains on the London to Inverness via Edinburgh and Glasgow services, and by Citylink (☎ 0870-550 5050) buses between Glasgow, Edinburgh and Inverness. Buses run to Buckie from Aberdeen and from Keith, both on the train line connecting Inverness and Aberdeen. Several intermediate towns have bus services from major centres.

SOUTHERN CAIRNGORMS

Morrone

Morrone (859m) dramatically presides over Braemar from the south-west and offers a good introduction to the area, with fine views of Braeriach, Ben Macdui and much more. Well-made and waymarked paths (extensively rebuilt during 2000) make the climb relatively easy. The communications tower on the summit isn't overly intrusive and makes possible a good round walk, following the gravel road built to construct and maintain it.

To reach the start of the walk, turn off the Linn of Dee road on the western edge of Braemar along Chapel Brae, signposted to 'Forest Walk'. There's a large car park at the end of the sealed road, beside a small lochan. The first part of the walk goes through the Morrone Birkwood, a National Nature Reserve protecting an unusual community of birch, juniper and lime-loving herbs. From the summit go down the road on the eastern flank of the mountain to a minor road. Follow this north for almost 1.2mi to a narrow gravel road on the left; beyond a large stone house and in open ground, fork right and continue to Chapel Brae and back to the start. Allow about three hours for this 7.5mi (12km) walk. You'll need OS Landranger 1:50,000 map No 43 *(Braemar & Blair Atholl)*.

Loch Muick & Dubh Loch

If cloud and strong winds rule out doing Lochnagar, then a circuit of Loch Muick, with a side trip to mysterious and dramatically beautiful Dubh Loch, is a very worthy substitute. The walk starts and finishes at the Spittal of Glenmuick car park (see the Lochnagar walk on page 238) and is best done clockwise, heading out on the vehicular track along the south-eastern shore of Loch Muick, then the path from Black Burn to the head of the loch.

The path to Dubh Loch takes off from the north-western corner of Loch Muick – at the point where the main path turns east to follow its north-western shore. The Dubh Loch path climbs above tumbling Allt an Dubh-loch, past a spectacular waterfall on Stulan Burn. It can be very boggy above Dubh Loch but it is possible to reach the loch's wild and rocky western end. The Loch Muick circuit involves very little ascent and 7mi (11km) horizontally; the Dubh Loch extension adds about 5mi (8km), making a reasonable day's walk. The visitor centre at Spittal of Glenmuick (see the Lochnagar walk) has plenty of information about the area, including a *Loch Muick Circuit Walk* leaflet; carry OS Landranger 1:50,000 map No 44 *(Ballater & Glen Clova)*.

Highland Glens

Highland and glens are two of the most evocative words associated with Scotland – touchstones for images of misty, rugged mountains and long, lonely valleys (or glens). These are, in fact, the essential features of the area covered in this chapter, extending from Glen Garry and Glen Spean in the south to Strathconon in the north, and west from the Monadhliath Mountains to the east coast. This extensive area contains several beautiful and very different glens and straths (broader valleys); scores of mountains of all shapes and sizes; waterfalls, lochs and tumbling rivers; and, of course, dozens of first-class walks at high and low levels. This chapter offers an introduction to a wealth of riches: Scotland's newest long-distance path; another long and wilder walk in Glen Affric; and day walks around Glen Shiel, Glen Spean and Glen Garry. There are also some suggestions for Other Walks in this area.

Highlights

PHILIP GAME

Locks, between lochs, on the historic Caledonian Canal at Inverness.

- Striding along the Caledonian Canal and wondering about the legend of Loch Ness on the Great Glen Way
- Traversing the Five Sisters: the slender, scenic ridge above dramatic Glen Shiel
- Mountain-filled panoramic views from the summit of magnificent, ice-sculpted Creag Meagaidh.
- Wandering through Caledonian woodland in beautiful Glen Affric and following the footsteps of early travellers over a narrow pass

NATURAL HISTORY

Putting it simply, these mountains were formed when two enormous plates of the earth's crust rammed together and the plates were bent and folded into peaks and ranges. Much later, ice sheets and glaciers, which accumulated in successive ice ages, enlarged the glens and sculpted the mountains.

To the north and north-west of the Great Glen, the rocks are almost universally metamorphic (altered sediments), of ancient origin and known as schist. This produces poor soil, which supports vast tracts of heather and grass moorland. Small remnants of the native Caledonian woodland survive, mainly in Glen Affric (see the boxed text 'Caledonian Woodland Restored' on page 257). You're never very far from a conifer plantation anywhere, although none are of any great size.

CLIMATE

Depressions moving in from the Atlantic Ocean, and westerly and south-westerly winds passing over the relatively warm waters of the Gulf Stream define the area's climate. Consequently, it's wet in the west with an average annual rainfall of around 400cm, in some years more than 500cm. Dampness decreases as you move eastward, down to 120cm on the North Sea coast. The driest months are May and June; August is much wetter. The 'hills' and glens are often snow-covered in winter, although snow only lies for prolonged periods on high ground.

Summer temperatures vary little across the glens, averaging between 12°C and 14°C, although temperatures in the 20s are not uncommon when high pressure areas linger over the north Atlantic and warm southerly winds prevail. The warmest months are July and August. In winter western areas usually enjoy milder temperatures.

For walkers the direction and strength of the wind is crucial. The prevailing winds are from the south-west and west, although relatively cold northerlies often intervene. At about 900m a gentle sea-level breeze may have trebled in strength and the temperature dropped by several degrees.

INFORMATION

Maps

For overall planning, the best bet is the OS Travelmaster 1:250,000 map No 2 *(Northern Scotland)*.

Books

The most comprehensive guide to the area is the Scottish Mountaineering Club's *The Northwest Highlands* by DJ Bennet & T Strang in the District Guide series. The club's two guides to the Munros and the Scottish Rights of Way Society's *Scottish Hill Tracks* are also useful.

For historical background, James Hunter's books are fired by a passionate commitment to devolution of power to Scotland. *Last of the Free: A Millennial History of the Highlands and Islands of Scotland* and *Scottish Highlanders* is stimulating reading.

Information Sources

The Met Office forecast for the western Highlands is available on ☎ 09068-500441 or fax 09060-100405.

A useful Web site for Highlands transport information is Ⓦ www.hi-ways.org. Highland Council publishes a set of four comprehensive transport guides to the region, of

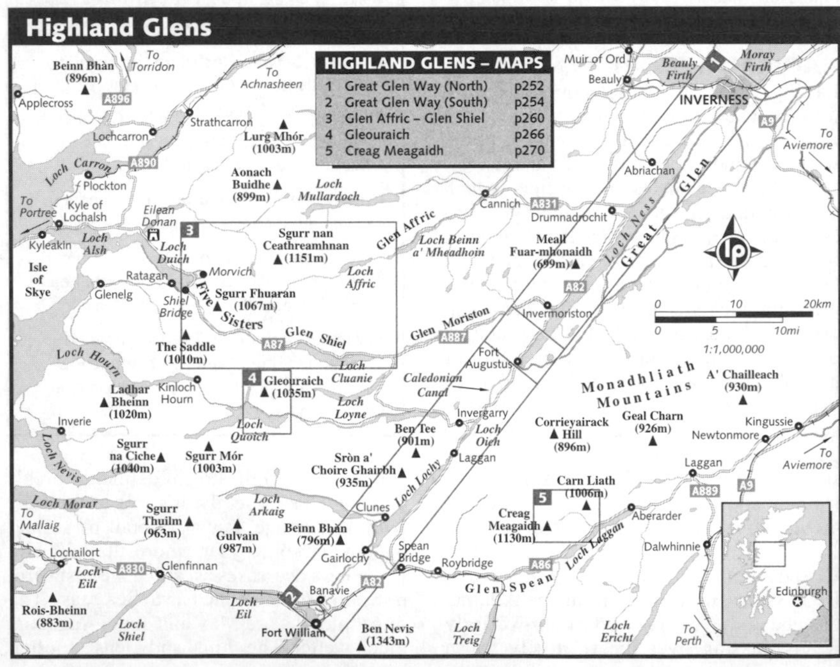

which *South Highland & Inverness* cover the area in this chapter. They're most readily available from local TICs.

The Northern Constabulary (☎ 01463-715555) encourages walkers to register details of extended walks, in particular through the Web site **W** www.northern.police.uk (go to The Hills page) or by a form available from TICs, some outdoor gear shops and youth hostels.

Place Names

For some walks in this chapter, the recommended map is published by Harvey at 1:25,000. Inevitably this gives more place names (and topographical detail) than the OS Landranger 1:50,000 map for the same area. For occasional and minor variations in spelling of place names, the OS version has been used.

GATEWAY

Inverness

Scenically located on the shores of the inner Moray Firth, Inverness is the bustling capital of the Highlands and provides all the services and facilities needed before you disappear into the more remote and sparsely populated hinterland.

The main TIC for the area is in Inverness (☎ 01463-234353, fax 710609, **e** info@host.co.uk, **W** www.host.co.uk); it's open daily (except Sunday from late October until Easter). The Web site includes an online booking service. Internet/email facilities are available at the TIC for a nominal fee.

The town is well served by outdoor equipment shops, including a branch of Tiso's (☎ 01463-716617), 41 High St, and Clive Rowland Mountain Sports (☎ 01463-238746), 9–11 Bridge St. In addition, bookseller James Thin, at 29 Union St, has a good selection of guidebooks, maps and books about Scotland.

Drop in at the Highland Council Library (☎ 01463-236463, fax 237001) in Farraline Park (next to the bus station) for free Internet access; the only catch is you must book a half-hour session in advance. The library is open Monday to Saturday until at least 5pm and later on Thursday and Friday.

Places to Stay & Eat Purpose-built, ***Inverness SYHA Hostel*** *(☎ 01463-231771, fax 710349)*, Victoria Drive, charges from £13.25, including a continental breakfast, and some rooms have en suite facilities. Cafeteria meals are provided. The hostel also has an Internet kiosk; the hourly rate is £5. ***Eastgate Backpackers Hostel*** *(☎/fax 01463-718756)*, in the centre of town, has small dorms (£8.90) and twin rooms (£11) in an older, homely and clean building. Internet access is available. ***Bught Caravan & Camping Site*** *(☎ 01463-236920)*, between the Aquatic Centre, sports fields and nearby housing, is conveniently located (on the Great Glen Way); a pitch costs around £3.50. Details of B&Bs and guesthouses in and near the town are given in the Highlands of Scotland Tourist Board's guide *The Freedom of the Highlands*.

Inverness has several good Italian restaurants, including lively ***Pazzo's*** *(☎ 01463-226686)*, on Ness Walk overlooking the river, where you can fill up on traditional pizzas (£4.30 to £7.30). Downstairs is the more upmarket and indisputably Italian ***Riva Bistro*** *(☎ 01463-237377)*, with a menu in which genuine Italian ingredients are used as far as possible; pasta dishes range up to £9, fish to £13. Across the river is ***Shapla Tandoori*** *(☎ 01463-241919)* with an extensive menu featuring tandoori dishes (£7 to £12) and biryani (£6.50 to £11). There are also numerous pubs in town for bar meals.

There's a ***Safeway*** supermarket next to the train station, a good health food shop in Baron Taylor's St, and an excellent delicatessen, ***The Gourmet's Lair*** in Union St, specialising in Scottish products.

Getting There & Away Several ScotRail (☎ 0845-755 0033) and GNER (☎ 0845-722 5225) trains arrive in Inverness from London, Glasgow, Edinburgh and Aberdeen. A middle-of-the-range, return fare from Glasgow Queen Street or Edinburgh (via Aviemore) is £32, and from Aberdeen £16. From London, you can travel with GNER for as little as £50 return or you can arrive in style on a ScotRail sleeper, having paid £109 for an Apex ticket.

National Express (☎ 0870-580 8080) and Scottish Citylink (☎ 0870-550 5050) buses also serve Inverness. With Citylink the standard return fare from Glasgow is £21.50 and from Edinburgh £22.50; with National from London the return is £40.50.

EasyJet (☎ 0870-600 0000) operates flights from London Luton Airport to Inverness; the return fare is £50, less than half the single fare. British Airways (☎ 0845-773 3377) flies to Inverness from London Gatwick. A round-trip ticket from London costs £115.50 and must be booked at least seven days in advance. There are British Airways flights from Edinburgh and Glasgow. A Highland Rover ticket provides for a minimum of five separate flights on Scottish routes; the cost is £169 and additional (but different) sectors can be purchased for £40. Maximum duration is three months.

Inverness Airport is at Dalcross about 6mi (10km) north-east; Highland Country Buses (☎ 01463-222244) operates daily services between Inverness post office and the airport. The single fare is £2.05.

The main arterial roads to Inverness from Glasgow are the A82 via Fort William and the M80 then A roads and motorways via Stirling to the A9. From Edinburgh take the M9/A9 via Perth and Pitlochry. The A96 links Inverness with Aberdeen.

Great Glen Way

Duration	4 days
Distance	70mi (113km)
Standard	medium
Start	Inverness
Finish	Fort William
Nearest Towns	Inverness, Fort Augustus, Fort William, Drumnadrochit
Public Transport	yes

Summary A magnificently scenic walk through the Highlands' most famous glen, above three superb lochs, beside an historic canal and through woodlands.

The Great Glen is the wide, deep trench that almost severs the Highlands from the rest of Scotland. With Ben Nevis and the Nevis Range at the south-western end, Loch Ness and the Moray Firth at the north-eastern outlet, and the superb Loch Lochy and Loch Oich and several fine 'hills' in between, it's magnificently scenic. The whole glen is rich in historical associations dating from prehistoric times. It's a natural route for a long-distance path, and the Great Glen Way is set to become Scotland's fourth official long-distance path, linking Inverness on the shores of the Moray Firth in the east and Fort William on the west coast.

The Great Glen Way was officially opened and waymarked in April 2002. It can be walked in either direction but by starting from Inverness you are walking towards the best of the views, to the high peaks around Loch Lochy and beyond to Ben Nevis, so this is the direction described. Although the prevailing wind is from the south-west, it's as likely to be coming from the north or north-east, so this isn't a decisive factor.

The Way is about 70mi long; spread this over four or five days and you will have a reasonably comfortable walk. Most of the ascent is at the north-eastern end, from Inverness up to the Abriachan plateau, and between Drumnadrochit and Invermoriston. The Way follows long stretches of the historic Caledonian Canal's towpath, sections of the Great Glen Cycleway, an old railway formation, and quiet roads and tracks. Some sections are shared with cyclists and trail bike riders, so you need to keep alert on the narrower paths. There's relatively little walking along sealed roads, most of this being across the Abriachan plateau and around Drumnadrochit.

Alternatives If you don't have time to do the whole walk, any one of the sections described (or parts of them) could be done as a day walk, making use of the good bus services through the glen.

There are many great side trips to tempt you to extend the walk to a week or more. There's a scenic network of mainly woodland paths at the southern end of the Abriachan plateau (developed and maintained by

Scenic splendours abound on the **Isle of Skye** – the Black Cuillin provides sublime mountain and ocean views; a spectactular winter day on Am Basteir (935m) and Sgurr a' Fionn Choire (930m) in the Black Cuillin (inset). *Main photo: Gareth McCormack. Inset: Graeme Cornwallis.*

Beauty and mystery in the **Highland Glens** – Barrisdale Bay from Ladhar Bheinn (1020m) in the wild and rugged Knoydart; walking the upper reaches of Glen Affric (top inset); Urquhart Castle (bottom inset) on Loch Ness, standing guard over Scotland's greatest mystery. *Main photo: Graeme Cornwallis. Top Inset: Colin Hood. Bottom Inset: Dennis Johnson.*

the community-owned Abriachan Woodland Trust). From Drumnadrochit you can wander through the woodlands overlooking the village (see under Other Walks on page 272 for a route to Glen Affric from there). Meall Fuar-mhonaidh (699m), meaning 'hill of the cold moor' and pronounced me-awl foor-vonee, is the highest point overlooking Loch Ness, offers extraordinarily wide panoramic views and is directly accessible from the Way (see Day 2). Fort Augustus (Day 2) isn't far from the start of the track over the Corrieyairack Pass, and the clutch of Munros and Corbetts above Loch Lochy is easily accessible from the Way. There are also several short walks in various Forest Enterprise-managed forests. And lastly, Fort William is at the northern end of the West Highland Way (see the West Highland Way on page 173), so now there's the opportunity for a really long journey of about 170mi (274km) linking Inverness to Glasgow!

HISTORY

There's plenty of evidence of prehistoric occupation of the Great Glen, most visibly as Iron Age forts (duns); Torr Dhuin near Fort Augustus (and in view from the Way) is an excellent example. Perhaps the earliest recorded visitor was St Columba, the Irish Christian missionary, who travelled through the Glen in AD 565 (see the boxed text 'Loch Ness – Legend & Science'). A few castles gaze down on the lochs, most much reduced from their original dimensions; both Invergarry Castle (destroyed in the 18th century) and Urquhart Castle near Drumnadrochit (dating from about the 13th

Loch Ness – Legend & Science

The Great Glen Way provides an unrivalled opportunity to contemplate the famous and mysterious Loch Ness, from the shore to several hundred metres above, right along its length of 22.6mi (36.6km).

Although St Columba is said to have repelled a large creature in the River Ness in AD 565, it wasn't until the 1930s that claims of sightings of large, plesiosaur-like creatures were publicly made, hoaxes were perpetrated and the name 'monster' was first used in print. The excitement bubbled for a year or two, then died away until the 1960s. A vigil was mounted along the loch in 1962 but, after many years, merely strengthened scepticism about the chances of a large creature living in the deep, dark waters. Since the 1970s, the legend has been sustained with regular sightings of 'Nessie' (totalling around 1000 by the year 2000) and the founding of a Loch Ness Monster Fan Club.

Scientific interest in the loch, first formally expressed early in the 20th century with the making of a remarkably accurate underwater map, has intensified. The loch's habitats have been accurately described, down to the icy-cold depths where tiny creatures, relics of the ice age, survive the enormous pressure. Comparatively few aquatic species live in the loch, the largest of which is the wild salmon. It's been shown that the loch simply doesn't contain enough food to support even one sizable reptile, let alone a small family of them. The Rosetta Project during the 1990s extracted cores from the loch bed which revealed 10,000 years of environmental change – a fascinating chart of the loch's history.

The Loch Ness 2000 exhibition in Drumnadrochit (☎ 01456-450573) delves into this intriguing story in more detail and is worth a visit as you pass through.

CLINT CURÉ

century and destroyed 400 years later), can be seen from the Way.

Jacobite disturbances raged up and down the Great Glen and led to the building of military roads along its eastern side to link forts near Inverness, at Fort Augustus and Fort William; even now, 250 years later, the formation is still clear in many places. The Caledonian Canal, planned by Thomas Telford to make the glen navigable from end to end, opened for through traffic in 1822. For many decades it provided the main means of transport through the glen, until roads made for faster and easier travel. A Great Glen railway seemed a logical development but the dream fell foul of inter-company wrangling and underfunding; only a line from Spean Bridge to Fort Augustus (part of which the Way follows) carried trains, from 1903 until the 1930s.

In the glen, substantial industries have been few; an aluminium smelter operated at Foyers for more than 60 years until 1967. A hydroelectric power station at Foyers is now one of the few sizable buildings, and probably the ugliest, on any loch shore.

NATURAL HISTORY

The Great Glen is essentially an enormous trench wrought along a fault in the earth's crust hundreds of millions of years ago. It was widened and deepened during the last ice age. This trench is largely filled with water – Loch Ness, Loch Oich and Loch Lochy, all joined by short rivers. Both sides of the glen rise steeply, particularly in its central section; a series of roughly parallel and quite large glens breach the western side but the streams entering from the east cut smaller, narrower valleys. Quite extensive areas of deciduous woodland are scattered along the Way and on the rugged eastern slopes in view between Drumnadrochit and Fort Augustus. Pine plantations also feature, but not for unduly prolonged stretches.

PLANNING

This is one walk in Scotland that can be done at almost any time of the year; indeed, it offers the opportunity to see the magnificent spectacle of snow-covered mountains, especially Ben Nevis, during winter. The only serious hazard at that time could be ice on the paths and tracks.

Maps & Books

OS Landranger 1:50,000 maps No 26 *(Inverness & Loch Ness)*, No 34 *(Fort Augustus)* and No 41 *(Ben Nevis)* cover the route.

At the time of writing there was no official guide or leaflet to the Way; contact the Great Glen Way manager (☎ 01320-366633) for up-to-date information. In the meantime, two leaflets from Forest Enterprise (☎ 01320-366322) are worth chasing, *The Great Glen* and *Cycling in the Forest: Great Glen*, which between them cover a fair bit of the Way. An unofficial guide, *The Great Glen Way* by Heather Common & Paul Roper, does not follow the official route in its entirety and its deviations are best ignored. *The Caledonian Canal* by Anthony Burton is a multipurpose guide for waterborne travellers, cyclists and walkers, and has plenty of background information. Rucksack Readers' guide (also unofficial) *The Great Glen Way* has detailed maps and a handy format.

Other Information

For up-to-date information about development of the Way, check the official Web site at **W** www.greatglenway.com.

The Highland Council Ranger Service (☎ 01463-724260) runs guided walks around Loch Ness throughout the year.

NEAREST TOWNS

Drumnadrochit & Around

Famed for its association with the Loch Ness Monster, the village has much more to offer, with abundant accommodation and several pubs. A small TIC (☎ 01456-459076) in the central car park, open Monday to Saturday year-round and on Sunday during July and August, has details of local B&Bs. The bank, open Monday, Wednesday and Friday morning, also has an ATM.

Loch Ness Backpackers *(☎ 01456-450807)*, about 200m east of the A82 in East Lewiston, charges £9 for a bed in a smallish dorm. ***Borlum Farm Caravan & Camping Park*** *(☎ 01456-450220)*, beside the A82 about 1mi south of the village, charges £4 for a pitch in an open field.

Drumnadrochit Hotel *(☎ 01456-450202)*, just above River Enrick bridge, has budget accommodation in four-person 'travelodges' where a bed costs £11.25; breakfast (£4.25) and evening meals are served in the bar-restaurant. A drying room is available for anyone in need, not only hotel patrons.

In the centre of the village, ***Fiddlers Restaurant*** *(☎ 01456-450678)* knows how to feed hungry walkers, from a menu featuring Scottish fare; expect to pay around £8 for a main course (and there's more than one vegetarian choice).

There's a small ***supermarket*** (with an ATM) on the main road and the ***post office shop*** has groceries. See Getting to/from the Walk for transport options.

Fort Augustus

This large village straddles the Caledonian Canal and offers plenty of accommodation. The TIC (☎ 01320- 366367), next to the car park by the main road at the northern end of town, is open from April to October. There is an ATM at the petrol station nearby. The lone bank (between the canal and the A82) is open Monday, Thursday and Friday but doesn't have an ATM.

Right beside the Way as you approach Fort Augustus is ***Thistle Dubh*** B&B *(☎ 01320-366380)* with comfortable, en suite rooms in a modern bungalow from £20. At the other end of the town, beside the canal, is ***Tigh na Mairi*** *(☎ 01320-366766)*, where the B&B tariff starts at £16.

To reach ***Fort Augustus Caravan & Camping Park*** *(☎ 01320-366618)* you have to walk along the A82 to the southern edge of the town. It's a spacious, well-grassed site and costs £4 per person, including a shower.

There are several pubs and bars to choose from; overlooking the canal are two worth trying. ***The Lock Inn*** *(☎ 01320-366302)* offers good, traditional bar suppers from £6. Close to the road bridge is ***The Bothy*** (it doesn't take bookings), which has a rather carnivorous menu with just one vegetarian item; expect to pay at least £6.

There are two small supermarkets, both are north of the canal, as well as a ***butcher-green grocer*** on its south side. See Getting to/from the Walk for transport options.

Fort William

For details on Fort William, see Gateway in the Lochaber & Glen Coe on page 192.

GETTING TO/FROM THE WALK

To reach Inverness Castle and the start of the walk, from the train and bus stations walk east along Academy St to the pedestrian crossing near Marks & Spencer. Cross over and follow the short street ahead (Inglis St) to the pedestrianised high street and turn right. Continue to a T-junction with a pedestrian crossing on the left; cross here and walk uphill along Castle St for about 250m to the castle entrance on your right.

Scottish Citylink (☎ 0870-550 5050) and Highland Country Buses (☎ 01463-222244) operate services through the Great Glen, stopping at the villages along the A82.

THE WALK

Day 1: Inverness to Drumnadrochit

7–7½ hours, 18.6mi (30km)

From Inverness Castle walk down past a large church to the riverside street of Ness Bank. Follow footpaths upstream for just over half a mile to the footbridge leading to the wooded Ness Islands. Pleasant paths and footbridges then lead to a bridge over the River Ness. Turn left and follow a riverbank path to Whin Park then bear right and walk out of the park. Continue along the minor road to the A82. Cross the road and the Tomnahurich bridge over the Caledonian Canal, and stay beside the A82 to General Booth Drive. Turn right, cross the road and walk along the roadside footpath for 500m to a path on the left; this generally skirts a housing estate and leads to the ridge near a large pond (about 1½ hours from the start). There are excellent views from here back over Inverness and the Moray Firth.

Forest tracks, initially following the route of an old drove road, generally skirt a conifer plantation for nearly 2mi. The Way then

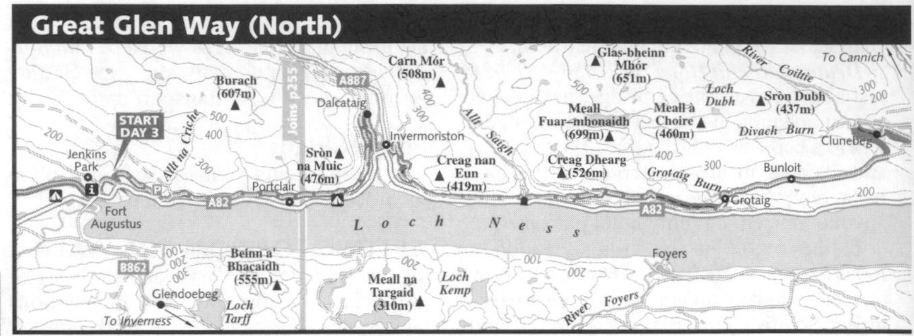

dives into the plantation for another mile or so and emerges at a minor public road at Blackfold (about 1½ hours from the pond). You then set out on the longest stretch of road walking on the Way; fortunately it's a quiet road and the views westward of mountains and deep glens are superb. From the cottages at Ladycairn the road passes through a plantation. Back in the open, the Way leaves the road and follows an old right of way to a minor road near Lochlait (about two hours from Blackfold). Cross over and continue on a gravel road through a pine plantation for about 1mi. With open ground on your right, leave the road along a path to the left, which leads up around the edge of, then through, a plantation and out into open moorland. The direction is generally south-eastward, past the end of an old vehicular track at Corryfoyness and into another plantation. Paths and forest roads take you south through the pines and, after about 1.5mi, steeply south-east to the A82, just above Loch Ness. A short distance along to the right, a roadside footpath leads into Drumnadrochit (about two hours from Lochlait).

Day 2: Drumnadrochit to Fort Augustus

7½–8 hours, 19.2mi (31km)

Walk through Drumnadrochit and, just over the bridge spanning the River Coiltie, turn off the A82 along the road signposted to Bunloit. At the first bend continue ahead, following the river on a dirt road to Clunebeg Farm. Go up past the farm and continue on a path, which winds around to the left, steeply up through the trees to the Bunloit road. Soon it emerges into high moorland and fields and Meall Fuar-mhonaidh dominates the view ahead. The quiet road undulates along for 2mi, relieved by two sections of roadside path; a short distance past a small car park on the right (used by walkers heading for Meall Fuar-mhonaidh), turn off the road to the left (about 1½ hours from Drumnadrochit).

The Way heads down towards Loch Ness via a path beside Grotaig Burn, then through oak woodland and a succession of gates to a forest road; turn right. The road gains height to another junction; continue in the same direction to the end of the road. A path leads on with superb views unfolding to the south, down the Great Glen, to distant hills beyond Fort Augustus and across Loch Ness to the Monadhliath Mountains. After about 20 minutes the path meets a forest road, which rises to the highest point on this section about half an hour further on. Turn left at a forest road junction and descend into conifers to reach another junction (nearly two hours from the Bunloit road). Here a forest road to the left leads to the SYHA's ***Loch Ness Hostel*** *(☎ 01320-351274)*. The hostel is open from March to October; it's a few miles to the nearest shops in Invermoriston so you'll need to bring your own supplies.

Continue straight on at the junction, across cascading Allt Saigh, up past a track leading away to the right. The forest road pursues an undulating route across the very steep slope. About half an hour from Allt

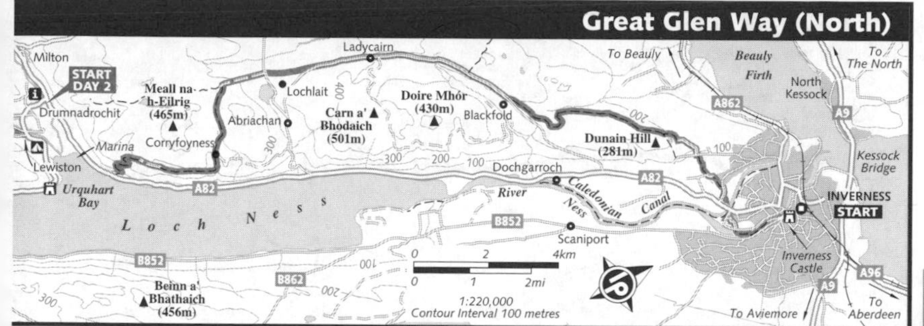

Saigh, a track down to the A82 branches to the left, but the Way continues below the vertical cliffs of Creag nan Eun, still mainly in the open. Farther on, there's a signposted **'Stone Cave'** beside the road – a small overhang converted to a shelter by the skilful use of dry-stone (cement-free) stone work. From the end of the road, a path winds up north between conifers and birch to another forest road. Nearby to the right, a short, signposted path leads up to a curious **stone seat** with a fine view of the 'hills' on the other side of Loch Ness. Continue on the main track to another junction and turn left, soon into conifers and along to a crossroads. Turn left and descend the steep, sealed road to the A887 in Invermoriston (about 1½ hours from Allt Saigh).

The village ***shop*** on the A82 corner is open daily. ***Glenmoriston Arms Hotel*** *(☎ 01320-351206)* has comfortable rooms from £35, and a highly regarded restaurant or the Tavern & Bistro for bar meals. ***Invermoriston Tea Room & Restaurant*** *(☎ 01320-351352)*, beside the A887, is open all day for snacks and evening meals.

To continue, walk beside the A82 towards Fort Augustus briefly then turn right and cross the river on an old stone bridge; walk through the chalet park grounds to a minor road leading to Dalcataig.

Along here you'll pass ***Burnside B&B*** *(☎ 01320-351262)*, which offers very comfortable accommodation from £18. About 20 minutes' walk brings you to the turn-off left along a forest road. It gains height up to a junction; keep on generally upwards around the steep slopes of Sròn na Muic towering above. An hour or more from Invermoriston, and with the forest road now leading southward, a road branches left and down to the A82 close to ***Loch Ness Caravan & Camping Park*** *(☎ 01320-351207)*, which has good loch-side pitches.

The road can't decide whether to consistently descend or ascend, as it passes above the wooded headland of Portclair and on to the car park at Allt na Criche. Continue along the forest track to a minor road on the left and go down to the A82; turn immediately right along a minor road and follow it, past a junction on the right, and back down to the A82 on the edge of Fort Augustus (about three hours from Invermoriston).

Day 3: Fort Augustus to Laggan

4–4½ hours, 10.3mi (16.5km)

The first part of this easy day's walk is very straightforward – along the towpath on the northern side of the canal, shortly passing British Waterways' Canal Heritage Centre (admission is free). Near Kytra Lock you can glimpse the cliffs of Torr Dhùin to the north – on top of which is a fine example of an Iron Age fort. Around another bend, the canal straightens out and leads past Cullochy Lock to the road bridge where the river and canal merge with Loch Oich (about two hours from Fort Augustus). Nearby is the splendidly preserved **Bridge of Oich**, built in 1849, a pioneering, half-suspension half-cantilever design.

Cross the road and the bridge, and follow a path beside the loch shore around to the

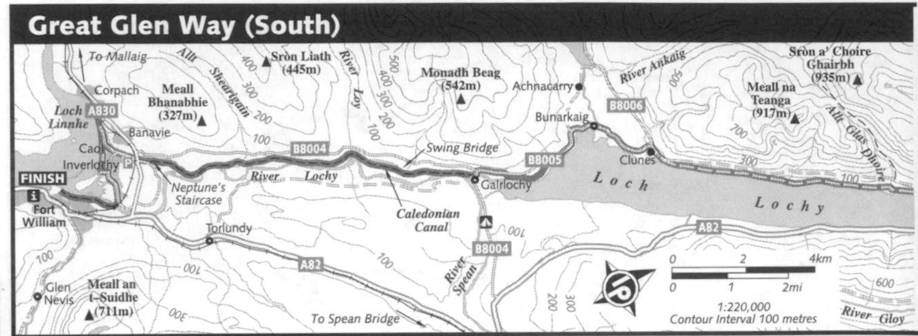

old railway bridge near Aberchalder Farm, then continue along the woodland path. Look out for views of Invergarry Castle from a small clearing at Leitirfearn, nearly 2mi from Aberchalder. A mile farther on the Way joins the formation of the old train line to Fort Augustus and follows it, over a tunnel, to the Great Glen Water Park, emerging from the trees near its ***bar***.

Follow a minor road to the A82; turn right for 30m and then left, walking down to a path on the canal bank, immediately below Laggan Swing Bridge. The path meets a gravel road, which you follow briefly then continue along the path with fine views down the canal to the mountains above Loch Lochy. A few hundred metres farther on, a short detour to and along the road is necessary to cross a bridged stream. From here accommodation is no more than 200m along the road (about 1½ hours from Aberchalder).

Lilac Cottage *(☎ 01809-501410)* offers B&B from £17 and DB&B from £30. ***Loch Lochy SYHA Hostel*** *(☎ 01809-501239)* nearby is open March-October; a bed in a largish dorm costs £9.25. The nearest ***shop*** is more than 1mi away, about 400m north of Laggan Swing Bridge.

Day 4: Laggan to Fort William

7½–8 hours, 21.9mi (35km)

Return to the canal and follow the path to Laggan Locks. Cross the canal via a lock gate and, beyond the canal-side buildings, pick up a minor road. This road leads along the shore of Loch Lochy, past some holiday chalets, to a junction; turn left. The sealed road ends at Kilfinnan Farm, about half a mile farther on. Continue on the gravel road and through a forest gate. Shortly, bear left at a junction and descend slightly on a vehicular track. The track keeps close to the shore of Loch Lochy, below towering peaks and with superb views towards the Nevis Range, for nearly 6mi to a public road and the settlement of Clunes.

Follow the road south-west, crossing the River Arkaig bridge, for about 2.5mi to a superb shoreline path, which starts about 500m past the side road leading to Achnacarry. The path meets the road again near the end of the canal. Walk along the road to **Gairlochy** – a handful of houses, the canal lock and moorings (about 4¼ hours from Laggan).

Cross the bridge and set sail down the canal towpath – a magnificently scenic walk overlooking the River Lochy to Ben Nevis and neighbours. Continue beside the canal to **Neptune's Staircase**, the spectacular flight of eight locks at Banavie (two to 2½ hours from Gairlochy). Cross the A830 and follow the towpath to the end of the canal at Corpach. From here a path leads east along the shore, past the playing field and houses of Caol, and around to a minor road (B8006). Follow it to a footbridge beside a railway and, on the far side, the final stretch of the walk is along a path through houses, past a sports stadium and then a fast food joint. Cross the road to the end of the Way at the old fort beside Loch Linnhe (about an hour from Banavie).

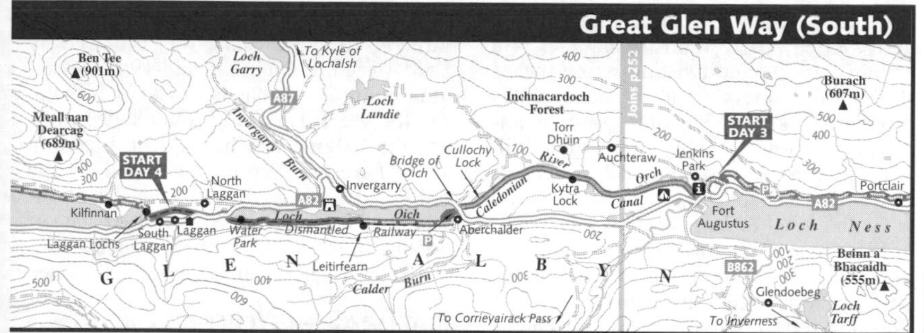

Great Glen Way (South)

Glen Affric

Duration	2 days
Distance	17mi (26km)
Standard	medium
Start	Loch Affric car park
Finish	Morvich
Nearest Towns	Cannich, Shiel Bridge
Public Transport	no

Summary One of the finest long-distance walks in Scotland; through beautiful, untouched Glen Affric, across a dramatic pass to the shores of Loch Duich and past some tempting Munros.

Glen Affric could be called the brightest and best star in the Highland Glens constellation. Its claim to first place is strong: no public roads; the superbly beautiful Loch Affric is not compromised by a dam wall; the small area of conifers has made way for a major Caledonian woodland revival; it's traversed by a public right of way; and it has one of the very few youth hostels you can't drive to. With Loch Cluanie and Glen Shiel to the south and remote Loch Mullardoch and Glen Cannich to the north, it's centred in a magnificent, road-free area extending north to Strathcarron in Wester Ross.

This remote and rewarding walk through the glen follows public footpaths virtually all the way, although it isn't waymarked. While it's described from Loch Affric in the east to Loch Duich in the west (from the mountains to the coast), it can just as well be done in the opposite direction, although this would involve more ascent, starting from a lower level. The height gained going east to west is a negligible 70m to the hostel and 230m over Bealach an Sgàirne.

The overall distance can easily be walked in a long summer day (indeed, it's part of an annual charity marathon, the Highland Cross, from Morvich to Beauly). However, the opportunities for side trips and to stay in remote Glen Affric Youth Hostel (or camp locally) easily justify the longer duration.

Alternatives Two alternative Day 2 routes from the hostel are also described. Gleann Lichd, immediately south of the main route, is perhaps a little less dramatic but beautiful nonetheless, flanked by the Five Sisters of Kintail (see page 262) on one side. It also leads to Morvich (by Loch Duich) and involves only 100m of ascent, although it's slightly longer than the more northerly route. The other route takes you south through a broad pass and down An Caorann Mór to the A87 near Cluanie Inn. It's the shortest route, with 150m of ascent (190m in the opposite direction), but has by far the worst going underfoot – bogs and morasses joined by short dry bits of path.

With time on your side, you could do a Grand Affric Tour. Walk to Morvich (Loch Duich) from Loch Affric as described. Stay there overnight, then return to the hostel via Gleann Lichd and back to Loch Affric car park via the south side of the loch, along the road from Athnamulloch (see later in this section). The total distance is 34mi (55km).

Two of several possible side trips are also described. Sgurr nan Ceathreamhnan

(1151m, 3775ft) is the third-highest peak above Glen Affric (and, of course, is a Munro). Its tongue-twisting name means 'hill of the quarters' (land divisions) and is pronounced **kay**-ravan, although colloquially it's known as chrysanthemum hill. Secondly, the Falls of Glomach is perhaps the most spectacular waterfall in the country with a total drop of 123m.

It's also possible to experience much of the beauty and remoteness of Loch Affric on a day walk around the loch, starting and finishing at the Loch Affric car park. Follow the route described below along the northern side of the loch to the junction of the path with a vehicular track. Walk down this to Athnamulloch, and cross a small stream on stepping stones to a path beside the River Affric. This leads to the forestry road along the south side of the loch and back to the car park. The distance is 10.4mi (16.5km).

HISTORY

There's little, if any, definite evidence of prehistoric settlement in the glen. It's likely that the Irish missionary St Dubhthach (Duthac) crossed Bealach an Sgàirne during the 11th century in the course of travels between his parishes in Kintail and Tain (on the southern shore of Dornoch Firth, north of Inverness). The bealach appears on a map dated 1725 and was the main route from Kintail eastward until the military road was built through Glen Shiel after 1746.

As you walk through the glen, you can't miss the many low rectangles of stones – the remains of small cottages, some with adjacent stone-walled enclosures (for sheep and cattle) and probably dating from the early to mid-19th century. These are particularly prominent above Loch Affric and in Gleann Gnìomhaidh, west of the hostel. A substantial survivor is Camban Bothy. It was used by a shepherd as early as 1839 and was later occupied by stalkers; the last residents left in 1920. More recently, the bothy has been restored by the Mountain Bothies Association. People were living at Alltbeithe in 1841; there has been a hostel there since 1949, although the present premises are much modified from the original.

Glen Affric was cleared of sheep and farmers after the estate was acquired by Lord Tweedmouth in the mid-19th century, after being in the hands of Clan Chisholm for 400 years. He turned it into a deer 'forest' for stalking and built Affric Lodge in 1870. Forest Enterprise purchased a large holding in 1951; the National Trust for Scotland acquired the West Affric Estate of 3650ha in 1993 and, with its adjacent Kintail Estate, is now a major local landowner.

NATURAL HISTORY

In marked contrast to Glen Shiel, just over the mountains to the south-west, Glen Affric is relatively broad and flat-bottomed. It is also flanked by towering peaks; less jagged but no less beautiful in a grand, majestic style. The main reason for this difference is believed to be that during the last ice age, the glen (and others to the north) sheltered beneath an ice cap, safe from gouging glaciers.

This walk traverses Glen Affric from the River Affric and crosses the watershed to Loch Duich. The River Affric merges with streams from neighbouring glens and eventually flows into the Beauly Firth and thus the North Sea. At the other end of Glen Affric, streams feed Loch Duich, which ultimately is one of the inner reaches of the Atlantic Ocean.

Glen Affric harbours one of the largest surviving remnants of native Caledonian woodland, which is benefiting from a long-term project for its restoration and expansion, led by Forest Enterprise (see the boxed text 'Caledonian Woodland Restored'). Glen Affric became a National Nature Reserve early in 2001.

PLANNING

When to Walk

The ideal times for this walk are from May to early June and from mid-September to mid-October. Snow can lie on the ground to quite low levels until early April, and some stream crossings could be tricky during early spring. The midges are very keen but once they've gone, autumn is particularly beautiful around Loch Affric.

Caledonian Woodland Restored

Glen Affric Caledonian Forest Reserve is one of several reserves established by Forest Enterprise to ensure the future of the fragile remnants of Caledonian woodland that once covered vast areas of Scotland. In the Highlands these reserves will double the area of Caledonian forest during the early 21st century.

The Glen Affric reserve is the largest in northern Scotland and covers more than 14,150ha. Here the unusually varied woodland of Scots pine, birch, aspen, alder, rowan and holly is being expanded from its surviving core of only 1560ha, mainly by natural regeneration. Some exclosures (to keep out deer) have been established to protect seedlings, which will ultimately provide a seed source. Deer numbers are carefully managed to ensure that regeneration elsewhere is successful.

To promote the health and purity of the woodland, all introduced conifers (planted during the 1950s) have been felled and many left in situ as the most efficient and economic way of dealing with them. Some areas of Scots pine have been thinned using horses to remove the timber, to minimise ground disturbance.

Forest Enterprise is working in partnership with the charity Trees for Life (which is also busy in the National Trust for Scotland's West Affric Estate), as well as Scottish Conservation Projects, Scottish Wildlife Trust and other local landowners. The large amounts of cash needed to make it all work have come from the European Union (EU) LIFE program and the National Lottery-funded Millennium Forest for Scotland project.

By the late 1990s the core area of remnant woodland had been doubled in area, and Glen Affric's outstanding natural importance was recognised by Scottish Natural Heritage, which acknowledged its potential for designation as a National Nature Reserve.

For more information about Glen Affric Caledonian Forest Reserve, and a copy of a free brochure, contact Forest Enterprise (☎ 01320-366322).

Stalking The greater part of this walk is within the National Trust for Scotland's West Affric Estate; public access is unaffected by stalking activities. The eastern part of the walk, above Loch Affric, passes through North Affric Estate; provided you keep to the path (a public right of way) you shouldn't encounter any problems during the stalking season (mid-August to mid-October).

Maps

The coverage of the excellent Harvey 1:25,000 *Kintail* map extends west from Allt Coulavie, near the western end of Loch Affric, and so misses most of the first day of this walk. It also stops short of the descent to the Falls of Glomach from Bealach na Sroine. For both of these you'll need OS Landranger 1:50,000 map No 25 *(Glen Carron & Glen Affric)*; map No 33 *(Loch Alsh, Glen Shiel & Loch Hourn)* covers the western part of the walk.

Guided Walks

Forest Enterprise (☎ 01320-366322) runs a series of guided walks in Glen Affric, with a special emphasis on wildlife, from late April to late October.

NEAREST TOWNS

Cannich

The village of Cannich, at the start of the only road to Loch Affric, was originally established to house forestry workers in the 1950s.

Places to Stay & Eat Open March to October, ***Cannich SYHA Hostel*** *(☎ 01456-415244)* charges £8.25. ***Cannich Caravan & Camping Park*** *(☎ 01456-415201)*, off the road to Drumnadrochit, has a sheltered, well-grassed area for tents; the tariff for two people is £6.50. Six-berth static vans are available for around £27 per day. Amenities are clean and well maintained. ***Comar Lodge*** *(☎ 01456-415251)*, just west of the village, is a very comfortable B&B in a listed building dating from 1740. The tariff starts at £18 and all rooms are en suite.

For a meal, the choice is between the old-style ***Glen Affric Hotel*** *(☎ 01456-415214)*, which specialises in local game (and provides accommodation), and the more basic but cheerful ***Slaters Arms*** *(☎ 01456-415215)*, which offers bar meals, including a better than average choice for vegetarians.

The small ***post office shop*** (an off-licence) has a good range of supplies; it's open daily.

Getting There & Away Highland Country Buses (☎ 01463-222244) operates a daily service (except Sunday) to Cannich from Inverness via Drumnadrochit. Ross's Minibuses (☎ 01463-761250) has a more limited service between Inverness and Cannich via Beauly.

Cannich is on the A831 between Drumnadrochit and Beauly.

Shiel Bridge & Around

At the end of this walk there are three hamlets, Morvich, Ault a' chruinn and Shiel Bridge, which offer a reasonable choice of accommodation and restaurants. Glenshiel TIC (☎ 01599-511264), beside Kintail Lodge Hotel south of Ault a' chruinn, is open from Easter to the end of September.

Places to Stay & Eat Closest to the end of the walk is secluded ***Morvich Caravan Club Site*** *(☎ 01599- 511354)*, where the tariff is £2.60 per person plus £2 per tent on well-grassed pitches.

About 1.5km south of Morvich at Ault a' chruinn is ***Glomach House B&B*** *(☎ 01599-511382)*. It is in a superb location overlooking Loch Duich and charges from £17.50. Nearby on the main road (A87), ***Port Bhan Restaurant*** *(☎ 01599-511347)* offers a small menu in pleasant surroundings and has a takeaway service. There's an off-licence close by.

Another mile south on the A87 is ***Kintail Lodge Hotel*** *(☎ 01599-511275)*, where walkers are particularly welcome at the Trekkers Lodge, which costs £23.50 for B&B; the hotel's bar suppers are better than average.

A bit farther south, in Shiel Bridge, there's the small ***Shiel Bridge Caravan & Campsite*** *(☎ 01599-511211)* with simple and clean facilities; the tariff is £3 per person plus £1 per tent.

The nearest hostel is the SYHA's ***Ratagan*** *(☎ 01599-511243)*, where the tariff is £9.25. To reach the hostel, turn off the A87 at Shiel Bridge; the hostel is 1.5mi along the Ratagan road.

For a meal in Shiel Bridge, ***Five Sisters Restaurant*** *(☎ 01599-511211)* has a rather imaginative menu, including a vegetarian choice, and serves Black Isle and Isle of Skye beers. The adjacent ***shop*** has a good range of supplies.

Getting There & Away Scottish Citylink (☎ 0870-550 5050) buses on the Edinburgh and Glasgow to Uig services via Fort William stop at Shiel Bridge, as do Citylink's buses on the Inverness to Portree service. All services have at least three departures daily.

You can reach Shiel Bridge by train and bus, travelling to the last station on the scenic Inverness to Kyle of Lochalsh line, then catching a bus to Shiel Bridge. There are at least three ScotRail (☎ 0845-755 0033) trains Monday to Saturday.

Shiel Bridge is on the A87 trunk road, which branches from the A82 at Invergarry.

GETTING TO/FROM THE WALK

To the Start

From Cannich a single lane road winds its way westward for 10mi (16km) to the car park at its end, where there are toilets and picnic tables. There is no bus service beyond Cannich but there is a taxi service (☎ 01456-415300); Mr Noble will take you out to Loch Affric for around £12.

From the Finish

From the end of the walk at Morvich, it's 1.5mi to the A87 and just over 1mi farther south along the A87 to Shiel Bridge. Buses to/from Shiel Bridge (see Getting There & Away under Shiel Bridge & Around) also stop at Cluanie Inn near the end of alternative route B.

THE WALK

See map page 260

Day 1: Loch Affric car park to Alltbeithe

3½–4 hours, 8.5mi (13.5km)

Set out along the gravel road leading westward and shortly bear right at a fork. The road follows the course of the broad River Affric to the access road to private Affric Lodge and the nearby house. From here a path, signposted to Kintail and the hostel, continues in the same direction. A few hundred metres along, a single, creaky plank crosses a small stream and from here you can see the impressive Affric Lodge, backed by tall Scots pines, gazing down Loch Affric. Farther on, the path passes through a fenced pine regeneration area. The path maintains a good height above the loch, revealing wonderful views westward to the mountains around the hostel.

Succeeding streams are crossed by stepping stones and footbridges, and the path rises across the steep slope, passing vigorously regenerating clumps of birch and scattered remains of stone buildings. A substantial bridge takes you across Allt Coire Leachavie (a short distance west a cairned path leads into the corrie – the route to Màm Sodhail and other nearby Munros), then it's generally down towards Loch Coulavie. On the way, the crossing of Allt Coulavie (which tumbles down via the fine waterfall of Sputan Bán) could be difficult after heavy rain. The path, now rather boggy and eroded, curves around Loch Coulavie and down to a vehicle track (2½ hours from the start).

The track leads west in undulating fashion, across the broad, flat-based glen of the River Affric, rising steeply on both sides. A substantial bridge over Allt Coire Ghaidheil marks the boundary of the National Trust for Scotland's West Affric Estate. The track continues close to the river and soon the reddish roof of the hostel and the wind turbine come into view. You should reach Alltbeithe and the hostel about an hour after meeting the vehicle track.

If you plan to stay at ***Glen Affric SYHA Hostel*** it's best to book ahead, if possible at least a week before your arrival. The hostel doesn't have a telephone, so contact central reservations (☎ 08701-553255); the tariff is £7.75. You'll need to take a sheet (blankets are provided) or standard sleeping bag. For its isolated location, amenities are luxurious – running water and a hot shower, electricity (thanks to a wind turbine) and gas for cooking. You'll need all your own food, a bag to carry out your rubbish and footwear for indoors. The hostel is closed from late October to mid-March. Alternatively, you can ***camp*** nearby.

Side Trip: Sgurr nan Ceathreamhnan

4 hours, 7.5mi (12km), 940m ascent

The path starts on the far side of the upper hostel building. Go up beside the burn for about 200m then head east to cross Allt na Faing, which could be difficult if it's in spate. The narrow, mostly clear path climbs beside the burn, passing through two gates in an exclosure, to Coire na Cloiche. Cross two burns flowing down from the left and continue up towards the headwall of the corrie via a series of broad 'steps', skipping past peat hags. The path fades in this potential morass, as the crags close in on the left, but it's easy enough to go up, just above the burn, to the unnamed gap on the main ridge (about 1¼ hours from the hostel).

The crags of Stob Coire na Cloiche seem to bar the way as you climb south-westward from the gap; the way over it is straightforward enough, just to the left then right, closer to the northern edge. The fine ridge then opens up ahead, rising to the graceful sgurr. Continue along the undulating ridge and up the final, steep pull to the summit of **Sgurr nan Ceathreamhnan** with its large cairn (1¼ hours from the gap). The all-round view is quite awesome: the Kintail and Affric hills, and multitudes more as far north as Torridon, and south across Glen Shiel to Knoydart (see page 271) and the 'hills' above Loch Quoich (see page 264).

If you decide to make this a circuit, rather than retracing your steps to the hostel, head west along the narrow ridge, cross a confined gap, then climb up a gully to the right to the broad summit of Ceathreamhnan's

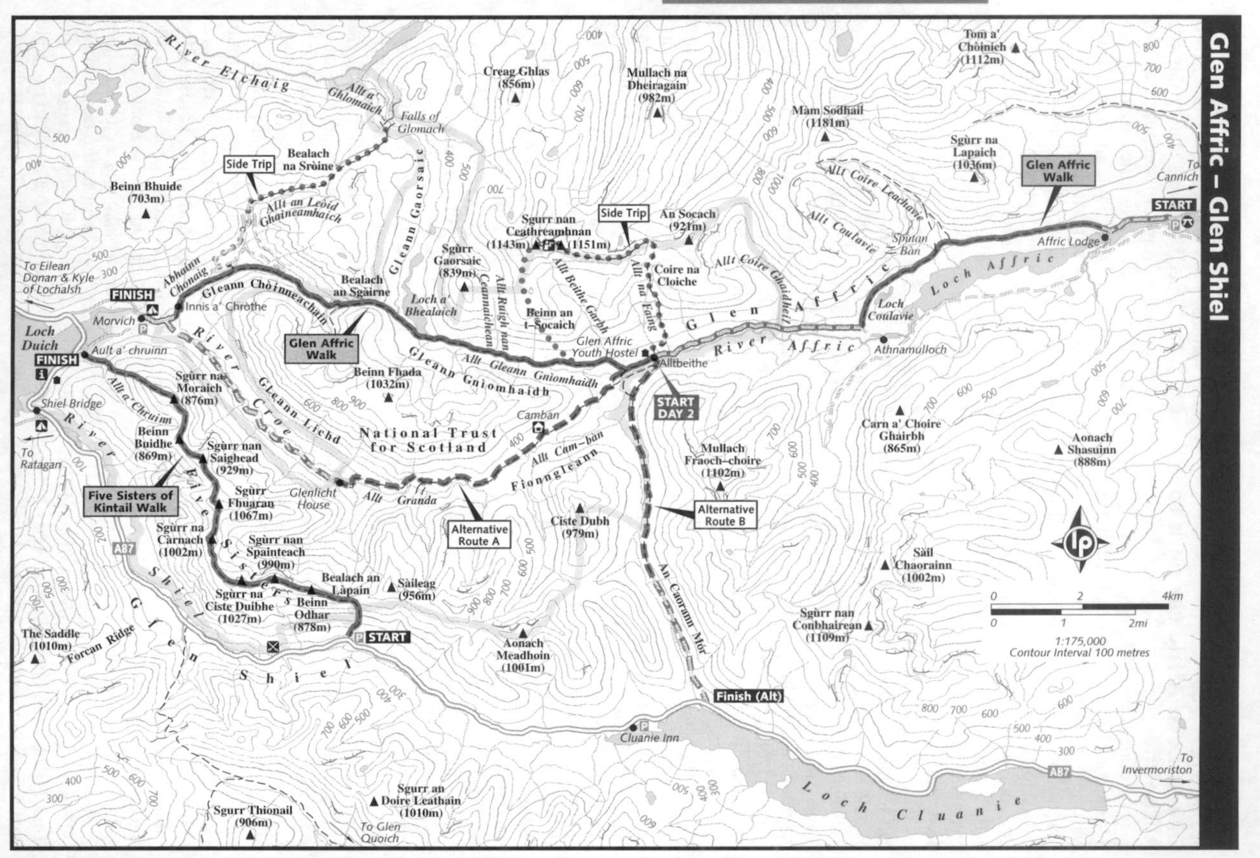

Glen Affric – Glen Shiel
River Elchaig
Allt a' Ghlomaich
Falls of Glomach
Creag Ghlas (856m)
Mullach na Dheiragain (982m)
Tom a' Chòinich (1112m)
Màm Sodhail (1181m)
Sgùrr na Lapaich (1036m)
Glen Affric Walk
To Cannich
START
Side Trip
Bealach na Sròine
Beinn Bhuide (703m)
Allt an Leòid Ghaineamhaich
Gleann Gaorsaic
Allt Coire Leachavie
Allt Coulavie
Sgùrr nan Ceathreamhnan (1143m) (1151m)
Side Trip
An Socach (921m)
Coire na Cloiche
Allt Coire Ghaidheil
Spùtan Bàn
Affric Lodge
Loch Affric
To Eilean Donan & Kyle of Lochalsh
Abhainn Chonaig
FINISH
Innis a' Chròthe
Morvich
Gleann Chòinneachain
Bealach an Sgàirne
Sgùrr Gaorsaic (839m)
Loch a' Bhealaich
Allt Ruigh nan Ceannaichean
Allt Beithe Garbh
Beinn an t-Socaich
Allt na Faing
Glen Affric
Loch Coulavie
Loch Duich
FINISH
Ault a' chruinn
Glen Affric Walk
Glen Affric Youth Hostel
Alltbeithe
River Affric
Athnamulloch
Shiel Bridge
Allt a' Chruinn
Sgùrr na Moraich (876m)
River Croe
Beinn Fhada (1032m)
Gleann Gniomhaidh
Allt Gleann Gniomhaidh
START DAY 2
Carn a' Choire Ghairbh (865m)
Aonach Shasuinn (888m)
River Shiel
To Ratagan
Beinn Buidhe (869m)
Sgùrr nan Saighead (929m)
Gleann Lichd
National Trust for Scotland
Camban
Allt Cam-bàn
Mullach Fraoch-choire (1102m)
Five Sisters of Kintail Walk
Sgùrr Fhuaran (1067m)
Glenlicht House
Allt Granda
Fionngleann
Ciste Dubh (979m)
Alternative Route B
Alternative Route A
Five Sisters
Sgùrr na Càrnach (1002m)
Sgùrr nan Spainteach (990m)
A87
Sàil Chaorainn (1002m)
Sgùrr na Ciste Duibhe (1027m)
Beinn Odhar (878m)
Bealach an Làpain
Sàileag (956m)
An Caorann Mór
Sgùrr nan Conbhairean (1109m)
The Saddle (1010m)
Forcan Ridge
START
Aonach Meadhoin (1001m)
1:175,000
Contour Interval 100 metres
Glen Shiel
Finish (Alt)
Cluanie Inn
To Invermoriston
A87
Sgurr an Doire Leathain (1010m)
Sgurr Thionail (906m)
To Glen Quoich
Loch Cluanie

satellite, only a few metres lower at 1143m. Head down, south-westward, generally keeping close to the rim of the spur on your left, and on to Beinn an t-Socaich. From here plot a route down to the path through Gleann Gnìomhaidh below, avoiding the extensive fencing. Once safely on the path, just follow it back to the hostel (about two hours from the summit).

Day 2: Alltbeithe to Morvich via Bealach an Sgàirne

4 hours, 8.5mi (13.5km)

Head towards the River Affric and follow a track upstream along the bank. Cross the bridge over Allt Beithe Garbh (meaning 'rough stream of the birches') and turn right on a stone-paved path, which follows the stream for a few hundred metres then turns west to head up Gleann Gnìomhaidh. The path is joined by a wide, eroded vehicle track. Although there is also a path of sorts close to the stream below, it's better to stick with the higher track, which is mostly grassed but wet in places and not consistently clear. Aim for a prominent circular stone enclosure (shown on the Harvey map) beside Allt Ruigh nan Ceannaichean (about an hour from the hostel). About 500m farther on, the path (as it is now) becomes clear and leads west, across the potentially hazardous stream draining beautiful **Loch a' Bhealaich** and round its southern shore. It's a steep climb on a good path up to dramatic, narrow **Bealach an Sgàirne** (1½ hours from the stone enclosure).

The descent through spectacularly rugged and steep-sided **Gleann Chòinneachain** is mostly on a good path. After about 3mi go through two gates in a fenced exclosure and continue downstream, above Abhainn Chonaig, past Innis a' Chrótha to the small bridge over the River Croe. On the far side of the bridge is the end of the road, which leads to Morvich (1½ hours from the top of the bealach).

Side Trip: Falls of Glomach

4 hours, 7.5mi (12km), 600m ascent

As you're coming down Gleann Chòinneachain from Bealach an Sgàirne, you pass through two gates in a fenced exclosure. Almost immediately beyond the second gate, bear right down the field to a path through trees, which leads to a bridge over Abhainn Chonaig. Go on up through a gate to a forest road, turn left and follow it to a car park.

Walk up the road signposted to 'Glomach Falls 4 miles'. Follow it through the plantation to a fork where you turn right (as signposted) and cross the stream. The track ends about 750m farther on at a bridge over Allt an Leòid Ghaineamhaich (45 minutes from Abhainn Chonaig). A footpath leads up and across the steep slope, then up the deep glen. It loses a bit of height then regains it up to the narrow defile that is Bealach na Sròine. Out onto open moorland, you soon start to descend gradually then steeply to Allt a' Ghlomaich (1½ hours from the last bridge). An eroded path descends beside the **Falls of Glomach** to truly breathtaking viewpoints of the thundering water. The falls plunge in two leaps; the uppermost enclosed between dark crags encrusted with mosses and ferns, the lower more open. The water crashes into a churning pool, from where the stream surges through a deep gorge.

Day 2A: Alltbeithe to Morvich via Gleann Lichd

4½ hours, 9.5mi (15.5km)

Head towards the River Affric and follow a track upstream along its bank. Cross the bridge over Allt Beithe Garbh and continue beside the river. A little farther on bear right along a narrow path, just before a ford on the main track and continue for about 200m to a footbridge. Rejoin the main track about 40m beyond the ford. Nearly an hour's walk from the hostel brings you to a short path leading to Camban Bothy.

Return to the main track, which soon becomes a narrow footpath and is well made for a few hundred metres. Climb to the watershed between Glen Affric and Gleann Lichd, marked by a large cairn. The path loses height gradually, across some boggy bits and some rocky ground, then climbs over a spur and wanders up and down to the top of the real descent into Gleann Lichd (an hour from Camban).

The path, much of it stone-paved, winds down the steep hillside. Pass a narrow gorge with a fine waterfall on Allt Granda, crossing the main stream and a tributary near Glenlicht House, a securely locked stone building. From here a vehicle track makes for easy walking down the scenic glen to the end of the sealed road near Morvich (about 1½ hours from Glenlicht House).

Day 2B: Alltbeithe to Loch Cluanie

2½ hours, 7mi (11.5km)

Follow a path beside the burn next to the hostel for a short distance south then swing left to the bridge across the River Affric. The path is vague across boggy ground but it becomes clearer as you climb fairly gently up the hillside. Keep to higher paths (not as wet) and press on across the gap and down to the start of the vehicle track through An Caorann Mór. Follow this for about 1.5mi to the A87; Cluanie Inn is 1mi west along the road.

Cluanie Inn (☎ *01320-340238)* offers comfortable rooms (from £30) and good food in the bar and restaurant.

Five Sisters of Kintail

Duration	6¾–7½ hours
Distance	7.5mi (12km)
Standard	hard
Start	Glen Shiel car park
Finish	Ault a' chruinn
Nearest Towns	Ault a' chruinn, Morvich, Shiel Bridge
Public Transport	no

Summary One of the finest ridge walks in Scotland – an arduous but immensely scenic walk over rough ground, traversing narrow ridges along mostly clear, well-used paths.

Travelling west to the Isle of Skye you pass through what appears to be impenetrable Glen Shiel. The winding road snakes between steep-sided, rock-encrusted mountains, soaring skywards to the north, and rising almost as steeply and ruggedly to the south. The western end of the long, spiky ridge to the north is known as the Five Sisters of Kintail, quite different in character from the more rounded, less dramatic chain of summits on the south side of the glen. The name Kintail comes from the Gaelic *cean da shaill* meaning 'head of the two seas', ie, Loch Duich and Loch Long, which in turn are inlets from Loch Alsh.

This chain of elegant, precipitous summits, separated by slits of passes (or bealachs), falls away vertiginously to Glen Shiel on one side and to the more remote and peaceful Gleann Lichd on the other. To the north-west, the ridge drops a little less steeply to the shores of beautiful Loch Duich. Three of the sisters are Munros (peaks over 3000ft/914m): Sgurr Fhuaran (1067m), Sgurr na Càrnach (1002m) and Sgurr na Ciste Duibhe (1027m). The other two, at the northern end of the ridge, are Sgurr nan Saighead (929m) and Sgurr na Moraich (876m). There are two peaks to deal with before you even reach the first or southernmost sister – Beinn Odhar (878m) and Sgurr nan Spainteach (990m); see the boxed text 'The Spanish Connection'.

The ridge commands fine views, with the Torridon 'hills' punctuating the horizon to the north-west, the Isle of Skye spreadeagled across the western skyline and the islands of Canna, Eigg and Rum sailing between the rugged peaks to the south-west – and much, much more. Far and away the better direction is from east to west – walking towards the views, starting at a higher point than where you finish, and with a slightly less steep and knee-jarring descent. The overall distance isn't unusually long but ascent of 1530m is nearly 100m more than a romp up Ben Nevis. Keep in mind that even when you've reached the highest point on the walk (Sgurr Fhuaran) the climbing isn't over – there are still two peaks to go.

Alternatives Once you're on the ridge, escape routes are few. People do go down to Glen Shiel via the spur from Sgurr Fhuaran but this is seriously steep. Routes to and from Gleann Lichd, on the other side, are feasible and, indeed, have much to recommend them. There is a clear path up to the ridge at Bealach an Làpain from Glenlicht House, and the long ridge thrusting eastward from Sgurr Fhuaran offers a fairly straightforward climb or descent.

PLANNING

When to Walk

The Five Sisters are very exposed and could be extremely hazardous in poor visibility, strong wind or rain, so it's worth waiting for the right day for this classic ridge walk. This is also important because there's a lot of loose rock along the ridge, especially on the descents into and climbs out of the bealachs, so considerable care is needed for your own and others' safety. For walkers the best times are May and June, and September to early October. The whole ridge is within the National Trust for Scotland's Kintail Estate, so access is open at all times.

Maps

Harvey's 1:25,000 map *Kintail: Glen Shiel* covers the Five Sisters and has some background information and local contacts. In the OS Landranger 1:50,000 series, the relevant map is No 33 *(Loch Alsh, Glen Shiel & Loch Hourn).*

NEAREST TOWNS

Shiel Bridge & Around

See under Nearest Towns on page 258.

GETTING TO/FROM THE WALK

To the Start

The walk starts at an informal car park on the A87 between Cluanie Inn and Shiel Bridge. The car park is distinguished by a vehicle height barrier and is immediately east of a small open area between pine plantations. Citylink (☎ 0870-550 5050) bus services to Shiel Bridge (see Getting There & Away on page 258) stop at Cluanie Inn, about 5mi (8km) east of the start.

From the Finish

The walk finishes in the hamlet of Ault a' chruinn, on the minor road (which branches off the A87, 1.5mi from Shiel Bridge) to Morvich. The closest parking area is at the nearby Port Bhan Restaurant.

THE WALK

See map page 260

Follow a narrow path leading from the western edge of the plantation adjacent to the car park, climbing the steep bracken- and grass-covered hillside. After a few hundred metres of ascent the path angles across to the right (east), to the northern edge of the plantation and parallels it for about 200m. You then turn north along a path leading straight up a subtly defined spur to meet the ridge at **Bealach an Làpain**. Suddenly you're in a wholly different world – surrounded by mountains and deep glens, for the moment out of earshot of the traffic on the road below.

Turn west along the ridge crest and follow the well-worn path up to a breezy arête and on over the twin bumps of Beinn Odhar. Then comes a shallow dip and a rocky climb to **Sgurr nan Spainteach** (see the boxed text 'The Spanish Connection'). A scrambly descent down the face of a bluff takes you to the amazingly narrow Bealach nan Spainteach.

Make your way up through the boulders to the neat summit cairn on **Sgurr na Ciste Duibhe** (peak of the black coffin), the first of the Five Sisters (2½ to three hours from the start). Here you can look east towards Glen Affric across the gap at the top of

The Spanish Connection

In the long struggle between government and Jacobite forces, which ended at the Battle of Culloden in 1745, a lesser known battle took place right here in Glen Shiel. In June 1719 Jacobite troops, including a Spanish regiment, landed at Eilean Donan castle beside Loch Duich. Government troops came from Inverness and the two sides met about 1mi west of the starting point of this walk (there is a National Trust for Scotland interpretive sign at the site). The government side routed the Jacobites, of whom the last to flee were the Spanish who dashed up the hillside to the pass now called Bealach nan Spainteach, and down into Gleann Lichd.

HIGHLAND GLENS

Gleann Lichd and, in the opposite direction, contemplate the serrated skyline of the Isle of Skye beyond Loch Duich.

The ridge changes direction, leading north-west down to Bealach na Craoibhe. Keep to the highest ground in the absence of a clear path. The line of ascent then turns northward, climbing to **Sgurr na Càrnach** (rocky peak), the second Sister. From here new features in the panorama include Lochs Affric and Beinn a' Mheadhoin to the east. The first bit of the descent is down a narrow cleft to the left, then bear right to regain the line of the ridge and go down to Bealach na Càrnach. A steep, rocky and twisting path takes care of the climb to **Sgurr Fhuaran** (peak of the springs or small stream), the highest point on the ridge and the third Sister. From here the view is no less absorbing than those from her siblings (about 1½ hours from Sgurr na Ciste Duibhe).

Leaving the summit cairn take care to head north-west then north on this awesome and spectacular descent to Bealach Buidhe. The path then traverses above the dramatic sheets of cliffs leading up to **Sgurr nan Saighead** (arrows peak), Sister number four. The ridge now changes character with more small, rocky knobs to negotiate on the way down and then up to Beinn Buidhe. A rough path drops down to a narrow gap, with fine views of Gleann Lichd below. Climb straight up and soon the path follows a more even course among rocky outcrops and across grass (for a pleasant change) and finally up to **Sgurr na Moraich** (mighty peak), Sister number five (two hours from Sgurr Fhuaran).

Having led north-west from the summit, straight towards Skye Bridge, the path fades into insignificance. Keep well to the left of the broad spur, generally north-westward (or about 300 degrees magnetic) as you descend very steeply over grass and heather, steering away from the small cliffs bristling on the crest of the spur. Keep your eye on the crags on the western side of Allt a' Chruinn as a guide to the best route down to a narrow path high above the stream. Follow it down to a stile over a fence and continue to a water treatment works. Turn right along a vehicle track, which becomes a sealed road and meets the Morvich road in Ault a' chruinn, about 200m from its junction with the A87 (about an hour from Sgurr na Moraich).

Gleouraich

Duration	5–5½ hours
Distance	7.5mi (12km)
Standard	medium-hard
Start & Finish	Loch Quoich car park
Nearest Town	Invergarry
Public Transport	no

Summary An exhilarating traverse of a narrow mountain ridge with awesome views of multitudes of peaks, near and far.

Glen Garry reaches westward from the village of Invergarry in the Great Glen. It contains two large lochs, Loch Garry and Loch Quoich, both enlarged for hydroelectric power generation. Between Glen Shiel to the north, and Glen Kingie and Loch Arkaig in the south, it lies in the heart of a large, sparsely populated and mountainous area.

There are plenty of excellent mountains around the head of Glen Garry, mostly above both sides of Loch Quoich. The highest, Gleouraich (1035m, 3395ft), which means 'roaring' or 'bellowing' (a reference, perhaps, to the autumnal roaring of red stags during the rut or mating season), and its neighbour Spidean Mialach (996m), probably meaning 'peak of the deer', are both Munros. Together they make a top-class round walk.

Their rugged, linking ridge and the spurs extending generally south towards Loch Quoich enclose three coires (Coire Peitireach, Coire Mhèil and Coire Dubh) and Loch Fearna, perched on the spur below Spidean Mialach; a remarkably varied cluster of scenic features in a relatively small area. While Loch Quoich can betray its artificial size during summer when its level drops, it still provides a fine foreground. So, with little Glen Quoich to the west and the South Kintail mountains to the north, this walk has as scenic a setting as you'll find anywhere.

The best way to do the circuit is clockwise, so you can enjoy climbing the superbly engineered stalkers' path up the western spur, which makes the ascent relatively painless. The path stops short of the final climb to the summit but the way is clear enough – it's quite a popular mountain. The narrow ridge linking the two summits drops precipitously to the north, so good weather is a must for this one. It's not a particularly long day, although it does involve 1180m of ascent and so, a medium-hard grading.

Alternatives There are two possible routes down from Spidean Mialach; one on the western side of Allt a' Mhèil and the other following the spur on its eastern side. It is best to avoid the western route during stalking season.

The walk could be cut short by descending into Coire Dubh, west of Spidean Mialach, or you could simply return to the start from Gleouraich, leaving Spidean for another day.

A footpath from Alltbeithe in Glen Quoich (west of Gleouraich) crosses the South Kintail ridge via Bealach Duibh Leac and goes down to Glen Shiel, between the Cluanie Inn and Shiel Bridge – another walk to put on your list.

PLANNING

When to Walk

Like so many Scottish 'hill' walks, this is one for spring and early summer, before the midges congregate. The ridge is definitely a serious mountaineering route under snow.

Stalking Stalking takes place in the Glenquoich Forest of Western Glenquoich Estate between 24 August and 10 October each year. During that time the estate requests that walkers refrain from using the path that crosses Allt a' Mhèil below Coire Mhèil.

Maps

Harvey's 1:25,000 *Kintail* map extends as far south as Loch Quoich so is ideal. For identifying peaks to the south and west (and for local use), OS Landranger 1:50,000 map No 33 *(Loch Alsh, Glen Shiel & Loch Hourn)* is the one to have.

NEAREST TOWN

Invergarry & Around

Invergarry is a small village with only limited facilities.

Places to Stay & Eat Mr & Mrs Wilson's well-appointed ***Ardgarry Farm B&B*** *(☎ 01809-501226)*, in a peaceful location just west of the village, offers excellent value at £21 for dinner, bed and breakfast.

Royal Glen Quoich Lodge

Only the massed thickets of rhododendrons and a few tall pines on the shores of Loch Quoich give any clue of previous habitation. So it needs a considerable leap of the imagination to 'see' a large two-storey building, with others nearby, right on the shore where Allt Coire Peitireach enters the loch.

The lodge was well established by 1872 and it had at least 10 bedrooms, many with a dressing room attached. The walls of the billiard room were decorated with heads of stags shot on the estate (a common practice in those days). Nearby were a large cottage, coach house, carpenter's shop and gardeners' 'bothies'. There was even a school room for a handful of local pupils.

The lodge was clearly fit for a king, as a fragment from the *Glen Quoich Stags Log Book* (itemising the number of stags shot during the stalking season) for the 1904 season reveals. The tally for the North Forest, directly above Loch Quoich, was 77 stags, of which 'The King' (George V) shot three, and Grand Duke Michael of Russia nine.

However, royal patronage ultimately counted for nought in preserving the lodge – it was eventually demolished and the site drowned by the rising waters of an enlarged Loch Quoich, part of a hydroelectric power scheme in the late 1940s.

Nearby, a great deal of thought has gone into the excellent facilities at ***Faichemard Farm Campsite*** *(☎ 01809-501314)*; the £6 pitch price covers a car, tent and two adults.

In the village, bar meals are served at the ***Invergarry Hotel*** *(☎ 01809-501206)* and at ***The Garry*** self-service restaurant. There's a small ***shop***, which also serves snacks, at the service station beside the A82, about 220m from the A87 junction towards Inverness.

On the minor road through Glen Garry, the renowned ***Tomdoun Hotel*** *(☎ 01809-511244)* is more than a century old. The tariff for dinner, bed and breakfast starts at £39; the hotel is open for bar meals at lunchtime and during the evening.

Getting There & Away Invergarry is on the junction of the A82 and A87, 7mi (11.3km) south-west of Fort Augustus, and 15mi (24.3km) north of Spean Bridge. Buses on the Scottish Citylink (☎ 0870-550 5050) Fort William to Inverness service stop here at least five times daily.

GETTING TO/FROM THE WALK

From Invergarry drive west along the A87 for 5.3mi (8.2km) to a junction signposted to Tomdoun and Kinloch Hourn. Follow this single-lane road (look out for wandering sheep which don't have much time for cars) for about 15.3mi (24.6km) to an informal car park on the south side of the road, close to the bridge over Allt Coire Peitireach. The walk starts and finishes here. A postbus (☎ 01463-256228) goes from Invergarry to Kinloch Hourn and back, passing the start and finish of this walk, on Monday, Wednesday and Friday. However, you'd have to be prepared to camp in the area for two nights to take advantage of this service.

THE WALK

The path leads away from the road through an intimidating tunnel of rhododendrons for about 200m, then emerges onto open, grassy moorland, climbing fairly gently. Once on the narrow crest of the spur the view northward takes on new and dramatic dimensions as the mountains of the South Kintail ridge take shape. The path skirts the rocky crest of the spur on its western side to reach a shallow saddle, from which the final and steeper climb starts; ignore a large cairn by the path. Here you can look down to lonely Alltbeithe Cottage beside the River Quoich far below. The stalkers' path ends at a stone shooting butt (a low, roofless shelter used by stalkers). Continue straight up the steep slope, mostly over rocky ground but on a clear path, to the neat summit cairn of **Gleouraich** (about 1¾ hours from the start). On a good day you can easily see Ben Nevis to the south-east.

Continue along the rocky crest for about 100m then lose a bit of height before going up and over a secondary summit (Creag Coire na Fiar Bhealaich). Here you join a well-made path to descend to a bealach above rugged Coire Dubh to the south and steep cliffs on the northern side (about 45 minutes from the top). The ensuing climb to the next summit (977m) isn't unduly steep. From here a narrow ridge, with near vertical cliffs below on the left, leads to the final climb to the sprawling cairn on **Spidean Mialach** (40 minutes or so from the bealach above Coire Dubh). The stunning

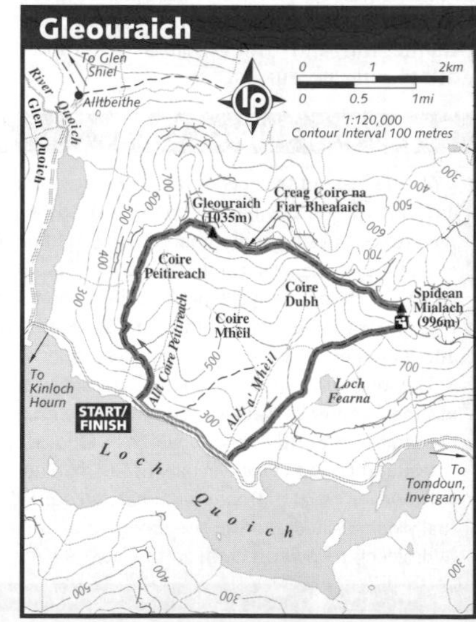

view extends as far as Ben Nevis to the south-west, west to Skye's Cuillins, and to the dramatic corries scooped out of the South Kintail mountains nearby.

The descent southward starts straight away along a clear path on the south side of the cairn, heading towards Loch Fearna over shattered slabs then grass. Head generally west across the slope, intersected by several boggy burns, to a well-defined spur. Follow the spur on its eastern side over grass and scattered rocks and continue down to the road just east of Allt a' Mhèil. Turn right to return to the start, another 0.75mi. The descent, from where you joined the spur, takes about an hour.

Creag Meagaidh

Duration	7–7½ hours
Distance	11.8mi (19km)
Standard	hard
Start & Finish	Aberarder
Nearest Towns	Roybridge, Laggan
Public Transport	yes

Summary A strenuous but immensely rewarding and very scenic circuit of a magnificent mountain massif in one of Scotland's finest National Nature Reserves.

Glen Spean extends south-west to north-east for around 25mi (40km); from Spean Bridge at the southern end of the Great Glen, along the River Spean and through to the head of Loch Laggan, close to the divide between the glen and Strathspey to the north-east. Along its southern side two groups of sprawling, high mountains are separated by Loch Treig. On the opposite side of the glen, above Loch Laggan, is a smaller cluster of peaks, dominated by Creag Meagaidh. The mountain, in the Creag Meagaidh National Nature Reserve (owned and managed by Scottish Natural Heritage), offers one of Scotland's classic horseshoe walks.

The walk can be done in either direction, depending on whether you prefer to reach the highest point, Creag Meagaidh (1130m, 3706ft), after a longish ridge walk or before it. That said, probably the more popular direction is anticlockwise, climbing generally north from Allt Coire Ardair to Carn Liath (1006m), the easternmost summit on the ridge. Although it's not a particularly long walk, the 1240m of ascent easily puts it in the hard class, as does the roughness of the ground on the long southern spur over Sròn a' Ghoire (1001m) and down to Allt Coire Ardair. The route gives Munro baggers three summits: Carn Liath, Stob Poite Coire Ardair (1053m) and Creag Meagaidh, which is pronounced krayk megee and means 'crag at the bog'.

Alternatives If Creag Meagaidh alone will satisfy your desires, then the quickest approach is the mostly good path (along which railway sleepers keep you out of most of the bogs) all the way from Aberarder to Lochan a' Choire in Coire Ardair. From there an informal path skirts the northern side of the lochan and wriggles up the steep, scree-filled gully to the gap between Stob Poite Coire Ardair and the summit massif. This entails around 900m of ascent and can take up to six hours.

If the weather isn't suitable for a high-level walk (which it often isn't) or if there's too much snow on the ridge for your tastes, you can walk to Lochan a' Choire and back (10mi/16km, 370m ascent). The view of the corrie's cliffs, likely to be crawling with ice climbers, is well worthwhile. Coire Ardair's cliffs offer some of the best snow and ice climbing in Britain and have attracted climbers since the end of the 19th century.

NATURAL HISTORY

Creag Meagaidh is a spectacular example of a landscape moulded by snow and ice, created by two million years of advancing and retreating glaciers and ice sheets. Coire Ardair is a classic glaciated corrie, with its almost sheer headwall cliffs, the lochan below and the wavy mounds of glacial debris or moraine in the glen of Allt Coire Ardair. The stream is almost encircled by the ridge, which this walk traverses. The massif, crowned by Creag Meagaidh, is more

Caring for Creag Meagaidh

The importance of Creag Meagaidh's superlative glaciated landscape was officially recognised by the declaration of the area as a Site of Special Scientific Interest in 1975. Nearly a decade later the threat of a conifer plantation on the lower slopes prompted the Nature Conservancy Council (Scottish Natural Heritage's predecessor) to buy the land and the adjacent mountainous ground, covering about 3948ha; it became Creag Meagaidh National Nature Reserve in 1986.

Most of the Aberarder farm buildings, at the eastern entrance to the reserve, date from the 19th century, a time of intensive sheep grazing. This dwindled after 1918 and never really recovered, apart from a brief revival in the late 1940s. All surviving sheep were taken away after the National Nature Reserve was created.

In 1986 the remnants of native woodland were very sparse and the Nature Conservancy Council committed itself to restoration. This has been outstandingly successful and has also shown that nature conservation can provide a worthwhile number of jobs. This success is partly due to the substantial reduction of the red deer population.

The way deer are managed in the reserve, with heavy culling, is a fairly radical departure from traditional methods. However, despite the drastic reduction, deer (very territorial creatures) from neighbouring estates have not moved into Creag Meagaidh's less populous grounds. For walkers a crucial aspect of this new approach is Scottish Natural Heritage's open access policy. It has been shown that big culls can be achieved while walkers continue to visit the reserve and walkers are far more likely to accept any minor changes when the need for deer management is explained.

The full story of Scottish Natural Heritage's work at Creag Meagaidh is told in the publication *Revival of the Land* (see Maps & Books).

complex, with corries gouged out on all sides and ridges fanning out from the summit, from the west round to the east.

The National Nature Reserve protects a diverse range of plants and wildlife, from woodlands to the near arctic, tundra-like summit plateau. One of Scottish Natural Heritage's aims is to restore the native birch woodland. The results of reducing the number of grazing animals can be seen in the dense regrowth along the lower reaches of Allt Coire Ardair (see the boxed text 'Caring for Creag Meagaidh'). There are also plenty of rowan and willow, some alder and hazel, and many smaller flowering plants.

On the high ground camouflaged ptarmigan are common, although it's more difficult to spot a dotterel, a rare species in Scotland; golden plovers, with their evocative lonely call, are a more likely sighting.

PLANNING

When to Walk

Snow can lie on the ridge until well into spring but usually the best times for this walk are from mid-May until mid-June and September. In poor visibility finding your way across Creag Meagaidh's relatively featureless summit plateau can be difficult, so take particular care to check the forecast when planning this walk.

Stalking Scottish Natural Heritage staff carry out an annual deer cull between July and February, but access within the reserve is open at all times – the policy is that people come first.

It may happen that you'll be asked to consider an alternative route but not to leave. Contact Scottish Natural Heritage (☎ 01528-544265) at Aberarder for more information.

Maps & Books

The OS Landranger 1:50,000 map No 34 *(Fort Augustus)* covers the walk.

The Scottish Mountaineering Club's Hillwalkers Guide *The Munros*, edited by Donald Bennet, is useful but the best sources of information about Creag Meagaidh are two leaflets produced by Scottish Natural Heritage – a *Guide* to the National Nature Reserve, and *Revival of the Land*. The latter actually introduces a major publication of the same title describing Scottish Natural Heritage's work at Creag Meagaidh. The leaflets are available locally from Scottish Natural Heritage and the book from Scottish Natural Heritage Publications Branch (☎ 01738-627921) or online at W www.snh.org.uk.

NEAREST TOWNS

Laggan

Laggan is a small village 10mi (16km) north-east of Aberarder. The Community Office (☎/fax 01528-544383) serves as a TIC and has maps and local guidebooks, including a folder *Walks in and around Laggan* with notes for 10 walks in the area; it's generally open daily.

Places to Stay & Eat At Caoldair Pottery, ***The Pottery Bunkhouse*** *(☎/fax 01528-544231,* e *lynda@potterybunkhouse.fsnet.co.uk)*, on the A889 just east of the village centre, is a well-designed place with bunk beds and en suite family rooms. The tariff is £9 plus £1.50 for bedding or £45 for a room sleeping up to five. The facilities are excellent and include a hot tub with mountain views. The adjacent coffee shop serves first-class cakes, filled rolls and hot drinks.

The ***Monadhliath Hotel*** *(☎/fax 01528-544276)*, close to The Pottery, has en suite rooms from £20 and serves decent bar meals.

The village ***shop*** (☎ 01528-544257), open daily (hours vary), has a good range of supplies.

Getting There & Away Highland Country Buses' (☎ 01463-222244) Munro Bagger service (Fort William to Cairngorm) stops in Laggan twice daily between late May and the end of September.

Laggan is on the A86 (Spean Bridge to Newtonmore road), 29mi (47km) from Spean Bridge and 7mi (11.3km) from Newtonmore.

Roybridge

Roybridge is a larger village on the A86, 16mi (26km) south-west of Aberarder.

Places to Stay & Eat Beside the River Roy, ***Bunroy Holiday Lodges*** *(☎ 01397-712332,* e *bunroy@roybridge.esesurf.co.uk)* is about 300m south of the main road. You can pitch a tent in the spacious grounds for £4; facilities are well maintained.

There is a small ***shop*** in the village and bar meals are served at the two hotels, notably the ***Stronlossit Hotel*** *(☎ 01397-712253)*, which also has en suite rooms from £25.

Between Roybridge and Aberarder is one of the best bunkhouses, ***Station Lodge*** *(☎/fax 01397-732333,* e *info@stationlodge.co.uk)* at Tulloch station on the Fort William to Glasgow train line. The tariff is £10 for a bed in well-appointed bunkrooms; meals are available from a varied menu, with main courses around £5.50 and the lodge is licensed.

Getting There & Away The Munro Bagger bus service (see Getting There & Away for Laggan) stops in Roybridge, which is about 4mi east of Spean Bridge. ScotRail (☎ 0845-755 0033) trains between Glasgow and Fort William (including an overnight sleeper service from London Euston) stop at Roybridge and Tulloch daily.

GETTING TO/FROM THE WALK

The walk starts at the car park beside the A86, near Scottish Natural Heritage's Aberarder office, nearly 20mi (32.4km) from Spean Bridge and 10mi (16km) from Laggan. The Munro Bagger bus (see Getting There & Away for Laggan) stops here.

THE WALK

From the car park walk north-west along the vehicle track, passing to the right of the white-painted, two-storey house and a small information shelter. A well-made track, with sections of railway sleepers across boggy ground, leads towards Allt Coire Ardair. After about 500m it swings away northward to climb the partly wooded hillside, soon entering densely regenerating birch. Just over half a mile farther on and a few metres past an old metal fence post on the right, a narrow, informal path, marked by a small cairn, leads uphill and generally follows the

HIGHLAND GLENS

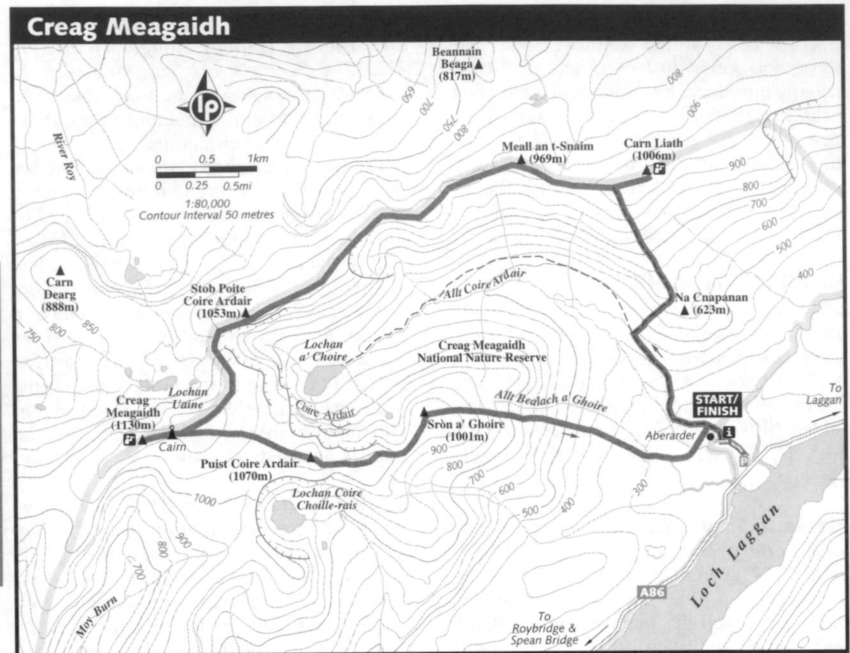

intermittent line of posts up to the crest of the spur just north-west of Na Cnapanan (623m). From here the clear path climbs steadily to the main ridge, over mainly rocky ground. Diverge to the east, over shattered rock, for a few hundred metres to the sizable cairn on the summit of **Carn Liath** (1006m; almost two hours from the start). The very fine panorama takes in scores of 'hills', notably the Glen Shiel ridge to the north-west and part of Ben Nevis to the south-west; the Cairngorms are draped across the eastern skyline.

Descend the broad ridge, soon leaving the rocky ground for grass, skirt a narrow gap on the left and then wander over a string of small bumps. The way is still down to a deep, narrow gap, from where there's a good view of Loch Spey, at the head of the River Spey in the glen far below to the north. Inevitably a climb follows, leading to a fine, narrow ridge and on to Stob Poite Coire Ardair (1½ hours from Carn Liath).

Then it's steeply down into the divide between the ridge and the main mountain massif, hitting the lowest point on the north side of the twin gaps here. A not too steep pull takes you up to the sprawling summit ridge. Here the path keeps to the northern edge, past the huge, mysteriously named Mad Meg's Cairn, to the summit of **Creag Meagaidh** (about 45 minutes from the Stob). The extraordinary view includes Loch Ericht and the Glen Coe and Nevis Range 'hills' to the south.

Return to Mad Meg's Cairn then descend eastward and across a shallow, dry valley. Go over Puist Coire Ardair, crowned with a small cairn, and on to the cliff edge path, which yields excellent views of Loch Laggan and upper Strathspey. Then comes a steep descent to skirt a corrie cradling a tiny lochan; a discontinuous path leads on and up to Sròn a Ghoire. Then it's down with a vengeance – keep well to the right (south) for the best way around the small streams and marshy ground on the hillside. Aim to reach a pair of old fence posts from where a fairly clear path leads generally eastward, across Allt Bealach a' Ghoire and marshy ground. At a distinct path intersection turn right and continue to a bridge across Allt Coire Ardair. A few hundred metres farther on ignore a track leading towards the Aberarder buildings and continue towards the stone wall ahead to join the main path, about 100m west of the information shelter. You should reach the car park about 2½ hours after leaving the summit.

Other Walks

There are scores of other first-rate high- and low-level walks in the Highland Glens. On top of the following suggestions, browse the references given under Books on page 246 to find out more about: the South Kintail ridge, a fine, fiercely undulating string of mountains opposite the Five Sisters; Glen Dessary, west of Loch Arkaig, an excellent low-level walk leading to the remote and beautiful shores of Loch Nevis and overlooked by several great mountains, notably Sgurr na Ciche; and Strathfarrar, north of Glen Affric, with plenty of both 'hill' and glen walks. Lastly, not quite within the scope of this chapter but one that can't be overlooked, is Ben Wyvis, the big sprawling mountain dominating the view westward from Inverness. It is similar to the Cairngorms with its spacious, undulating summit plateau and affords magnificent panoramic views.

STRATHCONON

This long broad valley reaches west along the River Conon from near Dingwall on the Cromarty Firth. A public road through the strath passes two artificial (dammed) lochs, scattered farms and woodland, and follows the River Meig as far as Scardroy, a lone, large house. The 'hills' on either side are relatively unassuming until you reach Scardroy and the start of a right of way into the mountains.

Scardroy to Glen Carron

This path follows the River Meig generally westward through Gleann Fhiodaig to its head deep in the mountains, near Glenuaig Lodge. It then descends through a spectacular gorge beside Allt a' Chonais and a plantation to a bridge over the River Carron, near the hamlet of Craig on the A890 (Achnasheen to Lochcarron) road. Gleann Fhiodaig is overlooked by towering peaks on both sides, including several fine crag-girt hills, notably the formidable Maoile Lunndaidh (1007m) and Sgurr a' Chaorachain (1053m) to the south. The low-level walk is about 13mi (21km) one way and you'll need OS Landranger 1:50,000 map No 25 *(Glen Carron & Glen Affric)*. The most useful references are the Scottish Rights of Way Society's *Scottish Hill Tracks* and the Scottish Mountaineering Club's *The Munros*. There's a bunkhouse at Craig, otherwise the nearest accommodation is at least 10mi (6km) farther west at Lochcarron. A postbus service from Beauly goes right through to Scardroy; trains on the Inverness to Kyle of Lochalsh line stop at Achnashellach, about 2.5mi west of Craig. For more information contact the Inverness TIC (☎ 01463-234353, ⓔ info@host.co.uk).

KNOYDART

Knoydart is a wild, rugged, virtually road-free area on the west coast, between Loch Nevis to the south and Loch Hourn to the north, and west of Loch Quoich at the head of Glen Garry. It's defined as much by these lochs and its remoteness as it is by the marvellous glens leading into and within its confines, notably Glen Dessary and Glen Barrisdale. After long years of mismanagement and conflict, Knoydart is now set to be cared for sympathetically by a group of landowners comprising the Knoydart Foundation (on behalf of the local community), the John Muir Trust and private individuals. Contact the Fort William TIC (☎ 01397-703781) for more information. Several Web sites feature the area including Ⓦ www.road-to-the-isles.org.uk/knoydart, which has details of numerous accommodation places, activities and the ferry from Mallaig to Inverie, Knoydart's port. Mallaig, in turn, is served by trains and buses from Fort William.

Kinloch Hourn to Inverie

This route follows a public right of way, generally along the southern shore of Loch Hourn to Barrisdale Bay, then across the pass of Mam Barrisdale and down to the village of Inverie overlooking Loch Nevis. From the pass it's possible to climb the magnificent peak of Ladhar Bheinn (1020m, 3346ft), pronounced larven, and its southern neighbour Luinne Bheinn (939m). The distance for the through walk, without side trips, is 15mi (24km). OS Landranger 1:50,000 map No 33 *(Loch Alsh, Glen Shiel & Loch Hourn)* covers the area and the Scottish Mountaineering Club's Munros book is your guide. There's a good bothy at Barrisdale Bay and a choice of accommodation at Inverie.

GLEN URQUHART

Drumnadrochit, roughly midway along the north-western side of Loch Ness, is famously associated with the legendary Loch Ness Monster and is a staging point on the Great Glen Way. It's much less known as the 'capital' of Glen Urquhart, and as the crucial link to a string of forest paths and tracks leading to Loch Affric and through to Loch Duich (see the Glen Affric walk description on page 255).

From the western edge of the village, paths lead through Craig Mony woodland to forest tracks, which go westward along the south side of beautiful Glen Urquhart to Corrimony. Then, farm and hill tracks lead up the River Enrick's glen, and generally west to the village of Tomich (about 16mi/26km from Drumnadrochit). The route continues generally south-west along forest roads past Plodda Falls and Cougie to a forest road on the south side of Loch Affric, from where the car park is about 1.5mi north-eastward (about 11mi/18km from Tomich). Alternatively, sections of this route can be done as day walks from local bases.

Accommodation is available around Balnain and Shenval in Glen Urquhart, and at Tomich; otherwise it's OK to camp in Forest Enterprise areas, for one night at a time. David Peck's guide *Fifty Walks Extended to Sixty-four* is very helpful. The walk is covered by OS Landranger 1:50,000 maps No 25 *(Glen Carron & Glen Affric)*, No 26 *(Inverness & Loch Ness)* and No 33 *(Loch Alsh, Glen Shiel & Loch Hourn)*. A bus service from Drumnadrochit to Tomich goes through Glen Urquhart Monday to Saturday. Contact Forest Enterprise (☎ 01320-366322) for more information.

Isle of Skye

The Isle of Skye boasts what is, arguably, the greatest concentration of scenic splendour and variety in Britain, a quality that has attracted writers, bards, artists and travellers to the island for centuries. These days walkers and climbers also flock to Skye to experience spectacular mountain travel and soak up some of the mystical island ambience, which still pervades despite the new road bridge and an explosion of tourism. This chapter is divided into two sections, covering the contrasting landscapes and styles of walking to be found in the Cuillin mountains and the Trotternish peninsula.

The Black and Red Cuillin are all about strain and challenge, with sublime views of mountains and ocean. They rate highly in terms of physical demand, but also offer a huge sense of reward and satisfaction. The skills required for some of the Black Cuillin are beyond the scope of this book, but there are a few routes onto the main ridge that give the thrill of being in the domain of mountaineers without the risk. Two such routes are described here, plus a route up the great fin of Bla Bheinn, a giant outlier of the main Black Cuillin ridge. Some of the routes involve scrambling – see the boxed text 'Scrambling' on page 299.

To the north of the Cuillin, beyond the island's capital of Portree, is Trotternish, a peninsula with an undulating spine of crumbling escarpments and pinnacles. The walking here is over gentler gradients and the terrain is mostly grassy. Progress on and off the paths is fast and the scenery is unique and iconic – many people will have seen photos of the Old Man of Storr long before they ever see it in person.

Highlights

GRANT DIXON

Wild and beautiful, Loch Coruisk is the jewel in the crown of the Black Cuillin.

- Scrambling on the airy, knife-edged ridges of the Black Cuillin – Britain's most spectacular mountain range
- Cooling off under one of many waterfalls in the Cuillin after a hot, summer ascent
- Walking into the hidden mountain sanctuary of Loch Coruisk on the Coast & Cuillin route
- Exploring the weird pinnacles of The Storr and Quiraing on the Trotternish peninsula

CLIMATE

When it comes to weather, Skye does not have a good reputation. Summer can be glorious but the proximity of the Atlantic, which ensures such incredible views on clear days, also ensures there are a good number of days with low cloud, mist and rain. On average July and August are the warmest months with an average maximum of 17°C, while May is the driest. Winds, mostly from the south or west, can be strong, sweeping in straight from the ocean to give real problems on the Cuillin ridge. The proximity of the ocean means winters are generally relatively mild – the average daily maximum in January is 6°C, and snow does not accumulate so much at a given height as it does in the Cairngorms or central Highlands.

INFORMATION

Maps & Books

For a topographic overview of the island try OS Travelmaster 1:250,000 map No 3 *(Western Scotland and the Western Isles)*.

Skye & the North West Highlands by John Brooks & Neil Wilson includes 16 varied walks on Skye. Hamish Brown's *25 Walks: Skye & Kintail* also describes 16 walks on the isle, while *50 Best Routes on Skye & Raasay* by Ralph Storer has a wide selection of mountain and coastal outings. *The Isle of Skye* by Terry Marsh has a feast of 85 walks. There is also *Selected Walks – Northern Skye*, *Selected Walks – Southern Skye* and *Walks from Glen Brittle* by Charles Rhodes (all locally produced in English and German). The Ramblers' Association's *Guide to the Isle of Skye* by Chris Townsend includes nine routes in the Cuillin. For those wishing to do some scrambling on the Black Cuillin, *Skye Scrambles*, published by the Scottish Mountaineering Club, is worth a look.

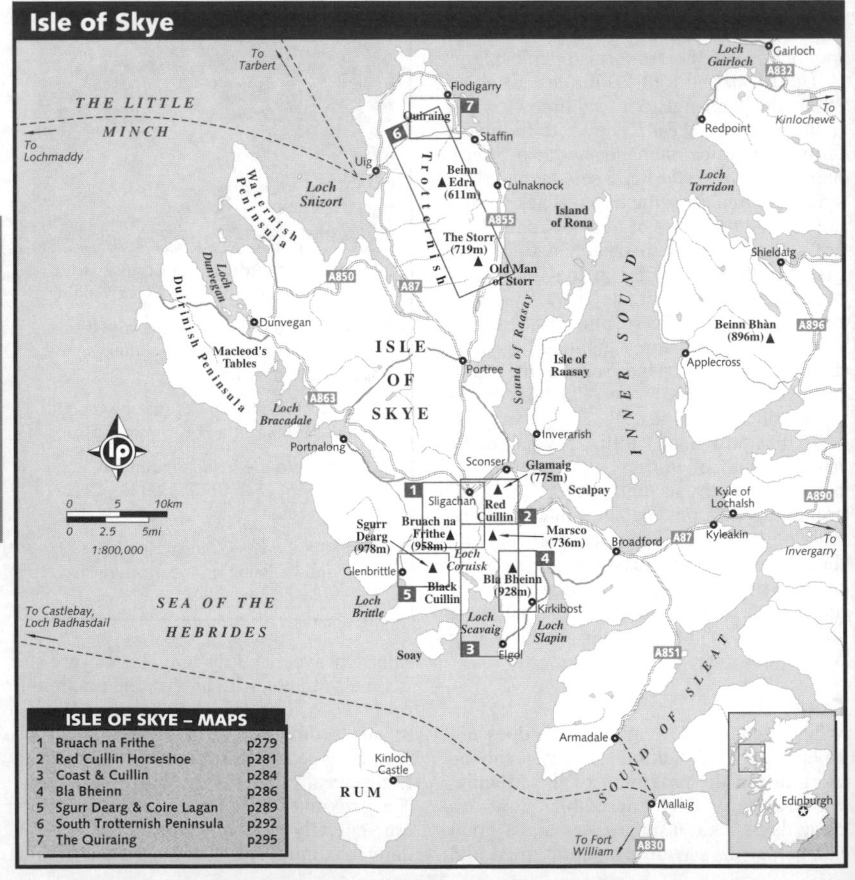

Information Sources

The Highlands of Scotland Tourist Board (☎ 01997-421160, W www.host.co.uk) can send you accommodation listings, brochures and timetables for Skye. A good Web source can be found at W www.skye.co.uk, a community site with accommodation, event and transport information.

The mountain weather forecast for the western Highlands (which includes Skye) is available from ☎ 0891-500441 or fax 0336-500441.

A useful Web site for transport information in the Highlands (including the Isle of Skye) is W www.hi-ways.org. The Highland Council publishes a set of four comprehensive transport guides to the region, including *Skye & Western Isles*. They're available from local TICs.

In case of an emergency, call Portree police station on ☎ 01478-612888. Don't forget about the 'Let Someone Know Before You Go' form, available from W www.northern.police.uk.

Guided Walks

The environmental centre in Broadford (☎ 01471-822487) runs guided walks and wildlife tours. Skye also has a long tradition of professional guiding dating back to the 19th century. Most guides will be able to help with anything from an easy Black Cuillin introduction walk to the complete traverse of the Cuillin ridge or an ascent of the Inaccessible Pinnacle. If you are unsure of your scrambling ability on steep, exposed ground, the Black Cuillin might be more safely explored with a guide.

Skye Mountain Guides (☎ 01478-612682) and Skye Highs (☎ 01471-822116) provide guiding on the Black Cuillin ridge, as do Blaven Guiding (☎ 01478-613180), Cuillin Guides (☎ 01478-640289) and George Yeomans (☎ 01478-650380).

GATEWAY

Portree

The capital of Skye, Portree is the largest settlement on the island. Spread between a central market square and a picturesque fishing harbour, it has all the facilities that could be expected of a capital town. There is a wide array of shops, petrol stations, grocery stores and supermarkets. There are two banks with ATMs, a post office and several places offering foreign exchange facilities. Skye Thematics Centre (☎ 01478-612983) offers Internet access, although it is not very central, located on the A87 towards Dunvegan, soon after Portree Backpackers. For outdoor gear there is Island Outdoor on Bridge Rd and Janesport on Wentworth St.

Information Portree TIC (☎ 01478-612137, e portree@host.co.uk), just off Somerled Square, is open all year (seven days a week from May to October). It has a fax weather forecasting service, and sells maps and walking guides.

Places to Stay & Eat Portree has a wealth of accommodation options and it can seem as though every second house is a B&B. Nonetheless, visitors in peak season do a good job of filling the spaces and booking ahead is advisable in summer.

Portree Independent Hostel *(☎ 01478-613737)* is centrally located near the TIC and charges £9.50. ***Portree Backpackers*** *(☎ 01478-613641)* has a homely atmosphere and costs £9, but is 1mi away from the town centre on the A87 towards Dunvegan and Uig. There is also camping here for £4. ***Torvaig Campsite*** *(☎ 01478-612209)*, 1mi up Staffin Rd, charges £3.

Granary Bakery on Somerled Square serves tasty snacks and light meals all day. There are several takeaways around the town centre. For something more substantial try the ***Caledonian Hotel***, Wentworth St, where bar food starts at £3.

Getting There & Away There are two main ways to get to Portree from the mainland. One is to take the ferry from the mainland port of Mallaig to Armadale on Skye. The ferry service is run by Caledonian MacBrayne (☎ 01475-650100) and costs £15.25 for cars (excluding passengers) and £2.70 for foot passengers. ScotRail (☎ 0845-755 0033) train services from Glasgow tie in with the Mallaig ferry to Armadale, as does a Citylink (☎ 0870-550 5050) bus from Fort William. From Armadale, Highland Country Buses (☎ 01463-222244) has connections to Portree several times daily.

The other way to get to Portree is to travel to Kyle of Lochalsh (on the mainland) by bus or train. There are four trains daily (two on Sunday) to Kyle of Lochalsh from Inverness. Two of these trains come right through from Edinburgh and Glasgow. From Kyle of Lochalsh you can pick up a Highland Country Buses service to Portree. Citylink also travels from Glasgow and Inverness to Kyle of Lochalsh, continuing directly on to Portree (two buses daily).

If you have your own transport you could drive across the controversial Skye Bridge (opened in 1995) between Kyle of Lochalsh and Kyleakin, paying a hefty toll of £5.80 each way for cars.

The Cuillin

The mountains of the Black and Red Cuillin dominate the landscape of southern Skye. The name Cuillin (pronounced coolin) is derived from the Norse *kjollen*, meaning 'keel-shaped'.

The Black Cuillin is visually the most impressive mountain range in the British Isles and is also the most technically challenging. The main ridge runs for 7.5mi (12.2km), averages about 700m in height and is often knife-edged. The traverse of this ridge, an ultimate mountain challenge, is aspired to by many walkers (see Other Walks on page 296). However, there are a few places where more cautious walkers with some mountain experience can get 'Skye-high'.

The nearby Red Cuillin mountains, by contrast, are more rounded, and the red granite, which gives them their name, also appears somewhat friendlier than the black gabbro of their neighbours.

From a base on the moor at Sligachan, you can walk up into Fionn Coire and onto the summit of Bruach na Frithe, the easier of the two Black Cuillin peaks described in this chapter. The summit affords stupendous views in either direction along the ridge. By taking a different path from Sligachan you can climb onto the Red Cuillin horseshoe or, if the cloud is down or you fancy a low-level walk, you can start in Elgol and walk back to Sligachan via the grandeur of Loch Coruisk.

From near Elgol you can also climb the great fin of gabbro known as Bla Bheinn (Blaven), a superlative viewpoint for both the Black and Red Cuillin. Finally, from remote Glen Brittle you can scramble to the summit of Sgurr Dearg and experience some of the most airy and exhilarating walking in Scotland.

Conservation on Skye

A good deal of south Skye and the Cuillin is owned and managed by the John Muir Trust, a conservation body which manages other areas on the Scottish mainland (see the boxed text 'John Muir Trust' on page 197). A combination of three separate estates total some 12,100ha of mountainous and rural Skye. The estates also hold several small and active crofting communities who provide representatives for a joint management committee.

The first land was bought in 1991 with the purchase of the Torrin Estate, which lies within the Cuillin National Scenic Area. In 1994 the much larger Strathaird Estate was purchased from Iain Anderson (of Jethro Tull fame), which ensured the preservation of land running to the heart of the Cuillin, and included Glen Sligachan, Loch Coruisk and the peaks of Bla Bheinn, Marsco and Ruadh Stac. The recent addition of the Sconser Estate has brought more summits in the Red Cuillin under the Trust's control.

Perhaps the major deficiency in the Trust's Isle of Skye portfolio is the Black Cuillin mountains themselves, the current and future ownership of which is the subject of a controversial debate (see the boxed text 'Black Cuillin for Sale' on page 278). For further details contact the John Muir Trust (☎ 0131-554 0114, e jmt_admin@compuserve.com, w www.jmt.org).

NATURAL HISTORY

Millions of years after violent volcanic activity created what was to become the Cuillin, Skye experienced the great ice age of the Pleistocene epoch. Glaciers formed on the highest parts of the island and sculpted the landscape, carving deep basins from the gabbro rock.

Both the Black and Red Cuillin are igneous formations but their mineral compositions are very different. The Black Cuillin rock is mainly gabbro, with sections of smooth basalt on the surface. The gabbro is a coarse crystalline rock, which is rich in iron and magnesium and dark in colour. The basalt has eroded more readily than the hard gabbro, leaving gullies and chimneys. At the same time glacial action has carved corries out of the rock, and the end result is a finely sculpted, jagged ridge line. A peculiar property of the rock is a localised magnetic influence – a rather important consideration if you're intending to navigate by compass! The Red Cuillin mountains are a product of later igneous activity. They comprise granite and quartz, with flakes of pink feldspar providing the characteristic red colour.

Arctic and alpine flowers grow at unusually low altitudes in the Cuillin. In summer the hillsides and glens are a riot of colour, with the purple of heather species and the yellow of bog asphodel predominant. Glen Sligachan is also a good place for spotting the most regal of birds, the golden eagle. Sightings are common (the birds usually nest on north-facing mountain crags) but it is also easy to confuse the eagle with the buzzard, a smaller bird of prey. Eagles typically have a lazy, soaring flight pattern, while buzzards fly in tighter circles and flap their wings more vigorously.

PLANNING

When to Walk

All walks in this section are best attempted in clear weather with the mountains free of snow and ice. This generally means between late spring and late autumn. All the mountain walks described include rocky summit ridges, and these can become dangerously slippery if wet or icy.

Warning

Due to the magnetic properties of the Black Cuillin gabbro rock, compasses give distorted readings. Map-reading skills alone must be relied on for navigation on cloudy days. If your abilities in this area are not reliable, the summit walks should only be attempted in good weather and, even then, extreme caution is necessary as the mountain climate is notoriously changeable.

What to Bring

On all routes bring the usual gear for a mountain walk, including warm clothing, waterproofs and strong boots, plus a map, torch and compass. Water is generally plentiful at lower levels but scarce higher up.

Maps

OS Landranger 1:50,000 map No 32 *(South Skye & Cuillin Hills)* and OS Outdoor Leisure 1:25,000 map No 8 *(The Cuillin & Torridon Hills)* cover all the routes described in this section. In addition, Harvey's Superwalker 1:25,000 map *Skye: The Cuillin* covers all routes except the Coast & Cuillin walk. The latter includes a 1:12,500 enlargement of the Cuillin ridge, and probably gives the clearest picture of the complex terrain.

Bruach na Frithe

Duration	6–8 hours
Distance	8.5mi (13.5km)
Standard	medium-hard
Start/Finish	Sligachan
Nearest Towns	Portree, Sligachan
Public Transport	yes

Summary A fine but strenuous mountain walk with spectacular views of the Black and Red Cuillin. An alternative route on the north-west ridge provides exciting scrambling for more adventurous walkers.

Situated on an apex of the main Black Cuillin ridge, Bruach na Frithe (958m, 3142ft) is a superlative viewpoint from

Black Cuillin for Sale

During the early part of 2000, John MacLeod (chief of the Clan MacLeod) put the Black Cuillin mountains of Skye on sale for an asking price of £10 million. Environmental and outdoor interest groups had only just defeated plans for scenic flights to be operated over the same mountains from Sligachan, and were horrified by rumours that wealthy foreigners had expressed interest in purchasing the range. Some feared the Black Cuillin would be turned into a mass-tourism theme park or the long history of public access to the mountains would be threatened. The move prompted an even stronger reaction from islanders who were more than a little peeved by MacLeod's assumption of title – a suggestion at a public meeting that the government would buy the estate for the people was booed. Their view was that MacLeod should not profit from the sale and it was unclear whether he actually owned the mountains. MacLeod, on the other hand, stated that he simply needed the money for repairs on the roof of Dunvegan Castle, one of the island's leading tourist attractions.

Later in the year the property was withdrawn from the market pending an investigation by the Crown Estate Commission, which looks after state-owned land, into legal title to the mountains. If the commission found that MacLeod did not own the estate then title would fall to the Crown and, hence, become public property. However, the commission decided not to contest MacLeod's claim to the title and, despite the strength of feeling, MacLeod put the estate back on the market. In July 2001 MacLeod announced that he was prepared to look at proposals to take either Dunvegan Castle or the land including the Cuillins into public ownership, at the right price. It was not clear whether the land would be taken off the commercial market while these new proposals were being considered.

With the sale late in 2000 of An Teallach (see the boxed text 'Sale of An Teallach' on page 303), a serious debate has been prompted into the stewardship of Scotland's wild mountains.

which to appreciate the outstanding rock architecture of this amazing range, without getting involved in the serious scrambling normally associated with the Black Cuillin. From Sligachan good paths are followed right into Fionn Choire from where a short and steep, but very straightforward, ascent leads to the summit. This may be the easiest peak in the Black Cuillin to reach, but it still requires considerable effort and has a total ascent of more than 900m. On the whole navigation in poor conditions is not difficult for the experienced, but remember that map reading rather than compass work should be relied on given that the gabbro rock can interfere with compass bearings. An alternative route ascending via the north-west ridge is described for those wishing to spice up the walk with some easy scrambling, in keeping with the normal flavour of Black Cuillin 'walks'.

NEAREST TOWN
Sligachan

Sligachan is a minimalist sort of place, consisting mainly of a large hotel, a bus stop and a camping site. However, it has also been a gateway to the Cuillin for over a century and thrives throughout the summer. There is no shop (except for very basic supplies available at the camping site reception), so all supplies need to be brought with you.

Places to Stay & Eat The centre of activity, ***Sligachan Hotel*** *(☎ 01478-650204)* charges from £35 for B&B (£40 during July and August). Adjacent Seamus's Bar has food until 9pm, including a hearty 'camper's breakfast' served from 7.30am to 10am. The ***Sligachan Campsite*** *(☎ 01478-650303)* is opposite the hotel, has laundry facilities and charges £4.

Getting There & Away Highland Country Buses (☎ 01463-222244) operates between Portree and Broadford via Sligachan seven times daily in each direction (except Sunday). Citylink (☎ 0870-550 5050) buses travelling to Portree from Glasgow, Inverness and Kyle of Lochalsh also stop at Sligachan (two buses daily).

THE WALK

From Sligachan Bridge (just east of the hotel), walk west along the A863 towards Dunvegan for a little over 500m. Take the track on the left, signed 'Footpath to Glenbrittle', that heads towards Alltdearg House. Just as you approach the house a signed footpath diverts around the grounds to the north, crossing over a stretch of boggy ground. The firmest route keeps close to the fence on the left.

You soon pick up a stony path that runs alongside Allt Dearg Mór, a burn that tumbles down a series of rock ledges, forming some beautiful pools and small waterfalls that invite a swim on a hot day. After 2mi the path begins to level out in Coire na Circe. Continue on, fording a sizable tributary to reach a large cairn. Here the path for Bruach na Frithe (much fainter than the one you've been on) forks left across boggy ground and crosses another burn some 200m after the cairn. If the weather is clear you will be able to see the summit of Bruach na Frithe and grassy, boulder-strewn slopes running up into Fionn Choire. Follow the ascending path for about 30 minutes, keeping Allt an Fionn Choire (a burn

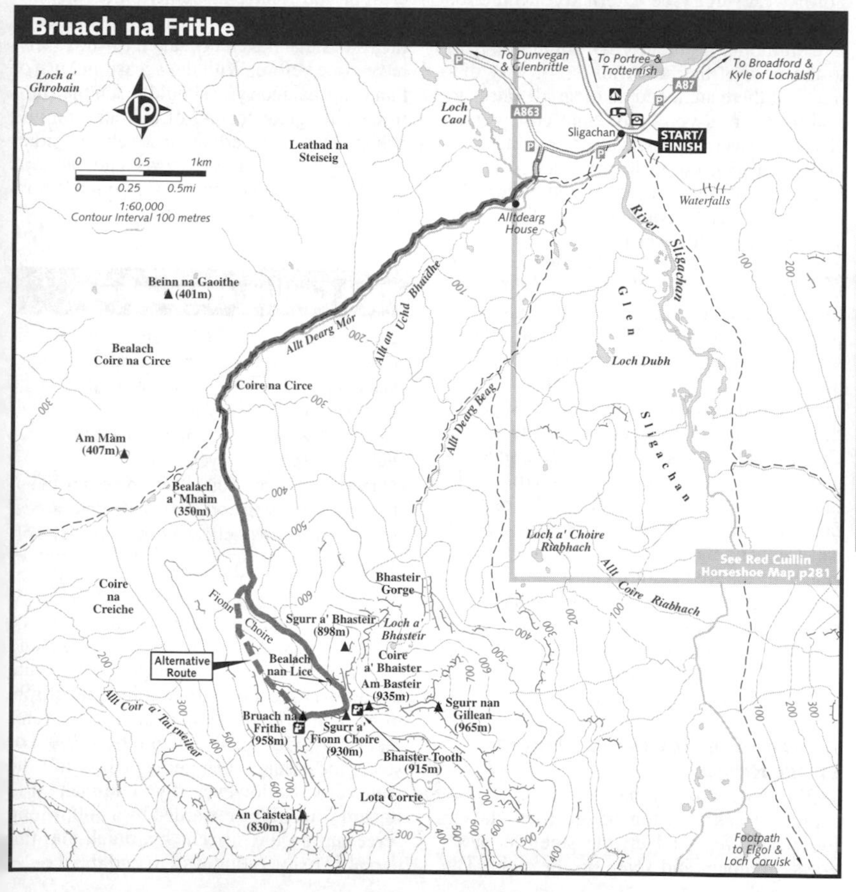

ISLE OF SKYE

with small waterfalls pouring from the corrie above) on your left, until you reach a substantial cairn on top of a rock slab. This is a good place for a rest while you decide which route to take to the summit.

Fionn Choire has not been gouged out as deeply as most Scottish corries and does not hold a lochan. Nonetheless, it is a beautiful and impressive place. You should be able to make out a path climbing the steep scree on the corrie headwall to reach Bealach nan Lice, just east of the summit. This is the normal route. To your right a grassy shoulder leads up onto the jagged and impressive north-west ridge (see Alternative Route for details of this more adventurous route).

Continuing on the normal route, the path to the base of the headwall is not very distinct but there are a couple of small cairns to look out for as you tend south-east, gently climbing over easy terrain. Cross a small gully and pick up an intermittent path that leads towards the steeper ground, where the path again becomes quite distinct. From here a short steep climb brings you to the dramatic Bealach nan Lice in the shadow of Am Basteir and Bhasteir Tooth. Turn right and follow a distinct trail around the base of a pinnacle and onto the final, rocky ridge leading to the summit of **Bruach na Frithe**. The peak is marked by a trig point and the view on a clear day is one of the best on Skye. To the west the main section of the Black Cuillin ridge cuts back on itself in a spectacular z-shape, ending in the prominent thumb-like summit of Gars-bheinn. To the east the fang of rock rising above Am Basteir is Sgurr nan Gillean, and beyond it the bright scree slopes of the Red Cuillin can be seen.

The easiest way back to Sligachan is to reverse the route of ascent. Alternatively you can continue past Am Basteir and drop into Coire a' Bhasteir for a more direct but more difficult descent back to Sligachan.

Alternative Route: via North-West Ridge

2–2½ hours, 2mi (3km)

From the cairn on top of the rock slab in Fionn Choire, head up the steep slope of grass, boulders and scree on the right. The bearing is south-south-west and there are occasional cairns to guide you. Climb the steep slope up to the left and join a more obvious path (which has come up from Bealach a' Mhaim). This zigzags up steep scree and grass to a narrowing of the ridge and a brief easing of the angle of ascent.

There is a short, steep ascent before an almost horizontal, narrow section of about 150m. This is a superb situation for those with a head for heights. At the end of this the main ridge scramble begins. Difficulties encountered near the ridge crest can be avoided on the right, but don't drop too far below the crest or you'll have difficulty climbing back up farther on. There is plenty of evidence of the routes that have been taken by those who have gone before. With the occasional use of hands for balance you should reach the summit with a great feeling of exhilaration and achievement (or perhaps just relief). Either way, enjoy the superb views and perhaps check your compass to see for yourself how the gabbro affects the needle.

Red Cuillin Horseshoe

Duration	6–7 hours
Distance	7.5mi (12km)
Standard	medium-hard
Start/Finish	Sligachan
Nearest Towns	Portree, Sligachan
Public Transport	yes

Summary A surprisingly demanding mountain horseshoe crossing rocky summits and steep, scree-strewn slopes, offering expansive views of the entire island.

This walk makes a circuit of the main Red Cuillin peaks. Although access is easy and the distance covered is not great, the route has a total ascent of 1207m. The final climb, in particular, is demanding, and if you don't feel happy with the idea of climbing 300m of steep, loose scree then perhaps this isn't the walk for you. However, if you do make it to the top you will be rewarded by a 500m-long scree-run on the descent – a quick and undeniably exhilarating way to end the day.

In recent years the route has become the subject of a local race, with competitors finishing the circuit in around 1½ hours. Mere mortals can count on taking a little longer. The Gaelic meaning of the mountains on the circuit is also worth noting. Beinn Dearg Mheadhonach and Beinn Dearg Mhór can be translated as 'middle red mountain' and 'big red mountain' respectively. The meaning of Glamaig itself is slightly more incongruous – translation theories vie between 'deep gorge mountain' or, more suggestively, 'greedy woman' (on account of her ballooning shape maybe?).

NEAREST TOWN

Sligachan

See Nearest Town under Bruach na Frithe on page 278.

THE WALK

Cross the old stone bridge east of Sligachan Hotel and pass through the metal turnstile on the other side, following the path signed to Loch Coruisk. After approximately 200m, the gorge of the Allt Daraich comes up on the left. Leave the main path here and follow a smaller path along the southern rim of the ravine. The gorge soon dwindles in height and the path strikes out across open moor towards the shoulder of Sròn a' Bhealain. This section can be boggy but the path can be seen zigzagging encouragingly up drier slopes ahead.

The ascent of the shoulder is initially steep and passing feet have cut high steps into the muddy ground. The gradient eases as you climb higher, until you join the grassy, undulating terrain of the Druim na Ruaige ridge. Several cairns mark the crest of the ridge and there is an excellent perspective over the circuit of peaks ahead. The peak of Sgurr Mhairi (775m), on the Glamaig massif to the north, looks ominously steep.

Leaving the ridge the path enters the stone and scree-covered terrain that makes up most

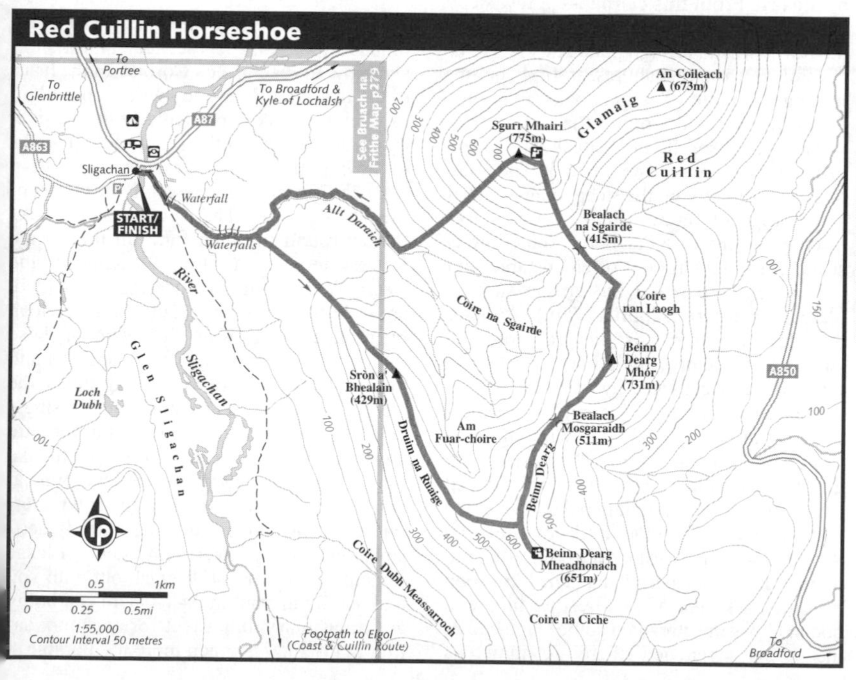

of the high ground of the circuit. Zigzag up the loose rock to a cairn at the top. The official summit of **Beinn Dearg Mheadhonach** (651m) is actually a short detour to the south-east, but the views from both cairns are impressive. MacLeod's Tables and the Trotternish peninsula lie to the north-west, while the peaks of Glen Shiel and The Great Wilderness are clearly visible on the mainland. The dark, barren peaks of the Black Cuillin dominate the scene to the south.

Return to the cairn that marked your arrival on the summit ridge and continue northward, following a faint path over easy ground to the col between Beinn Dearg Mheadhonach and Beinn Dearg Mhór. The path becomes more obvious as it climbs up the other side over steeper, rocky ground to reach **Beinn Dearg Mhór's** (731m) summit cairn. Finding the descent from here can be tricky and care is required in poor visibility. Follow the northern spur of the mountain for around 500m to a subsidiary rise marked by a cairn. From this cairn take a few steps backwards (south) and drop steeply down to the north-west. A rough path descends over several worn scree chutes at first, before joining a jumble of larger rocks and boulders towards the bottom of the slope.

The grassy saddle of Bealach na Sgairde offers a short break from the rock. The route then goes directly up the steep, crag-studded scree slope of Sgurr Mhairi, roughly following the line of a dry burn. The climb is sustained and the rock is often unstable, and it is a relief to reach the grassy summit plateau of **Sgurr Mhairi** (775m). Another excellent panorama is viewed from the large summit cairn, including a bird's-eye view of the Isle of Raasay.

Descend from Sgurr Mhairi in a south-westerly direction, sliding down long scree slopes to the grass below. The best way to descend scree chutes is with the pronounced use of the heels to maintain balance over the sliding rocks. Continue until you meet the Allt Daraich, then turn right to follow a faint path along its northern bank. The burn soon becomes a series of picturesque falls and pools. Cross the stream at some stage before the ravine is reached (there are numerous crossing places) and continue down the opposite bank. You will rejoin the path that you started the day on and from here it doesn't take long to retrace your initial steps back to Sligachan Hotel.

Coast & Cuillin

Duration	2 days
Distance	14mi (22.5km)
Standard	medium
Start	Elgol
Finish	Sligachan
Nearest Towns	Portree, Sligachan, Elgol, Kirkibost
Public Transport	yes

Summary A spectacular, low-level route that penetrates the heart of the Black Cuillin to reach the shores of Loch Coruisk via 'The Bad Step', a short, exposed rock section, which some walkers might find problematic.

This low-level route combines coastal paths, mountain views, glen scenery and a short scramble to reach Loch Coruisk in the heart of the Black Cuillin. The section from Elgol to Loch Coruisk is particularly impressive, and provides one of the finest coastal walks in the country.

Loch Coruisk is the jewel in the crown of the Black Cuillin. The jagged ring of peaks that surround the loch form an impressive fortress and a wild setting for its clear blue water. Without mountaineering skills there are only three possible routes into the loch by foot, and this walk links two of those routes (the other path is more tenuous and leads in from Glenbrittle camping site, to the west). The walk can be completed in a single day (allow eight to nine hours), but for pure appreciation of the scenery it is good to take two days. The experience of camping at Loch Coruisk is unique, but this is wild terrain and you will need to be entirely self-sufficient with overnight gear. Please remember to carry all rubbish out with you and leave minimal impact. There is a bothy at Camasunary, but a tent for accommodation at the loch is much more memorable.

Despite its high quality, the route described involves one section of scrambling that may not be to everyone's liking. The Bad Step, about 500m before Loch Coruisk is reached, is a 6m-long, 60-degree slab with a narrow ledge for the feet and small handholds for support. It is exposed but is situated about 8m above deep water, so is not necessarily dangerous if you can swim well! It should be within the capabilities of most fit walkers, but a cool head is required and heavy packs may also increase the difficulty.

Alternatives If the idea of The Bad Step is too daunting, then it is possible to take a linear route from Elgol to Sligachan straight up Glen Sligachan, avoiding Loch Coruisk altogether. There is a sign on the wall of the house at Camasunary that directs you up the valley and the path is very good all the way. This option covers a total distance of 11mi (17.5km) and should take about six hours to complete.

Alternatively you can take a boat to Loch Coruisk and then walk out. Bella Jane Boat Trips (☎ 01471-866244) charges £10 to take you from Elgol across Loch Scavaig to the landing steps near Loch Coruisk. From here you can join the route and walk the 8mi out to Sligachan. This option would fit easily into a single day and make for a very memorable trip.

NEAREST TOWNS

Sligachan

See Nearest Town under Bruach na Frithe on page 278.

Elgol

This is a very small fishing village with an incredible view of the Cuillin.

Places to Stay & Eat There are a limited number of places to stay in the village, and most of them are closed during the winter months. There's a B&B at ***Rowan Cottage*** *(☎ 01471-866287, ⓔ Rowan@rowancott.demon.co.uk)*, which charges from £18 with evening meals available. ***Coruisk Guesthouse*** *(☎ 01471-866330)* has an excellent tearoom and licensed seafood restaurant, and also does B&B for about £25. There is a small ***shop***, a post office and the friendly ***Cuillin View Coffee Shop***, which serves snacks and meals.

Getting There & Away There is a postbus (☎ 01246-546329) service between Broadford and Elgol post offices. On weekdays it leaves Broadford at 10.45am and 3.40pm, and Elgol at 8.07am and 2.30pm. On Saturday only the morning services operate and on Sunday there is no service. Broadford has numerous bus connections to Sligachan and Portree – see Getting There & Away for Sligachan on page 278.

Kirkibost

The tiny village of Kirkibost consists of a couple of buildings and is 3.5mi from Elgol towards Broadford. Walkers are welcome at ***Strathaird House*** *(☎ 01471-866269, ⓔ jkubale@compuserve.com)*, which offers B&B from £25. Lunch and evening meals are available at the ***Hayloft*** restaurant. The Broadford-Elgol postbus (see Getting There & Away for Elgol) drops off and picks up in Kirkibost five minutes before reaching and after leaving Elgol.

GETTING TO/FROM THE WALK

The walk begins about 400m south of the Elgol post office and 600m north of the village jetty, where a lane leads off to the north from the B8083 road. The lane is clearly signposted as a footpath to Camasunary and Sligachan.

THE WALK

Day 1: Elgol to Loch Coruisk

4–5 hours, 6mi (9.5km)

Walk up the lane signposted to Camasunary and Sligachan. The road soon disappears, leaving a dirt track that ends at two houses. A footpath, signed to Loch Coruisk, continues directly ahead between the fences of the houses. It crosses through a gate and leads out onto open hillside. The views are immediately impressive; the small isles of Soay, Eigg, Rum and Canna lie to the south, while the Black Cuillin dominate the skyline to the north-west.

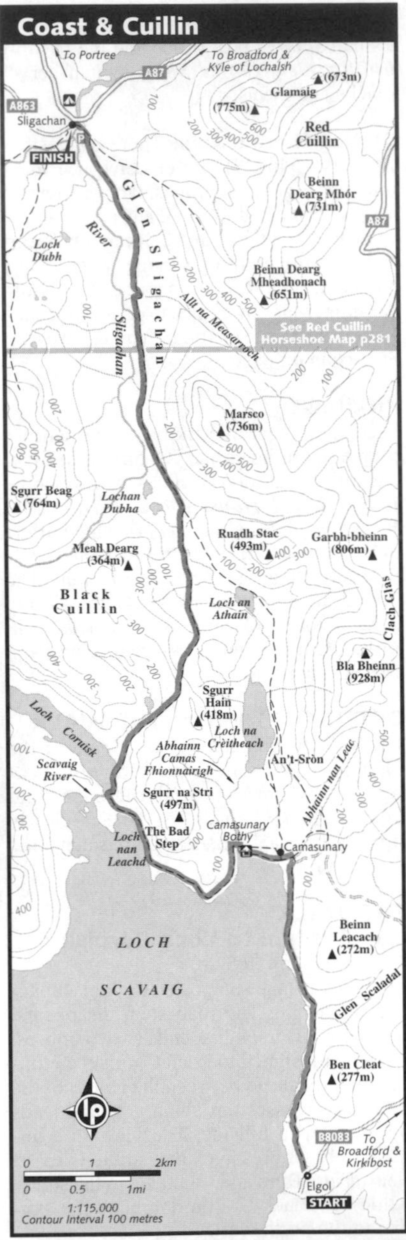

The well-trodden path basically contours across grass and heather slopes all the way to the beach at Camasunary, with views becoming better all the time. The drop-off to the west is steep in places as the lower slopes of Ben Cleat and Beinn Leacach are passed, and care is required over these sections. At Glen Scaladal a stile is crossed before descending to a pebbly cove. A steep climb from the back of the beach leads to the broken cliff top. Duck under the branches of a grove of stunted trees, and watch out for a place where the old path has eroded away in a landslide and a new track skirts past the drop by climbing slightly higher up the cliff. Easier ground then leads down to the bridge over the Abhainn nan Leac and a substantial junction of paths, about 3mi from Elgol.

Of the two buildings at Camasunary, the larger house near the bridge is privately owned. The smaller building 500m farther west is a ***bothy*** belonging to the Mountain Bothies Association, providing free accommodation for hillwalkers. At the junction of paths, the 4WD track descending from the shoulder to the east leads to Kirkibost, 1.5mi away. The path that forks right, between the bridge and house, leads directly up the glen to Sligachan, avoiding Loch Coruisk.

To continue to Loch Coruisk take the path leading west along the top of the beach, passing in front of the bothy. Ford the Abhainn Camas Fhionnairigh by following its banks upstream for 100m or so and then cross on stepping stones. The path on the other side soon climbs slightly to contour around the craggy lower slopes of Sgurr na Stri. The terrain is rougher than previously, and several rock steps and angled slabs are crossed. As you round the headland another wonderful vista greets the eye; rocky islands nestle in the azure water at the mouth of the Scavaig River, backed by the looming Cuillin.

The slabs become more frequent as the path veers north and care must be taken not to lose the main trail as it splits in various places. Continue towards the white sand and turquoise water of Loch nan Leachd cove. The notorious **Bad Step** is the very last slab that needs to be negotiated before the beach. A cairn marks the stony path that descends to the difficulties. (It could be a good idea to undo pack straps if you are worried, just in case of a slip into the water below.) Duck under an overhang and scramble out onto the seaward rock face. Pull yourself up to balance on a ledge that skirts around the slab, using handholds for support. Shuffle along, taking care to drop diagonally down to the boulders at the beach rather than continuing up the slab at a convergence of fault lines.

Cross the boulders to the sand of Loch nan Leachd beach, and follow the path inland across the low saddle at the back of the cove. **Loch Coruisk** is suddenly revealed in all its glory and its banks make a fine rest-spot. If you are spending the night here, flat ground for camping can be found just over the stepping stones that cross the Scavaig River.

Day 2: Loch Coruisk to Sligachan

3–4 hours, 8mi (13km)

The path from Loch Coruisk to Sligachan leads around the south-eastern shore of the loch and climbs up the right-hand side of the burn that can be seen tumbling down from a smaller loch above. It is a climb of over 300m to the saddle itself and the terrain is rocky towards the top. A large cairn marks the saddle and there are fine views west over the serrated north Cuillin ridge. Veer north-west along the ridge to a second cairn 20m away, where a wide, stony trail drops down the other side. The path from Camasunary to Sligachan can be seen winding along the valley below. The descent to join it is fairly steep for a section and then evens out, becoming rather wet at the valley floor. Join the main Sligachan path at a large cairn, from where there is a great perspective of Bla Bheinn and the Clach Glas ridge to the south-east.

From the junction of paths it is about 3.5mi along the valley to Sligachan. The terrain is largely flat and the going easy. Although the Sligachan Hotel soon comes into view, it can seem like a long time before it moves much closer. The final 500m of the route is along a well-benched path and you exit the mountains at a metal stile. Turn left across the old bridge to arrive at the hotel.

Bla Bheinn

Duration	6–7 hours
Distance	7.5mi (12km)
Standard	medium-hard
Start/Finish	Kirkibost
Nearest Town	Kirkibost, Elgol
Public Transport	yes

Summary A long and strenuous ascent to an impressive Black Cuillin summit and tremendous views across the mountains of southern Skye.

Bla Bheinn (928m, 3045ft), or Blaven as it is often called, is an impressive mountain from any angle. Buttresses, gullies and sheets of scree suggest an ascent would be technically difficult, and the classic traverse to Bla Bheinn across Clach Glas (the skyline ridge as seen from the shores of Loch Slapin) is indeed one of the hardest 'walking' routes on any mountain in Britain. It requires rock climbing ability to at least D (difficult) standard (British grades). However, the south-west ridge provides straightforward access as far as the south-west summit (924m), from where a short but exposed scramble leads to the main summit (928m). A steep descent is made from the south-west summit to reach a small bealach, from where the rest of the descent across Slat Bheinn is very pleasant when dry.

The mountain is potentially serious with steep and dangerous ground all around. Although the passage of many boots has created paths to follow in mist, a snow shower and lowering of the cloud base could turn the descent into a nightmare if your map reading is not up to scratch. Much of Bla Bheinn is made up of gabbro, which can make compasses unreliable (see the Warning box on page 277).

Alternatives An alternative and popular approach is from Loch Slapin, following a good path up Coire Uaigneich to the bealach previously mentioned. From there the line of descent, which is described for this route, is used to reach the summit. Most walkers then retrace their outward journey.

NEAREST TOWNS
Elgol & Kirkibost

See Nearest Towns on page 283.

GETTING TO/FROM THE WALK

The walk starts and finishes at a parking area just south of Kirkibost, on the Broadford to Elgol road, 3.5mi north of Elgol. Park opposite the prominent gate and track that leads to Camasunary. The postbus to Elgol can also drop you here – see Getting There & Away for Elgol on page 283.

THE WALK

From the parking area, cross the stile on the opposite side of the road and follow the 4WD track west, following the sign for Camasunary. Cross a small burn and then climb steadily for 20 minutes to reach the gap of Am Màm, where a grand vista of Loch Scavaig and the Black Cuillin comes into view and the great winging south-west ridge of Bla Bheinn is increasingly revealed.

Descend gradually for around 800m to a hairpin turn in the 4WD track. A small cairn marks the start of a narrow path continuing north over the Abhainn nan Leac. Five minutes after crossing the Abhainn nan Leac, a small cairn marks the junction with another narrow path that climbs onto the south-west ridge. Follow this over steep ground to the foot of the first rock outcrops. The path swings to the right around the crags, and gains the shoulder of the ridge after a steep climb through a gully. The effort to reach this point is rewarded by some fine views across the Black Cuillin ridge and down Glen Sligachan.

From the shoulder the path becomes indistinct but intermittent sections are easily followed between here and the summit, keeping mainly to the right of the most awkward ground. The climb continues steadily for 30 minutes, before a brief descent leaves you at the base of a steeper, rockier climb. Once over this another brief descent brings you to the final climb, weaving a line between jumbles of boulders and rock outcrops. The **south summit** (924m) is reached some two to 2½ hours from the base of the south-west ridge. The views from here reach across to the summits of Knoydart and even as far as Ben Nevis on the mainland.

A little distance to the north-east, a cairn and trig point mark the slightly higher main summit of Bla Bheinn, but getting to it is not straightforward. A 20m descent into a notch on the ridge requires a short but exposed scramble. This is best taken directly along the crest of the ridge where the rock is more solid. At the final rise, move out to the right across some exposed sloping ledges and a straightforward walk then leads to the main summit of **Bla Bheinn** (928m). The views north across Garbhbheinn and the Red Cuillin are stunning. From just north of the summit you can also appreciate the difficulty and exposure of the

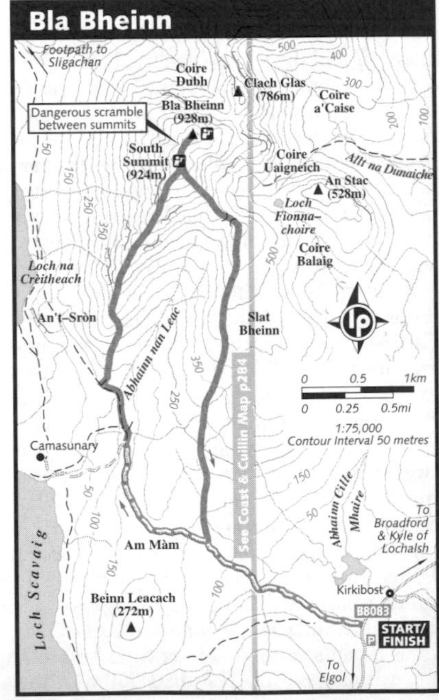

ridge between Bla Bheinn and Clach Glas. This is one of the most demanding scrambles in Britain.

Return to the south summit and follow a distinct path steeply towards the bealach above Coire Uaigneich. The going underfoot is treacherous. About halfway to the bealach the gradient steepens and the path becomes indistinct, but it is still possible to see where people have been. As long as the mist is not down you can aim for the prominent lochan on the bealach. Lower down keep left of a prominent gully and pick up a re-established path to reach the bealach, where you can relax for a while with all the difficult ground behind you. Climb steeply out of the bealach to the summit of Slat Bheinn (624m) and then descend gently southward for 1.5mi to rejoin the 4WD track. Turn left and follow the track back to the start.

Sgurr Dearg & Coire Lagan

Duration	5½–6½ hours
Distance	5mi (8km)
Standard	hard
Start/Finish	Glen Brittle Hut
Nearest Town	Glenbrittle
Public Transport	yes

Summary A challenging and exhilarating ascent of a peak on the main Black Cuillin ridge, involving some scrambling. A tricky descent leads to the shores of Loch Coire Lagan and one of Britain's most impressive corries.

Earlier in this chapter the classic 'easy' outing into the Black Cuillin was described (see page 277). The route to Bruach na Frithe is a stroll by the standards of some Black Cuillin walks. In fact most summits in the Black Cuillin cannot be reached by walking alone – scrambling and occasionally rock climbing in positions of great exposure are sometimes necessary just to progress along the line of least resistance. The route described here is a step up from the Bruach na Frithe route, and gives a good flavour of Cuillin 'walking' without being as technical or serious as other routes on the main ridge.

The route takes in the summit of Sgurr Dearg (978m, 3208ft), scuttles around the base of the Inaccessible Pinnacle and then descends an exhilarating scree chute into Coire Lagan. Along the way some of the most impressive rock scenery in Scotland can be seen, so impressive, in fact, that those who are new to the Cuillin may well feel quite intimidated. This is a challenging and potentially very serious route. However, as long as it is tackled in good conditions and the described route is adhered to, then most fit and experienced walkers with a head for heights will be up to the task. Total ascent for the route is 990m.

It is important to carry plenty of water on the mountain and it should be remembered that the magnetic properties of the gabbro rock will interfere with compass bearings.

NEAREST TOWN
Glenbrittle

Little more than a hamlet, Glenbrittle has very limited facilities and accommodation options.

Places to Stay & Eat The ***SYHA Hostel*** (*☎ 01478-640278*) has a friendly manager and dorm beds cost £8. The ***camping site*** (*☎ 01478-521206*), down by Loch Brittle, charges £4 per person with a surcharge for cars. The camping site has a small shop stocking basic supplies. Both the hostel and camping site are only open between April and October.

Glen Brittle Hut, marked on the OS maps at the start of this walk, is not open to the public.

Getting There & Away Highland Country Buses (☎ 01463-222244) runs a daily service (except Sunday) from Portree to Glenbrittle via Sligachan, with two buses in each direction during summer months only (from mid-May to the end of September). The first bus leaves Portree at 9am and arrives in Glenbrittle at 9.55am. The last bus leaves Glenbrittle at 2.15pm.

Early Ascents in the Black Cuillin

Standing on the summit of Bruach na Frithe or Sgurr Dearg on a good summer's day, it is difficult to imagine how impregnable the Black Cuillin were considered as recently as the early 19th century. Today, with people regularly making the traverse of the entire Cuillin ridge and some people making nonstop traverses of the Greater Cuillin (including Bla Bheinn), it is remarkable how much difference attitude has made. It is not modern equipment, boots or clothing that has made the difference, but quite simply the pioneering of a different approach to the mountains. Most of the summits were considered unclimbable until 1835 when The Reverend Lesingham Smith and local forester Duncan MacIntyre visited Loch Coruisk and returned to Sligachan by scrambling across the ramparts of the Druim nam Ramh ridge into Harta Corrie. The following year Professor James Forbes hired MacIntyre and together they made the first (recorded) ascent of Sgurr nan Gillean by the now popular (but still tricky) south-east ridge.

With the psychological barrier broken, local men quickly knocked off the other peaks in the Cuillin, with Sheriff Alexander Nicolson claiming the first ascent of Sgurr Alasdair, the highest summit on Skye. Many of these local men became guides to members of the Alpine Club and John Mackenzie became the first local professional guide on the island. In 1859 an Admiralty surveyor, Captain Wood, mapped the south Cuillin and identified a pinnacle at 986m as being unclimbable. The Inaccessible Pinnacle, as it is now known, had its first ascent shortly afterwards and its first female ascent a few years after that. Today it is one of the most popular climbing challenges in the Black Cuillin, requiring an easy pitch of rock climbing and a short abseil. Another popular climbing challenge today is The Cioch on the face of Sron na Ciche above Glen Brittle, which was first climbed by Norman Collie (a scientist credited with the first X-ray photograph) and John Mackenzie. The first traverse of the Black Cuillin ridge fell to Shadbolt and Maclaren in 1911, taking nearly 17 hours. It has since been completed in a staggering four hours.

THE WALK

Cross the road from Glen Brittle Hut, just north of the village, and use a footbridge to cross the Allt Coire na Banachdich. A well-defined path climbs gently over the bog to reach a lookout above the Eas Mor waterfall after five to 10 minutes. Continue to follow the main path as it climbs to the south-east, passing under the west spur of Sgurr Dearg. At any stage here you can leave the path and strike out towards the spur, crossing rough and sometimes wet ground. The gradient soon steepens as you climb onto the spur and the terrain becomes rockier. Paths appear, zigzagging around outcrops until you reach a short, steep section. Either bypass this on the left (north) or scramble easily up a prominent gully to emerge on a flat and partially grassy shoulder with great views westward out to sea (one hour from the start).

The ascent continues at a steady gradient along a broad ridge until you reach another short, steep section. A little easy scrambling brings you to the top of this and within sight of the summit of Sgurr Dearg. Between you and the summit, however, is a section of knife-edge ridge, which constitutes the crux of this route. The scrambling across it is straightforward but the exposure is considerable. An easier option can be found just to the right (south) side of the ridge crest. Once over the difficulties, a short climb leads to the sharp summit of **Sgurr Dearg** (978m), three hours from the start.

Even sharper than the summit of Sgurr Dearg is the adjacent Inaccessible Pinnacle (986m), a great fin of rock whose top is a mere 50m as the crow flies from the top of Sgurr Dearg. It is often referred to as the 'In Pin' and can only be reached with a rock climb up its crest. The In Pin was once thought to be the highest summit on Skye (that honour goes to Sgurr Alasdair by 7m) and is the hardest Munro to climb – even Munro himself didn't get to its summit. Farther afield the stunning view takes in the northern sweep of the main Cuillin ridge,

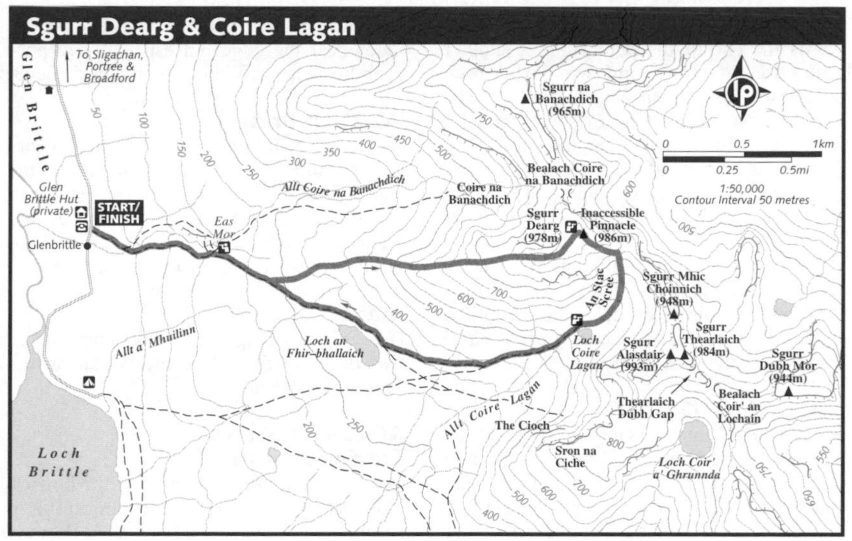

with an impressive knife edge rising to the summit of Sgurr na Banachdich and continuing beyond to Sgurr a' Ghreadaidh. To the south there is a tremendous view across Coire Lagan to Sgurr Alasdair and Sgurr Mhic Choinnich.

Great care must be taken to find the correct route down into Coire Lagan. A prominent ramp runs down to the right (south) of the In Pin. Descend along this, dropping down from the main ridge beneath the cliffs of An Stac. Take care on the slabs, where loose gravel and stone act like ball bearings underfoot. Round a corner to the left, passing beneath the cliffs, and contour for a short distance to the top of a scree slope (the An Stac Scree) that runs down from the Bealach Coire Lagan. You should be able to see a clean run down to Loch Coire Lagan, but if the cloud is down and you can't see the bottom, proceed with great caution. The scree is best descended with a pronounced use of the heels to maintain balance among the sliding rocks. With balance and nerve you can be on the loch shore within a few minutes.

Coire Lagan is one of the most impressive corries in Britain, with cliffs of more than 300m falling directly from the summit of Sgurr Alasdair. Impressive also is the Great Stone Chute, a massive scree run allowing a super-fast (or tortuous depending upon your frame of mind) descent to Coire Lagan from Sgurr Alasdair. The massive gabbro slabs holding the loch reinforce the alpine atmosphere of your surroundings.

A well-defined path descends steeply from the rim of Coire Lagan. After a few hundred metres you'll reach a fork in the path marked by a small cairn. Turn right and follow the smaller path (rough and boggy in places) past the shores of Loch an Fhir-bhallaich back to the start at Glen Brittle Hut (one to 1½ hours from Coire Lagan).

Trotternish

Trotternish is a huge thumb of mountainous land protruding from the north-east corner of Skye. The mountains are not as large, nor as dramatic, as the Cuillin, but a very particular geology has created escarpments, pinnacles and landslides that give the peninsula a unique and iconic landscape. The single most famous pinnacle on the peninsula is the Old Man of Storr, visited on The

Storr route. The Quiraing, farther north towards the end of the peninsula, is another collection of weird and wonderful rock sculptures. Its hidden charms include The Table, a magical plateau of short grass set above crumbling pinnacles and cliffs. The undulating terrain of the Trotternish ridge runs between The Storr and the Quiraing, with escarpments along the length of its eastern edge.

The three walks described in this section are generally easier and less serious than those in the Cuillin, but they should still be treated with respect and may present navigational difficulties in mist.

NATURAL HISTORY

Some 150 million years ago Trotternish was a coastal lagoon colonised by dinosaurs and sea reptiles. Dinosaur footprints have been found on the east of the peninsula and fossils can be seen in abundance along the shore. Then the whole peninsula was covered, up to 1300m deep, in lava from huge volcanic eruptions farther south on the island. The incredible weight of basalt bore down on the softer, more pliable Jurassic rocks, causing them to crack and slip. The Trotternish ridge and its chaotic crags are the result of this huge landslide, and the geological upheaval is still ongoing today. The 2300m-long landslide that runs from the scarp on Meall na Suiramach (the peak above the Quiraing) down to Staffin Bay is the largest single slip in the British Isles. It is generally stable, but the road at Flodigarry still moves occasionally. It is under such conditions that pinnacles of rock have sheered off from the main cliff face and been squeezed and eroded into positions that seem to defy natural laws.

PLANNING

When to Walk

These walks can be completed at any time of the year, although experience of walking across slopes in winter conditions is recommended if there is snow on the ground. The most dangerous time to attempt all three routes is in mist and low cloud; the cliffs are precipitous and steep gullies frequently cut their way inland. Caution is needed at all times near the edge but especially in poor visibility, when navigation could be difficult.

What to Bring

Warm and waterproof clothing and plenty of food and water is a must for all of the walks described in this section. Although the Quiraing and The Storr routes are mainly on paths, strong boots are still advised to cope with the rockier sections.

Maps

Use OS Landranger 1:50,000 map No 23 *(North Skye)* for all of the walks on the Trotternish peninsula.

ACCESS TOWNS

Staffin & Around

Staffin is a compact group of white houses. The nearest post office is north of Staffin in Brogaig and the nearest bank is in Portree. There is Internet access at Colomba 1400 in the centre of Staffin.

Places to Stay & Eat On the southern edge of the village, ***Staffin Caravanning & Camping Site*** *(☎ 01470-562213)* is open from May to September and charges £7.50 per pitch.

Glenview Inn and Restaurant (☎ 01470-562248), 1.5mi south of Staffin in Culnaknock, is an attractive house maintained in traditional style and charges from £25 for B&B. There are also several B&Bs in Staffin itself – contact the TIC in Portree for a full listing. In the centre of Staffin, ***Colomba 1400***, a very modern sort of community centre, has excellent snacks and meals from 9am to 8pm Monday to Saturday, and 11am to 3pm on Sunday.

Also in Staffin, there is a small ***shop*** with a laundrette (open 9am to 5pm from Monday to Saturday). Another, even smaller, ***shop*** with a petrol pump can be found 1mi north along the A855 at Stenscholl.

Getting There & Away Highland Country Buses (☎ 01463-222244) has a service that runs around the Trotternish peninsula from Portree six times daily (except Sunday). All services pass through Staffin and Flodigarry, with half the services travelling around the peninsula in a clockwise direction and half travelling anticlockwise.

Flodigarry

Flodigarry is a quiet village strung out along the coast near the northern tip of the peninsula. The main draw for visitors is the hotel and hostel, next door to each other on the north side of the village. The village's most famous daughter is Flora MacDonald, who lived here from 1751 to 1759. A Scottish heroine, Flora helped the Young Pretender (Prince Charles) escape to Skye after his defeat at the battle of Culloden (1746). Her cottage is now part of the hotel.

Places to Stay & Eat Overlooking Staffin Bay, ***Dun Flodigarry Hostel*** *(☎ 01470-552212)* is a large building in a beautiful position. Staff are friendly and helpful and can provide photocopied maps marking various walking routes up to the Quiraing and around the coast. There is also a drying room, Internet access, a basic shop and the option of breakfast for £1.50. It costs £8 to stay in the hostel or £4 to camp.

The adjacent ***Flodigarry Country House Hotel*** *(☎ 01470-552203)* has many awards to recommend it, and charges from £55 for B&B, with a set dinner available for £32. The public bar offers food and snacks.

Getting There & Away See Getting There & Away for Staffin.

The Talisker Distillery

If you fancy a dram of the hard stuff to warm your cheeks after a blustery day on the hills you probably won't go far wrong with a taste of Talisker. Described as warming and 'outdoors' in style, Talisker is Skye's only malt whisky and has a very distinctive flavour. The distillery was built at Carbost in 1830 by the Macaskill brothers and saw numerous changes in ownership as its fortunes fluctuated over the decades. Even from an early stage Talisker was a sought-after malt: Robert Louis Stevenson described it in 1880 as 'the King o' drinks'. Today it is aged for 10 years before being bottled for sale, this being judged to be its optimum condition.

The flavour is peaty, a taste derived from the peat fires that are used to roast the barley and the peat-stained water of Carbost Burn, used to produce Talisker. Ten years in an oak cask, slowly infiltrated by the sharp sea-air, also gives the whisky a spicy finish that is evocative of the seashore. The Talisker Distillery (☎ 01478-640314) is open to the public from July to September, Saturday and weekdays, with guided tours costing £3.

The Storr

Duration	4–5 hours
Distance	5.5mi (9km)
Standard	medium
Start/Finish	Old Man of Storr parking area
Nearest Towns	Portree, Staffin
Public Transport	yes

Summary A beautiful route around one of Skye's iconic landmarks. Although there is a good deal of ascent and descent, the terrain is kind and there are picture-postcard views of the Old Man of Storr.

The tottering cliffs and pinnacles of The Storr (from the Norse *staur*, meaning 'stake') must be one of the most distinctive landscapes in Scotland, photographed countless times and a popular attraction. Many tourists are happy with a stroll around the Old Man of Storr but walkers will want to catch the airy views from the summit of The Storr (719m, 2358ft) itself. The walk is surprisingly undemanding, given the ascent involved; much of this has to do with the easy terrain and the good paths. Fit walkers will easily cover the route in half a day and could go on to walk the Quiraing in the afternoon (see The Quiraing walk description on page 294). The first half of this route is also followed by walkers traversing the Trotternish ridge (see page 293).

ISLE OF SKYE

PLANNING

Despite the relatively straightforward nature of this route, it must be remembered that it is a mountain walk and there is some very dangerous ground adjacent to the route. In low cloud and snow a walker could easily go straight over the main cliff edge! Bring plenty of water as there is not likely to be any running water on The Storr.

GETTING TO/FROM THE WALK

The walk starts from a prominent and busy parking area on the A855, 6.5mi north of Portree. Highland Country (☎ 01463-222244) operates buses daily along this road in both directions (except Sunday) and drivers will stop at this parking area on request. See Getting There & Away for Staffin on page 290.

THE WALK

From the A855 parking area follow a well-constructed path through the forest plantation, steadily gaining height. After 15 to 20 minutes you should reach the forest edge and be greeted by a close-up view of the **Old Man of Storr**, the prominent pinnacle set beneath the main cliffs. Follow a path up the grassy slopes to the right of the Old Man, gradually gaining the classic perspective of the pinnacle from a position slightly above it and to the north. Follow the path to a fence on a rocky spur. Cross the fence and continue on a well-defined path around to the west where a short, steep climb leads to the grassy bowl beneath the northern cliffs of The Storr. The path becomes fainter as it leads around the bowl and onto the broad, skyline ridge, where the views of Trotternish really begin to open out. From here a short climb south of 20 minutes should see you on **The Storr** (719m) summit.

The panoramic views extend across most of Skye. The long line of cliffs of the Trotternish ridge stretches northward to the Quiraing. You can also look south-west across the bleak moors of Sleat and south to the jagged profile of the Cuillin. To the east, across the waters of The Minch, the mainland mountain ranges of Torridon, Applecross, Glen Shiel and Knoydart stretch

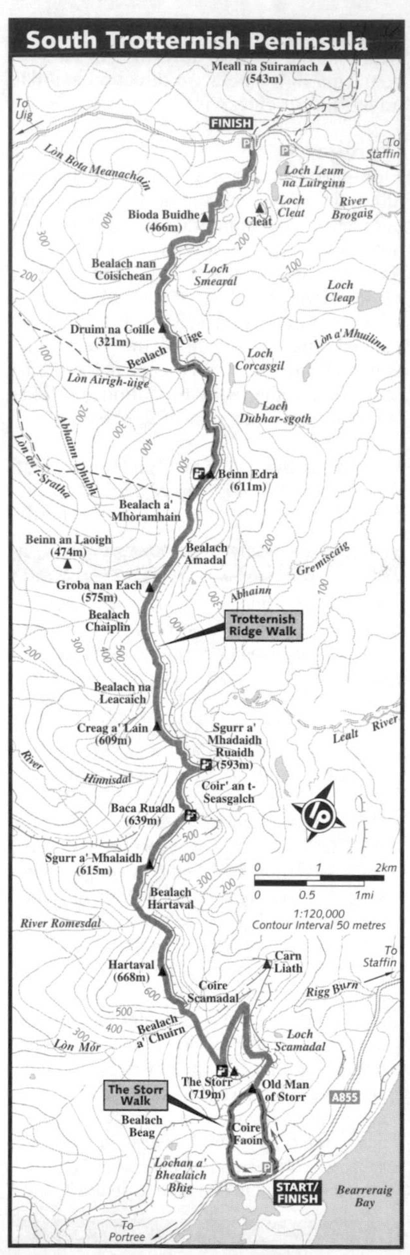

across the horizon. More immediately there is a dizzying view across the cliff edge to the Old Man of Storr and the pinnacles of Coire Faoin 300m below.

Descend from The Storr by the route of ascent. It is possible to descend a small gully to the north of the summit. This option is steep at the top and takes you directly into the grassy bowl described earlier. Once back in the vicinity of the Old Man you can explore the base of this pinnacle and follow various small paths to the many intricate hollows and pinnacles south of the Old Man. Eventually you can descend steeply to the western edge of the forest plantation and follow a well-defined path to the road. Turn left at the road and walk the short distance back to the start.

Trotternish Ridge

Duration	7–8 hours
Distance	14mi (22.5km)
Standard	medium-hard
Start	Old Man of Storr parking area
Finish	Loch Leum na Buirginn parking area (Staffin-Uig road)
Nearest Towns	Staffin, Flodigarry
Public Transport	yes

Summary A long ridge walk exploring some of the best landscapes along the Trotternish peninsula. Lots of ascent and descent but the views from the escarpments are well worth the effort.

The classic Trotternish ridge route begins in Portree and follows the line of the ridge all the way to Duntulm on the north coast of the peninsula. It is a challenging two-day backpacking route, covering 26mi (42km) and 2410m of ascent. The walk described here offers a single-day excursion along the best section of this longer route.

The day begins with an ascent of the highest peak on the ridge, The Storr. It then continues north along the cliff line to Hartaval, the second-highest peak in the area, and on over Beinn Edra, the northernmost 600m peak on Skye. The walk ends just short of the Quiraing, which is another section of the ridge that is well worth exploration and is described on page 294. There is no obvious path for much of the walk but the cliff line offers guidance.

Alternatives For those who prefer to end the walk on the western side rather than the eastern side of the peninsula, there is a path 3mi before the end of the walk that leads from the ridge down to Uig.

GETTING TO/FROM THE WALK

To get to the start, see Getting to/from the Walk for The Storr on page 292.

The route ends at a parking area near Loch Leum na Buirginn on the Staffin-Uig road. From here it is a 1.5mi walk east to the A855 at Brogaig, where you can pick up any of the Highland Country (☎ 01463-222244) buses that operate around the Trotternish peninsula.

THE WALK

See map page 292

Follow the directions given earlier for The Storr as far as the summit. From the summit cairn, cliffs of the Trotternish ridge can be seen stretching away to the north. Descend to the north-west down a steep slope to Bealach a' Chuirn, where the broad grassy back of Hartaval (668m) rises up ahead. The ascent is continuous and the upper slopes become slightly craggy before the rock-strewn summit is reached.

Descend along the cliff line to Bealach Hartaval. A short, steep climb now leads back up onto the ridge; follow up the right side of an animal pen and scramble up a short gully to the top. The terrain is now flatter as the rises of Sgurr a' Mhalaidh and Baca Ruadh are passed. The impressive tongue of cliff that is **Sgurr a' Mhadaidh Ruaidh** juts out from the ridge to the east; it is possible to walk to the very end of it for views back along the main cliffs.

The ridge now veers to the west and a descent, a climb and then another descent brings you to Bealach na Leacaich. There is an old stone wall and a newer wire fence on the bealach. Follow the fence away from the cliff edge for 100m to find a stile. Cross this and continue over three more tops before the more significant peak of **Beinn Edra** (611m) is reached. There are paths leading off west towards Uig from the bealachs just before and just after Beinn Edra; the more southerly route is preferable if you are heading in that direction because the ground to the north is more arduous.

North of Beinn Edra the terrain is difficult for around 2.5mi. The ground is boggy and covered by thick heather, and numerous peat hags need to be crossed. Keep close to the cliff edge for the easiest ground. The steep slope up to the summit plateau of Bioda Buidhe is also covered in thick tussock grass, but the thought that this is the last climb of the day is a consoling one. The Staffin-Uig road soon comes into view over the other side, and the pinnacles of the Quiraing can be clearly seen beyond that. Veer away from the cliff edge to avoid a crag on the descent, then return to the ridge to join a worn path that will guide you down to the parking area at the end of the route.

The Quiraing

Duration	4–5 hours
Distance	5.5mi (9km)
Standard	easy-medium
Start/Finish	Flodigarry
Nearest Towns	Flodigarry, Staffin
Public Transport	yes

Summary An exploration of the weird and wonderful pinnacle formations of the northern Trotternish ridge.

The pinnacles, cliffs and landslides of the Quiraing (pronounced kweer-yng and meaning 'pillared enclosure') are a compact and easily explored example of the features that make the Trotternish peninsula so unique. A network of generally easy paths gives access to the base of the escarpment and to the summit of Meall na Suiramach (543m, 1781ft). For those wanting the easiest of 'hill' walks, or for those with young children, this will be enough. However, a trip to the Quiraing would not really be complete without a visit to The Table, a flat plateau of sheep-cropped grass hidden among the pinnacles and cliffs. It is a tradition that on New Year's Day, local men come up to The Table to play shinty (a sort of rough hockey) – it's that flat! Half the challenge of reaching The Table is finding it. You can, however, look down on it from near the summit of Meall na Suiramach and get an impression of this special place, without needing to cover the steep and unstable ground that is required to actually set foot on it. Bring water with you as there are no major streams higher up on the hill.

GETTING TO/FROM THE WALK

The walk starts from a small parking area on the A855 about 900m south of Flodigarry hostel. Highland Country Buses (☎ 01463-222244) operates daily along this road in both directions (except Sunday) and drivers will stop at the parking area on request. See Getting There & Away for Staffin on page 290.

THE WALK

Follow the 4WD track that leads inland from the A855 just south of the parking area, and pass around the northern shores of Loch Langaig. The track turns into a wide grassy path that cuts through the heather and climbs gently, passing over a stile to skirt around Loch Hasco. The terrain becomes slightly steeper as you gain a rise just in front of the main cliff face. Several pinnacles can be seen to the right. Head up to the cliffs and take the main path to the left, proceeding along the base of the ramparts in a southerly direction.

Continue along this path for around 900m. The path then turns a corner to the right and an old wire fence is crossed. This is the sign that you are arriving at the **Quiraing** proper. The large lump of rock in front of you to the left is The Prison and the tall thin spire to the right is The Needle. There is a large cairn at the side of the path just below The Needle, marking the ascent to The Table. From your position in front of The Needle, the easiest way to The Table is to climb up the dirt and scree slope just to the left of the pinnacle. The slope is steep, loose and significantly more tricky than previous terrain. Climb past and around to the back of The Needle, keeping to the left to continue up to the top of a small but steep mud and grass ridge. You are now among a maze of towering outcrops and the atmosphere of the place begins to make itself felt.

Descend down the other side of the ridge, veer left and then right on the path, and you will be brought to the magical plateau of **The Table**. Rock stacks surround the hidden plateau and between towers the sea can be seen far below. The cliff that makes up the back wall of the enclave is the main escarpment of the Trotternish ridge, and the summit of Meall na Suiramach is only about 60m away above you. There is no way up the sheer rock walls, however, and the summit can only be reached via a wide circuit to the west.

When you have spent enough time wandering around The Table, retrace your steps to The Needle and rejoin the main path. Turn right and continue west, following the well-worn path along the hillside. The cliffs lose height and the path climbs up and over the shoulder of the escarpment, heading towards the large parking area on the Staffin-Uig road (the finish of the Trotternish Ridge route described, see page 294).

About 500m before the road is reached, an indistinct path leaves the main path and turns sharply to the right, beginning the climb up the grassy shoulder to Meall na Suiramach. Follow this path north, climbing steeply at first and then more gradually along to the cliff edge. Care is needed in mist because the sheer drop comes up quite suddenly after a section of contouring across gentler slopes. There are fine views over the pinnacles of the Quiraing and onto The Table, and the wider panorama encompasses the east coast, the mountains of the mainland, the Western Isles and the Trotternish ridge to the south.

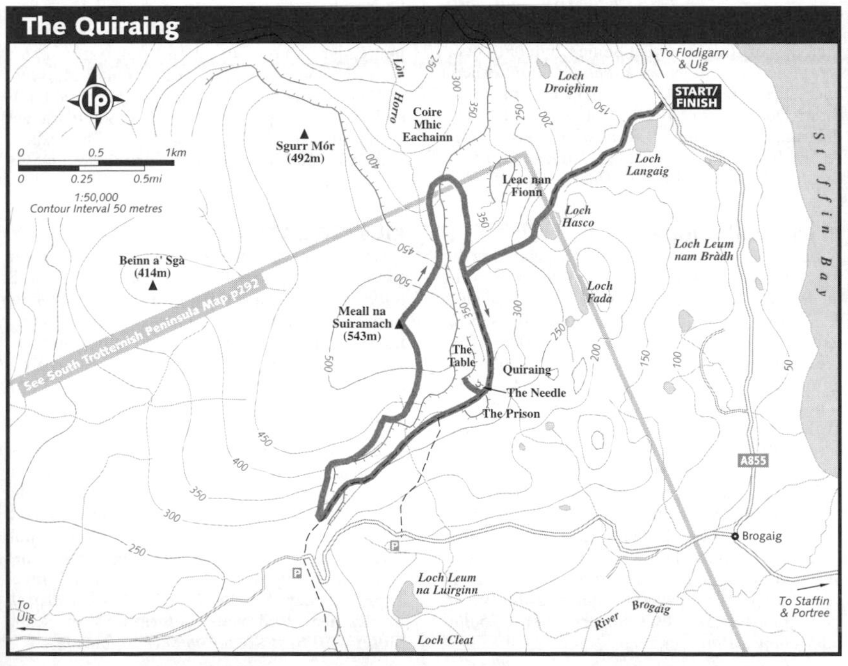

The Meall na Suiramach summit itself is flat and unspectacular, marked almost arbitrarily by a summit cairn. Continue carefully along the cliff edge, descending over the rocks of an escarpment and bearing off to the north-east. At a small hollow, a section of fencing on the cliff top marks the descent route. Cross over the wooden stile and follow the path as it veers right, descending easily into a basin below the main cliff face. Follow this path over a rise and around a shallow basin to rejoin the path that you climbed up on at the start of the walk. Turn left and retrace your steps down past the two lochs and back to the A855.

Other Walks

THE CUILLIN

Sgurr Alasdair

At 993m (3257ft), Sgurr Alasdair is the highest peak in the Black Cuillin and on Skye. Situated close to the south end of the Black Cuillin ridge it is quite easily accessed from Glenbrittle. The easiest ascent is via Coire Lagan, ascending and then descending the Great Stone Chute. For good scramblers and those with rock climbing experience, the round of Coire Lagan encompassing Sgurr Dearg, Sgurr Mhic Choinnich, Sgurr Alasdair and Sgurr Sgumain is one of the classic ridge scrambles in the British Isles. Consult Harvey's Superwalker 1:25,000 map *The Cuillin*.

Black Cuillin Ridge

A step up from the round of Coire Lagan (see the Sgurr Alasdair description above), the traverse of the Black Cuillin ridge is possibly one of the most aspired-to expeditions for walkers/climbers in Britain. The traverse involves over 4200m of ascent, 40 separate summits and unavoidable rock climbing to VD (Very Difficult – British grades). It begins from Glenbrittle, heads for Gars-bheinn at the south end of the ridge and then proceeds across all the intervening summits to Sgurr nan Gillean, before descending to Sligachan. Most parties start late in the evening, bivouacking for a few hours, before continuing for the whole of the next day. The route demands great fitness, route-finding skill and technical ability on rock. In winter conditions the route becomes one of the most demanding mountaineering routes in the British Isles. Consult Harvey's Superwalker 1:25,000 map *The Cuillin*.

Garbh-bheinn

Garbh-bheinn (806m, 2644ft) must be one of the most impressive overlooked mountains in Britain. It is part of the Bla Bheinn massif and is normally passed over in favour of Bla Bheinn itself. The rock is gabbro and the appearance and character of the mountain is all Black Cuillin. The circuit of Garbh-bheinn and Belig (702m) does not involve any real scrambling, but the ridges are fine and rocky giving tremendous views of the Black Cuillin. The route starts from the A87 about halfway between Broadford and Sligachan. Consult Harvey's Superwalker 1:25,000 map *The Cuillin*.

MACLEOD'S TABLES

On the peninsula of Duirinish in western Skye is a large and rugged expanse of wild and windswept moorland dominated by the unusual, flat-topped summits of Healabhal Mhor (MacLeod's Table North) and Healabhal Bheag (MacLeod's Table South). These twin tops are commonly referred to as MacLeod's Tables. Myth has it that the chief of the MacLeod clan once hosted a banquet on the summit of Healabhal Bheag in order to prove the superiority of his dining hall! Both tops can be visited on a 7mi (11km) circuit starting and finishing from a small stream about three-quarters of a mile north of Orbost on the road to Dunvegan. The route should take around 5½ hours to complete and involves 800m of ascent over some steep, rough ground. Wear good boots and take waterproofs. Consult OS Landranger 1:50,000 map No 23 *(North Skye)*. The walk is detailed in Ralph Storer's *50 Best Routes on Skye & Raasay*.

ISLE OF RAASAY

Raasay is the quiet island sandwiched between Skye and the mainland. The bulk of the island is undulating upland and forest, and a circuit taking in the best features can be made in around seven hours from the pier where the ferry docks near Inverarish. The circuit is 11mi (18km) and involves 570m of ascent to the top of Dún Caan (443m), from where there are excellent views of the Cuillin, Trotternish and the mainland ranges. There are also several options for shorter walks. There is a hostel, a camping site, a hotel and a small shop on the island. Caledonian MacBrayne (☎ 01475-650100) operates a ferry to the island from Sconser (near Sligachan). There are nine sailings daily (except Sunday) during summer and six in winter. Consult OS Landranger 1:50,000 map No 24 *(Raasay & Applecross)*. You'll also find walk descriptions in Ralph Storer's *50 Best Routes on Skye & Raasay*.

Wester Ross

For serious walkers Wester Ross is heaven. This is a remote and starkly beautiful highland area, with lonely glens and lochs, an intricate coastline of rocky headlands and white sand beaches, and some of the finest mountains in Scotland. The emptiness that is integral to this area's charms can make logistics difficult for walkers on short visits, but for those who have the time and inclination, the effort will be well rewarded. If you are lucky with the weather, the clear air will provide rich colours and great views from the ridges and summits. In poor conditions the remote nature of the area makes walking a much more serious proposition. Whatever the weather, the walking can be hard, so this is no place to begin learning mountain techniques. But if you are a fit, competent and well-equipped walker, Wester Ross will not disappoint.

Highlights

GRAEME CORNWALLIS

Dramatic, double-tiered Slioch (980m) – a Wester Ross landmark and walking mecca.

- Enjoying lofty scrambling manoeuvres on the exposed ridges of An Teallach and Liathach
- Crossing the remote and beautiful heart of The Great Wilderness and taking in the stunning scenery
- Exploring the Caledonian woodland of the Beinn Eighe National Nature Reserve
- Ascending the Horns of Beinn Alligin for panoramic views of the west coast of Scotland

CLIMATE

Wester Ross has a typically changeable coastal climate, with the prevailing winds blowing weather straight off the sea to the west. Near the coast, in particular, thick mist and rain can sweep in and settle over the area for days at a time, and often the weather comes in much faster then walkers can get off the mountain. Winds are often strong and many of these routes will be problematic if the wind is even moderate in the valleys – the pinnacles, gullies and steep flanks of the mountains compress the airflow and can make winds across the ridges twice as strong as forecast. There is no guarantee of good weather at any time, so you should allow extra days for sitting out poor conditions.

INFORMATION

Maps & Books

OS Travelmaster 1:250,000 map No 3 *(Western Scotland)* provides an excellent topographic overview of the region.

Walking books include *Best Walks in Wester Ross* by Richard Hallewell, *West Coast Walks: Knoydart, Skye & Wester Ross* by Pamela Clark and *Skye & the North West Highlands* by John Brooks & Neil Wilson, which describe a range of low-level and easy routes in the area. More challenging mountain walks are generally included in books covering a wider geographical area, such as the Scottish Mountaineering Club's *The Northwest Highlands*.

Information Sources

The Highlands of Scotland Tourist Board (☎ 01397-703781, W www.host.co.uk) is a good port of call for accommodation listings and planning information. On the Web try W www.scotland-info.co.uk/wester-ross.htm for a range of planning information and links. For details on local bus timetables use W www.celticfringe.org.uk/postbus.htm.

The mountain weather forecast for the western Highlands is available on ☎ 09068-500441 or fax 09060-100405.

The Highland Council publishes a set of four comprehensive transport guides to the region, including *North Highland & Orkney*, which covers the area in this chapter. The guides are most readily available from the local TICs in Ullapool (☎ 01854-612135), Gairloch (☎ 01445-712130) and Lochcarron (☎ 01520-722357).

In case of an emergency in the mountains of Wester Ross, the number to call for assistance is Dingwall police station on ☎ 01349-862444.

In terms of mountain safety, don't forget about the 'Let Someone Know Before You Go' form, available from W www.northern.police.uk.

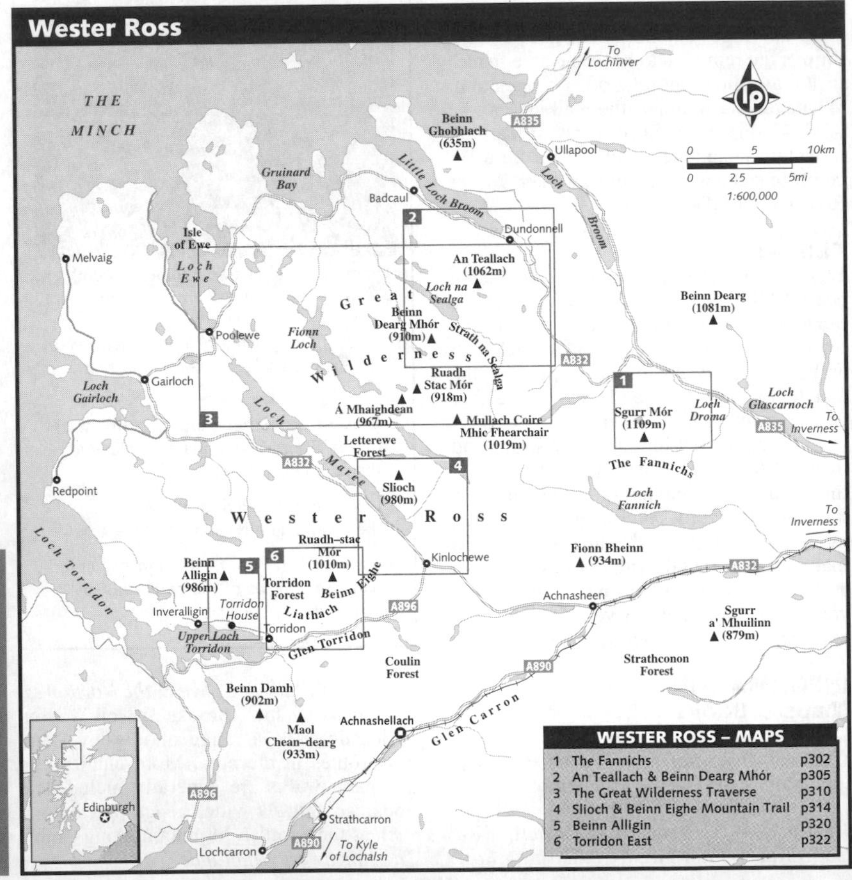

Scrambling

Between the world of walking and the world of rock climbing, there is a grey area of increasing exposure, increasing verticality and increasing adrenaline. Scrambling is the term used for sections of a route that require the significant use of hands for balance and/or upward movement. It may be a small rock-step on an otherwise easy ridge, it might be a knife-edge narrowing on a ridge or, at the extreme end, it could be several hundred feet of quite steep rock. Essentially, scrambling ends where technical rock climbing begins, although most walkers may feel frightened and insecure long before this point. Mostly it depends on your head for heights, and previous climbing experience helps a great deal. Most scramblers go without ropes but some parties will benefit from the reassurance offered by a rope on harder moves. Bear in mind though, there is a skill in using a rope correctly.

A few routes in this book, and in particular this chapter, necessarily involve some scrambling: Liathach and An Teallach; Aonach Eagach (Lochaber); and routes on Skye's Black Cuillin. For an introduction to scrambling try the Ring of Steall walk, or the Beinn Alligin horseshoe. Any route will be that much harder if the rock is wet or the wind is strong. Pick dry, calm days for scrambles and enjoy the friction. Hiring a guide might also be a good introduction, especially if you know nothing about rope work on steep ground. For more information, *Classic Mountain Scrambles in Scotland* by Andrew Dempster is worth a look.

Guided Walks

Celtic Horizons (☎ 01854-612429) offers private guided walks in the mountains of The Great Wilderness and Inverpolly, and also runs outdoor skills courses and activity holidays.

GATEWAYS

Ullapool

Ullapool is a picturesque fishing town situated on Loch Broom. It is the main departure point for ferries going to the Western Isles and has a relaxed atmosphere. Ullapool is the largest town in Wester Ross and, as such, has all the necessary facilities for walkers.

Information The TIC (☎ 01854-612135, ⓔ ullapool@host.co.uk), on Argyle St, is open daily from May to September. The town's only bank is on Ladysmith St and the post office is on West Argyle St. There is public Internet access at the West House Hostel (see Places to Stay & Eat). Mountain Man Supplies, opposite the post office, has a good selection of outdoor gear and an outside board where mountain weather forecasts are posted. The Ullapool Bookshop, opposite The Seaforth Inn, also has a large range of walking books and maps.

Places to Stay & Eat Homely ***West House Hostel*** *(☎ 01854-613126)*, West Argyle St, has excellent facilities and charges £10 for a dorm bed. A separate building a couple of streets away offers double rooms with televisions and coffee making facilities for £12.50 per person, although you have to go to the main hostel for kitchen facilities.

On the harbour front, ***Ullapool SYHA Hostel*** *(☎ 01854-612254)*, Shore St, costs £9.25. ***Broomfield Holiday Park*** *(☎ 01854-612020)*, Garve Rd, reaches down to the sea and costs £5 for a backpacker and tent, with cars costing £3 extra.

There are numerous cafes, pubs and restaurants in the town. ***The Seaforth Inn***, Quay St, is opposite the pier. It is a lively,

Warning

All the routes in this chapter are described for summer. In Scotland that means May to September, although weather conditions can be bad at any time of the year. Many of the walks described are of a serious nature, and snow and ice will turn them into graded mountaineering routes. They should only be attempted in winter conditions by walkers with mountaineering experience.

central place with an excellent bar-food menu and live music a couple of nights a week during summer. There is also a good ***chip shop*** next door. For breakfast or lunch, the ***cafe*** upstairs at Mountain Man Supplies is hard to beat.

There are several grocery stores and a large ***Safeway*** supermarket at the top of the town, to the north of Seaforth Rd.

Getting There & Away Scottish Citylink (☎ 0870-550 5050) and Rapson's Coaches (☎ 01463-222244) both operate two or three services daily (not Sunday) in each direction between Ullapool and Inverness, 1½ hours away. Inverness is on the main bus and train networks, and there are frequent connections between it and most other major Scottish towns.

Kinlochewe

Kinlochewe is a compact village situated on a junction of roads that give access to the mountains of southern Wester Ross. It has a small but well-stocked outdoor shop (beside the post office in a wooden shed) that is not open all the time. The owners (☎ 01445-760234) will open on request.

Places to Stay & Eat In the village centre, ***Kinlochewe Hotel*** *(☎ 01445-760253)* charges from £22.50 for B&B. It has basic bunkhouse accommodation for £8, a restaurant and bar meals from £6. The very basic ***Beinn Eighe Campsite*** is situated 1.5mi north of the village along the A832 and a tent pitch costs £3.

There is also a variety of B&B and self-catering accommodation, including ***Cromasaig B&B*** *(☎ 01445-760234)* and central ***Kinlochewe Mountain Chalets*** *(☎ 01445-760334)*. The latter has wooden cabins that sleep four for £145/£225 per week in the winter/summer and offers individual accommodation for £10 per night whenever there are cabins available.

The village has a ***shop*** and post office (open daily). The ***cafe*** attached to the shop offers mediocre snacks and meals during the day. There is also a petrol station with another ***shop***.

Getting There & Away Westerbus (☎ 01445-712255) has a service between Gairloch and Inverness via Kinlochewe. It runs on Tuesday, Thursday and Friday, leaving Kinlochewe post office at 9.05am and returning from Inverness at 5.05pm.

The nearest train station is at Achnasheen, 12mi to the east. The station is on the Kyle of Lochalsh–Inverness line, with four ScotRail (☎ 0845-755 0033) trains passing in each direction from Monday to Saturday and two on Sunday. From Achnasheen there is a daily (except Sunday) postbus (☎ 01246-546329) service to and from Kinlochewe, which leaves Kinlochewe post office at 11.10am and returns from Achnasheen post office at 12.10pm. On Tuesday, Thursday and Friday the Gairloch-Inverness Westerbus service also stops at Achnasheen.

If you're coming from Ullapool on a Tuesday, Thursday or Friday, you can take the bus to Garve on the Ullapool-Inverness route (see Getting There & Away for Ullapool) and then connect with the Westerbus Inverness-Gairloch service in Garve. On all other days (except Sunday) it is necessary to take the bus from Ullapool to Garve, the train from Garve to Achnasheen and then the postbus from Achnasheen to Kinlochewe. This makes for a complicated route but it is still possible to complete the journey in one day in both directions.

The Fannichs

Duration	7–8 hours
Distance	10.5mi (17km)
Standard	medium-hard
Start/Finish	Parking area on the A835, 2.5mi east of Braemore Junction
Nearest Town	Ullapool
Public Transport	yes

Summary A mountain circuit on the highest peak in Wester Ross, involving few technical difficulties and offering great views.

This circuit explores a fine mountain loch and the three Munro summits that surround it. The Fannichs is a compact mountain range with no less than nine of the summits achieving Munro status. The shapely peak of Sgurr Mór (1110m, 3641ft) is the highest in this chapter but receives a lot less attention than the jagged mountains of Torridon and The Great Wilderness to the west. The Fannichs have been described in many guidebooks as 'rounded', but they have some fine corries and high buttresses, which add to the overall feeling of airiness and space.

Alternatives Walkers have the option of modifying this route to take in extra summits such as Sgurr nan Clach Geala (1093m, 3585ft), or cutting out the high ground completely by simply visiting Loch a' Mhadaidh and returning on the stalkers' path. This second option gives a scenic walk of three to four hours and an easy-medium grade. The presence of a rough footpath along the summits will make summer navigation in poor visibility quite straightforward, but solid map reading skills are still necessary.

PLANNING

When to Walk

This walk is accessible throughout the summer season. At other times of the year the névé on the slopes below Meall a' Chrasgaidh may be tricky until late in the spring and large cornices can form on the cliff edge south-west of Sgurr Mór.

Stalking The area covered by this walk is in the Loch Luichart Estate (☎ 01997-414242). The main time for stalking on estate ground is from mid-August to 21 October. Contact the estate office for route advice if walking during this period.

Maps

Use OS Pathfinder 1:25,000 map No 120 *(An Teallach & Dundonnell)*.

GETTING TO/FROM THE WALK

The walk starts at a small, unmarked parking area on the A835, 12.5mi south-east of Ullapool and 2.5mi east of Braemore Junction. When approaching from that direction you will pass a conspicuous parking area on the right, east of the junction. About 0.75mi farther on, a track leaves the road on the left and there is room to park several cars.

Buses on the main Ullapool-Inverness route use the A835 and pass by the start/finish point for the walk. Contact bus operators to discuss possible drop-off and collection (see Getting There & Away for Ullapool on page 300).

THE WALK

From the parking area walk west along the road for 100m to where you can see a small building in the field to the south. Strike out across rough ground, crossing the Abhainn Droma to reach the north-east corner of that field. Although the OS 1:50,000 map shows the stalkers' path beginning from the road, it does not form properly until here. Pick up the path and cross the Allt a' Mhadaidh on a wooden bridge before beginning to climb gently around the base of Meall Breac, with the river running through a small gorge below. Twenty minutes from the start the path joins a 4WD track (the junction is marked with a small cairn), which is followed for the next mile to where it ends just above the Allt a' Mhadaidh. Again the OS map errs by showing this section as a path.

A good path continues from where the track finishes and descends across the stream before climbing past a cairn and onto gentle slopes. After 15 minutes the path swings to the west and crosses the Allt a' Mhadaidh. The terrain becomes much rougher as you climb more steeply along the north bank of the stream, reaching the shores of **Loch a' Mhadaidh** after 20 minutes. The lake shore is a good spot for a break if the midges aren't out.

Now without a proper path, follow the lake shore around to the north for a short distance and then climb diagonally across rough ground towards the north-east spur of Meall a' Chrasgaidh. Once on the spur you should be able to pick up a small path that runs along a ramp beneath the crags and outcrops of Meall a' Chrasgaidh, giving easy access to the broad, grassy col beyond. If you want to bag the summit of Meall a'

The Fannichs

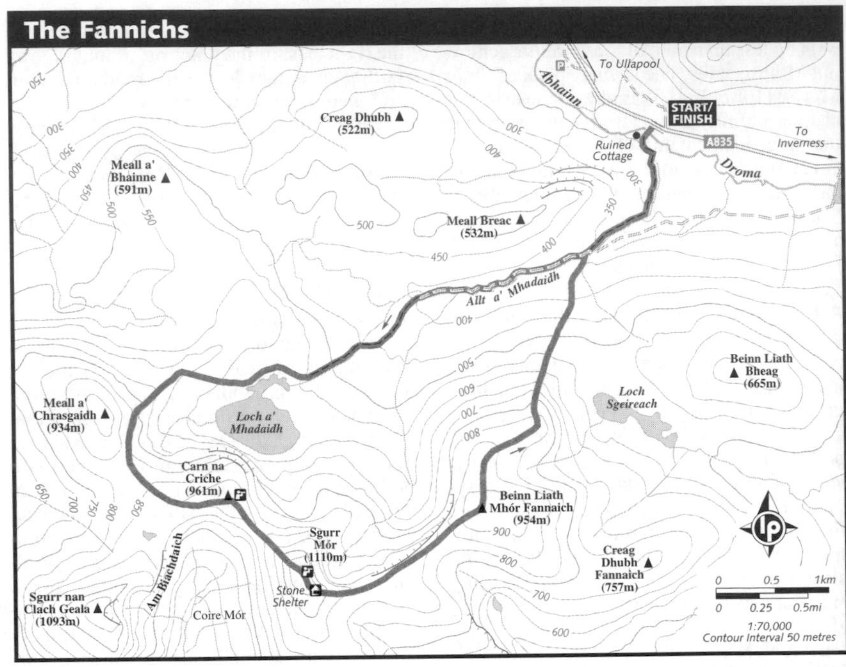

Chrasgaidh (934m), simply continue along the north-east spur, climbing steeply up through outcrops, adding an extra 45 minutes to the route. Meanwhile, from the col, there is also the option of heading south past a lochan and up the lovely sweeping ridge to Sgurr nan Clach Geala, which will add an hour to the route.

Back on the col a path climbs steadily along a broad ridge to the small summit cairn of **Carn na Criche** (961m), roughly 1½ hours from the shores of Loch a' Mhadaidh. The views from the summit are stunning, encompassing the wild ranges of Torridon and The Great Wilderness to the west, and the distant ranges around Glen Affric and Loch Mulladoch to the south. To the north the great bulk and stony wastes of Beinn Dearg rise above a cluster of ridges. Nearer at hand, Sgurr nan Clach Geala shows off the wonderful buttresses of its east face, in particular the clean sweep of rock of Am Biachdaich. The summit of Sgurr Mór looks very close, although the ridge to the summit is not as steep as it looks.

Descend gently from Carn na Criche and immediately begin the steady climb of 210m to the top of **Sgurr Mór**, from where views open out across the eastern Fannichs. The top is marked with a substantial cairn. From here descend steeply around the cliff line to reach a broad ridge, which curves around to Beinn Liath Mhór Fannaich. A good path exists, beginning at a small stone shelter and cutting around the south side of a small rise before climbing around the eastern slopes of Beinn Liath Mhór Fannaich, just below the summit. Continue around onto the broad northern shoulder from where you can easily turn back south and scramble over the boulder field to the summit of **Beinn Liath Mhór Fannaich** (954m).

The descent back to the Allt a' Mhadaidh and the 4WD track is quite strenuous. The easiest option is probably to continue along the gentle northern shoulder and then turn to the north-east for a while before dropping off to the north on steep slopes. The descent is more gentle here, but there are still awkward boulders and deep heather to negotiate before you reach the 4WD track just above the junction with the stalkers' path. The descent to here from the summit of Beinn Liath Mhór Fannaich should take about one hour. Retrace the outward journey to reach the main road.

An Teallach

Duration	7½–8½ hours
Distance	11.5mi (18.5km)
Standard	hard
Start/Finish	Corrie Hallie
Nearest Town	Dundonnell
Public Transport	yes

Summary A long, tough mountain walk involving a scramble along an airy, pinnacled ridge. An impressive and challenging route for experienced hillwalkers only.

The jagged ridgeline and rock pinnacles of An Teallach are a landmark of Wester Ross and the mountain is a true classic of Scottish walking. It is also one of the country's more serious propositions and negotiating the pinnacles involves some scrambling along a very exposed ridge. Several walkers have fallen to their deaths from the ridge and it is, undoubtedly, a mountain for experienced walkers. However, if you are up to the challenge that it presents, you will be justly rewarded by one of the finest days that it is possible to have in the Scottish 'hills'. The walk also makes for a strenuous day out, with a total ascent of 1370m.

An Teallach (pronounced an chelluck) means 'the forge', a name which bears no relation to its shape but comes from the mountain's red, Torridonian sandstone, which glows like a smithy's fire when lit by the setting sun. This sandstone is also a scrambler's delight, offering plenty of friction. The most difficult part of the ridge is the notorious 10m-high 'bad step', a very steep and committing section. At the same time, it is possible to avoid almost all the scrambling if desired. Paths lead around the base of the pinnacles, and it is basically possible to chose if, and when, you wish to venture onto the rocky ridge itself. Even by taking the most cautious paths, however, it is not possible to complete the walk without crossing some steep and exposed ground.

The route described here makes a circuit of the ridge, although it is also possible to descend to the village of Dundonnell (see Alternative Finish on page 306). The traverse is described in a clockwise direction, which means scrambling up, rather than down, the most difficult parts of the ridge. The popularity of the mountain means that extensive paths have formed on the high ground making navigation in mist (but not snow) relatively straightforward.

Sale of An Teallach

Ownership of the 2350ha Eilean Daroch Estate, which contains most of An Teallach, changed hands in late 2000 for a cool £1.7 million. It is thought that the good access, which the public has traditionally enjoyed, will not be affected. It was hoped that the John Muir Trust could have made a bid, but the organisation was already too far stretched by the Ben Nevis purchase (see the boxed text 'John Muir Trust' on page 197).

PLANNING

When to Walk

The ridge is narrow and exposed, so best tackled in fine, calm weather. Strong winds, wet rock and slippery ground make the route a much less secure proposition.

Stalking An Teallach is part of the Eilean Daroch Estate and stalking has traditionally taken place in the area between mid-August and mid-October.

With the sale of the estate, the future of stalking activity is uncertain. The best advice is to check the updated situation with the Mountaineering Council of Scotland (☎ 01738-638227) before walking at any time near the traditional season.

What to Bring
There is little water on the ridge so bring plenty with you. A short walking rope (and knowledge of how to use it properly) could offer extra security. You will also be grateful for boots that offer as much friction as possible. The weather on the mountain is notoriously changeable, so bring clothes in anticipation of all weather conditions.

Maps
OS Landranger 1:50,000 map No 19 *(Gairloch & Ullapool, Loch Maree)* has sufficient detail for navigation.

NEAREST TOWN
Dundonnell & Around
Dundonnell is a small village, and most accommodation and facilities are spread between it and neighbouring villages.

Places to Stay & Eat The ***Dundonnell Hotel*** *(☎ 01854-633204)* has rooms from £50 per person; there is also a restaurant and a bar with good food from £5. ***Sàil Mhór Croft Hostel*** *(☎ 01854-633244)* is 2mi west of Dundonnell in Camusnagaul, on the side of the A832. It is family-run and oriented towards walkers (the owners are very knowledgeable about the surrounding mountains), and charges £8.50 for a dorm bed. Cooked breakfasts are available for £3.50 and evening meals for £4 to £5.

Northern Lights Campsite, 3mi farther on at Badcaul, is basic and not very flat, and charges £4 per pitch plus £1 per person.

In Dundonnell there is a petrol station with a small ***shop*** (open seven days), opposite the hotel, but the larger shop and post office at ***Dundonnell Stores*** are actually 5.5mi west at Durnamuck on a side road off the A832. The stores are open Monday to Saturday.

Getting There & Away Dundonnell is one of the stops on the Ullapool-Gairloch and Inverness-Gairloch services operated by Westerbus (☎ 01445-712255). The service to Ullapool operates on Thursday only, leaving Dundonnell at 10.05am and returning from Ullapool at 1.15pm. The service to Inverness runs on Monday, Wednesday and Saturday, departing from Dundonnell at 9am and returning from Inverness at 5.05pm. The scheduled stop is outside the Dundonnell Hotel, but the driver will drop off and pick up farther along the road if requested.

GETTING TO/FROM THE WALK
Corrie Hallie parking area is 2mi south of Dundonnell village beside the A832. The bus services mentioned in Getting There & Away for Dundonnell will drop you off, if arranged in advance with the driver.

THE WALK
See map page 305

From Corrie Hallie cross the road and take the vehicle track signposted to Kinlochewe. Pass through a gate and follow the track up through a grove of silver birch. The track fords a stream and there is a wooden footbridge if water levels are high. The ground becomes steeper, the stream forms into a series of picturesque waterfalls and the track zigzags up the hill beside it. The top of this climb is marked by a cairn, and views of The Great Wilderness open out in front of you.

About 100m after the cairn, two smaller cairns mark a path to the right. This path is well-worn and heads towards the bothy at Shenavall. After 0.75mi or so it crosses a hollow, and here the most direct route up An Teallach leaves the established path and heads off east over open ground. Make for Lochan na Bradhan, just out of sight over the top of the grass and slabs. Walk around the loch, then head straight up the shoulder of Sàil Liath. The scree can be avoided by following a grassy slope towards the north of the shoulder. This route is steep and slippery in wet conditions, and a slightly more gradual line can be taken farther to the south if necessary.

Join the ridge and turn north-west, following the rocky slope up to the **Sàil Liath** (954m) summit cairn. From the top there is a wonderful panorama over Beinn Dearg Mhór and The Great Wilderness, as well as an excellent perspective of An Teallach with Loch Toll an Lochain set far below the impressive amphitheatre of buttresses. A path worn by passing feet marks the route along the ridge from here. Descend to the west and the ridge is immediately steep, narrow and exposed; a taste of things to come. Drop down to a narrow gap, with an excellent view over the length of Loch na Sealga to the west, climb to a minor peak and then descend once more into Cadha Gobhlach, a pass from where it is possible to descend very steeply down to the beautiful Loch Toll an Lochain. This path offers an escape route off the ridge if needed.

Another steep ascent is made to the start of the difficulties on the ridge. A wall of slabs blocks progress directly along the main ridge, but a path skirts around to the left to bypass all of the difficulties between here and Sgurr Fiòna. For those happy to scramble, the first slabs are best taken slightly around the corner to the left, leaving you on a ledge beneath the 'bad step'. Any progress back to the right along the true ridge line is barred by a very steep and intimidating rock step. The easiest route lies straight up across more slabs and rock steps, which would be very tricky to descend. Once past this an easy scramble places you on top of the first of the **Corrag**

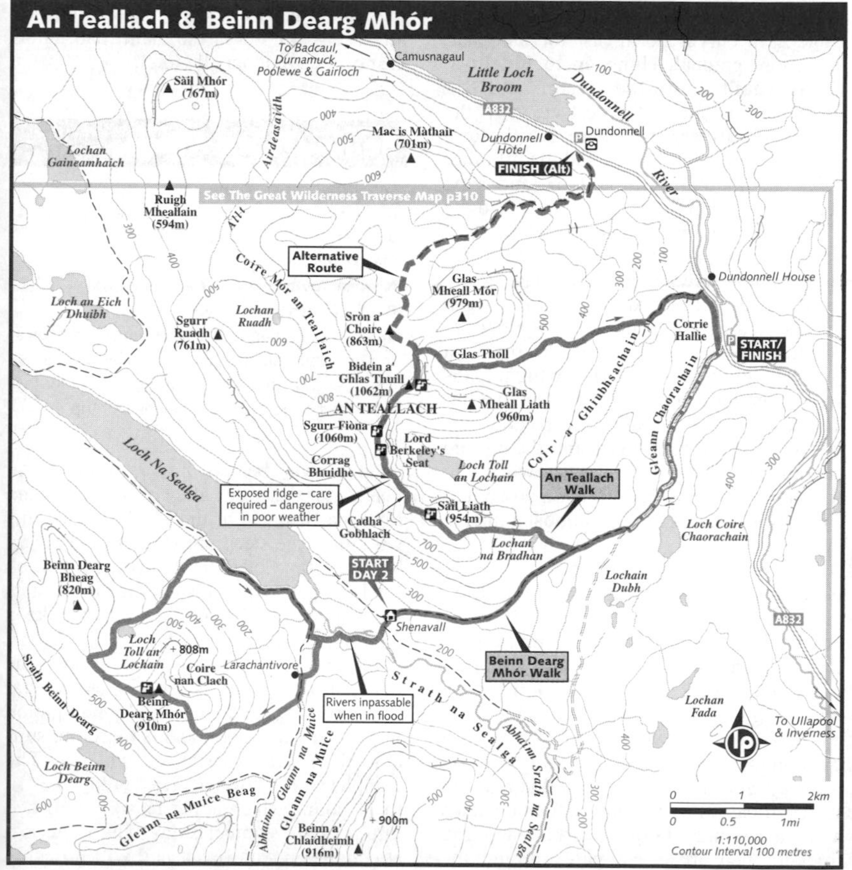

Bhuidhe pinnacles. From here to Sgurr Fiòna, narrow paths on the left bypass all of the difficulties, but it is relatively easy to scramble up each of the pinnacles for views back over into Coire Toll an Lochain. The last pinnacle is the vertiginous and overhanging prow known as Lord Berkeley's Seat, again passed innocuously on the left. You should allow at least an hour for the traverse from Corrag Bhuidhe to Lord Berkeley's Seat.

The ground becomes slightly easier with the final ascent to the cairned summit of Sgurr Fiòna. From here the path descends over easier ground, although the terrain underfoot is still loose and steep. Keep to the ridge as it curves north-east for the final, and more gradual, climb up to **Bidein a' Ghlas Thuill**. From the summit and trig point there is one of the best views of the circuit; on a clear day all of the Western Isles are visible out to sea and, on all other sides, an incredible mountain landscape seems to go on indefinitely. This is also the classic viewpoint for the ridge just traversed, and a fine place to take a break and reflect on the excitement of the day.

Descend northward over more steep ground to a col. Immediately at the bottom of the descent take a path to the east (marked by a small cairn), which leads steeply down a gully to the glen of Glas Tholl. The top of the path is steep and loose, but the gradient soon eases and the ground becomes solid. Steps have been worn into the short grass and they lead you down into a beautiful, secluded valley almost alpine in character.

Networks of subterranean streams gurgle beneath you and eventually join up to form the beginnings of a larger burn. Follow the left bank of the burn downhill and a path that is intermittent at first soon becomes continuous. Stick close to the burn and it will bring you all the way down to the road, passing through several small gorges and over numerous picturesque waterfalls on the way. Shortly before the road is reached the path passes over some sandstone slabs and then tunnels through a rhododendron thicket. There are several paths through the dense bushes; take care to follow the wooden stakes to arrive at the road. Turn right along the road and, after about 600m, arrive at Corrie Hallie car park.

Alternative Finish: Dundonnell

2–2½ hours, 5mi (8km)

If you intend to end the day at Dundonnell, an alternative route can bring you directly down to the village. Follow the walk description as far as the summit of Bidein a' Ghlas Thuill then continue northward, passing over a minor peak before veering northwest to the summit of Sròn a' Choire. Descend the ridge to the north and join a path about halfway down that will eventually bring you out at the main road, 300m east of the Dundonnell Hotel.

Beinn Dearg Mhór

Duration	2 days
Distance	16mi (25.5km)
Standard	medium-hard
Start/Finish	Corrie Hallie
Nearest Town	Dundonnell
Public Transport	yes

Summary A long and challenging circuit of a remote and spectacular peak; river crossings, steep slopes and a night at Shenavall Bothy make this a real Highland wilderness trip.

Hidden away behind the vast bulk of An Teallach is the wide valley of Shenavall and Loch na Sealga. On the south side of this wild glen, the steep crown of Beinn Dearg Mhór (910m, 2985ft) rises resplendent. A finely chiselled massif standing tall from its flat surrounds, the mountain rises like a beacon to walkers.

Its ascent is a challenge that involves the negotiation of some steep slopes, several river crossings and some tricky navigation if the weather is poor, and is therefore suitable for more experienced walkers. The complete circuit from Corrie Hallie takes 10 to 11 hours, which could feasibly be fitted into a single summer's day. The route is a strenuous one, however, and will probably be better appreciated split over two days with night at Shenavall Bothy.

PLANNING

When to Walk

The route involves the crossing and re-crossing of two rivers that are impassable in high water, so avoid walking during or after heavy rain. Navigation on the summit ridge can also be difficult in adverse weather conditions. The steep slopes of Beinn Dearg Mhór itself make this route very serious in winter conditions.

Stalking The route passes through the Eilean Daroch Estate – see Stalking on page 303 for details.

What to Bring

Bring all the normal gear for a two-day mountain walk, including all equipment and food. A spare pair of socks might also be appreciated after the two river crossings.

Maps

Use OS Landranger 1:50,000 map No 19 *(Gairloch & Ullapool, Loch Maree)*. Note that Beinn Dearg Mhór has been misspelt Beinn Dearg Mór on this map.

NEAREST TOWN

Dundonnell

For details of facilities and accommodation in Dundonnell, see Nearest Town under An Teallach on page 304.

GETTING TO/FROM THE WALK

See Getting to/from the Walk under An Teallach on page 304.

THE WALK

See map page 305

Day 1: Corrie Hallie to Shenavall

2 hours, 4mi (6.5km)

From Corrie Hallie cross the road and take the vehicle track signposted to Kinlochewe. Pass through a gate and follow the track up through a grove of silver birch trees. The track fords a stream, and there is a wooden footbridge if water levels are high. The ground becomes steeper, the stream forms into a series of picturesque waterfalls, and the track zigzags up the hill beside it. The top of the climb is marked by a cairn and views of The Great Wilderness.

About 100m after the cairn, two smaller cairns mark a path to the right. This path is well-worn, although after about 0.75mi it passes the shoulder of Sàil Liath and the ground becomes wetter and rougher. Pick your way alongside a stream as the path descends through a narrow valley to reach Shenavall and the bothy.

Shenavall Bothy is maintained by the Mountain Bothies Association and is open and free for all mountain users. It is simply a shell of an old stone house and has no facilities except a fireplace. It can be used as an alternative to camping, although all camping gear (sleeping mats/stove etc) is still necessary. If you do stay in the bothy (or camp near it), be sure to walk well upstream before collecting water – the bothy sees fairly heavy use and there are no toilet facilities, so the water nearby is unfit for consumption.

Day 2: Shenavall to Corrie Hallie via Beinn Dearg Mhór

8 hours, 12mi (19km)

The first challenge is to cross the two rivers in the valley that snake towards Loch na Sealga. If the rivers are in spate crossing will be impossible, but generally the water is calf- to knee-deep in the shallow sections and wading is cold but not difficult.

Leave Shenavall and cross the Abhainn Srath na Sealga just to the south-west of the bothy. Stick to the river bank on the other side to avoid the worst of some very wet ground between the two rivers, then cross the bog to the Abhainn Gleann na Muice. Follow this river's bank south and cross in front of the private Larachantivore cottage. Once on the western bank of the Abhainn Gleann na Muice, join a path that passes in front of the cottage and follows the river upstream. Follow this path for a few hundred metres until the steep eastern flanks of Beinn Dearg Mhór are in view. Leave the path and cross rough ground to reach the foot of the slopes north of the prominent gully and stone chute. Climb steeply towards the chute and follow it to where it is bounded on the left by some small crags. Cross the chute and traverse left above the crags, ascending gradually across boulder fields and heather to reach easier ground at the lip of a corrie. This should take about 1½ to two hours from Larachantivore cottage. The route to the summit is now quite apparent and straightforward, but a promontory on the summit ridge hides the top. Immediately in front of you is an impressive cleft, where a few hardy ash trees grow from ledges in the rock walls.

Climb steadily north-west to reach the summit ridge in 20 to 30 minutes. The ground falls away abruptly here, with buttresses, gullies and overhanging prows of rock dropping away for 300m into the corrie below. The pinnacled ridge of An Teallach stands framed beyond Loch na Sealga. You can turn right here and follow the ridge out to the east summit (15 minutes return). From where you reach the ridge, a short, steep climb brings you to the summit of **Beinn Dearg Mhór** (910m). An Teallach dominates the views to the north while to the south the complex ridges, valleys and summits of The Great Wilderness hold the eye.

Walk south from the summit for a couple of hundred metres and pick up an eroded path that zigzags north-west down the steep, stony slope towards the bealach between Beinn Dearg Mhór and Beinn Dearg Beag. Below and to the right the waters of Loch Toll an Lochain are your next goal, but don't be tempted to descend directly. It is easier to continue along the bealach almost to the beginning of the ascent to Beinn Dearg Beag and then follow grassy slopes north-east down to the lake shore.

Skirt around the western shores of the lochan and descend gently at first and then more steeply along the west bank of the burn that drains it. Cross over the burn where the descent begins to ease, and then cut across rough ground to pick up a good path on the shores of Loch Sealga. Follow this path south-east until it reaches Gleann na Muice, where you should be able to ford the waters without walking too far upstream. Cross the Strath na Sealga in front of Shenavall Bothy and then follow the path out to Corrie Hallie.

The Great Wilderness Traverse

Duration	2 days
Distance	23mi (37km)
Standard	medium
Start	Corrie Hallie
Finish	Poolewe
Nearest Towns	Dundonnell, Poolewe
Public Transport	yes

Summary A long, scenic low-level route crossing the beautiful and isolated heart of The Great Wilderness.

The Great Wilderness is a particularly remote area of the western Highlands, stretching from Little Loch Broom in the north to Loch Maree in the south, and from the Fannichs in the east to the west coast village of Poolewe. The area covers about 180 sq mi. For visitors from countries where wilderness areas are a bit larger, this title may seem exaggerated but, by British standards, this is wilderness indeed.

The landscape is mountainous, with some fine, austere peaks. Between the mountains there are lochs of all shapes and sizes, rivers and waterfalls, peat bogs and grassy valleys. The one thing that the landscape lacks is trees, so it may seem a bit strange when you see Fisherfield Forest, Letterewe Forest and Dundonnell Forest on the map. Forest, as used here, means hunting ground and these boundaries delineate different estates.

The route itself follows well-trodden, although unmarked, paths for its entirety. It involves one ascent of 500m to a mountain plateau that is roughly half the height of the major peaks surrounding it. It is a long route but, for the second half, the terrain is largely flat and the going is quick. While it could conceivably fit into one long summer's day, it is well worth taking your time and splitting the route over two days, both for the sake of your leg muscles and to fully appreciate the beauty and atmosphere of your surroundings. There are two shelters for the use of walkers along the route: the bothy at Shenavall and a rough, shed-type building at Carnmore. Alternatively, it is possible to camp anywhere along the route (see the boxed text 'Wild Camping and the Letterewe Estate' on page 312). It can be walked in either direction, although it is best walked as described so the river crossings can be made early on.

Alternatives A variant of the route is the Dundonnell-Kinlochewe traverse, which follows the same paths for half the distance and then branches southward at Fionn Loch, to eventually join the path along Loch Maree that is used for access to Slioch (see the Slioch route description on page 313). The trail is clearly marked on the OS map. The total distance covered is roughly the same as the route described here, although a second ascent and descent of around 500m is necessary.

PLANNING

When to Walk

The route involves the crossing of two rivers that are impassable in high water, so avoid walking during or after heavy rain. Although there aren't any major navigation problems, it is worth waiting for good weather; almost all of the joy of the route is in the stunning scenery and it would be a shame not to be able to see any of it! As this is a low-level route, it has a longer season than the more difficult mountain ascents in the area. It makes for a beautiful winter walk although the harshness of winter weather, short daylight hours and navigating when paths are obliterated by snow makes it a much more serious proposition.

Stalking The route passes through the Letterewe Estate (☎ 01445-760207). The main time for stalking on the estate is weekdays between 15 September and 15 November. Walkers are asked to contact the estate for route advice during this period. The route also passes through the Eilean Daroch Estate – see Stalking on page 303 for details.

What to Bring

Bring all the normal gear for a two-day mountain walk, including all equipment and food. A spare pair of socks might also be appreciated after the two river crossings.

Maps

Use OS Landranger 1:50,000 map No 19 *(Gairloch & Ullapool, Loch Maree)*.

NEAREST TOWNS

Dundonnell

See Nearest Town on page 304.

Poolewe

A compact village situated on the shores of Loch Ewe, Poolewe has a good array of facilities and accommodation. Slioch outdoor clothing factory has a retail store (open Monday to Friday), located between the swimming pool and Poolewe Hotel.

Places to Stay & Eat Right at the end of the walk, ***Poolewe Camping and Caravanning Club Site*** *(☎ 01445-781249)*, charges £12.50 for two backpackers with a tent, and £14.90 for two people with a car and tent.

There is a wide range of B&B and hotel accommodation in the village, including ***Poolewe Hotel*** *(☎ 01445-781241)*, which offers B&B from £25. This hotel and the ***Pool House Hotel*** are the two main hotels in town, and both offer bar food. ***Achtercairn Hostel*** *(☎ 01445-712131)*, 5mi south on the outskirts of Gairloch, is the nearest hostel and charges £8.50.

In Poolewe there is a ***shop*** and post office (Monday to Saturday), and a ***coffee shop***.

Getting There & Away Westerbus (☎ 01445-712255) runs a daily (except Sunday) service between Poolewe and Inverness, travelling via Dundonnell on Monday, Wednesday and Saturday, and via Kinlochewe on Tuesday, Thursday and Friday. Buses leave from Poolewe post office on all days at 8.15am and return from Inverness at 5.05pm. The same company also has a service between Poolewe and Ullapool on Thursdays only, departing from Poolewe at 9.20am and leaving Ullapool at 1.15pm.

GETTING TO/FROM THE WALK

The walk starts at Corrie Hallie – see Getting to/from the Walk on page 304. It finishes in Poolewe – see Getting There & Away on page above.

THE WALK

Day 1: Corrie Hallie to Shenavall

2 hours, 4mi (6.5km)

See Day 1 of the Beinn Dearg Mhór route description on page 307.

Day 2: Shenavall to Poolewe

8–9 hours, 19mi (30.5km)

The first challenge is to cross the two rivers in the valley that snake towards Loch na Sealga. If the rivers are in spate crossing will be impossible, but generally the water is calf- to knee-deep in the shallow sections and wading is cold but not difficult.

Leave Shenavall and cross the Abhainn Srath na Sealga just to the south-west of the bothy. Stick to the river bank on the other side to avoid the worst of some very wet ground between the two rivers, then cross the bog to the Abhainn Gleann na Muice. Follow this river's bank south and cross in front of the private Larachantivore cottage. Once on the western bank of the Abhainn Gleann na Muice, join a path that passes in front of the cottage and follows the river upstream. Pass the slopes of Beinn Dearg Mhór and the valley of Gleann na Muice Beag opens up to the west. A burn runs

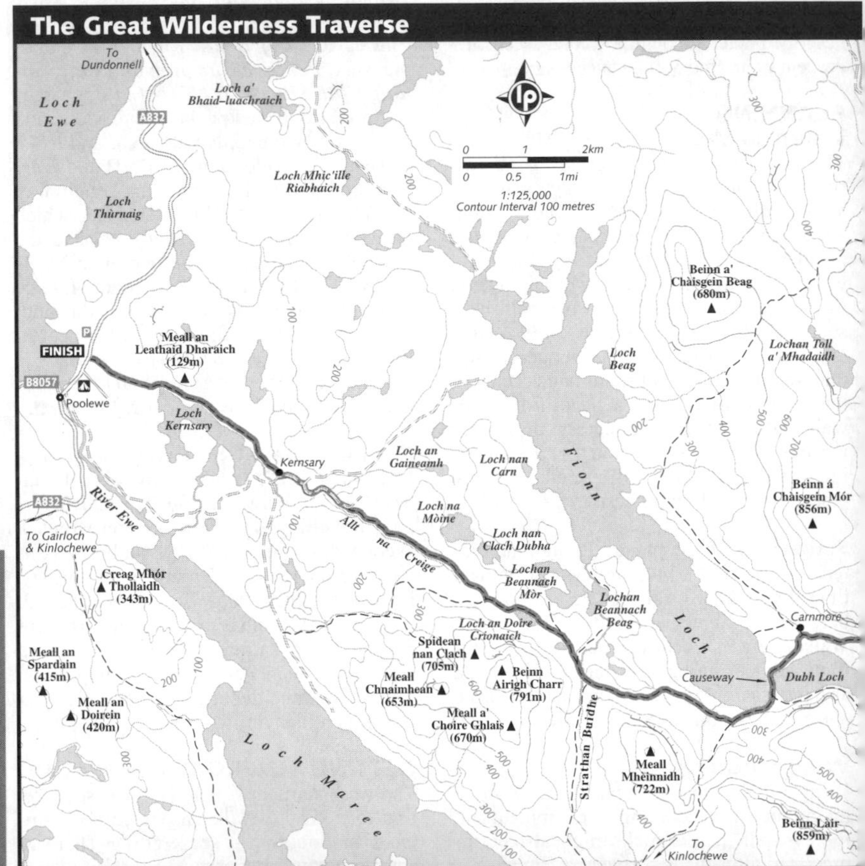

down the centre of the steep-sided valley; you should take the path that leads off to the right about 50m before the confluence of this burn with the main river.

This path is smaller and drier than the previous one. Follow it up the northern bank of the burn, which cascades down steep rock walls at the head of the valley. The path zigzags its way up the side, passing the beautiful **Loch Beinn Dearg** halfway up. Gain the plateau and the path is fairly flat for the next 1.5mi as it leads past numerous lochans. As you reach the western side of the plateau there is a fork in the path; keep right and begin the descent towards Carnmore. Just as you leave the plateau the most stunning view of the route opens up ahead; Allt Bruthach an Easein is framed in the perfect bowl of a glacial valley, then drops suddenly away to reveal the steep walls of the massif opposite. As you descend slightly farther and round a corner towards the west, another vista is spread before you and Dubh Loch and Fionn Loch lie stretched out below.

The descent is fairly gentle as the path contours down the steep slope towards the buildings at **Carnmore** (about 8mi from

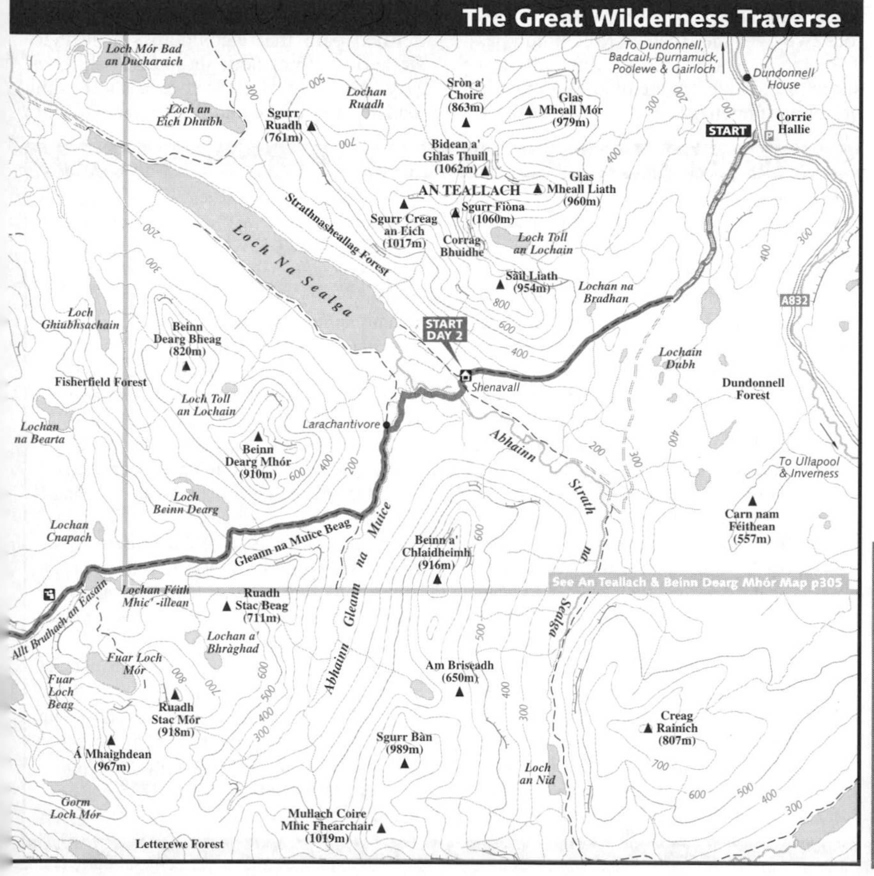

Shenavall). These buildings are part of the Letterewe Estate and are not maintained by the Mountain Bothies Association, but climbers and walkers are welcome to use the barn (always open and without charge) situated 50m north-west of the main house. The shelter is very rough, however, with a dirt floor, and would not be a first choice for accommodation.

The trail veers to the south-west at Carnmore and leads down to a rock and concrete causeway crossing the lochs. Follow round the top of a series of pebble beaches on the opposite (southern) shore of Fionn Loch. The path forks about 0.75mi beyond the causeway. The left fork leads to Kinlochewe over the Bealach Mheinnidh pass. Take the right fork and continue along the shore of the loch, where there is a great impression of open space. Bear away from the loch slightly and pass several small lochans. At a cairned fork, 1.5mi beyond the Kinlochewe junction, keep right and cross directly over the Srathan Buidhe burn (a path amendment not marked on the OS map). The trail from here is relatively new and offers well-benched, level walking.

Continue along the obvious route to a forestry plantation. Pass through a turnstile and join a vehicle track at a cairn. Turn left along the track and follow it through the trees, and then bear left downhill. The track will bring you to a farm at Kernsary, where a sign directs you right along the side of farm enclosures. Cross a stream, veer left across a small field and join a more well-defined path that leads across a heathery slope on the northern shore of Loch Kernsary. At the end of the loch a short climb leads to a turnstile and Poolewe comes into

Wild Camping and the Letterewe Estate

Wild camping has long been a necessary and immensely satisfying way for walkers to access the more remote areas of the Scottish Highlands. As such, the Mountaineering Council of Scotland embraces the right for hillwalkers to camp anywhere beyond boundaries of cultivated land and issues guidelines encouraging walkers to camp with minimal environmental impact.

The issue of wild camping is a complicated one, as are many access issues in Scotland, because laws exist that stipulate one thing, while current practice dictates another. In this case the 1865 Trespass Act and 1994 Criminal Justice Act both prohibit some of the practices of wild camping; the Mountaineering Council of Scotland is currently campaigning for amendments to both pieces of legislation.

The convolutions of the issue are illustrated by events that have taken place on the Letterewe Estate, the estate through which both The Great Wilderness Traverse and the Slioch routes pass. In 1993, the Letterewe Accord was signed by Paul Van Vlissingen, the Dutch millionaire owner of the estate, and a range of conservation and mountaineering groups. It was considered a progressive agreement that might be used as a basis for future access legislation and permitted minimal-impact camping on the estate.

It is therefore strange to come across signs in the estate asking walkers and outdoor users to protect the wilderness by refraining from camping. Mr Van Vlissingen explains these notices by saying 'no camping' does not actually mean camping is not allowed, it simply protects him from being held liable for any health and safety issues arising from people camping on his land. So opens another chapter in Scotland's contorted access laws.

Despite their convoluted current state, it can only be positive that these issues are beginning to be debated and, hopefully, there will soon be a solution to the quagmire of access legislation in Scotland. In the meantime, do not be misled by any signs suggesting that minimal-impact wilderness camping is not permitted – it is and the Mountaineering Council of Scotland is prepared to fight to prove it.

For more information or a copy of *Wild Camping: A Guide to Good Practice?*, contact the Mountaineering Council of Scotland at The Old Granary, West Mill St, Perth, PH1 5QP (☎ 01738-638227), or check its Web site at W www.mountaineering-scotland.org.uk.

view. Pass through another gate before joining the A832. Turn left along the road and the centre of Poolewe is just a couple of minutes' walk away.

Slioch

Duration	8 hours
Distance	12mi (19km)
Standard	medium-hard
Start/Finish	Incheril parking area
Nearest Town	Kinlochewe
Public Transport	yes

Summary A beautiful approach along the shores of Loch Maree leads to a compact mountain horseshoe with excellent views.

The dramatic, double-tiered Slioch (980m, 3214ft) is a landmark of Wester Ross. Eight hundred metres of red Torridonian sandstone rise out of a bed of rounded, grey gneiss, and when the flanks of the mountain reflect the evening sunlight, the effect is dramatic.

This walk follows the picturesque Kinlochewe River to Loch Maree and then turns away from the valley, climbing over wild moorland to the cluster of peaks that make up the Slioch massif. From the summit ridge views range from the remote heart of The Great Wilderness to the Western Isles. The walk is not technically demanding, but it does involve a total ascent of 1160m and crosses some very rough ground.

PLANNING

When to Walk

This route crosses some wet ground and is best avoided after very heavy rain. Navigation will be difficult in poor visibility, so try and walk on a clear day.

Stalking The route passes through the Letterewe Estate – see Stalking on page 309.

Maps

Both the OS Landranger 1:50,000 map No 19 *(Gairloch & Ullapool, Loch Maree)* and OS Outdoor Leisure 1:25,000 map No 8 *(The Cuillin & Torridon Hills)* cover this route.

GETTING TO/FROM THE WALK

The circuit starts and finishes at the Incheril parking area, about 1mi from Kinlochewe. To get there follow the A832 east from Kinlochewe for about 0.5mi, then take a left turn signed to Incheril. Continue straight to the large car park at the end of the road.

THE WALK

See map page 314

Pass through the turnstile at the northern end of Incheril parking area and turn left, following signs for Letterewe and Poolewe. After a short section on a vehicle track the path crosses two sheep fields, passing through a gate on the way. Keep the high deer fence to your left and, when the fields come to an end, a more obvious path leads on across several bracken-covered rises. This leads to another gate, beyond which is a wide wooden bridge that crosses the Allt Chnàimhean. The well-worn path now climbs slightly to contour along the hillside above Kinlochewe River, passing over several small tributary streams before dropping back down to continue along the river bank itself. This section along the river to the loch is very beautiful and the terrain is easy.

Veer right through some reeds, cross over two smaller rivers, and the path becomes better defined again. Loch Maree opens out in front of you, and the path splits just ahead of a dense thicket of bracken. A small, stony path leads up to the right through the bracken, while a wide, grassy track leads along the loch shore. Stick to the left; both routes lead to the same place but the route along the shore passes over much easier, drier terrain. The track crosses a pebble beach and then passes through a silver birch grove before reaching the **Abhainn an Fhasaigh**. A wooden footbridge takes you over the raging white water and several impressive waterfalls can be seen upstream.

Cross through a gate on the other side of the bridge and immediately turn right along the path that follows the river upstream. After 150m the path forks at a cairn; take the left fork up and over some rock slabs to join a small tributary stream. The path diverges again at this stream – one path continues along the western bank, while another, larger path crosses the river and makes its way along the other side. Again, both lead to the same place. If you cross the stream watch out for another cairned fork after 0.75mi, where the route to Slioch veers left. Both paths eventually pick their way alongside the burn that can be seen dropping down the shallow depression between Meall Each and Sgurr Dubh.

At the col between Meall Each and Sgurr Dubh, the main path veers west around the bottom of Sgurr Dubh directly towards Slioch. Leave the path at the col and strike out over open ground across Coire na Sleaghaich towards the grassy eastern slopes of Sgurr an Tuill Bhain. Cross the stream that runs down the centre of the corrie and climb the heathery, lower slopes of the mountain. Veer west to gain easier ground on a rocky shoulder and then climb up to the **Sgurr an Tuill Bhàin** (934m) summit cairn, where there is a wonderful view north over Lochan Fada to the remote heart of The Great Wilderness.

Pick up a path from the summit and follow it west, dropping down onto an enjoyably narrow ridge. The ridge widens as it climbs towards the northern summit of **Slioch**. In

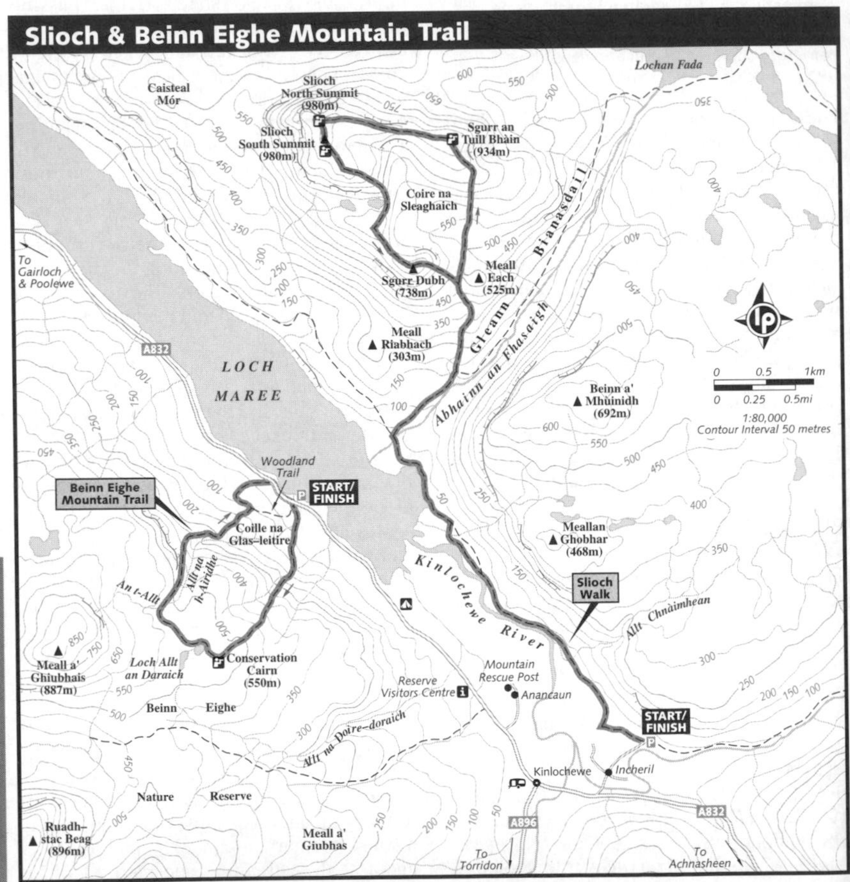

poor visibility stick to the northern edge of the ridge and you will be guided to the top. The northern and southern summits are actually the same height, although the south summit has been granted official recognition as the true summit. Views from both points are stunning, with a panorama of Loch Maree stretching out to the Atlantic below you and the Western Isles visible on the horizon beyond that. From the northern summit make a major change in direction south, swinging slightly east around the top of a steep drop, to reach the trig point on Slioch.

From the summit descend south-east on a grassy slope. The path becomes confused by rocky ground, but cross a rise and then veer farther east to drop down the left side of a steep rock spur. Arrive at the col below, just east of two lochans. The main path heads east into Coire na Sleaghaich. If you want to complete the entire horseshoe, climb the rise to the south of the lochans, veering west slightly to locate the path that descends down to the broad col before Sgurr Dubh. A straightforward climb up the shoulder ahead will bring you to the summit of **Sgurr Dubh** (738m). To descend cross to the north-east of the summit plateau and go down steeply in the direction of Meall Each. Rejoin the main path at the bottom, turn south and retrace your route back to Loch Maree and the Incheril parking area.

Beinn Eighe Mountain Trail

Duration	2½–3½ hours
Distance	2.5mi (4km)
Standard	easy-medium
Start/Finish	Glas Leitir parking area
Nearest Town	Kinlochewe
Public Transport	yes (inconvenient)

Summary A short, steep walk that explores the beautiful woodland and wild mountain terrain of the Beinn Eighe National Nature Reserve.

Beinn Eighe (pronounced ben ay) National Nature Reserve was established in 1951, the first such reserve to be created in Britain. It was created to help safeguard the largest remnant of ancient Caledonian woodland in the western Highlands, and covers 4750ha between the shore of Loch Maree and the mountain massif of Beinn Eighe. The whole reserve, managed by Scottish Natural Heritage, is open to the public. Two walking trails have been created to take visitors through the best of the area's habitats. The Mountain Trail is longer and ventures higher up the slopes of Beinn Eighe for some great views; the Woodland Trail is only 1mi long and explores the Caledonian woodland bordering Loch Maree. Both trails are maintained by volunteers and are well marked by stone cairns. Some of the cairns along the trails also encompass 'indicator points', marking features of interest that are fully explained in the trail guidebooks (see Information Sources on page 316).

The Mountain Trail leads up from the shores of Loch Maree, through Scots pine, to the bare and rocky mountain slopes above. Despite its relatively short length and waymarked character, the walk's level of difficulty should not be underestimated; terrain covered is steep and hands are necessary to help mount high rock steps in several places. In one section 320m is gained in height in just over 500m of path. The trail offers an ideal introduction to mountain walking, an informative and exciting place to bring older children or an interesting afternoon's activity when the higher mountain peaks of the area are cloud covered.

PLANNING

When to Walk

The quality of the trail means the path can be walked at almost any time, although rocks will be slippery in wet or icy conditions.

Stalking The waymarked trails in the reserve are open to the public throughout the year, although signs will request no deviations from the paths for one or two weeks of the stalking season. Contact the visitor centre (☎ 01445-760254) with any queries.

What to Bring

The trail climbs over halfway up Beinn Eighe and passes over steep, mountainous

Scots Pine

Beinn Eighe National Nature Reserve and the area around Torridon is home to some of the rare surviving fragments of the 'Great Wood of Caledonia', the dense forest that once covered most of highland Scotland. Perhaps the most distinctive and evocative reminder of the lost native woodland is the Scots pine. These stately trees were almost wiped out in Scotland by the last ice age, but managed to survive in a small enclave in the south-west of the country. When the temperature began to rise 10,000 years ago, scattered seeds began to take hold again and by 8000 years ago the species was well established once again.

Once home to bears, wild pigs, deer and wolves, this forest was gradually cleared to make way for crops and livestock. Heavy grazing by sheep and deer has prevented the woodlands from regenerating. With such a limited amount of the natural woodland remaining, it is impressive to walk among the fragments that have managed to survive.

Scots pine typically have long, straight trunks and narrow crowns, a shape that evolves as the saplings reach high to compete for light. The Caledonian woodlands in this area consist of several 'granny trees' – seed trees up to 350 years old with broad crowns and shorter, gnarled trunks that grew in open, light conditions after a huge forest fire cleared the slopes. Now dwarfing these parent trees is a dense growth of younger, taller Scots pine. The trunks of the trees have an orange bark, which glows beautifully when caught by the evening sun.

LPP

terrain that is exposed to bad weather. Strong walking boots are essential for negotiating the rocky terrain, and warm and waterproof clothing is also needed. Food and water are also necessary because of the strenuous nature of the climb.

Maps

The Mountain Trail is marked on the OS Landranger 1:50,000 map No 19 *(Gairloch & Ullapool, Loch Maree)*. For more detail use the OS Outdoor Leisure 1:25,000 map No 8 *(The Cuillin & Torridon Hills)*.

Information Sources

Beinn Eighe National Nature Reserve Visitor Centre is 0.75mi north of Kinlochewe along the A832. It is open daily from May to September, has displays about the park's habitats, and sells maps and natural history guides.

Scottish Natural Heritage produces a trail guide entitled *Beinn Eighe National Nature Reserve: Mountain Trail*, which is available at the visitor centre, from a vending machine in Incheril parking area and from local outlets. This guide not only provides a wealth of interesting information about the reserve and the trail, but also has a basic map of the route on the inside cover. This reproduction map, in addition to the excellent waymarking along the trail, should be sufficient to guide you around the route.

GETTING TO/FROM THE WALK

Glas Leitir parking area marks the beginning and the end of the route, and is situated about 2.5mi north of Kinlochewe along the A832. Westerbus runs a service that passes along this road (see Getting There & Away on page 300) but, unfortunately, it doesn't operate at convenient times for completing the walk. You may be lucky enough to be offered a lift with other walkers in the area, otherwise the 2.5mi walk should take about an hour to complete.

THE WALK

See map page 314

From the information board at the Glas Leitir parking area, cross under the road on a walkway beside the river. Keep left at the trail junction just after the tunnel, following the direction of the mountain symbol on a marker post. The stony path follows along the banks of the Allt na h-Airidhe burn for a short time, before veering away to cross through a silver birch grove densely carpeted with bracken. The trail begins its ascent almost immediately, although the gradient is easy at first. As you climb, the bracken is interspersed by heather and the silver birch gives way to Scots pine.

The path joins up with a tumbling burn and climbs more steeply up its banks on stone steps, before crossing it on a wooden footbridge. The steps become more continuous as the trees dwindle in size and the path emerges onto open slopes. Views of Loch Maree and Slioch open up to the north. The rock steps gradually give way to natural slab and loose stone and the terrain becomes wilder. Just beyond the 305m marker cairn some very steep ground must be negotiated, and hands are needed to help mount one or two rock ledges.

As you climb, views of the Beinn Eighe massif open up ahead and the steepest section of ascent is now over. The path weaves its way uphill between craggy outcrops of rock and finally reaches a sprawling pile of stones – the **Conservation Cairn**. At 550m this is the high point of the trail and there is a real feeling of being in the heart of the mountains. A 360-degree panorama is spread before you; the steep, compact summits of Torridon gathered to the south-west and the lofty landscape of The Great Wilderness spread out to the north. In good visibility a total of 31 Munros (mountains over 914m/3000ft) can be seen from this excellent vantage point.

The trail drops down to the west and weaves its way past several beautiful lochans. An t-Allt is crossed on stepping stones and the path turns north to follow the burn and begin the descent. Thankfully the terrain is more gently graded than it was on the climb up. The burn soon disappears into a gorge to your right and as you descend farther there are impressive views into the deep, sheer-sided chasm.

After a right bend and small rise the path leads to the rim of the gorge; care is needed on this section because the drop to the burn below is sheer. Continue on and re-enter the forest below. The path joins up with the Woodland Trail and turns left, soon reaching a wooden conservation cabin and a trig point. You are then led back through the gentle environment of the silver birch, over a planked walkway above a marsh, and back to the road. Both trails now cross the road and pass through trees to a beautiful pebble beach on the shore of **Loch Maree**. Turn right and walk along the top of the beach, crossing a wooden bridge, to find yourself back at the parking area.

Torridon

The 6450ha Torridon Estate was purchased in 1967 by the National Trust for Scotland and encompasses some of the most impressive peaks of Wester Ross. The massifs of Beinn Alligin and Liathach and parts of Beinn Dearg and Beinn Eighe all nestle within the estate's boundaries. Impressive and imposing peaks all of them, the Torridon area is renowned for its deep corries, imposing buttresses, airy pinnacles and magnificent views.

For the walker, much of the high ground is of a serious nature, although there are also several low-level routes that explore the deep valleys between the mountain massifs. Whatever the route, given a little luck with the weather, this is an area that is sure to leave quite an impression.

PLANNING

Maps

Most of the walks within the Torridon Estate are covered by OS Landranger 1:50,000 map No 24 *(Raasay & Applecross)*, although this map overlaps with OS Landranger 1:50,000 map No 19 *(Gairloch & Ullapool, Loch Maree)* on Beinn Alligin. The OS Outdoor Leisure 1:25,000 map No 8 *(The Cuillin & Torridon Hills)* neatly covers the whole area and is much more useful, as is Harvey's 1:25,000 Superwalker map *Torridon*.

Geology of Torridon

Many of the peaks of Wester Ross have exposed, rocky flanks and summits, and the geological processes that made up the region can be clearly seen. The old base of the region is made up of Lewisian gneiss, which was formed up to 2500 million years ago. This rock base was subsequently eroded and then, when the area was situated south of the equator around 800 million years ago, was drowned beneath an accumulation of desert sediment up to 4mi thick. This sediment hardened to form a rock so specific to the area that it has been named red Torridonian sandstone. The mountain of Slioch, with its famous double tiered silhouette, is a prime example of this, with a broad, grey base topped by an 800m-high mound of red sandstone.

Much of this relatively soft sandstone layer has since been eroded (largely by successive ice ages and the weather) and has been sculpted into wonderful pinnacle formations on high mountain ridges. The pinnacles of An Teallach and the Horns of Beinn Alligin are wonderful examples of this process, and today the sandstone's friction offers scramblers a perfect rock playground.

The third main geological component of the area, Cambrian quartzite, was formed by the sediments laid down by tropical seas after the desert of the sandstone era was flooded, some 600 million years ago. The famous scree of Beinn Eighe is made up of this rock.

Books

The National Trust for Scotland produces *Torridon*, a guide to the estate that includes historical information and descriptions of several walking routes. The guide is available from the Countryside Centre and local outlets. In addition, *Torridon – A Walkers Guide* by Peter Barton gives details of low- and high-level routes.

Information Sources

For information check the Torridon Estate Web site at W www.torridon-estate.co.uk. TICs in the area are at Gairloch (☎ 01445-712130 e gairloch@host.co.uk) and Lochcarron (☎ 01520-722357).

Guided Walks

National Trust for Scotland rangers, based at the Countryside Centre (☎ 01445-791221) in Torridon, organise day walks on and around peaks within the Torridon Estate. Guided walks are run three times a week during July and August, cost £5, and leave the centre at 10am. One walk is a high-level walk but does not climb any mountains, while the other is a Torridon ridge walk.

Mountain guides based in Wester Ross (at Lochcarron) include well-known and experienced guide Martin Moran (☎ 01520-722361, W www.moran-mountain.co.uk). Daily rates for walks and climbs on the Torridon mountains start at £130 per day, reasonable if shared between a small group. Discover Torridon (☎ 01445-791218) also offers guided walks in the area.

ACCESS TOWN
Torridon

The village of Torridon is the main settlement in the area. The nearest bank is 31mi away in Gairloch, although the shop may be able to provide a cash-back service for small amounts from UK bank cards. There is free Internet access and petrol pumps at the Ben Damph Lodge (see Places to Stay & Eat).

Information The National Trust for Scotland Countryside Centre (☎ 01445-791221) is at the entrance of the village, just off the A896. It is open Monday to Saturday, and on Sunday afternoon. It sells maps and walking books relating to the local area, and has displays and information about the landscape and wildlife. There is also a nearby Deer Museum. Mountain weather forecasts are available at the Countryside Centre and the SYHA Hostel.

Places to Stay & Eat *Torridon Campsite (☎ 01349-868486)* is opposite the Countryside Centre and is run by a friendly local woman who arrives to collect fees (£3 per tent) on a moped, which is sure to wake the heaviest sleeper. It is basic, but has water, toilets and a coin-operated shower. Nearby ***Torridon SYHA Hostel*** *(☎ 01445-791284)* is open between February and October and costs £9.25; the staff can be pedantic.

Ben Damph Lodge *(☎ 01445-791296)* is in the village of Annat, just across the other side of Loch Torridon. B&B prices range from £46 for a single to £18 per person for six people sharing. There is an excellent bar menu that includes a hearty breakfast and main courses from £5. The bar is the centre of activity in the area during the evening.

Torridon has a small but well-stocked ***shop*** and post office, open daily with limited Sunday hours (10am to noon, 4pm to 6pm).

Getting There & Away Torridon village lies at the eastern end of Loch Torridon, on the A896 between Kyle of Lochalsh and Kinlochewe. The nearest train station is at Strathcarron, which is on the Inverness–Kyle of Lochalsh line. ScotRail (☎ 0845-755 0033) runs four trains a day in both directions (two on Sunday). A postbus (☎ 01246-546329) leaves Strathcarron at 9.55am for Torridon, connecting only with the first train from Kyle of Lochalsh. Alternatively Duncan Maclennan (☎ 01520-755239) runs a bus service from Strathcarron station to Torridon via Lochcarron and Shieldaig. It waits for the trains from both Kyle and Inverness that get in at around 12.35pm, and runs daily (except Sunday) during summer, and on Monday, Wednesday and Friday in winter. Going the other way, this bus leaves Torridon about 10am, arriving at Strathcarron in time for the 12.35pm trains to Kyle and Inverness. The times and services can change, especially in winter, so check with the bus operator or a local TIC.

It is also possible to get to Torridon via Achnasheen train station. A postbus service leaves Achnasheen daily (except Sunday) at 12.10pm and arrives at Torridon at 2.55pm. This service also makes the journey from Torridon to Achnasheen in the morning, leaving Torridon post office at 10.35am and arriving at Achnasheen at 11.25am.

Beinn Alligin

Duration	6½ hours
Distance	6mi (9.5km)
Standard	medium-hard
Start/Finish	Torridon House Bridge
Nearest Town	Torridon
Public Transport	yes

Summary A difficult but immensely rewarding circuit of a horseshoe ridge with two major summits, involving several steep and exposed sections and some scrambling.

The circuit of ridges and peaks of Beinn Alligin is one of the most popular mountain walks in the north-west. A steep ascent allows access to excellent, airy walking and the traverse of the Horns of Alligin offers a small amount of scrambling with some exposure. This route is a good 'warm-up' for the difficulties encountered on An Teallach and Liathach. If you find Beinn Alligin difficult then don't consider the other two; Liathach, in particular, is much more difficult. Most of the scrambling on the horns can be bypassed, but this option is still exposed and will not be a pleasant experience for walkers who dislike heights.

Beinn Alligin means 'the mountain of jewels'. It is definitely a gem – a mountain that allows walkers to get a feel for the high and wild Scottish peaks, without having to be a mountaineer or cover long approaches. This route involves a total ascent of 1190m and has only a few cairns to mark the way, so map and compass knowledge is essential. In places you will find a well-defined path on top, formed by the erosion of many feet, but this should not be followed blindly as side-paths can also lead to dead-end lookouts and other potential difficulties.

PLANNING

The walk can be completed at almost any time during the summer, although the rocks will be slippery in the wet.

There is little water on the ridge so bring plenty with you. The weather is also notoriously changeable, so bring clothes in anticipation of all weather conditions.

GETTING TO/FROM THE WALK

The walk starts from Torridon House Bridge, about 2mi west of Torridon village on the road towards Inveralligin. Torridon House is just below the road in the trees and there is a busy parking area beside the bridge. A postbus (☎ 01246-546329) service runs between Torridon village and Torridon House Bridge (on the way to Diabaig) in the morning (except Sunday), leaving Torridon SYHA at 9.25am. This service returns at around 5pm.

THE WALK

From the bridge, a path signposted for Coire Mhic Nòbuil leads up through a small wood on the east bank of the Abhainn Coire Mhic Nòbuil and then onto open moorland. Straight ahead is the blunt western wall of Beinn Dearg. To the right is the western end of Liathach and to the left is Beinn Alligin. The path crosses a footbridge and aims roughly north, towards the eastern end of the horseshoe ridge.

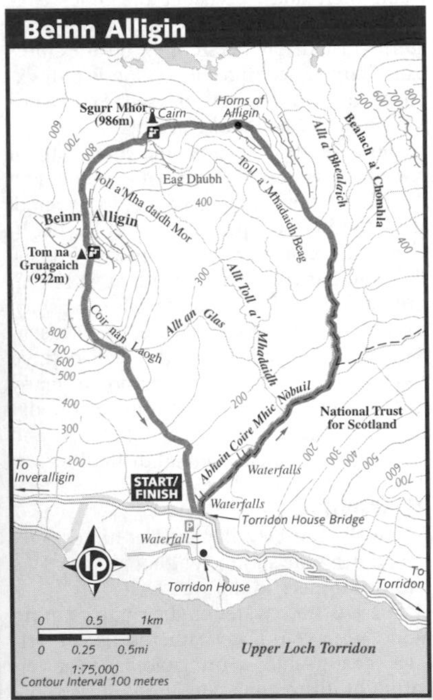

As you get higher the path becomes indistinct, but continue up the crest of the broad and very steep ridge, using your hands to help negotiate some rocky steps, aiming for the three **Horns of Alligin**. You reach the base of the first horn about 1½ to two hours from the start. You can scramble over this and the next two rocky peaks (taking care on the steep descent of the first pinnacle) or follow the path on the left that skirts their south side. After the third horn drop to a small col then climb again, swinging to the north-west to keep the steep drop down into the corrie on your left. To your right (north-east) the view really begins to open out; a beautifully jumbled mosaic of lochans, moors and smaller peaks, with Loch Maree beyond and the town of Gairloch visible on the coast.

It is a short distance to the summit of **Sgurr Mhór** (986m), about three to four hours from the start. With the extra height your view is almost 360 degrees, with range upon range of wonderful peaks, too numerous to mention, spread out in all directions. Most notable to the south-west are the Cuillin 'hills' on the Isle of Skye and, to the east, the summits of Beinn Eighe, where exposed quartz makes them appear eternally snowcapped.

From the summit head north-west down a grassy slope, keeping the corrie edge to the left. If the visibility is poor take particular care on this section as the top of Eag Dhubh, the giant gash that dominates the view from below, is hereabouts, just waiting to trap the unwary walker in mist. If, however, the day is clear, the cliffs on either side of the gully frame the view of the glen far below; one of Scottish walking's many classic vistas. (Don't try to descend this way.)

After Eag Dhubh go steeply up again, over large boulders, to reach the summit and trig point of **Tom na Gruagaich** and more good views, about one to 1½ hours from the summit of Sgurr Mhór. The descent is steep but straightforward. Walk south into Coir nan Laogh, dropping steeply on an eroded path with several small streams gurgling along beside. The steep walls of the corrie funnel you down to a rocky plateau, where the descent eases briefly before descending steeply again towards the parking area and bridge. The path splits twice on the way down but quickly rejoins, so don't worry when you meet junctions – everything is going to the finish. The last section of path is quite rough and feels difficult after the efforts of the day, passing through an area fenced for native forest regrowth. The descent from Tom na Gruagaich to the finish will take around two hours.

Liathach

Duration	7–8 hours
Distance	6mi (9.5km)
Standard	hard
Start/Finish	Allt an Doire Ghairbh parking area
Nearest Town	Torridon
Public Transport	yes

Summary A sensational but serious route with lots of exposed scrambling on one of Scotland's most challenging mountains. The positions and views make this a truly memorable day.

Immediately to the north of Loch Torridon, a massive, 3mi-long wall of rock pinnacles and buttresses sweeps up to an average height of over 900m. The south face of this massif is littered with crags and boulder fields, and has no obvious line of weakness. On the northern side the situation is even more intimidating, with several brooding corries ringed by cliffs. This is Liathach (pronounced lee agagh) and the traverse of its ridge is one of the Scotland's classic mountain challenges.

The ascent is steep and unrelenting, and the main ridge is often exposed. The crux of the route is negotiating Am Fasarinen's Pinnacles, which are reached after the ascent of Spidean a' Choire Léith (1055m, 3460ft), the main summit of the massif.

PLANNING

The traverse of Liathach's ridge should be reserved for a dry summer day with good visibility and light winds. Wet ground can make the mud paths and rock treacherous.

There is little water on the ridge so bring plenty with you. You will also be grateful for boots that offer as much friction as possible and a walking rope will lend confidence to those unnerved by exposure. The weather is notoriously changeable, so bring clothes in anticipation of all weather conditions.

GETTING TO/FROM THE WALK

The walk starts and finishes at a parking area opposite the Allt an Doire Ghairbh on the southern side of the A896. This is about 2.5mi east of Torridon village and 700m east of Glen Cottage. A postbus (☎ 01246-546329) service runs between Torridon and Kinlochewe in the mornings and can drop off at the parking area if requested. The service departs from Torridon post office at 10.35am daily (except Sunday). To return to Torridon at the end of the walk turn right along the road instead of left and you will be back in the village after just 1mi of road walking.

Warning

This is arguably the most demanding route in this book in terms of exposure and steep ground. The traverse of the Am Fasarinen Pinnacles requires skill, confidence and route finding ability on rock, and should be left to those with prior scrambling or rock climbing experience.

The pinnacles can be avoided via a narrow goats' track on the left, which contours across extremely steep and exposed slopes. While the scrambling on the pinnacles is avoided, the exposure is considerable and a simple trip would be disastrous almost anywhere.

If in doubt try one of the easier scrambles in this chapter such as Beinn Alligin or An Teallach first. Alternatively, you could go as far as the pinnacles and, if in doubt, retreat along your line of ascent.

THE WALK

See map page 322

From the parking area walk east along the main road for 100m and turn left onto a prominent path. Above you can see the path zigzagging up the steep slopes on the right of the Allt an Doire Ghairbh. The climb begins almost immediately and, although the path is well constructed, there are a couple of short scrambles over rock outcrops. An hour of steep ascent will bring you onto gentler slopes in Coire Liath Mhór, where the encircling buttresses, terraces, gullies and scree slopes seem to offer no easy access to the ridge above.

From this point the path is no longer constructed but continues quite distinctly as an eroded trail. The gradient soon increases again as you climb steadily north under the impressive eastern face of Spidean a' Choire Léith. Swing abruptly back to the east under a prominent gully and climb steeply along grass slopes for a short distance. Then turn north and climb directly through rock outcrops (care is required in places) to reach the ridge at a bealach just west of Stùc a' Choire Dhuibh Bhig (915m). This should take around two to 2½ hours from the start. If the ascent to here proves difficult and worrying then do not continue beyond Spidean a' Choire Léith, using the line of ascent to return to the parking area.

It is worth climbing east along the ridge as far as the cairned summit of Stùc a' Choire Dhuibh Bhig for the superb view of Beinn Eighe's sweeping ridges and scree. The view

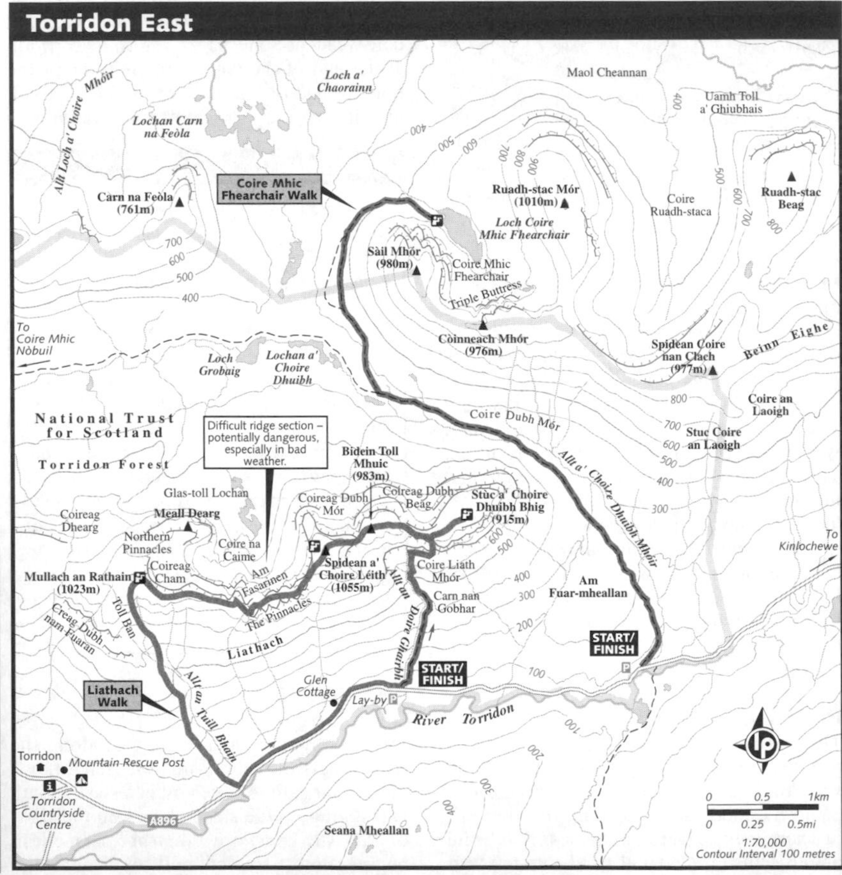

back to the west to Spidean a' Choire Lèithe is a classic photopoint on Liathach. Allow an hour return for this detour.

From the bealach where you arrived at the crest, follow the ridge easily west to where it narrows just before the first of the two tops between here and Spidean a' Choire Lèithe. Either scramble easily along the crest of this short, knife-edged section or traverse just beneath on a path to the south. Climb easily across the two tops and descend steeply to a notch in the ridge where steep gullies meet at a sharp point. The easiest route down into the notch is along the crest of the ridge, but paths do run out to the right before contouring back left into the notch along a worrying and tremendously exposed ledge.

The climb from the notch to the summit of **Spidean a' Choire Léith** is quite straightforward, the last section crossing large slabs and blocks. The views are superb, encompassing all the summits of Torridon to The Great Wilderness beyond and culminating in the jagged spine of An Teallach. To the south the rugged quartzitc summits of the Coulin Forest seem like foothills, while beyond these the summits of Glen Affric and Mulladorch stretch across the horizon. On a very clear day you can make out the distant whaleback of Ben Nevis.

Back on Liathach, descend from Spidean a' Choire Lèithe to the south-west, crossing awkward scree slopes to reach a grassy shoulder just before **Am Fasarinen's Pinnacles**. At this point a path begins to contour across the southern slopes just below the top of the ridge, while another stays on top to meet the first difficulties head on. The first path can be followed all the way around the pinnacles and is certainly the easiest option, despite the exposure. Care is required as a simple slip could be fatal.

Meanwhile, the direct line of the ridge is entertaining without being unduly difficult until a notch is reached at the halfway mark. The contouring path also passes this notch and those wishing to save a bit of time, while still tackling the most difficult scrambling, could take that path as far as here. There are two options for getting out of the notch and onto the easier ridge above, neither of them easy. There is either a passable, sloping stone gully around to the left or a route up the rock wall to the right. The scramble out of this notch is more akin to an easy graded rock climb. It should not be attempted by anyone who is not competent and relaxed on steep and exposed rock.

Once past the pinnacles, a steady climb brings you to the summit of **Mullach an Rathain** (1023m), with more good perspectives over the other Torridon summits. Don't be tempted to scramble out onto the northern pinnacles as they are difficult and the rock is quite loose. The descent into the Toll Ban runs south-west down a stony ridge before turning to the south-east and following an eroded path very steeply down scree slopes. The rest of the descent to the A896 follows this path and is remarkably easy considering the ruggedness of the surroundings. You should reach the road in 1½ to two hours from the summit of Mullach an Rathain. Turn left at the road and continue for 1mi to return to the parking area.

Coire Mhic Fhearchair

Duration	4½ hours
Distance	8mi (13km)
Standard	medium
Start/Finish	Coire Dubh parking area
Nearest Town	Torridon
Public Transport	yes

Summary A beautiful, low-level walk to one of the most outstanding corries in Scotland. Impressive mountain valleys, wild moorland and potential sightings of red deer add flavour to the journey.

Hollowed out of the west end of the Beinn Eighe massif by the glaciers of the last ice age, Coire Mhic Fhearchair is one of Scotland's most impressive and well-known corries. The walk to it takes you through the wild heart of Torridon and offers views of mountains not normally seen by road-bound tourists. In particular, the brooding buttresses and pinnacles of Liathach's north face are company for most of the journey.

The walk follows paths that have been constructed and maintained by the National Trust for Scotland, which owns and manages most of the country you'll pass through except Coire Mhic Fhearchair itself.

The route's medium grading is merited mainly because of the difficulty of the paths. Despite the fact that a considerable amount of labour has been put into their construction, the paths still conspire to tire ankles and knees, almost more than walking the same distance over open mountain terrain. They do, however, make navigation a straightforward affair. The total ascent for the route is 510m.

Alternatives The walk returns along the same route, although those with two cars can vary the return trip and finish by walking down through Coire Mhic Nòbuil. Keen mountain walkers will probably want to return over Beinn Eighe (see Beinn Eighe in Other Walks on page 325).

PLANNING

When to Walk

The walk can be done at any time of the year. The ground is generally passable in winter conditions, although paths may be either obliterated by snow or very icy.

Stalking The walk into Coire Mhic Fhearchair itself is not affected by stalking activities, but between August and October you should check with the Torridon Countryside Centre (☎ 01445-791221) if you wish to explore north into Glen Grudie.

GETTING TO/FROM THE WALK

The walk starts and finishes at Coire Dubh parking area on the A896, 3.5mi east of Torridon village. The parking area is on the left, just before a bridge, marked by a signpost for the 'Public Footpath to Coire Dubh Mór'. A postbus (☎ 01246-546329) service runs between Torridon and Kinlochewe in the mornings and can drop you off at the parking area if requested. The service departs from Torridon post office at 10.35am daily (except Sunday). A return service to Torridon passes the car park at around 2.20pm, but you will have to walk very quickly to make the connection. Alternatively allow 1½ to two hours for the walk back to Torridon.

THE WALK

See map page 322

Follow the well-constructed path away from the parking area and begin to climb steadily towards Coire Dubh Mór, the prominent cleft between Liathach and Beinn Eighe. The path stays well above Allt a' Choire Dhuibh Mhoir, which thunders down through a small gorge to the right. About 40 minutes of steady climbing brings you to a flatter section right under the massive eastern prow of Liathach. In another few minutes you reach Allt a' Choire Dhuibh Mhoir, which is crossed on good stepping stones. This may be difficult and potentially dangerous if the river is in full spate, in which case you'll need to follow the south bank of the river to ford it close to the junction with the path going up to Coire Mhic Fhearchair.

A gradual ascent passing several small lochs then brings you up through Coire Dubh Mór to reach a path junction marked with a small cairn. Already you have fine views of the northern corries and buttresses of Liathach, which stretch in an unbroken line of impregnability for almost 3mi. Particularly prominent are the northern pinnacles of Meall Dearg.

Turn right at the junction (the other path continues down into Coire Mhic Nòbuil) and begin climbing steadily around the western flank of Sàil Mhór. The path, although constructed, is quite strenuous in places but the views opening out across Coire Mhic Nòbuil and Beinn Dearg more than compensate for the effort. After about 40 minutes the path swings around to the east and climbs steeply beneath impressive cliffs. A series of waterfalls drops down on the left and a final steep climb brings you suddenly onto the boulder-strewn rock slabs on the shores of **Loch Coire Mhic Fhearchair** (two to 2½ hours from the start).

From this point you can take in the view or explore farther along the rough ground on either side of the lake. The alpine atmosphere of this place is quite special, with the imposing 300m-high Triple Buttresses at the very back of the corrie taking pride of place. Not long after WWII a Lancaster bomber crashed into the west buttress, killing the crew. Parts of the wreckage can still be seen in the far west gully. To the north and west there are excellent views across the wilderness of lochans and bog between Beinn Dearg, Baosbheinn and Beinn an Eoin. When you are ready, retrace your steps back to the parking area.

Other Walks

THE GREAT WILDERNESS

Á Mhaighdean & Ruadh Stac Mór

These two Great Wilderness peaks are considered to be the most remote in Britain, requiring a walk of at least 10mi (16km) from the nearest road just to reach the foot of the mountain. Á Mhaighdean (967m, 3172ft) and Ruadh Stac Mór (918m, 3011ft) are both Munros and, not surprisingly, are two of the stiffer Munros to 'bag'. Everyone has their own preferred style of ascent. Some, the very fast and very fit mainly, will use a pre-dawn start and, carrying only a daypack, make the ascent in a single day (27mi in 14 hours!). The majority of walkers will camp at Carnmore, and carry a day-pack on the climb itself. The route starts and finishes in Poolewe, although if you are planning a two-day ascent it may be worth thinking about starting at Corrie Hallie and using The Great Wilderness Traverse (see page 308) as a jumping-off point for the climb. Either way, the north-west ridge of Á Mhaighdean provides superb walking in a remote setting. The ascent to Ruadh Stac Mór from the intervening col is not long but requires a positive approach to work up through the scree. Use OS Landranger 1:50,000 map No 19 *(Gairloch & Ullapool, Loch Maree)*. The route is described in more detail in Ralph Storer's *100 Best Routes on Scottish Mountains* and an excellent personal account can be found in *The Big Walks*, edited by Richard Gilbert.

TORRIDON

Beinn Eighe

The Torridon giant Beinn Eighe is a sprawling mass of deep corries and scree-covered ridges, with no less than seven summits achieving Munro status. It is possible to reach all of these in a single day, however, the demands of this will be too much for most walkers. A good (although still strenuous) alternative is to visit the peaks on the western half of the massif, which are also the highest and most impressive. Starting from the A896, halfway between Torridon and Kinlochewe (near Loch Bharranch), a path can be used to reach Coire na Laoigh, just beneath the summit of Spidean Coire nan Clach (977m). After an interesting ascent to that summit, a fine ridge can be followed west to reach the peaks encircling Coire Mhic Fhearchair (see the walk description on page 323): Ruadh-stac Mór (1010m), Còinneach Mhór (976m) and Sàil Mhór (980m). Descend into the corrie before following the path out through Coire Dubh Mór. Total distance is around 12mi (19.5km) and total ascent is 1300m. Allow at least eight hours. Consult OS Outdoor Leisure 1:25,000 map No 8 *(The Cuillin & Torridon Hills)*. The route is described in more detail in Ralph Storer's *100 Best Routes on Scottish Mountains*.

THE NORTH-EAST

Beinn Dearg

In the north-east corner of Wester Ross, the grey, scree-covered dome of Beinn Dearg (1081m, 3556ft) rises above the sea of ridges and peaks that stretches east for some 13mi. It is a popular mountain but in poor weather navigation on its featureless summit plateau can be difficult. The route is also quite remote. Start from a parking area on the A835 Ullapool-Inverness road at the south-east end of Loch Droma. The approach uses an old track, no longer marked on the OS map, and climbs through two corries to ascend Cona' Mheall by its south-east ridge. Descend to the col above the headwall of Coire Ghranda from where a straightforward climb leads to the summit of Beinn Dearg. Allow seven to eight hours for the 11mi (17.5km) route. Use OS Landranger 1:50,000 map No 20 *(Beinn Dearg & Loch Broom)*.

THE SOUTH

Maol Chean-dearg

The peaks of the Coulin Forest are largely overshadowed by the giants of Torridon just to the north across Glen Torridon. However, the Coulin peaks offer a wilder and more intricate walking experience, with fewer people. The highest Coulin summit, Maol Chean-dearg (933m, 3060ft), is easiest approached from the south. Begin at the A890 where it crosses the Fionn-abhainn river, just east of Lochcarron. This village has accommodation and a shop and the Inverness–Kyle of Lochalsh line is about 1mi away at Strathcarron. The route is 10mi (16km), has a total ascent of over 900m and should take eight hours. Although the walk follows good paths for a considerable portion, navigation on the higher ground can be a real challenge. Use OS Landranger 1:50,000 map No 25 *(Glen Carron & Glen Affric)*

Western Isles

The Western Isles (Eilean Siar) – the very name expresses beyondness, difference and mystery, qualities which soon become real, almost tangible. There's always something special about travelling to islands and you soon realise these isles are strikingly different from each other; from the peatlands of north Lewis and the rocky mountains of Harris, to the mosaic of water and land in the Uists, and the compactness of Barra. However, they all share two qualities, an extraordinary sense of space (the vast sky and the limitless ocean) and a feeling of stretched time. Western Isles communities are lively and dynamic, but there is a relaxed feeling of unhurriedness. On a practical level, getting around is surprisingly easy (by public or private transport) and accommodation (except formal camping sites) is plentiful, although well spaced. Waymarked walks with strong historical and natural history themes can be found throughout the isles, and there are enough hills, long glens, extensive rocky coasts and vast sandy beaches for months of exploration on foot. This chapter features walks in north Lewis, north Harris, North and South Uist and Barra, with some suggestions for other walks in Harris and Barra.

Highlights

GRANT DIXON

A sea of rock and water from the isles' highest peak, Clisham (799m).

- Revelling in the wild, rugged mountainscapes of Harris
- Gazing down at the extraordinary water and rock patchwork landscape from peaks in North and South Uist
- Wandering along vast white sandy beaches
- Soaking up the tranquility and peace of the islands

NATURAL HISTORY

The 10 populated islands that make up the Western Isles form a chain about 130mi (209km) long on the western edge of the British Isles. By far the greater part of the islands consists of greyish Lewisian gneiss, the oldest rock type in north-western Europe, and altered by heat and pressure countless times since it was formed. Extensive outcrops of pink and white granite are found in the mountains and on the coast of Harris. The last ice age honed the narrow mountain ridges, sculpted corries and U-shaped valleys in hilly areas, and left behind masses of glacial material in valleys and on flat ground. Particularly in northern Lewis, large areas are covered with peat, dark soil composed of dead vegetation; although of great botanical importance, the peatlands and blanket bogs are not walker-friendly.

There are two distinct types of coastal landscape. Dramatic cliffs with deep inlets can be found mainly on the east coasts, where the formation of The Minch, the stretch of water between the isles and the mainland, was responsible for the emergence of the coastal cliffs. Long sandy beaches and machair on the Atlantic coasts

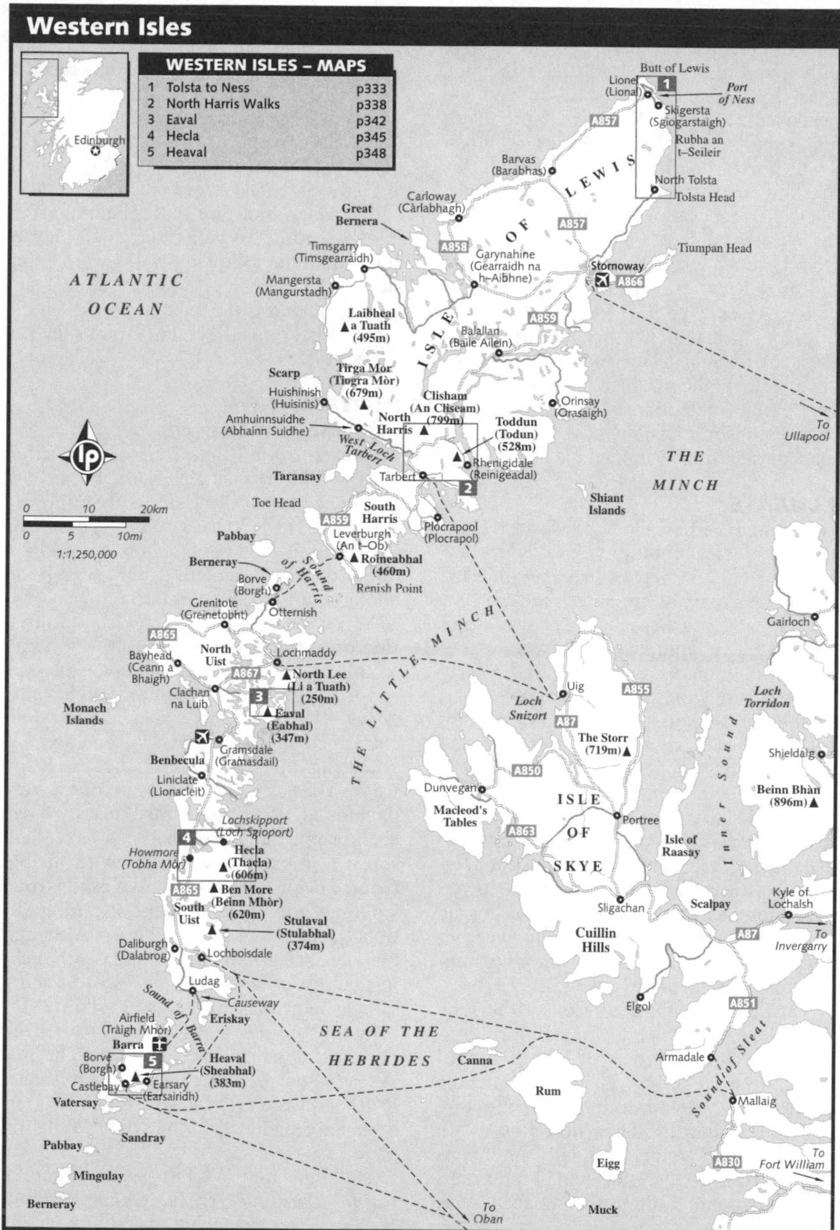
Western Isles
WESTERN ISLES – MAPS
1 Tolsta to Ness p333
2 North Harris Walks p338
3 Eaval p342
4 Hecla p345
5 Heaval p348
Edinburgh
Butt of Lewis
Lionel (Lional)
Port of Ness
Skigersta (Sgiogarstaigh)
Rubha an t–Seileir
North Tolsta
Tolsta Head
Barvas (Barabhas)
ISLE OF LEWIS
Carloway (Càrlabhagh)
Great Bernera
Timsgarry (Timsgearraidh)
Garynahine (Gearraidh na h–Aibhne)
Tiumpan Head
Stornoway
ATLANTIC OCEAN
Mangersta (Mangurstadh)
Laibheal a Tuath (495m)
Balallan (Baile Ailein)
Scarp
Tirga Mor (Tiogra Mòr) (679m)
Huishinish (Huisinis)
Clisham (An Cliseam) (799m)
Orinsay (Orasaigh)
Amhuinnsuidhe (Abhainn Suidhe)
North Harris
Toddun (Todun) (528m)
West Loch Tarbert
Rhenigidale (Reinigeadal)
To Ullapool
Taransay
Tarbert
THE MINCH
Toe Head
South Harris
Shiant Islands
Pabbay
Leverburgh (An t–Ob)
Plocrapool (Plocrapol)
Berneray
Roineabhal (460m)
Sound of Harris
Borve (Borgh)
Renish Point
Grenitote (Greinetobht)
Otternish
Gairloch
North Uist
Lochmaddy
THE LITTLE MINCH
Bayhead (Ceann a Bhaigh)
North Lee (Li a Tuath) (250m)
Clachan na Luib
Uig
Loch Torridon
Monach Islands
Eaval (Eabhal) (347m)
Loch Snizort
The Storr (719m)
Gramsdale (Gramasdail)
Benbecula
Shieldaig
Liniclate (Lionacleit)
Dunvegan
Beinn Bhàn (896m)
Macleod's Tables
ISLE OF SKYE
Portree
Inner Sound
Lochskipport (Loch Sgioport)
Howmore (Tobha Mòr)
Hecla (Thacla) (606m)
Isle of Raasay
Ben More (Beinn Mhòr) (620m)
South Uist
Sligachan
Scalpay
Kyle of Lochalsh
Stulaval (Stulabhal) (374m)
Cuillin Hills
To Invergarry
Daliburgh (Dalabrog)
Lochboisdale
Ludag
Sound of Barra
Causeway
Elgol
Eriskay
Airfield (Tràigh Mhòr)
SEA OF THE HEBRIDES
Barra
Heaval (Sheabhal) (383m)
Armadale
Sound of Sleat
Borve (Borgh)
Canna
Castlebay
Earsary (Earsairidh)
Rum
Mallaig
Vatersay
Sandray
Pabbay
To Fort William
Eigg
Mingulay
Berneray
To Oban
Muck
0 10 20km
0 5 10mi
1:1,250,000
A857
A858
A859
A866
A865
A867
A855
A87
A850
A863
A851
A830

originated after the last ice age when skeletons of innumerable marine creatures were pulverised into sand. Machair is the flat, coastal plain, where a mixture of sand and peat produces fertile, flower-rich grasslands and supports numerous species of birds. Traditional, small-scale cropping of the machair is an integral part of its life cycle.

Of the four National Nature Reserves in the Western Isles, only one is on an inhabited island – Loch Druidibeg in South Uist (see the boxed text 'Loch Druidibeg National Nature Reserve' on page 343). More than 40 Sites of Special Scientific Interest protect areas of botanical and zoological importance, notably the machair. The Royal Society for the Protection of Birds' Balranald reserve in North Uist includes beach, dune, machair and freshwater habitats.

CLIMATE

One thing is certain about the Western Isles' climate – its variability from day to day, hour to hour and between areas within the isles. The two major influences are the Gulf Stream, which carries relatively warm water from southern latitudes, and its accompanying mild, moisture-laden south-westerly winds. These winds expend the greater part of their energy and load on the western coast, with relatively little left for sheltered eastern parts. Processions of depressions from the south-west bring cloud and rain, and wind-shifts from the south-west round to the north-west. Approaching fronts can usually be seen across the vast sky, presaged by 'mare's tail' clouds, then lower, hazy cloud and sheets of rain streaking the horizon. Interludes of dry, calm weather correspond with easterly air, bringing summertime warmth and winter frost.

The driest months are from April to July, when the average monthly rainfall for Stornoway, on the east coast of Lewis, ranges from 55mm to 70mm. The wettest months are from October to December with monthly totals exceeding 125mm. These figures are higher farther south, especially in mountainous Harris, where the annual total rainfall is around 1400mm compared with Stornoway's 1100mm.

July and August are the warmest months – the average daily temperature is around 13°C and the maximum only occasionally touches 20°C. Winter is relatively mild, with a daily average temperature of around 4.5°C. Snow certainly falls but usually thaws quickly; March has the highest snowfall.

Gales are most prevalent in December and January, and rare during summer (although a force 10 gale interrupted play in June when the following walks were being surveyed!). Windless days are almost unknown – wind is the most important single factor likely to affect your plans in the Western Isles.

INFORMATION

Information Sources

There are two full-time Tourist Information Centres (TICs) in the Western Isles; both are open Monday to Saturday. Stornoway TIC (☎ 01851-703088) and Tarbert TIC (☎ 01859-502011) both stock an excellent range of maps (including OS maps) and books about the Western Isles.

You can use the Western Isles Tourist Board's informative Web site **W** www.witb.co.uk to book accommodation and purchase maps, books and guides. Another site, **W** www.hebrides.com, covers Skye as well, and is best for background information.

During the 1990s more than a dozen waymarked, low-level walking routes were developed throughout the Western Isles, each mapped and described in an excellent series of inexpensive brochures (available from TICs). Several involve some road walking, while others make use of traditional routes closed to vehicles. Although maintenance is variable, they're worth seeking out as an enjoyable means of learning more about local history and wildlife. Information boards and car parks have been provided at the main access points. The Tolsta to Ness walk in Lewis and the old track to Rhenigidale are featured in this chapter; others are included in the Other Walks on page 349.

Highland and Western Isles Council's *Public Transport Travel Guide: Skye & Western Isles*, available at TICs, contains timetables and contact information for travel to and within the isles.

The best sources of information about the weather are the Met Office (☎ 09068-500441) mountain area service for the western Highlands, including the islands, and the *West Highland Free Press*, published in Skye but an informative source for the Western Isles too.

In an emergency, the number for the local mountain rescue service is the Stornoway police station on ☎ 01851-702222.

Maps

For planning and familiarisation, there's a choice between the official tourist map *Western Isles* at 1:125,000, not topographical but with much useful information, and the OS Travelmaster 1:250,000 map No 3 *(Western Scotland & the Western Isles)*.

Books

A trilogy, *The Hebrides: A Habitable Land?*, *The Hebrides: A Natural Tapestry* and *The Hebrides: A Mosaic of Islands* by JM Boyd & IL Boyd, comprehensively surveys the human and natural history of the entire Outer Hebrides. The Scottish Mountaineering Club's hillwalkers' guide *The Islands of Scotland* by DJ Fabian, GE Little & DN Williams includes the Western Isles. June Parker's *25 Walks: The Western Isles* is outdated on some points of detail, but the clear walk descriptions hold good. *Walking in the Hebrides* by Roger Redfern has several walks in the Western Isles.

Place Names

On street and roadside direction signs, Gaelic names either stand alone or are shown more prominently than the English version. Similarly, the OS Landranger 1:50,000 maps show Gaelic names almost exclusively, with English equivalents only for the major towns. In this chapter, the English place names are followed, wherever possible, by the Gaelic names.

Other Information

The walks described in this book follow defined and/or recognised routes where access is unrestricted. Elsewhere, as a general rule, you shouldn't strike any problems with access to the coast and hills. Always take care with fences – find a gate or stile, or step over with minimal strain on the wires. Nevertheless, if there's a house nearby, it's worth calling in and checking that there aren't any problems. The same applies to camping 'in the wild' – ask first, then leave your site as you find it (see Responsible Walking on page 64). On Barra and Vatersay much of the countryside is fenced for grazing; it is best to seek out unfenced ground on the

Sunday in the Western Isles

The Western Isles is the stronghold in Scotland of the Free Church, which was founded in 1843 following a schism in the Church of Scotland about the appointment of ministers. The Free Church has since split, and split again, and among these smaller churches are the Free Presbyterian Church and United Free Presbyterians.

Free Church congregations have built many remarkably large churches, on Lewis and Harris in particular, standing solidly four-square against the elements. Their deep attachment to the Bible requires observance of the Lord's day, Sunday, as a day of rest and devotion. Consequently, there are no public transport services (including to and from the mainland), shops and petrol stations are closed, and only a handful of hotels provide meals for nonresidents. You'll also see signs prohibiting sport and even the use of children's playgrounds.

Attempts by the ferry company CalMac to operate a Sunday service to Tarbert in Harris have been fiercely opposed, although it's likely that one will have started by the time you're reading this.

Things are quite different on South Uist and Barra, where most people adhere to the Roman Catholic faith.

In today's materialistic world, the Free Presbyterians' beliefs may seem anachronistic but the people of the Western Isles, nonetheless, deserve visitors' respect for their beliefs and practices.

machair (coastal grasslands) where camping should be OK.

Guided Walks

At the time of writing, there was no Countryside Ranger Service providing guided walks in the Western Isles. North-West Frontiers (☎ 01854-612628, e NWF@compuserve.com), a well-established company, has coast and mountain walks in Harris, Barra and the Uists. Locally based Mike Briggs Sports (☎ 01859-502376) offers guided day walks, mainly in Harris.

Lewis

Lewis (Leodhas) is the most populous of the Western Isles, with Stornoway on the east coast and several villages sprawled along the west. The empty hinterland of north Lewis is dominated by almost featureless peatlands; in the south the countryside becomes rockier and more hilly. All around the coast is the scenic highlight – cliffs punctuated by narrow inlets, bays and sandy beaches. The relatively smooth profile of the coast breaks up the farther south you go, the crumpled lines extending into Harris.

GETTING AROUND

There are several car hire companies in and around Stornoway. Hiring may be more economical than bringing a car on the ferry if you are staying only a few days. Arnol Car Rental (☎ 01851-710548, e arnolmotors@aol.com) charges £18 a day for a small car over seven days or more. Mackinnon Self Drive (☎ 01851-702984, e mackinnonhire@hotmail.com) charges £130 to hire a small car for a week.

Lewis has a surprisingly good network of bus services to outlying areas, although you need to study the timetable carefully to ensure you are not stranded (remember – no buses on Sunday).

ACCESS TOWN

Stornoway (Steornabhagh)

Far and away the largest town on Lewis, Stornoway is anything but a metropolis and still has a country town feel about it. When making your plans, remember that some B&B hosts prefer not to welcome or farewell guests on Sunday (see the boxed text 'Sunday in the Western Isles' on page 329). Shops are closed on Sunday and many also close for part or all of Wednesday each week.

Stornoway TIC (☎ 01851-703088), in the town centre at 26 Cromwell St, stocks an excellent range of maps and books, and is open Monday to Saturday.

One of the very few places in the Western Isles where you can buy gas canisters for camping stoves is Sportsworld (☎ 01851-705464), 1–3 Francis St, open Monday to Saturday.

The public library, Leabharlainn nan Eilean Siar (☎ 01851-703064), in Cromwell St, offers Internet access. The charges are £2 for 30 minutes or £3.50 per hour, and you probably need to reserve a slot. The library, open Monday to Saturday, has its own coffee shop.

You'll find an ATM opposite the TIC and at the Co-op supermarket (see Places to Stay & Eat).

Luggage can be left during the day at the bus station in Shore St for £1 per large item. It's open from 8.30am to 6pm.

Places to Stay & Eat About 1.5mi north of Stornoway is ***Laxdale Holiday Park*** *(☎ 01851-703234)*. It has plenty of space for campers; the cost is £3.50 for a tent and £2 per adult. The modern, compact bunkhouse has four-person rooms and a kitchen with a barbecue area nearby; the tariff is £8.50. ***Stornoway Backpackers*** *(☎ 01851-703628, 47 Keith St)* is centrally located in a traditional cottage. The £9 tariff includes breakfast. Of the B&Bs, Mrs Macleod's ***Ravenswood*** *(☎ 01851-702673)*, in a fine, 19th-century home in Matheson Rd, is very comfortable indeed, from £20.

Apart from the several pubs, which all serve bar meals, Stornoway is surprisingly cosmopolitan with the excellent ***Thai Cafe*** *(☎ 01851-701811, 27 Church St)*. It's open Monday to Saturday and offers a wide range of curries and Thai dishes; expect to pay around £9 for a delicious meal. You can bring your own drinks. There's also the ***Stornoway Balti House*** *(☎ 01851-706116, 24 South Beach St)*, open Sunday, offering an extensive menu of curries from £6.

For self-caterers there are several bakeries and butchers in the town centre and a small ***health food shop*** in Cromwell St. There's a ***Safeway*** supermarket near the ferry terminal and a ***Co-op*** supermarket at the northern end of town.

Getting There & Away British Airways Express (☎ 0845-773 3377) operates flights from Glasgow and Inverness at least once daily Monday to Saturday. The return economy fare from Glasgow is £107.70 and from Inverness £80. British Airways offers a Highland Rover ticket, which provides for a minimum of five separate flights on Scottish routes, including the Western Isles. The cost is £169; additional (but different) sectors can be purchased for £40. The maximum duration of this ticket is three months. Flights also operate between Stornoway and Benbecula (£79 return) and Barra (£119.80 return). You have to catch a taxi from Stornoway airport (4mi east of the town) – there's no bus service.

Sailing from Ullapool on the mainland at least twice daily, Monday to Saturday, is Caledonian MacBrayne's (CalMac; ☎ 01475-650100) car ferry *Isle of Lewis* . It's wise to book well in advance if you're taking a car during the peak summer season (July and August); foot passengers can normally expect to travel without advance booking. A five-day return ticket costs £21.75 plus £101 for a standard-sized car.

If you're travelling around the islands, the Island Hopscotch and Island Rover tickets are a good investment. There are many to choose from, such as the Hopscotch ticket (valid for a month) for travel from Ullapool to Stornoway, Leverburgh to Otternish, Lochboisdale to Castlebay and back to Oban for £37 per person plus £158 for the car. A 15-day Rover ticket costs £61 plus £307 for the vehicle, and allows unrestricted travel on all CalMac services. Tickets can be booked online at ⓔ reservations@calmac.co.uk or ⓦ www.calmac.co.uk.

Scottish Citylink (☎ 0870-550 5050) runs connecting services to the ferries at Ullapool from Edinburgh (£26.50 return), Glasgow and Inverness (£11 return). Rapson's (☎ 01463-710555) and Macdonalds (☎ 01870- 620288) also operate between Inverness and Ullapool to connect with the ferry.

Tolsta to Ness

Duration	4–4½ hours
Distance	10mi (16km)
Standard	medium
Start	Garry Beach
Finish	Skigersta
Nearest Towns	Stornoway, Ness
Public Transport	yes

Summary Spectacular coastal scenery, remains of summer shielings, superb views of Sutherland mountains and abundant seabirds.

This walk is inspired by the waymarked route from Garry Beach (Tràigh Ghearadha), north of the village of New Tolsta (Bail' Ur Tholastaidh), northward to the district of Ness (Nis) and the village of Skigersta (Sgiogarstaigh). The greater part of the waymarked route stays well inland from the cliff tops, as it crosses the peaty moorland. Thus it misses the very fine coastal scenery of cliffs, stacks, rock islets and deep inlets (geos). The walk described here leaves the waymarked route early on and stays close to the cliffs, but take care, they drop vertically into the sea 50m or more below. Although there isn't a continuous path, on the whole the going underfoot is across grassland with only a few boggy patches. At either end of the walk the way is along minor vehicular tracks, used for access to peat diggings or for gathering sheep. The walk can be done in either direction – there's not much to choose.

Alternatives As an alternative, an out-and-back walk from Garry Beach to Dibidale (Dhiobadail) would take in the best of the coastal scenery and the easiest going underfoot. The distance is 10mi (16km), for which you should allow at least four hours.

HISTORY

During this walk you can see evidence of some strikingly different aspects of Lewis' history. Precariously situated on cliff tops are the remains of at least two Iron Age promontory forts – Dùn Othail and Dùn Filiscleitir (around 500 BC). Similarly located, on top of a rock stack at the southern end of Garry Beach, is Caisteal a' Mhorair (Mormaer's Castle), probably dating from the 13th century.

Shieling settlements have long been an integral part of island life, although less so nowadays. Shielings (small stone cottages), some quite elaborate and some providing only the roughest of shelter, were built on the coast and in remote mountain country. People lived here while fishing or tending and gathering sheep. There are three shieling villages – Dibidale, Filiscleitir and Cuiashader (Cuidhsiadar), and several isolated shielings along the way.

Lord Leverhulme, a wealthy English magnate, bought Lewis and Harris in 1918 and launched ambitious plans to provide jobs for all, mainly by developing the fishing industry. One of his many projects was building a road from Tolsta to Port of Ness, but it only got as far as Abhainn na Cloich, barely 3mi along the way. Two fine bridges survive as memorials to the scale of his vision. Even Leverhulme's wealth couldn't cope with the costs of his projects, on an island far from big mainland cities. He also ran into opposition from landless soldiers returning from WWI, for whom possession of land was more important than modern fishing ports. Confronted with severe financial difficulties, Leverhulme offered Lewis to its people but, apart from Stornoway, there were very few takers. He died in 1925.

NATURAL HISTORY

The fractured, indented coastline, composed mainly of various types of gneiss, is the highlight of this walk; inland the relatively featureless peat moorlands, dotted with lochs, stretch to the horizon. Here and there peat is still cut for use as domestic fuel. Seabirds are constant companions – stiff-winged fulmars, skuas, gulls and cormorants. Seals can often be seen basking on the rocks at the foot of the cliffs and, out to sea, gannets dive for fish.

PLANNING

The best weather is between April and September but it's always windy, even along the east coast of Lewis, which is relatively sheltered from prevailing winds.

Carry food and drink for the day; sheep graze the moorlands and the chances of there being an upturned sheep in any of the burns is high.

Maps & Books

The OS Landranger 1:50,000 map No 8 *(Stornoway & North Lewis)* covers the walk and shows the waymarked route.

The Western Isles Walks leaflet *Tolstaidh – Nis*, available from Stornoway TIC, contains excellent background information; this is reproduced in summary form on a board at the start of the walk. June Parker's *25 Walks in the Western Isles* describes the coast walk as far as Dibidale.

NEAREST TOWN
Ness (Nis)

Ness is a district rather than a particular village, with several villages scattered along the last few miles of the A857 where facilities are few.

Places to Stay & Eat Beautifully restored, the ***Galson Farm Guest House*** *(☎ 01851-850492)* is a short distance from the A857, 6mi (10km) south-west of Lionel. B&B starts at £29 and evening meals are available (DB&B from £45).

Closer to the end of the walk is Ms Macleod's B&B ***Eisdean*** *(☎ 01851- 810240)* at Five Penny Ness (Coig Peighinnean), where B&B costs £19 and DB&B £28.

The nearest hostel is ***Garenin Gatliff Trust Hostel***, about 1mi beyond the village of Carloway (Càrlabhagh) on the west coast and about 25mi (40km) south-westward. The tariff in the restored, thatched traditional cottage is £6.50; you'll need to bring your own bedding. Bookings aren't accepted – it's first come, first served (see the boxed text 'Herbert Gatliff – Visionary' on page 336).

The nearest ***shop*** to the end of the walk is a licensed grocer at Swainbost (Suainebost), about 1.5mi south-west along the A857 from its junction at Lionel (Lional) with the B8015 (Skigersta road).

Getting There & Away Galson Motors (☎ 01851-840269) runs buses between Stornoway and Port of Ness Monday to Saturday. Maclennan Coaches (☎ 01851-702114) operates a service from Stornoway that goes through Carloway; some buses connect with the Port of Ness bus at Barvas (Barabhas) Junction.

GETTING TO/FROM THE WALK

To the Start

Western Isles Council (Comhairle nan Eilean Siar; ☎ 01851-709721) operates a bus service from Stornoway to the village of New Tolsta, from Monday to Saturday starting at 7.45am.

By car drive north along the A857 from Stornoway town centre for just over 1mi to Newmarket. Turn right along the B895 and follow it to the car park above Garry Beach, about half a mile beyond New Tolsta.

From the Finish

From the car park at the end of the walk near Skigersta, it is 2mi along the B8015 to the junction with the A857 at Lionel. Galson Motors (☎ 01851-840269) buses stop at Lionel en route to Stornoway at 3.55pm Monday to Saturday.

THE WALK

From the car park at Garry Beach set out along the rough, sealed road as it dips down to cross the incongruous Bridge to Nowhere across River Garry (Abhainn Ghearadha). Past the river the road becomes more of a vehicle track heading to the coast. From here, on a clear day, some of the Sutherland peaks can be seen across The Minch – Suilven stands out as a graceful spire (see Other Walks on page 368). Beyond the concrete bridge across **Abhainn na Cloich** (where the waterfall is best seen slightly downstream), the route is marked by green posts with a yellow band. After about 50m the driest

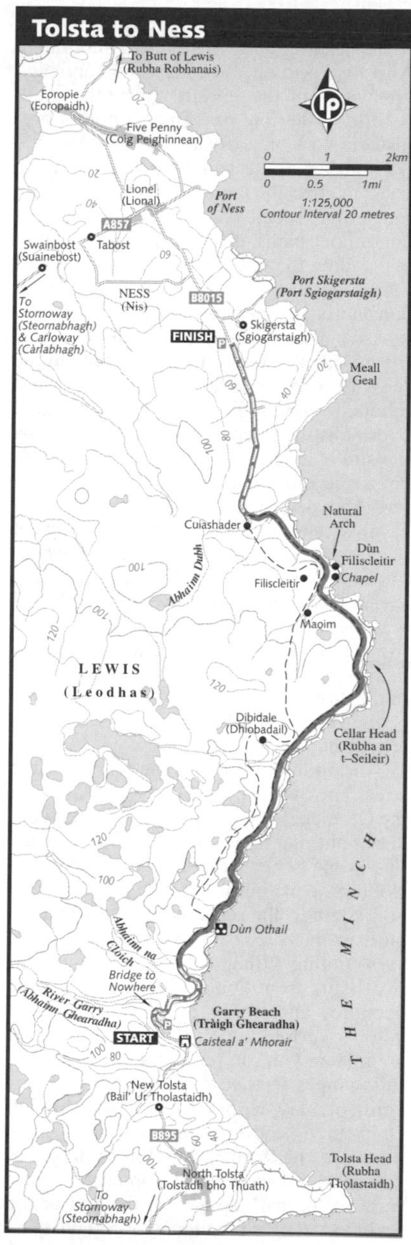

ground should be upslope from the marked route, leading north-east across moorland. Aim for a post on a heathery knoll and pick up the path on the seaward side of the knoll. A little farther on, past **Dùn Othail**, a prehistoric fort on a rocky promontory, the waymarked route swings away from the coast to cross the moor. Instead, stick to the much more scenic coast where more or less continuous paths, made by sheep and walkers, follow the cliff tops. The panorama of mountains across the eastern skyline changes constantly as you move north.

After nearly 2mi of fine walking above the crinkled coastal cliffs, you come to the ruins of a stone cottage on a grassy knoll (about 1¾ hours from the start). The knoll overlooks the steep-sided glen of Dibidale, the site of a shieling village. Drop down to cross the burn at a confluence, following red-topped, green waymarker posts, and climb steeply up the other side to a cluster of ruinous shielings. The marked route continues its inland course. If you're pursuing the independent coastal way, you'll find that the path of sorts is much less obvious from here, across grassland and above the many spectacular geos (narrow rocky inlets) in the cliff line. A couple of hundred metres beyond Cellar Head (Rubha an t-Seileir) the coast trends north-westward.

Turn inland to cross the next sizable stream below the place shown as Maoim on the OS map. Here you might find, and wonder about, the remains of a cluster of curious stone structures built into the steep slope near the burn. Up the other side and you come to the remains of a tiny **chapel**, built in the 1920s for the residents of the surrounding village of Filiscleitir (about two hours from Dibidale). Dùn Filiscleitir occupies an improbable site at the cliff edge, overlooking a spectacular natural arch. Here you can rejoin the marked route following a vehicle track, which leads inland, or stay with the coast to Abhainn Dubh then head west to reach the vehicle track at the former shieling village of Cuiashader. From here it's about an hour's walk to the parking area at the end of the sealed road near the village of Skigersta.

Harris

Harris (Na Hearadh) adjoins Lewis, occupying the southern third of their island. Its name probably comes from an old Norse word that means 'the higher parts'. The Lewis/Harris boundary runs through Loch Seaforth, across Loch Langavat's southern end and west along the top of Loch Resort.

Rock is the overwhelming feature of the landscape – there's plenty of water too, in freshwater and sea lochs, but it's the surreal, glaciated moonscapes that distinguish Harris from the rest of the isles. The north of Harris is wilder and more mountainous, with Clisham (799m), the highest peak in the Western Isles, and several others topping 700m towering over long, deep glens and remote lochs.

South Harris has plenty of respectable although lower mountains, and is known for the magnificence of its west coast beaches and machair.

This section describes two walks in north Harris, one following a historic path to an isolated settlement, with high- and low-level options, and the other to Clisham. There are suggestions for more walks in Other Walks on page 349.

PLANNING

When to Walk

Being the most mountainous part of the Western Isles, Harris is prone to walker-unfriendly weather. The best times are May to early June and September. Snow can fall on the highest peaks in most months and may lie for some time during winter.

Stalking Clisham is within the North Harris Estate; any stalking activities are unlikely to affect access. However, if you contemplate venturing into the mountains to the west of Clisham between mid-August and mid-October, check about access by calling ☎ 01876-500329.

Maps

All the walks on Harris described here are covered by OS Landranger 1:50,000 map No 14 *(Tarbert & Loch Seaforth)*.

ACCESS TOWN
Tarbert (Tairbeart) & Around

The capital of Harris, Tarbert straddles a narrow neck of land between north and south Harris. Tarbert TIC (☎ 01859-502011), in Pier Rd above the ferry terminal, stocks an excellent range of maps and books, and is open from Monday to Saturday. The Harris Tweed shop also has a good selection of maps and books. The one bank in Tarbert is open Monday to Friday but doesn't have an ATM. Internet access is available in the public library on the high school campus towards the western end of Tarbert. It's open Monday to Friday and Saturday morning, and the charge is £2 per 30 minutes or £3.50 for an hour.

Places to Stay & Eat Walkers are welcome at ***Avalon B&B** (☎ 01859-502334)*, on the western side of Tarbert, where B&B starts at £20 and evening meals are available. ***Drinishader Bunkhouse** (☎ 01859-511255)* in the crofting village of Drinishader (Drinisiadar), on a minor road that branches from the A859 about 3mi south of Tarbert, is very congenial and homely; the tariff is £7. There's a basic ***camping site*** at Plocrapool, which is about 1mi south of Drinishader; contact ☎ 01859-511207.

For a meal and a drink, and accommodation, it's the ***Harris Hotel** (☎ 01859-502154, ⓔ Cameronharris@btinternet.com)* in Tarbert, about 500m north-west of the ferry terminal. B&B starts at £25 and the bar suppers are good value. During summer ***First Fruits Tearoom***, near the TIC, is open until 6.30pm (otherwise 4.30pm) and does good light meals, home baking and teas.

Tarbert Stores, opposite the TIC, has a limited range of gas canisters for camping stoves. Well-stocked ***Munros*** off-licence supermarket has a butcher's section.

Getting There & Away CalMac (☎ 01475-650100) runs a ferry service Monday to Saturday from Uig on the Isle of Skye to Tarbert. A five-day return ticket costs £14.20 per person and £67 for a vehicle. Coming from the Uists, you'll need the CalMac ferry across the Sound of Harris from Otternish to Leverburgh; it operates Monday to Saturday and the single fare is £4.60 per person plus £21.35 for a car. See Getting There & Away under Stornoway on page 331 for details on Island Hopscotch and Rover tickets.

Harris Coaches' (☎ 01859-502441) bus service between Stornoway, Tarbert and Leverburgh provides five departures each way Monday, Wednesday and Friday.

Tarbert is 37mi (59.5km) from Stornoway along the A859, the greater part of which is a good two-way road.

Rhenigidale Path

Duration	4 hours
Distance	7mi (11km)
Standard	medium
Start & Finish	Lacasdale Lochs bridge
Nearest Towns	Tarbert, Rhenigidale
Public Transport	yes

Summary Follow a historic path through magnificent mountain and coast scenery to the isolated hamlet of Rhenigidale; explore a deserted village or climb the rugged peak of Toddun.

Until 1990 Rhenigidale village (Reinigeadal) could only be reached on foot via rough paths, which were hazardous in winter, or by boat. The new road over the mountains made life much easier for the residents, but perhaps took away some of the magic of the place for visitors. Most of the old path from the west survives and provides an outstandingly scenic walk up and over a rugged ridge and steeply down to the shores of Loch Trolamaraig. The path is easy enough to follow, although boggy in places. Around 400m of ascent is involved; this, with the occasional roughness of the track, merits a medium grading. This walk is described in an informative leaflet *Cuairt Reinigeadail* in the Western Isles Walks series, available from TICs.

Alternatives Using Rhenigidale as a base, there's scope for at least two walks in the vicinity. This first is to Toddun (Todun; 528m); wedge shaped and precipitous, but a surprisingly approachable mountain overlooking Rhenigidale. Standing apart from the main north Harris mountains, Toddun affords spectacular all-round views. The climb can take just a couple of hours up and back from the old path (see Side Trip: Toddun on page 337).

You can make it a full day by descending west from Toddun, about 150m north of the summit. From the glen below continue over An Reithe, from where a broad gully, cutting diagonally across its western face, leads down to the southern end of Loch an Reithe. Then it's over Stralaval (Strathabhal; 389m) and down to the path in lonely Glen Lacasdale, which provides an easy stroll down to the Tarbert-Scalpy road, about half a mile west of the start of the path to Rhenigidale. This option takes six hours to cover the 11mi (18km) and involves 1010m of ascent.

Another possibility is to visit the deserted settlement of Molinginish (Molingeanais), perched above Loch Trolamaraig opposite Rhenigidale (see Side Trip: Molinginish on page 338). This walk could be incorporated in the return to Lacasdale Lochs, in which case the overall distance is 8.5mi (13.5km).

HISTORY

Rhenigidale originated in the 1820s as a new home for crofters evicted from the Forest of Harris (estate) – the area along the Huishinish (Huisinis) road (B887) west of Tarbert. Early in the 20th century around 90 people lived in Rhenigidale, occupying 17 houses, most of which are still standing. They were expert boat handlers as all their supplies, including peat (for fuel) and seaweed (for fertiliser), had to be shipped in from Tarbert. Isolation came to an end in 1990 with the completion of 5mi of sealed road; the first warden of the Rhenigidale Hostel, Roddy Macinnes, led the campaign to have the road built.

Molinginish was settled around the same time as Rhenigidale; at least 12 families lived there – enough to support a school. The village was abandoned in 1965 although two cottages are still occupied from time to time.

NATURAL HISTORY

Rhenigidale sits on the northern shore of Loch Trolamaraig and close to the entrance to Loch Seaforth, which bites deep into the

Herbert Gatliff – Visionary

Herbert Gatliff, an Englishman born near the end of the 19th century, dedicated most of his life to young people and the youth hostel movement. He discovered the Western Isles in the late 1940s and was completely captivated; annual visits followed for the next 20 years. Convinced that the isles were the ideal place to establish simple hostels he tried, but failed, to persuade the SYHA to become involved.

Undaunted, Gatliff seized an opportunity to open a hostel at Rhenigidale. An empty, thatched cottage was soon made ready and opened in Easter 1962 – when access was only on foot or by boat. Howmore hostel, also a thatched cottage, followed in 1964. The next year a hostel was opened on the island of Scarp (off Harris' west coast) but closed in 1969 when the island was deserted. During the 1970s piped water and toilets were bestowed on Rhenigidale and Howmore, and Berneray hostel was opened.

Herbert Gatliff died in 1977; his work is carried on by the Gatliff Trust, which works in partnership with the local crofters who own the hostel buildings. In 1987 the SYHA agreed to bring the crofters' hostels into their system, the main benefit being better publicity. Running of the hostels stayed with the crofters and Gatliff Hebridean Hostels Trust.

There are now four crofters' hostels: Garenin, Rhenigidale, Berneray and Howmore. Despite the imposition of the Scottish Tourist Board's grading system, the hostels still provide no-frills accommodation with basic facilities, including heating (although not central heating), and an indefinable atmosphere of camaraderie and freedom. For more information about the Trust, check the Web site at W www.gatliff.org.uk or contact The Secretary at 30 Francis St, Stornoway HS1 2ND.

interior of Harris. The old path crosses the rugged, rocky ridge between East Loch Tarbert and Loch Trolamaraig. In the sheltered north-western corner of the latter loch is an oasis (in Harris terms) of luxuriant plant life (willow, aspen and fragile primrose), protected from the wind and nourished by a rushing stream.

NEAREST TOWN
Rhenigidale (Reinigeadal)

The only place to stay is the ***Rhenigidale Hostel***, simple accommodation with a special tranquillity. The tariff is £6 and you need to come self-contained with a sleeping bag and supplies; there isn't a shop in the village, although the warden who lives nearby keeps a stock of basic items. As a Gatliff hostel (see the boxed text 'Herbert Gatliff – Visionary'), bookings are not accepted – first come, first served. The nearest telephone is at the Maaruig (Màraig) junction, less than 1mi down the Rhenigidale road from the A859 and 2.5mi from Rhenigidale.

Getting There & Away Rhenigidale is at the end (about 3mi) of a minor road, which branches south from the A859 between Ardvourlie (Aird a' Mhulaidh) and the B887 junction.

Harris Car Services (☎ 01859-502221) operates a limited taxibus service between Rhenigidale and Tarbert Pier Monday to Saturday with connections to the Stornoway bus. Seats are limited and must be booked the night before for the morning run or by 3pm for the late afternoon service. The bus operator is happy to carry large rucksacks to Rhenigidale from Tarbert TIC or vice versa. A more expensive taxi service is available by arrangement.

GETTING TO/FROM THE WALK

The walk starts and finishes at a car park on the road from Tarbert to Scalpay (Scalpaigh), just across the bridge over the stream flowing out of Lacasdale Lochs, 2mi (3km) from Tarbert.

Scalpay Community Minibus (☎ 01859-540356) does the run between Tarbert and Scalpay, passing the start of the walk, Monday to Friday; on Saturday the service is provided by Harris Car Services (☎ 01859-502221), generally running between 9.30am and 4.30pm.

THE WALK

See map page 338

From the car park the track starts to climb almost straightaway, beside the tumbling Abhainn an t-Sratha, crossing and recrossing it in the process. After about 40 minutes you reach a fairly broad saddle on the long ridge between Beinn a' Chaolais to the south and Trolamul to the north. As you start to descend, note a cairn on the right, marking the start of the path to Molinginish. The Rhenigidale path copes with the extremely steep drop to the shore of Loch Trolamaraig in a series of extraordinary zigzags, through broken cliffs lower down. You soon reach a bridge across Abhainn Cheann a' Locha, the stream in rugged Glen Trolamaraig, with a delightful shingle beach nearby (25 minutes from the saddle).

Although there is a low-level path onwards from here, it's little used and in poor condition. The better route rises sharply from the bridge but soon heads back down across the spur to a gated stream crossing. Continue past the silent remains of the village of **Garry-aloteger** (Gearraidh Lotaigear), with substantial stone cottages and stone-walled enclosures. The low, parallel ridges in the nearby fields were lazy beds – humps laboriously created by hauling loads of seaweed to enrich the poor soil for the cultivation of potatoes and animal fodder. From here it's a short distance along the narrow, grassed path cut into the slope, up to the road. Rhenigidale is barely half a mile down the road (about 50 minutes from the shingle beach). Return to Lacasdale Lochs bridge by the same route.

Side Trip: Toddun

3 hours, 4mi (6.5km), 550m ascent

From the road west of Rhenigidale, follow the path signposted to Urgha and Tarbert (the path followed on the main walk), through the remains of Garry-aloteger, across a bridge

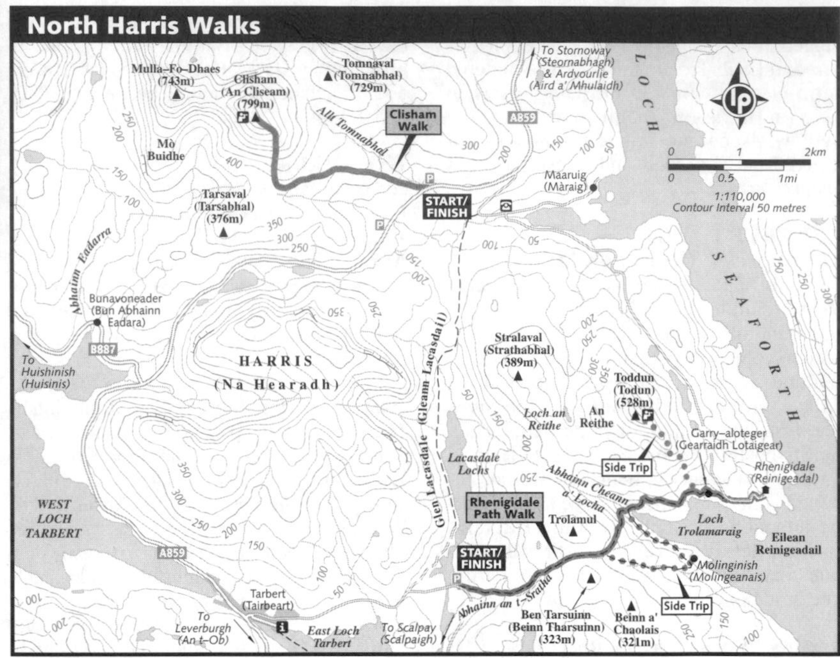

and leave the path 10m farther on. Walk northward up the broad spur to a fence; bear left and follow it generally west until you meet a fence running north-south. Cross this fence then climb to the well-defined ridge and follow it generally north-westward, shortly crossing another fence. Keep to the highest ground – it's surprisingly easy to find a way up through the scattered crags to the summit ridge. Go on to the survey cairn sheltered by a circular stone wall on **Toddun's** summit (an hour from the main path). Among many other places, you can gaze upon the mountainous massif to the north, dominated by Clisham; the Shiant Islands to the east; and the South Uist 'hills' to the south. Eventually, retrace your steps to Rhenigidale.

Side Trip: Molinginish

3 hours, 5mi (8km), 150m ascent

Follow the old path from the road west of Rhenigidale, down past Garry-aloteger, and on to the bridge over Abhainn Cheann a' Locha. The Molinginish path takes off a short distance up from the shingle beach, and soon becomes clear as it cuts across the precipitous slope; it's narrow, rocky and boggy in places. The second stream crossing needs *great care*, making use of slender rocky ledges. After about 35 minutes the path starts to descend and suddenly the ruinous and roofed cottages of **Molinginish** materialise, crammed into a small, partly sheltered glen right down to the edge of the shingle beach, with the lazy beds above.

For the walk through to Lacasdale Lochs (or to make a round walk back to Rhenigidale), cross the burn and pick up the track through a large gap in the fence across the slope. The track is wide and still in good condition, with few bogs to negotiate as it rises westward across the moorland. Allow about 30 minutes up to the saddle and the junction with the main Rhenigidale path, marked with a large cairn.

Clisham

Duration 3½–4 hours
Distance 4mi (6.5km)
Standard medium
Start & Finish Allt Tomnabhal bridge
Nearest Town Tarbert
Public Transport yes
Summary The Western Isles' highest peak – a steep, rocky, straightforward ascent for superb, all-round views of peaks, lochs and deep glens.

Clisham (An Cliseam; 799m, 2622ft) is the only peak that draws Corbett baggers to the Western Isles (there are no Munros), and it is well worth climbing for the exceptional views on the clear, not too windy, days that do happen on Harris. The meaning and derivation of its name is uncertain, but an educated opinion has it being of Norse origin and possibly meaning 'rocky cliff'.

The conventional approach up the south-eastern ridge from the A859 is straightforward, although almost unrelentingly steep; the total ascent is 640m. There is a clear enough path over some of the lower, boggy ground and high on the main ridge.

Alternatives Experienced and agile walkers can take a different approach, from Bunavoneader (Bun Abhainn Eadara) on the Huishinish road, via Mó Buidhe, Mulla-Fo-Dhaes (743m) and the scrambly ridge east to Clisham, returning via Tarsaval.

NATURAL HISTORY

Clisham dominates a complex array of narrow, granitic ridges and peaks rising steeply from the western shore of Loch Seaforth and overlooking West Loch Tarbert to the south. To the west, Clisham's massif is separated from another magnificently rugged group of peaks by a long deep glen aligned north-south.

GETTING TO/FROM THE WALK

The walk starts at a parking area on the northern side of the A859 at the Allt Tomnabhal bridge, about 1mi west of the turn-off to Rhenigidale. Harris Coaches' (☎ 01859-502441) bus on the Stornoway-Tarbert-Leverburgh service stops at the Rhenigidale turn-off (see Getting There & Away for Tarbert on page 335).

THE WALK

See map page 338

From the car park a slightly muddy path leads generally north-west, tending westward, above Allt Tomnabhal. To steer well clear of the cliffs guarding the eastern approaches to the summit, make a rising traverse of the broad spur on the left, aiming to reach the really steep southern slopes north of a saddle. Climb towards a big drift of scree to the left of some small cliffs. Continue up, mainly over rock and, higher up, small patches of grass.

Once the ridge narrows and becomes distinct, a clear path materialises and leads along the slender rocky spine to **Clisham's** compact summit; the survey (trig) cairn is surrounded by a sheltering stone wall (about 1½ hours from the start). On a good day, there isn't much of the Western Isles you can't see from here, and the view extends east to the more prominent peaks in Wester Ross and Sutherland. Return to the start by the same route – more or less!

North Uist

At first North Uist (Uibhist a Tuath) seems to comprise merely water, separated by scraps of rock and soil. But there is actually lots of dry ground (mainly in the north-western quarter); some small but attractive mountains, miles of magnificent beaches on the north coast and a rugged eastern coastline. Beyond the principal town of Lochmaddy (Loch nam Madadh), which takes its name from the extraordinary, island-studded sea loch, there are a few villages on the western side, and many houses and crofts scattered in between. North Uist's identity as an island is perhaps slightly compromised by the modern, but extremely convenient, causeways linking it to Berneray (Bearnaraigh) in the north, and Grimsay (Griomasaigh) and Benbecula (Beinn na Faoghla) in the south.

PLANNING

Information Sources

The community-based Web site W www.uistonline.com is a useful source of information about the island.

GETTING THERE & AWAY

British Airways Express (☎ 0845-773 3377) inter-island flights land at Benbecula airport (between North and South Uist) Monday to Friday; the return fare from Stornoway is £79 and from Barra £40.80. There are also flights direct to Benbecula from Glasgow, Monday to Saturday; the return economy fare is £108.60.

Hebridean Coaches' (☎ 01870- 620345) Ludag to Lochmaddy, via Clachan na Luib, service calls at the airport and operates Monday to Saturday.

ACCESS TOWN

Lochmaddy (Loch nam Madadh)

The TIC (☎ 01876-500321), in Pier Rd, is open from early April to mid-October. The Bank of Scotland (near the ferry terminal) has an ATM.

Places to Stay & Eat In a handsome white building, ***Stag Lodge*** *(☎ 01876-500364)*, offers comfortable B&B accommodation from £20 and, conveniently, has a small restaurant. ***The Old Bank House*** *(☎ 01876-500275)* has a range of rooms; the B&B tariff starts at £20.

Lochmaddy Hotel *(☎ 01876-500331)* has a particularly good restaurant specialising in seafood (to £18) and serves bar meals. The ***post office shop*** has an adequate range of supplies.

Getting There & Away CalMac (☎ 01475-650100) operates a daily ferry between Uig on the Isle of Skye and Lochmaddy. A five-day return ticket costs £14.20 per person plus £67 for a car. Coming from Harris, you catch the small CalMac vehicle ferry from Leverburgh to Otternish on the northern tip of North Uist and next to the Berneray causeway. The ferry operates Monday to Saturday; a five-day return ticket costs £7.80 per person and £36.50 for a standard car.

Various bus companies operate between Otternish and Lochmaddy; for details pick up a copy of the Highland and Western Isles Councils' *Public Transport Travel Guide: Sky & Western Isles*, available at TICs.

Travelling from South Uist, it's possible to catch the Hebridean Coaches' (☎ 01870-620345) Ludag, Lochboisdale and Howmore to Lochmaddy and Otternish service – see the *Public Transport Travel Guide: Sky & Western Isles*.

By road, Lochmaddy is on the A865, 6mi (9.5km) from Otternish and 50mi (80.5km) from Lochboisdale.

Eaval

Duration	3½–4 hours
Distance	8mi (13km)
Standard	medium
Start & Finish	Drim Sidinish
Nearest Towns	Clachan na Luib, Lochmaddy
Public Transport	yes

Summary The highest peak in North Uist gives a superb, panoramic view of the maze of lochans and land that comprise the Uists, and as far south as the Isle of Rum.

At 347m (1138ft), Eaval is on the route of the Western Isles Challenge, an annual team marathon from Barra to Lewis, involving running, sailing and canoeing. Consequently, there's a clear, if often muddy, path all the way from the end of the Locheport road at Drim Sidinish (Druim Saighdinis). The walk described involves 350m of ascent and is a simple out-and-back route.

Alternatives Alternatively, with suitable transport arrangements, a through walk is possible, descending south-westward from the summit to the shore of the narrow strait between North Uist and Grimsay. You can then, work your way around the long, deep inlet of Oban nam Muca-mara and finally cross-country to the end of a minor road at Cladach Chairinis, which is about 1mi from the A865.

NATURAL HISTORY

Eaval's name, from two Norse words *ey fjall* meaning 'island fell' or 'hill', accurately describes its situation. With the waters of Loch Obisary (Obasaraigh) and several smaller lochs on three sides, and Loch Eport (Euphort) and the open sea also nearby, Eaval is almost an island. Rising steeply on all sides, the mountain dominates the south-easternmost corner of North Uist. It is also the highest of a chain of rocky peaks along the east coast, including the twins South Lee (281m) and North Lee (250m) immediately north of Loch Eport.

PLANNING

This walk could be done at almost any time, although clear weather is essential for the views and to avoid the steep cliffs on Eaval's northern face. The causeway that must be crossed not far from the start should be dry except after heavy rain and at very high tide. The waters of Loch Obisary are brackish, so carry all the drinking water you'll need.

Maps & Books

Eaval is on the OS Landranger 1:50,000 map No 22 *(Benbecula & South Uist)*; the adjoining map to the north, No 18 *(Sound of Harris & St Kilda)*, is useful for orientation and identification of local landmarks.

NEAREST TOWN

Clachan na Luib & Around

Clachan na Luib is a scattering of houses around a major road junction (A867 and A865), at a point where North Uist is almost split in two. There's plenty of accommodation to the north-west, along the A865, and south towards Grimsay and Benbecula. The following is just a tiny selection. The nearest place where you can access the Internet is in the village of Urachadh-Uibhist on the Bayhead Industrial Estate (☎ 01876-510777) about 5mi (8km) north-west of Clachan na Luib on the A865, but only during the day on Tuesday and Thursday.

Places to Stay & Eat A comfortable bunkhouse, ***Taigh Mo Sheanair*** *(☎ 01876-580246, e sheanair@hotmail.com)* is at Carnach (west of Clachan na Luib) and is in (literally) the owner's grandfather's house. Each of the two bunkrooms is en suite; the tariff is from £9 and hire of bedding is £2. Alternatively you can camp for £4. Access along minor roads from the A865, about 1mi south of Clachan na Luib, is signposted.

The modern ***Carinish Inn*** *(☎ 01876-580673)*, beside the A865 about 2mi south of Clachan na Luib, does B&B from £35 and DB&B starting at £45.

The ***licensed store and grocer*** at Clachan na Luib is well stocked and sells sandwiches. There is a larger ***Co-op*** supermarket at Sollas on the north coast.

Getting There & Away From Monday to Saturday, Hebridean Coaches' (☎ 01870-620345) operates a Ludag to Lochmaddy service, via Clachan na Luib and the airport. Clachan na Luib is 7.5 mi (12km) from Lochmaddy.

GETTING TO/FROM THE WALK

The walk starts at the end of the B894, which branches off the A867 half a mile north-east of the A867/A865 junction at Clachan na Luib, or 6.7mi (11km) south-west along the A867 from its junction with the A865 near Lochmaddy. The road end is 5mi (8km) from the A867.

A postbus (☎ 01876-500330) leaves Clachan na Luib at 9.55am and returns from Sidinish (Saighdinis), about half a mile west of the end of the B894, at 2.15pm Tuesday, Thursday and Saturday.

THE WALK

From the car park go through a gate beside the nearby cottage. Cross a field, through another gate and then follow an old track, which leads down to a small cove with an old stone pier on Loch Eport. Head east on a grass track to a larger cove, with a ruined cottage on the far shore, and on to a boulder causeway. From here continue south-eastward towards the prominent bulk of Buraval (Burabhal). A path, easy to follow most of the way, leads above the very convoluted shores of Loch Obisary and across the lowermost slopes of Buraval. Near the

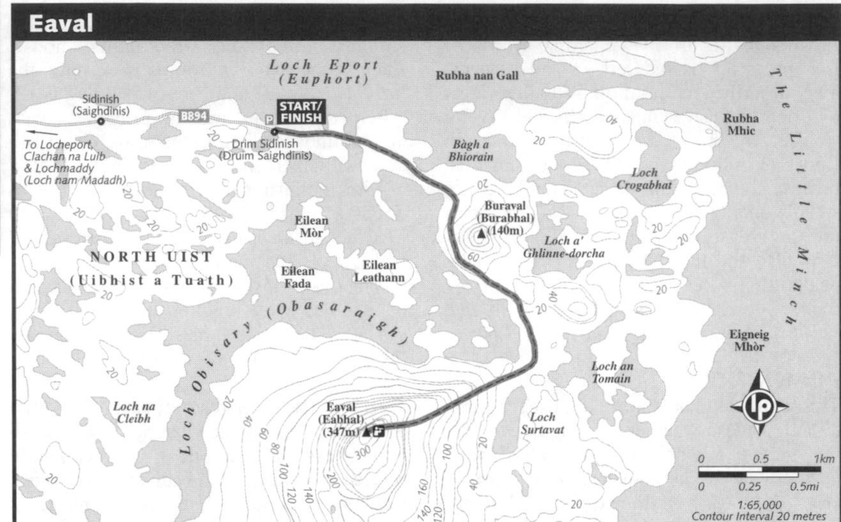

small, orange-sand beaches at the loch's south-easternmost corner, a deer was seen swimming from one of the islets to the eastern shore of the loch when this walk was being surveyed.

Cross the boggy ground between the northern end of Loch Surtavat and the corner of Loch Obisary to the foot of the spur falling precipitously to the north. Broad ribs of rock make for a surprisingly easy, although consistently steep climb. About two hours from the start you should reach the trig point on the summit of **Eaval**. The panoramic vista takes in an extraordinary range of features – the north Harris 'hills', the Black Cuillins on Skye, and an incredible mosaic of rock, grass, water and scattered houses.

On the return it's much easier to pick the best route than it was on the way up; continue around Loch Obisary and back to the start (about 1½ hours from the summit).

South Uist

With a remarkably smooth western coast and crumpled eastern shore, South Uist (Uibhist a' Deas) is quite unlike the other isles because of its long, slender shape. There is much to interest walkers here; numerous rugged peaks, the wild and remote east coast, and the long, long beaches of the Atlantic coast. Causeways link the isle to Benbecula in the north and Eriskay (Eiriosgaigh) in the south. South Uist's population is scattered along the main road, which runs the length of the island. This road demarcates the settled western fringe from the rugged, almost empty country of rock, water and peat to the east. Lochboisdale (Loch Baghasdail), the main town, is near the southern end of the island.

PLANNING

Information Sources

For information about the island, check the community-based W www.uistonline.com.

GETTING THERE & AWAY

See Getting There & Away under North Uist on page 340.

ACCESS TOWN

Lochboisdale (Loch Baghasdail)

Lochboisdale is the principal town of South Uist and is a somewhat unimpressive place, focused on the ordinary business of island life. Thc Lochboisdale TIC (☎ 01878-700286), which is near the pier, is open Monday to Saturday from early April to mid-October. There's a bank but it doesn't have an ATM.

Places to Stay & Eat With an excellent location overlooking the harbour; nearly all the rooms at ***Lochboisdale Hotel*** *(☎ 01878-700332)* are en suite and the B&B tariff ranges up from £36. Bar suppers are good value. Mrs Macdonald's ***Kilchoan B&B*** *(☎ 01878-700517)* is about 1mi from the town centre; B&B is from £17.

There's a ***Co-op*** supermarket at Daliburgh near the junction of the A865 and the B888 to Ludag (and the Eriskay causeway).

Getting There & Away CalMac (☎ 01475-650100) operates a daily ferry service between Oban and Lochboisdale, and via Castlebay (Barra) on some days. There's also a run between Lochboisdale and Mallaig on Tuesday and Wednesday. The five-day return fare from Oban to Lochboisdale is £31.50 and £110 for the car. The fares are slightly cheaper between Mallaig and Lochboisdale.

Hebridean Coaches (☎ 01870-620345) has a Monday to Saturday service between Lochmaddy and Lochboisdale, via the airport, with five buses between 8am and 5.25pm.

Hecla

Duration	7–7½ hours
Distance	10.4mi (16.5km)
Standard	hard
Start & Finish	Lochskipport
Nearest Towns	Howmore, Lochboisdale
Public Transport	no

Summary A challenging and highly rewarding walk to the second-highest peak on South Uist with fantastic, wide-ranging views.

Hecla (Thacla; 606m, 1988ft) is of Norse origin and means 'serrated' or 'comb-like'. It's only a few metres lower than its southern neighbour Beinn Mhòr (620m); if climbing this, the highest peak on the island, appeals, it must be said that Hecla offers a more interesting and equally scenic outing. The walk described here is a fairly straightforward out-and-back route from Lochskipport (Loch Sgioport) to its north. Involving 600m ascent, it's graded hard in recognition of the rough ground traversed and the intricate route finding through broken cliffs. There's a track along the shore of Loch Skipport and indeterminate paths on higher ground, but no beaten highways.

Alternatives There is scope for varying this route. A round walk is possible via the long spur extending north-west from Hecla's

Loch Druidibeg National Nature Reserve

Within its 1660ha, this reserve, managed by Scottish Natural Heritage, protects most of the habitats readily found in the Uists. A self-guided walk is the ideal way to find out for yourself – and to occupy a day when the mountains are clouded in.

The reserve extends from the machair grassland on the west coast, across a brackish lagoon to the loch and surrounding peaty moorland. Extensive and shallow, Loch Druidibeg is dotted with islands. On some of these you can see a relatively rare sight in the Western Isles, trees (juniper, willow and rowan). On one of the islands there is a colony of heron. One of Scotland's few native populations of greylag geese live around the loch. Beside the Lochskipport road a small plantation includes the only mature Scots pine in the Uists; if you're here in early spring you might just hear one of the local cuckoo. On the moorland, red grouse and deer are likely sightings, and it's easier to hear the lonely piping of the golden plover than to see the bird itself.

For more information visit Scottish Natural Heritage's office at Stilligarry (Stadhlaigearraidh), beside the A865, or call ☎ 01870-620238.

summit to Maoil Daimh, then (having negotiated the not-too-formidable crags) north-east across the lochan-strewn moor to the shore of Loch Skipport. The full round of South Uist's highest peaks, taking in Beinn Corradail en route to Beinn Mhòr, is a challenging walk, covering a lot of rough ground and narrow ridges on near Beinn Corradail.

NATURAL HISTORY

Built of Lewisian gneiss, Hecla stands at the northern end of a very rugged cluster of peaks and ridges in central South Uist, between Loch Skipport in the north and Loch Aineort in the south. It rises very steeply from the sea and tapers westward to the flat coastal plain. Two fine corries, reflecting the work of glaciers during the last ice age, bite deep into its northern face.

A Resting Place for Clan Chiefs

Howmore is one of several places in the Western Isles associated with the early history of Christianity. From around the 6th century, Irish monks, disciples of St Columba, spent time in many areas explaining their beliefs and introducing improvements in agriculture and education.

At Howmore the remains of two chapels and two churches enhance and deepen the feeling of tranquillity and peace that pervades the nearby hostel and its surrounds. It's an inspirational experience to sit outside the hostel on a summer evening, gazing across the chapels to Hecla and Beinn Mhòr changing colour with the westering sun.

The remains of the chapels and churches stand within a stone wall. Another was completely demolished in 1866. The largest, Teampall Mòr, probably dates from the 13th century – only its eastern wall is still standing. One of the chapels, built in 1574, is closely associated with Clan Ranald – the site was for long a burial place for the clan chiefs.

The Howmore chapel group is cared for by Historic Scotland, the government agency responsible for protecting the country's cultural and built heritage.

To the north-west is Loch Druidibeg National Nature Reserve, one of the major conservation reserves in the Western Isles (see the boxed text 'Loch Druidibeg National Nature Reserve' on page 343).

PLANNING

May to September is the best time for Hecla, although it could be climbed at almost any time of the year – weather permitting. Snow isn't unknown but it doesn't last for long. Mist and cloud can descend on the mountain very quickly, so a compass is essential on this walk to ensure you don't end up on top of a precipitous cliff.

Maps

The OS Landranger 1:50,000 map No 22 *(Benbecula & South Uist)* is the one to carry.

NEAREST TOWN

Howmore (Tobha Mòr) & Around

Howmore is a typically diffuse village along and west of the A865, roughly midway between the northern and southern coasts and almost directly west of Hecla.

Places to Stay & Eat Less than 1mi west of the A865 is ***Howmore Hostel***. It's run by the Gatliff Hebridean Hostels Trust (see the boxed text 'Herbert Gatliff – Visionary' on page 336) and offers simpler accommodation than the standard SYHA hostel. Occupying traditional stone cottages (one of them thatched), it has perfectly adequate facilities (including a shower) but you'll need to bring your own sleeping bag. Bookings are not accepted – it's first come, first served. The warden, a local crofter, calls each evening to collect fees – £6 per night. There's also plenty of space around the cottages to pitch a tent (for only £3).

The nearest B&B is ***Mr & Mrs MacRury*** *(☎ 01870-620321)* at Stoneybridge (Staoinebrig), 2mi south and then west of Howmore. Evening meals are available on request and the B&B tariff is from £16.

The ***post office shop*** at Howmore (just south of the turn-off to the hostel) is a well-stocked licensed grocery.

Wester Ross is a remote and starkly beautiful highland area – wild flowers and the enticing three horns of Beinn Alligin (992m); the jagged ridge line and rock pinnacles (inset) of An Teallach (1062m) offer a classic mountain walk. *Main photo: Graeme Cornwallis. Inset: Grant Dixon.*

'Rugged',' tranquil' and 'individual' best describe the **Western Isles** – a typical Harris view of lochs and sea from Clisham (799m), the highest point in the isles; the isolated hamlet of Rhenigidale (inset) on Harris. *Main photo: Grant Dixon. Inset: Graeme Cornwallis.*

The nearest pub is ***Orasay Inn*** *(☎ 01870-610298)* at Lochcarnan (Loch a' Chairnain), off the A865 in the north-eastern corner of South Uist. The inn's bar meals, highlighting seafood, are justifiably renowned. B&B rates start at £27.

Getting There & Away Howmore is about 6.7mi (10.5km) south of the Benbecula causeway and about 12mi (19.5km) north of Lochboisdale.

The two main operators of bus services that stop at Howmore garage (next to the post office shop) are Hebridean Coaches (☎ 01870-620345), between Ludag and Lochmaddy, and Royal Mail (☎ 01878-700313) for the Lochboisdale to Benbecula postbus. Both services run Monday to Saturday between 8am and 5.25pm.

GETTING TO/FROM THE WALK

The walk starts and finishes at Lochskipport, at the end of the B890, which branches off the A865 about 2mi (3.5km) north of Howmore. Lochskipport is 4mi (6.5km) from the A865. There is no formal car park at Lochskipport, just several grassy patches beside the road.

THE WALK

Follow the road to a point about 120m beyond the end of the sealed section and turn off right (south) along a wide path, opposite an old letter box. The path is clear enough as it skirts the shore of Loch Skipport to the ruinous stone buildings on the western side of Caolas Mòr. From here, keep close to the shore and cross the stream issuing from Loch Spotail. Go up the slope on its far side then head south-eastward across moorland, over a small stream draining a tiny, diamond-shaped lochan, and on to cross the burn from Loch Bèin just below the outlet (about an hour from the start).

Keep seaward of the cliffs above Loch Bèin and a surprisingly easy line of ascent opens up, through the crags of Maol Martaig. Cairns, not always in line of sight, mark the way over the highest ground, although there's no continuous path, up to Beinn na h-Aire. Once you reach this rocky eyrie the rest is relatively easy, over not such rough ground to the minor summit of Beinn Scalabhat (1½ hours from Loch Bèin). Traverse the southern slope of the ridge to reach the next cairn-crowned top (564m), then dip across the bealach and go

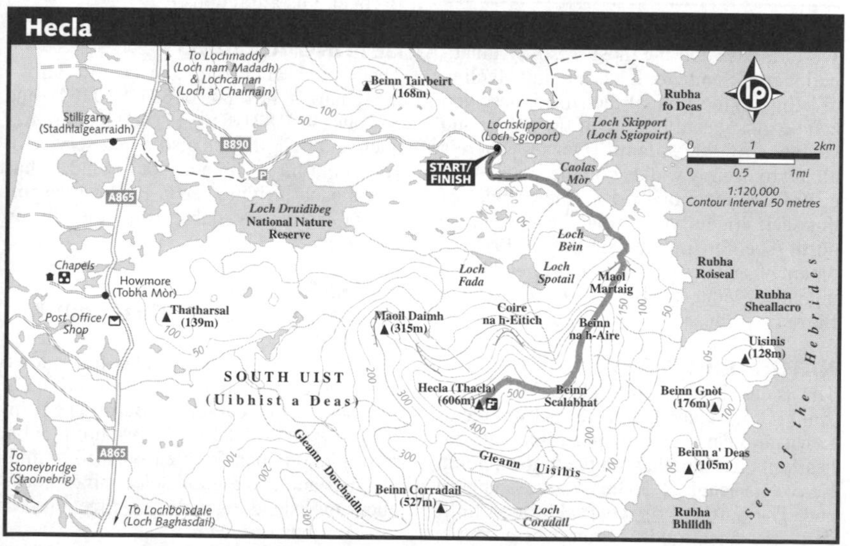

up to **Hecla's** rock and grass summit (35 minutes from Beinn Scalabhat). There's a veritable feast of islands and mountains in the view, notably Skye's Red and Black Cuillins and flat-topped MacLeod's Tables to the east, and the Harris 'hills' in the north.

The descent is much easier – threading together a line of grass, rock and heather, down to Maol Martaig. From here drop down to the west initially, then swing northward, to avoid the almost unbroken cliffs on the north face of this bump, and go on to the north shore of Loch Bèin (nearly two hours from the top). The direction is then north-westward, past two small lochans and across Loch Spotail's outlet stream; a path of sorts leads to the next small inlet. Continue generally close to the shore, past another tiny bay on the western shore of Caolas Mòr, then head west through a shallow valley. Pass the substantial ruin of a stone cottage, cross another shallow valley, then the track which you followed earlier in the day becomes clear. Follow it back to the start (1¼ hours from Loch Bèin).

Barra

Barra (Barraigh) is the southernmost of the Western Isles and the most westerly inhabited part of Scotland. It has a unique feeling of being on the edge of the world; here you can be most keenly aware of the power and vastness of the Atlantic Ocean. There's plenty to occupy walkers on the island – the central mountainous ridge (the subject of this section), outlying 'hills', beaches in the north (see Other Walks on page 349), and mountain and beach walks on the neighbouring isle of Vatersay (Bhatarsaigh), linked to Barra by a causeway.

NATURAL HISTORY

The island is about 8mi (13km) long and 7mi (11km) wide. A rugged, rocky ridge of Lewisian gneiss extends north to south for nearly its full length, with the highest point, Heaval (Sheabhal; 383m) at the southern end. The northern tip, centred around Eoligarry (Eòlaigearraidh), comprises a couple of mountains and a tract of machair. It is joined to the rest of the island by two vast beaches (one serving as the island's airfield) and a slender strip of dry land. In the south-west corner, Ben Tangaval (Beinn Tangabhal; 333m) forms a spectacular bulwark against the Atlantic Ocean. Typical in the Western Isles, the east coast is rocky, indented and relatively sheltered, and the west coast is graced by superb beaches and fine stretches of machair, carpeted with wild flowers during summer.

PLANNING

Barra's season extends from April to October; the weather is often stormy outside that time but fine spells aren't unknown. Accommodation may, however, be more limited. Unfortunately, there's neither a hostel nor formal camping site on Barra.

Maps & Books

The island has its own OS Landranger 1:50,000 map, No 31 *(Barra & South Uist)*.

Information Sources

The island's Web site W www.isleofbarra.com provides an interesting introduction to Barra and its attractions.

GETTING AROUND

There's no real need to take a car to Barra – the island's bus (☎ 01871-810262) and postbus (☎ 01871-810312) services are frequent enough, there's also a taxi service or you could hire a bike to get around. A bus meets each arriving ferry. Public transport timetables are available from the TIC in Castlebay.

ACCESS TOWN
Castlebay (Bagh a' Chaisteil) & Around

Castlebay, a large village rather than a town and huddled around the sheltered harbour in the south, is the 'capital' of Barra. The helpful TIC (☎ 01871-810336), just north of the ferry pier, is open from early April to mid-October and has a good selection of books about the island, as well as a timetable for the local bus service.

The one bank is open Monday to Friday but doesn't have an ATM. Internet access is available at the Social Services office (☎ 01871-810401), near the pier, Monday to Friday; the charge is £2.50 per half-hour.

Places to Stay & Eat Chrissie Beaton's ***Ocean View B&B*** *(☎ 01871-810590)* at Borve (Borgh) is a great place for watching sunsets and enjoying good breakfasts. The tariff starts at £14 or for DB&B around £25.

Mrs MacKechnie's ***Ravenscroft B&B*** *(☎ 01871-810574)* at Nask (Nasg) overlooks Castlebay harbour; B&B costs from £15 and DB&B from £25.

Isle of Barra Hotel *(☎ 01871-810383)*, a modern establishment overlooking beautiful Tangasdale Beach, does good bar suppers featuring local scallops and several vegetarian choices. The four-course dinner in the dining room is good value at £20. The hotel has en suite rooms from £32 for B&B.

Two traditional pubs in Castlebay, the ***Castlebay Hotel*** and the ***Craigard Hotel***, serve bar meals. There's a good ***Co-op*** supermarket, a ***Spar*** supermarket and Barra's community shop ***Co-Chomunn Bharraidh***.

Getting There & Away The timetable's warning 'Barra Flights are subject to Tide' isn't a joke. Barra's airport is Tràigh Mhòr (big beach), where British Airways Express (☎ 0345-222111) flights (operated by Loganair) from Glasgow land Monday to Saturday; the return economy fare is £134. There's also an inter-island service between Barra, Benbecula (£40.80 return) and Stornoway (£119.80 return). The island's bus service meets flights at the terminal, where there's a good tearoom open all day. The single bus fare from the airport to Castlebay is £1.

CalMac (☎ 01475-650100) ferries from Oban and from Lochboisdale (en route to Oban) call at Castlebay several days weekly. The five-day return fare Oban-Castlebay is £31.50 and £110 for a vehicle. During summer, ferries sail between Mallaig and Castlebay, leaving Mallaig on Sunday and Castlebay on Monday. The five-day return fares are £22.95 and £82 for a vehicle.

With the opening of the South Uist to Eriskay (Eiriosgaigh) causeway, a new ferry service from Eriskay to Northbay (Bagh a' Tuath), on the north-east coast, is expected to start in 2002 and will replace the old tide-dependent ferry from Ludag. Contact the TIC for timetables. The Barra bus meets all arriving ferries.

Heaval

Duration	4–4½ hours
Distance	5.5mi (9km)
Standard	medium
Start	Craigston
Finish	Castlebay
Nearest Town	Castlebay
Public Transport	yes

Summary A varied walk to Barra's highest peak, crowning the central ridge, with unsurpassed views; the walk passes a traditional black shieling house and a prehistoric burial cairn.

It's easy enough to dash up and down Heaval (Sheabhal; 383m) from the road crossing the southern foot of the mountain, but the approach described here, along the island's central spine, is more scenic and varied, and involves less seriously steep climbing. Although it is quite a popular walk, there isn't a defined path, nor any cairns other than on the summits; most of the going is over grass and broken rock. The total ascent is 555m.

Near the start of the walk, you'll pass a restored, thatched cottage (*dubharaidh* in Gaelic), which houses a museum about island life; it's open most days in summer. Farther on, the route takes you past Dùn Bharpa, a Neolithic (Stone Age) chambered burial cairn, built around 5000 years ago. High on the steep southern slopes of Heaval stands Our Lady of the Sea, a marble statue of the Madonna and child, symbolising the islanders' main religious faith; it's not easy to find, being off the best line of descent.

Alternatives It would be possible to extend this walk by starting farther north along the ridge, most conveniently from the main road where it crosses a gap between Beinn Chliaid to the north and Beinn Bheireasaigh to the south, adding about 1mi, 230m of ascent and nearly an hour to the walk described.

GETTING TO/FROM THE WALK

The walk starts at the end of the minor road through the village of Craigston (Baile na Creige), where there is an informal car park. Alternatively, catch a Castlebay-Eoligarry bus (roughly hourly from 7.30am), get off at the junction on the main road and walk nearly 1mi (1.4km) to the start. If you need a taxi, call John Beaton (☎ 01871-810590).

THE WALK

From the end of the sealed road continue along the vehicular track to a point opposite the black shieling on the right. Go through a gate and head up the hillside with a fence on your left; following it north-eastward, then north for a short distance. Look out for a prominent waymarker post up to the right; continue to it then go on to the obvious **Dùn Bharpa**, crossing a stile over a fence en route (about 45 minutes from the main road). Sitting in a shallow gap in an east-west ridge, the dun is a large, sprawling mound of small stones, with a huge capstone (or lid) on top.

Go back over the stile then head east across flattish moorland to the foot of the very steep western side of the central ridge. Climb up a broad, grassed gully to the obvious gap on the ridge then southward and up to the summit of Grianan (294m), about an hour from the dun. Descend steeply to Beul a' Bhealaich, taking care not to overshoot and finish up east of and below the gap. From the gap, angle up the steep, grassy and rocky hillside, south-eastward then south to a minor summit at 353m (marked with a miniature cairn). Then go sharply down, across a narrow slit as the ridge bends markedly to the west, and up to the main top of Hartaval (Thartabhal; 358m), an hour from Grianan. From here the ridge

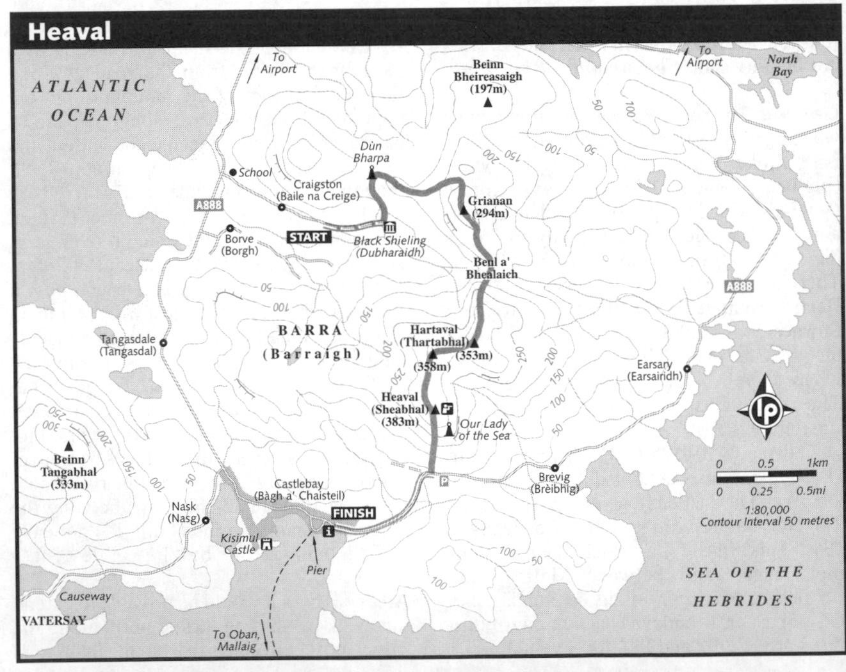

regains its north-south orientation as you dip across a gap then quickly dispose of the final climb to the survey cairn on **Heaval** (Sheabhal; 383m). The view is unsurpassed – from the mountains of Harris to the southernmost isles of Mingulay and Berneray (both uninhabited), and with Castlebay and Kisimul Castle (ancestral home of the Clan Macneil) at your feet.

The descent is extremely steep and unrelenting, over grass and rock. Heading south and south-eastward, aim for a prominent car park on the south side of the road about 200m east of a sharp bend. This should lead you to a weakness in a long fence across the lower slopes, where many other people have crossed before, close to the road. The centre of Castlebay is less than 1mi downhill from here (about an hour from Heaval).

Other Walks

HARRIS

Scalpay (Scalpaigh)

Scalpay guards the entrance to East Loch Tarbert. A scenic, 8mi (13km) circuit of the island starts at a car park above North Harbour. It follows the west coast to Lag na Laire, heads east to the lighthouse at Eilean Glas, then north-west over Ben Scoravick, past Loch an Duin and back to the start. Waymarking is variable, but with the OS Landranger 1:50,000 map No 14 *(Tarbert & Loch Seaforth)* and the descriptive leaflet *Cuairt Eilean Scalpaigh* in the Western Isles Walks series, it's easy enough to follow. A Scalpay bus service operates from Tarbert between 8.30am and 4pm.

Hushinish (Huisinis)

The peninsula at the south-western extremity of north Harris, sheltering Hushinish, offers scenic, low-level walking. The B887 branches from the A859 (2.5mi north of Tarbert) and continues for 14mi (22.5km) to a car park above the eastern end of Hushinish Bay. From here you can walk along the shore, climb Cnoc Mòr (84m), then head cross-country (use stiles or gates to negotiate fences) and down to the pier on the Kyle of Scarp. From near here, a remarkable old path crosses the steep slopes of Husival Beag, then drops over Gresclett to Tràigh Mheilein. You can then climb the low hill, Meilein, skirt Loch na Cleavag and return to the start via the old path. On a good day you could add Husival Beag (306m), easily reached via the gully on its northern side, then descend to the road. All this could take up to five hours. Use OS Landranger 1:50,000 map is No 13 *(West Lewis & North Harris)*. During school term a Western Isles Council (☎ 01859-502213) bus to and from Tarbert runs Monday to Friday; out of term the bus runs only on Tuesday and Friday.

Luskentyre Ridge (Losgaintir)

The ridge rising from the southern shore of West Loch Tarbert and overlooking Luskentyre beach to the south, offers a fine traverse. Start from a car park beside the A859, 8mi south-west of Tarbert, and 0.5mi west of the Luskentyre turn-off. Follow an old road up past Loch Laxdale to the A859 and start climbing the ridge from there. Descend from the highest point, Beinn Dubh (506m), to Tràigh Rosamol. Walk along the beach to near the village of Luskentyre and follow the road to the start. This 14mi (22.5km) walk should take seven hours. Use OS Landranger 1:50,000 map No 14 *(Tarbert & Loch Seaforth)*. Harris Coaches' (☎ 01859-502441) Stornoway-Tarbert-Leverburgh service stops at the Luskentyre road junction Monday to Saturday between 9am and 6pm.

Toe Head (Goban Tobha)

Toe Head offers a variety of walks: an easy ramble to a tiny chapel on the southern shore; a longer and rougher walk around the east and north coast to Toe Head; and a climb to Chaipaval (365m). Use OS Landranger 1:50,000 map is No 18 *(Sound of Harris & St Kilda)*. These walks are approached from the village of Northton, 2mi north-west of Leverburgh. There's a bus service Monday to Saturday between Stornoway, Tarbert and Leverburgh with at least five runs both ways. The Web site Ⓦ www.leverburgh.co.uk has details.

BARRA

Eoligarry (Eolaigearraidh)

The northern tip of Barra has two of the island's most important historical sites. Here a 6mi (9.5km) waymarked walk, Cuairt Eólaigearraidh, starts and finishes at the former South Uist ferry pier. It leads past the remains of St Barr's Chapel (Cille-Bharra), dating from early Christian times, to Dun Scurrival (Dùn Sgùrabhal), an Iron Age fort. Then it's over Ben Eoligarry (102m) and down to the long Tràigh Eais and back past the airfield. It's possible to extend the walk, skirting Scurrival Beach (Tràigh Sgùrabhal) to reach Ben Scurrival. The leaflet for the walk should be available from the TIC in Castlebay (☎ 01871-810336). Use OS Landranger 1:50,000 map is No 31 *(Barra & South Uist)*. The island's bus service will take you to and from Eoligarry (hourly departures between 7.30am and 7.30pm).

The North-West

The north of Scotland, beyond a line joining Ullapool in the west and Dornoch Firth in the east, is the most sparsely populated part of the country. The north-west (Sutherland) is graced with a generous share of the wildest, most remote coast, mountains and glens. At first sight, the bare 'hills' (more rock than earth) and the maze of lochs and waterways may be alien and unattractive. But the very wildness of the rockscapes, the isolation of the long, deep glens, and the magnificence of the indented coastline can exercise a seductive fascination. What's more, intrusive developments are few, and many long-established paths lead into the mountains and through the glens.

This chapter focuses on the north-west; a coast walk in the farthermost corner, two contrasting mountain walks, Scotland's highest waterfall and a long, rugged glen, as well as some suggestions for other walks in the area.

Highlights

SANDRA BARDWELL

Wild and rugged moorland in Glen Canisp provides some spectacular walking.

- Walking along the pristine sands of Sandwood Bay, en route to the towering cliffs at north-westernmost Cape Wrath
- Venturing deep into a rocky wilderness to visit Scotland's highest waterfall
- Savouring the magnificent mountain and moor coast-to-coast views from rugged Ben More Assynt

CLIMATE

Sutherland is very much at the mercy of the steady procession of depressions moving across the country from the south-west and west. However, in the north-west, annual rainfall is generally lower than it is farther south – from about 70cm up to 140cm at Cape Wrath.

Temperatures are slightly cooler with a July average of about 13°C but a relatively mild winter, with the January average 4°C. July and August are the mildest months, but wetter than May and June, which, with September and early October, are the best times to visit this area.

Wind is the most critical factor for walkers – calm days are rather uncommon in the north-west; strong winds and gales blow in most months, and frequently in winter. Cold, biting northerlies prevail from time to time but usually bring dry weather. Snow falls throughout the area, although only on the higher ground does it last for any length of time.

INFORMATION

Maps

For route planning and general orientation the OS Travelmaster 1:250,000 map No 2 *(Northern Scotland)* is ideal.

Books

Scottish Mountaineering Club's guide *The Northwest Highlands* by DJ Bennet & T Strang is authoritative and captures the magic of the area. Tom Strang, also the author of *Walk Sutherland: 50 Graded Walks* and

Hillwalkers Guide to Sutherland, lives locally; his reliable guides are alive with enthusiasm for Sutherland. *Making More of Assynt* by the Assynt Mountain Rescue Team contains notes on a variety of walks and local wildlife. *Exploring the Far North West of Scotland* by Richard Gilbert was published in the early 1990s and has good descriptions by a Sutherland devotee. The Pathfinder guide *Skye and the North West Highlands* by John Brooks & Neil Wilson has 13 walks.

Sutherland's landscape is rich in evidence of its past – prehistoric and historic. *Sutherland: An Archaeological Guide* by Robert Gourlay describes a range of sites, many easily accessible. *Sutherland: An Illustrated Architectural Guide* by Elizabeth Beaton has lots of photos and plans.

Information Sources

There are two TICs in the area, Durness (☎ 01971-511259), open year round, and Lochinver (☎ 01571-844330), open from mid-April to late October. A useful Web site is W www.undiscoveredscotland.co.uk.

Scottish Natural Heritage (☎ 01854-666234) has a turf- and timber-roofed interpretive centre at Knockan, beside the

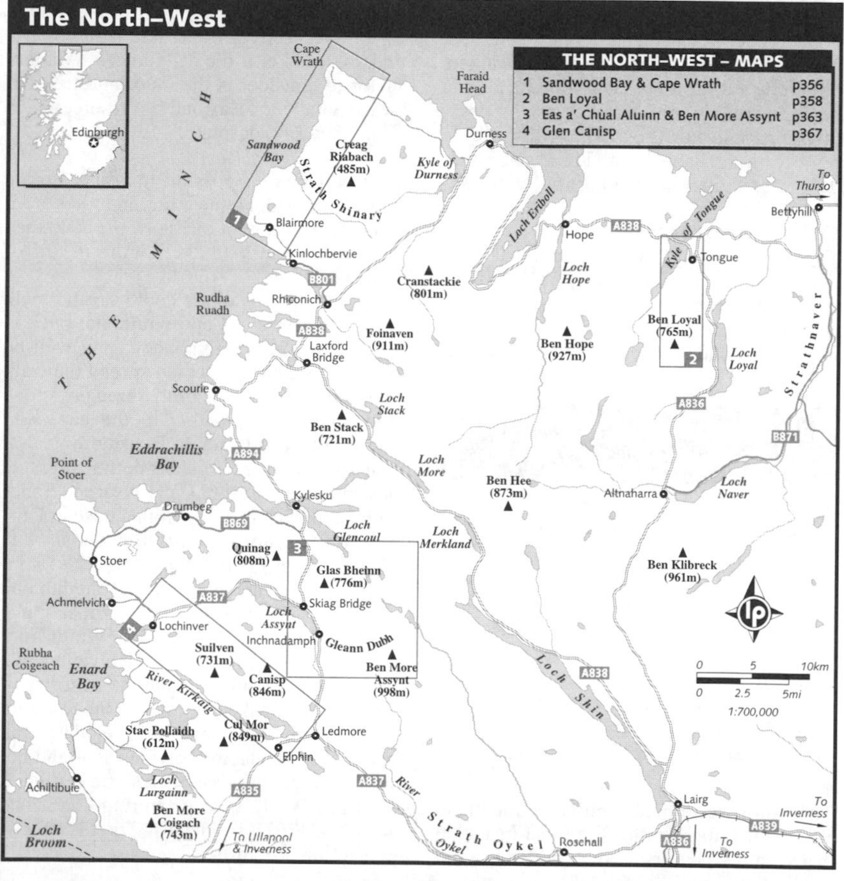

A835 about 2mi south of Elphin. It's open all year and has displays interpreting the landscape through geologists' eyes.

The Highland Council's *Public Transport Travel Guide: North Highland and Orkney* is invaluable and available from TICs. It also gives details of the Northern Explorer Ticket, which provides seven days travel on major bus lines around the north-west, Inverness to Inverness, for £25.

The Met Office forecast for the western Highlands is available on ☎ 09068-500441 or fax 09060-100405.

The Northern Constabulary (☎ 01463-715555) encourages walkers to leave details of extended walks; you must let the police know when you have safely returned. This is a useful service for visiting walkers who have no local contacts. Itineraries can be registered through the Web site W www.northern.police.uk (go to The Hills page) or by a form available from TICs, some outdoor gear shops and youth hostels.

Other Information

The only important camping item that's difficult to find in the region is gas for portable stoves; the nearest supplies are in Inverness (see under Gateway on page 247) and Ullapool (see under Gateways on page 299).

Sandwood Bay & Cape Wrath

Duration	6½–7 hours
Distance	14mi (22.5km)
Standard	medium
Start	Blairmore
Finish	Cape Wrath
Nearest Towns	Durness, Kinlochbervie
Public Transport	yes

Summary Scotland's finest coastal walk; from an incomparable beach to the north-westernmost tip of the country, through a remote and uninhabited area of great beauty and wildness.

The north-westernmost point of mainland Scotland (Cape Wrath), the most beautiful beach in the country (Sandwood Bay) and the long stretch of magnificent, unspoiled coastline between them are the evocative and irresistible highlights of this finest of coast walks. This is also lonely and remote country – not a soul lives anywhere near the route, except at its southern extremity in the crofting town of Blairmore, north of Kinlochbervie. An extensive area around Sandwood Bay and nearby Sandwood Loch is owned and managed by the John Muir Trust in partnership with the local community.

The recommended direction is south to north, arriving at the dramatic landmark of Cape Wrath after several hours along the coast. You may feel, however, it is better to start from the relatively civilised, although forlornly deserted, Cape Wrath lighthouse and to walk into the wilderness. Another factor to consider is the moorland trek between Sandwood Bay and Blairmore, which some may find desolate.

Alternatives It's possible to follow a more coastal route along the moorland track from Sheigra (0.6mi west of Blairmore) and then go cross-country to the southern end of Sandwood Bay.

Although fit walkers could do the walk from Blairmore to Cape Wrath and back in a day, camping at Sandwood may well be preferable. Thus you could spread the walk over a much more leisurely three days: one into Sandwood, another to the cape and back, and a third back to Blairmore.

In midsummer, transport permitting, it is possible to walk from Cape Wrath to Sandwood and back in a day from a base in Durness on the north coast; the distance is 19.5mi (32km) with 300m ascent.

There is yet another option, although one needing even more careful organisation – walking along the road to Cape Wrath from the Kyle of Durness ferry. However, this means you're going through the Ministry of Defence's Balnakeil Bombing Range where live ammunition is fired fairly regularly and unexploded shells lurk on the moorland beside the road. 'Activity dates' are posted at the Durness TIC or you can ring Freephone ☎ 0800-317071 for details. The distance is about 10mi (16km).

HISTORY

Cape Wrath's name comes from the Norse word for 'turning point' – it was clearly a crucial landmark for the Vikings during their incursions in the north and west between the 9th and 13th centuries.

The hazards involved in navigating the often stormy seas around here were long recognised and led to the building of the lighthouse at the cape by Robert and Alan Stevenson in 1828. The last keepers left by 1997 when people were replaced by automatic equipment; the once-handsome buildings are now sadly neglected.

Less peaceably, part of the Balnakeil Estate on the moorland east of the cape is owned by the Ministry of Defence and has served for decades as a bombing range where live ammunition is used. The ministry claims, nevertheless, that wildlife flourishes and the landscape has been preserved.

People evicted from their lands on the north coast settled around Sandwood (and Sheigra to the south) in the 1820s, but their descendants were ejected in 1847 and the area given over to sheep. The land was returned to local people 50 years later. Sandwood House, built during the 19th century (now roofless but stable), was used by shepherds until the 1950s. The John Muir Trust purchased the 4650ha Sandwood Estate in 1993. It extends from Sandwood Loch and Strath Shinary south to Loch Clash at Kinlochbervie and inland for up to 6mi (10km). Essential to the management of the estate is the participation of local crofting communities through a special committee.

NATURAL HISTORY

Along the coast, the cliffs, deep inlets (geos) and the offshore stacks and islets are predominantly sandstone, mixed into ancient gneiss, the most widespread rock type. At Cape Wrath the red gneiss cliffs soar to a height of about 120m. A few miles east, at Kervaig, are reputedly the highest coastal cliffs in Scotland at 284m. Glaciers and ice sheets left their mark in sculpting the river

Where Not to Camp

CLINT CURÉ

The shore of Sandwood Loch seemed an idyllic camping site – right beside a fresh water supply, where we could also take a dip after a warm day's walk. But we were still pretty naive about camping in Scotland during summer – we'd heard about midges but hadn't much idea about where they lived.

So we pitched the tent beside the tranquil, reed-fringed loch then spent the day walking up to Cape Wrath and back. We returned to the tent in the early evening and the breeze that had kept us cool on that warm July day had died. We lit the stove for a brew but, within a minute, were reduced to futile, flailing anguish as the black clouds of voracious insects swarmed upon us – even into our mouths.

Clearly, cooking a meal would be impossible, so instant relocation was the only answer. All the unpacked gear was frantically stuffed into the packs and we ran across the dunes to the beach and midge-free expanses of bare sand. All that remained was the dome tent, its inner already lying in a heap on the sand. So, we pulled out the pegs, crawled inside and picked it up, and once again ran for the beach, seeing the way through the tent's cream panels. Our only regret was that someone didn't arrive with a camera, or preferably a video recorder, to immortalise the sight of a dome tent with four brown legs, moving at high speed through the Sandwood dunes.

Sandra Bardwell

valleys; large gneiss boulders perched on sandstone platforms were left behind by retreating glaciers.

The peatlands, sand dunes and machair, from Sandwood to Sheigra, and the dunes and machair between Sheigra and Oldshoremore (all within the John Muir Trust's Sandwood Estate), are protected in two Sites of Special Scientific Interest. The machair, found only in relatively few places along the west coast and in the Western Isles, comes alive between late June and August, with carpets of globeflower, bell flower, vetch, knapweed and orchid.

PLANNING

When to Walk

Since the ferry across Kyle of Durness only operates between May and September, it's impossible to do this walk from north to south at any other time. Although these are the best months, the season for this walk could extend from March to November. The earlier and later months have the extra advantage of being outside the midge season.

What to Bring

If you're planning to camp at Sandwood Bay, a fuel stove is an absolute must, as are a trowel (there are no toilets) and a bag to carry out all your rubbish. Water containers will be handy – there are camping sites close to the limited supplies of fresh water but they're midge havens in summer. For more information contact the manager of Sandwood Estate on ☎ 01971-521459.

Maps

The walk is covered by the OS Landranger 1:50,000 map No 9 *(Cape Wrath)*.

Information Sources

A leaflet about the Sandwood Estate is available from the estate manager (☎ 01971-521459) and from a leaflet box by the start of the track at Blairmore.

Guided Walks

If you are interested in exploring the area with an expert, Highland Council's Ranger Service (☎ 01971-511756) runs guided walks to the coast near Cape Wrath, Faraid Head (near Tongue) and around Scourie (to the south, beyond Rhiconich).

NEAREST TOWNS

Durness

A surprisingly large, spread-out village on the coast, Durness lays unbeatable claim to being the most north-westerly village in Britain. The TIC (☎ 01971-511259) is at the eastern end of the village and is open year-round. There's an ATM at the supermarket.

Places to Stay & Eat Overlooking the ocean, ***Durness SYHA Hostel*** *(☎ 01971-511244)* is about 1mi east of the village on the main road; the tariff is £6.75. ***Sango Sands Camping Site*** *(☎ 01971-511761)*, near the TIC and beside the main road, has plenty of grassy pitches, a small campers kitchen and uninterrupted ocean views. The cost per adult is £4; you need tokens that cost 50p for the showers. ***Puffin Cottage B&B*** *(☎ 01971-511208)*, just west of the village centre, has well-appointed rooms (one en suite) from £17.

For a meal, you can't go past ***Loch Croispol Bookshop & Restaurant*** *(☎/fax 01971-511777)* in unique Balnakeil Craft Village, about 1mi west of Durness. Here you can enjoy the very civilised experience of being surrounded by books as you sup from a menu featuring Scottish products, especially wild Sutherland salmon, and cheeses. You'll pay £9.50 for two courses or £12 for three. The shelves are lined with Scottish titles, and the restaurant is open daily for lunch, plus Friday to Monday evening. There's also ***Sango Sands Oasis*** *(☎ 01971-511222)*, next to the camping site, a popular place serving bar meals.

There's a ***Mace*** supermarket (open Monday to Saturday) and a licensed ***grocer*** close to the camping site, open daily.

Getting There & Away Highland Country Buses (☎ 01463-222244) operates a summer service from Thurso, which conveniently departs after the early morning ScotRail (☎ 0845-755 0033) train from Inverness has arrived. Alternatively, the same train from

Inverness connects with a postbus service (☎ 01463-256228) from Lairg station to Durness via Kinlochbervie. Also only in summer, Tim Dearman Coaches (☎ 01349-883585) runs a once-daily Monday to Saturday service from Inverness to Durness via Ullapool and Kinlochbervie (£10 single).

Kinlochbervie

Principally a fishing village, Kinlochbervie has large, purpose-built port facilities around the sheltered harbour.

Places to Stay & Eat Beside the minor road from Kinlochbervie to Sheigra, the ***Oldshoremore Camping Site*** *(☎ 01971-521281)* is a small, sheltered site (effectively a large front lawn), costing £6.70 for two people and tent; facilities are simple but adequate. ***Kinlochbervie Hotel*** *(☎ 01971-521275, ⓔ klbhotel@aol.com)* occupies a scenic position on the Sheigra road, just north of the village. It has comfortable rooms from £45 for B&B or £65 DB&B; fresh local seafood and Scottish foods generally feature on the dinner menu. In the adjacent bunkhouse, a bed costs £15 for B&B or £20 in an en suite room.

Bervie Stores is open Monday to Saturday for supplies and snacks; it's an off-licence. The ***Royal National Mission to Deepsea Fishermen***, beside the port, has a cafe and takeaway service.

Getting There & Away See Getting There & Away for Durness on page 354.

GETTING TO/FROM THE WALK

To the Start

The walk starts at Blairmore, a hamlet on the Kinlochbervie-Sheigra road; there is a car park and a public telephone. Blairmore is 3.4mi (5.4km) from Kinlochbervie.

A subsidised taxi service serving the Kinlochbervie area can take you to (and from) Blairmore. Call ☎ 01971-521477 the evening before to arrange a pick-up. This service is only available at certain times on selected days; full details are given in the Highland Council's *Public Transport Travel Guide: North Highland and Orkney*, from TICs.

From the Finish

Kyle of Durness ferry (☎ 01971-511376) operates daily from May to September; trips are most frequent in July and August starting at 9.30am. The fares are £2.20 (single) and £3.65 (return). The ferry departs from the jetty at Keoldale, at the end of a minor road, which branches off the A838 about 2mi south of Durness.

All sailings connect with the Cape Wrath minibus service (☎ 01971-511287), which bounces along the rough road to the lighthouse; the single fare is £4.50 and return costs £6.50. If you're walking north from Sandwood Bay, contact the ferry and bus operators in advance to ensure they are waiting for you.

THE WALK

From the Blairmore car park, set out along the unsealed road signposted to Sandwood. This road, used by crofters tending their sheep, leads across the rather featureless moorland, which is enlivened by several nearby lochs. It becomes a path at Loch a' Mhuilinn. Little more than 1mi farther on, the path (much of it repaired and built by John Muir Trust volunteers) curves round a steep-sided hill on the left and starts to descend, affording the first glimpse of the beach at Sandwood Bay.

A flat, grassed area, with old, stone-walled enclosures, is a possible ***camping site***. Water should be available from the small burn near the roofless cottage about 200m to the south; otherwise you'll have to go right down to peat-dark **Sandwood Loch**, although it may be slightly brackish. The shore of Sandwood Loch may seem like an idyllic camping site but beware the midges (see the boxed text 'Where Not to Camp' on page 353).

The path leads down through marram grassed dunes to the beach at **Sandwood Bay**, a superb sweep of pinkish-cream sand (about 1¾ hours from the start). The towering rock stack of **Am Buachaille** stands guard close to the cliffs extending west from the sands.

Walk along the beach, cross the outlet from Sandwood Loch on stepping stones

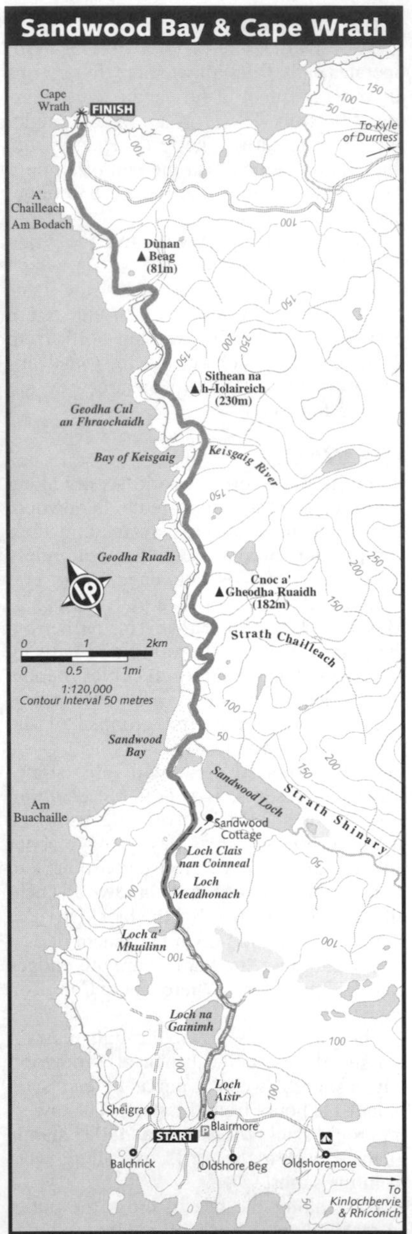

and go up the steep, sandy slope ahead, through a gap in the low cliffs. Cross a patch of grass and make your way through the jumble of rock slabs and boulders down to a shallow valley, then along the cliff edge to Strath Chailleach.

Cross the stream at the top of the cascades and follow the spur leading north-east for about 500m then turn generally north to skirt the steep-sided Cnoc a' Gheodha Ruaidh on its seaward side. Keep close to the cliff edge, across a dip above Geodha Ruadh and up past the next hill.

At the top of the long slope down to the Keisgaig River, there's a good view of a remarkable rock stack on the northern side of the bay, its profile resembling a rather sullen face. Just above the river is a low, turf-roofed stone shelter, a bit the worse for wear (2¼ hours from Sandwood Bay). There's space for a tent or two nearby if you want to ***camp***.

Cross the river just above the cascade coursing down onto the shingle beach and climb up the very steep slope. Steer a course west of Sithean na h-Iolaireich to overlook the superb, vertical, dark-pink cliffs in **Geodha Cul an Fhraochaidh**.

Continue along the cliff tops, mainly across bare, stony ground for 1mi or so, to the top of the next descent to the unnamed burn immediately south of Dùnan Beag. Detour inland (north-eastward) around the cliffs lining the seaward reaches of the burn to a small stream junction; cross over and head back towards the cliffs.

There's a potential ***camping site*** at the next stream crossing (north of Dùnan Beag), a short distance inland. A bit farther on the two remarkable rock stacks **A' Chailleach** and **Am Bodach** (the old woman and old man) dictate a photo stop. If you look back (south) from here, Sandwood Bay is visible – on a clear day.

Continue across a small burn towards the lighthouse, keeping close to the cliffs. Skirt the walled enclosure around the buildings, which are now forlornly deserted, to reach the courtyard in front of the tower and the end of the walk (about 2½ hours from the Keisgaig River).

Ben Loyal

Duration	6–6½ hours
Distance	8mi (13km)
Standard	medium
Start & Finish	Ribigill turn-off
Nearest Town	Tongue
Public Transport	yes

Summary A steep climb to one of the most attractive and interesting peaks in the north, with fine views in all directions.

Ben Loyal is often called 'The Queen of Scottish Peaks'. It's thought that the name Ben Loyal comes not from some dutiful subject but from the Norse *laga fjall* meaning 'law mountain' – where laws were once promulgated. Whether or not you think any mountain should be female rather than male, let alone royal, it is indeed a fine peak. Standing proudly alone above rather desolate moorland to the south, its spectacular, cliff-lined western flank majestically overlooks the Kyle of Tongue and the coast to the north. At 765m (2509ft), Ben Loyal's summit, An Caisteal, grants it the status of Corbett. However, the mountain is well worth climbing for its own sake, irrespective of its title and designation.

The most popular approach is from the village of Tongue to the north. Farm tracks and rough, discontinuous moorland paths lead up onto the mountain where the going is much easier. Having gained the summit, you could spend time exploring the individual summits and peering down into the rugged corries on the western face of the mountain. The walk involves 750m ascent which, combined with the intermittently rough going, justifies the medium grading.

Alternatives It is possible to descend the extremely steep north-western slope but only with great care. From the gap between Sgòr a' Bhatain and Sgòr Chaonasaid, head down to the edge of a scattered line of birches fringing Ben Loyal's north-western lower slopes. Make your way generally north-eastward through this attractive woodland, then across open ground to rejoin the path followed earlier in the day, not far from the lonely cottage at Cunside. Reckon on taking about the same time for the return leg as for the outward journey.

Approaches to Ben Loyal from the south-east, across boggy moorland, have nothing to recommend them.

NATURAL HISTORY

With a longish, gracefully, undulating summit ridge, crowned by clusters of granite tors, five separate summits make up Ben Loyal: Sgòr Chaonasaid (712m), Sgòr a' Bhatain (708m), An Caisteal (the castle; 765m), and two southerly tops, Beinn Bheag (744m) and Carn an Tionail (716m). There are also two outliers above the western crags – Sgòr a' Chleirich and Sgòr Fhionnaich.

Consisting of granite (specifically syenite), Ben Loyal stands alone in an area consisting principally of schist and sandstone. The belt of birch trees fringing the western slopes is also unusual in the north, so much of which is treeless.

PLANNING

When to Walk

The season for this mountain is usually quite long – it does see snow but it normally doesn't last. May and June are the best months, before the midges settle in.

Stalking During the stalking season, from mid-August to mid-October, walkers are asked to avoid areas where stalking activities are taking place on a particular day. The number to phone to find out what's happening is ☎ 01847-611291.

Maps

The OS Landranger 1:50,000 map No 10 *(Strathnaver)* is the one to have.

NEAREST TOWN

Tongue

A largish village, Tongue overlooks the Kyle of Tongue. Seemingly in the middle of nowhere, the village is itself dramatically overlooked by Ben Loyal. The one bank in Tongue opens Monday to Friday but does not have an ATM.

THE NORTH-WEST

Places to Stay & Eat Originally a hunting lodge built by one of the Dukes of Sutherland, ***The Tongue Hotel*** (☎ *01847-611206*), has spacious, tastefully furnished rooms from £25. Bar suppers feature seafood and venison (and limited vegetarian dishes) or you can splash out and enjoy the £25 set menu in the dining room. More economical, kindly ***Mrs Macintosh*** (☎ *01847-611251, 77 Dalcharn*), east of the village, does B&B from £13. ***Kincraig Caravan & Camping Site*** (☎ *01847-611281*), just south of the village centre, has grassy pitches with excellent views and charges £6 for a tent and car or £4 tent only; facilities are basic. ***Tongue SYHA Hostel*** (☎ *01847-611301*), near the causeway across the Kyle of Tongue, features welcoming open fires; the tariff is £8.25.

For supplies, there's ***Tongue Stores & Post Office*** (closed on Sunday), which also has a small coffee shop, and ***Burr's Shop*** at the northern end of the village; it's licensed and open daily although only briefly on Sunday.

Getting There & Away It's possible to reach Tongue by public transport from Inverness, Monday to Saturday. The first stage is to Lairg, either by the early morning ScotRail (☎ 0845-755 0033) train on the Inverness to Thurso and Wick line or by Stagecoach (☎ 0870-608 2608) bus. From Lairg a postbus (☎ 01463-256228) goes to Tongue, arriving mid-afternoon.

By road, Tongue is at the junction of the A838 from Durness and the A836 from Thurso in the east and Lairg to the south.

GETTING TO/FROM THE WALK

You can walk or drive the 3mi (5km) south from Tongue along a minor road to the entrance to Ribigill Farm (there's a sign 'Ribigill' on the farm gate), where there is very limited roadside parking.

THE WALK

From the turn-off to Ribigill Farm head south along the private road. Bear left at the first fork (after about 600m) then, on a bend with a large derelict stone cottage on

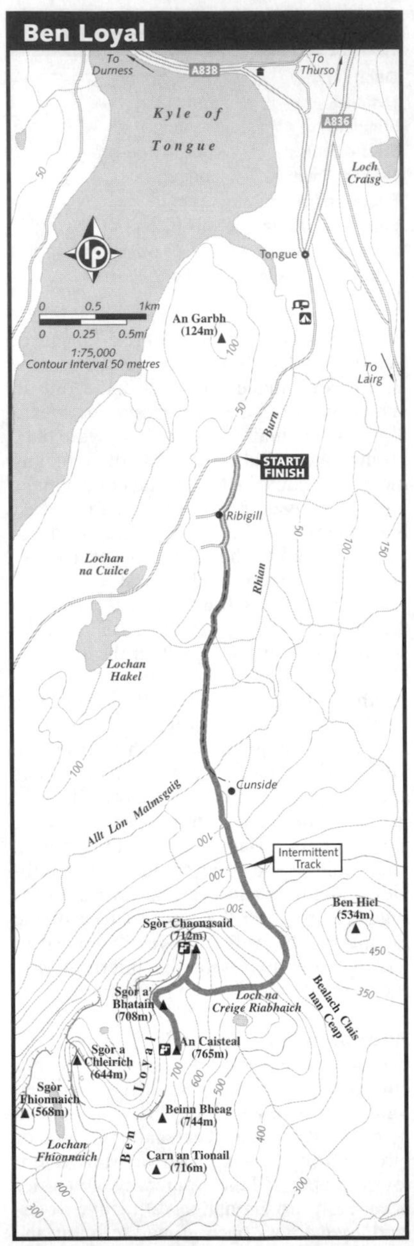

the left, continue straight on along a farm track towards Ben Loyal. As the track starts to cross the low spur, ignore another track to the right and continue south. The track is clear enough across the moorland, where there are some boggy patches. Stepping stones take you across Allt Lòn Malmsgaig. Just before you reach stone-built Cunside cottage at the foot of Ben Loyal's northern slopes, a path leads south along a narrow bank. It fades as you start to gain height steeply up the grassy moorland slope with a small stream on the left. Cross this stream after a while and continue up to the broad gap in the ridge, Bealach Clais nan Ceap. A fairly clear path leads up the slope on your right (west), above the morass in the bealach, towards a cluster of low, broken cliffs. Again the path fades; evidently walkers make various ways up the steep slope. It's best to avoid the wettest ground close to the cliffs, making your way up to the wide, shallow valley cradling Loch na Creige Rhiabhaich. From here continue generally north-westward up to the main ridge where a path leads north to **Sgòr Chaonasaid**. Here there's some entertainment to be had, scrambling around the small tors on the summit to find the best outlook across Tongue and the Kyle of Tongue (about 2½ hours from the start near Ribigill).

Retrace your steps down the ridge and continue along it, keeping to the highest ground – the path is more or less continuous. Gain height past the twin knobs of **Sgòr a' Bhatain** then go steeply up to a low cliff, where a rocky ramp provides an easy way up to the well-made cairn on the summit of **An Caisteal**. On a clear day you can see as far east as Duncansby Head, west to the towering cliffs beyond Durness and south to the peaks of Assynt.

There is a path southward along the ridge from here – you could walk to the western side of the next summit, Beinn Bheag (744m), for views down into the rugged corrie below An Caisteal. To return to Ribigill and Tongue, you simply retrace your steps – appreciating the very different outlook on the way.

Assynt

Assynt, the legendary practice ground for mountain building Norse gods, is a distinct geographical and cultural area in the north-west. Its northern boundary is Loch A' Chairn Bhain and its eastward extensions Lochs Glendhu and Glencoul; the eastward limit is along the watershed of Beinn Uidhe, Conival and Breabag (and, for practical purposes, Ben More Assynt although it's actually east of that divide); to the south, Loch Veyatie, Fionn Loch and the River Kirkaig separate Assynt from the district of Coigach. The coast forms its western boundary. The two possible meanings of Assynt, 'rocky' from a Norse word or 'in and out' from the ancient Gaelic, neatly summarise the area's unique landscape of rock and water, a fascinating and wildly beautiful walkers' heartland.

PLANNING

Maps

All the walks in this section are covered by the OS Landranger 1:50,000 map No 15 *(Loch Assynt)*.

Guided Walks

Inchnadamph Lodge (see Places to Stay & Eat under Inchnadamph on page 360) is the base for the Assynt Field Centre, which runs guided walks and courses in the local geology and wildlife. Assynt Visitor Centre (see under Lochinver on page 361) is also the Assynt base for the Highland Council's Ranger Service (☎ 01571-844654), which runs a varied program of guided walks in summer.

ACCESS TOWNS

Kylesku

This is a tiny settlement off the A894 near the Kylesku bridge; until the bridge was built in the 1980s, a ferry crossed the strait between Kylestrome and Kylesku.

Places to Stay & Eat Built in 1883 and overlooking the old slipway, ***Kylesku Hotel*** *(☎ 01971-502231)* charges from £35 for B&B; it's open from March to the end of

Assynt is Different

Within its relatively small area, Assynt has an extraordinary array of rock types and strikingly clear evidence of major geological processes. In the late 19th century, geologists from around the world journeyed to Assynt to argue about, and finally agree on, an explanation for the evolution of the landforms around them. Assynt continues to be of interest to geologists and naturalists generally.

Lewisian gneiss, an ancient rock, is the main component of the landscape, forming a platform on which sit eroded sandstone mountains (notably Suilven) and huge masses of shattered quartzite capping the ridges and peaks. Schist (highly altered rock) occurs in the east while limestone is found mainly around Inchnadamph.

The most important geological process was the displacement of vast sheets of rock – the evidence of which can be seen in thrust planes (collectively in the Moine Thrust Zone) in the western half of Assynt. The pitted plateaus and deep valleys of the area graphically reveal the erosive forces of ice during the last ice age.

Against this stark background, Assynt lost many of its people during the 19th-century clearances and later, as farming and fishing declined. However, the strong tradition of valuing possession of land above all else survived. In 1993, after a determined and at times dramatic campaign, a group of Assynt crofters purchased the North Lochinver Estate. Agitation for land reform was growing during the 1990s and this achievement – returning the land to the people – was hailed as a landmark victory. Since then, communities elsewhere have had similar success; another local group, Culag Community Woodland Trust, purchased the Little Assynt Estate in 2000.

To find out more about Assynt's geology, *Assynt: Geological Motor Trail* by DR Shelley is a good starting point; *Suilven's World* by Peter & Janet Sprent covers social and natural history; *Historic Assynt* by Malcolm Bangor-Jones is more detailed about social history; and *We Have Won the Land* by John MacAskill recounts the North Lochinver Estate saga.

October. ***Newton Lodge*** *(☎ 01971-502070)*, about 1.5mi south of Kylesku, offers modern accommodation with spectacular views over Loch Glencoul. The lodge has B&B from £30 and DB&B is £45. ***Kylesku Backpackers*** *(☎ 01971-502003)*, on the western side of the A894 near the village, offers twin rooms in purpose-built lodges from £12. They are well equipped for self-caterers. The nearest shop is in Scourie, 9mi north.

Getting There & Away Tim Dearman's (☎ 01349-883585) summer-only Inverness to Durness service calls at Kylesku Monday to Saturday. A postbus service (☎ 01463-256228) from Lochinver to Scourie also stops at Kylesku Monday to Saturday.

Inchnadamph

Inchnadamph is not even a village – simply the hotel, bunkhouse and a handful of houses, all by themselves beside the A837 north of Ledmore Junction.

Places to Stay & Eat Facilities in the superbly renovated ***Inchnadamph Lodge*** *(☎ 01571-822218, ⓔ assynt@dial.pipex.com)*, dating from 1821, are first rate. The lodge offers either dorm accommodation for £8.50 (breakfast included) or B&B in private rooms from £13. There's a small ***shop*** nearby, which sells groceries, frozen food, beer and wine.

Close by is historic ***Inchnadamph Hotel*** *(☎ 01571-822202)*, which has simply furnished, comfortable rooms (some en suite) from £35. The generous bar suppers are superbly cooked and excellent value; you can eat your fill for £10, including local fish from £5, and there are vegetarian choices.

Getting There & Away A bus service operated by Rapson's (☎ 01463-710555) and Spa Coaches (☎ 01977-421311) from Inverness to Ullapool connects with a service to Drumbeg, which calls at Inchnadamph twice daily Monday to Saturday. There's also a postbus (☎ 01463-256228) from Lairg station, which meets the morning ScotRail (☎ 0845-755 0033) train from Inverness, and stops at Inchnadamph en route to Drumbeg.

Lochinver & Achmelvich

Lochinver is a sizable village on the sheltered upper reaches of Loch Inver; originally a fishing village it is now also the centre for the lively tourist industry. The TIC is the Assynt Visitor Centre (☎ 01571-844330), in the main street, open from mid-April to late October. It has an excellent range of books about the area, first-class displays about local history and wildlife, and a natural history reading room, ideal for a wet day. The one bank in Lochinver is open Monday to Friday (except Wednesday) but doesn't have an ATM; the nearest is in Ullapool.

Achmelvich is a hamlet on the coast a few miles north-west of Lochinver.

Places to Stay & Eat Mrs Macleod's ***Polcraig B&B*** *(☎ 01571-844429)* has a fine outlook over Loch Inver; the tariff in the large modern bungalow is from £20.

The nearest hostel is ***Achmelvich SYHA*** *(☎ 01571-844480)*, close to the beach; the tariff is £6.75. With no showers you'll have to hope it's warm enough to go for a swim. Nearby is ***The Shore Camping and Caravan Site*** *(☎ 01571-844393, e enquiries@shorecaravansite.co.uk)*, which definitely does have showers and plenty of space for tents right on the shore. Backpacker tariff is £4.50, or £7 for two people and a car. In summer there's a small, on-site ***shop***.

In Lochinver the celebrated place to eat is ***Riverside Restaurant*** *(☎ 01571-844356)*, in the main street. It's famous for its savoury and fruit pies (which you can take away or even have posted home) and specialises in locally caught fish (up to £15). Servings are extremely generous and the restaurant is also very good at vegetables. Anticipate paying around £15 for two courses. You can eat a little more economically in the Riverside's bistro-coffee shop.

There is also a ***Spar*** off-licence supermarket, which is open daily, as well as a ***butcher*** and a ***greengrocer***.

Getting There & Away Tim Dearman's (☎ 01349-883585) once-daily, summer bus service from Inverness to Durness diverges to Lochinver, Monday to Saturday. See Getting There & Away under Inchnadamph for Rapson's and Spa Coaches seasonal service from Ullapool to Drumbeg via Lochinver. A morning postbus (☎ 01463-256228) from Lochinver to Drumbeg calls at Achmelvich Monday to Saturday. Lochinver is on the A837, 10mi (16km) west of the Skiag Bridge junction with the A894.

Eas a' Chùal Aluinn

Duration	5¾–6¼ hours
Distance	10.4mi (16.5km)
Standard	medium-hard
Start	Loch na Gainmhich car park
Finish	Inchnadamph
Nearest Towns	Kylesku, Inchnadamph, Lochinver
Public Transport	yes (limited)

Summary A ruggedly scenic walk to the top of the highest waterfall in Scotland, in one of the wildest corners of Sutherland.

Eas a' Chùal Aluinn (which means 'beautiful slender waterfall') is the highest waterfall in Scotland with a drop of 204m, most of it in three long streams with a broad cascade at the base. It may lack the sheer dramatic force of the Falls of Glomach (see Side Trip on page 261) but the setting is wild and beautiful in a strangely compelling and desolate way.

The path to the falls from the A894 is well trodden, across rough, rocky ground, boggy in places, giving the walk its medium-hard grading, along with the amount of ascent (650m) and the distance. On a fine day you could spend an hour or more exploring the cliff tops and seeking out better vantage points for the falls. Although an out-and-back walk from the road is the simplest arrangement, a through route, deeper into the wilderness, is described here, finishing at Inchnadamph and mostly on clear paths.

Alternatives Between the waterfall and Inchnadamph the route crosses a high pass between Glas Bheinn (776m) to the west and Beinn Uidhe (740m) to the south-east. The walk to the former peak, which provides very fine views, is described briefly as a Side Trip on page 364.

Another possibility to make a round walk involves following a road, built in the early 19th century for the transport of marble from a quarry near Ledmore to the Kylesku harbour, to Loch na Gainmhich. It is shown on the OS map and is still in fair condition. It starts 1.3mi (2km) north of Inchnadamph as the access road to Achmore Farm and runs north along the western slopes of Glas Bheinn. The distance is 14.6mi (23.5km) with about 910m ascent.

NATURAL HISTORY

Essentially the walk is a crossing of the rocky ridge, pockmarked with lochans and encrusted with cliffs and scree, rising precipitously from the shores of Loch Glencoul and Loch Beag, and its tributary Abhainn an Loch Bhig, in the north and east. On the western side the ridge rises from north-flowing Unapool Burn and from the many streams that empty southward into Loch Assynt.

Eas a' Chùal Aluinn spills over a weakness in the long line of cliffs rising from Abhainn an Loch Bhig. Miraculously, in an otherwise almost treeless area, spindly birch cling to the cliffs, permanently dampened by the fall's spray.

PLANNING

When to Walk

Allowing that this walk could be quite hazardous in very windy conditions, its season is quite long – from April to late October.

Stalking During the stalking season (mid-August to mid-October) walkers are asked to avoid areas where stalking is taking place on the day, although access remains open on the main paths. Information about activities and recommended walking routes in the area are available from Inchnadamph Estate on ☎ 01571-822208.

GETTING TO/FROM THE WALK

The walk starts at a signposted car park on a sharp bend in the A894, above the north-western corner of Loch na Gainmhich. Tim Dearman's (☎ 01349-883585) summer bus service between Inverness and Durness goes past the start at 12.15pm – a bit late for the full walk but not for a simple out and back to the falls. Another option is to contact the Lochinver taxi service (☎ 01571-844607).

THE WALK

See map page 363

From the car park walk south along the road for about 200m and diverge down an old track to the left. It crosses a small stream then rises to meet an east-west path; turn left. The path descends to and parallels the shore of Loch na Gainmhich to its feeder stream, then goes up the rocky slope to the right and crosses Allt Loch Bealach a' Bhuirich. Shortly it meets a not as well-defined path on the left. Continue up the northern side of a rugged, rocky valley, with fine views of the corries on the north face of Glas Bheinn, and on to dark, peaceful **Loch Bealach a' Bhuirich** (1¼ hours from the start). The bealach itself is above the loch to the east.

The path, now cairned, wastes no time in losing height down to a nameless tributary of Abhainn an Loch Bhig. Cross the burn on stepping stones and continue beside it downstream (not on the northern side as shown on the OS map). Go across very peaty ground, through a line of low cliffs and down to near the edge of the main cliff, high above Abhainn an Loch Bhig. Continue to the right (south-east) for about 250m to a good vantage point for **Eas a' Chùal Aluinn** – it's next to impossible to safely get a good, close-up view (1¼ hours from Loch Bealach a' Bhuirich). A series of graceful, steep cascades fall to the green, flat-floored glen of Abhainn an Loch Bhig, meandering into tranquil Loch Beag and overlooked by cliffs on its far side.

Return almost to the stepping stones and, in a peaty spot between two crags (the left one topped with a cairn), turn left. A path materialises in a very short distance and rises south-eastward then south up a rocky spur. It crosses a shallow valley and continues rather deviously to overlook a pair of lochans, the northern one little more than a puddle. Turn right at a cairned path junction and go between these lochans then up the wild, rocky glen feeding them towards the cliffs ahead (south). The views of the spires and scree on Glas Bheinn to the west and the crags of Beinn Uidhe above are awesome. The path, clear enough on the ground, is sparsely cairned. Take care to find a right-hand turn in the path, then cross a stream on mossy stepping stones and continue up to a rock shelf at the base of the steep, scree-strewn slopes.

The path zigzags up to **Bealach na h-Uidhe** (1¾ to two hours from the waterfall) – a fine lookout embracing all the country southward as far as the big 'hills' east of Ullapool (see Side Trip on page 364).

The path drops straight down from the gap. On the edge of the scree on the steep slope to the left, the path bends left (south-east) across a rocky shoulder, then south down to Loch Fleodach Coire, becoming increasingly clear and intermittently cairned. Continue across two burns entering the loch. A stake marks the position of a decrepit footbridge across the burn flowing from the

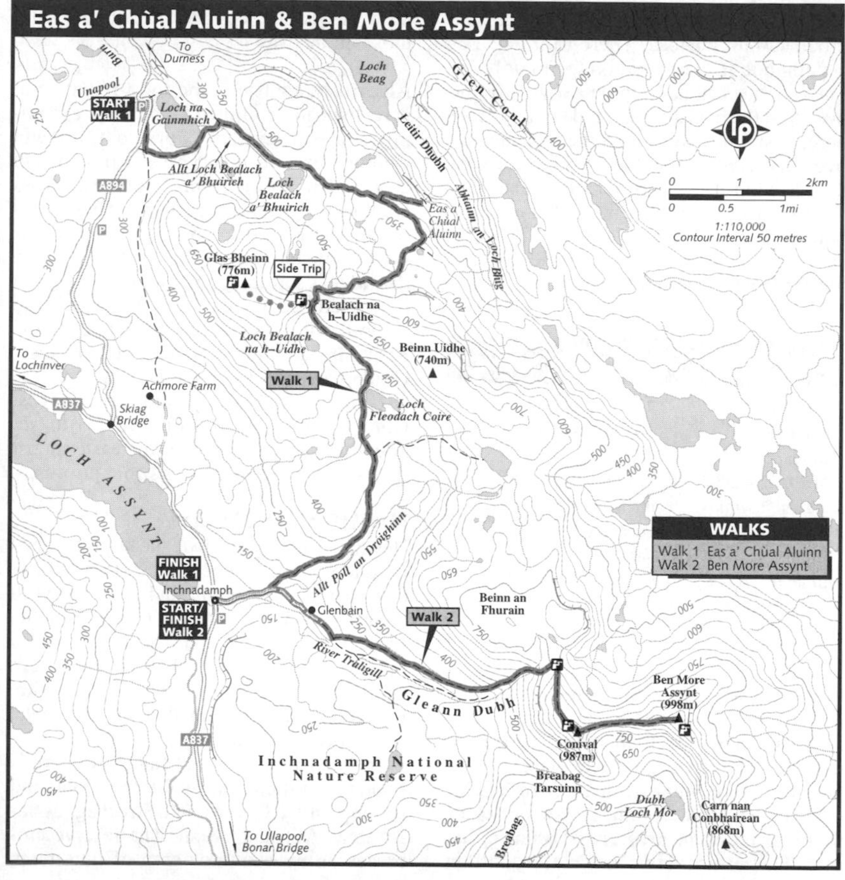

loch. Make your way through a maze of peat hags up to a broad spur, past a small lochan and on to a path junction where there's a stone shelter, used by stalkers. From here the path makes a well-graded descent into the glen of Allt Poll an Droighinn and on to meet the Gleann Dubh vehicle track near a bridge. Turn right and walk down to the Inchnadamph car park (1¾ to two hours from the bealach).

Side Trip: Glas Bheinn

1–1¼ hours, 2mi (3km), 150m ascent

From a large cairn at **Bealach na h-Uidhe**, head west up over grass, then scree and some boulders on the narrow ridge, to the broad summit plateau. There isn't much of a path but it's easy walking, mainly on grass, to a subsidiary top on a low cliff line bisecting the plateau. Descend slightly from here, past a tiny lochan on the left, then up over shattered rock to the 2m-high cairn on **Glas Bheinn**. The views of Quinag and Suilven are truly awe-inspiring; all the mountains to the north can be seen and the view east, on a good day, extends to Ben Wyvis, not far from Inverness.

Ben More Assynt

Duration	7–7½ hours
Distance	10.4mi (16.5km)
Standard	hard
Start & Finish	Inchnadamph
Nearest Towns	Inchnadamph, Kylesku, Lochinver
Public Transport	yes

Summary A fairly strenuous walk to the highest peak in the far north-west, in the heart of wild, rocky Assynt and with coast-to-coast views.

From the west, Ben More Assynt (998m, 3273ft) hides behind its satellite Conival (987m) – they seem to merge into one huge mass of shattered quartzite. Doing both peaks (they're Munros) in a day makes for a fairly long and strenuous but outstandingly scenic walk involving 1100m of ascent. The rewards are considerable; on Ben More it's easy to feel you're deep in wild, lonely country made up of little other than rock and water. Ben More's name means 'great mountain of Assynt' and Conival translates roughly as 'joined-on mountain'.

From Glenbain, east of Inchnadamph, a well-used and often boggy path takes you up Gleann Dubh; on the mountain massif there's little respite from rocky going underfoot. The ridge linking the two peaks is quite narrow although, with care, not seriously exposed. Nevertheless, this is definitely not a place to be in wind, rain or mist.

The walk is described as a there-and-back trip, usually not the ideal but the views on the way back are completely different from those on the way up.

Alternatives The scope for a round walk is realistically confined to the ridge extending south from Ben More to Carn nan Conbhairean, from where it's possible to drop to Dubh Loch Mòr, head west across the corrie to Breabag Tarsuinn (the gap between Conival and Breabag), then northwest to join the Gleann Dubh path. However, the ridge is seriously narrow and exposed in places, and demands a head for heights and scrambling experience (described in the Scottish Mountaineering Club's District Guide – see Books on page 350).

If time is short you could settle for just Conival, reducing the time to 5½ to six hours and sacrificing only the easternmost limits of the view that Ben More affords.

NATURAL HISTORY

Ben More and Conival are the highest points on a long, high, rugged ridge, with numerous peaks above 600m and speckled with countless lochans, extending south from the shore of Loch Glencoul to the upper reaches of Glen Oykel, east of Elphin. Both peaks are capped with masses of fractured quartzite, which gleams white in the sun and looks like snow from a distance.

Inchnadamph National Nature Reserve is bounded in the north by Gleann Dubh and in the east by Conival and Breabag, as far south as Allt nan Uamh. The reserve embraces an extensive outcrop of limestone, riddled with underground caverns and subterranean streams, and rich in limestone-loving plants. The presence of this rock explains why Gleann Dubh (despite its name, meaning 'dark glen') is so green, in a landscape where the most obvious vegetation is grey-green (and purple) heather.

PLANNING

When to Walk

The mountain is exposed and often cloud-capped, so it's worth waiting for a good day – conditions could be hazardous on the narrow ridge between Conival and Ben More Assynt in strong winds and mist. Snow is common in winter, making the best time for this walk between April and early October.

Stalking This walk is in the Inchnadamph Estate – see Stalking on page 362.

GETTING TO/FROM THE WALK

The walk starts and finishes at the car park adjacent to the entrance to the Inchnadamph Hotel, beside the A837.

THE WALK

See map page 363

From the car park walk north along the road a short distance and turn right along the road leading to Inchnadamph Lodge. Follow it past the boundary of Inchnadamph National Nature Reserve and, farther on, across a causeway. Here the track divides and either way will do – the track to the right is just slightly longer. The two tracks soon merge and go on to Glenbain (a stone cottage). Not far beyond Glenbain, the track forks; bear left and soon it becomes a path. Fork left again just before crossing a burn, then follow the muddy path through a narrow belt of conifers and across the grass and heather slope. The path is clear enough in between the patches of soft ground (the bogs near the conifers are the wettest of the day), as it climbs Gleann Dubh with the scree on Conival's slopes soaring skywards ahead.

The gradient steepens as you climb into the narrowing glen, turning north-eastward and beside a tumbling stream. Cross a wide, shallow bowl, with the stream cascading down its rocky headwall. Ford the stream at the foot of a broken crag and follow a sinuous route up to the foot of the low cliffs. The way up is easy, using natural rock steps (there's also a line of cairns, more useful for the descent) into a wide corrie. From here the path leads up through the scree, then crosses rock and grass to a low point on the skyline – the bealach (gap) on the main ridge (2½ hours from the start). The views of the impressive cliffs of Beinn an Fhurain nearby to the north are particularly fine, and the Western Isles sit along the horizon.

A clear path leads south up the spur, across scree to the broad summit ridge and on to the cairn marking the summit of **Conival** (30 minutes from the gap). Here you can add Ben Hope (north-east) to the tally of peaks in the wide view. Descend the eastern ridge on shattered rock, high above the deep corrie sheltering Dubh Loch Mor; it's narrow in places but not really exposed. Skirt a small pinnacle on the left then tackle the final climb to the top – toss a coin to decide which of the two rocky knobs is actually the summit of **Ben More Assynt** (about 45 minutes from Conival). On a clear day, you can see right across Scotland. The Dornoch Firth can be made out to the east and the Western Isles in the opposite direction. Allow at least three hours for the return.

Glen Canisp

Duration	6½–7 hours
Distance	14mi (22.5km)
Standard	medium-hard
Start	Ledmore River bridge
Finish	Lochinver
Nearest Towns	Elphin, Inchnadamph, Lochinver
Public Transport	yes

Summary An outstandingly scenic walk across wild and rugged moorland, beside remote and beautiful lochs, and past two of the north's prominent landmarks, Canisp and Suilven.

This low-level walk follows an established public footpath through wildly beautiful country. It can be done in either direction – there's little to choose as the views would be equally spectacular. Accommodation and transport, available near each end, could be the deciding factors. As little as 220m of ascent is involved but the distance, the roughness of the path in places and at least one potentially difficult stream crossing justify the medium-hard grading.

Alternatives The walk could be split into two, to simplify transport arrangements, perhaps making Lochan Fada or Loch na Gainimh the turn-around points. From either direction, an ascent of Canisp at 846m or Suilven at 731m (see Other Walks on page 368) could be added if you're prepared for a long day. Alternatively, Suileag Bothy could provide a comfortable base for more leisurely exploration of the area. The bothy's owner, Assynt Estate, asks walkers not to stay overnight during the stalking season (1 August to 21 October).

NATURAL HISTORY

Water is an ever-present feature of this walk, fortunately not always underfoot, but in lochs, lochans, burns and rivers that punctuate and dissect the landscape. In the early stages the route passes indented Cam Loch, the waters of which find their way into the River Kirkaig, which enters the sea south of Lochinver. Across a broad ridge, the route generally follows the chain of lochs and streams flowing into Loch Inver.

Surprisingly, perhaps, there are isolated stands of birch in the most sheltered corners of the area – out of reach of grazing animals. Elsewhere heather and moorland grasses dominate the scene.

PLANNING

Since fording the outlet stream from Lochan Fada can be hazardous after a day or two's rain, when the stepping stones can be about half a metre (2ft) under water, keep this walk for a fine, dry spell, preferably during May and June or September.

Stalking The walk passes through the Glen Canisp Estate. During the stalking season (mid-August to mid-October) walkers are asked to avoid areas where stalking is taking place on the day; contact the estate on ☎ 01571-844219.

NEAREST TOWN

Elphin

Elphin is a small village spread out along the A835, with a spectacular mountain backdrop, near Ledmore Junction.

Places to Stay & Eat Superbly appointed ***Birchbank Holiday Lodge*** *(☎ 01854-666215, e tomraystrang@btinternet.com)* is a modern establishment near Elphin. The B&B tariff is £20 and most rooms are en suite. A four-course meal can be turned on, complete with superb views of Suilven, for £15. There's a small ***camping site*** nearby where you can pitch a tent for £3.50. Birchbank is run by Tom and Ray Strang; Tom is the author mentioned in Books on page 350 and, as Assynt Outdoor Holidays, he organises guided and self-guided walks.

If you're just passing through Elphin, the ***Elphin Tea Rooms***, beside the main road, is open daily until 6pm for light meals and snacks.

Getting There & Away The postbus service from Lairg to Drumbeg (see Getting There & Away for Inchnadamph on page 360) stops, by request only, at Elphin from Monday to Saturday. Rapson's summer service from Ullapool to Drumbeg (again, see under Inchnadamph) calls at Elphin, Monday to Friday.

Elphin is on the A835, about 15.3mi (24.5km) north of Ullapool and 2.4mi (4km) west of Ledmore Junction and the A837.

GETTING TO/FROM THE WALK

The walk starts 100m east of the bridge over the Ledmore River, about 1.2mi east of Elphin on the A835. There is no formal car park nearby but there is space for three cars beside a gate 300m east of the bridge.

The walk finishes at a junction with the A837, marked by a public footpath sign to Ledmore, at the southern end of Lochinver. There is a car park about 200m to the right.

THE WALK

Go through a gate in the fence and follow a rough track that skirts the hillock ahead (rather than crosses it, as on the OS map) to the shore of Cam Loch. Make your way generally east to a small inlet and cross a burn (not mapped). From the shingle beach the path then becomes clear, leading into the heather and uphill. It soon crosses a burn and then goes through a gated deer fence. After a couple of ups and downs, the path decides to stick with the shore of Cam Loch. Immediately beyond the stream draining Loch a' Chroisg, a cairn marks the path's continuation north-westward, uphill and gradually away from Cam Loch. Having crossed a minor burn, continue up on rocky ground, taking care to turn north with the cairned path as the ground steepens to your left (west). It's a steady climb, in eerily beautiful country. With Loch a' Chroisg below to the right, the path turns north-westward and reaches its **highest point**, overlooking Lochan Fada (about two hours from the start). Then it's down, across several burns, with superb views of Canisp's southern flanks, to the north-western end of Lochan Fada.

Cross the outlet on small stepping stones and pick up the path along the north side of Allt a' Ghlinne Dhorcha. Continue through a deep, narrow gorge and out into the open with the expansive Loch na Gainimh and its grassy flats ahead and Suilven as the spectacular backdrop. The path is now easier to follow and improves further from a track junction, where a path heads away generally east towards Canisp. A bridge crosses Abhainn na Clach Airigh, from where the path becomes a vehicular track. About 250m along, a cairned path on the left takes off towards Suilven. About half a mile farther on, the track recrosses the tumbling stream and continues north-westward beside or above the sinuous stream and its many pools. The side track leading to ***Suileag Bothy*** diverges at a sharply angled junction, 1.3mi from the second bridge (1½ hours from Lochan Fada).

For the best part of 2mi the track then wanders up and down and levels out as

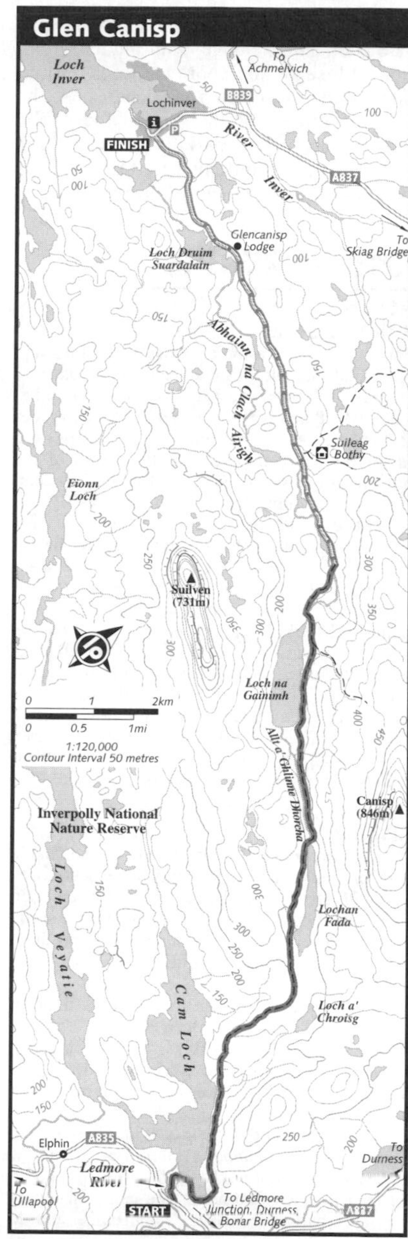

gorse, bracken and old fences announce private Glencanisp Lodge, well hidden in tall trees, close to the shore of Loch Druim Suardalain. A sealed road leads past the lodge's entrance to the start of the public road and a small car park. It's easy walking then for the last mile or so into Lochinver (1½ hours from Suileag Bothy).

Other Walks

ASSYNT

Point of Stoer

For a fairly easy walk, on a day when mist and low cloud rule out the mountains, the spectacular coastal cliffs north-west of Lochinver, on either side of the Point of Stoer and its Old Man of Stoer (a towering rock stack close to the cliffs) are ideal. Whatever the weather, the views of the mountains of Assynt and beyond are magnificent. An easy-medium 5mi (8km) round walk from Stoerhead lighthouse takes you along the cliff tops to the point then back over two grassy, heathery 'hills' – Sidhean Mòr and its nameless satellite, topped by a communications tower.

There are well-used paths as far as the closest point to the Old Man, beyond which the path is less clear. The road to the lighthouse is well signposted from the B869 coastal road, about 6mi (10km) north of the turn-off from the A837 near Lochinver. The nearest places for refreshments are at Lochinver or Drumbeg, about 8mi east along the B869. The OS Landranger 1:50,000 map No 15 *(Loch Assynt)* covers this walk.

Quinag

Quinag (pronounced **koon**-yak, from the Gaelic for 'milking pail') is a uniquely Y-shaped mountain with terraced sandstone cliffs between Loch Glencoul and Loch Assynt. It dominates the scene west of the Ben More Assynt massif. It has three distinct tops: Spidean Coinich (764m) on the southern leg of the Y, separated from Sàil Gharbh (808m) on the north-eastern arm and Sàil Gorm (776m) to the north by deep Bealach a' Chornaidh. The usual approach is from a parking area on the A894 between Skiag Bridge and Kylesku and up the broad, south-eastern ridge leading to Spidean Coinich.

The full round of all the peaks involves around 10mi (16km) with about 1100m of ascent; allow at least eight hours. By following a path to Lochan Bealach Chornaidh you can concentrate on Sail Gharbh, or strike a compromise and do Spidean and Sail Gharbh, descending to Lochan Bealach Cornaidh from the bealach. Use OS Landranger 1:50,000 map No 15 *(Loch Assynt)*. The contact for information about stalking activities between mid-August and mid-October is the Quinag Estate on ☎ 01854-666238.

Suilven

Suilven (731m) is perhaps the icon for the north-west – its extraordinary terraced sandstone dome looming over Lochinver is a staple of calendar publishers. It's quite a complex mountain, however, with a longish, bristly ridge tapering away from the dome, Caisteal Liath – its highest point.

The main approach is from Lochinver, along the road to Glencanisp Lodge, then the vehicular track south-eastward as far as the southern end of Loch na Gainimh (see the Glen Canisp walk on page 365). An all too well-used path goes up to Bealach Mor from where the summit is easily reached; a full traverse of the ridge, south-east from the bealach, calls for some scrambling and a head for heights. The walk is covered by OS Landranger 1:50,000 map No 15 *(Loch Assynt)*. The Scottish Mountaineering Club's guide *The Northwest Highlands* has a useful description. For information about access during the stalking season ring ☎ 01571-844219.

Stac Pollaidh

Stac Pollaidh (612m), or Stac Polly, is perhaps the most distinctive among the remarkable group of mountains north of Ullapool, and the most accessible. An isolated, comb-like peak west of Elphin, it rises precipitously above Loch Lurgainn to the south and from a maze of lochs and rock to the north, in extensive Inverpolly National Nature Reserve. It affords panoramic views as fine as those from many peaks hundreds of metres higher. A major footpath repair and construction project by The Footpath Trust, costing £500,000 and partly funded by public donations, was completed in 2000. It replaced the dangerously eroded gutters up the south face with an excellent path round the steep eastern flank and up to the top from the north; a western extension makes a round walk possible.

The path starts at a formal car park beside the single-track road to Achiltibuie, which branches from the A835 between Ullapool and Elphin. Achiltibuie, a small village overlooking the Summer Isles in outer Loch Broom, is the nearest town and another good base for walks in the area. Allow about three hours for this walk, which is covered by OS Landranger 1:50,000 map No 15 *(Loch Assynt)*.

Northern Isles

Although collectively referred to as the Northern Isles, the island groups of Orkney and Shetland are quite distinct and separated by 60mi of stormy North Atlantic Ocean. Orkney is close to the Scottish mainland and has a pastoral feel, while Shetland is bleaker, more remote and has a stronger Norse influence. What the islands do have in common is their superb coastal scenery, a plethora of archaeological sites and the greatest concentrations of seabirds in Europe. Add the occasional display of the *aurora borealis* (the northern lights) and endless hours of light during summer, and you have two inspirational walking destinations.

All walks are coastal, cross relatively easy terrain and pose little difficulty in terms of navigation. As such they provide much easier walking than many of the more mountainous regions of mainland Scotland. There is no deer culling in the Northern Isles, so all the routes are unaffected by stalking activity.

Highlights

BRYN THOMAS

Skara Brae, on the Yesnaby Coast, provides a unique insight into Stone Age Orkney.

- Walking on the edge of some of Britain's highest sea cliffs on Hoy
- Visiting Skara Brae, Scotland's best-preserved Neolithic village, on the Yesnaby Coast
- Watching the puffins and gannets at Hermaness Nature Reserve
- Getting dive-bombed by skuas on Hoy and by arctic terns on Westray

INFORMATION

Maps

For a topographic overview of Orkney and Shetland, use OS Travelmaster 1:250,000 map No 2 *(Northern Scotland)* or you can pick up a copy of the 1:128,000 *Official Tourist Map – Shetland & Orkney*, available from TICs and local bookshops.

Permits

In the Northern Isles, it is illegal to wilfully disturb the red-throated diver and a permit is required to photograph them. Contact the Royal Society for the Protection of Birds (☎ 01856-791298) for more information.

Place Names

Many place names in the Northern Isles have a strong Norse influence. When the Norse settlers arrived around AD 800 the previous Pictish and Gaelic languages largely disappeared and a version of Old Norse, called Norn, developed. This language has only begun to decline over the last two or three hundred years, and even today the accent and colloquial words used by the people of the Northern Isles bear evidence of Norn influence.

On maps, the Norn influence is even more evident with geos (narrow inlets), voes (sounds), gloups (holes in cliffs) and wicks (bays) liberally scattered across the landscape.

Warning

All of the routes in this chapter involve some walking along the edge of high sea cliffs. The cliff tops are generally unfenced and sometimes have loose and crumbling edges. There is an inherent danger in this sort of walking, especially when nesting seabirds invite closer observation from the cliff edge. Be careful and err on the side of caution, especially if the wind is strong. In particular, accidents have occurred when people wearing waterproof trousers and coats have slipped on steep slopes above the cliffs – the combination of shiny fabric and wet grass can be lethal in such situations.

Orkney

There is something almost mystical about the wild and beautiful Atlantic archipelago of Orkney. Just 6mi north of mainland Scotland, 70 islands (16 inhabited) stretch north-east towards Shetland. Many of the islands are flat or have low, gently-sloping hills, patchworked with fields and bog. Hoy is the exception, having a more rugged feel, with steep-sided mountains reaching an altitude of 479m and some of the highest vertical sea cliffs in Scotland (and Britain). It is this landscape that is the focus of the Old Man of Hoy circuit, a route that includes a visit to Scotland's most famous sea stack.

The islands also boast the greatest concentration of prehistoric archaeological sites in Europe and many of these can be visited on walking routes. The Yesnaby Coast walk takes in Skara Brae, a 5000-year-old Neolithic stone village and perhaps the finest archaeological site on the islands. Sea cliffs are also a strong visual theme on all of the walks, although on Westray it is the seabirds that take centre stage during the trip along the island's western cliffs.

CLIMATE

Considering its northerly latitude, Orkney experiences a very temperate climate, with mild winters (average daily maximum 6°C) and cool, wet summers (average daily maximum 15°C). Wind is the most predictable part of daily weather – the islands are very exposed to ocean gales. A familiar pattern is for a storm to sweep in from the west or south-west, bringing a day of wet and windy weather. This is typically followed by a day of cold north-westerly winds accompanied by squally showers of rain or hail. These showery days can make for exhilarating walking, with stormy seas sparkling under crystalline blue skies. Snowfall is common throughout winter but never accumulates for long at low altitudes.

PLANNING

Books

Walking guides specific to Orkney, available locally, include *Orkney on Foot* by Kate Barrett, which has a foreword by none other than Bill Bryson. However, the sketch maps are quite poor. *Walks in Orkney* by Mary Welsh is better presented, but the majority of walks are really short strolls (around 3mi). A *Walks in Orkney* pamphlet is also available from local TICs; 19 walks are described briefly and shown on a map of the islands.

A wide range of books provides extra background information on Orkney, most of which are available in Stromness and Kirkwall. *The Orkney Guide Book* by Charles Tait has some good detail on history and natural history. *Orkney – A Historical Guide* by Caroline Wickham-Jones is worth a look, and *The Mammals of Orkney* by Chris & Jean Booth is a small, illustrated guide to both the marine and terrestrial mammals of the islands.

Information Sources

For preliminary planning contact Orkney Tourist Board in Kirkwall (☎ 01856-872856, W www.orkney.com), which will mail out leaflets, timetables, accommodation listings and a background guide, *The Islands of Orkney*.

The Highland Council publishes a set of four comprehensive transport guides to the region, including *North Highland & Orkney*, which are most readily available from the local TICs.

In case of an emergency in Orkney, call Kirkwall police station (☎ 01856-872241). Don't forget to fill out the 'Let Someone Know Before You Go' form, available from W www.northern.police.uk.

GETTING AROUND

Orkney Bus (☎ 01856-870555) runs a service between Kirkwall and Stromness, with numerous buses each way Monday to Saturday and no service on Sunday. The trip costs £2 and takes around 30 minutes. In Stromness buses arrive and depart from outside the Stromness Hotel (on Victoria St, opposite the port), while the Kirkwall bus station is at the junction of Pickaquoy and Great Western Rds. Flights within Orkney are operated by Loganair (☎ 01856-872494).

ACCESS TOWNS

Stromness

With its old stone houses, cobbled alleyways and fishing harbour backed by the 'hills' of Hoy, Stromness makes an atmospheric base for exploring Orkney. Although smaller than Kirkwall, the capital of Orkney, Stromness is the first port of call for most visitors arriving on the islands by sea.

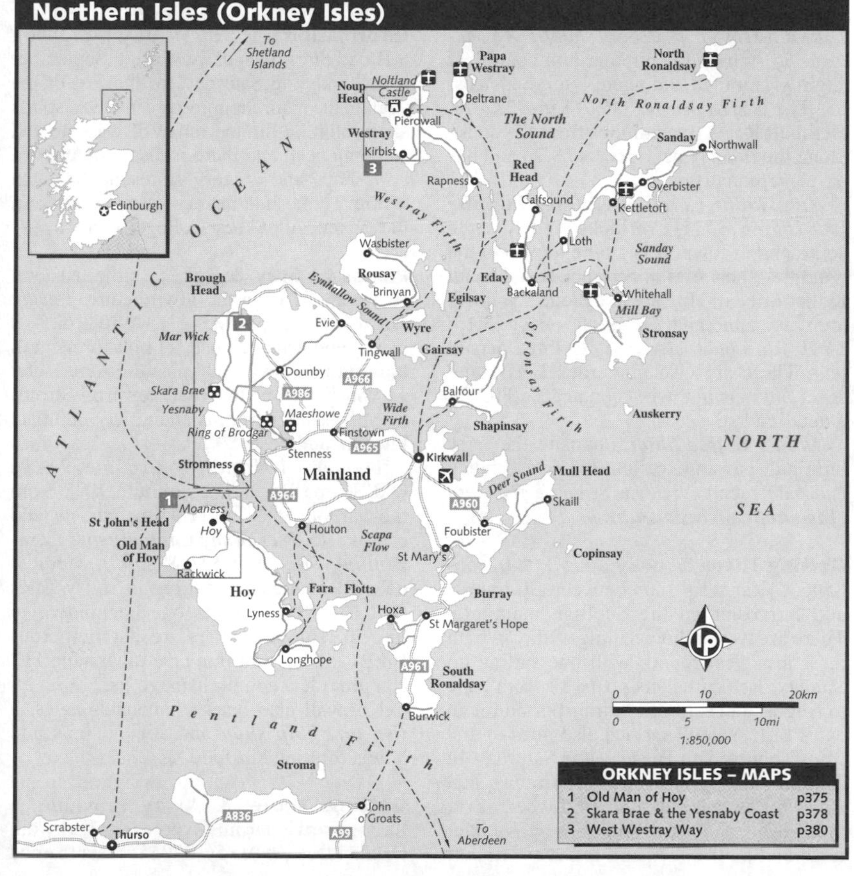

Information The TIC (☎ 01856-850716) is inside the P&O ferry terminal on the main quay and is open daily. It sells all of the Orkney OS maps and a good selection of guidebooks. During the very busiest periods it also opens to greet passengers from late ferries. There is a Royal Society for the Protection of Birds office (☎ 01856-850176) on North End Rd, a Royal Bank of Scotland ATM in Victoria St and a laundry at 20 Ferry St. There are several grocery stores and a bookshop in the town centre, but nowhere to buy outdoor gear. Public Internet access is available at the CESS office in John St.

Places to Stay & Eat Open all year, ***Brown's Hostel*** *(☎ 01856-850661, 45 Victoria St)* is friendly, popular and central, if slightly cramped and aged; bunk beds cost £8. The ***SYHA Hostel*** *(☎ 01856-872243)*, Hellihall Rd, is five minutes from the docks along the main street. It costs £8.25 and has an 11.45pm curfew.

Ness Point Caravan & Camping Site *(☎ 01856-873535)* overlooks the bay at the south end of town. It is a bit exposed to the wind, but the views of Stromness and south to the 'hills' of Hoy are excellent. Facilities are reasonable and tent pitches cost £3.15/£4.20 for a one person/two to three person tent. There are also numerous B&Bs and several hotels in town – contact the TIC for a detailed list.

Julia's Coffee Shop, opposite the ferry terminal, has an excellent breakfast, lunch and cafe menu. Victoria St has a ***fish and chip shop*** and ***restaurant***.

NORTHERN ISLES

Getting There & Away A P&O (☎ 01856-850655) car ferry runs between Stromness and Scrabster on the Scottish mainland. There are two or three sailings a day in both directions year-round, with one sailing on Sunday. Return tickets cost £32 from June to August and cars can be transported for an extra £81. A P&O service also goes to and from Aberdeen on Tuesday and Saturday. In summer this service costs £84 return and £201 for a car, although mid-week saver fares offer a 20% discount on passenger fares and a 50% discount for vehicles. For details on ferry services linking Orkney and Shetland, see Getting There & Away for Lerwick on page 383.

Note that a company called Northlink will take over from P&O as the main shipping-service provider to the Northern Isles from October 2002; routes, timetables and fares may change considerably as a result.

Kirkwall

Although it is the capital of Orkney, Kirkwall does not have the charm of Stromness. However, it does have a better selection of shops and facilities, and good ferry and air connections to other islands in the group.

Information The TIC (☎ 01856-872856), 6 Broad St, is open daily April to September and Monday to Saturday for the rest of the year. In the main shopping precinct is a sports shop selling a limited range of walking and camping gear, and there is also a number of bookshops and grocery stores in the town centre. Public Internet access is available in the evening at Orkney College, East Rd.

Places to Stay & Eat Near the harbour, five minutes from the town centre, ***Peedie Hostel*** *(☎ 01856-875477)*, Ayre Rd, is a small, unobtrusive hostel. Look for a small blue sign on a wall just past the Ayre Hotel as you head out the road towards Stromness. It has new rooms and a very compact kitchen, and costs £9.50.

The ***SYHA Hostel*** *(☎ 01856-872243)*, Old Scarpa Rd, is a 20-minute walk from the harbour, has an 11.45pm curfew and costs £8.75. ***Pickaquoy Camping and Caravanning Site*** *(☎ 01856-879900)*, Muddisdale Rd, is adequate but can be noisy. Sites cost £3.15/£4.20 for a one person/two to three person tent. There are also numerous B&Bs and hotels around the town – the TIC can provide a comprehensive list.

Kirkwall also boasts numerous cafes, a ***fish and chip shop*** and several inns and hotels offering bar food.

Getting There & Away Providing a through service from Inverness to Kirkwall, Orkney Bus (☎ 01856-870555) has teamed up with the passenger-only ferry run by John O'Groats Ferries (☎ 01955-611353, W www.jogferry.co.uk). One or two departures leave daily from May to September and a return ticket costs £39. Booking in advance is recommended.

British Airways/Loganair (☎ 0845-773 3377) runs scheduled flights daily (except Sunday) between Kirkwall and Aberdeen, Edinburgh, Glasgow, Inverness and Shetland, with connections to all main UK cities. As a guide to fares, a return Glasgow-Kirkwall ticket costs £224 and Kirkwall-Sumburgh (Shetland), £89. Kirkwall airport is 2.5mi from the town centre; there are taxi connections.

Old Man of Hoy

Duration	2 days
Distance	12mi (19km)
Standard	medium
Start/Finish	Moaness Pier
Nearest Towns	Hoy, Stromness
Public Transport	yes

Summary A magnificent coastal walk along some of Britain's highest sea cliffs. Highlights of the walk include the Old Man of Hoy sea stack and magnificent views over the Orkneys from the summit of Cuilags.

Hoy, the second largest island in Orkney, is by far the most mountainous. This walk makes a relatively strenuous circuit of north Hoy, taking in the Royal Society for the Protection of Birds' North Hoy Nature Reserve and the line of massive sea cliffs running from St John's Point to the Old Man of Hoy. The cliffs at St John's Head fall just over 300m plumb vertical to the ocean, making them among the highest in Britain. The Old Man of Hoy is perhaps the centrepiece of the walk, an iconic 137m sea stack photographed countless times and the focus of a live BBC broadcast in the 1960s, when British mountaineer Chris Bonnington led the first ascent.

The terrain is a mixture of sealed roads, stony tracks and open moor, and the ascent to the summit of Cuilags (433m, 1420ft) is quite strenuous. Watch out for the great skuas when crossing between Cuilags and St John's Head – see the boxed text 'Beware of the Bonxie' on page 374. The walk can be covered in a day but Rack Wick is a fine place to spend a night. Alternatively, you could walk directly to the Old Man of Hoy via Rack Wick and then return the same way to reduce the grade of the walk to easy-medium.

NATURAL HISTORY

Topographically the Old Man of Hoy is the most interesting walk in Orkney. It has two deep, U-shaped valleys formed by past glacial action, the most notable being the gap between Cuilags and Ward Hill. The cliffs, which have eroded spectacularly at St John's Head and Old Man of Hoy, are comprised of old red sandstone.

The 4000ha North Hoy Nature Reserve was purchased by the Royal Society for the Protection of Birds in 1983 and is a Site of Special Scientific Interest. Four hundred pairs of great skua (bonxie) nest on the uplands and around 22,500 pairs of fulmar nest on the cliffs along with good numbers of puffin, guillemot, razorbill and kittiwake. Sharing the uplands with the skua are dunlin and golden plover, with rare red-throated diver inhabiting the small mountaintop lochans. High densities of smaller birds such as stonechat, wheatear and meadow pipit are also present.

PLANNING

When to Walk

Winter conditions can make the mountainous section of this walk difficult and the steep ascent of Cuilags can be dangerous under snow. May to September is the best time to see seabirds along the route.

What to Bring

The terrain across Cuilags and St John's Head can be quite rough, so strong boots are in order. Bring plenty of warm and waterproof clothing and possibly a stick or pole for distracting diving skua (see the boxed text 'Beware of the Bonxie' on page 374).

Beware of the Bonxie

The great skua *(Catharacta skua),* known as a bonxie in the Orkneys, is one of the most formidable and aggressive seabirds in the world. Surpassed only by the great black-backed gull in terms of size and power, the great skua commonly attacks other birds in flight to force them to give up their catch. They even attack and kill gannets, hanging on to a tail or wingtip until the gannet has to ditch. Until 90 years ago their only breeding colonies in the British Isles were on Unst and Foula in the Shetlands. They have since spread to other locations in the Orkneys and northern Scotland. If you have the misfortune of straying too close to a skua nest (they nest on the ground), you're quite likely to be dive-bombed. The huge birds approach out of a dive at speeds of up to 50mi/h but rarely make direct contact. Still, it can be an unnerving experience and it is normal to hold a stick or pole above your head to ward off sharp beaks. If you happen to stray into a colony you could find yourself under attack from all sides!

MARTIN HARRIS

On Hermaness Nature Reserve in Shetland (see the Hermaness & Muckle Flugga walk on page 384), skua have become accustomed to human presence and will rarely attack. Of the other seabirds you're likely to encounter in the Northern Isles only terns are as aggressive in defending their nests, often making contact with their small but very sharp beaks. The best idea is to skirt all ground-nesting bird colonies. You have been warned!

If you plan to split the walk over two days you'll need to bring a sleeping bag for the hostel at Rackwick, some change to call the warden and all necessary provisions.

Maps

Use OS Landranger 1:50,000 map No 7 *(Orkney – Southern Isles)*.

NEAREST TOWN

Hoy

Hoy is the general name for the scattering of cottages and farms on the hillsides above Moaness Pier. The Royal Society for the Protection of Birds has a ranger (☎ 01856-791298) on the island who looks after the reserve. By prior arrangement he will meet visitors off the boat and conduct tours. The Society's Web site (W www.rspb.co.uk) has more information about the reserve.

Places to Stay & Eat Fifteen minutes' walk uphill from the pier, just to the left of the obvious church, is ***Hoy Outdoor Centre*** *(☎ 01856-873535, ext 2404, office hours only)*. Dorm beds cost £8 and it is advisable to book in advance. The ***Hoy Inn*** *(☎ 01856-791313)* serves bar meals; follow the signpost from the pier (five-minutes' walk).

Getting There & Away Orkney Ferries (☎ 01856-872044) makes the 30-minute crossing between Stromness and Moaness Pier. On weekdays ferries depart Stromness at 7.45am and 10am, with the last service returning from Hoy at 4.30pm. There are two later evening runs on Friday, and one morning and one evening crossing on Saturday and Sunday. A return ticket costs £5.

THE WALK

Day 1: Moaness Pier to Rackwick

5–6 hours, 8mi (13km)

From Moaness Pier follow the small sealed road west, round the Bay of Creekland. Follow this road for 1.5mi, ignoring left and right turns, and climb gently at first and then more steeply past a church on the right. The gradient eases as you leave the greener fields behind and begin to pass over rougher, heather-clad ground. At the top of the hill (40 minutes from the start) the road swings sharply to the right and a good track continues straight on towards the gap between Cuilags on the right and Ward Hill on the left. Follow the track to **Sandy Loch**, where the track becomes little more than a wide path. You may see skua gathered together on the loch, washing and socialising.

Fifty metres past the mouth of the loch, leave the track and begin to climb the rough slopes to the west. The gradient is very steep and you should allow 45 minutes to reach the summit of **Cuilags** (433m), with its panoramic views of the other Orkney isles to the north and east. To the south you can see right down through the Glens of Kinnaird to the cliffs flanking the east side of Rack Wick.

Leaving the summit of Cuilags, descend gently over boulder-strewn ground in a north-westerly direction. From here to St John's Head watch out for skua, which nest

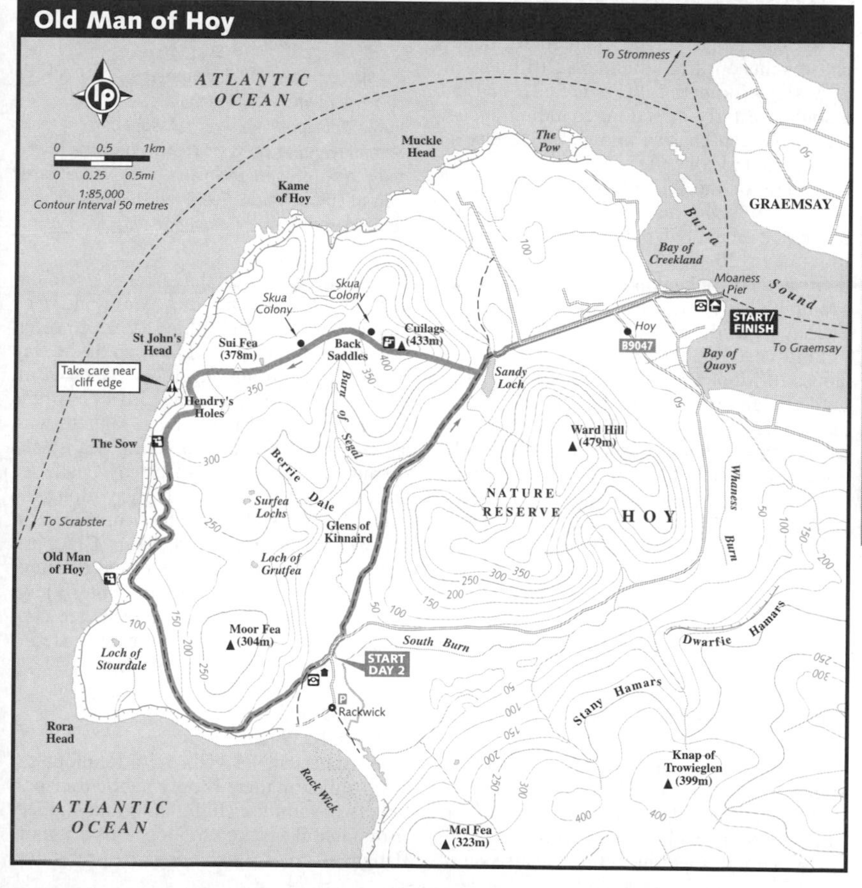

in considerable numbers in the boggy col. Try to steer around nests and create as little disturbance as possible, although even this probably won't save you from being dive-bombed once or twice. From the col swing back to the west and climb gently past a couple of lochs where you may see red-throated divers. It is illegal to disturb these rare birds and a permit is required to photograph them (see Permits on page 369).

Cross the broad Sui Fea summit (378m), which is marked by a trig point surrounded by a stone wall, and descend gently to the west to reach the dizzying cliff edge at **St John's Head.** From here the drop to the ocean is almost 350m. Close by, a prominent, wedge-shaped headland flanked by deep chasms juts out from the main cliff line.

A rough footpath follows the cliff line in a south-westerly direction, rounding spectacularly deep chasms known as Hendry's Holes. Round a gentle slope and get your first view of the **Old Man of Hoy** jutting proudly from the main cliff line. Descend towards it on a rough path to reach the main lookout in 20 to 30 minutes. From here there are not only good views of the Old Man but also views back along the cliffs to St John's Head.

Follow a good path south around the slopes of Moor Fea (304m) for 30 minutes, until you are overlooking the scattered hamlet of Rackwick and Rack Wick. This section can be muddy after wet weather. Pass through a gate and follow the path around two cottages to emerge through a gate at ***Rackwick Hostel*** *(☎ 01856-873535, ext 2404, office hours only)*. This small, eight-bed hostel has a kitchen, a hot shower and the option of camping outside. You may need to phone the warden to get in if there is no one else there, even if you have been prudent enough to book. There is a phone box beside the hostel.

Day 2: Rackwick to Moaness Pier

2–3 hours, 4mi (6.5km)

From Rackwick follow the sealed road to a signpost for Moaness Pier. Turn left and follow a path along the banks of a small river to a bridge with a plaque of engraved poetry. Cross a footbridge and climb gently onto the lower slopes of Ward Hill. The small gully of Berrie Dale on the other side of the valley is wooded with dwarf birch, and has the distinction of being the most northerly native woodland in the British Isles. Climb steadily for another 45 minutes to one hour to reach Sandy Loch, and then retrace your outward journey back to Moaness Pier.

Skara Brae & the Yesnaby Coast

Duration	7–8 hours
Distance	12.5mi (20km)
Standard	easy-medium
Start	Skara Brae
Finish	Stromness
Nearest Town	Stromness
Public Transport	yes (seasonal)

Summary An impressive route along the shattered cliffs of west Mainland, with an optional visit to Europe's best-preserved Neolithic village and views of Yesnaby Castle sea stack.

This route explores the most spectacular section of coastline that Mainland (the largest island in the Orkneys) has to offer, starting at the wide sandy sweep of the Bay of Skaill and following the west coast all the way to Stromness. The cliff line of this part of the island is wild and jagged, with sheer-sided geos and towering sea stacks dominating. The famous Yesnaby Castle sea stack is about a third of the way along the route. The walk also has an historic flavour: the World Heritage site of Skara Brae, just near the start, and the ruins of the Broch of Borwick are passed along the route. Views of Hoy are excellent and seabirds are constant companions. As always, care is needed when walking along the cliff tops.

PLANNING

When to Walk

This route can be walked throughout the year, although there is only public transport access in summer. High winds and slippery ground could make cliff-top walking more dangerous, so dry, calm days are preferable.

NORTHERN ISLES

The North-West is graced with a generous share of the wildest coast, mountains and glens – climbers atop the Old Man of Stoer near Lochinver; scanning east from 612m Stac Pollaidh (top inset) north of Ullapool; the extraordinary terraced sandstone dome of Suilven (731m) looming over Loch na Gainimh (bottom inset). *Main photo: Graeme Cornwallis. Insets: Grant Dixon.*

Archaeological sites and nesting sea birds abound in the **Northern Isles** – northern Europe's best preserved Neolithic village, Skara Brae (Orkney); a gannet chick (left inset) and a clownish puffin (right inset), just two of the attractions at Hermaness Nature Reserve on Shetland's northern tip. *Main photo: Bryn Thomas. Left inset: David Tipling. Right inset: Bryn Thomas.*

Skara Brae – World Heritage Site

Skara Brae is a 5000-year-old village that had been covered by sand until it was exposed by a severe storm in 1850. It is the best-preserved Neolithic village in Europe and offers an incredible insight into the thriving communities that existed in Stone Age Orkney. For this reason it has been classified as part of a World Heritage site.

A visit to the site, managed by Historic Scotland, makes a wonderful, thought-provoking start to the walk. It is open 9.30am to 6.30pm Monday to Saturday, and 2pm to 6.30pm on Sunday in summer (April to September), but closes at 4.30pm in winter. Entry costs £4.50/£3.30 in summer/winter. The visitor centre (☎ 01856-841815), at the entrance to the site, has informative displays and a sizeable shop; various publications about Skara Brae are among the many available.

What to Bring

Stout boots are recommended for extra friction and support over the rocky shore towards the end of the route. The cliffs are exposed to the notorious Atlantic weather, so bring plenty of warm clothing.

Maps

Use the OS Landranger 1:50,000 map No 6 *(Orkney – Mainland)*.

GETTING TO/FROM THE WALK

Orkney Bus (☎ 01856-870555) runs a summer service that connects Skara Brae, at the start of the route, with both Kirkwall and Stromness. The service operates Monday to Friday from 5 June to 9 September. Buses depart Kirkwall at 9.30am and 1.30pm and cost £2.25. Departures from Stromness are at 11.15am and 4.15pm and cost £1.30. Alternatively a taxi (☎ 01856-850750/850973) from Stromness costs £8.

THE WALK

If you wish to visit **Skara Brae** (highly recommended; see the boxed text), go through the visitor centre first and then drop onto the beach to join the walk. Otherwise, reach the beach directly on the track from the Bay of Skaill parking area. Follow the beach south and clamber over the rocks at the end, passing a ruined stone building. A faint path leads along the edge of a field and soon a stone stile allows you to cross the fence and climb onto the open cliff tops.

As soon as you have gained height, there is a fine view to the north of Kitchener Memorial (from WWI) on top of Marwick Head. The first coastal feature you come to is **Yettna Geo** – an impressive, sheer-sided gorge that echoes with the cries of the soaring birds. Thousands of guillemots can be seen crowding ledges on the walls of the cleft. Climb to the large cairn at **Row Head** (59m), and views south open up. The entire south-western coastline lies stretched before you and, beyond, the cliffs of Hoy rise from the sea with the Old Man of Hoy himself (see the Old Man of Hoy walk on page 373) silhouetted off the western shore.

A faint path descends gradually along the cliff tops, passing another large geo and a guillemot colony. The grassy terrain is interspersed by rock-slab paving, sometimes arranged in beautiful geometric formations. Pass another small geo and cross a stile. The path now descends to the **Broch of Borwick**, the remains of a tower-like structure similar to many others on Orkney, probably dating back to the 1st century. Although it is now half-ruined, it is still possible to duck through the entranceway to have a look at the double-walled construction.

Skirt around the inlet, cross a stile and climb up the other side inside a fence. You will be rewarded by a fine 180-degree panorama at the top. The cliff line becomes more shattered and the ground rockier as you near the WWII pillar boxes that mark your arrival at Yesnaby. This is perhaps the most beautiful section of cliff line in Orkney, adorned with thrusting headlands, jagged caves, natural arches and the weathered tower of **Yesnaby Castle**.

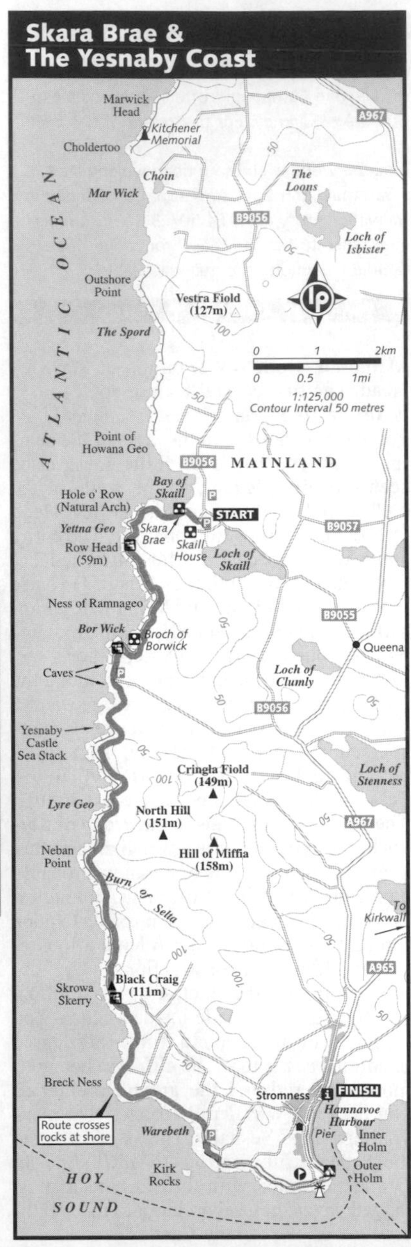

Continue past the sea stacks and through a wooden turnstile. Grassy ground rises to the headland and then remains fairly level, with precipitous drops to seaward. The cliffs of St John's Head on Hoy are resplendent ahead. Go past more geos, through another turnstile and you soon reach the picturesque **Burn Of Selta**, which disappears over the cliff and falls dramatically to the sea. Follow the next fence inland a little way and pass through a gate at the top. The ground now rises to Black Craig. Take care because the cliffs are reaching their highest and the terrain slopes seaward. Cross the stile in front of the concrete lookout marking the summit. The views across Hoy Sound and Scapa Flow to Orkney are excellent.

Descend heathery slopes towards farmland. Keep to the shore to avoid the fields as you follow the coast to Stromness. The rock slabs of the shore often make for the easiest going. After about 1.5mi you come to the sandy beach of **Warebeth**, where a well-trodden path at the back of the beach is signed to Stromness, just over 1mi away. Follow the path past a graveyard and along a shore littered with the rusty remains of ships that have foundered in the dangerous waters leading to Scapa Flow. The path becomes a sealed lane, passes Stromness golf course and arrives at the camping site on the peninsula, just south of the town. Follow the road north to reach Stromness.

West Westray Way

Duration	5–6 hours
Distance	9.5mi (15km)
Standard	easy-medium
Start	Kirbist
Finish	Pierowall
Nearest Town	Pierowall
Public Transport	no

Summary A coastal walk along the top of vertical sea cliffs teeming with different species of seabird and a chance to see puffins up close.

Westray is the largest of Orkney's northern islands and about 20mi north of Kirkwall.

The island's Noup Head Nature Reserve, administered by the Royal Society for the Protection of Birds, is perhaps the best place in Orkney to watch the many species of seabird that visit during summer. It is one of the largest seabird colonies in the British Isles. A faint path runs from the croft at Kirbist north along the island's western sea cliffs before sweeping round in a north-westerly direction to reach the reserve and lighthouse at Noup Head. Return to Pierowall along a track and then a small, sealed road, passing Noltland Castle. The walk's main interest is the birds, although the arches and caves in the sheer and sometimes overhanging cliffs are also impressive. Be careful if venturing close to the crumbling cliff edge, especially in windy weather.

NATURAL HISTORY

The horizontal bedding in the old red sandstone sea cliffs of west Westray has been weathered and exposed by the elements, creating perfect nesting sites for several hundred thousand seabirds. The numbers are staggering: at the height of the breeding season these cliffs are home to around 60,000 guillemots (known as aaks in Orkney), 30,000 pairs of kittiwake, 3000 pairs of fulmar, several thousand puffins (known as the tammy norrie) and 1700 razorbills. Just inland from the cliffs, on the exposed coastal heath, about 20,000 arctic terns and 1000 pairs of great skua have nests. In midsummer the overall effect of noise and movement, not to mention the smell, makes for a sensual overload.

PLANNING

When to Walk

The optimum time for seeing birds is June and July although the whole summer and early autumn are worthwhile. In winter, stormy seas might make the trip equally spectacular.

What to Bring

Although terrain covered by the route is dry, some sections are rough and rocky so boots are recommended. Otherwise bring as much warm clothing and protective gear as you would on a mountain walk – the route is very exposed to wind and rain. Bring binoculars if you have them.

Maps

Use OS Landranger 1:50,000 map No 5 *(Orkney – Northern Isles)*.

Information Sources

For information on the Noup Head Nature Reserve, contact the Royal Society for the Protection of Birds in Stromness (☎ 01857-644240), 14 North End Rd, or check the Web site at W www.rspb.co.uk.

NEAREST TOWN

Pierowall

Pierowall is the largest village on Westray. It is a friendly place, with traditional stone cottages (complete with stone roofs) gathered around a sandy bay. There's a post office and a bank open Wednesday and Friday.

Places to Stay & Eat Exceptionally well equipped, ***The Barn*** *(☎ 01857-677214)* is a renovated stone barn, complete with stone roof in traditional Westray style. The owners are very welcoming and will probably be driving the minibus that picks you up from the ferry in Rapness. It costs £11.75 for a bed in a shared room and camping is available for £3. ***Pierowall Hotel*** *(☎ 01857-677208)* is in the centre of the village and serves fish and chips renowned throughout Orkney. Accommodation starts at £38 for a double room with breakfast. There are also several B&Bs, charging around £18, including ***Arcadia*** *(☎ 01857-677283)* and ***Sand O'Gill*** *(☎ 01857-677374)*.

The upmarket ***Cleaton House Hotel***, 1mi outside Pierowall, offers extensive dinner and bar-food menus.

There are two main ***shops*** with reasonable supplies of groceries. Between them they are open from 9am to 10pm Monday to Saturday and on Sunday afternoon.

Getting There & Away Orkney Ferries (☎ 01856-872044) runs two or three services daily from Kirkwall to Rapness on the southernmost tip of Westray. The return crossing costs £10 and cars can be transported for £22.40 return. There is nothing at the ferry terminal in Rapness, so inform the ferry crew if you want the local minibus (☎ 01857-677211) to transport you to Pierowall. The 6mi trip costs £2.50 and a return journey can be arranged.

Loganair (☎ 01856-872494) has two flights a day between Westray and Kirkwall, with one fight on Saturday and none on Sunday. A return ticket costs £30.

GETTING TO/FROM THE WALK

There is no public transport between Pierowall and Kirbist, at the start of the walk, but there are several options for avoiding the 4.5mi (1½ hour) walk along the road between the two villages. Westray Tours (☎ 01857-677355) will take walkers to Kirbist; the price depends on the size of the group. You could also try the island's taxi (☎ 01857-677220), although the service is a bit informal and might not always be available. Failing that, inquire where you are staying and they might be able to organise a lift.

THE WALK

Kirbist is a loose collection of old crofts, most of which appear derelict. At the gatepost where the road becomes a farm track there is a weathered signpost for the West Westray Way. You won't see any more of these until you reach the lighthouse at Noup Head; the large and frequent stiles are your main route guide.

From the end of the farm track strike out north across fields, using the makeshift gates or crossing the fence where stones have been piled up. Already you may hear the shrill 'peeps' of oystercatcher and see them wheeling overhead. The concentration of bird life increases as you turn to the north-west into the col between Skea Hill and Fitty Hill. **Fitty Hill** (169m) is the highest point on the island and gives good views of Westray and the southern Orkney group. A detour to the top will take 20 minutes return. There may be a small colony of arctic tern nesting on the northern slopes of Skea Hill; if so you will need to detour around them. Never walk into the colony as you might harm the chicks. Even from the fringes of a tern colony, it is impossible to ignore the low passes and occasional dive-bombs of these beautiful but aggressive birds.

A short descent from the col leads to the cliff edge, where you cross a stile and get your first view of the seabird colonies on the ledges below. This very first section of cliffs offers perhaps the best opportunity to view puffin up close, although the largest concentrations of other birds are farther on towards the cliffs of Noup Head. Walk north along the cliff tops, passing a large cleft, and continue across a flat, grassy heath and over a couple of stiles. After 0.75mi the cliffs sweep around, reaching a height of almost 70m and providing a good opportunity to see the guillemot crammed onto the narrow ledges below. Cross a wobbly stile and continue towards a bay and low shoreline, which sweeps around to the north-west.

The route skirts the rims of some deep sea inlets and it is possible to look back over some spectacular sea arches and overhanging promontories. Keep an eye out for seal in the bay as you cross another stile and begin to climb steep grass slopes towards

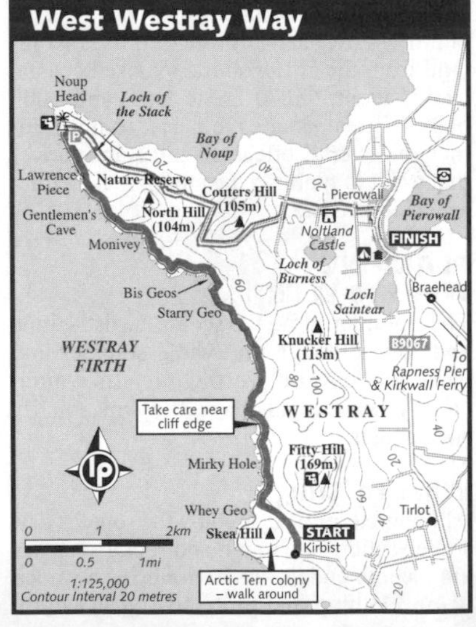

Noup Head. As you come over the crest of the climb the sound (and smell!) of seabirds in their thousands wafts on the breeze. At this point a corner with sheer walls on either side provides good views of several hundred pairs of guillemot and kittiwake. To the south the eye is drawn to the distant 'hills' of Hoy. Continue to follow the cliffs as they become higher and more impressive, reaching the lighthouse in 20 minutes.

To reach Pierowall follow the obvious track from the lighthouse. Within 15 minutes you'll arrive at a gate beside a farm, where the track becomes a minor road. Follow the road over the crest of a small hill and then descend past Noltland Castle (built in 1560 for Gilbert Balfour), reaching Pierowall in around one hour from the lighthouse.

Shetland

The Shetland isles are the most northerly land masses of the British Isles and consist of more than 100 islands, about 15 of which are inhabited. The largest island is Mainland, which has ferry or air connections to all other inhabited islands.

Shetland is closer to Norway than to mainland Scotland and the isles were once an outpost of Viking civilisation. They remained Norse territory until 1469, when they were presented to Scotland as part of the dowry of a Danish princess. A strong Scandinavian influence is evident throughout the islands, and can be found in Norn words and place names as well as local myths surrounding the creation of the lands.

The history of Shetland stretches back further than this; there are many archaeological sites and remains from the Iron Age and back as far as Neolithic civilisations. Ancient villages and burial sites at Sumburgh Head, on the southern tip of Mainland, have been found to contain bones and artefacts dating back to 3200 BC.

NATURAL HISTORY

In general the terrain of the islands is remote, boggy, undulating and sparsely populated, and the impression can be bleak in poor weather. However, the islands are world-famous among bird enthusiasts and the seabirds are probably the main attraction for walkers. The walk to the Royal Society for the Protection of Birds' Hermaness Nature Reserve on Unst visits perhaps the best bird habitat on Shetland. If you have no interest in raptor, Shetland is a long way to come for good but not spectacular cliff and

Life on the North Atlantic

Until the discovery of the Brent oilfields in 1971, fishing was the mainstay of Shetland's economy. As far back as the 14th and 15th centuries, islanders traded split, salted and beach-dried whitefish with German merchants. Later, Dutch *busses* (17th-century versions of factory ships) began to catch herring in huge numbers, processing the fish onboard. The French destroyed the Dutch fishing fleet in 1703, after which the industry fell into decline. Things were made worse in the 18th century when the British government banned imported salt, which the traders relied upon to get produce to market in an edible state.

Gradually Shetland landlords developed another, albeit iniquitous, fishing industry of their own, employing their tenants to fish for them. Crofts were subdivided to increase the numbers of available fishermen. Equipment had to be hired from the landlord and fish also had to be sold to the local merchant at a price fixed by the landlord. The Truck System, as it was known, was highly exploitative and was eventually banned.

Conditions for the men who worked in this way were appallingly dangerous. The far haaf (deep water) was good for cod and other valuable whitefish, but took a great toll in lives. With no weather forecasts to warn of approaching storms, summer fleets were sometimes caught out 40mi (60.5km) offshore by bad weather, where their *sixerns* (six-oared boats) gave little protection against big seas. In 1832 alone, 31 boats went down with the loss of 105 men from North Mainland. Today memorials to such disasters can be found all over Shetland.

coastal walking! The intricate coastlines of the islands mean it is impossible to get more than 3mi from the sea. Jagged cliff lines and secluded sandy bays are inherent features of the shoreline, and the other walks described explore some of the best coastal scenery Shetland has to offer.

CLIMATE

Being on a latitude of 60 degrees north, you wouldn't expect Shetland to have great weather. However, the islands are surrounded by the warming influence of the Gulf Stream, and generally have cool, wet summers and relatively mild winters (rarely below 0°C during the day). Being on the track of Atlantic weather systems, they do see a good deal of overcast and drizzly weather, but the absence of any high ground means that rainfall is not as high as you might expect (the annual average for rainfall is 102cm, only half the average for the western Highlands). Wind is something that these islands do see a lot of, with gales almost daily in winter.

In midsummer (June and July – when the bird numbers are also at a peak) the days are almost endless, with up to 19 hours of light and five hours of semi-darkness constituting

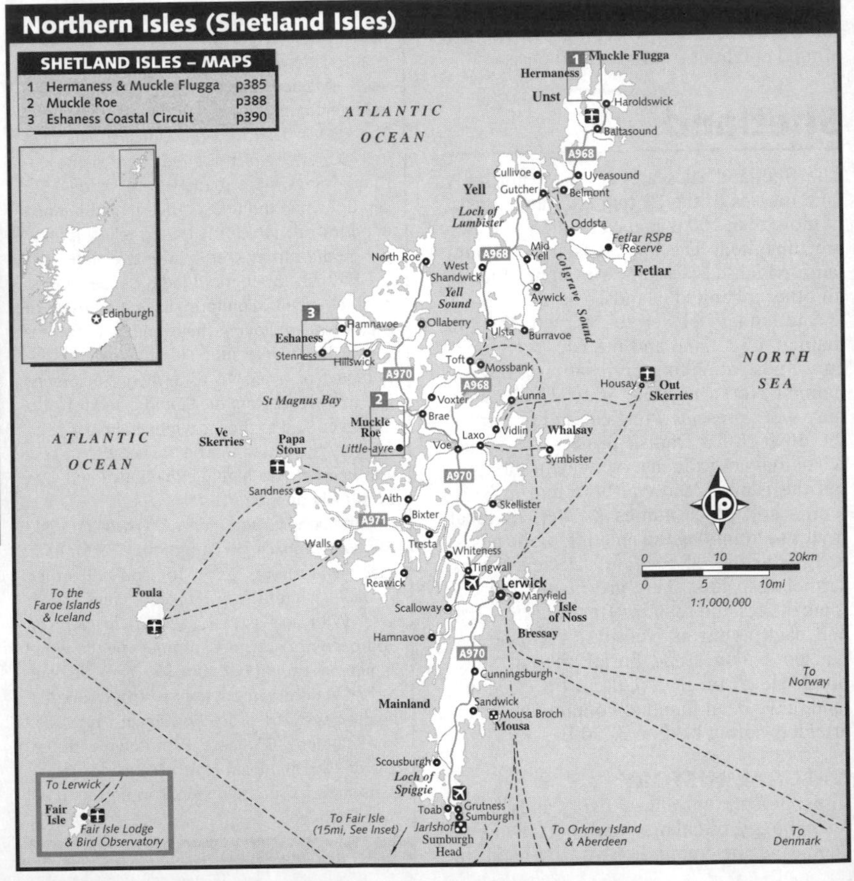

'night'. This period is locally referred to as the simmer dim. Storms can also make a winter visit exhilarating, but the combination of poor weather and short hours of daylight may prove too much for some.

PLANNING

Books

A Guide to Shetland's Breeding Birds by Bobby Tulloch is a well-respected field guide for birdwatching. Local walking guides include *Walks on Shetland* by Mary Welsh and *Walking the Coastline of Shetland* by Peter Guy. The former covers a multitude of short walks with sketch illustrations, while the latter covers the entire coastline in six small volumes with useful background information. The *Official Tourist Guide* published by Shetland Islands Tourism is particularly good for historical background.

Information Sources

Shetland Islands Tourism (☎ 01595-693434, W www.visitshetland.com) is a good information source for trip planning. It can provide accommodation listings and organise reservations. For those with an interest in wildlife, W www.wildlife.shetland.co.uk has some useful information and links.

In case of an emergency in Shetland, call Lerwick police station (☎ 01595-692110). Don't forget to fill out the 'Let Someone Know Before You Go' form, available from W www.northern.police.uk.

Walking Festivals

Shetland holds a walking festival every summer, generally around the beginning of September. Walks are led by local guides and cover a range of levels of difficulty. Check the Shetland Islands Tourism Web site for more details (see under Information Sources). The booklet produced for the festival lists 11 walks with all necessary details and is worth getting hold of.

GETTING AROUND

Hiring a car can greatly facilitate transport around the islands as public transport to walking areas in Shetland is often infrequent and/or at inconvenient times. Several car hire companies are based in Lerwick. Try Star Rent-A-Car (☎ 01595-692075), 22 Commercial St or Bolts Car Hire (☎ 01595-693636), 26 North Rd. For details on public transport options, see Getting There & Away and Getting To/From the Walk under the individual walks.

ACCESS TOWN

Lerwick

The capital of Shetland, Lerwick is by far the largest settlement of the islands. It is also the first port of call for the vast majority of visitors to the island chain. The town is centred around its port and fishing harbour, and has a thriving commercial centre with all necessary shops and facilities.

Information The town centre and Lerwick TIC (☎ 01595-693434), in Market Cross, are immediately opposite the old harbour. The high street boasts plenty of grocery shops, an outdoor store and several bookshops. There is public Internet access at the SYHA Hostel (see Places to Stay & Eat) and at Isleburgh Community Centre opposite.

Places to Stay & Eat Large ***Lerwick SYHA Hostel*** *(☎ 01595-692114)*, King Harold St, sets a high standard with its facilities and costs £9.25. An 11.45pm curfew applies. ***Clickimin Caravan and Campsite*** *(☎ 01595-741000)* is on the lochside behind the leisure centre and charges £6.30 to pitch a small tent.

Lerwick also has numerous B&Bs, charging between £18 and £30, and five hotels, all charging around £45. A complete accommodation listing is available from the TIC.

There are plenty of places to eat, with several takeaways in Commercial St. ***Caffe Latte***, at the side of the Westside Pine building on Mounthooly St, has an excellent cafe menu, while ***Monty's Deli & Bistro***, nearby on the same street, serves more substantial meals all day (except Sunday) and has an evening menu from around £8.

Getting There & Away P&O Ferries (☎ 01856-850655) has a regular service linking Shetland to mainland Scotland. There are four or five sailings per week between Lerwick and Aberdeen (£104/£116 return in winter/summer). P&O also operates one or two sailings per week between Lerwick and Stromness in Orkney (£78 return). From May to September Smyril Line runs a weekly service connecting Lerwick with Bergen (Norway), Torshavn (Faroe Islands), Seydisfjordur (Iceland) and Hanstholm (Denmark). Further details can be obtained from P&O Ferries. A company called Northlink will take over from P&O as the main shipping service provider to the Northern Isles from October 2002; routes, timetables and fares may change considerably as a result.

Shetland's main airport is at Sumburgh, 25mi from Lerwick on the southern tip of Mainland. British Airways (☎ 0845-773 3377) has almost daily connections between Sumburgh and Kirkwall in Orkney, and the major mainland airports. As a guide, a return Edinburgh-Sumburgh ticket costs £247. Leask's Buses (☎ 01595-693162) runs six services between the airport and Lerwick on weekdays, fewer on Saturday and Sunday. A single ticket costs £1.90. Taxis and hire cars are available at the airport.

Hermaness & Muckle Flugga

Duration	3 hours
Distance	5.5mi (9km)
Standard	easy
Start/Finish	Hermaness Nature Reserve parking area
Nearest Towns	Haroldswick
Public Transport	no

Summary A short, waymarked circuit visiting one of Europe's foremost seabird colonies and overlooking the northernmost point of the British Isles.

This walk makes a circuit of the Hermaness Nature Reserve and visits the cliffs that are the breeding site for more than 100,000 seabirds. Species of birds that are rare throughout the world are found in abundance here, perhaps because of the site's very special location. Unst is Britain's most northerly inhabited isle and Muckle Flugga lighthouse, on a rock outcrop just north of the cliffs of the nature reserve, is the first and last signal on British land. North across the sea is nothing but the Arctic Circle.

The walk is well maintained and waymarked, although it crosses open moor and follows the top of sheer cliffs, so care is still needed. Allow plenty of time for watching the antics of the birds.

NATURAL HISTORY

Conservation at Hermaness began in 1831, when the laird noted that the great skua population had been reduced to single figures by zealous egg collectors and taxidermists. He mounted a personal campaign to watch over the remaining birds and the protection he offered became official in 1907 when the Royal Society for the Protection of Birds took over the job.

Great skua have thrived as a result and Hermaness is now home to the world's third-largest colony of these flying pirates (for an account of the dangers of walking near these birds see the boxed text 'Beware the Bonxie' on page 374. Skuas nest on the bog-covered hills of the reserve, but the granite and gneiss cliffs of Hermaness, which rise to a height of 170m at Neap, are also teaming with bird life. Around 25,000 pairs of puffin, 14,000 pairs of gannet (Britain's largest seabird, with a wingspan of up to 2m) and 20,000 guillemots also nest within the reserve.

PLANNING

When to Walk

Most of the seabirds visit Hermaness for the breeding season only, from May to August, peaking in June and July, so this is the optimum time to walk. The moorland crossed by the route can be boggy in places, so dry conditions are preferable.

What to Bring

The open moor and cliffs are exposed to the changeable weather that sweeps off the Atlantic, and fog and high winds can occur at any time. Plenty of warm and waterproof clothing, as well as sturdy footwear, are required. Bring binoculars if you have them.

Maps

Use the OS Landranger 1:50,000 map No 1 *(Shetland – Yell, Unst & Fetlar)*.

Information Sources

Hermaness Visitor Centre (☎ 01957-711278) is a couple of minutes' walk from the start of this circuit, and is well worth a visit to find out more about the flora and fauna of the area. Entrance is free and the centre is open daily from late April to mid-September.

NEAREST TOWN

Haroldswick & Around

Haroldswick is a small collection of buildings gathered around a stony bay. It is home to Unst Boat Haven (a collection of old fishing boats, open every afternoon, admission free). The nearest post office is at the island's main village of Baltasound, 2.5mi south.

Places to Stay & Eat In Haroldswick, ***Joan Ritch*** *(☎ 01957-711323)* offers B&B for £15 and can provide evening meals. ***Baltasound Hotel*** *(☎ 01957-711334)* is the nearest hotel (and the most northerly in Britain), 2mi south of Haroldswick on the outskirts of Baltasound village. It charges from £29.50, and has a restaurant and a bar with food. ***Gardiesfaud Hostel*** *(☎ 01957-755259)* is the only hostel on Unst and is 10mi south of Haroldswick at Uyeasound; it costs £8. Haroldswick also has a ***shop*** with a cafe.

Getting There & Away Although it is possible to travel from Lerwick to Belmont (the ferry port of Unst) by bus, there is no real service from there to Haroldswick and getting around the island is not easy without your own transport. However, it is possible to hire a car in Lerwick and drive the 55mi (88.5km) to Haroldswick (see Getting Around on page 383). Ferries cross every half hour between Mainland and Yell, and Yell and Unst; each crossing costs £3 for a car and driver, and £1.25 for additional passengers. Vehicles can be booked on ☎ 01957-722259.

Loganair (☎ 01595-840246) has four flights a week between Tingwall Airport on Mainland (with bus connections to Lerwick) and Baltasound Airport on Unst. Flights cost £42 return.

It is then a few miles by taxi (☎ 01957-711666) to Haroldswick.

GETTING TO/FROM THE WALK

No public transport services cover the 3mi between Haroldswick and the start of the walk at Hermaness Nature Reserve, so walking or a taking a taxi (☎ 01957-711666) are the only access options.

THE WALK

From the parking area follow the signs through two turnstiles and join the well-worn path that climbs a hill alongside the Burra Firth inlet. The rocky path is broken by tussocks of grass and is almost immediately exposed to the wind. Wooden posts splashed with green paint mark the way

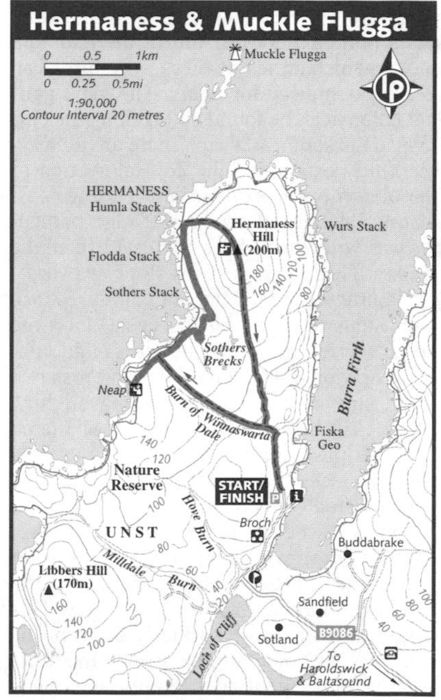

every 100m or so and there are wooden walkways across the boggiest sections.

The path becomes less obtrusive as it drops down the other side of the hill and crosses the Burn of Winnaswarta Dale, and is generally a line of trodden grass from here. Soon after the stream is crossed a marker post signals a parting of the path and the two arms of the circuit go their separate ways. Take the left fork and follow the burn up the open hillside. This moorland is the home of the great skua, and many of the large, brown birds can be seen both on the ground and in the sky. Although there is a real danger of being dive-bombed if you make them feel threatened (see the boxed text 'Beware the Bonxie' on page 374), these particular birds seem used to the number of visitors and are largely tolerant of passing walkers.

As you come to the top of the hill (approximately 45 minutes from the start), it is a surprise to discover what lies on the other side – nothing but air filled with soaring birds! These cliffs are approximately 2mi from the car park. A large **puffin colony** nests immediately in front of the path and the clownish antics of these little birds can keep you amused for hours. The main **gannet colony** can be found 800m along the cliff tops to the south, at Neap. There are no waymarking posts along the coastal section of the circuit but there is a faint path in most places. Take care along the cliff edge, particularly as you climb to the highest cliffs of the walk at Neap as some tops slope seaward.

Having visited the gannet colony, retrace your steps north along the coast. Pass the point where you joined the cliffs and continue onwards, dropping down to cross two small streams and then climbing slightly. The rocky cliff line is wonderfully shattered and you pass numerous offshore outcrops and sea stacks. The upper slopes of the cliff are peppered with puffin burrows. The grass becomes tussocky and there are several wet patches, until you mount a rise and the lighthouse at **Muckle Flugga** (built in 1857 and now automated) comes into view. This is not quite the most northerly point of the country – as you continue around the cliffs another outcrop of rock comes into view slightly farther to the north-east. This jut of gneiss is Out Stack, the official northern end of the British Isles. Another large gannetry is spread over five pyramid-shaped rocks below.

The waymarking posts begin again about 1.5mi north of Neap and a well-trodden path leads inland to the summit of **Hermaness Hill** (200m). From the top, on a clear day, there is a view over most of Unst. The myriad of bog pools and small lochs of Sothers Brecks are spread out below, and the path weaves its way through these as it descends from the hill. Rejoin the rocky access path that you came up on and retrace your initial steps to the parking area.

Muckle Roe

Duration	4–5 hours
Distance	7.5mi (12km)
Standard	easy-medium
Start/Finish	Little-ayre
Nearest Town	Brae, Little-ayre
Public Transport	yes (limited)

Summary A rugged and intricate coastal walk with excellent views north and south along the west Shetland coastline. Offers plenty of scope for extra exploring.

Divided from Mainland by a narrow channel, the island of Muckle Roe used to be reached via stepping stones. Now this delightfully rugged area of red granite hills and cliffs can be reached by a modern bridge. An exploration of the island's west coast begins at the roadhead in Little-ayre and uses a 4WD track to reach North Ham then returns along the tops of the sea cliffs. Distant views of the coast of Shetland to both the north and south are superb, as is the scenery closer at hand. The variety of seascapes is matched inland by the many lochs that are hidden in every dip and hollow. On paper this appears to be a very short route, but the intricacy of the terrain on the return leg is time consuming and invites walking a substantial extra distance to reach the end of each promontory and headland.

The distance can be increased by taking in the summit of South Ward (169m) on the way to North Ham.

PLANNING

Any time of year is suitable for this route, but you'll see much more bird life between May and September.

Although the going is largely dry and firm underfoot, the roughness of the terrain along the cliff tops would merit wearing strong boots. Bring plenty of warm and protective clothing. Binoculars would be beneficial for studying birds.

Maps

Use OS Landranger 1:50,000 map No 3 *(Shetland – North Mainland)*.

NEAREST TOWNS

Brae

The village of Brae houses workers from the nearby oil refinery at Sullom Voe and isn't particularly attractive. However, this is the largest settlement in the area and does have a post office and several accommodation options.

Places to Stay & Eat Family-run ***Valleyfield Guest House*** *(☎ 01806-522563)* is 2mi south of Brae on the road to Lerwick. The owners offer home cooking and singles/doubles cost from £30/£50. It is also possible to ***camp*** close to the house.

Busta House Hotel *(☎ 01806-522506)*, 1.5mi south-west of Brae, is a luxurious country-house hotel charging £70/£90. The restaurant is considered to be one of the best in Shetland.

Brae has a ***supermarket*** for self-caterers.

Getting There & Away Whites Coaches (☎ 01595-809443) operates daily services (except Sunday) between Lerwick and Brae. Buses leave Brae at 8.10am and 10.30am, and return from Lerwick at 5.10pm. The journey costs £1.50 each way.

Little-ayre

Right at the start of the walk, Little-ayre is only a collection of houses with one B&B. ***Westayre B&B*** *(☎ 01806-522386)* has singles from £17 with good sea views. For details on how to get to Little-ayre see Getting to/from the Walk.

GETTING TO/FROM THE WALK

The walk starts and finishes at Little-ayre, 4.5mi from Brae on a small road with little traffic. Johnson Transport (☎ 01806-522443) runs a bus service between the two places but, unfortunately for walkers, this leaves Brae in the evening (5.50pm) and returns from Little-ayre in the morning (7.45am). If you are relying on the bus you'll have to stay in Little-ayre or camp wild somewhere along the route. The alternative is to arrange with a local taxi (☎ 01806-242501) to drop you off and collect you at the end of the walk.

THE WALK

At the end of the sealed road in Little-ayre, the B&B is on the right and a small farm is on the left. A track runs between the two buildings. Follow the track and pass through a gate into a field. Continue as the track curves round and goes through another gate. Ignore side tracks running off to the right and follow the main track as it climbs steadily onto open moorland, passing through another gate and then climbing more steeply to reach a col with a small loch on the left (0.75mi from Little-ayre). Walk over the col to a view of Burki Waters in a hollow to your right. East of this loch, heather-clad slopes rise to the summit of South Ward (169m), which can be added as a one-hour side trip.

Descend across a small bridge and then climb onto the eastern side of a small valley, framing a view of the headlands at North Ham and, beyond, the famous sea stacks known as The Drongs. Continue to a junction near a small sheet-metal building, where the main track veers to the west and a smaller track passes through a gate to the right of the building. Follow the right-hand track to the prominent headland just south-west of North Ham. Note that the track actually runs to the west of Town Loch and not to the east as shown on the OS map. By climbing onto the headland you can get good views across the inlets and promontories to the east.

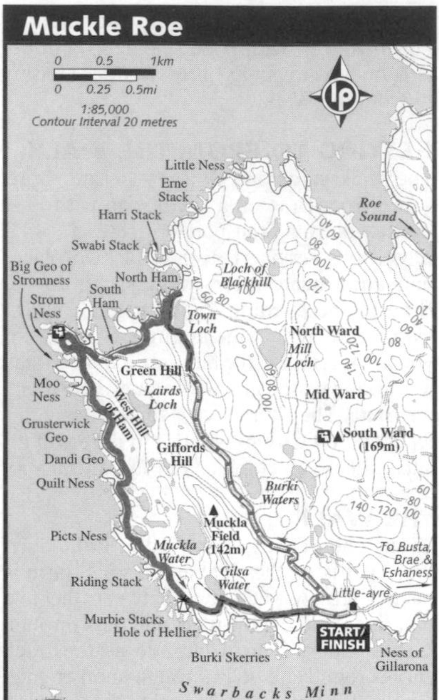

Descend off the headland and walk west past the remains of an old stone cottage, probably once used as a shelter for herring fishermen (see the boxed text 'Life on the North Atlantic' on page 381). Cross a small storm beach, pick up the track from Little-ayre and follow it the short distance to South Ham. Cross a stile and climb onto Strom Ness, from where there are good views back to the east. You can walk right out to the end of **Strom Ness** or simply cut across it to the cliffs on the other side and then turn south passing the impressive inlet called the Big Geo of Stromness.

Continue along the cliff line, climbing steeply to **West Hill of Ham**, from where there are good views back to the north-west across a prominent sea stack with a narrow arch. To the south-east there is a myriad of lochs, outcrops and boulders. Pass around Dandi Geo and a small loch and contour around to the west of some craggy hills, passing another loch, to eventually come into sight of a small headland and lighthouse. Descend steeply and cross some rough ground to reach the headland. Either walk out and back to visit the lighthouse or cut straight across to pick up the obvious track. Follow this around the southern shores of Gilsa Water to a smaller loch, which often has red-throated divers (note that it is illegal to disturb these birds). Continue along the track to reach Little-ayre in 20 to 30 minutes.

Eshaness Coastal Circuit

Duration	5 hours
Distance	8mi (13km)
Standard	easy-medium
Start/Finish	Braehoulland junction
Nearest Town	Hillswick
Public Transport	yes (limited)

Summary A circular route that explores the traditional culture and shattered coastline of this beautiful, outlying peninsula.

The peninsula of Eshaness juts from the west coast of Mainland and has been shaped by millennia of violent winds and seas. Huge natural arches, big enough for a boat to pass through, have been chiselled by pounding waves – see, for example, the island of Dore Holm towards the start of the walk. Long clefts have been cut inland along fault and joint lines and, at the Holes of Scraada, the sea extends underground 300m inland from the cliffs. In other places huge blocks of rock have sheared off the cliffs and been hurled inland by gales and storms – the Grind of the Navir is an awesome example of such natural power.

The area is also renowned for its long history of settlement and traditional croft farming. In the village of Tangwick, near the start of the circuit, is the Tangwick Haa museum. A haa is the house of a laird (master of an estate) and this one was built in the late 17th century. It has interesting photo displays and artefacts of many aspects of Eshaness social and natural history, and makes a good start to the walk. It is open daily from May to September and entry is free.

The Braer Oil Disaster & Hillswick Wildlife Sanctuary

In January 1993 the *Braer*, an oil tanker registered in Liberia, broke up on the rocks at Garth's Ness on the southern tip of Shetland, spilling a cargo of 84,000 tons of North Sea crude oil into the ocean. The quantity of oil released was twice that spilt by the *Exxon Valdez* when it devastated a section of the Alaskan coastline a few years previously. An ecological disaster was predicted and, indeed, the spill had severe short-term effects. High winds blew oil and spray across fields and houses, coating everything in an oily, toxic slime. Fish farms were ruined and people developed sore throats from the minute but irritating particles of oil in the air. However, it was the very storm that forced the *Braer* onto the rocks that helped minimise the damage. Five more days of strong gales dispersed the slick widely enough for the predicted disaster to be averted. Local seabird and marine mammal populations were not critically affected and today there is no discernible trace of the spill.

The incident did, however, benefit the cause of conservation on the islands. The Hillswick Wildlife Sanctuary had been operating since 1978, when Jan Morgan, the owner of The Booth (an historic building and at that time the local pub in Hillswick) began taking in injured seals, otters and birds. When the *Braer* broke up The Booth became the centre for oiled animals and its basic facilities were quickly upgraded with injections of cash. In total 37 seals and seven otters were treated after the spill and almost all of them survived. Since then Jan has closed the pub and made The Booth a full time charity.

She also runs a cafe-restaurant serving vegetarian and vegan food, the proceeds going to the sanctuary. Visitors can help nurse some of the sick animals. For more information contact Hillswick Wildlife Sanctuary (☎ 01806-503348).

KRAIG LIEB

Seals, and other injured animals, have benefitted from the efforts of the Hillswick Wildlife Sanctuary.

The route crosses generally grassy terrain but involves several fence crossings between fields. For a shorter option that takes in the best of the cliff scenery, start and finish at the parking area of Eshaness lighthouse and make a circuit along the cliffs to the north.

PLANNING

This route is suitable for walking at any time of the year, although watch out for strong winds as the cliffs are very exposed to the changeable and at times violent weather from the north and west, and mist can blow in at any time. Bring plenty of warm and waterproof clothing.

Maps

Use OS Landranger 1:50,000 map No 3 *(Shetland – North Mainland)*.

NEAREST TOWN
Hillswick & Around

Hillswick is a pleasant village on the shores of Ura Firth. It's a quiet place but ideally situated, not only as a base for this walk but also for a circuit of the Ness of Hillswick, the promontory that bulges out from the town itself (see Other Walks on page 392).

Places to Stay & Eat The most impressive building in the village is ***St Magnus Hotel*** *(☎ 01806-503372)*. It was prefabricated in

Norway using traditional pine wood and re-erected in Hillswick in 1902. It has bar food and a restaurant, and rooms cost from £24.

Mrs Williamson *(☎ 01806-503261)* offers B&B from £17 and can provide evening meals. ***The Booth***, Hillswick's only cafe, is vegetarian. It is attached to the wildlife sanctuary on the waterfront and is unlicensed, so bring your own wine.

Another accommodation option is in Hamnavoe, a 1.5mi walk from the start of this circuit. ***Johnny Notion's Camping Bó'd*** is named in honour of the local man who invented his own inoculation against smallpox. It is basic (no electricity) and costs £5.

Hillswick has a petrol pump and a ***shop*** with a post office that is open Monday to Saturday (although closed for lunch), and from noon to 3pm on Sunday.

Getting There & Away Whites Coaches (☎ 01595-809443) operates daily services (except Wednesday and Sunday) between Lerwick and Hillswick. Buses leave Hillswick in the morning (7.35am and 10am) and return from Lerwick at 5.10pm. The journey costs £1.90 each way.

GETTING TO/FROM THE WALK

The circuit starts and finishes at Braehoulland junction on the B9078. Whites Coaches (☎ 01595-809443) operates a bus service to Eshaness from Hillswick (a continuation of the Lerwick-Hillswick service), leaving Hillswick at 6.25pm and returning from Stenness (the end of the main road on the Eshaness peninsula) at 7.15am and 9.40am. The bus will stop as requested along the road. However, the timing of these services are of little use for a day trip from Hillswick.

Alternatively, there are two taxi services in the area: John Halcrow (☎ 01595-859369) and Terry Scott (☎ 01595-859444) both operate from Hamnavoe, and it is possible to organise return transport from Hillswick to Eshaness with them.

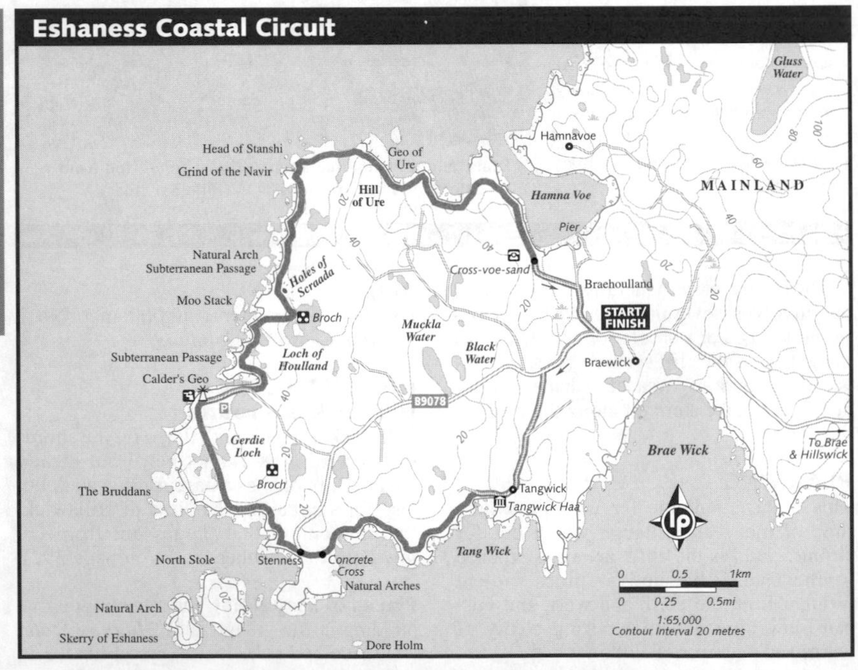

THE WALK

Continue west along the B9078 from the Braehoulland junction and turn left to Tangwick after 400m. Continue to the end of the road, past the Tangwick Haa museum, and down the rough track towards the pebble beach. At the ruined stone building at the back of the beach turn left, cross over a stone wall and begin to follow the short grass west around the shore. The red cliffs of the Ness of Hillswick and the jagged spires of The Drongs are resplendent offshore to the south-east.

The low-lying rocks of the shoreline are already the deep red and black of volcanic deposits, and seals can often be seen basking in this area. Pass through a turnstile and cross several stiles and fences to contour around the top of a cove. The island of Dore Holm, half hollowed to form a huge arch, lies out from the middle of the bay. Climb up a rise on the other side of the cove to a concrete cross, erected by the lighthouse commission to guide vessels into the Sound of Stenness. There is a particularly good panorama seawards from this point.

Descend from the hill north-west, towards the farm of Stenness that can be seen across a field. Cross another couple of stiles and pass in front of the farm, through a gate, to join the sealed road for 20m or so before crossing through another gate on the left and regaining open grassland. Keep close to the shore as the ground descends slightly to cross a stream, and soon afterwards climb inland towards a rocky crag. As you mount this rise Eshaness lighthouse comes into view ahead; head straight for it. Pass several small lochs and you soon reach the beautifully twisted shape of Gerdie Loch. There are stepping stones over the narrowest part of this. Take care; there is an arctic tern colony nearby during the summer and you are liable to be dive-bombed if you disturb them. Continue over the remaining ground to the lighthouse, which is reached approximately 3mi from the start.

Eshaness Lighthouse (built in 1929 and now automated) sits on top of a 70m-high cliff, and signals the start of a wild and rugged section of coastline. A deep-cut geo with towering black walls is the first obstacle, and you will have to retreat some distance inland to pass it. Once back at the cliff tops, a real perspective can be gained northward over the jagged red shoreline and numerous offshore outcrops. Keep close to the cliffs, pass several small lochs and use a stile to cross a stone wall. Follow this wall inland and you will come to the Loch of Houlland, with the remains of an Iron Age broch built out into the water.

Leave the broch and head north-west, and within 300m or so you reach the **Holes of Scraada**. This is a subterranean sea cavern whose roof has collapsed, revealing a deep, narrow chasm with the sea at the bottom. Head back to the cliff edge and follow the coast north again. Pass over several stiles and you will arrive at the **Grind of the Navir**, a stairway in the rock that has been blasted by huge westerly storms, with large boulders being lifted by the sea and deposited 200m inland. The route now bears east along the exposed northern shore of the peninsula.

Pass through a gap in a stone wall and climb over a rise to a jumble of boulders between the shore and a small loch. Scramble over these and climb once again to cross the Hill of Ure. Drop down to round a bay and continue over the next rise, which is steeper and slopes seawards, so take care. From the top, the calm waters of Hamna Voe contrast with the turbulent seas below.

Cross the peninsula over marshy ground and pass through a gate. Several ruined stone buildings are passed and shortly before Cross-voe-sand beach the path follows a narrow strip of ground in front of a fence. This path is eroded in places so take care. Pass round the front of a farm to join a sealed lane. Follow this lane inland for 800m to join up with the B9078 where you started.

Other Walks

ORKNEY

Stronsay

This peaceful farming island has broad sandy beaches, a bird reserve, impressive rock formations and some good coastal walking. The Odin

Bay footpath is in the south of the island. It encompasses heritage sites, a Norse harbour and the Vat of Kirbuster, Orkney's most spectacular natural arch. The footpath is 4mi, but the complete circuit from Whitehall (the island's capital) is 10mi. Orkney Ferries (☎ 01856-872044) runs ferries to Whitehall from Kirkwall. Use OS Landranger 1:50,000 map No 5 *(Orkney – Northern Isles)*.

Sanday

Sanday is an island of pristine white-sand beaches that might be more at home in the Caribbean. The island is almost entirely flat and hosts several impressive archaeological sites, including a 5000-year-old chambered cairn. A signposted walk makes a 3.5mi (5.5km) circuit around Backaskaill Bay in the east of the island. For further information, get *The Sanday Trail* from TICs in Stromness and Kirkwall. Orkney Ferries (☎ 01856-872044) runs regular ferries to the island from Kirkwall. Use OS Landranger 1:50,000 map No 5 *(Orkney – Northern Isles)*.

SHETLAND

Ness of Hillswick

This spectacular headland is just south of Hillswick village. A short but very scenic route passes good cliff scenery and Neolithic and Bronze Age remains; you may also see otters in the more sheltered waters. The walk starts and finishes in Hillswick and it should take around two hours to complete the 5mi (8km) circuit. Use OS Landranger map No 3 *(Shetland – North Mainland)*.

St Ninian's Isle

On this island you'll find the ruins of a 12th-century church and may also see puffins and skuas near the cliff tops. Another very short but extremely scenic route, the main feature of this walk is the beautiful sand and shell isthmus that gives access on foot to the island. The walk starts and finishes at Bigton on south Mainland and will take only a couple of hours for the 3.8mi (6km) circuit. Use OS Landranger map No 4 *(Shetland – South Mainland)*

Language

Scottish Gaelic (Gàidhlig – pronounced **gaa**-lik in Scotland) is spoken by about 60,000 people. Its heartland is the Highlands and Islands, but nearly half this number now live elsewhere in Scotland. A member of the Celtic group in the Indo-European family of languages, its closest relatives are Irish and Manx Gaelic. Welsh, Cornish and Breton are more distantly related.

Scottish Gaelic is Scotland's oldest living language. Gaelic speaking Celts (Gaels) arrived from Ireland from the 4th to the 6th centuries AD and initially settled on the west coast, where their name is perpetuated in Argyll, from the Gaelic Earra-Ghaidheal, meaning coastline of the Gaels. The Irish settlers, known to the Romans as Scotti, eventually gave their name to the entire country. As they moved about, so did their language and from the 9th to the 11th centuries Gaelic was spoken throughout Scotland. For hundreds of years the language was the same as the language of Ireland; there is little evidence of any divergence before the 13th century.

Gaelic culture flourished in the Highlands until the 18th century and the Jacobite rebellions. After the Battle of Culloden in 1746, many Gaelic speakers were driven from their ancestral lands by poverty, indifferent governments and landlords keen to replace them with more lucrative sheep and/or cattle. Although still studied at academic level, the spoken language declined; it was regarded as a mere peasant language of no significance. The neglect of Gaelic in the 1872 Education (Scotland) Act, providing for universal public education, was a severe blow. As late as the 1940s, children who spoke Gaelic at home were punished for using it at school in preference to English.

It was only in the 1970s that Gaelic began to make a comeback, as a new generation of young enthusiasts emerged who were determined that it should not be allowed to die. However, despite a long campaign for Inbhe Thèarainte (Secure Status), Gaelic still does not enjoy official status in Scotland, as does Welsh in Wales. Hopes that a post-devolution Scottish administration would do this have so far been dashed.

All is not lost, however; the language is being encouraged through some government agencies and the European Union (EU). Gaelic medium education is available in some centres, from playgroups to tertiary level, but mainly in a steadily growing number of primary schools (60 in 2000), where education is primarily in Gaelic, at least in the early years. The children become comfortably bilingual, but their number is still too few to replace the number of older Gaelic speakers dying. Even in the Western Isles, where the language is strongest, barely one-third of children take on Gaelic medium education.

The renaissance is perhaps strongest in the fields of music and literature, in cultural events such as *fèisean* (festivals) and in broadcasting. Daily television programs are spread among the main channels. BBC Radio nan Gaidheal, the Gaelic broadcasting arm of BBC Radio Scotland, is on the air for part of each day in most areas. Some local community radio stations also broadcast partly in Gaelic.

The majority of place names on OS maps of the north and west are Gaelic, and the OS maps of the Western Isles give Gaelic names for all towns and villages, with the English equivalent of only the principal places. For a comprehensive list of Gaelic words with English translations that you're likely to encounter while doing the walks in this book, see the Glossary.

Using the Gaelic greetings and basic conversational phrases listed later in this chapter will be appreciated by Gaelic speakers – but there'll be no need to (try to) conduct an elaborate discussion!

Pronunciation

Stress usually falls on the first syllable of a word. The Gaelic alphabet has only 18 letters. When Gaels adopted the Latin alphabet, they named their letters after trees, a practice which, sadly, hasn't survived; Gaels now name their letters in the English manner.

Vowels

There are five vowels: **a**, **e**, **i**, **o** and **u**; **a**, **o** and **u** are known as broad vowels, **e** and **i** are known as slender vowels. A grave accent indicates that a vowel sound is lengthened, eg, *bata* (stick), *bàta* (boat).

Consonants

There are 12 consonants: **b**, **c**, **d**, **f**, **g**, **l**, **m**, **n**, **p**, **r**, **s**, **t** and the letter **h** (used only to change other sounds).

Consonants may be pronounced in different ways depending on the vowel beside them. The spelling rule in Gaelic is 'broad to broad and slender to slender'. This means that if, in a word, a consonant is preceded by a broad vowel, it must be followed by a broad vowel, and if it is preceded by a slender vowel, it must be followed by a slender vowel. Consequently, there are broad consonants and slender consonants, eg, *balach* **bal**-ach (boy) and *caileag* **kal**-ak (girl).

Broad consonants sound approximately the same as their English equivalents. Slender consonants are sometimes followed by a 'y' sound, eg, *cailleach* **kal**-yach (old woman).

c always a hard 'k' sound, never an 's' sound
d when broad, thicker than English 'd'; when slender, as the 'j' in 'jet'
l, ll when broad, as in 'bollard'; when slender, as in 'long'
n, nn when broad, similar to the 'n' in English 'no'; when slender, as in 'new'
s when broad as in English 'see'; when slender, as 'sh'
t when broad, thicker than English 't'; when slender, as the 'ch' in 'chin'

When consonants are followed by 'h', a change of sound occurs:

bh, mh as 'v'
ch when broad, as in *loch* (not 'lock'!); when slender, as in German *ich*; close to 'h' in English 'hue'
dh, gh when broad, voiced at the back of the throat; when slender, as 'y' – there's no English equivalent
fh silent
ph as 'f'
sh as 'h' if before a broad vowel
th as 'h'

Certain Gaelic sounds, especially vowel combinations and consonantal changes caused by the addition of the letter **h**, cannot be reproduced satisfactorily in English. A fluent speaker will be an invaluable help with learning these.

Greetings & Civilities

Good morning.
madding va
Madainn mhath.
Good afternoon/Good evening.
feskurr ma
Feasgar math.
Good night.
uh eech uh va
Oidhche mhath.
How are you?
kimmer uh ha oo?
Ciamar a tha thu?
Very well, thank you.
gley va tappuh leht
Glè mhath, tapadh leat.
I'm well, thank you.
ha mee goo ma tappuh leht
Tha mi gu math, tapadh leat.
That's good.
sma shin
'S math sin.
Please.
mahs eh doh hawl eh
Mas e do thoil e.
Thank you.
tappuh leht
Tapadh leat.

Many thanks.
moe ran ta eeng
Mòran taing.
You're welcome.
sheh doh veh huh
'Se do bheatha.
I beg your pardon.
bal-yuv
B'àill leibh.
Excuse me.
gav mo lishk yal
Gabh mo leisgeul.
I'm sorry.
ha mee dooleech
Tha mi duillich.

Small Talk

Do you speak Gaelic?
uh vil gaa lick ackut?
A bheil Gàidhlig agad?
Yes, a little.
ha bake-an
Tha, beagan.
Not much.
chan yil moe ran
Chan eil mòran.
What's your name?
jae an tannam uh ha orsht?
De an t-ainm a tha ort?
I'm ...
is meeshuh
Is mise ...

Good health! (Cheers!)
slahntchuh va!
Slàinte mhath!
Goodbye. (lit: blessings go with you)
byan achk leht
Beannachd leat.
Goodbye. (lit: the same with you)
mar shin leht
Mar sin leat.

Useful Phrases

It's warm today.
ha eh blaah un joo
Tha e blàth an diugh.
It's cold today.
ha eh foo ur un joo
Tha e fuar an diugh.
It's a beautiful day.
ha un la bree a uh
Tha an latha brèagha.
It's wet.
ha e flooch
Tha e fliuch.
It's raining.
ha un tooshku a woon
Tha an t-uisge ann.
It's misty.
ha k yaw a woon
Tha ceò ann.
It's snowing.
ha shnee-uchk a woon
Tha sneachd ann.

Glossary

Some English words and phrases commonly used in Scotland will be unknown to visitors from abroad, even if they regard English as their first language. There are also many walking and geographical terms used in Scotland, often derived from ancient and endemic languages, which you are likely to come across during your travels. We have translated some of these terms here. For those seeking a more in-depth introduction to the British English language, Lonely Planet also publishes a *British phrasebook.*

AA – Automobile Association
abhainn – river; stream
ABTA – Association of British Travel Agents
achadh – field
allt – river; stream
aonach – ridge
arête – narrow or sharp ridge separating two glacial valleys
ATM – automatic teller machine; cash point
Aurora Borealis – waves of light or arches of colour in the far northern night sky, caused by high-speed solar particles entering the earth's atmosphere; *Northern Lights*
aye – yes; always

B&B – bed and breakfast
bag – to reach the top of a mountain or hill
bàn – white
bank holiday – public holiday (when banks are closed)
beag – small
bealach – pass between hills
beg – small
beinn – mountain
ben – mountain
bhàn – white
bidean – peak
biel – shelter
binnean – peak
birk – birch tree or wood
bitter – type of beer; ale
bitumen – road surfacing material; asphalt; Tarmac
bonxie – great skua (a bird – Orkney Islands)
bothy – simple hut in the hills used by walkers (and shepherds and others)
brae – hillside; mountainside
broch – ancient circular, dry-stone tower large enough to serve as a fortified home
BT – British Telecom
burgh – town
burn – stream

cairn – pile of stones to mark path or junction; peak
caisteal – castle
CAMRA – Campaign for the Protection of Real Ale
carry out – takeaway food or drink
ceilidh – informal evening entertainment and dance
clachan – village
clan – group of people claiming descent from a common ancestor
cleuch – small valley
chips – hot, deep-fried potato pieces, traditionally eaten with fish; fries
cnoc – rounded hillock
coire – high mountain valley; cirque; *corrie*
col – the lowest point of a ridge connecting two peaks
contour interval – vertical distance between contour lines on a topographical map
Corbett – hill or mountain between 2500ft and 2999ft high
corrie – semicircular basin at the head of a steep-sided valley, usually formed by glacial erosion; cirque; *coire*
crack – good conversation; discussion
crag – rocky outcrop
craig – rocky outcrop
creag – crag; cliff; rocky peak
crisps – salty flakes of fried potato in a packet (chips to the rest of the world)
croft, **crofting** – plot of land and adjacent house, worked by occupiers
cull, **culling** – systematic reduction of deer population as part of a wildlife management program
DB&B – dinner, bed and breakfast

dearg – red; reddish
derg – red; reddish
doddle – something easily accomplished
doire – copse; wood
Donald – Scottish lowland hill between 2000ft and 2499ft high
dram – whisky measure
dreich – wet; dull; cool (weather)
drochaid – bridge
druim – ridge
dubh – dark; black
duibh – dark; black
dùn – fortress; fort
duvet – warm bed cover; quilt; doona
dyke – stone wall

eas – waterfall
eilean – island
en suite room – bedroom with its own bathroom
estate – large (usually) area of landed property
EU – European Union
exclosure – fenced enclosure to protect internal trees from external grazing stock

fank – enclosure for animals
farm shop – shop that sells farm produce, usually cheese, smoked meat and other delicacies, but sometimes also fruit and vegetables, eggs and home-made cakes
FE – Forest Enterprise
fells – hills (in southern Scotland)
fionn – white
firth – river estuary
fraoch – heather

geal – white
gendarme – large block (of rock) barring progress on a narrow ridge
geo – very narrow coastal inlet or chasm
GGW – Great Glen Way
glas – grey; grey-green
gleann – valley
glen – valley
gloup – blowhole (Northern Isles)
GNER – Great North Eastern Railway
gorm – blue
GR – grid reference on maps
gully – small, steep-sided valley
haa – house of a *laird* (Northern Isles)
hag – mound of peat, usually in bogs
half – half a pint of beer, as in 'half of bitter'
hamlet – small settlement
headwall – wall at the head (top) of a valley
hillwalker – person who enjoys walking in the 'hills' of Scotland
Hogmanay – New Year's Eve
horseshoe – curved or circular route up one ridge and down another, round a valley
HS – Historic Scotland

inch – island
inn – pub, usually with accommodation
inver – river mouth

jam – jelly; conserve
JMT – John Muir Trust

ken – head (noun); know (verb)
kin – head (noun); know (verb)
kirk – church
kissing gate – swinging gate in fence, built to allow people, but not animals or bicycles, through
kyle – narrows; strait

laird – estate owner
lairig – pass (mountain)
law – round hill
lay-by – parking place at side of road
lazy beds – long, generally parallel ridges and furrows, dug by hand (in most cases centuries ago), with seaweed placed in the furrows to enrich the soil
LDP – long-distance path
links – golf course
linn – waterfall
linne – pool
loch – lake
lochan – small lake
lock – section of canal that can be closed off and the water level changed to raise or lower boats
lùb – bend
lùib – bend

machair – area of sandy, calcium-rich soil, confined to the west coast, extending inland from the beach and very rich in summer wild flowers
màm – rounded hill; pass in the hills

MBA – Mountain Bothies Association
MCoS – Mountaineering Council of Scotland
meadhan – middle; central
meadhon – middle; central
meall – lumpy, rounded hill
mercat – market
mheadhain – middle; central
mheadhoin – middle; central
mhor – big; great
midge – minute, biting insect, irresistibly attracted to humans in damp, moist areas on dull, still days
MoD – Ministry of Defence
moor – high, open, treeless area
mor – big; great
moraine – ridge or mound of debris deposited by retreating glacier
morass – swampy, low-lying land
moss – bog; morass; mire
motorway – freeway
muckle – big
muirburn – seasonal burning of heather to encourage new growth
mull – promontory
Munro – mountain over 3000ft high
Munro bagger – someone who deliberately sets out to reach the top of a *Munro*

ness – headland
névé – mass of porous ice, formed from snow, not yet frozen into glacier ice
NNR – National Nature Reserve
Northern Lights – see *Aurora Borealis*
NP – National Park
NSA – National Scenic Area
NTS – National Trust for Scotland

off-licence – shop selling alcoholic drinks to take away
OS – Ordnance Survey

passing place – area beside a *single-track road* where vehicles can wait for others to pass, allowing the smooth flow of traffic in remote areas
path – trail; walking track
pavement – sidewalk; roadside path
peat – compact brownish deposit of partially decomposed vegetable matter saturated with water, and used as a fuel when dried; see also *hag*
Pict – early Celtic inhabitant
pint – about 0.75L
pitched – surfaced with flat stones (on a walking path)
postbus – mail delivery van, which also carries passengers
private bathroom – designated bathroom for use by *B&B* guests, separate from the bedroom
pub – short for public house, a bar usually also serving food and possibly providing accommodation

RA – Ramblers Association
RAC – Royal Automobile Club
ramble – relatively short, easy walk
real ale – any beer that is allowed to ferment in the cask, contains no chemicals or additives and, when served, is pumped up without using carbon dioxide
reive – to go on a plundering raid (historic)
rhinn – headland
ride – originally a path made for riding on horseback
rig – furrow (usually ploughed); steep-sided ridge (in southern Scotland)
rin – headland
RSPB – Royal Society for the Protection of Birds
rubha – headland
rudha – headland

SAC – Special Area of Conservation
sàil – long mountain slope; heel
scrambling – using hands for balance and/or to enable movement upwards on rock
sea stack – pillar of rock rising from the sea
sealed road – road surfaced with *bitumen*
self-catering – type of accommodation that includes a kitchen for guests' use
sgorr – pointed hill or mountain
sgurr – pointed hill or mountain
shieling – traditional stone cottage used in summer for fishing or tending herds in remote areas
shinty – Scottish sport, similar to hockey and Irish hurling in outward appearance, but played with a different stick (called a caman) and with different rules
single-track road – sealed road, one-lane wide with regularly spaced *passing places*

SMC – Scottish Mountaineering Council
sneachd – snow
snell – cold; bitter (used to describe wind)
SNH – Scottish Natural Heritage
spittal – old guesthouse or hospice
sròn – ridge running off mountain top; nose
SROWS – Scottish Rights of Way Society
SSSI – Site of Special Scientific Interest
stalking – hunting of deer for sport and/or to control population
STB – Scottish Tourist Board
steading – farm building; sometimes the farm itself
steall – spout of liquid; waterfall
stell – small corral for sheep etc
stile – set of steps enabling crossing of a fence or stone wall
stob – peak
strath – broad, flat river valley
SUW – Southern Upland Way
SWT – Scottish Wildlife Trust
SYHA – Scottish Youth Hostels Association

teallach – forge; hearth
teashop – cafe, usually in country areas
TIC – Tourist Information Centre
topograph – plate, usually installed on a mountain, showing direction or bearing of all visible landscape features, with towns and villages not necessarily visible
torr – small hill
tràigh – beach
tree line – altitude above which trees cannot survive
trig point – survey pillar or cairn
true left/right bank – side of the river as you look downstream
tryst – cattle market

uamh – cave
unco – unfamiliar, strange or odd; remarkable or striking; very; extremely

VAT – value-added tax
verglas – thin coating of ice on rock
voe – large bay or sea inlet (Northern Isles)

Way – walking trail
whiteout – zero visibility in blizzard, fog or mist when ground is snow-covered
WHW – West Highland Way
wick – bay (Northern Isles)
woodland – forest

LONELY PLANET

You already know that Lonely Planet produces more than this one guidebook, but you might not be aware of the other products we have on this region. Here is a selection of titles that you may want to check out as well:

Scotland
ISBN 1 86450 157 X
US$16.99 • UK£10.99

Edinburgh
ISBN 1 86450 378 5
US$12.99 • UK£8.99

Cycling Britain
ISBN 1 86450 037 9
US$19.99 • UK£12.99

Britain
ISBN 1 86450 147 2
US$27.99 • UK£15.99

Walking in Britain
ISBN 1 86450 280 0
US$21.99 • UK£13.99

Europe on a shoestring
ISBN 1 86450 150 2
US$24.99 • UK£14.99

Walking in Ireland
ISBN 0 86442 602 X
US$17.95 • UK£11.99

Western Europe
ISBN 1 86450 163 4
US$27.99 • UK£15.99

Edinburgh City Map
ISBN 1 74059 015 5
US$5.99 • UK£3.99

Diving & Snorkeling Scotland
ISBN 1 55992 094 7
US$14.95 • UK£7.99

British phrasebook
ISBN 0 86442 484 1
US$5.95 • UK£3.99

Available wherever books are sold

Index

Text

For a list of walks, see the Table of Walks (pp4–7)

Bold indicates maps.

Bold indicates maps.

Boxed Text

MAP LEGEND

BOUNDARIES

International
Regional
Disputed

HYDROGRAPHY

Coastline
River, Creek
Loch/Lake
Intermittent Lake
Salt Lake
Canal
Spring
Waterfall
Swamp

ROUTES & TRANSPORT

M8 Motorway
A1 Primary Road
A77 Main Road
B4530 Secondary Road
One-Way Road
Unsealed Major Road
Unsealed Minor Road
4WD Track
Lane
Tunnel
Train Route & Stations
Disused Railway
Chair Lift/Ski Lift
Described Walk
Alternative Route
Side Trip
Walking Track
Ferry Route

AREA FEATURES

National Park
National Trust For Scotland
Beach
Cemetery
Urban Area

MAP SYMBOLS

CAPITAL National Capital
CAPITAL Regional Capital
CITY City
Town Town
Village Village
Hamlet/Farm Settlement

Bothy/Hut
Camping Site
Lookout
Place to Eat
Point of Interest
Shelter
Youth Hostel

Airport/Airfield
Battle Site
Castle
Cathedral/Church
Cliff or Escarpment
100 Contour
Embassy
Gate
Golf Course
Hospital
Lighthouse
Mine
Monument
Museum

Park or Reserve
Parking
Pass/Saddle
Peak or Hill
Picnic Area
Post Office
Pub
Ruin
+100m Spot Height
Stately Home
Stone Row
Telephone
Tourist Information
Trigonometric Point

Note: not all symbols displayed above appear in this book

LONELY PLANET OFFICES

Australia
Locked Bag 1, Footscray, Victoria 3011
☎ 03 8379 8000, fax 03 8379 8111
e talk2us@lonelyplanet.com.au

USA
150 Linden St, Oakland, CA 94607
☎ 510 893 8555, TOLL FREE: 800 275 8555
fax 510 893 8572
e info@lonelyplanet.com

UK
10a Spring Place, London NW5 3BH
☎ 020 7428 4800, fax 020 7428 4828
e go@lonelyplanet.co.uk

France
1 rue du Dahomey, 75011 Paris
☎ 01 55 25 33 00, fax 01 55 25 33 01
e bip@lonelyplanet.fr
w www.lonelyplanet.fr

World Wide Web: w www.lonelyplanet.com *or* AOL keyword: lp
Lonely Planet Images: e lpi@lonelyplanet.com.au